David Hay Fleming

Mary Queen of Scots, from her Birth to her Flight into England

A Brief Biography: with Critical Notes, a few Documents hitherto unpublished, and an Itinerary

Elibron Classics
www.elibron.com

Elibron Classics series.

© 2005 Adamant Media Corporation.

ISBN 1-4021-7275-3 (paperback)
ISBN 1-4212-8448-0 (hardcover)

This Elibron Classics Replica Edition is an unabridged facsimile
of the edition published in 1897 by Hodder & Stoughton,
London.

MARY QUEEN OF SCOTS

Mary Queen of Scots

From her Birth to her Flight into England: A Brief Biography: with *Critical Notes, a few Documents hitherto unpublished, and an Itinerary by* David Hay Fleming

London: Hodder and Stoughton

27 Paternoster Row. MDCCCXCVII

Edinburgh : T. and A. CONSTABLE, Printers to Her Majesty

PREFACE

So long ago as 1773 one of the most capable and most cautious of Scottish historical students expressed the opinion that the Marian controversy had already become too angry and too voluminous. Its subsequent tone was not sweetened by such writers as Whitaker and Chalmers. If in recent years it has become much less acrimonious, it has also become so much more voluminous that comparatively few readers can afford the requisite time to master a subject so intricate, and of which nearly all the details have been keenly contested for three centuries. Too many of the literary combatants have been content to derive their materials at second, third, or even fourth hand, with the result that mere opinions and conjectures have frequently been borrowed and repeated as well-established facts. Not a few of these 'fictitious facts,' as well as other blunders more or less blameworthy, have been exposed or exploded in the following pages; but they will doubtless be again resuscitated by those who are more anxious to uphold theories than to ascertain truth.

PREFACE

My aim has been to state—fairly, briefly, and clearly
—all the more important and more interesting events
in Mary's life up to the date of her flight into England,
without attempting to suggest or sustain any theory.
The text has been almost entirely drawn from the State
Papers, the official records, and the letters of the period,
and from the contemporary histories and chronicles.
Controverted points are freely dealt with in the Notes ;
and there special attention has been paid to the works
of two of the Queen's most recent and best-known
biographers—Father Stevenson and Mr. (now Sir John)
Skelton.   It will be seen that the former has dimmed
his great reputation as an historical student by prejudice, partiality, and perversion ; and that the latter
not only rivals him in these faults, but is so reckless
in matters of fact and so careless in quotation that no
reliance can be placed on his statements, no weight on
his opinions.

The *Hamilton Papers*, the Calendars of Venetian and
Spanish State Papers, and the documents printed by
M. Philippson, have been examined, as well as the Foreign
and Domestic Calendars, and the Reports of the Historical MSS. Commission.   Fresh material has also been
derived from the forthcoming volume of the *Register of
the Scottish Privy Council*, edited by Professor Masson ;
and from unpublished original documents in the Register
House—of which documents a selection is printed in the

PREFACE

Appendix. For the period of Mary's personal reign in Scotland, I have also gone somewhat carefully through the *Register of the Privy Seal*; and the whole of its evidence regarding her movements is for the first time tabulated in the Itinerary. Scattered through Record and Club publications and privately-printed books there are many of her letters and other documents which are not in Labanoff's *Recueil*. A list of these has meanwhile been held over; but, in so far as they bear on her movements in Scotland, they have been utilised in the Itinerary.

Although great care has been taken to ensure absolute accuracy, it would be too much to expect that it has been actually attained. Having so frankly pointed out the lapses of my predecessors, I hope, with becoming humility, to accept reproof for my own.

This volume—the result of three years' hard, almost incessant, work—would not have been undertaken but for the long-continued and urgent pressure of Dr. Robertson Nicoll. For much valuable help most ungrudgingly given, my warmest thanks are due to Mr. W. A. Craigie, Dr. Mark Anderson, Dr. Thomas Dickson, the Rev. Walter M'Leod, and the Rev. J. A. Milne; and also to Mr. Maitland Thomson and the Rev. John Anderson for the kindness and aid which rendered my work in the Register House a pleasure and delight.

In another volume I purpose to deal with Mary's life

PREFACE

in England, and in connection with the conferences at York and Westminster the Casket Letters will be discussed. In this volume there is no reference whatever to them, either in text or notes. The other volume will contain an index to both.

The editions of the works which I have used are distinguished in the references; and when a document of any importance is printed in more than one book, reference is usually made to each. In citing the various Calendars, the page has uniformly been given—not the number of the document.

D. H. F.

St. Andrews, *July* 1897.

CONTENTS

ix

CONTENTS

CHAPTER VI

CHAPTER VII

CHAPTER VIII

CHAPTER IX

CHAPTER X

CHAPTER XI

CHAPTER XII

CHAPTER XIII

CONTENTS

LEADING DATES

CHAPTER I

1542-1548

MARY STUART was born on the 8th of December 1542 in the palace of Linlithgow.[1]   Both time and place are quite certain, although on neither have her biographers and historians been unanimous.[2]   In the state papers the coming event cast its shadow before.   Rumours there were that ' the Skottishe Quene ' had borne a son on the 30th of November, and that this had been proclaimed at Jedburgh on the 2nd of December.   Later despatches were more uncertain—there being ' sundre tales ' on the matter : some said that it was a son, some said a daughter. The message passed that the child was dead, then that it was ' vary wayke,' and again that it was ' alyve and good liking.'   Her name was reported to be Elizabeth, but this mistake was soon corrected.[3]   In the malevolent gossip of the time doubts were whispered concerning her parentage.[4]

Only four and a half years had elapsed since Mary of Guise had landed at Fifeness, and been married to James the Fifth in the cathedral of St. Andrews.[5]   Their two sons had both died.   The King, despondent and

A   I

heartbroken over the rout of Solway Moss,[6] had retired
to Falkland, where the tidings of his daughter's birth
reached him. Far from being uplifted by the news, his
thoughts reverted to Marjory Bruce, through whom the
throne had come to the Stuarts, and, according to Knox,
he exclaimed: 'The devil go with it! It will end as it
began; it came from a woman, and it will end in a
woman.'[7] Or, as Pitscottie has it, ' It came with a lass,
and it will pass with a lass.'[8] Mary was born on a Friday,
and next Thursday 'at xii. of the cloke at nyght,' her
father died[9] not without the suspicion of having been
poisoned.[10] Lisle, the Lord Warden of the Marches,
stayed active proceedings against the Scots on hearing
of James's death, deeming it inconsistent with Henry's
honour to make war 'upon a dedd bodye, or uppon a
wydowe, or on a yonge sucling,' especially at the time of
the King's funeral; yet on the 30th of December he takes
care to explain to Henry that, in Alnwick, the weather
hath been such—the snow stopping all passages and
knowledge of ways—that little or nothing can be done to
the annoyance of the enemies.[11] This incidental reference
shows that Mary was born not only in stormy political
times, but that tempestuous weather speedily followed, if
it did not accompany, her birth. Next month the frost
was so intense that it was impossible to release the
ships from the ice in the haven of Newcastle.[12]

Trying and troublous times had been experienced in
previous minorities; and with the impetuous and unscrupulous Henry the Eighth on the English throne, the
prospect for Scotland was by no means bright. The

machinery of the state, however, was kept in motion. On the strength of a fraudulent will, Cardinal Beaton had himself and several of the leading nobles proclaimed Governors of the realm; [13] but this arrangement was soon set aside, and Arran was proclaimed Governor on Wednesday the 3rd of January.[14]

As the scheming for the governorship had begun before the King was actually dead, so plans were being laid for the marriage of the infant Queen before she was many days old. On the 24th of December Lisle wrote to Henry that some of the best sort of gentlemen of the Scottish Borders wished that he had their Princess for his Prince; and on the 1st of January he wrote to the English Council that there was a rumour that the Cardinal wished Arran's son to have the Princess, 'and,' he adds, 'many other devices the people have of her marriage.'[15] Henry at once saw the desirability of marrying her to his son, and determined to get her and the principal fortresses of Scotland into his hands. To carry out his plans, the Solway prisoners and the Douglases were sent back to Scotland.[16] When Sir Ralph Sadleyr, who was afterwards sent with the same object, arrived in Edinburgh on the 18th of March, he found that the Scots Parliament had been prorogued on the previous day.[17] His Instructions—recently printed for the first time by the Lords of the Treasury—are characterised as a revelation of 'the unprincipled designs of Henry,' which 'fully justify the temporising policy of Arran.'[18]

While in session, the Scots Parliament had considered the proposed marriage between Mary and Edward. The

Instructions then drawn up for the Scots Ambassadors [19] jealously guard the independence of Scotland.   They also provide for Mary's safety.   She was to be kept in Scotland until she was marriageable; kept and nourished principally by her mother, and four lords of the realm least suspected and chosen thereto.   For the more sure keeping of her person, one or two honourable English knights, with as many ladies of honour, and their servants might remain with her at Henry's expense.   As she was 'sa tender of aige,' it was thought expedient that she should remain in the palace of Linlithgow, where she had been born, or in the castle of Stirling, at her mother's pleasure, with the advice of the Governor and Council. If her mother died or left the kingdom, some of the most noble and virtuous ladies of Scotland were to be chosen to abide with her; and if, after marrying Edward, he died before her, without leaving lawful heirs by her, she was to be delivered again to Scotland free, unmarried to any other.[20]

In Sadleyr's interview with the Queen Dowager, at Linlithgow, on the 22nd of March, she professed to be anxious for the English marriage, and that her daughter should be forthwith delivered to Henry—professions at such variance with what he had learned from the Governor and Sir George Douglas, that he perceived there was juggling somewhere.   She also exhibited the little Queen to him, causing the nurse 'to unwrap her out of her clowtes,' that, as Miss Strickland says, 'he might see her in her native loveliness'; and he thus expressed his opinion to Henry: 'I assure your Majesty, it is as goodly a

4

child as I have seen of her age, and as like to live, with the grace of God.'[21]

Other two Ambassadors, Glencairn and Sir George Douglas, were sent to England early in May.[22] Douglas soon returned with a Memorial[23] of the English desires, requiring Mary's delivery to Henry or Edward, at the age of eight or ten at the furthest; and her marriage by twelve at the latest. Early in June the Scots nobles and members of council somewhat modified the original Instructions. Hostages were to be given, and Mary was to be delivered at ten, provided the marriage was made by procurators before she left Scotland.[24] The double treaty of peace and marriage was formally concluded between the Scots Ambassadors and the English Commissioners at Greenwich on the 1st of July.[25] It was ratified in the Abbey-Church of Holyrood, by the oath of the Governor, in the name of the Queen and Three Estates, on the 25th of August, 'at the high-mass solemnly sung with shalms and sackbuts.' Sir George Meldrum of Fyvie, 'a right honest gentleman,' whose revenue was nearly five hundred merks—'a greate lyvyng in this countrey,'—was at once despatched to procure Henry's confirmation, and to explain the difficulty of promptly sending hostages.[26] Henry, however, looked upon the hostages as 'the knot of the holl treatie,' and declined to confirm it until they were produced.[27]

Meanwhile events were not developing in Scotland exactly as Henry wished. He had been dissatisfied from the very first with Arran's appointment as Governor— desiring to have him, as well as the Cardinal and the

infant Queen, in his hands; he had been anxious to prevent his confirmation as Governor by the Scots Parliament, and longed to see him overthrown.[28]   He tried,
nevertheless, to use him in furthering his designs; but
although Henry was powerful and Arran pliant,[29] there
were difficulties in the way which could not be readily
overcome.   Not only had the dubious motives of the
nobles to be reckoned with, but so had the strong
national feeling of the people;[30] and the instability of
the Governor did not always tend to Henry's advantage,
nor was his sincerity undoubted.[31]   Despite English
remonstrances, Beaton, who had been imprisoned, was
transferred from Blackness to his own castle at St.
Andrews, and soon set at liberty.[32]   Lennox was neither
intercepted by the way nor repulsed at his arrival in
Scotland, though he came with the intention it was said
of marrying the Queen Dowager, and so asserting his
claim—a claim supported by the French—as 'rightfull
enheritour' of the Scots crown after Mary.[33]   The Abbot
of Paisley, Arran's bastard brother and future Archbishop
of St. Andrews, was allowed to return to Scotland, in the
hope that he would strengthen the Governor's hands; but
it was speedily found that he too was in the interest of
France.[34]   On the 25th of July, representatives of the
English and French parties met, and amicably arranged
that Mary should be cared for by four of the lords
formerly named by Parliament — Montrose, Erskine,
Livingston, and Lindsay. Glencairn, who had taken a
leading part in making this agreement, assured Sadleyr
that Beaton and his party, and all the nobles, were now

perfectly satisfied with the treaties of peace and marriage.[35]
But, in a fortnight, Sadleyr was able to send Henry a copy
of ' a secret band,' which had been entered into by Beaton
and his party on the 24th of July, to prevent Mary's
removal to England.[36]   On the 26th of July, Mary and
her mother were taken from Linlithgow Palace to Stirling
Castle, and proclamation made at Edinburgh of the treaty
of peace with England[37]—a peace to be too soon and
rudely broken.

On the 2nd of July, Sadleyr had been informed that
Mary could not be conveniently removed from Linlithgow,
as she was ' breeding of teethe.'   In his opinion the
Governor was then as anxious concerning ' her health,
preservation, and surety, as if she were his own natural
child.'[38]   Before she had been quite a fortnight at
Stirling, Sadleyr saw her, when the Queen Dowager
' praised the ayre aboute the house,' and said ' that her
daughter did grow apace, and soon . . . would be a
woman, if she took of her mother,' who, indeed, Sadleyr
adds, ' is of the largest stature of women.'   Mary, who
had had small-pox, was now perfectly recovered, and
Sadleyr pronounced her to be ' a right fayre and goodlie
child.'[39]

The early days of September were signalised by the
reconciliation of Arran and Beaton[40]—a reconciliation
fraught with momentous results ; and immediately followed by the coronation of the infant Queen, ominously
enough, on the thirtieth anniversary of Flodden.[41]

Henry's offers to Arran—his offer to make him King
of Scotland beyond the Forth, his offer to marry the

Princess Elizabeth to his son [42]—had been made in vain.
His attempts to get Mary into his own hands—the hands
of 'her father-in-lawe,' as he described himself [43]—
were less likely than ever to be successful.   He had
advised her removal to Tantallon. [44]   He had wished to
part her from her mother, and to have more of his own
people about her than the stipulated number. [45]   He had
instructed Sadleyr to 'grope the Governour,' as to whether
he would deliver, in gage for the £5000 he wished to
borrow, the fortresses on the south side of the Forth, or
'convey the yong Quene into our handes.' [46]   He had
complained that she had not been brought to Edinburgh
Castle. [47]   He had suggested that Arran should get
possession of Stirling Castle, and take her to a nearer and
safer place ; or else remove the adverse lord-keepers, and
place her and the castle in such hands that 'there shuld
be no doubt but she shalbe furthecummyng.' [48]   On the
29th of August—four days after Arran had solemnly
ratified the treaties, eleven days before Mary's coronation—
the English Privy Council directed Suffolk to select sixteen
or twenty thousand men who would be ready to receive the
fortresses from the Governor, or 'to woorke any other
exployt ther' which his Majesty might think convenient. [49]
Five days after the coronation, Henry informed Suffolk
that he thought he might pass into Scotland with eight
thousand horsemen, on the pretence of making a raid on
the Humes and Carrs, and by a rapid march surprise
Edinburgh, seizing, if possible, the Governor and Cardinal ;
or, failing this, to burn the town, and, as they returned,
to waste 'the countreyes of suche as be our ennemyes,

sparing as niegh as you can our freendes and their adherentes.' [50]

The relations between the two countries were already sufficiently strained. Henry's impolitic seizure of the Scottish ships, before the treaties were ratified by the Governor,[51] was hotly resented by the Edinburgh merchants. Sadleyr had to report, on the 1st of September, that the inhabitants of the capital, both men and women, were threatening with oaths to avenge themselves on him —to burn his house over his head 'so that one of us shulde not escape alyve.' [52] Rumours of the projected English invasion speedily reached Scotland; and at the same time there arrived at Dumbarton a French fleet, 'with money, munytion, and powder.' A Papal Legate and two French Ambassadors were also on board. 'Verey like it is,' wrote Sadleyr, 'that the cummynge of thies Frenche shippes woll make a grete chaunge here.' [53]

Not wishing to be on the same side as his rival, Lennox had left the Cardinal's party not long after the Governor joined it; and, although he had not yet declared himself, was understood by Sadleyr to be no longer 'a good Frencheman,' but 'a good Englisheman.' [54] Hints there were of a proposed marriage between him and Lady Margaret Douglas [55]—the daughter of Angus, the niece of Henry,—a marriage from which the ill-fated Darnley was destined to spring. Lennox was at Edinburgh with the lords of the English party when, on the 6th of October, he received letters announcing the arrival of the French fleet. He and Glencairn were at once despatched to get the arms and money lodged in Dumbarton

Castle—a diplomatic enterprise which they successfully carried out.[56] It was not enough, however, in Henry's opinion, that the supplies sent for the French party should be used in his service, he advised the seizure of the Papal Legate; but that desire was not complied with.[57] The changes of parties staggered Sir George Douglas. 'The worlde is so full of falsehood,' he said, 'he knewe not whome he myght trust'! Yet he thought that 'Lynoux, although he be a yonge man, was more constant and assuryd then the Governour.'[58] Little did Douglas dream how he himself was to be chastised by the English for his inconstancy and falsehood.

There was much intriguing, and wire-pulling, and wild rumour[59] before the Scots Parliament met on the 3rd of December 1543; but on the 9th of that month the Estates declared, that neither those who had assembled for conveying 'our Soverane Lady' from Linlithgow to Stirling, nor those who, at that time, had convened with the Governor at Edinburgh, had committed any crime.[60] Two days later the same Parliament further declared, that, as the peace had been broken by the English seizing and retaining the Scottish merchants, with their ships and goods; and as King Henry had refused to ratify the treaties, these had consequently expired, and were not to be kept on the part of Scotland. Immediately thereafter the two French Ambassadors—La Brosse and Mesnaige —explained that their King (Francis the First) had sent them, that the ancient leagues might be renewed, and to promise help against the King of England. Their proposals were accepted, as the Act bears, 'with ane

consent and assent,' after seeing 'all contractis past
betuix the Kingis of France and Scotland sen King
Robert the Bruce.'[61]

In Stirling Castle Mary was in comparative safety.
Sir George Douglas told Sadleyr, barely a month after
her coronation, that he did not think that Henry's Scottish
friends could take her by force; but they were quite
willing to try, provided his Majesty 'wolde advance a
convenient summe of money.' Douglas further said that
her keepers, being charged with her safety on peril of
losing their lives and lands, would take her, if they
thought fit, into 'the High-lande which is not farre from
Sterlinge, where it is not possible to come by her.'[62]
Next May (1544), Hertford, who had arrived with
Henry's ruthless Instructions,[63] sent the cheering news
to his sanguinary master that he had desolated the
country to 'within six myles of Sterling'; and in the
same despatch he says that Mary had been conveyed to
Dunkeld.[64]

Hertford's merciless devastation of the Borders[65] in
September 1545—a devastation which it was feared
might be repeated in 'the inwart partis of the realme'—
determined the Scots Parliament on the 2nd of October
to enact that a thousand horsemen should lie on the
Borders for resisting 'our auld inymeis of Ingland.'[66]
And three days later the Governor and Lords of Council
declared, that although Lords Erskine and Livingstone[67]
had undertaken, in the previous April, 'the keiping of
our Soverane Ladeis persoun, in cumpany with the Quenis
Grace hir moder, under the pane of tynsale of lif, landis,

and guidis,‛ yet they should not incur any pains if pursued and invaded by an army of Englishmen, or Scots fortified with Englishmen, whom, in spite of 'thair detfull diligence,' they could not resist.[68]

If true love is to be ascertained and measured by the roughness of its course, the love in this marriage-suit must indeed have been intense. Nor did the boisterous courtship cease with Henry's death.[69] Dethick, Norroy King of Arms, was instructed to explain to the Queen Dowager and the Scots Council in the autumn of 1547 that the Protector's invasion was only to bring to good effect the godly purpose of the marriage between Edward and Mary; to show them the advantage of the match; and to tell them that, if they did not yield to the Protector's amicable proceedings, he would accomplish his purpose by force.[70] The third invasion by Hertford—now known as the Lord Protector Somerset—culminated on Saturday the 10th of September in the disastrous battle of Pinkie.[71] It was at this time that Mary was removed to Inchmahome.[72] She was then four years and nine months old; and Bishop Lesley's narrative implies that she only remained in that lovely and secluded isle about three weeks;[73] yet there, her admirers allege, 'she first laid the foundation of her knowledge in the Latin and French, the Spanish and Italian tongues';[74] there too she is said to have learned history, geography, tapestry-work, and embroidery;[75] and there also, we are asked to believe, she found time for child-gardening.[76] When, nineteen days after Pinkie, the English army re-crossed the Tweed, it was not with the idea that the last

card had been played in a difficult and dubious game.
Recourse was again to be had to intrigue,[77] to the sword,[78]
to the prayers of the Church;[79] but all in vain, as the
Scots, in their deepened hatred of their 'auld inymeis,'
were to throw themselves into the arms of their ancient
allies of France.

Ever since Mary's coronation there had been occasional
rumours of a design to marry her in France.[80] Her
mother had long yearned for such an arrangement;[81] and
now it was to be definitely settled. In the spring of 1547
Francis the First had been succeeded by Henry the Second,
who was anxious to be on good terms with the Scots.[2] To
him they appealed for aid against the English, proposing
at the same time to send their young Queen into France
that she might be brought up there and married to the
Dauphin.[83] In response he sent six thousand men—' as
good men of warr,' in Sir Thomas Palmer's opinion, ' as
any be cownttyd in Crystondome, and of dyvers nacions '
—who, a fortnight after landing at Leith, began on the
30th of June 1548 the arduous and prolonged task of
ousting the English from Haddington.[84] A week later the
Scots Parliament met at the neighbouring Abbey,[85] when
D'Essé, the lieutenant-general, explained that his master,
'the maist Christin King of France'—moved by the
ancient league, and by 'the mortall weiris, crudeliteis,
depredatiounis, and intollerabill injuris done be our auld
enimeis of Ingland '—had ' set his haill harte and minde
for defence of this realme'; and, for the more perfect
union and indissoluble amity of France and Scotland,
desired that Mary and the Dauphin might be married,

13

'to the perpetuall honour, plesour, and proffeit of baith the realmes.' The Queen Dowager, the Governor, and the Estates of Parliament 'all in ane voice' approved the desire as 'verray ressonabill'; and gave their consent, on condition that the King of France should keep, maintain, and defend Scotland, with its lieges, laws, and liberties, as he did his own realm, and as Scotland had been kept and defended by its own noble kings in bypast times.[86]

In the preceding January there had been rumours of a proposed marriage between Mary and the young Earl of Kildare;[87] and, in April, between her and a brother of the King of Denmark.[88] Of Mary herself, during this period, little is gleaned. In March it was rumoured that she was dead.[89] She was certainly ill at that time in Dumbarton. Huntly heard that she had small-pox;[90] La Chapelle, then in Edinburgh, said it was measles.[91]

To evade the English fleet,[92] the French galleys passed round the north of Scotland, skirted the west coast, and reaching Dumbarton took the young Queen and her retinue[93] on board about the end of July.[94] 'Lack of wether' kept them lying in the Clyde for several days;[95] but on the 13th of August she was safely landed in Brittany.[96] According to a contemporary Scottish chronicler, she 'past to France to be brocht up under the feir of God';[97] but, according to Knox, 'to the end that in hir youth she should drynk of that lycour, that should remane with hir all hir lyfetyme, for a plague to this realme, and for hir finall destructioun.'[98]

CHAPTER II

As Henry the Second was on a progress through his
frontier towns when Mary Stuart arrived in his kingdom,
she was, after a short rest, honourably convoyed to St.
Germain-en-Laye, where she was enthusiastically welcomed, and appointed meanwhile to remain with the royal
children with whom she was to be educated. A train and
household were chosen for her from the lords, ladies, and
gentlemen who had accompanied her from Scotland ; but,
about two years later, most of them were superseded by
Frenchmen.[1] In her new home Mary speedily became
a favourite.[2]

A few months after her departure from Scotland,
Luttrell, the English commander at Broughty Ferry,
and Fisher were instructed to confer with Argyll and
other Scots nobles regarding her return from France, and
her marriage with Edward [3]—a project which the English
were loath to relinquish. Nine months later (January
1549-50), the Commissioners, appointed by Edward to
treat with the French concerning peace, were directed to
demand, in recompense for Boulogne, that the treaties

15

between Henry the Eighth and the Scots should be fulfilled, and Mary delivered in order that the marriage then
covenanted might be performed.[4] Again, in May 1551,
the Marquis of Northampton and the other Commissioners to France were ordered to claim the young Queen
of Scots in marriage with the King of England; and, in
the event of that being refused, to solicit for him the
hand of the Princess Elizabeth, the daughter of the
French monarch.[5] The application for Mary was declined
on the ground that she was affianced to the Dauphin;
and in July the marriage with Elizabeth was agreed to.[6]

Accompanied by many of the Scots nobles, Mary of
Guise sailed, in September 1550, for France.[7] She wished
to see her daughter, and eagerly desired to secure for
herself the regency of Scotland held by Arran, now
Duke of Chatelherault.[8] Ere the Prior of Capua left
France to fetch her, he provided above a thousand ells
of white damask wherewith to apparel the slaves and
mariners of his galleys. Great preparations were also
made for her reception; and, a month before her arrival,
the flower of the French nobility went to Dieppe to meet
her.[9] Before the end of September she met her daughter
with the French King at Rouen;[10] and with her accompanied the French Court from place to place.[11] The
Dowager Queen of Scots was almost worshipped as a
goddess;[12] and Henry, anxious to strengthen his hold
of Scotland, ingratiated himself with the nobles in her
train.[13] By the following May, however, the English
Ambassador perceived that the whole Court was weary
of her, as 'an importunate beggar' for herself and her

16

chosen friends; that 'the King would fain be rid of her;
and she, as she pretendeth, would fain be gone.'[14]   While
in France she was vexed by various occurrences, and not
least by a plot to poison her daughter—a plot which was
fortunately discovered and frustrated.[15]   At length, bidding her daughter and the French Court farewell, the
Dowager visited her widowed mother at Joinville, and
afterwards sailed from Rouen.[16]   By the 22nd of October
she reached Portsmouth; and in passing through England
was kindly received by Edward,[17] who, it is alleged,
pressed her ' in most effecteous maner' to persuade the
French King to break off the marriage between the
Dauphin and her daughter, in order that 'he mycht
marie hir, according to the first appointment.'[18]   By the
end of November 1551, the Queen Dowager was again in
Scotland.[19]

Mary's education was not neglected in France.   After
making due allowance for the flattery and exaggeration
likely to be evoked in such a case, it is evident enough
that she neither lacked brains nor assiduity.   While
her linguistic attainments were above the average, she
apparently excelled in music, in needlework, in dancing,
and in horsemanship.[20]

The Court of Henry the Second was distinguished for
its learning, its luxury, and its licentiousness.   Writers
of very different schools have, with wondrous unanimity,
denounced its unblushing profligacy.[21]   Hence, no doubt,
the frequent and persistent attempts to minimise Mary's
connection with it; and hence, too, the denial of its
influence over her for evil.[22]   A young and unsuspecting

girl must have incurred grave danger at least, when thrown into such a vortex of vice,[23] where several of the worst sinners were the friends and protectors she was taught to love and honour.[24]

The Cardinal of Lorraine, in writing to the Dowager Queen of Scots, on the 25th of February 1552-3, speaks very highly of her daughter, who, attended by her usual train, was expected at St. Germain with the other lords and ladies. He refers to the advisability of now providing her with an establishment of her own, towards the expense of which he did not expect France to contribute. The postscript of the letter is in the Cardinal's autograph, and thus concludes:—'I forgot not to remind her to keep a guard upon her lips, for really some who are in this Court are so bad in this respect that I am very anxious for her to be separated from them by the forming of an establishment of her own.'[25] It was nearly a year later (9th January 1553-4) before the English Ambassador reported that Mary kept a separate establishment to show that she was of age to govern.[26] This new arrangement, however, did not detach her from the Court. Giovanni Capello, the Venetian Ambassador, mentions, on the 30th of June, that Mary, the Dauphin, and the Princess Elizabeth had been sent to Rheims; and that they were to be followed by Catherine de Medici, who had remained behind because her eldest daughter had been suddenly seized with a slight indisposition. Capello and the English Ambassador were also going to Rheims.[27] It was at this time that Mary there wrote the first four of her *Latin Themes*,

so carefully edited by Montaiglon. The fifth was written
at Compiègne, on the 26th of July; the sixtieth, at St.
Germain, on the 8th of January, 1554-5. This little
volume shows that during that period, Mary was travelling
with the Court from one royal residence to another.[28]
On the 10th of the following March, the Bishop of Ely
and Viscount Montagu, then on their way to Rome, were
received in Catherine de Medici's chamber of presence at
Fontainebleau, by Catherine herself, her two daughters,
and Mary. Next day, Mary very courteously received, in
her own chamber of presence, some in the Ambassadors'
train who wished to see her—calling them her countrymen.[29]

The young Queen of Scots was beloved and befriended
by Diana of Poitiers, who thus wrote to Mary of Guise :
—' As to what concerns the Queen, your daughter, I will
exert myself to do her service more than to my own
daughter, for she deserves it more.'[30]   That Diana
showed her much kindness is certified by Mary herself,
who, in telling her mother in 1555 of the kindness of
her uncles, says :—' It is incredible how careful they are
of me; I do not say less of Madame de Valentinoys.'[31]
Again, in 1557, she writes:—' You know how I am
bound to Madame de Valentinois, to do for her and hers,
for the love which more and more she shows to me.'[32]

The French Parliament had presumed to decide that
Mary having entered her twelfth year, Scotland should
thenceforth be governed in her name, that is, as Teulet
explains it, by French delegates.[33]   In a Parliament held
at Edinburgh, on the 12th of April 1554, the regency

was formally transferred from the Duke of Chatelherault to the Queen Dowager, on whose head— in Knox's opinion—it was as seemly a sight to place a crown 'as to putt a sadill upoun the back of ane unrewly kow.'[35] The head of the Papal Hierarchy in Scotland was even more indignant than the plain-spoken Reformer. Archbishop Hamilton, however, was moved neither by religion nor by patriotism, but by family ambition; and his anger found vent in language more forcible than Knox's, and much less polite.[36]   The Dowager began too soon, as the Bishop of Ross testifies, to follow the counsel of the resident French agents, rather than that of the Scots nobles, who from the first were thus made jealous of her government[37]—a government which, instead of binding Scotland, as Henry the Second expected, more closely to France, was destined to be the means of breaking up the old alliance, and of throwing the Scots into the arms of the English.[38]

The marriage of Mary and the Dauphin, though agreed on before she left Scotland, did not meet with universal approval in France.   On the 30th of December 1550, Sir John Mason, then at Blois, informed the English Council that, among other marriages 'muttered' is that of the Dauphin with the Queen of Scots.[39]   From Tours, on the 10th of the following May, he reported that there had been much consultation concerning this marriage; that the Constable and the Chancellor wished it to be deferred; and that, during the debate, words passed between M. de Guise and the Constable.[40]   The French Ambassador at Brussels threatened, in July 1556, that if

the King of Spain purposed marrying the Archduke
Ferdinand to Elizabeth Tudor, Henry the Second would
give Mary Stuart—though betrothed to the Dauphin—to
Lord Courtenay, to prevent the House of Austria from
establishing itself in England. Two months later, Courtenay's death in Padua disposed for ever of this threat.[1]
In the spring of 1558, 'in the gret hall of the palice of
the Louver,' says Lesley, 'the fianzeillis, utherwyis callit
the hand fastinge,' of 'the excellent young prince Frances'
and Queen Mary—'ane of the farest, most civile and
verteous princes of the hoill world'—was celebrated by
the Cardinal of Lorraine 'with gret solempnitie, triumphe,
and banquating.'[42] This was on Tuesday, the 19th of
April.[43] Next Monday, one who had been present thus
wrote:—' On the day of the hand-giving, after performance of that ceremony, during the first dance, danced
by the princes in company with the King, one of the
dancers being the King of Navarre, he, in the act of
passing before me, whispered in my ear, " Ambassador,
thou this day seest the conclusion of a fact which very
few persons credited until now ": thus confirming what
was said to me a few days ago on the same subject by the
Cardinal of Lorraine, that the King's chief reason for
wishing the marriage to take place was that he might
no longer be pestered, whenever the agreement was discussed, with proposals for some other matrimonial alliance ;
as now, no one could any longer hope to thwart or impede this result, and that they would consequently turn
their thoughts to something else ; hinting also at the Constable amongst the other opponents of the marriage.'[44]

Mary was publicly married to the Dauphin on Sabbath, the 24th of April 1558, in the Cathedral of Notre Dame. Lesley refers to the eloquent and learned sermon, the profuse scattering of gold and silver, the 'magnifique solempniteis,' the sumptuous dinner, the princely dancing, the continued banqueting, and the marriages then made at Court.[45] Giovanni Michiel mentions that 'these nuptials were really considered the most regal and triumphant of any that have been witnessed in this kingdom for many years'—in respect of the personages assembled, the jewels and apparel, the grandeur of the banquet, the stately service of the table, the costly devices of the masquerades and similar revels. 'Nothing whatever that could possibly be desired was wanting for the embellishment of such a spectacle,' he says, 'except jousts and tournaments, which were reserved for a more convenient opportunity, either at the end of the war, or when any agreement shall be made.' 'Henceforth,' he adds, 'the Dauphin will no longer be styled simply "the Dauphin," but "the King Dauphin" (and thus was he proclaimed by the heralds), and the Queen in like manner will be called "the Queen Dauphiness," the two crowns of France and of Scotland being united in their arms.'[46]

The marriage was marked by a transaction of deep duplicity. The Commissioners sent by the Scottish Parliament to France, 'for completing of the mariage of our Soverane Lady with my Lord Dolphin,' were charged with Instructions intended to protect Mary's interests on the one hand, and to safeguard the liberties of her country on the other.[47] Accordingly, for the latter pur-

pose, on the 15th of April—nine days before the marriage
—she acknowledged, over her own seal and signature,
and over those of her curator, the Duke of Guise, that
the Scottish Acts, Articles, and Instructions were for the
evident advantage of herself and her kingdom ; and she
bound herself and her successors, by her 'royal word,'
faithfully to observe and keep the laws, liberties, and
privileges of Scotland, to all the subjects of that kingdom,
as they had been kept by their most illustrious kings.[48]
On the 30th of April—six days after the marriage—a
similar document was signed by Francis and Mary as
'King and Queen of the Scots, Dauphin and Dauphiness
of France.'[49] On the 26th of June, Francis, as King of the
Scots, declared that he not only wished to preserve their
prerogatives, immunities, and ancient liberties intact and
inviolate ; but also to increase, amplify, and strengthen
them.[50] Over and above these documents, Henry and
Francis promised, in their letters-patent of 19th April
1558, that they would maintain the liberties of Scotland ;
and that, should Mary die without issue, the nearest heir
should succeed to the Scots crown without hindrance.[51]

Nevertheless, Mary had been induced, on the 4th of
April, to sign secretly three documents of a very different
kind. In the first of these, in the event of her leaving
no issue, she made over to the King of France, by free
gift, the kingdom of Scotland, and all right which she
had or might have to the kingdom of England. In the
second, with the advice of her uncles—the Cardinal of
Lorraine and the Duke of Guise—she made over to the
French King, in the like event, the kingdom of Scotland,

until he was repaid a million of money, or such other sum as should be found due for the defence of that country. In the third, she referred to the Scottish intention of assigning her kingdom—in default of heirs of her body—to certain lords of the country, as a depriving her of her liberty of disposing of it; and protested that, whatever assent or consent she had given or might give to the Articles and Instructions sent by the Estates of her kingdom, she willed that the dispositions made by her in favour of the kings of France should be valid, and have full effect. This last is signed by Francis as well as by Mary.[52] The young Queen—only in her sixteenth year —probably signed these deeds without fully realising their import. If so, her heedlessness gives a rude shock to the panegyrics of those apologists who speak of her precocity as phenomenal.[53]

CHAPTER III

MARY's marriage-contract not only provided that the
Dauphin should have the title of King of Scotland; but,
in accordance with another of its provisions, the Commissioners, in name of the Scots Estates, swore allegiance to
him during the subsistence of the marriage.[1] This, however, was not enough. The Commissioners were asked to
endeavour to have the Scottish crown immediately sent
to France that the Dauphin might be crowned with it.
Their spirited objection led to a softening of the demand
into a request for the matrimonial crown.[2] The patriotism of the Commissioners was—rightly or wrongly—
supposed to have some connection with the mysterious
malady which effectually prevented four of them from
returning to Scotland.[3] After the Scots Parliament had,
on the 29th of November 1558, signified its satisfaction
with the way in which the Commissioners had discharged
their duties, the four who had returned declared that
Mary wished her Three Estates to consent to her honour-
ing her husband, 'the King Dolphine, with the crowne
matrimoniale be way of gratificatioun during the mariage,

25

without ony maner of prejudice to hir Hienes self, the
successioun of hir body, or lauchfull successioun of hir
blude quhatsumevir; and this crowne to be send with
twa or thre of the lordis of hir realme; to the entent
that the maist Cristin King and King Dolphine, hir
husband, may understand with quhat zele and affectioun
hir subjectis ar myndit to observe and recognos hir said
spous.' The Queen Dowager and Three Estates 'thocht
and declarit the said desire gude and ressonabill and
consentit thairto during the mariage allanerlie'; and
ordained 'A. B. C., or ony of thame, sick as plesis the
Quenis Grace to name,' to go to France 'with the said
crowne to the effect foirsaid allanerlie.'⁴ The crown,
however, was never sent.⁵

On the 17th of November 1558—twelve days before
the Scots Parliament agreed to send the crown to France,
barely seven months after Mary Stuart married the
Dauphin—Mary Tudor died; 'and in hir place,' says the
Bishop of Ross, 'ane beutifull and verteous princess,
Lady Elizabethe, was proclamed Quene of Inglande.'
The Bishop goes on to tell how the French King, considering the claims of his daughter-in-law as 'just
heritour of the realme of Inglande,' had her publicly
proclaimed in Paris as 'Quene of Inglande, Scotlande,
and Ireland,' and caused her and the Dauphin to assume
the English arms.⁶ When the treaty of Château Cam-
brésis was being negotiated (February 1558-9) the
Cardinal of Lorraine and others said they doubted
whether they should treat with any for England, save
with the Dauphin and his wife.⁷ On the 28th of June

1559, two days only before Henry met Montgomery in
the fatal tilt, the Dauphin's band, which began the jousts,
was preceded by two heralds 'fair set out with the King
and Queen Dauphins' arms, with a scutcheon of England
set forth to the show, as all the world might easily
perceive; the same being embroidered with purple velvet
and set out with armory upon their breasts, backs, and
sleeves.'[8]   Henry succumbed to his wound on the 10th
of July;[9] and by next day Throckmorton was informed
that Mary had already written to Scotland that, notwithstanding the malice of her enemies, she was now Queen
of France and Scotland, and trusted to be Queen of
England too.[10]

Even in happy France, Mary had her own share of
illnesses and troubles.   A modern writer, more glowingly
than truly, says :—'There was nothing fragile or hectic
about her; the youthful Mary was hardy as a moun-
taineer, and she seems as a rule to have enjoyed perfect
health.'[11]   Only seven months after her arrival in France,
Sir John Luttrell, the English commander at Broughty
Ferry, heard that she was dead ; but was soon assured
that she was still alive, and had recently recovered from
measles.[12]   In the early part of September 1550, she was
'so dangerously ill of the prevailing flux that her recovery
was doubted.'[13]   About a year later a report reached
Augsburg that she was dead.[14]   In April 1554 the Cardinal informed her mother that she was troubled with a
faintness at the heart; when, to satisfy her good appetite,
she sometimes ate a little too much.[15]   She herself has
recorded that she had toothache on the 29th of the

following November.[16] In 1556 she had a long illness. On the 14th of August the Venetian Ambassador reported that she was 'rather better'; but, on the 23rd of September, he said that she had not ' yet recovered her health.' [17] In November it was stated that she was 'ill of a quartan ague'; but, writing from Poissy on the last day of that month, Wotton informed Mary Tudor that she seemed to be meetly well amended and was soon expected at Court.[18] Before her marriage she had another attack of small-pox. By skilful treatment, however, Fernel — Henry's physician — saved her beauty.[19] In March 1558-9, eleven months after her marriage, Sir John Mason wrote to Cecil :—' The Queen of Scots is very sick, and these men fear she will not long continue. God take her to Him so soon as may please Him.' [20] After seeing her on the 24th of May, Throckmorton wrote :— ' Assuredly, sir, the Scottishe Quene, in myne opinion, loketh very ill on it, very pale and grene, and therewithall short breathed; and it is whispered here amongs them that she cannot long live.' [21] On the 18th of June she was so ill in church that to prevent her swooning they were fain to bring her wine from the altar. Throckmorton had never seen her look so ill before.[22] Three days later she did swoon.[23] Six days afterwards, writing from London, Bishop Quadra informed Philip that Mary was 'suffering from a certain incurable malady.' [24] In August her weakness and sickness daily increased. She was ill after her meals, swooned, and had to be revived ' with *aqua composita* and other things.' [25] Perhaps, as in her girlhood, her appetite was better than her digestion.

In September she felt herself well, 'contrary to her wont';
but, on receiving unwelcome news from Scotland, again
fell sick.[26] Early in October it was reported in Stras-
burg that Francis was suffering from an incurable disease,
and that Mary was in a consumption.[27]   In November
she felt very ill, and looked very pale ;[28] but, in the same
month, declared that she was determined to run the
hart, and for that purpose desired English geldings.[29]   In
December a Scot, named Thomas Stewart, was imprisoned
for, among other things, imprudently wishing that Mary
was in heaven ;[30] and next day she had a narrow escape
in the hunting-field.[31]   When, in April 1560, she heard
of the danger her mother was in, and of the risk there
was of losing Scotland, she refused to be comforted by
her husband, her mother-in-law, or her uncles ; shed
most bitter tears incessantly ; and at length, from anguish
and sorrow, took to her bed.[32]   It was known in France
on the 18th of June, that the Queen Dowager of
Scotland had died in Edinburgh Castle a week before ;
but not until the 28th was the bad news broken to
Mary.[33] Giovanni Michiel, the Venetian Ambassador in
France, testifies that she 'loved her mother incredibly '—
much more than daughters usually do—and showed such
signs of grief that during the greater part of next day
' she passed from one agony to another.' [34]

By this time Mary had been Queen of France for nearly
a year. When Henry the Second died, she lacked five
months of being seventeen, and her puny husband was
fully a year younger. [35]   Catherine de Medici—now
called *la Reine Mère*—took the authority, though not the

name, of Regent; but the government was really in the
hands of Mary's uncles. [36]   Mary, however, was no cipher.
Three days after the death of her father-in-law, Throckmorton wrote from Paris:—'The Quene of Scotland . . .
is a great doer here, and taketh all upon her.'[37]   Already
she had requested the Duchess of Valentinois—now
debarred from the Court—' to make accompt of the French
King's cabenet and of all his jewels.'[38]   Mary was Queen
of France for barely seventeen months—a short period
not devoid of trouble and excitement.   The 'conspiracy
of Amboise' revealed in some degree the power and pluck
of the oppressed Huguenots, as well as their distrust and
detestation of the Guises.[39]   Nor was the dissatisfaction
confined to the persecuted Protestants.[40]

These internal troubles of France enabled the Scots—
with the help of the English [41]—to throw off the tyranny
of their old allies and the yoke of the Papacy.   The
Treaty of Edinburgh—6th of July 1560—provided, *inter
alia*, that all the French soldiers save six score should
leave Scotland; that neither Francis nor Mary should
order peace or war in Scotland without the advice
and consent of the Three Estates; that the members of
Council to be chosen by the Queen should be selected
from twenty-four nominated by the Estates; and that
a Parliament should be speedily summoned.[42]   On the
17th of the following August, this Scottish Parliament
ratified a Protestant *Confession of Faith*, and on the 24th
not only abolished the Pope's jurisdiction, but prohibited
the celebration of mass under pain of death for the third
offence.[43]

It had been foreseen that the power of Mary's uncles was bound up with hers; but it became only too patent when Francis ascended the throne.[44] During his brief reign, Mary and her mother-in-law are frequently associated in the contemporary diplomatic correspondence.[45] If at this time the Guises and their royal niece were hated by Catherine de Medici, the wily Florentine veiled her feelings.[46]

In the middle of November, 1560, the weather, which had been extremely mild, like that of spring, suddenly became bitterly cold. To this was attributed the last illness of the weakly Francis, who had taken no precautions against the change. From the day that he was seized, contradictory rumours were rife regarding him. While, on the one hand, it was reported that he had only taken to his bed to please his mother, whose fears arose from 'too much female tenderness,' it was alleged on the contrary that his malady was serious, that it was underrated by those interested, that his constitution was defective, and that according to an astrological prediction his life would not exceed eighteen years.[47] His real condition was known to few;[48] but, three days before the end came, the Venetian Ambassador learned that he could only live a few hours.[49] A little before midnight on Thursday, the 5th of December, poor Francis passed away.[50] Mere boy though he was, many were ready to rejoice at his death, few to mourn his premature end. While it was openly hailed by the Huguenots of France and the Protestants of Scotland as a providential deliverance from persecution and oppression, it was by others regarded with quiet satisfaction.[51]   It was even suspected that his mother had shortened his days ; [52] and sorrowful as Mary appeared at the time,[53] it was declared long afterwards, by one of her staunchest friends, that, as he understood, she was not innocent in the matter.[54]

CHAPTER IV

1560-1561

MARY, 'immediately upon her husband's death,' says
Throckmorton, 'changed her lodging,[1] withdrew herself
from all company, and became so solitary and exempt
of all worldliness that she doth not to this day [31st
December 1560] see daylight, and so will continue out
forty days.'[2] Her grief may have been as genuine as it
seemed acute and crushing; but, if contemporary rumour
was right, 'the thoughts of widowhood at so early an
age'[3] took at once a practical turn. A few hours after
she lost her husband, Throckmorton was able to tell
what he understood her own feelings to be in the matter
—to marry one who could uphold her greatness.[4] Her
alacrity was probably stimulated, if not caused, by the
knowledge that the statesmen of so many countries were
keenly interested in the matter.[5] Before the forty days
of mourning were ended, Throckmorton had learned that
the Guises were using every effort to marry her to Don
Carlos ; and that the King of Navarre and the Constable
were doing their utmost for Arran.[6] Three days after her
period of seclusion had expired, Throckmorton reported

c

that she was presently sending four of her gentlemen
to Scotland to obtain the consent of her Estates ' to
marry where and whom she lists,' notwithstanding the
clause to the contrary in her contract with Francis.[7]   By
the 23rd of February, Bishop Quadra was able to inform
Philip that Lady Margaret Lennox was trying to marry
her son—the youthful Darnley—to the Queen of Scots,
and was not without hope of success.[8]   It does not appear
that Mary's thoughts of another marriage lowered her
in Throckmorton's eyes.   On the contrary, several of his
statements show that in the early days of her widowhood she rose greatly in his estimation.[9]

Within two or three days after the forty of mourning
were ended, Mary removed two leagues out of Orleans,
where she was visited every other day by the King, the
Queen-mother, and the Princes of the Court.   There, too,
the Spanish Ambassador and his wife were very often with
her.[10]   Up to this time at least, if her letters-patent are
to be trusted, she was still on good terms with her
mother-in-law.[11]   The Court left Orleans on the 3rd of
February for Fontainebleau;[12] and when Bedford and
Throckmorton arrived there on the 16th, Catherine
directed the Duke of Guise to conduct them to Mary's
chamber, where they found her ' with the Bishop of
Amiens and divers other French bishops, and many
gentlemen and ladies.'   Bedford having conveyed Elizabeth's commendations, letters, and condolence unto her,
' she answered, with a very sorrowful look and speech,
that she thanked the Queen for her gentleness in comforting her woe when she had most need of it; and con-

sidering that the Queen now shows the part of a good
sister, whereof she has great need, she will endeavour to
be even with her in goodwill; and though she be not so
able as another, yet she trusts that the Queen will take
her goodwill in good part.'[13] Bedford and Throckmorton had interviews with Mary again on the 18th and
19th, when they desired her to ratify the Treaty of Edinburgh. It was in vain, however, that they reiterated and
pressed this desire. No doubt the Duke of Guise was at
hand; but she had not the Cardinal of Lorraine, nor any
of her Scots nobles to advise with, and on this plea she
firmly, though courteously, declined.[14] She did not leave
the Court quite so soon after this as she had intended; and
for her 'stay' the Earl of Bedford took credit.[15] Not
until after the middle of March did she quit Fontainebleau;[16] and scarcely had she left ere an Ambassador
from Denmark arrived with a proposal to marry her to
his King.[17] Reaching Paris on the 20th, she spent a day
there examining her robes and jewels,[18] and then, accompanied by the Archbishop of Glasgow, the Abbot of
Dunfermline, and D'Oysel, she 'took her way straight
towards Rheims.'[19] On arriving there, on the 26th of
March, she was received by her uncles—the Cardinals of
Lorraine and Guise, the Duke D'Aumale, and the Marquis D'Elbœuf—and her grandmother, the old Duchess
of Guise. There, too, was the Duchess of Arschot, who
had come eight days before on purpose to meet the young
widow—an indication to Throckmorton that there might
be something on hand for the Prince of Orange, as the
Duchess was his sister.[20] For Mary's hand, rumour was

industriously supplying other candidates, likely and unlikely. Failing Arran — whom it was said she had
definitely resolved to reject—many of the Scots preferred
the reputedly 'wise and virtuous' King of Sweden to
the 'dissolute and insolent' King of Denmark, albeit a
Protestant.[21] There were, besides, the Prince of Spain,[22]
the Duke of Ferrara,[23] and the Emperor's sons—Charles
and Ferdinand.[24] If Mary and her uncles were anxious
to select the one who could best uphold her greatness,
her mother-in-law and Elizabeth Tudor were as anxious
to checkmate her, should the future interests of their
respective countries appear to be imperilled.[25]

In April, Mary was on her way from Rheims to Nancy
in Lorraine, when she was waited on by two representative Scots—John Lesley, afterwards Bishop of Ross ;
and the Lord James, afterwards the Regent Murray. By
Lesley's own account, he first met her at Vitry on the
14th, while the Lord James only overtook her next day
at St. Dizier, or, as Lesley's translator quaintly renders it,
'the toune of haly desyre.'[26] From these chosen representatives of the old Church party and of the Protestant,
she received very different counsel. The burden of
Lesley's advice—backed up by the strongest arguments
he could urge—was that she should beware of the Lord
James, who was attacking the Catholic religion in every
way with the intention of utterly overthrowing it, and
had even cast his eye on her crown. She ought either to
detain him in France until she had personally ordered
matters in Scotland ; or she should land at Aberdeen,
where her Catholic nobles would meet her, and with twenty

thousand men convoy her to Edinburgh.[27] Dalrymple
makes Lesley assure Mary that they expected her, when
she returned to Scotland, to 'ouerschadwe' them 'with
her presence'; and, like a new-risen sun, 'to skail and
skattir the cloudis of al tumulte schortlie fra the myndes
of her subjectes.'[28] Lesley's diplomacy and representa-
tions, however, were practically fruitless. If the Lord
James, by his apparent frankness and sincerity, did not
win her entire confidence, she resolved at least to follow
his advice on some points, and to recognise the Protestant
party for a time.[29] In connection with this episode,
much abuse—as virulent as unmerited—has been showered
upon the Lord James.[30]

Three of Mary's uncles—the Cardinals of Lorraine and
Guise, and the Duke D'Aumale—accompanied her to
Nancy;[31] and he who was afterwards to prove her evil-
genius is said to have been also in her train, but the
evidence for this is not satisfactory.[32] On the borders
of Lorraine, she was received by Christina of Denmark,
niece of Charles the Fifth, and by her son Charles, the
young Duke of Lorraine, who, with 'ane honorabill companye,' convoyed her to Nancy, 'his principall citye and
strenth.' For her entry, 'ane magnifique triumphe' had
been made; the cannons on the city walls were discharged; and by her sister-in-law, the young Duchess of
Lorraine, she was heartily welcomed.[33] Various reasons
have been assigned for this lengthened journey—to avoid
her mother-in-law,[34] to see her kinsfolk and friends,[35] to
enjoy that quiet rest which could only be found in a
community of religious women,[36] to attend the baptism of

De Vaudemont's young child,[37] to lament the death of her mother and husband,[38] and to arrange for another marriage.[39] In Nancy her time was spent pleasantly enough, for there she ' was weill intertenit, sumtymes in hunting on the feildis, and uther quhills seing and behalding plesant farces and playes, and using all kinde of honorabill pastymes within the palice.'[40] Despite the farces and festivities, Mary was seized with a tertian fever, of which when her grandmother heard she hastened to her, and by easy stages took her back to Joinville,[41] which she was unable to leave until the latter part of May, when she went to Rheims, but not in time for the coronation of Charles the Ninth.[42] Not until the 10th of June did she arrive in Paris, there receiving an honourable welcome from the King, his mother, and the nobles.[43]

In vain had Throckmorton sent Somer to Nancy after Mary in April, in vain had he sent him to Rheims in May.[44] Now that she was within his own reach, he lost little time in waiting upon her—hopeless as the object seemed[45]—again to demand the ratification of the Treaty of Edinburgh. When he had audience, on the 18th of June, she told him that she was not yet in perfect health; but it was quite apparent that she had all her wits about her. With becoming candour she informed him that she meant to delay her resolute answer until she had the advice of the Estates and nobles of her own realm; that she intended going there very shortly, embarking at Calais;[46] that she was to send D'Oysel[47] to Elizabeth, with a message which she trusted would satisfy her, and to require of her those favours that princes use to do in such cases. Beyond this she would not commit herself, though she assured him that she was desirous of amity with Elizabeth. In the course of this conversation, she declared that she did not intend to constrain any of her subjects in matters of religion, and hoped that his Queen would not help them to constrain her.[48] When D'Oysel reached the English Court he was promptly, if not angrily, informed by Elizabeth that she would not grant Mary a safe-conduct unless she ratified the Treaty of Edinburgh; and he was requested—instead of proceeding to Scotland—to go back to France with this message.[49] Keen as Elizabeth had been, and still was, to secure the ratification, this refusal of a passport was no mere device on her part to extort the reluctant approval of a document which might weaken Mary's claim to the English crown. Elizabeth and her Council had thought —as did Throckmorton and the Lord James—that Mary should be encouraged to return to her own country, in the interests of England as well as of Scotland;[50] but now they found, or thought they found, that the prospect of her speedy return was exciting such feelings beyond the Tweed that her stay in France should, if possible, be prolonged.[51]

Meanwhile, Mary had had another attack of tertian fever at the French Court; and when Throckmorton saw her there, on the 9th of July, he perceived that it had 'somewhat appaired her cheer,' though she made 'no great matter of it, the worst being past.' He also perceived that she was very desirous of her safe-conduct.

39

' She prayed him as soon as he had word of it to advertise
her, and said that her going would be about the beginning of August.'[52]   He understood she was to go by
Fécamp, ' to make her mother's funeral, and from thence
to Calais to embark.'[53]   It was eight days later before
Throckmorton received Elizabeth's reply; and Mary,
who was at Dampierre with her uncles, appointed him an
audience on the 20th at St. Germain.[54]   For this audience,
as for previous ones, she was doubtless well primed by the
Guises.[55]   Throckmorton found that as usual she was
prompt and sagacious, courteous but inflexible.   She
regretted that she had asked a passport which she did
not require.   Had she not reached France in safety
despite the attempt of the late King[56] of England to
intercept her? and she might have as good means to
help her home again.   It was useless of Elizabeth to say
that if she ratified the Treaty she would not only get a
free passage, but would be welcome to pass through
England.   How could she ratify it at present?   She was
bound neither in honour nor conscience to perform what
her late husband had commanded.   Since his death the
French Council had ceased to advise her, and her uncles[57]
were standing aside.   Elizabeth herself had said that she
ought rather to follow the counsel of her own realm ;
and now when she wished to hasten home, that the
matter might be so answered, the Queen of England tried
to prevent her.   She, the Queen of Scots, had never done
Elizabeth wrong in word or deed, nor meant her harm ;
and did not ' practise' with her subjects, though some of
them were ' inclined enough to hear offers.'   As for the

IV]   THE SAFE-CONDUCT

assumption of the English arms and title, that was done by the order of her husband and father-in-law; and since their death she had neither borne the arms nor used the title.[58]

Next day, Catherine de Medici informed Throckmorton that she not only approved of Mary's decision regarding the ratification; but that both she and the King, her son, were sorry that Elizabeth had refused the safe-conduct; and hinted that such a refusal might prove a cause of war. On the same day, after seeing the King of Navarre and the Constable, Throckmorton repaired again to Mary—professedly to take his leave of her—in reality that he 'might the better decypher' whether she meant 'to continue her voyage.' She frankly addressed him thus:—' *Monsieur l'Ambassadour*, if my preparations were not so much advanced as they are, peradventure the Queen your Mistriss's unkindness might stay my voyage; but now I am determined to adventure the matter, whatsoever come of it: I trust the wind will be so favourable as I shall not need to come on the coast of England; and if I do, then, *Monsieur l'Ambassadour*, the Queen your Mistriss, shall have me in her hands to do her will of me; and if she be so hard-hearted as to desire my end, she may then do her pleasure, and make sacrifice of me; peradventure that casualty might be better for me than to live: in this matter God's will be fulfilled.'[59]

It was on the 25th of July that Mary left St. Germain, taking 'hir leif of the King, Quene, and hoill nobilitie, with gret honour, favorabill and loving interteinment,

and most frendlie amyte.'[60]   There was still some
mystery as to the port from which she would sail.
Some indeed thought that even yet she would not go
at all, though 'all her stuff' was 'sent down to the sea.'
It was deemed probable that she would go to Calais,
'there to hover and hearken'; and, according to Elizabeth's doings, go or stay.[61]   On the 3rd of August, she
was yet at Beauvais waiting the return of one of Navarre's
secretaries who had been sent to England.[62]   As she
wished to see Throckmorton again, he followed her to
Abbeville, where he found her on the 7th; and there he
again took his leave of her next afternoon, after which
'she rode five leagues' in the evening[63] to the abbey of
Forest Monstrier.   She had determined to send the Lord
of St. Colms and Arthur Erskine to Elizabeth, as she
meant to take nothing unkindly at her hands, and was
content to 'redoubbe' and amend past faults.[64]   It was
suspected that there was a trick in this final appeal, and
that she intended to embark without awaiting Elizabeth's
response.[65]   If a device, it was successful; the safe-
conduct was at length obtained, but Mary had sailed
without it.[66]   In the hurry and anxiety of departure, she
had forgotten to give Throckmorton a parting present;
but hers was no niggardly nature, and the temporary
oversight was speedily and amply atoned for.[67]

Of her six uncles who had accompanied her to Calais,[68]
three—the Duke D'Aumale, the Grand Prior, and the
Marquis D'Elbœuf—embarked with her for Scotland, as
did also 'many ladies and gentillwomen, speciale the four
maidis of honour quha passit with hir Hienes in France,

of hir awin aige, bering the name everie ane of Marie.'[69]
About noon on Thursday, the 14th of August, one of
Throckmorton's servants saw her galleys and ships leaving
Calais.[70] 'Fra that'—says Lesley, who was with her—
'making saill, and rowing throw the seys with prosperous
weddir, bot allwayis (as God wald haif it) covered with
mist all the way,[71] so that the Quene of Inglandis shippis,
quha was awating upoun that pray, culd nevir gett sicht
of the gallayis quhill thay war past the coist of Ingland,[72]
and happely arrivit in the raid of Leith with all hir
Majesteis cumpanye.'[73]

Though the real author of the touching lines, beginning

      'Adieu, plaisant pays de France,'

has been frequently pointed out,[74] they are still per-
sistently attributed to Mary by those who ought to know
better.[75]

CHAPTER V

1561

ON Tuesday morning, the 19th of August,[1] Mary arrived in Leith Road. She landed in the forenoon, and, after resting a short time in ' Andro Lambis hous,'[2] was convoyed to Holyrood Palace.[3] She had not been expected so soon,[4] but the cannons of the galleys soon brought out crowds of people, and the enthusiasm of her reception is vouched for by writers of all shades.[5] The staid Scots did not confine their expressions of welcome to crowding and gazing. ' Fyres of joy,' says Knox, ' war sett furth all nyght, and a cumpany of the most honest, with instrumentis of musick, and with musitians, geve thair salutationis at hir chalmer wyndo. The melody (as sche alledged) lyked hir weill; and sche willed the same to be contineued some nightis after.'[6] If Mary appreciated the melody, the gay Brantôme, who had come in her train, certainly did not. He complains bitterly that, when she wished to go to bed in the evening, five or six hundred knaves of the town came under her window, with wretched fiddles and small rebecs,[7] and sung psalms so badly and out of tune that nothing could be worse.[8]

44

Not content with bonfires and music as expressions of their joy, the Magistrates and Town Council of Edinburgh, with the deacons of the crafts, entertained the Queen's uncles to a banquet, on Sabbath, the last day of August. They also gave her an enthusiastic reception at her entry into the city on Tuesday, the 2nd of September.[9] After dining in the Castle at mid-day, she rode down the Castle Hill, where she was met by a convoy of fifty young townsmen disguised as Moors, their bodies and thighs covered with ' yeallow taffateis,' their arms bare and blackened, as were also their legs from the knees downwards, black hats on their heads, ' blak visouris ' on their faces, rings garnished with ' intellable precious staneis ' in their mouths, and chains of gold round their necks, arms, and legs. A pall of ' fyne purpour velvet lynit with reid taffateis, freinyiet with gold and silk,' was carried over her head by a band of ' the maist honest men of the toun, cled in velvot gownis and velvot bonettis.' A cart followed with ' certane bairnes ' and a coffer containing ' the copburd and propyne ' for her Grace. Preceded by the nobles and mock Moors she reached the Butter Tron, where, on a temporary wooden gateway, ' certane barneis ' sung ' in the maist hevinlie wyis '; and, as she passed through this painted port, a cloud opened from which ' ane bony barne . . . discendit doun as it had bene ane angell, and deliverit to hir Hienes the keyis of the toun, togidder with ane Bybill and ane Psalme Buik coverit with fyne purpourit velvot.'[10]   On a double stage at the Tolbooth were four fair virgins, ' in maist precious attyrement,' representing the virtues.   At the Cross there were

45

other ' four fair virgynnis cled in maist hevenlie clething,'
and from the spouts of the Cross itself wine ran in
abundance.   At the Salt Tron, Korah, Dathan, and
Abiram were burned on a scaffold;[11] and at the Nether
Bow a dragon suffered the same fate.   Besides the loud
hum of the great crowd, sounds of many kinds greeted
Mary's ears in her triumphal procession.   As she left the
Castle ' the artailyerie schot vehementlie,' at various stages
there were speeches, recitations, and psalm-singing, at
the Cross there was ' the noyiss of pepill casting the
glassis with wine.'   Having at length reached Holyrood,[12] ' the bairneis, quhilk was in the cairt with the
propyne, maid some speitche concernyng the putting
away of the mess'; and the honest men desired her to
receive the ' copeburd quhilk wes double ourgilt.'   She
returned thanks for the gift, which had cost the donors
two thousand merks, ' and sua the honest men and convoy' returned to Edinburgh.[13]

This display of Edinburgh enthusiasm was not rendered
less remarkable by the unpremeditated outburst by which
it was preceded.   As a contemporary chronicler has it, the
Lords of the Congregation were ' grittumlie annoyit' at
Mary's causing mass to be said in the chapel of Holyrood
House,[14] on the first Sabbath after her arrival.   Until
that morning there was, says Knox, nothing save ' myrth
and quyetness'; but the ominous preparations pierced
the hearts and loosened the tongues of the faithful, who
exclaimed :—' Shall that idoll be suffered agane to tack
place within this realm ?   It shall not ! '   The Master of
Lindsay, the Fife gentlemen, and others cried out in the

court-yard, that the idolatrous priest should die the death.
The servant who carried in the candles was 'evill effrayed';
and no wonder, for one in the crowd seized and broke the
candles, or, as one writer says, pulled them and some
other altar ornaments from the bearer, ' and trode them
in the myre.' No Frenchman or Papist ventured a
whisper in defence of the service; but the Lord James
—'whom all the godlye did most reverence'—took
charge of the chapel door, and kept the vehement Protestants outside. There were few inside with her Majesty
save her uncles and her household; yet the English Ambassador reported that the French priest who officiated
was almost overcome with nervous fear, 'when he had
his god at the highest.' After the service, he was, to
the scandal of Knox, convoyed to his chamber by two
Protestants—the Lord John and the Lord Robert, the
respective commendators of Coldingham and Holyrood,
the Queen's natural brothers. In the afternoon great
companies of the people went to the Abbey, and made it
known that they could not abide the re-introduction of
the mass.[15]

This comedy occurred on St. Bartholomew's day, eleven
years before the tragedy which has for ever rendered that
day memorable. The results of this Scottish St. Bartholomew's—when royal wax-candles were sacrificed un-
canonically—were immediately apparent. Next day, 25th
August, Mary issued a Proclamation declaring that she
intended, as soon as convenient, with the advice of her
Estates to take a final order, which she hoped would
content all, for pacifying the differences in religion;

and meanwhile, to prevent tumult or sedition, charging
her lieges 'that nane of thame tak upoun hand, privatlie
or oppinlie, to mak ony alteratioun or innovatioun of the
state of religioun, or attempt ony thing aganis the forme,
quhilk hir Majestie fand publict and universalie standing
at hir Majesteis arrivall in this hir realme, under the
pane of deid'; and further commanding, by advice of
her Privy Council, 'that nane of thame tak upoun hand
to molest or trouble ony of hir domestic servandis or
personis quhatsumevir, cumit furth of France in hir
Grace's cumpany at this tyme, in word, ded, or countenance, for ony cause quhatsumevir, either within hir
Palice or outwith . . . under the said pane of deid.'[16]
When this Proclamation was first made at Edinburgh,
Arran publicly protested against the Queen's servants
being allowed under its shelter, to say, participate in,
or defend the mass, any more than if they had committed murder, 'seing the ane is mekle mair abhomin-
able and odiouse in the syght of God then is the other.'[17]
Despite the vigour of Arran's protest, Mary re-issued this
Proclamation on various occasions, and on the 23rd of
May 1567—eight days after her marriage with Bothwell,
'hir derrest husband'—she refers to it as having, more
than anything, nourished the public quietness and kept
her subjects in due obedience.[18]

Indignant as the Lords of the Congregation were at
Mary's first mass, her blandishments soon took the 'fyre-
edge' off their zeal; there being about her, as the godly
Kinyeancleuch supposed, 'some inchantment whareby
men ar bewitched.' Next Sabbath, Knox, 'inveighing

against idolatrie,' said ' that one messe (thair war no mo
suffered at the first) was more fearful to him then gif ten
thousand armed enemyes war landed in any pairte of
the realme, of purpose to suppress the hoill religioun.'
But those who were then guiding the Court mocked his
fear as unfounded, and his warning as ' a verray un-
tymelie admonitioun.'[19]   Before Mary left France, Throckmorton understood that she regarded Knox as the most
dangerous man in her realm, and that she was determined
to banish him, or else assure her people that she would
not dwell in the country while he was there.[20]   Now she
sent for the uncompromising Reformer, and he has preserved a graphic account of this their first interview.[21]
With him there was no toleration of evil; no dubiety as
to ' the Quenis Kirk ' being ' that Romane harlot '; no
hesitation as to the right of the people to deprive their
princes of the sword; when in blind zeal they would
murder God's children.[22]   With her it was a grievous
fault that he had taught the people a religion the princes
could not allow ; nor could that religion be of God,
seeing He commands subjects to obey their princes.
With her there was no doubt as to the Kirk she ought
to nourish—not that of Knox, but that of Rome—as
' the treu Kirk of God.'   In this first encounter with
Knox, Mary learned something of the difficulties which
stood in her way.   He too formed an opinion of her
—an opinion which he never relinquished—' If thair be
not in hir a proud mynd, a crafty witt, and ane indurat
hearte against God and his treuth, my judgment faileth
me.'[23]   For his outspoken faithfulness at this and sub-

D   49

sequent interviews, the Reformer has been bitterly blamed on the one hand, and highly extolled on the other.[24] There are learned men and cultured women who fail to find that rude insolence on his part with which he has been so often charged.[25]

It was at this time that Randolph assured Cecil that the voice of Knox was able in one hour to put more life in them than five hundred trumpets continually blustering in their ears.[26] And yet, with all his sternness and remorseless logic, so anxious was he for the public peace, so loth to offend the leaders of whom he had formed a good opinion, that, instead of encouraging the zealous 'to put thair handis to the Lordis work,' he endeavoured 'to slokin' in them 'that fervencye that God had kyndled.'[27] Within a few weeks he was accusing himself that he 'did not mor zelouslie gainstand that idol at the first erecting';[28] and afterwards he acknowledged that in this he had 'done most wickedlie.'[29] The cause of Knox's self-reproach shows the sincerity and intensity of his convictions. Though he had privately advised earnest and zealous men to refrain from forcibly opposing the celebration of mass, he had never ceased to witness against and denounce the rite both in private and in public. Had he not at his first interview with Mary—a week after her arrival[30]—characterised it as 'an abominatioun befoir God'? Had he not condemned it next Sabbath from the pulpit with all that vehemency of language of which he was such a master?

On the 8th of September, a doctor of the Sorbonne preaching before Mary 'spoke more good words of the

mass than it was worth '; [31] but, if the echo of his words
was heard beyond the walls of Mary's chapel, it did not
render his contention palatable. The Act and Proclamation of the 25th of August had been penned and put
in form by Protestants; 'for,' says Knox, 'in the Counsall then had Papistis neather power nor vote.'[32] The
Lords had thus shown themselves amenable to her influence; but the municipal rulers of Edinburgh had,
eight days afterwards, mingled with the display of their
enthusiastic loyalty to her unmistakable demonstrations
of their hostility to her religion. Soon she was to witness
demonstrations of a somewhat similar kind in other
Scottish towns; soon to have fresh proof of the influence
of Knox's doctrine in her metropolis.

After spending three weeks in Holyrood she set out
for Linlithgow,[33] which two days later she left for
Stirling, where she narrowly escaped being smothered in
bed—a lighted candle having set the curtains and tester
on fire while she was asleep.[34] Short as was her stay in
Stirling it was marked by another incident. On Sabbath
the 14th of September her 'devout chaplains' intended to
sing high mass in the Chapel-Royal: but 'the Earl of
Argile and the Lord James so disturbed the quire, that
some, both priests and clerks, left their places with
broken heads and bloody ears. It was a sport alone for
some that were there to behold it. Others there were
that shed a tear or two, and made no more of the
matter.'[35]   At Perth 'thair wes ane honourable entrie
maid to hir.' But although 'she was well received and
presented with a heart of gold full of gold,' yet 'she liked

nothing the pageants there; they did too plainly condemn the errors of the world. As she rode in the street
she fell sick, and was borne from her horse into her
lodging, not being far off, with such sudden passions as
. . . she is often troubled with after any great unkindness or grief of mind.'[36] From Perth she went to
Dundee, 'quhair she was honourablie ressavit,' and presented with a 'princely propyne.' There, however, she
appears to have been offended by the insanitary condition
of the town; for 'when the council met a few days
afterwards, their first business was to promulgate an
imperative edict against the middens, and to order the
officers to inspect them daily under heavy penalties.'[37]
When in St. Andrews, on Sabbath, the 21st of September,
there seems to have been a religious squabble of some
kind, for a rumour reached Edinburgh that a priest had
been slain.[38] All these towns, says Knox, 'sche polluted
with hir idolatrie.'[39]

By the end of September the Queen was back in Holyrood. 'She hath beene in hir progresse, and hath considered the mindes of the people for the most part to be
repugnant to her devilish opinioun; and yitt in her
appeareth no amendement, but an obstinat proceeding
frome evill to worse.'[40] So Knox wrote on Thursday,
the 2nd of October. That very day the magistrates,
town council, and deacons of crafts took a step at which,
in the words of a contemporary, 'the Quenis Grace
was verry commovit.'[41] They re-issued a Proclamation,
which they had made in her name six months before
—'chargeing all monkis, freris, preistis, nonnys, adul-

teraris, fornicatouris, and all sic filthy personis to remove thameselffis of this toun and boundis thairof within xxiiij houris, under the pane of carting throuch the toun, byrning on the cheik, and banessing the samyn for evir.' The Queen showed how 'verry commovit' she was by promptly sending a macer to the Town Council, with her written order 'to convene incontinent,' to deprive the provost and bailies of their office, and to choose others in their room.⁴² A counter Proclamation was made that the town should be patent to all the Queen's lieges. 'And so,' says the relentless Knox, 'murtheraris, adulteraris, theavis, hooris, drunkardis, idolateris, and all malefactouris, gatt protectioun under the Quenis wyngis, under that cullour, becaus thai war of hir religion. And so gatt the Devill fredome agane, whair that befoir he durst nott have bene sene in the day-lyght upoun the commoun streatis.' ⁴³

Mary might depose her magistrates, she might order them into ward, she might throw open her city-gates to all her lieges, but she could not overcome the repugnance of her people to the central rite of her church. A few days later Randolph writes :—'Her masse is terrible in all men's eyes.' ⁴⁴ On All Hallow day (1st of November) she had 'a songe masse.' That night one of her priests was rewarded with a sound beating by one of Lord Robert's servants.⁴⁵ The 'myscheivous solempnitie' of this celebration—apparently her first high mass—so roused the preachers that the nobles were 'sufficientlie admonished of thair dewiteis,' duties which they were loth to lay to heart. A meeting of the leaders of

Church and State was held in the house of the Clerk
Register to consider the question—Whether subjects
might suppress the idolatry of their Prince. In the
midsummer of 1564 the same practical question was to
be again discussed, and again the discussion was to
prove abortive. While the statesmen contended that the
Queen's subjects could neither take the mass from her
nor punish her as an idolatress, they were apparently at one
with the preachers as to the idolatry of the mass itself.[46]
This national abhorrence of the mass was manifested not
only in the Acts of Parliament, in the Proclamations of
the magistrates,[47] in the declamations of the preachers,
but in the phraseology of the lawyers,[48] and in the
popular ballads of the people. The sarcasm of the latter
was biting enough :—

> ' Give* God was maid of bittis of breid,
>   Eit ye nocht ouklie† sax or sevin,
> As it had bene ane mortall feid,‡
>   Quhill§ ye had almaist heryit Hevin?
> Als mony Devillis ye man devoir,||
>   Quhill Hell grow les.
> Or doutles we dar nocht restoir
>   Yow to your Mes.

> ' Give God be transubstantiall
>   In breid with *Hoc est corpus meum,*
> Quhy war ye sa unnaturall
>   As tak him in your teith, and sla him?
> Tripairtit and devydit him
>   At your dum dress ;
> Bot God knawis how ye gydit him,
>   Mumling your Mes.' [49]

---

* If.   † Weekly.   ‡ Feud.   § Till. || Must devour.

54

Before setting out for France to see his widowed Queen and sister, the Lord James had been warned that if he agreed to her having the mass, either publicly or privately in Scotland, he would thereby betray the cause of God and expose religion to the utmost danger. He declared that he would never consent to her having it publicly; but who, he asked, could hinder her from having it secretly in her own chamber.[50] On the Lord James and on Lethington, Knox laid the chief responsibility of tolerating the Queen's mass.[51] That the Act and Proclamation of 25th August might be passed, it had been urged upon recalcitrants that she should be so far humoured for a little, in the hope that by and by she would be won to Protestantism[52]—a hope which some continued to entertain for a considerable time.[53] Knox, however, was not deceived. As he put it, the Cardinal of Lorraine's lessons were so deeply imprinted on her heart that the substance and the quality were like to perish together;[54] or, as the most picturesque of modern historians has it, she returned to her country ' to throw herself alone into the midst of the most turbulent people in Europe, . . . to use her charms as a spell to win them back to the Catholic church, . . . prepared to wait, to control herself, to hide her purpose till the moment came to strike; yet with a purpose resolutely formed to trample down the Reformation.'[55] This view has been laboriously, though unsuccessfully, contested[56] by one who has hazarded the reckless opinion that Mary was deterred from becoming a Protestant by Knox's narrowness, superstition, and fierce intolerance.[57] In returning to Scotland, her contemporary co-religionists gave her full credit for at least desiring to restore the old faith.[58] And, if she herself is to be believed, she never thought of becoming a Protestant, but steadily aimed at the recovery of her people from 'the new opinions and damnable errors' into which they had plunged.[59]

Before Mary's return, a 'knawin messe-mongare or pestilent Papist' durst not publicly show himself in any reformed town in Scotland.[60] If for the relaxation of such stringent Protestantism, Knox rates the nobles as backsliders, Lesley, on the other hand, praises these heretics for their clemency, saying that, 'at that time they exiled few Catholics on the score of religion, imprisoned fewer, and put none to death.'[61] This clemency was due more to Mary's personal influence than to any mere reluctance to inflict the penalties of the law, as was manifest at the Justice Court of Jedburgh, three months after her return, when more than a score of lawless Borderers were hanged right off, and twice as many brought to Edinburgh.[62]

In France, Mary had known something of popular tumult, as well as of religious bitterness; and in her own country she was not to escape the one any more than the other. The Scots of those days were a rude and ready people, impatient of restraint, and prompt to vindicate their privileges against magistrates or others who had the temerity to encroach upon them. On the very day of Mary's arrival, on her way to Holyrood, she was met by the triple-dyed 'rebellis of the craftis,' on whom she exercised her gentle prerogative of mercy, although in

56

their most recent riot—only a month before—they had
broken down the gallows on which a fellow-craftsman
was to be hanged, thrown open the prison doors, for five
hours besieged and assailed the provost and bailies in
the Tolbooth with stones, guns, and other weapons, and
extorted from their beleaguered rulers a written promise
that they would not prosecute them for their mis-
deeds.[63]

The unruly ' craftis childer '—the servants and appren-
tices of the craftsmen—were not allowed to monopolise
the pastime of fighting in the streets of the capital.
When, three months before the Queen's return, the
magistrates heard that there was ' sum variance ' among
the nobles then expected ' with greit companeis,' it was
deemed prudent to enlist ' thre score able men, hag-
buttaris,' to attend the provost and bailies night and
day.[64] Four months after her arrival, Edinburgh was
alarmed—the godly citizens horror-struck—by the out-
rageous invasion of Cuthbert Ramsay's house under
silence of night by D'Elbœuf, the Lord John, and
Bothwell. The outrage was quickly followed by a tumult
in which much blood would doubtless have been spilt had
it not been for the well-timed and vigorous action of
the Lord James, Argyll, and Huntly.[65] Even in Holyrood itself, Mary did not always feel secure. She had
been barely three months in Scotland when one Sabbath
evening, before she retired to bed, there was a sudden
alarm in the palace—the Lord James was at Jedburgh
taking order with the Borderers, and Edinburgh ' was
packed and pestered with Papists '—a rush was made to

arms, a watch set, and scouts sent forth. No sufficient
cause for the alarm could then be discovered—nothing
beyond a vague and apparently ill-founded rumour that
Arran had ' come over the water with a stark company'
to carry off the Queen. It afterwards transpired that he
had been heard to ask, ' Why is it not as easy to take
her out of the Abbey, as once it was intended to have
been done unto her mother?'[66] Towards the end of the
following March, Bothwell and Arran—who had long
been at bitter enmity, ' and could not be accorded by
all the means their Sovereign could devise'—were at
Bothwell's desire reconciled by Knox. Mary was justly
suspicious of their demonstrative friendship, and took
steps to obtain intelligence of their doings. Suddenly
and unexpectedly, Arran declared that Bothwell had
suggested that the Lord James and Lethington should
be slain, and the Queen forcibly taken to Dumbarton.
The heir of the House of Hamilton was evidently in a
frenzy ; but Bothwell was compromised by his own confession, and by the last day of the month both were in
ward.[67]

Notwithstanding the undying antipathy of the ardent
Protestants to the mass, the inflammable nature of the
rascal multitude, the fierce and fiery characteristics of
some of the nobles, and the evil designs of the frenzied
or too aspiring ones, the days of the youthful Queen were
not mainly spent in dread or displeasure. At the first
anniversary of her husband's death, the Scottish Court
seems to have been particularly joyous. On Sabbath,
the 30th of November, ' the Lord Robert, the Lord John,

58

and others ran at the ring, six against six, disguised
and apparelled, the one half like women, the other like
strangers, in strange masking garments. The Marquis
[D'Elbœuf] that day did very well; but the women,
whose part the Lord Robert did sustain, won the ring.
The Queen herself beheld it, and as many others as
listed.'[68] Next Saturday, she solemnly celebrated the
exequies of poor Francis;[69] and on the following day,
there was 'mirth and pastime upon the Sands of Leith.'
Here again there seems to have been running at the
ring; and here again Mary seems to have been present,
as Randolph rather irreverently expressed it, ' to signify
the sorrow of her heart after her soul-mass.'[70]   Four
days before and four days after that mass her mirth
is specially mentioned.[71]   Whatever the douce magistrates—who had so paternally warned the 'craftis childer'
of ' the punisment threatnit in Goddis word upoun the
braikaris of the Saboth'[72]—thought of these public
breaches of the fourth commandment, they at all events,
like honest men, wished to see their young Queen happy,
as is proved by the nature of their New-Year's gift—
three tuns of the best wine that could be got, irrespec-
tive of cost, and torches to boot.[73]   Even the Master of
Lindsay—who had so uncompromisingly withstood her
first mass at Holyrood—did not disdain, in her garden at
St. Andrews, to shoot with her at the butts against the
Lord James (then Earl of Mar) and one of her ladies.[74]
She was fond also of hawking and hunting;[75] and, if
her accusers are to be believed, when she ought to have
been wailing in secret, she played openly at golf and pall

mall.[76]   Her pleasures, however, were not confined to out-
door sports.   While in the Council Chamber—surrounded
by her Lords anxiously discussing the affairs of State—
her deft and nimble fingers were sometimes engaged in
congenial needlework.[77]   She had a good library, and
after dinner frequently read Latin with Buchanan.[78]   She
delighted in music;[79] and, as Knox has recorded, did
not neglect dancing.[80]   She played at cards,[81] at 'biles'
or billiards,[82] and at dice;[83] probably also at chess, and
at tables or backgammon;[84] and owned a puppet-show.[85]
She seems to have thoroughly enjoyed masques, banquets,[86] and such observances as those of Twelfth-day.[87]
Her behaviour was not always that of a conventional
Queen.   Although at the opening of Parliament, she
could appear in such grandeur that the preachers were
appalled at the 'styncken pryde of wemen,'[88] she could
on other occasions, to their scandal, wander through the
streets in disguise.[89]

When Mary left France, the royal exchequer there was
by no means overflowing; but she had come to a country
almost infinitely poorer in nearly every respect.   No doubt
she brought with her costly furniture, rich dresses, and
priceless jewels;[90] but these could not make up for the
magnificence, the lustre, and the refinement of the French
Court.   What was Holyrood[91] as a building, though
beautiful even in the eyes of Brantôme, compared to the
palaces she had left behind her?   These, it is true, had
to be quitted periodically because of the stench gener-
ated by occupation.[92]   The air of Paris itself was far
from perfect;[93] but the sanitary condition of the Scottish

capital was probably much worse. The merchants of
Edinburgh had been reproached by Dunbar in the days
of James the Fourth :—

> ' May nane pas throw your principall gaittis
> For stink of haddockis and of scaittis.
>
> .   .   .   .   .   .
>
> Tailyouris, soutteris, and craftis vyll,
> The fairest of your streitis dois fyll.' [94]

And there is abundant evidence that in Mary's time
there was still too much cause for the reproof. Ever
and anon the magistrates were constrained to issue orders
concerning the ' myddingis,' the evil-smelling occupations,
and more disgusting nuisances, by which not only the
principal street, but even the Church of St. Giles was
shamelessly defiled. [95]   It is not surprising therefore that
Mary did not like Edinburgh. [96]   Her other cities were
few and small, the country thinly populated, many of the
people poverty-stricken, still more of them restless and
unruly. The common Highlanders of the period are
represented as wearing tarred shirts and upper garments
of hide. [97]   Among her people, however, the spirit of
patriotism was not awanting. [98]   Nor was the love of
enterprise ever dormant, whether manifested in reiving
by the Borderers [99] and Highlanders, or in downright
piracy and honest commerce by the more civilised Low-
landers. The prowess of Scotch soldiers was not unknown on the Continent ; [100] and the skill and daring
of Scotch sailors were such that even the King of Spain
contemplated their enmity with some trepidation. [101]

61

Despite their religious zeal, their enterprise by land and sea, their street brawls, their family feuds, their dire poverty, the Scots had an innate love of sport and pastime, which the rulers tried not so much to repress as to guide into useful channels, and to keep within due bounds.[102] While Mary, like her predecessors, was ready to repress 'unleissum gammis,'[103] she showed—as her mother had done before her[104]—that she was interested in her poorer subjects, and wished them to obtain justice.[105] During her numerous progresses and hunting expeditions she visited many parts of her realm,[106] and had many opportunities of observing the condition and learning the wants of her people. It is not at all likely that she understood the language of the Highlanders—*sauvaiges d'Escosse*, as De Foix callously called them;[107] but though ignorant of Gaelic, she had a fluent command of the Lowland tongue.[108]

The Scots could hardly help being loyal to their young Queen. As one who did not always write smooth things concerning her said:—'Besides the interest excited by the varied perils of her lot, she was recommended by her exquisite loveliness of form, her blooming vigour of youth, and her elegant genius, which a courtly education had either increased, or at least rendered more engaging, by a specious colouring of virtue.'[109] She was, moreover, the representative of that long line of sovereigns—fabulous and real—of which they were justly proud.[110] And what was to some of them of much more importance, her throne would have been but poorly occupied by the niggardly, irresolute, and incapable head of the House of Hamilton, or by his frenzied son, who had shown signs of madness ere he charged Bothwell with inciting him to plot against the Queen.[111]

The leading statesmen, and Mary's bearing towards them, in the early months after her return, are portrayed by Randolph.[112] Chatelherault, he tells, had been among the first to leave the Queen after her arrival;[113] and in those of her own religion she did not find what 'she looked for'[114]—even Huntly, their head, in a short time 'utterly lost his credit.'[115] On the other hand, the Lord James and Lethington were 'above all others in credit.' With her 'the Lord James dealeth according to his nature, rudely, homely, and bluntly; the L[aird] of Lidington, more delicately and finely. Yet nothing swerveth from the other in mind and effect. She is patient to hear, and beareth much. The Earl Marischal is wary, but speaketh sometimes to good purpose; his daughter is lately come to this town; we look shortly what shall become of the long love (betwixt the Lord James and that lady). The Lord John of Coldingham hath not least favour with his leaping and dancing; he is like to marry the Lord Bothwell's sister. The Lord Robert consumeth with love of the Earl of Cassil's sister. The Earl Bothwell hath given unto him old lands of his father's in Teviodale, and the Abbey of Melross. The Duke's Grace [Chatelherault] is come to Kinneill, and purposeth not to come near unto the Court, except that he be sent for. . . . My Lord Arran purposeth not to be at Court so long as the mass remaineth.'[116] The conduct of the Lord James and of Lethington, being moderate, was displeasing to all zealots.

Ultra-Protestants 'imagine that the Lord James groweth cold, that he aspireth to great matters'; and regard Lethington as 'ambitious, and too full of policy.' 'In my conscience,' says Randolph, 'they are in the wrong to the Lord James; and whensoever Lidington is taken out of this place, they shall not find among themselves so fit a man to serve in this realm.'[117]   The Bishops from the opposite standpoint feared the influence of these two men.   'The Lord James,' say they, 'beareth too much rule; Lidington hath a crafty head and fell tongue.'[118] It was in connection with the Lord James that Randolph afterwards expressed the opinion that Mary's suspicious nature was her worst fault.[119]

CHAPTER VI

1562

IF Mary did not know whom to trust when she returned to Scotland, it was not the fault of her mother, who, shortly before she died, sent her a book containing lists of all the principal men in the realm—spiritual and temporal, baron and burgess—their good and bad behaviour being noted, and the dutiful subjects distinguished from the seditious.[1] She knew, therefore, what she was doing when—in accordance with the advice she received in France—she resolved to rely chiefly on her Protestant nobles.[2] These men had reason to fear their own Queen's return, knowing that Elizabeth would only support them and their religion so long as it served her own purpose to do so,[3] being also uncertain what Mary might do, if ever she had the opportunity or power to crush their party;[4] yet there is satisfactory proof that some of them at least wished to serve her loyally, and—for her advantage and their own security—to establish amity with England on a stable and honourable basis.

The letter which the Lord James wrote to Elizabeth eight days before Mary left France furnishes, in Patrick

Fraser Tytler's opinion, 'the key to the policy adopted by Mary during the first years of her government'; and 'proves that the Lord James was sincerely attached on this subject to the interests of his sister the Queen.'[5] In that letter, after referring to the wonderful conversion of the old enmity between the two nations into reciprocal good-will, and his earnest desire to see its continuance, he suggested, as a solution of the difficulty between the Queens, that Elizabeth's title to the English crown should 'remain untouched,' both for herself and her issue; that Mary's place should be reserved, as 'next in lawful descent of the right line of Henry VII.'; and that, in the meantime, 'this isle' should be 'united in a perpetual friendship.'[6] At the same time, he sent a copy of the letter to Cecil, that, if he thought proper, it might be kept back from Elizabeth.[7] The suggestion, however, was not new either to Cecil or Elizabeth.[8] It was afterwards said indeed that Mary was influenced by her knowledge of Cecil's favourable reception of this proposal, when, on the eve of leaving France, she sent for Throckmorton to propose a reconciliation with the English Queen.[9]

Thirteen days after her return, Mary despatched Lethington to Elizabeth to inform her of her safe arrival, hearty reception, and settled resolution to live in good neighbourhood with her, to keep peace and amity with England, and to increase the friendship by all possible means. He was also to negotiate, at the instance of the Scots nobles, for the declaration of the English succession.[10] So far as mere talent and diplomatic skill were concerned, Lethington was admirably qualified for

this mission. His contemporaries—like later historians
—might question his sincerity, but no one doubted his
ability. In the opinion of the Bishop of Aquila—no
mean judge in such a matter—he was a man who knew
well how to dissemble ;[11] and his enthusiastic apologist
admits that he was not destitute of 'politic pliancy.'[12]
In explanation of his conduct, he himself borrowed the
simile of the sailor who has to study wind and tide.[13] A
Scots rhymester of the period adopted a somewhat different
simile, but one not less expressive :—

> 'Thay say he can baith quhissill and cloik,
> And his mouth full of meill.'[14]

For his arduous and delicate task Lethington was
fortified by Instructions from the nobles, who, while
deprecating any misunderstanding or breach of amity
between the two Queens, plainly intimated that, if
Elizabeth treated their Sovereign discourteously, or
violated the present peace, they would stand by their
native Princess in her just quarrel.[15] It has been insinuated that the proposed settlement of the English
succession was purposely pressed by those Scots who
wished 'to foment jealousy, not friendship, between the
two Queens, and thereby pave the way for the utter
overthrow of their Sovereign.'[16] But it is now known
that the Duke of Guise and the Cardinal of Lorraine
were professedly quite as eager as the Lord James and
Lethington to carry out the compromise.[17] Elizabeth,
not enraptured by the proposal, told Lethington that
no prince had ever been asked to declare his heir-
apparent in his own time—a reasonable objection in

Lethington's opinion had the succession remained untouched according to law. To agree to his proposal would, she insisted, be simply to prepare her own winding-sheet, and make her grave ready.[18] Cecil foresaw difficulties in the proposal. Throckmorton, however, thought it more dangerous not to deal in the matter, especially if Elizabeth should happen to die without issue; and feared too that her emphatic answer to Lethington would forward the renewal of the old league between France and Scotland, and induce Mary to enter into a marriage of which England would not have cause to be glad.[19]

Sir Peter Mewtas was at once sent to Scotland to demand—what Elizabeth was so anxious to secure— what Mary had so long evaded—the ratification of the Treaty of Edinburgh.[20] Mary could no longer plead that she had not her nobles to advise with. Now she suggested to Mewtas that as there were divers things in the Treaty which concerned her late husband, it would be better to have a new meeting for such matters as concerned her only, and professed her readiness to name commissioners.[21] On the 7th of October, she wrote to Elizabeth thanking her for sending Mewtas to congratulate her on her safe arrival, and saying that she had so answered his message on every point that it would be apparent that she meant nothing more earnestly than a continuance of tender amity and good intelligence.[22] Her object, as Cecil perceived, was to have Lethington's succession proposal principally dealt with.[23] Several members of the English Privy Council were

68

inclined to 'hearken' to the idea of a new meeting; but, lest his motives might be misconstrued, Cecil feared to move in it.[24]

In her answer to Mary's letter, Elizabeth showed that she was not satisfied with the oral message brought by Mewtas from the Queen of Scots, and did not wish to treat anew by commissioners. She was willing to discuss Mary's reasons for refusing to ratify the Treaty, but wished to do so privately, either by Randolph or by letter. Elizabeth's answer is dated 23rd November 1561.[25] Mary did not reply until the 5th of next January, the reason being that Lethington was anxious to get Cecil's opinion as to how her reply should be framed. In vain he urged upon Cecil the reasonableness of Mary, and her wondrous love for Elizabeth; in vain he urged that Cecil must know why she could not ratify the Treaty, and so make herself, though 'so nygh off the blood off England,' to be 'as it were ane stranger from it'; in vain he urged that he hesitated to advise her—who was of 'soche a couraige and stomach'—to initiate the negotiations for the succession compromise, unless Cecil thought that her 'just demand' would not be finally repulsed; in vain he urged his readiness to hazard his own credit with Mary in advising her to follow Cecil's counsel.[26] As Cecil was too wary to commit himself even in response to Lethington's urgent and repeated appeals, Mary's reply had to be drawn without his advice,[27] and that reply reflects much of Lethington's skill and tact.

Mary cannot well imagine what lack Elizabeth had

found in her answer by Mewtas; but regards her dislike
to formal treating by commissioners as an infallible token
of her love. While waiving consideration of, she nevertheless hints at, various external circumstances of the
Treaty, the least of which are worthy of examination.
The Treaty itself is specially obnoxious, as it palpably
prejudices her title and interest to that which 'may fall'
to her as being of the same lineage; and because 'a
matter of sa greit consequence is wrappit up in obscure
termis.' Relying on Elizabeth's friendship and upright-
ness, she will at present have no other judge. She professes her willingness to perform everything in the Treaty
which can be reasonably required of her; or rather to
enter into a new one in favour of Elizabeth and her
lawful issue, providing her own interest in the succession
is properly secured. Thus the seed of dissension may
be eradicated, their amity increased, and the perpetual
peace of both realms procured. After referring to the
abundance of her love for Elizabeth, and her own earnest
desire for sincere and unceremonious dealing in the matter,
she expresses the hope that they may soon have a personal interview, when the unfeigned nature of her
good meaning would appear more clearly than in her
writing.[28]

Now that Mary had herself ventured to press the
succession compromise, would Elizabeth dare to test
her 'couraige and stomach' by refusing her 'just
demand'? For twelve weary weeks Mary had im-
patiently to await her reply—a reply which did not
object to the proposed personal interview, and which

satisfied her for the time being.[29]   Of this interview Mary was professedly exceedingly desirous, not so much as a means to perpetual amity, nor to win the recognition of her right to the English succession, as to gratify her longing desire to meet that sister Queen for whom she had so suddenly developed a vehement and unselfish love.[30]   She wished that either she or Elizabeth were a man;[31] she would have no husband but the Queen of England,[32] with the love of whom she was possessed.[33] Lethington was anxious for the interview, in so far as it might lead to that 'accord' of the Queens which he was bent on securing; but he was not without his misgivings, for he felt that if it did not promote this object it meant evil for himself; hence his efforts to commit Cecil.[34]   In Scotland, the Protestants seemed generally to approve of the interview, the Papists to distrust it.[35]   Patriotic reasons, however, were found for opposing it, not the least of which was the difficulty of raising the necessary funds—funds which would of course be left in England.[36] The French Court feared and opposed it;[37] the Duke of Guise favoured it; the Cardinal of Lorraine hesitated and ultimately wished to delay it;[38] the Spaniard 'practised' to hinder it;[39] most members of the English Council suspected or disliked it;[40] the weather was most unpropitious;[41] and Elizabeth's health was unsatisfactory.[42] But in spite of opposition—covert and open—in spite of the unfavourable circumstances, it seemed for a while that Mary was to have her own way.   The Scots Council would have preferred to have the succession compromise first agreed to,[43] but at length—19th May 1562—approved of the interview as a means for promoting the amity, cautioning Mary, however, as to the safety of 'her awin persone.'[44]   Within a week, Lethington was again despatched to the English Court,[45] where he found Elizabeth 'so earnestly bent to go forward to this voyage that she will sayle quhether the wynd blow or not.'[46]   Articles were agreed on for a meeting in autumn at York, or at Shrewsbury's Sheffield house—that castle which Mary was destined to know so well in later years —or at Nottingham;[47] arrangements for the journey were partly made,[48] when Elizabeth was constrained by the iniquitous persecution of the Huguenots in France to postpone the interview for a year.[49]   Mary received the announcement with great grief 'and watery eyes'; but was gratified by Elizabeth's continued amity, and accepted her reasons for delay as sufficient.[50]

If, as Throckmorton put it, the safety of England lay in neither of the parties in France being able to over- throw the other,[51] Elizabeth with all her caution could not avoid supporting Condé, especially after discovering that the Guises had 'practised' with her.[52]   Mary too had politic reasons for hoping that her amity with England would not be injured by the breach with her uncles.[53] Randolph testifies that, on her arrival in Scotland, one of the three things she found necessary to maintain her state, was to make peace with England.[54]

The Scots Council again consented to the interview, declaring, however, more emphatically than before, 'that thai wald na wyise gif hir [i.e. Mary] counsale to committ hir body in Ingland, and thairfoir referrit the place of the

meting and the securitie of hir awin persone to hir self.'[55]
But the two Queens were not destined to meet, though
the idea of an interview was yearly resuscitated;[56] though
royal presents,[57] as well as kindly wishes, were interchanged; and though the hope was continuously dangled
before Mary that the succession would be settled in her
favour if only she would marry to please Elizabeth.[58]
Was Elizabeth, in the language of her day, merely
' driving time'?[59] Was Mary only moved by a selfish
desire to seat herself on Elizabeth's throne?[60] It is
difficult to believe that they were perfectly sincere in
their extravagant protestations of mutual attachment.
To Mary, Lethington professed to believe that Elizabeth's
affection for her passed all measure; to Cecil and Randolph, that Mary was in earnest, and that he did not
over-colour her love for Elizabeth; but to the Spanish
Ambassador he told a somewhat different tale.[61] Randolph was sometimes inclined to think that the Queen
of Scots did mean all she said; at other times he had a
lurking suspicion that she did not altogether resemble
Nathaniel.[62] He knew that his own Queen was not over-
fastidious as to ways and means, when she had an object
to gain or a danger to avert. Mary's right of succession
to the English throne remained undeclared, and she did
not gratify Elizabeth and Cecil by ratifying that Treaty,
which he had helped so skilfully to frame, and in which
' a matter of sa greit consequence is wrappit up in
obscure termis.'[63]

CHAPTER VII

1562

It was on the 23rd of July 1562, that Sir Henry Sidney informed Mary in Holyrood that the interview with Elizabeth must be deferred for a year;[1] and by the 10th of August, the Queen of Scots had determined to enter on her long-projected[2] progress to the North—'a terrible journey,' as Randolph thought, 'both for horse and men, the country is so poor and victuals so scarce.'[3] She went by way of Stirling—where there were meetings of the Privy Council on the 14th and 15th of August[4]—by Coupar-Angus, Perth,[5] Edzell,[6] Glammis,[7] and before the end of the month was at Old Aberdeen. Randolph complains of the journey so far as being 'cumbersome, painful, and marvellous long; the weather extreme foul and cold; all victuals marvellous dear; and the corn that is, never like to come to ripeness.'[8]

A few days after her arrival in Aberdeen, it became known that she was so displeased with Huntly, that she would not go to his house, though 'within three miles of her way, and the fairest in the country.'[9] He seems to have previously fallen into disfavour, partly, perhaps, through his opposition to the interview with Elizabeth ; [10] and Mary's displeasure apparently increased from the day of her arrival in Aberdeen.   Instead of obeying her command—a command issued under pain of treason—to bring no more than a hundred men with him, he had come with fifteen hundred.[11]   His son, Sir John, though ordered, on the 1st of September, to ward himself in Stirling within seven days, under a similar penalty, had openly disobeyed ; and it was supposed that his disobedience was approved, if not prompted, by Huntly.[12]

When Mary reached Inverness, she intended to lodge in the Castle, but was refused admission ; and the garrison, when summoned, declared that it should not be delivered without the orders of Lord Gordon.   Next day, the people of the country gathered to help the Queen, the Castle was rendered, and the captain hanged.[13] ' In all these garboils,' says Randolph to Cecil, ' I assure you I never saw her merrier, never dismayed, nor never thought that so much to be in her that I find.   She repented nothing, but (when the lords and others at Inverness came in the morning from the watch) that she was not a man, to know what life it was to lie all night in the fields, or to walk on the causeway with a jack and a knap-schalle,[14] a Glasgow buckler, and a broadsword.' [15]

After spending a few days in Inverness she set out again for the South, by way of Spynie Castle—the seat of Patrick Hepburn, the dissolute Bishop of Moray, and uncle of the Earl of Bothwell—' well served of her nobles and obeyed of her subjects, and convoyed by great numbers both of horse and foot.' On her way north, Huntly had in vain entreated her to visit him. Now he kept his house, 'and would have it thought that this disobedience came through the evil behaviour of his sons.' The Queen was highly offended; and, so far as Randolph knew, no nobleman took his part. Alarmed at the royal charge to his son to ward himself in Stirling Castle, moved by the justice meted out to the garrison of Inverness, and fearing, perhaps, further proceedings against himself, Huntly assembled his forces, and put them under the command of that son who had so openly contemned the Queen's charge. It was intended to intercept her at the passage of the Spey—'a place where good advantage might have been had'—but their thousand horse and foot posted in the wood unexpectedly retired, ere Mary with a force three times as strong approached the river, on Sabbath the 20th of September. That night she reached 'a house of the Laird of Banke, where she was well lodged, and in good assurance.' On Tuesday the 22nd she was again in Old Aberdeen, and next day was honourably received into the new town, 'with spectacles, plays, interludes, and other things, as they could best devise.' She was presented 'with a cup of silver, double gilt, with 500 crowns in it'; and also with wine and wax and coals enough to serve her during her projected stay of forty days.[16]

With the advice of her Privy Council, Mary had already charged Sir John Gordon to render the houses of Findlater and Auchindoune;[17] but, as they were still held against her,[18] it was now resolved that if Huntly did

not submit himself and deliver up this rebellious son, the
utmost force would be used against him to the subversion
of his house for ever.　She accordingly levied 120 arquebusiers, and sent to the South for the Master of Lindsay,
for Grange, and for Ormiston.　Captain Hay was despatched, on the 25th of September, to Strathbogie to
order Huntly to transport the Queen's cannon—that
cannon which had overawed the Highlanders [19]—to a
place appointed ; and returned with the message that not
only her own cannon, but the Earl's body and goods, were
at her command.　With sobs and tears, he professed
to be innocent of his son's offences, and alleged that he
would be the first to hazard his life in taking the houses
held against her.　The Countess took the messenger
'into her holy chapel, fair and trimly hanged, all
ornaments and mass-robes ready lying upon the altar,
with cross and candles standing upon it'; and there
informed him that her husband was being oppressed,
because he would not forsake his God and his religion
'as those who are now about the Queen's grace and
have the whole guiding of her have done.'　Mary told
the Council that she did not believe a word either of
Huntly's message or of his wife's, whereat, says Randolph,
there has been much good pastime.　Of the nobles with
the Queen, only Atholl and Sutherland favoured Huntly,
and that quietly.[20]

It soon became evident to ' the authors of the troubles,'
as Randolph calls them, that they had gone so far that
they could not hope to win the Queen's favour again ; and
she was determined to proceed against them with all

severity. It was known that Huntly—although he feared to sleep at home, or to spend two nights in one place—still frequented his own house during the day. On the 9th of October, three bands—under Grange, the Lord John, and the Master of Lindsay—were sent to Strathbogie, on the pretext of discovering whether his rebellious son was harboured there, but in reality to apprehend himself. Bootless and swordless, Huntly escaped by a back gate. Two hours after Grange had left Aberdeen on this fruitless mission, a boy brought the keys of Findlater and Auchindoune ; but the Lord James and Lethington declined to receive them in such an ignominious manner; and Mary said that she had provided other means to open these doors.[21] On the 15th, she, with advice of her Privy Council, ordained that, if Huntly did not appear before her next day to answer for himself he should be outlawed and his strongholds taken from him.[22] On the night of the 15th Sir John surprised a detached party of the soldiers, who were besieging Findlater, and relieved them of fifty-six arquebuses and their captain.[23]

Huntly's eldest son, Lord Gordon, had now gone to Chatelherault, his father-in-law ; 'his purpose,' it was suspected, being 'either to persuade him to take part with his father, or else to remain with him as guileless of whatever shall be enterprised.'[24] Wild rumours were rife in the south of Scotland ;[25] but Knox and others did their best to keep that part of the country in peace during the Queen's absence in the North.[26]

On the 17th of October, Huntly was 'put to the horn.' He was ordered to deliver the House of Strathbogie ; but he refused to do so, and strengthened himself at Badenoch, hoping—with the help of the weather and the dearth of provisions—to weary out his opponents. Mary levied more soldiers; and several of the nobles who were with her sent for their tenants and friends. On the 20th the Countess of Huntly came near Aberdeen; but, on learning that the Queen would not see her, returned again to Strathbogie. Gordon gentlemen pledged themselves neither to leave Aberdeen nor to help their chief until these troubles were ended. Those who had been at feud with him—the Forbeses, the Leslies, the Grants, and the M'Intoshes—were set free to act against him.[27]

'Huntly, having assembled 700 persons, marched towards Aberdeen to apprehend the Queen and do with the rest at his will.' The Lord James, Atholl, and Morton were despatched, with a force three times as strong, to meet him. From his position on the hill top, Huntly was driven by shot of arquebus into the low, mossy ground, and forced by the horsemen into a corner from which there was no escape. At the first shock, the vanguard of his enemy fell back; but the Lord James and his company, seeing the danger, bore down upon them so fiercely that the vanguard speedily retrieved its honour and Huntly's force was completely overpowered. Two of Huntly's sons were among the prisoners—the enterprising Sir John, and Adam, a boy of seventeen. Huntly himself was also captured, but he, after being placed 'on horseback before his taker, suddenly fell from his horse stark dead.'[28] Such was the battle of Corrichie—'short, sharp, and decisive.'

Sir John was speedily brought to Aberdeen, tried, found guilty, and executed; but Adam was spared on account of his youth.[29] As Mary returned to the South she was met at Dundee by Chatelherault, who had come ' to demaunde pardon for his sonne-in-lawe, the Lord Gordon, whome hymself stayede by the Quenes commandement'; but in his suit he received little comfort.[30] On Thursday, the 26th of November—five days after Mary reached Edinburgh—the Duke, in obedience to her order, brought him to his 'lugeing in the Kirk of Feild Wynd,' and next Saturday he was committed to the Castle.[31] On the 8th of February he was tried for treason, found guilty, and condemned to 'be hangit quhill he wer deid, drawin, quarterit, and demanit as ane tratour at our said Soverain's plesour'—a sentence which was not to be carried into effect.[32] On the 28th of May (1563) Huntly's rudely embalmed corpse was arraigned in Mary's presence at the bar of Parliament—'the coffin was sette upright, as if the Earle stoode upon his feet'— when it was decerned that he was guilty of treason, that his lands, heritages, and goods were forfaulted, that his dignity, name, and memory were extinct, that his arms were cancelled, and that his posterity were thenceforth incapable of office, honour, or dignity within the realm.[33] On the same day the Earl of Sutherland was also condemned to death by Parliament—for 'art, part, and assistance' in Huntly's treason—but four years later he obtained reduction of the sentence.[34]

Whatever the object of Mary's progress to the North may have been — whether it was planned by the Lord

James for his own aggrandisement, as some Mariolaters affirm,[35] or intended by Mary for his destruction as Knox suspected,[36] or undertaken for her deliverance from his power and for her marriage to Sir John Gordon, as Huntly's grandson gravely records,[37] or occasioned merely by Mary's desire to see the country and to establish good order[38]—it had resulted in the disgrace, defeat, and death of the virtual ruler of the North, and in the utter ruin of his house for the time being.   Huntly's overthrow and Sutherland's condemnation had, moreover, greatly weakened the influence of that Church, which she was assuring the Pope—alike by legate and by letter—was the object of her undying devotion;[39] and she—the most fair rose among heretical thorns—had not scrupled to receive the rich ecclesiastical vestments seized at Strathbogie, some of which she was afterwards to hand over to the profligate Bothwell, and some to other profane purposes.[40] If the most powerful of the Popish nobles had suffered on the one hand, the most prominent of the Protestants had, on the other, reaped substantial advantages.   The Lord James had gone to the North as Earl of Mar,[41] he returned to the South as Earl of Murray;[42] and to him, too, there fell no mean share of the valuable spoils of Strathbogie.[43]

Up to the end of September—eight days after Mary had returned to Aberdeen from Inverness—Lethington was inclined to believe in Huntly's plea, that whatever was amiss was due to the youth and folly of his children, and that if there were any fault in him, it proceeded from too great simplicity rather than from craft or malice.[44] He soon, however, had cause to change his opinion.   The evidence of the Kers, the discovery of incriminating documents, the confession of Sir John—furnished keys to Huntly's conduct, and revealed the danger to which Mary and her ministers had been exposed at his hands.[45] On his way to the South Lethington wrote :—' I am sorry that the soil of my native country did ever produce so unnatural a subject as the Earl of Huntly hath proved in the end against his Sovereign, being a Princess so gentle and benign, and whose behaviour hath been always such towards all her subjects, and every one in particular, that wonder it is that any could be found so ungracious as once to think evil against her ; and in my conscience I know not that any just occasion of grudge was ever offered unto him. Well, the event hath made manifest his iniquity, and the innocence as well of her Majestie as of her ministers towards him.' [46]

It had been against the wishes of her Privy Council that Mary determined to decline Huntly's invitations to Strathbogie ; [47] misgivings she may have had at his death ; [48] but, when she learned the full extent of his projects, she appeared to regard her escape as providential.[49] It is now known that he had not only proved a trimmer immediately before her return from France,[50] but that, fifteen months after Pinkie, he had entered into a double compact with the Lord Protector of England, by which he was to be allowed to return to his own country—professedly on honourable terms—secretly to advance Edward's title to Scotland.[51] The proof of this compact unfortunately mars Bishop Lesley's picturesque story of the Earl's escape from Morpeth.[52]

CHAPTER VIII

1562-1565

ACCORDING to the report sent by the Jesuit priests in Scotland to Pope Clement the Eighth, 'no greater wound' could have been inflicted on the country than the overthrow of the Huntly family, which so weakened 'the power of the Catholics' that 'heresy made wide inroads, even in the northern districts.' 'The only remedy which seemed to remain' was 'the marriage of the Queen with some powerful Catholic prince, who could restore the exhausted energies of the Church'; and, say the Jesuit fathers, 'the effort was made to do this by all possible ways and means.'[1] One of Mary's biographers— also a Jesuit—alleges that she 'began, after the space of five years, to think of a second husband.'[2] It is true that, sixteen months after Huntly's death, Mary assured Randolph that the remembrance of her late husband was so fresh in her mind that she could not think of another, that her years were not so many that she could not abide, that she was neither sought nor desired of any; and that the polite Ambassador 'seemed' to believe her.[3] The numerous marriage projects of the Queen of Scots,

83

however, did not originate in the desolation caused by
Huntly's overthrow; nor did they require such incite-
ments as Hepburn's infamous insult,[4] or Chatelar's reckless attempt upon her honour.[5] As already mentioned,
the speculations had begun during the last illness of
Francis, her own feelings in the matter were reported the
day after his death, and the projects took definite shape
before the forty days of the girlish-widow's mourning
were ended.[6]

Morette—the ambassador from Savoy—on his way
back from Scotland in January 1561-2, was able to tell
the Bishop of Aquila in London, that Mary was determined to marry very highly, and did not dissemble about
Don Carlos.[7] During the next three years—ere she
finally committed herself—she was to have a score of
suggested suitors, ranging from the great princes of the
Continent, down to Elizabeth's English nobles.[8] 'The
mariage of our Queyn,' says Knox, 'was in all mannis
mouth. Some wold have Spaine; some the Emperouris
brother; some Lord Robert Dudlye; some Duck de
Nemours; and some unhappilie gessed at the Lord
Darnlye.'[9] Her attractions—personal and accessory—
were neither few nor despicable. These were apprecia-
tively set forth by Lethington, in the spring of 1563,
in urging on the Spanish Ambassador the desirability of
a match with Don Carlos. His words were thus reported
by De Quadra to Philip:—'This Queen [*i.e.* Elizabeth]
was in great fear of his [*i.e.* Don Carlos'] marriage, and
the Queen of France the same, with very good reason, as
if your Majesty listened to it, not only would you give

your son a wife of such excellent qualities as those possessed by his Queen, who was in prudence, chastity, and beauty, equalled by few in the world, but you also gave him a power which approached very nearly to monarchy, adding to the dominions already possessed by your Majesty two entire islands, this and Ireland, the possession of which by your Majesty would give no trouble whatever. . . . His mistress possessed property in France and Scotland of the value of 200,000 crowns a year derived from her dowry and her mother's property, and . . . had in money and jewels 800,000 crowns more.'[10]

By this time the marriage, which the Cardinal of Lorraine had been negotiating for his niece, with Charles the Archduke of Austria, was regarded by his father the Emperor and by others as certain.[11] In treating, the Cardinal of Lorraine, it was said, had not only affirmed that Mary was the inheritor of England, but had prompted the Emperor and his son to its recovery by arms.[12] With Du Croc, who had been sent by the Cardinal to Scotland, Mary returned thanks to the Emperor and his son; and requested the messenger 'to note well the personage of the Duke, to learn his nature and conditions, and his living and revenues.'[13] To the Spanish Ambassador, Lethington made light of this proposal to marry his Sovereign to the younger son of the Emperor. So far as he understood her thoughts and intentions, such a match would not satisfy her, since the Archduke had nothing in his favour but his relationship with Philip, and that alone, he said, was not sufficient

for the aims which she and her subjects had in view.
Unless, therefore, Philip promised 'great support and
effectual aid to the Archduke,' Lethington thought
'there was no chance of such a match being acceptable.'[14] Mary afterwards avouched that this was indeed
her opinion.[15]

De Quadra informed the Emperor that Lethington
had complained that the Archduke was not rich enough
to support the necessary state, and had suggested that
Philip should undertake his maintenance and give the
Scots 'an assurance that he would carry out the English
enterprise.' The Spanish Ambassador no doubt thought
that he was putting the whole question in a nut-shell,
when he assured the Emperor that 'the only thing they
will insist upon in Scotland is that the Archduke shall
have enough money to keep himself without looking to
them, and also that he is strong enough to establish his
right to this [*i.e.* the English] crown.'[16] The Emperor,
it was said, was so eager for the match, that he was
willing to provide a sufficient portion.[17]

Elizabeth's postponement of the interview, and her
continued aversion to agree to the succession compromise,
were leading Mary 'to seek a means of remedy in France,'
by 'such a marriage as would enable her to assert her
rights' in England 'by force, if they could not be
obtained by fair means.' So, at least, Lethington is
reported by De Quadra to have told him; and to him
he also said that if no satisfactory arrangement was now
made in England, he was going to France to propose,
through the Guises, the marriage of their niece with

86

Charles the Ninth.[18]   In Lethington's own report to Mary,
he informed her that De Quadra had become her affectionate servant, through the widespread accounts of her
beauty, great wit, and other excellent qualities; that
although he could not speak definitely of his master's
desire in the matter, he believed that Don Carlos was
already 'varay far in love' with her; and that he
thought she ought to keep one ear open for him, as
Philip would naturally do more for him than for the
Archduke, since 'his sark is narrere hyme nor his coit.'[19]

Lethington had led De Quadra to believe that the Scotch
Protestants would not object to the Don Carlos match;
and Raulet had assured him that even Murray was
extremely desirous of it.[20] Mary at least was anxious
for it.[21]   Philip hoped that it might be 'the beginning
of a reformation in religious matters in England,' and
accordingly 'decided to entertain the negotiation';[22]
but he was not altogether moved by unworldly motives.
He had substantial reasons for his interest in English
politics;[23] and it was principally the information about
the suggested match between Mary and Charles the
Ninth which induced him 'to take this business up, and
not to wait until the Emperor had been undeceived' as
to the marriage with the Archduke. Philip insisted
that, in carrying out the matter, the greatest secrecy
should be maintained, 'as all the benefit to be derived
from the affair depends absolutely upon nothing being
heard of it until it is an accomplished fact.' He authorised
De Quadra to encourage and console 'the Catholics and
good men in England'; but on no account to com-

promise himself.[24]   Over and above the King's injunctions,
the Duke of Alva also wrote, impressing on him the
necessity of inviolable secrecy.[25]   Thus enjoined, the faithful Ambassador, on the 17th of July 1563—eight days
after receiving Philip's Instructions—sent a cautious
message to Mary by a member of his own household, in
whom he had implicit confidence, and for whose journey
a harmless pretext was easily devised.[26]   When this
messenger—Luis de Paz—returned, he found the Bishop
of Aquila almost at the point of death, quite able to
understand and answer him, but grieving greatly that he
should drop from his work just when he hoped to succeed.
De Quadra expired with the words, 'I can do no more.'[27]

Despite the warnings of Philip and Alva, despite the
precautions of De Quadra, it was impossible to keep the
Don Carlos negotiations secret.   By the 20th of August
—four days before De Quadra died—Sir Thomas Smith,
then in Rouen, 'found that the French marvellously fear
a marriage to be made between the King of Spain's son
and the Queen of Scotland, which the Guisians take for
concluded.'   Smith believed that the intention of the
Pope and the Cardinal of Lorraine was to give England
in dowry to Don Carlos and Mary for reducing it to the
Romish Church, persuading themselves that in Scotland
and England their faction was strong enough to accomplish this.[28]   For such a purpose De Quadra had already
received liberal offers of help from several of the English
lords and gentlemen, some of them promising to serve
Philip in this with a thousand men, and others with
'things no less important.'   Their grievances were so

great, and the causes of discontent so numerous and so grave, that De Quadra marvelled that disturbances had not already broken out, especially as Elizabeth possessed neither power nor substance, being 'unpopular and despised, without troops, without money, and without harmony, at enmity with all the world.'[29]   But if Elizabeth was unpopular, poor, and despised, she at least had advisers of singular penetration and capacity.   Ere Lethington left London, on the 20th of June, he told De Quadra that Elizabeth had commanded him to inform Mary that if she married Don Carlos, the Archduke, or any member of the House of Austria, she could not avoid being her enemy, and therefore charged her to consider well her steps in such a matter, for, on the other hand, if she married to her satisfaction, she would not fail to be a good friend and sister to her, and would make her her heir.[30]

When Lethington returned to Scotland, he showed himself, says Knox, not a little offended that any rumour of the Spanish match should have arisen, and 'took upoun him that suche thing never entered in hir hearte.'   He was anxious to discredit Knox, who had prematurely if not recklessly affirmed, 'that such ane mariage was boyth proponit, and, upoun the parte of our Quene, by the Cardinall accepted.'   Foreseeing the danger to Scottish Protestantism, Knox had already sounded a vigorous alarm.   Seizing the opportunity when most of the nobles, who had flocked to Edinburgh for the Parliament, were in church, he preached a rousing sermon on God's mercy to the realm and the ingratitude of the people.   'Now,

my lordis,' he exclaimed, 'to putt end to all, I hear of
the Quenis mariage: Duckis, brethren to Emperouris, and
Kingis, stryve all for the best game; but this, my lordis,
will I say . . . whensoever the nobilitie of Scotland professing the Lord Jesus consentis that ane infidell (and all
Papistis are infidellis) shalbe head to your Soverane, ye
do so far as in ye lyeth to banishe Christ Jesus from this
realme, ye bring Goddis vengeance upoun the countrey,
a plague upoun your self, and perchaunce ye shall do
small comforte to your Soverane.' That very afternoon the preacher had to appear before his indignant
Queen in Holyrood, who 'in a vehement fume' cried out
that never Prince was handled as she was. 'I have,' said
she, 'borne with you in all your rigorouse maner of
speaking, bayth against my self and against my uncles;
yea I have sought your favouris by all possible meanes.
I offerred unto you presence and audience whensoever
it pleassed you to admonishe me; and yitt I cannott be
quyte of you. I avow to God, I shalbe anes revenged.'
Her voice was choked with 'owling' and tears. Knox ventured to explain that in 'the preaching place' he must
obey Him, who commanded him 'to speik plane, and to
flatter no flesche upoun the face of the earth.' Interrupt-
ing him, she demanded, 'But what have ye to do with
my mariage?' Most of the nobles, he replied, were so
addicted to her gratification that it became him to point
out their duty. But 'what have ye to do with my
mariage?' she insisted; or 'what ar ye within this
commounwealth?' Prompt was the answer, 'A subject
borne within the same, madam. And albeit I neather

be erle, lord nor barroun within it, yitt hes God maid
me (how abject that ever I be in your eyes) a profitable
member within the same.' To him, as much as to any,
he said, it appertained to forewarn of such things as
might prove hurtful; and therefore he now repeated to
her the warning he had given the lords. This plain
speaking was received with another outburst of 'owling'
and tears. Erskine of Dun—'a man of meak and gentill
spreit,' who had accompanied Knox to Holyrood—now
tried to mitigate her anger, by 'many pleasing wordis of
hir beautie, of hir excellence, and how that all the Princes
of Europe wold be glaid to seak hir favouris.' In vain
Knox assured her that he 'never delyted in the weaping
of any of Goddis creatures,' that he could 'skarslie weill
abyd' the tears of his own boys when he chastised them,
and that as he had only spoken the truth he must sustain
her tears rather than hurt his conscience or betray the
commonwealth. The Queen, more indignant than ever,
ordered him 'to pass furth of the cabinet.' After an
hour's merry speech in the outer chamber to the court
ladies, in 'thair gorgiouse apparell,' on the transient
pleasures of this life and the relentlessness of 'that knave
death,' he was permitted to leave the palace.[31] Had he
known of Lethington's negotiations with De Quadra, his
language would doubtless have been still more pointed
and more personal, both in 'the preaching place' and in
Holyrood.

Ere Randolph—with his Instructions of 20th August
—reached Edinburgh on the 1st of September, he learned
that Mary, having returned from the West Country,[32]

was at Craigmillar.   She received him very graciously,
and, without committing herself, interrogated him
thoroughly concerning his Instructions.   The substance
of these was, that, if she married in the Emperor's
lineage, the continuance of the amity between her and
Elizabeth would be impossible, and the concord between
the nations would be speedily dissolved; that, if no
English noble could be found to please her, she might
choose one from some other country who the English
might not have manifest cause to judge was sought for
their trouble; and in that case Elizabeth would show and
extend the goodwill she had for her.   Mary bade Randolph confer with Murray and Lethington on the matter,
and desired him to give her his Sovereign's mind in
writing.   He feared that she was 'more Spanish than
Imperial,' and found that many of the Scots were 'as evil
willing of the match' as were the English.[33]

Sir James Melville alleges that Randolph had a secret
commission to Murray and Lethington, 'to propon my
Lord Robert Dudly.'[34]   Five months before this, Lethington had told De Quadra that Elizabeth had said to him
'that if his mistress would take her advice and wished to
marry safely and happily, she would give her a husband
who would ensure both, and this was Lord Robert, in
whom nature has implanted so many graces that if she
wished to marry she would prefer him to all the princes
in the world.'   To which Lethington had replied 'that
this was a great proof of the love she bore to his Queen,
as she was willing to give her a thing so dearly prized by
herself, and he thought the Queen his mistress, even if

she loved Lord Robert as dearly as she (Elizabeth) did, would not marry him and so deprive her of all the joy and solace she received from his companionship.' Elizabeth had proceeded to say that she wished that 'the Earl of Warwick, his brother, had the grace and good looks of Lord Robert, in which case each could have one.' Yet 'Warwick was not ugly either, and was not ungraceful, but his manner was rather rough, and he was not so gentle as Lord Robert. For the rest, however, he was so brave, so liberal, and magnanimous, that truly he was worthy of being the husband of any great princess.'[35]

Besides the offer of good advice, the holding forth of vague promises, and even the generous surrender of him whom she held so dear, various expedients were open to Elizabeth to prevent Mary from marrying a powerful Prince. In the opinion of Guzman de Silva—who had succeeded De Quadra—she was quite fit to enter into marriage negotiations with such a Prince herself merely to oust Mary ;[36] and Sir James Melville alleges that such negotiations with the Archduke Charles led 'to inwart greffis and gruges betwen the twa Quenis.'[37]

Mary's prospects had been sadly spoiled by the assassination of the Duke of Guise, who, it was believed, would have done his utmost to place her on the English throne.[38] Besides the crooked policy of Elizabeth, she had to reckon with the intrigues and opposition of Catherine de Medici,[39] and had to study the temper of her own people—some of whom were implacable enough. After the autumn of 1563 it was noticed that she was occasionally greatly depressed, and wept when there was no

apparent cause. In December she took to bed and
complained of a pain in her right side. Some doubted
whether she would live. It was supposed that she had
over-fatigued herself by too much dancing on the twenty-
first anniversary of her birthday; she herself thought that
she had caught a chill through being too long in chapel;
but it was suspected that the real cause was her utter
despair of marrying to her mind—those abroad not being
very hasty in the matter, and her subjects at home not
very willing.[40]   It was not, however, until the 6th of
August 1564, that Philip instructed Guzman de Silva
that the proposal for Mary's marriage with Don Carlos
must be considered at an end.[41] A few weeks later, on the
rumoured death of the Queen of Spain, it was believed in
the French Court that Philip himself would marry the
Queen of Scots.[42]   Had the rumour proved true, it is
possible that he, who had been willing to marry Elizabeth
for the sake of religion,[43] would not have looked coldly
on her northern rival.   But poor Arran, once the hope
of the Protestants, offered to Elizabeth, scorned by Mary,
imprisoned and crazy, was still regarded by Catherine de
Medici as a suitable husband for her daughter-in-law,
in the hope that he would change his religion and revenge
himself on Murray. Mary's uncles, on the other hand,
were now said to be most earnest for the young Duke of
Guise.[44]

Randolph's Instructions of 17th November 1563 had
been as unsatisfactory to Mary and her advisers as those
of the 20th of August.   While 'the children of France,[45]
Spain, or Austria' were plainly objected to, Elizabeth's

indication of whom she wished her to choose was not
clear.[46]   After three months' consideration, Randolph
was told that, as his message was only general, Mary's
answer could only be uncertain.[47]   Elizabeth having at
length authorised him to offer the Queen of Scots her
choice of the English nobles, and in special to name the
Lord Robert, he did so before the end of March 1564.
'Upon this purpose they talked very long, and she heard
him with meetly good patience.'   Taken by surprise, she
was neither prepared to marry a subject, nor to reject one
who was so recommended by Elizabeth.   The English
Queen had previously proposed that her sister Sovereign
might send some of her trustiest servants to confer with
her.   Mary now suggested that Elizabeth might send
some one—Bedford, or any other with him—to Berwick,
to deal in the matter with those whom she would
appoint.[48]   Randolph set himself to arrange an interview between the two Queens in the summer of 1564, but
this was found impolitic or impracticable.[49]   By this
time a servant of Lennox had arrived at the Scottish
Court.   'Some in the countrey,' writes Knox to Randolph, 'look for the Lady and the young Erle er it be
long.   It is whispered to me that licence is allready
procured for thare hitther-cuming.   Goddis providence is
inscrutable to man, befor the ischew of such thingis as are
keapt clos for a season in His counsall.   But to be plaine
with you, that jorney and progress I lyke not.'[50]   Knox
was not the only one who already suspected the Darnley
match.[51]   In the previous month another correspondent
had written to Randolph that he believed that, whereso-

ever she hovers, and how many times soever she doubles
to fetch the wind, she will at length let fall her anchor
between Dover and Berwick, ' though perchance not in
that port, haven, or road that you wish she should.' [52]

According to Melville, it was because the Lord Robert's
name was not rapturously received that ' occasion wes
tane to geve leave unto Mathow Erle of Lennox, wha
dwelt in England for the tym, to pas in Scotland as
desyrous to se the Quen, and tak ordour with some of
his awen turnis ; whais eldest sone my Lord Darly was a
lusty young Prince, and apperantly was ane of the twa
that the Quen of England had tald me sche had in hir
head till offer unto our Quen, as born within the realm of
England.' [53]   Whatever Elizabeth's motive may have been
in interceding with Mary for the return of Lennox to
Scotland, she was constrained—by caprice or policy—to
regret her action ; and was ignoble enough to suggest
that Mary should take the blame by withdrawing that
permission which at her desire she had granted. [54]

On the evening of the 15th of September 1564, Mary
returned to Edinburgh after her second northern progress ; [55] and in writing to Cecil three days later, Lethington complains that no answer had been vouchsafed to
Mary's suggestion that a secret commission should be
given to Bedford that he might confer with some of
them at Berwick.   Personally he preferred the amity of
Elizabeth to that of any foreign prince ; and trusted that
the Queen of Scots would in her marriage as soon follow
her advice as that of any other friend she had, provided respect was had to honour and surety.   Randolph's

special overture had been 'propounded so nakedly that
the Queen had reason to know more before she should
answer it'; and Lethington did not dare to deal much
with her 'for any special person.'[56]   Elizabeth was in
dire perplexity, and besought Cecil to find out for her
delay some good excuse, which she might plead in
Randolph's despatches.[57]

Meanwhile, Sir James Melville was sent by Mary to
Elizabeth—'the persoun in the warld to whom,' next
herself, she wished 'maist gud luk and prosperite.'[58]
During the nine days he remained at the English Court,
he saw much of Elizabeth, having sometimes three conferences with her in one day, and seldom has an Ambassador recorded his experiences with such delightful
naïveté.   He had to stay until Lord Robert Dudley was
made Earl of Leicester, when he saw Elizabeth put her
hand on the neck of her kneeling favourite 'to kittle him
smylingly.'   'Then sche asked at me,' says Melville,
'how I lyked of him.   I said as he was a worthy subject, he was happy that had rencontrit a Princes that
culd dicern and reward gud service.   "Yet," sche said,
"ye lyk better of yonder lang lad"; pointing towardis
my Lord Darley, wha as nerest Prince of the bluid bure
the swerd of honour that day before hir.'   Melville, not
wishing her to think that he was favourably impressed
with Darnley,[59] answered 'that na woman of sprit wald
mak choise of sic a man, that was lyker a woman than a
man; for he wes very lusty, berdles and lady facit.'

Elizabeth owned that she was less offended at Mary's
angry letter concerning the proposal to prevent Lennox

going to Scotland, than ' that sche seamed to disdain sa
far the mariage with my L[ord] of Leycister, quhilk sche
had caused Mester Randolphe propon unto hir'; and
assured Melville that she did not intend to marry unless
she were compelled by the hard behaviour of the Queen
of Scots.[60]   Because she could not see Mary, ' sche delyted
oft to luk upon hir picture,' says Melville, ' and tok me in
to hir bed chamber, and oppenit a litle lettroum wherin wer
dyvers litle pictures wrapped within paiper, and wreten
upon the paiper, ther names with hir awen hand.   Upon
the first that sche tok up was wreten, " My lordis picture."   I held the candell and pressit to se my lordis
picture.   Albeit sche was laith to let me se it, at lenth I
be importunite obteanit the sicht therof, and askit the
same to cary hame with me unto the Quen ; quhilk sche
refused, alleging sche had bot that ane of his.   I said again,
that sche had the principall; for he was at the farthest
part of the chamber speaking with the Secretary Cicill.
Then sche tok out the Quenis picture and kissit it ; and
I kissit hir hand, for the gret love I saw sche bure to the
Quen.   Sche schew me also a fair ruby, gret lyk a racket
ball.   Then I desyred that sche wald eyther send it as
a token unto the Quen, or elis my Lord of Lecesters
picture.   Sche said, gene the Quen wald folow hir consaill, that sche wald get them baith with tym, and all
that sche had ; bot suld send hir a dyamont for a token
with me.'

   Mary had instructed Melville to ' cast in some purposes
of mirrines ' among his ' matters of gravite ' lest he ' wald
be tyred upon.'   He not only spoke to Elizabeth there-

fore of foreign customs, but forgot not ' the busking and clothing of the dames and wemen,' and which ' was best setten for gentilwemen to wair.' 'The Quen of England said sche had of dyvers sortis; quhilk every day,' while Melville was there, ' sche chengit; ane day the English weid, ane the Frenche, and ane the Ytalien, and sa of others,' asking him which of them ' set her best.' He said the Italian, ' quhilk plesit hir weill, for sche delyted to schaw her golden coloured hair, wairing a kell and bonet as they do in Italy.' ' Then sche entrit to dicern what kind of colour of hair was reputed best; and inquyred whither the Quenis or hirs was best, and quhilk of them twa was fairest.' The pawky Scot replied that ' the fairness of them baith was not ther worst faltes.' ' Bot sche was ernest with me,' writes Melville, ' to declaire quhilk of them I thocht fairest. I said, sche was the fairest Quen in England, and ours the fairest Quen in Scotland. Yet sche was ernest. I said, they wer baith the fairest ladyes of ther courtes, and that the Quen of England was whytter, bot our Quen was very lusome. Sche inquyred quhilk of them was of hyest stature. I said, our Quen. Then sche said, the Quen was ouer heych, and that hir self was nother ouer hich nor ouer laich. Then sche askit what kynd of exercyses sche used. I said that [when] I was dispatchit out of Scotland, that the Quen was bot new com bak from the Hyland hunting; and when sche had leaser fra the affaires of hir contre, sche red upon gud bukis, the histories of dyvers contrees, and somtymes wald play upon lut and virginelis.'

After demonstration, and in answer to Elizabeth's persistent inquiries, Melville had to own that she played better on the virginal than Mary; and that his Queen did not dance 'sa hich and disposedly.'[61]

Again and again Elizabeth spoke of her desire to meet the Queen of Scots, and 'used all the meanis she culd,' says Melville, 'to cause me persuad the Quen of the gret love that sche bure unto hir, and was myndit to put away all geleusies and suspitions, and in tymes comyng a straiter frendschip to stand betwen them then ever had bene of before.'[62]

To Leicester's question, what Mary 'thocht of him, and of the mariage that Mester Randolphe had proponit,' Melville, as instructed, 'answerit very cauldly.' 'Then he began to purge himself of sa proud a pretence as to mary sa gret a Quen, estemyng himself not worthy to deicht hir schone' [i.e. wipe her shoes]; alleging that it was the proposal of Cecil, his secret enemy; and praying Melville to request the Queen of Scots 'not to imput unto him that lourd falt, bot unto the malice of his ennemys.'[63]

Melville tells that Mary—for reasons not altogether unselfish—was greatly pleased with the result of his mission.[64] After hearing an account of all his proceedings, she asked, whether he thought Elizabeth really intended all that she professed towards her. Melville replied that, in his judgment, 'ther was nather plain dealing nor uprycht meanyng, bot gret dissimulation, emulation, and fear that hir princely qualites[65] suld ouer schone [i.e. too soon] chaise hir out and displace hir from the kingdome.'[66]

On the 19th of October 1564, Randolph again reached
Edinburgh fully primed with explanations [67] as to why
Elizabeth had not sooner acknowledged Mary's proposal,
and to state that Bedford and he were now empowered to
treat with any whom she might name. He found Lennox
at the Scots Court, honourably used of all men, and the
Queen liking his behaviour. The current rumour was
that Lady Lennox and Darnley were also coming, and
there was ' a marvellous good liking of the young lord.' [68]
Randolph expected that Murray and Lethington would
say something to him ' touching Lord Darnley '; but
they did not, although it was ' in the mouths of all men
that it is concluded in this Queen's heart, and that Lethington is wholly bent that way.' Mary willingly heard
now of marriage, and listened to all that Randolph
could say. [69] Murray and Lethington, by her appointment, had a private conference at Berwick, on the
19th of November, with Bedford and Randolph, which
proved unsatisfactory. [70] Mary seemed anxious to please
Elizabeth, but naturally wished to make her ground
sure. [71] Murray and Lethington tried hard to bring
matters to a point—' foreign practices ' were coming on
so quickly that long delay could not be suffered ; there
must be some resolution one way or other—but Elizabeth and Cecil were much too cautious to commit themselves. [72]

' The winter was never extremer ; [73] sickness, for the
time of year, never so many '; yet the Queen of Scots and
her Court ' were never merrier.' [74] In January they had
gone to Fife. [75] It was while she lodged in a merchant's

house in St. Andrews that Randolph directly asked her
how she liked Leicester's suit. She answered that she
ought not to mislike such an one to be hers whom the
Queen his mistress did so well like. 'Marry, what I shall
do it lieth in your mistresses will, who shall wholly guide
me and rule me.'[76]

While Mary was yet in Fife, Darnley—who, through
the influence of Cecil and Leicester, had obtained permission to visit Scotland[77]—met her on Saturday the 17th
of February 1564-5 at the house of the Laird of Wemyss.[78]
'Hir Majeste tok weill with him,' writes Melville, 'and said
that he was the lustiest and best proportionit lang man
that sche had sean; for he was of a heich stature, lang
and small, even and brent up; weill instructed from his
youth in all honest and comely exercyses.'[79] Having gone
to see his father, who was with Atholl at Dunkeld, he
returned to the South in time to cross the Queen's Ferry
with Mary on the following Saturday. Next Monday he
heard Knox preach, dined with Murray and Randolph,
and after supper danced a 'galiarde' with the Queen at
Murray's request. His behaviour was liked, and there
was great praise of him.[80]

The Cardinal of Lorraine was still seeking to marry
Mary in France;[81] while she was anxious to know when
Elizabeth would make up her mind decisively.[82] When,
on the 16th of March, Randolph did communicate his
Sovereign's resolution to her—that even though she
married Leicester, Elizabeth would not proceed to the
examination or declaration of her interest in the succession, until she herself had married or notified her deter-

mination never to marry [83]—Mary ' was more commoved
than for that present she spake,' and by next day he learned
that she was not only dissatisfied, but had ' wept her fill.'
She and as many as knew of the resolution were grieved
at heart.　Lethington neither would, nor could, counsel
her to delay longer, and Murray thought that further
unkindness would grow between the Queens.[84]　Hitherto
Randolph had not thought that Mary had any special
liking for Darnley; but did not now know what might
happen.[85]　A month later he not only feared that she
would marry him; but his chief care was how to avert the
suspicion that Elizabeth was a worker thereof.[56]　There
was in Scotland a suspicion—strong, general, and pertinacious—that Darnley had been sent to the North by
the Queen of England for no good purpose.[57]

Lethington had been despatched to Elizabeth, with
whom Mary did not yet wish to break;[88] but the
vehement love which she began to manifest towards
Darnley at Stirling, during his illness and convalescence,
soon made it apparent that she was determined to marry
him.[89]　Whatever Elizabeth's motives may have been—
and they at least lend themselves to an evil construction [90]—in sending Darnley to Scotland, she now did her
utmost to make it appear that she wished no such match.
The peccant youth and his father were recalled.[91]　Throckmorton was despatched to Scotland, only to find that his
persistence and tact [92] were as futile as Randolph's influence,[93] as Murray's counsel,[94] or Lethington's dubious
wrath.[95]　As on another occasion—similar though later
—various explanations of Mary's headstrong determina-

tion were suggested. Some thought that its foundation was laid in despite and anger;[96] others, that she had been bewitched.[97] She herself afterwards explained that it was because the match with Don Carlos—which she had steadily preferred—was broken off against her will, and because the Archduke, as a poor foreigner, would have been of no advantage to her kingdom, that she determined to please her subjects by taking a native of Britain; that Elizabeth had only offered Leicester to deceive her and keep off others; and that Lady Lennox had continually entreated her to marry Darnley as the next after her in the English succession, as a Stuart by name, as one of the same religion, and as one who would respect her according to the honour conferred upon him.[98]

The good opinion which had been formed of Darnley at his arrival had rapidly changed. His pride was now intolerable; his words, not to be borne; and the hatred towards him and his house was great. Looking forward, the dismayed Scots could 'find nothing but that God must send him a short end, or themselves a miserable life to live under such government as this is like to be.'[99]

Numerous as were the objections that could be, and were, urged against this match,[100] much could be said in its favour. Darnley's own claim to the English succession would strengthen Mary's,[101] and the favour with which the English Papists regarded him was a factor not to be despised.[102] The Cardinal of Lorraine was not in ecstasies;[103] but the approval of Charles the Ninth was speedily obtained.[104] Philip, too, was satisfied, knowing

that Darnley's parents were 'good Catholics,' and his
'affectionate servitors'; and promised that, if his advice
were followed, he would aid them at the proper time in
asserting their double claim on the English throne.[105]
Mary earnestly desired to be under Philip's protection,
and promised—in April by Lethington, in June by the
Commendator of Balmerino—to follow his wishes in every
respect.[106]   Heretofore, Cecil and Elizabeth had by skilful management obtained their desire, that Mary's affairs
should 'hang in an uncertainty';[107] now she was to marry
the man of her choice, either with their approval or without it.[108]   Even in April it was asserted that the
marriage had already taken place;[109] and again it was
said that they were secretly married in Holyrood on the
9th of July, not more than seven people being present.[110]
The banns, however, were not proclaimed until Sabbath
the 22nd of July; and on that day Darnley, who had
previously been made Earl of Ross, was raised to the
Dukedom of Albany.[111]   Next Saturday evening the
heralds announced that she intended to 'compleit the
band of matrimony in face of haliekirk,' and that she
ordained that—in respect of the marriage and during its
subsistence—Prince Henry should be 'namit and stylit
King of this our kingdome.'[112]   At six o'clock on the
following morning—the 29th of July 1565—they were
married 'in the chapell of Halyrudhous . . . with greit
magnificence';[113] although the Queen was 'all clothed in
mourning.'[114]   The Lords then in Edinburgh were all
present on Monday, when the heralds anew proclaimed
Darnley King, and announced that now—since the mar-

riage was 'fully solempnizat and compleit'—all letters should be set forth 'in the names of bayth thair Majesteis as King and Quene of Scotland conjunctlie'; but of the nobles no one so much as said 'Amen,' except Lennox, who cried aloud, 'God save his Grace!'[115]

CHAPTER IX

1565

MURRAY's repugnance to the Darnley match brought him into dire straits. When he left the Court at Stirling on the 3rd of April, it was whispered that he had 'gone hence with her Grace's disfavour';[1] when, towards the end of the month, he—having been sent for—returned, 'he had worse countenance than he looked for.'[2] When pressed by her, early in May, to give his written consent, he declined to commit himself for various reasons. 'Most of all, he would be loth to consent to the marriage of any such one of whom there was so little hope that he would be a favourer or setter forth of Christ's true religion, which was the thing most to be desired, and in him so few tokens that any good would be done, who hitherto had showed himself rather an enemy than a professor of the same.' Hereupon there arose 'great altercation' between Mary and Murray. 'She gave him many sore words. He answered with as great humility and humbleness.'[3] Perhaps she repeated—what he had, no doubt, heard she had said a few days before—that he wished to set the crown on his own head.[4] Though her misliking

107

of him does not appear to have decreased,[5] yet he was the first of those whom she named—in the Commendator of Balmerino's Instructions—as commissioners for removing Elizabeth's occasions of doubt and suspicion.[6]

Mary soon found that Murray was not the only one who was alarmed on religious grounds. The fears of the Protestants were increased, if not mainly caused, by her resentment of the treatment accorded to the priest who celebrated—and to the two men who confessed hearing— mass at Edinburgh in her absence.[7] She and her Council deemed it prudent, on the 12th of July, to issue an assurance that it had 'nevir enterit in hir Majesteis mynd,' 'to impede, stay, or molest' any of her good subjects, 'in using of thair religioun and conscience frelie.'[8] A mere assurance, however, she found was insufficient, as 'the untrew report' of her intentions had had such effect that 'a greit nowmer of hir liegis' had taken to arms. Three days later, therefore, it was resolved to proclaim anew that they would 'nocht be inquietit' for religion or conscience 'in ony tyme to cum'; and to charge all her subjects 'weill bodin in feir of weir' to appear in Edinburgh, and there to remain with her for fifteen days.[9]

The General Assembly had, on the 26th of June, shown its anxiety by despatching commissioners to Mary to obtain her approval of certain articles, the first of which was that the mass, 'with all Papistrie and idolatrie and Pope's jurisdictiouns,' be suppressed throughout the realm, 'not only in the subjects but also in the Queens Majesties awin person'; and that 'the sincere Word of God, and His true religioun now presentlie receivit,' might be established throughout the whole realm, 'alsweill in the Queens Majesties awin person as in the subjects.'[10]   The Queen's Majesty, however, was not disposed to give a prompt assent to such a demand; and by her delay the Protestant Lords felt constrained to convene in Stirling, to consider what they should do, if she endeavoured to overthrow their religion, or gave occasion to Elizabeth to invade Scotland.[11]   Dreading Mary's ire, Chatelherault, Argyll, and Murray—'the factious Lords' as Keith calls them—appealed to the bounty of Elizabeth, who had been blessed 'with that most honorable tytile to be, under God, Protectrix most special of the professors of the religion.'[12]   On the previous day, Mary had sent the Commendator of Balmerino and Crichton of Eliok to ask Murray and Argyll to declare plainly, in writing, the name of the reporter, and the details of that conspiracy which they alleged had been devised by Darnley and others, in 'the bak gallerie' of her Perth lodging, for Murray's slaughter.[13]   The Earl's reply that he was willing to come to her 'for declaratioun of the trewth of the report maid to him,' if assured of his life, not only evoked the required assurance, but also a peremptory order for his appearance.[14]   Murray, discreetly perhaps, neither availed himself of her assurance nor complied with her command.[15]   There was a counter allegation that the Lords had intended to intercept Mary and Darnley as they rode from Perth to Callendar House on Sabbath the first of July.[16]

Though the Queen would not change her religion to win the consent of her Protestant nobles to the Darnley

match,[17] she professed to be willing to 'hear conference
and disputation in the Scriptures'; and even 'to hear
publike preaching,' provided it was 'out of the mouth of
such as pleased her Majestie,' and, above all others, would
gladly listen to Erskine of Dun, who was 'a mild and
sweet-natured man.'[18]   At Callendar House—to which
she had ridden in fear and haste—she witnessed the Protestant baptismal service, saying to Lord Livingston
'that she would shew him that favour that she had not
done to any other before.'[19]

As the result of Mary's proclamations there was 'great
repair' to her 'of men in warlike manner.'   A week before
her marriage they numbered six or seven thousand, and
her power was daily increasing.   Bedford, who had just
returned from London to Berwick, soon found that 'the
Gospel and the chief professors of the same in Scotland'
were in 'great distress'; that the Protestant party, being
very weak and much afraid, were all in their castles.   He
was particularly sorry for Murray—the 'noble gentleman'
who was destined to be overthrown—and wished to deal
plainly, 'either by aiding them at this their great extremity,
or else by a flat denial.'   Lord Hume—who was now a
Councillor, and doing 'almost all with the Queen'—was,
like all of that surname, a sworn enemy to England.
Bedford was willing—if Elizabeth would allow him, as it
were without her knowledge—'to impeach the devices of
the men of the Middle March, who are Murray's greatest
enemies,' and so cause Hume and them to return to the
Border 'to look to their own things.'[20]

Elizabeth, at the end of July, despatched John Thom-

worth to complain to the Queen of Scots of her strange
dealings with her; and to urge her not to call Murray
before those 'whom he had cause to judge his mortal
enemies.'[21]   Two days before Thomworth received his
Instructions, Mary had sent another assurance to Murray;[22]
three days before the English Envoy reached Berwick,
the inflexible Earl had been peremptorily summoned
to present himself 'befoir thair Majesteis' under pain
of rebellion;[23] and on the 6th of August—the day
before Elizabeth's representative was admitted into
the presence of the Queen of Scots—her former chief
minister was denounced as an outlaw.[24]   Chatelherault,
Argyll, Murray, and Rothes were in Argyllshire, waiting
to see which way Elizabeth would 'bend her face.'   The
more Thomworth travailed for them at the Scots Court,
the worse they sped.   Mary he found to be 'marvellous
stout, and such as he never would have believed.'   She
was resolutely determined 'to pursue them to the uttermost,' and that Elizabeth should not 'meddle to com-
pound the controversies' between her and them.   So far
as Thomworth could perceive, they hated her as mortally
as she did them.[25]

Darnley and Mary offered, on certain conditions, to
promise to do nothing to the prejudice of Elizabeth's
title; to receive none of her disaffected subjects; to
enter into no league against her; to make a confederacy
with her and her realm; and to attempt no change in
the religion, laws, or liberties of England, 'albeit it sall
pleis God at ony tyme heireftir to call thame to the
possessioun of that to the successioun quhairof thai haif

interest.' Their conditions were, that Elizabeth should
establish the English succession—failing her own issue
—in Mary, and, failing Mary's issue, in that of Lady
Lennox; that she should neither practise with nor harbour disaffected Scots; and that she should not enter
into any league against the King, the Queen, or the
realm of Scotland.[26]

Mary strained every nerve to the utmost both in the
council chamber and in the field. Rothes and Kirkcaldy
of Grange had been ordered to ward themselves in Dumbarton Castle; the Provost of Dundee, in Dunbar; and,
not obeying, they also were outlawed.[27] Lord Gordon,
who had been long warded in Dunbar, was released;[28]
and Bothwell, long in disgrace, was recalled.[29] On the
22nd of August, the Proclamation of four years before, 'anent the estait of religion,' was again renewed.[30]
Darnley went to hear Knox preach, but did not altogether
relish the sermon.[31] As 'thair Hienessis' now intended,
'God willing, in propir personis to pas, serche, and seik'
the rebels, 'and to bring thame to obedience, or utherwyise to persew thame with fyre and swerd,' the inhabitants of the Lothians, of the central counties from Fife
to Renfrew, and of the south-west, were called out—
'undir the pane of tinsall of lyf, landis and gudis'—to
meet ' the King and Quenis Majesteis,' at Edinburgh, at
Almond Water, at Falkirk, at Stirling, at Kirkintilloch,
at Glasgow, and at Irvine on specified days, ranging from
the 25th to the 29th of August.[32] Provision was also
made for the heirs of those who might be wounded or
slain in the royal cause.[33]

Mary had left Edinburgh on Sabbath the 26th of August, declaring that she would rather lose her crown than not be revenged on Murray, who with his party was then at Ayr.[34]   At four o'clock next Friday morning, Chatelherault, Murray, Glencairn, Rothes, and Boyd rode with twelve hundred horse into Edinburgh.   There, however, they did not receive the support they had expected, for many of their friends were alienated through Lord Erskine turning the Castle guns upon the town ; and having learned that the Queen was hastily returning to entrap them, they quitted the metropolis at three o'clock on Sabbath morning.   As Argyll was not with them, her forces outnumbered theirs by five to one ; and while she had arquebusiers they had none.[35]   By way of Hamilton and Peebles they retired to Dumfries.[36]   Had the weather not been so foul on Saturday, she would probably have intercepted them.[37]   Before that she had followed them so closely that they found time to rest in no place.[38] Much as Knox was opposed to her, bitterly as he could write against her, he could not help admiring her pluck. His pen is recognisable in the description of the vehement tempest of wind and rain, when the little brooks became rivers, through which her troops that Saturday marched with great difficulty and no little danger, and when ' albeit the most part waxed weary, yet the Queen's courage encreased man-like so much that she was ever with the foremost.' [39]

Next day—the day on which the Lords left Edinburgh —Mary issued a proclamation from Callendar stating that she and the King were that night departing ' towart Striviling for reposing of thair Hienessis,' and charging 'thair liegis and subdittis presentlie convenit with thair Hienessis at this present raid ' to meet them next morning by sunrise at Kilsyth.[40] Notwithstanding this proclamation and its penalties, many of her forces—weary of the matter—were falling from her daily. She, it was reported, occasionally bore a pistolet; of her company, Darnley alone wore a gilt corselet; all the others, after their country fashion, were in jacks.[41] As Argyll was said to be in her neighbourhood, it was thought that she might possibly leave Glasgow sooner than she intended.[42] If Elizabeth would only wink at Bedford's procedure, he (the Governor of Berwick) did not doubt that 'things would pass in other sort than they do.'[43] Randolph was assured that one country might receive both the Queens erelong, and that £8000 or £10,000 would bring it to pass.[44]

Meanwhile Mary was not altogether idle in Glasgow. On the 5th of September she sent out two proclamations, by one of which all the fencible lieges throughout the realm were warned to prepare and hold themselves in readiness to meet their Majesties with twenty days' provisions, when summoned;[45] by the other, those in certain districts were ordered to meet them at Stirling on the last day of the month, 'weill bodin in feir of weir, with palyeonis[46] and uther neidfull provisioun to ly on the feildis.'[47] On the 6th of September, provision was again made for the heirs of those who might be slain or wounded in pursuit of the rebels;[48] Lennox was appointed Lieutenant-General of the western shires, from Stirling to the Solway;[49] and Chatelherault, Argyll, Glencairn, Boyd, Ochiltree, and others were summoned to appear before the King and Queen at St. Andrews in six days, under pain of being denounced rebels, put to the horn, and escheated.[50] From Glasgow she also sent an urgent message to the King of Spain, craving his help.[51] Before she left Edinburgh, Atholl had been appointed Lieutenant in the North, with power to search for the rebels, 'to assege thair houssis and strenthis, and to persew thame with fyre and swerd, quhill thai be opprest or brocht to obedience.'[52] On the 17th of September, Bothwell— having escaped the pirate who seized Sutherland—landed at Eyemouth, immediately went to Court,[53] and was appointed Lieutenant-General of the East, Middle, and West Marches.[54]

From St. Andrews on the 13th of September, Mary emitted a declaration to expose the designs of the Lords, who, 'undir pretence of religioun,' had raised 'this uprore,' in order that they might 'be Kingis thame selffis'; or, at least, might 'tak to thame selffis the haill use and administratioun of the Kingdom.'[55] A proclamation issued from Dundee on the 14th—summoning the fencible lieges to Stirling on the 30th—was followed by a declaration on the 15th, assuring her subjects that she was anxious to hold a Parliament to give perfect security to those professing the religion which she had found universally standing at her return.[56] With the inhabitants of Dundee and Perth—who were ready to send help to the Lords—she was greatly offended. Dundee she might have sacked; but lacking money to pay her soldiers

—for which purpose she had already pledged many of her jewels—the honest burghers bought their quietness for two thousand pounds Scots. From St. Andrews and Perth she also took ' a benevolence, with as evil a will of the givers as ever money was paid '; and from Edinburgh she extorted a loan.[57] The Queen was in straits; but the Lords were in desperation. They lacked shot; they lacked money; they lacked men.[58] If Elizabeth would support them as they wished, it was believed that Morton, Ruthven, Lethington, and many others would join them.[59] Robert Melville was despatched to the English Court to press their needs and claims,[60] only to elicit the tardy response that they should accept such conditions as might be devised, as Elizabeth could not give them open aid without declaring war against Mary; nevertheless, to save their lives, she would receive them into her protection.[61] She had previously sent them money secretly,[62] and had even authorised Bedford to let them have three hundred of his soldiers without notifying that he had any direction therein from her; but ere he could act upon this permission she withdrew it.[63] The Lords had already realised that her secret help would do them little good.[64] From Dumfries they had sent out an elaborate declaration, explaining their position, and justifying their conduct;[65] but their numbers went steadily down.[66]

So far as Mary was concerned, the persuasions and entreaties of Mauvissière—who had come from the French Court—proved as ineffectual as Elizabeth's proffered mediation.[67] Like Saul of old, she was ' yet breathing out

threatenings and slaughter.'   On the 8th of October, she
set out from Edinburgh for Dumfries, with one woman
and an army estimated at from six to twelve thousand.
It was now rumoured that she had 'a secret defence upon
her body, "a knape scall" for her head, and dagg at her
saddle.'[68]   Ere she left Edinburgh, the Lords, discouraged
and perplexed, had taken refuge in Carlisle; and from
thence they went by Hexham to Newcastle, where
they meant to remain till God should otherwise provide
for them, or Elizabeth's pleasure be made known.[69]
Mary's army—'unwilling and unserviceable'—made
great spoil of the country, as it marched to Dumfries;
and was so disorderly led that it might have been easily
overthrown by a much smaller number.[70]   Leaving a
considerable force under Bothwell at Dumfries, she
returned by Lochmaben;[71] and, having disbanded the
rest of her army, arrived in Edinburgh on the 18th
of October with not more than a hundred and forty
horse.[72]

Mary's anger was increased rather than diminished by
the flight of her Lords into England;[73] while they, in turn,
were still hoping that Elizabeth would send them the
help she had promised.[74]   Against the wishes of Bedford,
they despatched Murray to Westminster, to plead their
cause with the Queen of England, who had encouraged
them by false hopes and failed them in the time of need.[75]
Elizabeth sent a pressing order to stay him;[76] but ere the
messenger met him he was within forty miles of London.[77]
Had he known the reception he was to get, he would
probably have been content to return even then to the

friendly Bedford. Modestly dressed in black, and kneeling on one knee, in the presence of the English Privy
Council and of the two French Ambassadors—De Foix
and Mauvissière—Murray had to listen patiently to the
hypocritical oration of the imperious and unscrupulous
Queen, to submit quietly to her pointed interrogation
concerning his opposition to his Sovereign, and to receive
meekly the warning that he occupied a very grave position, and might justly be held as a prisoner.[78]

Had not the result of Murray's active opposition to the
Queen of Scots been somewhat dubious, it is not likely
that she would have allowed him to remain quietly in
Dumfries for a month before he took refuge in England.
The utter collapse of his enterprise was chiefly due to her un-
tiring energy, to her politic assurances concerning religion,
and to the unsteadfastness of the English Queen, though
she herself was afterwards pleased to give the glory to
Bothwell.[79] In this crisis, her attitude towards Elizabeth,
while courteous and firm,[80] had not been rigid. She tried
conciliation;[81] she tried remonstrance;[82] and, there is
reason to believe, tried the more effectual means of
stirring up trouble in Ireland[83]—a project suggested to
her, she alleged, by Elizabeth's own favourite, Leicester.[84]

Murray was still in the flesh, and still uncondemned
by Parliament; but otherwise his overthrow was as complete as Huntly's. Chatelherault made his submission,
agreed to go into exile for five years, and was pardoned.[85]
But Mary's aversion to Murray was slow to soften. In
November she had still been willing to lose half her realm
rather than see him restored to his former state.[86] He,

Argyll, Glencairn, Rothes, Ochiltree, Boyd, Kirkcaldy of Grange, and others were summoned in December, at the market-cross of Edinburgh, 'to compeir in the Parliament' on the 12th of next March, 'to heir and sie the dome of forfaltour ordourlie led aganis thame.' [57]

CHAPTER X

1565-1566

ONE of the grievances adduced in the Dumfries Declaration by the Protestant Lords, to justify their open opposition to Mary, was her ‘leaving the wholsom advice and counsell’ of her nobles and barons, and following instead that ‘of suche men, strangers, as have nather judgement nor experience of the ancient lawes and governance of this realme, nor naturall love toward her Majestie nor subjects therof’—these strangers, indeed, ‘being men of base degrie, and seeking nothing but their owne commoditeis.’[1] Of these base foreigners, the most obnoxious to the Lords was David Riccio, or Rizzio, ‘commounlie called among us Seigneur Davie.’[2] Melville, who knew him well, describes him as ‘a merry fallow and a gud mucitien’;[3] and the French still ‘ascribe to him the composition of several of their popular airs of uncertain parentage.’[4] Mary’s friends and enemies agree that he was by no means good-looking; but there is considerable diversity as to his age.[5] A native of Piedmont, he came to Scotland in the train of Morette, the Ambassador from Savoy, a few months after Mary’s

return to her own country;[6] and at first won her favour
by his musical skill.[7]

When, three years later, Raulet fell out of favour,
Riccio was advanced to be her secretary for French
affairs;[8] and as his influence in his new sphere increased,
so did the hatred of the nobles towards him. 'Some of
the nobilite wald glowm upon him,' says Melville, 'and
some of them wald schulder him and schut [i.e. shoulder
and shove] hym by, when they entrit in the chamber, and
fand him alwais speaking with hir Majeste. And some
again that had hard turnis to be helpit, new infeftmentis to
be tane, or that desyred to prevaill against ther ennemys
in court or session, addressit them unto him, and dependit
upon hym; wherby in schort tym he becam very rich.'[9]
Buchanan avers that it was to prepare a protection for
himself against the hatred of the nobles that he 'courted
by every species of flattery the youth destined for the
royal bed, and attained such familiarity, that he was
admitted to his chamber, couch, and most secret con-
sultations.'[10]   He at all events approved heartily of the
Darnley match, and did what he could to advance it.[11]
The great influence which he had gained over the Queen
before that marriage[12] did not decrease after it.[13]   Mary
knew that the Lords did not love him, and willed
Melville to be a friend 'unto Seigneur David, wha was
haited without cause.'[14]

It was not merely as a favoured foreigner that Riccio
was hated by the Protestant Lords.   He was regarded as
an emissary of the Pope,[15] craftily plotting the overthrow
of that religion which they valued, not only for conscience-

sake and duty toward God, but also because its sub-version would have rendered their lives and heritages liable to forfeiture for heresy.[16]   Despite Darnley's apparent in-difference,[17] and Mary's repeated assurances both before and after her marriage, the fears of the Lords were only too well founded.   Her Proclamation of 25th August 1561—in which they had been inclined to trust—had been renewed but not enforced.[18]   No doubt the Primate himself had been imprisoned for its flagrant breach, but when her immediate purpose was served he had been set at liberty;[19] while those Protestants, who zealously handled their ecclesiastical opponents for dis-regarding her Proclamation, were harshly dealt with by her.[20]   Great as the Lords knew the divergence between her proclamations and actions to be, and much as they may have suspected her sincerity, they probably did not fully realise her duplicity.

In view of her marriage, the Queen had in May made a promise to the Lords, at Stirling, concerning the public establishment of their religion.[21]   The Pope, on the other hand, granted a dispensation for the marriage on receiv-ing her promise and Darnley's 'that they would defend the Catholic religion to the utmost of their power.'[22] During the three weeks preceding her marriage, she had by three proclamations tried to quieten the fears of her Protestant subjects as to her intentions in matters of reli-gion;[23] and in less than a month after her marriage she had complained in another proclamation that her rebellious Lords were untruly representing her as trying to subvert their religion.[24]   Yet in less than other three weeks she

wrote to the King of Spain, imploring his aid in averting
the ruin of the Catholic religion in her kingdom, and in
frustrating the establishment of the unhappy errors which
she and her husband were resisting to the hazard of their
crown.[25]   Before another week had passed, she had given
her subjects clearly to understand—in the Proclamation
issued by her and Darnley from Dundee—that 'thair
Hienessis intendis to hald Parliament sa sone as the
occasioun will permit,' in order that 'all actis, lawis, and
constitutionis, canone, civill or municipall,' prejudicial to
the Reformed religion of Scotland, 'may be abolischit
and put away.'[26]   Three weeks after that Parliament
had been abruptly extinguished, she took care to inform
Archbishop Beaton—her Ambassador at the Court of
France—that at its opening one important step had been
taken 'tending to have done some good anent restoring the auld religion.'[27]   The Bishop of Dunblane—her
accredited Orator at the Holy See—assured the Pope
that one of the purposes for which that Parliament had
been convoked was 'the revival of the primitive Catholic
religion, which had all but faded out of the minds of the
inhabitants of that realm.'[28]

This course of duplicity may have been suggested by
Riccio, who as Mary's foreign secretary had no doubt a
hand in it; but, to borrow the words of one of her
apologists, the lessons which her uncles had taught
her as a child 'were never forgotten by the woman and
the Queen.'[29]   No matter how often, when in straits,
she might re-issue her tolerant proclamations and re-
iterate her assurances concerning religion, she had returned

to her own country not to strengthen Protestantism but to re-establish the Papacy. Of this great object she had never lost sight, and to Pius the Fourth had protested that she never would.[30] It was to extol her religious zeal and constancy, as well as to plead for substantial aid and encouragement, that Yaxley had now been despatched to Philip of Spain,[31] and the Bishop of Dunblane to Pius the Fifth.[32] If, soon after this, she did not actually join the Catholic League—as has been often asserted—it was neither because she was not asked to do so, nor because she was lukewarm in the cause of the Papacy.[33]

Within a fortnight after the Darnley marriage, it was perceived that Mary had a special reason for the intense dislike she was then manifesting towards Murray and the Lords who were acting with him.[34] The hints as to the cause of this intense bitterness gradually became less vague, until, on the 13th of October, Randolph plainly informed Cecil that she hated Murray, neither for his religion nor alleged ambition, but because he knew and detested her secret conduct—conduct 'not to be named for reverence sake.' From other references in the correspondence of the period, it is evident that Riccio was even then regarded as the one with whom she had dishonoured herself.[35]

Sir James Melville and Throckmorton advised Mary, in her own interests, to pardon the exiled Lords. Elizabeth had treated them badly; and if Mary, after having so thoroughly crushed them, would now deal gently with them, she would for ever detach them from the Queen of

England and secure their grateful and most loyal support. Such magnanimous behaviour would, moreover, greatly strengthen her party in England, and help them to obtain for her the Parliamentary declaration of the succession.[36] When Murray was in power, he had neither befriended nor flattered Seigneur Davie; and now the hated foreigner could not be expected to befriend him of whose increased antipathy he had no doubt received some hint. According to Melville, however, Throckmorton's arguments had great force, not only with Mary, but Riccio 'apperit to be also wone to the same effect,' until the message came from France that she ought 'in nawayes till agre with the Lordis Protestantis that were banissit, because that all Catholik Princes wer bandit to rut them out of all Europe.'[37]

Melville gives two reasons for Seigneur Davie's temporary approval of Murray's recall. The first, that Murray had besought him very earnestly, and more humbly than any man would have believed, with a repentant letter, a diamond, and fair promises for the future; the second, that Riccio perceived that Darnley now bore him little goodwill, and frowned upon him.[38] To Riccio's cost, to Mary's, and to his own, Darnley had at length become partaker of Murray's suspicions. The vehement love and self-sacrificing devotion shown by Mary towards Darnley, both before and after their marriage,[39] had speedily cooled, or at least become less demonstrative;[40] and, rightly or wrongly, the petulant husband laid the chief blame on Riccio.[41] Before Darnley had been more than five weeks in Scotland, he expressed the opinion that Murray's possessions were too great;[42] and, since his marriage, he had helped his royal spouse to drive this leading noble into exile ; but now, without her knowledge and against her will, he was to bring him back.

In Randolph's letter to Leicester of 13th February 1565-6, it is affirmed that Mary repents her marriage ; that she hates Darnley and all his kin ; that Darnley knows she is false to him ; that there are practices in hand, contrived between the father and the son, to obtain the crown against her will ; that if that take effect which is purposed, Riccio shall have his throat cut with Darnley's consent within ten days ; and that it was even said that something was intended against Mary's own person.[43] Twelve days later, Randolph informed Cecil that Lennox was shortly to meet Argyll, when the proposal would be made that if he and Murray would concur to give Darnley the crown-matrimonial, the King would take their part, bring them home, and establish religion as at Mary's return.[44] On the 6th of March, Bedford and Randolph wrote Cecil concerning a great attempt which was to be made, and with which they had promised to acquaint none, save Elizabeth, Leicester, and himself. They referred to the jars between Mary and Darnley as due partly to her refusing him the crown-matrimonial, and partly to his jealousy of him at whose apprehension and execution he had determined to be present.[45]

It was on Tuesday, the 12th of March, that Murray and the other Lords were ' to compeir ' in the Parliament, ' to heir thame decernit to haif incurrit the cryme of lese

majestie, and to haif tynt and forfaltit lyff, landis, and
gudis.'[46] On the previous Friday, Bedford and Randolph
wrote to Leicester and Cecil, that Morton [47] was in Edinburgh, and that Murray and his whole company would
be there on Sabbath evening: but that before their
arrival the intention towards him whom Cecil knows
would be carried out.[43]   The leading details of the
terrible scene enacted in Holyrood on the evening of
Saturday the 9th of March are well known—the little
supper-party, the unexpected intrusion, the upsetting of
the table, the dragging forth of the terror-stricken victim,
the savage murder, the mutual recrimination,[43] and the
commotion outside.[50]

According to Archbishop Spottiswoode, ' The Queen
. . . sent one of her maids to enquire what was become
of Davie, who, quickly returning, told her that he was
killed; having asked her how she knew it, the maid
answered that she had seen him dead.   Then the Queen,
wiping her eyes with her handkerchief, said, " No more
tears; I will think upon a revenge." Neither was she
seen after that any more to lament.'[51]

Quickly as the colours in a kaleidoscope did the stirring events of the next nine days follow one another—
Darnley's Proclamation discharging the Parliament,[52]
the arrival of Murray and his meeting with Mary,[53]
the negotiations of the Lords to obtain her pardon, her
detaching the wayward Darnley from them and regaining
complete ascendency over him, her skilfully planned and
daring escape from Holyrood, her long gallop to Dunbar
in the early hours of Tuesday morning,[54] the formal

appearance at the Tolbooth of Murray and the others who had been summoned for that day,[55] her Proclamation charging the inhabitants of certain districts of the Lothians and adjoining counties to meet her 'in feir of war' at Haddington and Musselburgh,[56] the departure of the Lords 'with dollorous hartis' from Edinburgh on the morning of Sabbath the 17th of March,[57] the departure of Knox in the afternoon 'with ane greit murnyng of the godlie,'[58] and her own triumphant return next day.[59] In the very crisis of the conspiracy, Mary had not only shown great courage and fertility of resource, but amazing coolness.[60]

In his wife's undue familiarity with Riccio, Darnley may have had some cause for jealousy;[61] but Ruthven's narrative reveals the youthful King as sensual, unstable, base, and brutal.[62] Nau's story of the midnight escape from Holyrood portrays him as cowardly, coarse, and callous.[63] He proves himself to have been shamelessly untruthful by his solemn declaration of the 20th of March, denying all knowledge of and complicity in the Riccio conspiracy, and owning merely that he had consented to the home-bringing of Murray and the others without Mary's cognizance.[64] She knew too much, however, to accept this declaration as entirely true; and she soon saw enough to convince her that it was entirely false. Darnley had thrown off his fellow-conspirators. They retaliated by sending to Mary the bond he had signed, 'not only showing his complicity, but that he had ordered the thing to be done.'[65] Within a fortnight after his declaration was issued, she had also seen the articles between him and the Lords, and was grievously offended that he had sought the crown-matrimonial by their means.[66]

It is not surprising that, as De Silva puts it, Mary again fell out with Darnley.[67] With his instability friends and foes were alike dissatisfied.[68] Had Lady Lennox been in Scotland, it was supposed that neither would he have been led astray nor would these disputes have taken place, as she was prudent and brave and he respected her more than he did his father.[69]

CHAPTER XI

1566

Two Edinburgh lawyers, John Johnston and James Nicolson, after conveying English gold to Mary's rebels, had fled from the Scottish capital on the 25th of August 1565. Their goods were confiscated, but Johnston, having received a remission, returned to Edinburgh in the following February, when he confessed, before Mary and her Council, that Randolph had given him three thousand crowns to convey to Lady Murray at St. Andrews. Randolph was confronted with Johnston, but denied his story, and was ordered to leave the country, which he did a week before Riccio's murder.[1] In announcing Randolph's dismissal, Mary professed an absolute belief in the sincerity of Elizabeth's protestations that she had not helped the Scots rebels; and therefore assumed that he had been acting without her knowledge and against her orders.[2] Elizabeth, in complaining that Randolph had been dismissed for an offence which had not been proved, intimated her intention of dismissing Robert Melville—whom Mary had just sent to her to intercede for Lady Lennox, and to see what Elizabeth would do in the matter of the succession, if favour were shown to Murray and his fellow-exiles—and threatened that if Mary would not receive Murray into favour, she could not help seeing him relieved in England.[3]

Whatever Mary's motives may have been at the time,[4] she afterwards alleged that she had taken the Lords of the Chase-about Raid into favour at Elizabeth's request.[5]

On the 19th of March—the day after Mary's triumphant return to Edinburgh—her Privy Council ordained that Morton, Ruthven, Lindsay of the Byres, and sixty-seven others, should be publicly summoned to appear before the King and Queen in Council, within six days, under pain of rebellion.[6] On the 2nd of April, Thomas Scott—the sheriff-depute of Perth—was hanged, drawn, and quartered at the Market Cross of Edinburgh, for warding the Queen in Holyrood. Mowbray and Harlaw—two Edinburgh burgesses, who had been condemned with him on the previous day to the same punishment—were released at the scaffold, as ' our Soveranis movit with mercie gaif thame thair lyffis.'[7]

On the very day that Mary had shown both justice and mercy at the Market Cross of Edinburgh, Randolph wrote from Berwick to Cecil that she was seeking by all means to quieten her country.[8] This was no easy task, and she could expect little help from her witless and unstable husband. Through his plotting one set of nobles had been brought back from exile; another set had been banished; Parliament had been broken up; and a supposed rival cruelly murdered. Because the Queen had hesitated to give him the crown-matrimonial,[9] he had tried to obtain it in spite of her; and now—distrusted and despised on all hands—he had made it impossible for his fellow-conspirators to fulfil their desperate promises. Before Riccio's murder, he had not been distinguished by his extreme devotion to state affairs;[10] and now he was not to have less leisure for his pastime.[11] Murray's restoration had been successively opposed by Darnley, by Riccio, and by Bothwell;[12] but now even Bothwell and Huntly were reconciled to Murray;[13] and Argyll, to Atholl.[14] Murray and Argyll having been called to Court to be received into full favour, Darnley rode to Stirling to meet them; but the Queen sent Robert Melville to warn them against dealing with him, and they obeyed her injunctions.[15] Mauvissière having meanwhile arrived from France, Darnley returned to Edinburgh; but the Envoy would only speak to him in presence of Murray, Argyll, and the Council. He thought to buttonhole Mauvissière as he returned from the hunting-field; but again he was baulked through a warning from the Queen. Yet to please Mauvissière, he consented—though reluctantly—to the release of Arran, who had endured four years' imprisonment. Mauvissière told De Silva— and De Silva thought he was truthful though a Frenchman—that Mary and Darnley 'did not trust each other, but they behaved as husband and wife and were together, and especially after his arrival the Queen had been more affectionate to her husband.'[16] As Sir James Melville has it, Darnley 'past up and down his allane, and few durst bear hym company. He was mislyked be the Quen and be all them that favorit secretly the lait banissit lordis.'[17]　There was bad feeling, too, between him and Bothwell.[18]

Though Murray and Argyll could not yet venture to plead with Mary for the exiled lords of the Riccio conspiracy, they were earnest with her for those gentlemen who had waited on their masters and were not present at the slaughter.[19]　As she had prayed Elizabeth not to receive her traitors, and in special to deliver up Morton,[20] the English Queen ordered Sir John Forster to signify to him and his companions that they must provide for their safety outside her realm.　Forster delivered the message, which they were slow to obey—not knowing where to go, and he owning that he could so secretly bestow them that it would not be known where they were.[21]　When Mary pardoned Argyll she had an eye to his league with Shan O'Neil[22]—England's vigorous Irish foe—and, now that Mary was herself negotiating with Shan, Argyll and Murray were willing to promise to Elizabeth that he should not only get no support, but that they would openly oppose him, if she would not be rigorous with their banished brethren, and be a means that religion should remain unaltered in Scotland.　To Elizabeth it seemed easier ' to have some portion of money by way of reward secretly bestowed '; but Shan's offers were so tempting that Murray and Grange had to confess that Argyll's determination was ' not so godly ' as they could wish.[23]

Not content with displaying great zeal against those who were prosecuted for the Riccio murder, Darnley scrupled to sign Lord Boyd's pardon, on the alleged ground that he was in the plot. Nevertheless, the mis-liking between Mary and her husband had so increased by the first week of May, that it was judged he could not long dwell safely in Scotland.[24] By another week Randolph learned that Argyll and Murray's dislike of him was exceedingly great;[25] but early in June, he and Mary were reconciled,[26] and Argyll and Murray were also with her in Edinburgh Castle.[27]

Within the Castle, too, was Sir James Melville, praying ' nycht and day for hir Majesteis gud and happy delyvery of a fair sonne.' Between ten and eleven in the forenoon of Wednesday, the 19th of June 1566, he was informed by Mary Beaton[28] that his prayer had been granted. As he took horse it struck twelve; that night he was at Berwick; and on Sabbath evening he delivered the good news in London.[29] There was great rejoicing in Edinburgh. ' All the artailzerie of the castell schot, and banefyris wer sett furth in all pairtis for joy of the samyn.' If the joy is to be estimated by the number of the bonfires, it must indeed have been great, for in Edinburgh alone there were said to be about five hundred.[30] Killigrew arrived in the Scottish capital on the same day that Melville arrived in London, and found Huntly, Argyll, Murray, Mar, and Crawford at the sermon. Bothwell, who, he reported, had more credit with Mary than all the rest, was on the Borders, with the Master of Maxwell, professedly to prevent the return of Morton; but in reality to avoid Argyll, Murray, Mar, and Atholl, who were linked together at the Court, and slept in the Castle.[31] On Monday afternoon Killigrew saw the Queen, when she spake faintly with a hollow cough. The Prince, only five days old, he saw as good as naked, and thought him well proportioned.[32]

Before the birth of the Prince, Mary had prepared for the worst by making her will, of which no copy is known to exist;[33] but fortunately a most interesting testamentary inventory of her jewels drawn up at that time has been preserved.[34] The will, as summarised by her accusers, reflected her regard for Bothwell and her disdain for Darnley. But that summary has been discredited in one important point by the testamentary inventory.[35] In its sixteen worn and water-stained[36] leaves are enumerated more than two hundred and fifty lots, and opposite many of these there are in Mary's handwriting the names of those to whom they were bequeathed. At the end she added that the bequests were only to take effect if her child died with herself, for if he lived he was to be heir of all.[37] The bequests to Darnley include a diamond ring enamelled in red, against which she has written, 'It was with this that I was married; I leave it to the King who gave it me.' Among those whom she remembered are the Earl and Countess of Lennox, her maternal aunt the Abbess of St. Peter's at Rheims, her uncle the Cardinal of Lorraine, Lord Robert of Holyrood, the Earls and Countesses of Argyll, Murray, Bothwell, Huntly, and Mar, the Dowager-Countess of Huntly, the Earl of Atholl, Bishop Lesley, the four Maries, Joseph Riccio,[38] a person whose name she would not write,[39] and the University of St. Andrews.[40]

During her convalescence, according to her accusers,

she seemed to loathe her husband, but showed great favour to Bothwell; and, before the end of July, she suddenly went to Newhaven, there—with some of Bothwell's servants, 'famous robberis and pyrates'—to embark for Alloa; where, during her stay, she indulged ' in mair than princely, or rather unprincely, licentiousnes'; and where she gave a chilling reception to Darnley, who, on hearing of her departure from Edinburgh, had hurriedly followed her by way of Stirling.[41] If the contemporary writers and records do not bear out the grosser charges, they at least corroborate some of the minor details. Bedford states that when Mary left Edinburgh Castle, Darnley knew nothing of it;[42] and Nau's narrative coincides with the *Detection* on two points—that Darnley arrived at Alloa after her, and only stayed a few hours.[43] Bedford had just learned that Bothwell carried all credit in the Court, and that he was the most hated man among the nobles in Scotland.[44] A few days afterwards, he wrote that Bothwell's insolence was so great that Riccio was never more abhorred; that Mary agreed rather worse than before with Darnley—seldom eating with him, and loving none who loved him—and that 'it cannot for modestie nor with the honour of a queene be reported what she said of hym.'[45] After the Alloa excursion, he notified that the disagreement rather increased, and that Darnley had gone to Dunfermline.[46]

Mauvissière, who had been sent from France to congratulate Mary on the birth of her son, was able to tell Bedford, on the 9th of August, as he returned through Berwick, that the Queen of Scots and her husband had

136

been reconciled;[47] but this reconciliation proved to be as temporary as it was superficial. Darnley was displeased that Murray should have so much of Mary's company; and again left the Court much aggrieved. 'He cannot bear that the Queen should use familiarity either with men or women, and especially the ladies of Argyll, Murray, and Mar, who keep most company with her.'[48]

By the middle of August, Mary was hunting in Megotland, with Bothwell, Murray, and Mar.[49] Buchanan charges her, while there, with nothing worse than behaving coyly, loftily, and disdainfully to her husband[50] —a calumny inconsistent, in Goodall's opinion, with her 'genteel behaviour.'[51] On the other hand, Nau tells a story, incredible enough, to show Darnley's heartlessness towards her at Traquair.[52] According to Nau, while on her way back to Edinburgh she resolved to remove her child to Stirling; and for this purpose raised four or five hundred arquebusiers, who on the journey surrounded the Prince's litter.[53] Before the end of August, they had a few days' hunting 'in lone Glenartney's hazel shade'; and there, Buchanan alleges, Mary's conduct to Darnley was the same as at Megotland.[54]

In September, Maitland was received into the Queen's favour, and by her reconciled with Bothwell.[55] During the same month, too, her accusers assert she was guilty, in Edinburgh, of gross immorality with Bothwell; and her amatory exploits in the Exchequer House are related with circumstantial fulness.[56] Had the Lords of her Privy Council then known and believed the scandalous story, they could hardly have reminded Darnley, on the last day of the month, that he ought to thank God for giving him so wise and virtuous a wife.[57] Had Darnley suspected her guilt, and been able to substantiate it, he had an excellent opportunity, when, in presence of Du Croc and the members of her Privy Council, she 'took him by the hand, and besought him for God's sake to declare if she had given him any occasion' for his resolution to go abroad, 'and entreated he might deal plainly and not spare her.'[58] While the oft-quoted letters of Du Croc and the Privy Council prove that Mary and Darnley were on bad terms, they confute Buchanan's assertion that Darnley followed her from Stirling to Edinburgh only to be again excluded 'with maist dishonourabill disdane.'[59]

For 'the fortificatioun of justice,' Mary and Darnley had intended to pass into Teviotdale in the beginning of August; but the project was delayed on account of the approaching harvest. On the 24th of September the Privy Council resolved to summon the lords, gentlemen, and yeomen from a large district to meet their Majesties at Melrose, on the 8th of October, 'weill bodin in weirlyke maner, with xx dayis provisioun eftir thair cuming to Jedburgh.'[60] The exact date of Mary's departure from Edinburgh is not quite certain;[61] but Darnley did not accompany her on this expedition. He was still speaking of going abroad;[62] and—as it was alleged, and as Mary believed—he was writing to France, to Spain, and to the Pope, complaining of her lukewarmness in the faith.[63] She may have been as far as Borthwick, on her way to Jedburgh, when she heard of Bothwell's serious misadventure with Elliot of the Park;[64] but she remained in Jedburgh five or six days before she set out on her wild ride to the Hermitage.[65]

It was at this time—the 15th of October—that Du Croc wrote from Jedburgh:—'There is not one person in all this kingdom, from the highest to the lowest, that regards him [*i.e.* Darnley] any farther than is agreeable to the Queen. And I never saw her Majesty so much beloved, esteemed, and honoured ; nor so great a harmony amongst all her subjects, as at present is by her wise conduct, for I cannot perceive the smallest difference or division.'[66]

Mary's alarming illness at Jedburgh has been ascribed to various causes—the long ride to and from the Hermitage, the night air, anxiety for Bothwell, grief that the Papal Nuncio had to linger in France, aversion to Darnley, and poison.[67] Perhaps all save the last had to do with it. 'A distinguished physician' infers from the recorded symptoms that she suffered from 'an attack of hæmatamesis, or effusion of blood into the stomach, subsequently discharged by vomiting; presenting also, possibly, hysterical complications, the whole induced by over-exertion and vexation.'[68] From Mary's declaration to Lethington, he understood that Darnley was the root of her trouble. 'Scho hes done him sa great honour without the advyse of her frends, and contrary to the advyse of her subjects, and he on the tother part hes recompensit her with sik ingratitude, and misusis himself sa far towards her, that it is ane heartbreak for her to think that he sould be hir husband, and how to be free

139

of him scho sees na outgait.'[69]   When Lethington thus
wrote, in confidence, to her Ambassador in France, he
thought she had passed the crisis of her illness; but that
very night she became much worse, and next morning (the
25th of October) she seemed to be actually dead—'eene
closit, mouth fast, and feit and armis stiff and cauld.'
The skill and persistence of her French physician—'ane
perfyt man of his craft'—were at length rewarded;[70] and
the public prayers of her people answered.[71]   Lethington's
statement as to Darnley's behaviour being the cause of
her illness is fully borne out by her 'godlie and vertuous
sayingis' during 'her extreme maladie' which were carefully noted down by Bishop Lesley.[72]

Darnley has been denounced for not appearing at
Jedburgh until the 28th; and Buchanan has been cen-
sured for saying that he hastened there on hearing of
her sickness.   When he did arrive his reception did not
induce him to stay long.[73]

Bothwell was there a week before him—having been
brought from the Hermitage in a horse-litter—and in a
few days Lesley had been able to report that he 'con-
valescis weill of his woundis.'[74]   Her accusers allege that
she had not only arranged for his transport from the
Hermitage to Jedburgh; but had him removed from his
lodging there to the house which she occupied, and to
the room under hers; where she kept company with
him 'in very suspitious maner,' as they who were
present perceived; and 'the warld in thay same dayis
begouth to speik of it, compairing Boithuillis inter-
tenyment with that quhilk the King hir husband res-

savit at hir handis quhen he come fra Streveling to visite
hir.'[75]

In Paris, genuine grief had been caused by the expected
death of 'a Princess personally the most beautiful in all
Europe, and of a most cultivated and candid disposition';
and her remarkable recovery elicited expressions of gratitude to God 'for preserving this most virtuous Princess.'
These feelings were not entirely due to her beauty and
accomplishments; but were partly evoked by the probable
fate within her realm of that religion of which she was
regarded as the champion amid her blinded subjects.[76]

By the 30th of October, Mary was able to give
peremptory orders for procuring silk, plaiding, taffeta,
velvet, canvas, and thread, from Edinburgh.[77] Perhaps
the urgency of her commands was due to the fire by
which she was that night driven from her lodging.[78]
When about ten days later, she left Jedburgh, she proceeded by Kelso,[79] Werk, Hume, Langton, and Wedderburn; and at the head of nearly a thousand horse viewed
Berwick-on-Tweed—Forster, the deputy-governor, having
met her by the way, and convoyed her not only to Halidon
Hill, 'and from that west the town,' but almost as far as
Eyemouth. Her route then lay by Coldingham, Dunbar,[80]
and Tantallon to Craigmillar, which she reached on the
20th of November.[81]

Mary had not been more than a week at Craigmillar ere
Darnley came to visit her. She was still in the hands of her
physicians, not at all well,[82] and his presence was no cordial.
Her disease, Du Croc writes to Archbishop Beaton, is
principally 'a deep grief and sorrow. Nor does it seem

possible to make her forget the same. Still she repeats these words, *I could wish to be dead.*' The expression was far from being in accordance with the pious resignation she had displayed during her illness at Jedburgh;[83] but apparently Du Croc was not greatly surprised. ' You know very well,' he says, ' that the injury she has received is exceeding great, and her Majesty will never forget it.' During Darnley's brief stay at Jedburgh, Du Croc had had a great deal of conversation with him; and now he had an interview with him in the vicinity of Edinburgh, only to find ' that things go still worse and worse.' To Beaton, Du Croc confidentially adds, ' I do not expect upon several accounts any good understanding between them, unless God effectually put to his hand. I shall only name two. The first is, the King will never humble himself as he ought; the other is, the Queen can't perceive any one nobleman speaking with the King, but presently she suspects some contrivance among them.'[84]

When at Jedburgh the Queen had been able to see ' na outgait'; at Kelso, it was alleged, she had expressed her determination to have one; and now the ways and means were to be discussed. According to the *Book of Articles*, she repeated at Craigmillar her desire, so bitterly expressed at Kelso, to get quit of the King;[85] and suggested to Murray, Huntly, Argyll, and Lethington that she might be freed by a divorce, which could be obtained by destroying the Papal dispensation; but, when it was pointed out to her that there would thus be a risk of bastardising her son, ' she utterlie left that consait and opinioun of divorce, and evir from that day furth imaginit

142

and devisit how to cut him away by death.'[86] But according to the so-called *Protestation* of Huntly and Argyll, the divorce was first broached by Murray and Lethington to Argyll; then Huntly was brought in; Bothwell was next approached; and, finally, the five proceeded to the Queen, to whom Lethington opened the matter, promising that if she pardoned Morton and the other Riccio offenders, means would be found to divorce Darnley. She, however, would only consent if the divorce could be lawfully obtained, and no prejudice done to her son. When Lethington suggestively said that they would find means to rid her of him without disadvantage to her son, and that Murray would ' looke throw his fingeris,' she answered that she willed them to do nothing by which a spot might be laid on her honour or conscience, and prayed them rather to let the matter rest till God remedied it; to which Maitland replied, ' Let us guyde the matter amongis us, and your Grace sall sie nathing bot gud, and approvit be Parliament.'[87] Although this *Protestation* was prepared, fully two years afterwards, partly to inculpate [Murray, chiefly to clear Mary, and was sent by her to Huntly for his signature and Argyll's,[88] yet it does not venture to represent her as being shocked at Lethington's significant suggestion.[89] Murray emphatically denied that anything was said at Craigmillar in his hearing ' tending to ony unlawfull or dishonourable end.'[90]

Before the little Solomon was three months old, there was some talk at Paris of his marriage to Philip's daughter.[91] Before he was baptized, Elizabeth, ever

jealous of her title, procured the imprisonment in France
of a Scot named Patrick Adamson, who had printed a
small book of Latin verse on the birth of the Prince of
Scotland, England, and Ireland.[92]

James was almost six months old when he was baptized
at Stirling, on Tuesday the 17th of December 1566.[93]
Brienne, the representative of the most Christian King,
reported on his return to Paris, that all the rites of the
Roman Church were observed to the great satisfaction of
the Scots Catholics, who for seven years had not seen a
bishop in pontifical habits.[94]   Long afterwards, James
insisted that the use of the spittle—'a filthy and an
apish tricke'—was omitted at the request of his mother,
who declared 'that she would not have a pockie priest to
spet in her child's mouth.'[95]   Archbishop Hamilton—
'the most abandoned of all Episcopal scoundrels,' as
Froude righteously calls him—officiated.   The Bishops of
Dunkeld, Dunblane, and Ross, the Prior of Whithorn,
and 'the haill college of the Chappell Royall' were there
in their robes.   Huntly, Murray, and Bothwell—as well as
the Earl of Bedford—stood outside the chapel, 'becaus it
was done against the poyntis of thair religioun.'[96]   Before
her son was six weeks old, Mary had prepared a new
chrismatory of gold.[97]   As godmother Elizabeth sent, by
the hands of Bedford,[98] a massive 'font of gold, curiously
wrought and enamelled, weighing three hundred and
thirty-three ounces,'[99] which reached its destination in
safety in spite of those who lay in wait near Doncaster
to intercept it.[100]   Bedford was instructed what to
'say pleasantly' as to its size, and its use on the next

occasion;[101] but within six months, on the eve of her ill-fated marriage with Bothwell, Mary sent it to the mint.[102]

By five in the afternoon the baptismal ceremonies were ended; and a supper in the Great Hall was followed by 'dansing and playing in haboundance.' On Thursday evening the Queen entertained the Ambassadors and Lords to a great banquet. 'Thair wes masry and playing in all sortis' before supper; and after it a display of fireworks.[103] The masque seems to have been arranged by Buchanan and Bastien, the future author of the *Detectio* providing the Latin verses, in which he did not forget to extol the Queen's virtue.[104] Bastien's satyrs unluckily offended the English by wagging their long tails.[105]

Darnley, though residing in Stirling at the time of the baptism and subsequent festivities, was present at none of these; and for his absence Elizabeth has been unjustly blamed.[106] Six days before the baptism, Forster wrote to Cecil that Bothwell was appointed to receive the Ambassadors, and that all things for the christening were at his appointment.[107] One of Mary's earliest and most ardent champions does not hesitate to say that, even up to this time and beyond it, her rigour to Darnley was only feigned, and 'from her hearte shee perfectlie loved him.'[108] In the eyes of such a writer, it could not be more than a coincidence that, six days after the baptism, she suddenly restored Archbishop Hamilton to his consistorial jurisdiction, a step which is now admitted by Mary's co-religionists to have been 'at once illegal and unwise'; and the motive of which is too readily suggested by the only use which the Primate is known to have made of his recovered

K

power—the promoting of 'the scandalous divorce which removed the last obstacle to Mary's marriage with Bothwell.'[109]

It was on the 24th of December—exactly a week after the baptism—that Mary pardoned Morton and more than seventy others of the Riccio fugitives, towards whom she had justly been so implacable.[110]   It has been pointed out that she did this ' on Christmas eve, as a deed of charity and benevolence suitable to that solemn festival.'[111]   Motives of a more practical and less kindly type have also been suggested.[112]   According to Cecil's *Diary*, it was on that day that Mary and Bothwell went to Lord Drummond's; and about the same time Darnley left Stirling for Glasgow, where 'he fell deadly seck.'[113]   In Stirling, says the *Book of Articles*, he had been forbidden to appear before the Ambassadors; they and the Scots nobles had been desired to ignore him; he had been stinted in his necessary expenses; his ordinary servants had been taken from him; his silver-plate had been exchanged for pewter; ere 'he had ridden half a myle' on his way to Glasgow, he had been seized with that grievous and 'uncouth seiknes,' the nature of which showed that he had been poisoned; he had received his food ' furth of the Quenis kitchene,' yet she refused ' to send hir medicinar or ypothicar to visite him.'[114]   Other accounts, at least as trustworthy, bear that he was suffering from small-pox;[115] and Bedford states that she did send her physician to him.[116]

The Queen herself did not hasten to see her suffering husband;[117] and, as Bedford said, the agreement between them was 'nothing amended.'[118]   She tells of rumours

she had heard—rumours which could not be substantiated
—that he intended to crown the Prince and take the
government upon himself. Whether she believed these
rumours or not, she wrote bitterly about him to Archbishop Beaton on the 20th of January.[119] On the 27th,
Beaton wrote informing her that Catherine de Medici saw
nothing now to hinder her prosperity, save the variance
between her and Darnley, which she desired God to
appease with the rest of her 'traversis and cummeris';
and Beaton warned her to take heed to herself, as he had
heard vague rumours that something was to be enterprised
against her.[120] Their letters crossed. A few hours before
Catherine's advice and Beaton's warning arrived in Edinburgh, Mary was again to be a widow;[121] and the bearer
of her letter—Du Croc—was destined to deliver with it
the tragic tidings.[122]

CHAPTER XII

THE DARNLEY MURDER AND THE BOTHWELL MARRIAGE

1567

MARY'S earliest apologist states that although she might justly have had Darnley convicted, condemned, and executed for his 'pageants,' yet, when she heard that he was repentant, sorrowful, and desirous to see her, she hasted to him without delay, 'to renew, quicken, and refresh his sprites, and to comfort his hart, to the amendment and repayring of his helth.'[1] Two contemporary chroniclers state that it was on the 20th of January—the very day on which she had written so bitterly about him to Archbishop Beaton—that she left Edinburgh for Glasgow to see him.[2] Whatever her motives may have been, she and Darnley were reconciled, and that in spite of the hints which he is said to have previously received concerning the Craigmillar 'band';[3] and he agreed to go with her to Edinburgh in spite of his alleged misgivings.[4]

By the end of January,[5] he was lodged at Kirk of Field, not in the house which belonged to Chatelherault,[6] but in what Lesley calls a 'humble building,'[7] in what Buchanan describes as 'ane hous, not commodious for ane seik

148

man, nor cumly for a King, for it was baith revin and ruynous.'[8]   She knew that at least some of her nobles were willing to despatch him;[9] and yet she had brought him to a house of which the key of one door was amissing, and of which another door had to be taken from its hinges to form a cover for his bath.[10]   One of his servants afterwards deponed that her economy did not end at the door, that she caused an old purple bed to be substituted for a new black one in Darnley's room, in case it were spoiled by his bath.[11]   So devoted had Mary now become to her wayward but repentant husband, that, not content with visiting him by day, she spent two nights in the lower room of this miserable house, beguiling the long evenings by going with Lady Reres into the garden, ' ther to sing and use pastyme.'[12]

Darnley had been professedly brought here as to ' a plaice of gud ayre, wher he mycht best recover his health;[13] bot many ane suspected,' says Melville, ' that the Erle Bodowell had some enterpryse against him,' though ' few durst advertise him, because he tald all again to some of his awen servandis, wha wer not all honest.'   Lord Robert of Holyrood, however, did venture to warn him that unless he quickly escaped from that place ' it wald coist him his lyf.'   Naturally, perhaps, the intended victim told his wife; and the Lord Robert, when challenged, denied that he had given any such hint.[14]   Long afterwards—just before his own execution—Morton gave as his reason for not warning Darnley of the plot against him that he ' knew him to be sic a bairne that thair was nothing tauld him but he wald reveill it to hir againe.' [15]

Never apparently had Mary been on better terms with Darnley than on Sabbath evening the 9th of February. She remained with him for hours, entertaining him ' verey familairlie,' and was to have stayed all night, when—suddenly remembering that she had promised to grace the masque for Bastien's wedding—she gave the King a ring in pledge of her love, and returned to Holyrood by torch-light.   Within an hour after her departure, Darnley retired to rest.[16]   As the murderers afterwards confessed, while she was upstairs with Darnley the gunpowder had been placed in the lower bedroom which she had previously occupied.[17]   About two in the morning—10th February 1566-7—the honest burghers of Edinburgh were awakened by an explosion, which, by Mary's own account, was so violent that ' the house quhairin the King was logit was in ane instant blawin in the air; . . . of the haill loging, wallis and other, thare is nothing remanit, na, not a stane above another, bot all other [i.e. either] carreit far away, or dung in dross to the very grund-stane.' [18]   Darnley's corpse, which was not found among the ruins but at a considerable distance in the garden, bore no trace of the explosion which had so completely razed his temporary abode.[19]   The unhappy victim—of whom few modern writers save Maidment have said a kindly word—had not reached the age of twenty-one.[20]

Writing to Archbishop Beaton on the very day of the murder, Mary tried to persuade him that the enterprise

150

had been intended for her destruction as well as her husband's; affirming her determination rather to 'loss life and all' than allow such a horrible deed to remain unpunished—a deed which God would 'never suffer to ly hid,' and which she meant to punish 'with sic rigor as sall serve for example of this crueltie to all ages to cum'; and expressing the thought that it was God and not chance that moved her to leave Kirk of Field for the masque at Holyrood.[21] On that Monday 'hir Majestie was sorrowfull and quyet,' so at least Bothwell told Sir James Melville.[22] She was nevertheless 'sa grevit and tormentit' that she could not then answer 'the particular heids' of Beaton's letter which had arrived that morning; and delayed doing so until the 18th, when she gave him pressing instructions about her money matters, and her desire to have her infant son appointed Captain of the Scots company of the men-at-arms.[23] In replying on the 11th March, the faithful Ambassador—though without a sou in his possession—warned her that nothing was so much talked of throughout Europe as herself and the present state of her realm, which most 'interpretit senistrelye.' He deemed it his duty to tell her all that he heard to her prejudice, that she might the better remedy it; but there was 'sa mekle evyll spokin,' and that so odious, that he neither could nor would rehearse it to her. He did tell her, however, that she was blamed as 'the motive princi-pall,' and that it was even said that all had been done by her command. He earnestly urged her to do such justice as would declare her innocence to the world, and give testimony for ever of the treason of those who had committed such an ungodly murder; otherwise, he said, it would have been indeed better that she had 'lossit lyf and all.'[24] Bastien, who soon found his way to France, represented her as making 'great dule,' and using much diligence to try the doers.[25] But Mary was not consumed with such zeal.[26] The advice of Beaton was in vain, as was the threat of Catherine de Medici,[27] the pleading of Lennox,[28] the entreaty of Elizabeth,[29] and the petition of the Protestants.[30]

Robert Melville told De Silva that he 'left the Queen confined to her chamber, with the intention of not leaving it for forty days, as is the custom of widows there';[31] and Killigrew found her, on the 8th of March, in a darkened room, so as he could not see her face, but by her words she seemed very doleful.[32] She had not, however, been all that time in a dark chamber. It was on Monday morning that Darnley was murdered. On Tuesday, Margaret Carwood, her favourite bed-chamber woman, was married in Holyrood to John Stewart, the Queen giving the bridal feast.[33] By the end of the week, Darnley was buried with little pomp or ceremony;[34] and on Sabbath —six days after the murder—Mary went to Seton.[35] In other twelve days, Drury learned that she and Bothwell had defeated Huntly and Seton in a shooting-match.[36] There, too, says the *Book of Articles*, she golfed and played at 'pallmall,' and gave rein to her criminal passion for Bothwell.[37]

It was only too plain that he who was most in favour with the Queen, and who had been the first to break to her the news of her husband's death, was himself the chief

culprit.[38]   Though it was no light matter at that time to
accuse such an one, her offer of a reward to the first who
should reveal the murderers [39] was not allowed to pass un-
heeded.   Within a week after the tragedy occurred, a bill
was set on the Tolbooth of Edinburgh, charging Bothwell
and others with the crime.   During the night voices
were heard crying in the darkness that Bothwell had
murdered the King.   Other bills were posted on the door
of St. Giles, on the Tron, on the Market Cross, on the
Abbey Gate of Holyrood, and on the ports of the city.
Portraits of Bothwell, drawn to the life, and bearing the
superscription, ' Here is the murderer of the King,' were
scattered through the streets.[40]   On the 25th of February,
he was in Edinburgh, where he declared that if he knew
who were the setters up of the bills he would wash his
hands in their blood.   ' His followers to the number of
fifty,' says Drury, ' follow him very near, their gesture as
his is much noted.   His hand, as he talks to any that
is not assured to him, upon his dagger with a strange
countenance.'   The bills were not becoming less personal
or more loyal.   Drury sent copies of some of them to
Cecil to show him ' how undutifully the doers behave
against their Sovereign.' [41]

It was discovered that James Murray, brother of the
Laird of Tullibardine, had ' devysit, inventit and causit
be set up certane payntit paperis upoun the Tolbuith dur
of Edinburgh, tending to hir Majesteis sclander and defamatioun.'   Mary charged him to compear before her to
answer for his treason ; and, knowing that he would flee,
she on the 14th of March ordered diligent search to be

made for him, and forbade all 'skipparis and marinaris' to receive him in their ships under pain of death.[42] In vain he besought her favour, offering to bring five or six with him, and to charge as many in the Court as the devisers of the cruel murder, and to try it with them ' either armed or naked.'[43]

Although the Queen of Scots knew that Bothwell was at least the reputed murderer of her husband, she allowed him to rule her Court,[44] and gave him fresh tokens of her favour.[45] At length she wrote Lennox—Anderson dates this letter the 24th of March, Labanoff the 23rd—that those whom he had named should be tried; and if found guilty condignly punished.[46] In the list which Lennox had sent, Bothwell's name stood first,[47] yet within eight days she presented him with three of her costliest church vestments of cloth of gold;[48] and he sat as a member of the Privy Council, on the 28th of March, to arrange for his own trial.[49] Already the people judged that she would marry him.[50]

Edinburgh was filled with Bothwell's supporters; but Lennox, as he averred, was forbidden to bring more than a handful of retainers; and, although he could not have the proof ready by the 12th of April, no delay was granted.[51] Mounted on Darnley's courser, so Drury writes, Bothwell—after looking up to Mary's window and receiving from her 'a friendly nod for a farewell'— set out from Holyrood for the Tolbooth, ' with a merry and lusty cheer,' attended through the crowded streets by two hundred arquebusiers, and four thousand gentlemen.[52] In the language of the time, justice was ' smorit and planelie abusit.'[53]   Sir James Melville alleges that the jury 'clengit him, some for fear, and some for favour, and the maist part for commoditie.'[54]   In Buchanan's expressive words, 'Bothwell was not clensit of the cryme, bot, as it wer, waschit with sowteris bleking.'[55]

Four days later, when the Queen rode to her Parliament in the same Tolbooth, Bothwell carried the sceptre.[56]   It was afterwards asserted by Mary, by the Lords who adhered to her, and by others, that Bothwell's acquittal was ratified in that Parliament;[57] but in its records—and it is one of the two Marian Parliaments of which the original records have been preserved—there is no such ratification.   The records, however, contain what may have been regarded as a virtual acknowledgment of his innocence—the ratification of the captaincy of Dunbar Castle to him on account of his 'gret and manifald gud service,' and the stringent Act concerning 'placardes and billis and ticquettis of defamatioun.'[58]

When Parliament was closed on Saturday the 19th of April, Bothwell bore the sword of honour back to Holyrood.[59]   That evening, after a supper to which he had invited them, he induced through fear or fraud a number of the Lords to sign a 'band' declaring their belief in his innocence; their determination to defend him against calumny; and their resolution, should Mary choose him as her husband, to further the marriage ' so farr as it may pleise our said Soverane Lady to allow.'[60]   Next day, Kirkcaldy of Grange wrote to Bedford that Mary was intending to take the Prince out of the Earl of Mar's hands to put him into Bothwell's, for whom, she had been heard to say, she cared not to lose France, England, and her own country, and that she would go with him to the world's end in a white petticoat ere she left him.[61]

On Monday she set out for Stirling to see her child;[62] and as she returned to Edinburgh, on Thursday (the 24th of April), Bothwell intercepted her, and carried her to Dunbar.[63]   Sir James Melville, who was with her, was told by his captor that 'it was with the Quenis awen consent.'[64]   Drury, too, writing three days after the event, said that, although the manner appeared to be forcible, it was known to be otherwise.[65]   It is quite certain that this was the common opinion at the time.[66]   Before the nobles signed the 'band' to Bothwell, De Silva had written to Philip that it was hinted in London that marriage with Mary was Bothwell's object in his intended divorce from his wife;[67] and, before the capture, the French Ambassador at the English Court felt certain that, if the divorce were effected, this marriage would take place.[68]   Nine days after the capture, De Silva wrote that as Bothwell's horsemen arrived near Mary, 'with their swords drawn, they showed an intention of taking her with them, whereupon some of those who were with her were about to defend her; but the Queen stopped them, saying she was ready to go with the Earl of Bothwell wherever he wished rather than bloodshed and death should result.'[69]   In the same letter to Philip, De Silva says:—'It is believed that the whole thing has been arranged so that, if anything comes of the marriage, the Queen may make out that she was forced into it.'   De Silva further tells his royal master that he received this information not only from Elizabeth and

Cecil, but also 'from the man who brought the news, who is a good Catholic, and an intimate acquaintance of mine.'[70]

No time was lost in entering and carrying through the double process for divorce. Within two days of the capture, Lady Bothwell lodged her libel in the Commissary Court, claiming divorce because of the Earl's adultery with one of her servants;[71] and next day, Archbishop Hamilton granted a commission to certain of his clergy to try the validity of the marriage.[72] On the 3rd of May, Lady Bothwell—a devout Romanist—obtained judgment from the Protestant Commissaries against her husband;[73] and, on the 7th, her professedly Protestant husband procured from the Papal Court the decision that their marriage had been null from the beginning for lack of a dispensation.[74] That there was collusion between Bothwell and his wife, her brother (Huntly), and Archbishop Hamilton seems certain enough.[75] So far as ability was concerned, the illegitimate Archbishop was the real head of the House of Hamilton, and a desire to advance the regal claims of that house probably explains his silence regarding the dispensation he had previously granted.[76]

On the day before the Papal Court gave its decision, Mary had returned to Edinburgh with Bothwell, Huntly, Lethington, and others. At their arrival, 'the artailyarie of the Castell schot maist magnificientlie; and thairefter [they] came in at the West Port of the said burgh, and raid up the Bow to the Castell, the said Erle Bothwill leidand the Quenis Majestie by the bridill as captyve.'[77]

157

The same day, if not before, Knox's colleague—the faithful and fearless Craig—was asked by Thomas Hepburn, in the Queen's name, to proclaim the banns of marriage between her and Bothwell. This the preacher pointblank refused to do without her writ. On Wednesday the 7th, the Justice-Clerk brought him a command signed by her, bearing in effect that 'sho was neither ravischit nor yet retainit in captivitie,' and charging him therefore to make proclamation. When constrained to do so, he publicly took heaven and earth to witness that he abhorred and detested the proposed marriage.[78] Next Wednesday—Bothwell having meanwhile been created Duke of Orkney, Mary placing the coronet on his head with her own hands[79]—the marriage-contract was concluded ;[80] and on Thursday (the 15th of May 1567) they were married, 'in the Palice of Halyrudhous, within the Auld Chappell, be Adame, Bischope of Orknay, not with the mess, bot with preitching, at ten houris afoir none,' and 'thair wes nathir plesour nor pastyme usit,' as 'wes wont to be usit quhen princes wes mariit.'[81] Some of her friends—anxious perhaps to save her religious reputation—averred that she and her husband heard a mass in the morning;[82] and from this possibly arose the statement of their enemies that they were married after both forms.[83]

Only three months and five days had passed since Darnley was so daringly murdered. Only fifteen months had elapsed since Bothwell and Lady Jean Gordon had been contracted with 'the advis and expres counsale' of the Queen of Scots, who had signed their marriage-contract, provided a marriage-banquet, and presented the bride with a wedding-dress of cloth of silver lined with white taffeta.[84]   Only one month more was to go by ere Mary was fated to part reluctantly and for ever from her third husband.

CHAPTER XIII

1567-1568

MARY's behaviour before and after Darnley's murder is, in the opinion of many, quite sufficient to establish her guilt. It is not easy to get over the incontrovertible outstanding facts, that she was on bad terms with him until the suspicious reconciliation, which was so quickly followed by his tragic death; that the favour which she had been showing to Bothwell continued to increase, although he was commonly and justly regarded as the chief murderer; and that, in spite of the remonstrances of her outspoken friends,[1] she married him so soon after the murder. Around these central facts are grouped multitudes of details, almost every one of which has been the subject of keen controversy. To one set of writers, the general drift of these details only shows more clearly Mary's infatuated love for Bothwell, and her determination to have him in spite of all obstacles. To another set, they furnish convincing proof that she was the unfortunate, if not helpless, victim of a huge conspiracy to hurl her from her throne. One of her most recent and most brilliant apologists is certainly not too severe on

her in holding that she was not entirely unaware of the
measures of the nobles to secure Darnley's removal; and
'that, if she did not expressly sanction the enterprise, she
failed, firmly and promptly, to forbid its execution.'[2]
The *Book of Articles* and the *Detection*, however, represent her part of the play as far from passive. According
to them, she was not only passionately enamoured of
Bothwell, but bent on being rid of Darnley, whom she
treacherously lured to his doom.[3]

Mary's apologists are hard put to it in trying to explain
or palliate her conduct in marrying Bothwell. Unfortunately, their most plausible excuses are refuted by
her own deeds or words; and the ardent zeal of one
apologist is occasionally under-cut by the bold assertion
of another. Blackwood—perhaps the most audacious of
her early champions—coolly asserts that she was made
to believe that Lady Bothwell was dead:[4] a statement
utterly inconsistent with Mary's own Instructions to the
Ambassadors she sent to France and England.[5] Claude
Nau escapes this difficulty in his narrative, by entirely
ignoring Lady Bothwell and the double divorce. Bishop
Lesley—unable to explain satisfactorily how Mary was
'induced to take a step so improper and unsuitable'—
wriggles and lies shamelessly in his perplexity;[6] and, as
the best excuse, can only repeat the general opinion,
that 'Bothwell threw the Queen's mind into a confused
state by means of magical arts.'[7] Yet the Jesuit priests,
in their report to Clement the Eighth, allege that Bothwell 'permitted himself to be led as the Queen pleased.'[8]
Others vigorously insist that she was under Bothwell's

power from the abduction to the marriage, and not being a free agent was irresponsible;[9] but over and above her statement to John Craig, that 'sho was neither ravischit nor yet retainit in captivitie,'[10] she appeared before the Lords of Session, three days before the wedding, declaring that she was at liberty, that she had forgiven Bothwell, and intended to promote him to greater honours.[11]   One champion, whose zeal far outstrips his knowledge, alleges that her being married in widow's-weeds was 'perhaps the strongest evidence she could give of her intense dislike and disgust at the whole affair';[12] but, if her garb on this occasion meant so much, what is to be inferred from her wearing mournings when she was married to Darnley?[13]

To her Dominican confessor—who had previously warned her against such a union—Mary's own excuse was that her object was by this means to settle religion.   This may have been an excellent reason to urge upon one who believed her to be 'not only a good but a very devout Catholic,'[14] although it is not quite apparent how she was to advance the interests of the Papacy by a husband who was at least nominally a Protestant.[15]   Despite all that has been said to the contrary, Bothwell was neither old nor ugly.   According to a contemporary account, he was then 'a young man twenty-five years old, of handsome presence';[16] or, as Bishop Lesley has it, a man 'endowed with great bodily strength and masculine beauty, but vicious and dissolute in morals.'[17]

It is not quite clear from Lesley's narrative whether he and his co-religionists objected so much to the marriage in itself as to the heretical mode of its celebration; but

to him she ' with many tears unlocked the secret of her
heart,' and showed many signs of repentance, promising
' that never again would she do anything opposed to the
rites of the Catholic and Roman Church, or permit any
such thing to be done in her presence, even if it should be
at the peril of her life.' Three days after her marriage,
' she publicly received the Eucharist after sacramental
confession, in order to repair by so excellent an example
of piety the mischief caused by her fault.'[18]

Mary's married happiness with Bothwell was far from
perfect, although they were occasionally merry together,[19]
and though in public he reverenced her as his sovereign.[20]
She was indeed frequently rendered miserable by his
jealousy;[21] yet it was alleged that he passed several days
a week with his divorced wife, regarding her still as his
lawful spouse and the Queen as his concubine.[22] Only two
days after the wedding she cried for a knife that she might
kill herself.[23] De Silva was inclined to explain her misery by
the maxim that ' an evil conscience can know no peace.'[24]

The Lords who had at length resolved on Bothwell's
overthrow[25] arrived at Borthwick Castle on the night of
the 10th of June.[26] Knowing that it could not stand a
siege, he slipped out and escaped.[27] Next night—in male
attire, booted and spurred—Mary also left Borthwick,
rejoined her husband, rode with him to Dunbar, and
helped him to raise an army.[28] Meanwhile the Lords
had entered Edinburgh, and, having proclaimed their
intentions, charged the subjects to assist in delivering
the Queen from thraldom, in preserving the Prince, and
in punishing the murderers of the King.[29]

On Sabbath, the 15th of June—exactly a month after the fateful wedding—the two armies met at Carberry. In point of numbers they were not unequally matched; but Mary's forces were half-hearted in the cause, many of them deserting while Du Croc was hopelessly trying to restore peace. She was eager to fight, but loth to allow Bothwell to engage in single combat. In the evening she persuaded him, says Beaton, 'to loup on horsebak and ryd his way,' and when he had covered 'twa myles or mair' she offered to render herself. She parted from him with many kisses and much grief; and was received in the other camp by Atholl's company and Tullibardine's shouting with one voice—'Burn the whore!' By ten o'clock on that summer Sabbath evening she arrived at Edinburgh, and, amid the fervid denunciations of the populace, was lodged in the Provost's house opposite the Market Cross.[30] That night, it was alleged, she wrote to Bothwell, 'calling him hir dear hart, whom sche suld never forget nor abandoun for absens,' assuring him that she had only sent him away for his safety, willing him to be comforted, and warning him to be on his guard. The keeper to whom she intrusted the missive was base enough to hand it to the Lords.[31]

The banner—with a representation of her murdered husband, and her fatherless infant crying, 'Judge and revenge my caus, O Lord! —which had waved before her at Carberry,[32] was now hung before her window, wherewith she seemed much offended.[33] Next day she came to the window, crying to the people that she was kept in prison by her subjects, who had betrayed her. 'Sche cam to the said windo sundrie tymes in sa miserable a stait, her hairs hingand about her loggs [*i.e.* ears], and hir breist, yea the maist pairt of all her bodie, fra the waist up, bair and discoverit, that na man could luk upon hir bot sche movit him to pitie and compassion. For my ain part,' says the sympathising Beaton, 'I was satisfiet to heir of it, and meicht nouch suffer to see it.'[34] Though her condition was so desperate and deplorable she was not dismayed.[35] She managed to send a secret message to the Captain of the Castle,[36] desiring him 'to keip a gud hart to hir,' and not to render the Castle to the Lords. That evening—Atholl on one side of her, Morton on the other, and the arquebusiers bearing the ubiquitous banner before her—she was convoyed to Holyrood; and from thence hurried off to Lochleven, which she reached on the following day, Tuesday, the 17th of June.[37]

This island castle was no new abode to Mary, who knew it well.[38] Once indeed she had had a discussion there with Knox, and not far from its shore she had had her one pleasant interview with him.[39] Now it was selected as her prison, say the nine lords[40] who sign the warrant for her captivity, because they found 'na place mair meitt nor commodious for hir Majestie to remane into.' Her deliverance from thraldom was one of the objects which the Confederate Lords professed to have in view when they marched to Carberry Hill. For now imprisoning her, they assigned the reason that, instead of agreeing as they proposed to punish Darnley's murderers, she rather 'apperit to fortefie and mantene' Bothwell and his accomplices in their wicked crimes; and as the realm would therefore be utterly ruined, if she were left 'to follow hir awin inordinat passioun,' it was 'thocht convenient, concludit and decernit that hir Majesties persoun be sequestrat fra all societie of the said Erll Boithuile, and fra all having of intelligence with him, or ony utheris quhairby he may have ony comfort to eschaip dew punisment for his demeritis.'[41]

Mary's ambitious projects were now hopeless,[42] her reputation blasted, her freedom gone; meanwhile, at least, all had been wrecked by what seemed to be an infatuated love for Bothwell.[43] Yet prisoner as she was, she still had a party, not despicable in power, though animated perhaps by selfish motives.[44] Elizabeth was averse to support those who had presumed to incarcerate a sister Sovereign;[45] but was eager to get the infant Prince into England, on the plea that he would be cared for by his grandmother[46] —that grandmother whom she had previously thought fit to imprison because her son had ventured to marry the Queen of Scots.[47] The French were also anxious to have the little Prince in their country.[48] But the Scottish lords—knowing too well how their own power depended on his presence—would not part with him.[49]

The captive Queen naturally resented the treatment to which she had been subjected. 'In this prison, and in the midst of such desolation,' says Nau, 'her Majesty remained for fifteen days and more, without eating, drinking, or conversing with the inmates of the house, so that many thought she would have died.'[50] By the fourteenth day, however, Drury had learned at Berwick that she 'better digests' her captivity, and 'uses some exercise.'[51]

When Throckmorton reached Edinburgh, before the
middle of July, he reported to Elizabeth that Mary was
in good health,[52] though kept very straitly[53] by Lord
Lindsay[54] and the Laird of Lochleven; that, so far as he
could perceive, this rigour was because she would neither
lend her authority for prosecuting the murderers, nor
abandon Bothwell as her husband—being willing rather to
quit crown and kingdom and to live with him as a simple
damsel, than suffer him to fare worse than herself; and
that the Lords, nevertheless, spoke of her ' with respect
and reverence,' and seemed to say that if she and Bothwell
were divorced they would restore her to liberty and
power.[55]   The chief of those then in Edinburgh, it was
thought, did not dare, for fear of the people, to show her
as much lenity as they might have done. ' The women
be moost furious and impudent against the Queen,' writes
the English Ambassador, ' and yet the men be mad
enoughe; so as a stranger ever busye maye soone be
made a sacrafyce amongest them.'[56]   Lord Ruthven,
whose father had played such a prominent part in the
Riccio tragedy, had been selected as one of her warders;
but already he had to be employed elsewhere, ' because he
began to shew favor to the Queen and to geve her in-
tellygence.'[57]   Apparently she still had that about her
' whareby men ar bewitched '; and it was soon found that
Ruthven was not the only one in Lochleven who was
susceptible to her charms.

Before the experienced Throckmorton had been ten
days in Scotland, he had to confess that he had never
before been ' in so busy and dangerous a legation.'   He

was bearing all the parties 'fayre in hande,' that he might the better discover their designs, though he liked 'nothinge of theyr doings.'[58] Elizabeth's wishes could not be carried out, as the Lords would neither set Mary free nor allow him to see her.[59] He found means, however, to let her know that he had been sent to Scotland for her relief, and tried to persuade her to agree to a divorce from Bothwell. This she firmly refused to do, saying she would rather die, as, 'takynge herselfe to be seven weekes gon with chylde, by renouncynge Bodwell she shoulde acknowledge herselfe to be with chylde of a bastarde, and to have forfayted her honoure.'[60] By the end of July Throckmorton expressed the conviction that he had in the meantime saved her life.[61] The tragedy he had thought might end violently in her person, 'as yt began in Dayves and her husbandes.'[62]

Elizabeth might threaten, but the Confederate Lords had gone too far to be easily persuaded to retrace their steps.[63] The heads of Mary's party—the Hamiltons, Argyll, and even Huntly—it was alleged would have offered no serious objection to her execution.[64] If Charles the Ninth wished to help his sister-in-law, he was effectually restrained by his mother.[65] Public opinion in Scotland was bitterly opposed to her;[66] and Knox was threatening the nation with the great plague of God if she were not condignly punished.[67]

On the 24th of July (1567), Mary was induced—through fear or policy or both—to sign three documents, by one of which she declared that her body, spirit, and senses, were, through the toil of governing, 'sa vexit, brokin and unquietit,' that she could no longer endure it; and therefore of motherly affection and of her 'awin motive will' renounced and demitted the government to her infant son, and authorised his coronation. By the second document she appointed Murray to act as Regent until her son was seventeen; and by the third she nominated Chatelherault, Lennox, Argyll, Atholl, Morton, Glencairn, and Mar, to act as Regents until Murray's arrival, or in case of his death, or to act with him if he refused the office singly.[68]

On the 29th of July—the second anniversary of Mary's marriage with Darnley—the Prince, now thirteen months old, was solemnly crowned in the parish church of Stirling, when Knox preached the sermon.[69] 'To honor the sayde coronation and to testefye greate joye, thys towne of Edenbroughe,' writes Throckmorton, 'made, the sayde 29 daye, at night verye neere, I thynke, a thousande bonefyers: the castell shot of 20 peeces of artyllerye, the people made greate joye, dauncyinges and acclamacyons; so as yt apperethe they rejoyced more at thinauguracyon of the newe Prynce then theye dyd sorowe at the depryvacyon of theyre Quene.'[70]

Though Mary had demitted the government, she was not kept less rigorously in Lochleven;[71] and within a few days was transferred to the tower of the Castle, where her liberty was even more restricted.[72] There were two reasons for this, as Throckmorton informed Elizabeth on the 5th of August: the first being that she had 'won the favour and goodwill of the house, as well men as women, whereby she had means to have great intelligence, and

169

was in towardness to have escaped.' The other reason was that she might be induced to relinquish Bothwell, of which Throckmorton did 'not now so much despair as heretofore.'[73]

Murray, after an absence of four months, reached Edinburgh on the 11th of August;[74] had long interviews with the Queen in Lochleven on the 15th and 16th;[75] and on the 22nd was proclaimed Regent.[76] On the 21st he told Throckmorton that he approved the action of the Confederate Lords; and that, although it should cost him his life, he intended 'to reduce all men to obedience in the King's name.'[77] Already some of the Queen's party were offering to make their peace with the Regent.[78]

Before Mary had been a day in Lochleven, at least two of Darnley's suspected murderers had been arrested.[79] One of these, Captain William Blacater, was, after his apprehension, nearly stoned to death by women and boys. On the 24th of June he was tried by a jury of Lennox gentlemen, found guilty, condemned as a traitor, and on the same day 'drawin backward in ane cairte frome the Tolbuith to the Crosse,' and there—despite his protestations of innocence—'hangit and quartred, for being on the King's murther.'[80] Two days later the Privy Council determined—as Bothwell's servants had now testified that he was not only the inventor and deviser of the murder, but 'the executor with his awin handis'—that proclamation should be made prohibiting the lieges to reset, supply, or support him, and offering a thousand crowns of the sun to any one who would bring

him into Edinburgh.[51]   On the 17th of July, he and
several others were publicly declared rebels and outlaws.[52]
He was, nevertheless, 'to the sklander and defamatioun
of this haill natioun,' sheltered in Spynie Castle, by his
aged relative, the incorrigible Bishop of Moray, whose
tenants, tacksmen, and feuars were therefore forbidden
to pay him any rents or teinds.[53]

Though Huntly still bore his former brother-in-law 'a
verye fayre countenaunce,' he now entered, it was said,
into a conspiracy with the captain of Spynie Castle,
and three of the Bishop's illegitimate sons, to murder
both the Bishop and Bothwell; but Bothwell slew one
of the sons, turned the Bishop's servants out of the
Castle, and committed the guard to his own followers.[54]

It had been already reported that the husband of the
Queen of Scots had fitted out four or five vessels, intending 'to allure the pyrates of all countreys unto hym,'
and 'to use the sea for hys uttermooste refuge.'[55]   He
and his pirates having turned their unwelcome attention
to the Orkneys, the Privy Council, on the 11th of August,
commissioned Tullibardine and Grange to pursue them
'with fyre, swerd, and all kynd of hostilitie, quhill thai
be apprehendit and brocht to justice.'[56]   Grange accepted
the task with alacrity, declaring that if he could only
encounter Bothwell, he would bring him to Edinburgh
dead or alive;[57] but a month later he returned with the
mortifying news that the prey had escaped his hands.[58]

Meanwhile, Murray had obtained Edinburgh Castle
from Sir James Balfour, and Grange was now made
captain.[59]   And on the 1st of October, Dunbar Castle,

which had been more faithfully held for Bothwell, was rendered after a short siege.[90]

In the Parliament, which met in December, Bothwell and six of his accomplices were forfaulted for treason and lese-majesty;[91] Mary's demission of the government was declared 'lauchfull and perfyte';[92] the Prince's coronation and investiture was held to be as valid as that of any of his predecessors, and as righteously done as if his mother 'had bene departit out of this mortall lyfe';[93] Murray's appointment as Regent was confirmed;[94] and the declaratory part of the Article—which had been prepared by the Lords and leaders who had taken arms at Carberry and imprisoned the Queen—was adopted and embodied in an Act, thus vindicating them, and condemning the Queen as 'previe, airt, and pairt, of the actuall devise and deid of the foirnamit murthour of the King hir lauchfull husband.'[95] In this Parliament sat the Bishop of Moray, who had been previously cleared of Darnley's murder and had submitted to the Regent's will for sheltering Bothwell.[96] There, too, were Huntly, Argyll, and Herries, who took the precaution to enter a protest—not in Mary's behalf, but in their own—that no fault should be imputed to them for what they had done since the 10th of June.[97] The Hamiltons were not present; and a protest in Chatelherault's name was peremptorily rejected by the Regent.[98] Among the many articles presented was one, bearing 'that in na tymes cuming ony wemen salbe admittit to the publict autoritie of the realme or function in publict government within the same.'[99]

On the 3rd of January, John Hay, younger of Tallo,

Hepburn of Bolton, Dalgleish, and Powrie, were executed, when, 'in presens of the haill peopill,' Hay declared that Huntly, Argyll, Lethington, and Balfour, had subscribed the 'band' for Darnley's murder. The Lords thus incriminated had remained in Edinburgh after the Parliament rose; but 'incontinent thai departit thairfra,' when public opinion became clamant that they too 'sould thole and suffer for thair demeretis.'[100]

In Lochleven, Mary seems on the whole to have enjoyed fairly good health,[101] to have met with kindness from those in charge of her,[102] to have indulged to a slight extent in pastime,[103] and to have been the object of more than one matrimonial project. The experienced Morton,[104] the youthful Methven,[105] the second son of Chatelherault,[106] the brother of Argyll,[107] and George Douglas[108] were deemed, by themselves or others, likely candidates for her hand.

The diplomatic attempts to set Mary at liberty utterly failed;[109] but the unswerving devotion of George Douglas was at length rewarded, when, on the evening of Sabbath, the 2nd of May 1568, she was rowed to the shore by Willie Douglas, who had adroitly secured the Castle keys and locked the gates behind them. With the aid of the Laird of Lochleven's horses, she was soon at Niddrie, from whence she sent several despatches, and then rode on to Hamilton,[110] where her supporters speedily rallied round her,[111] and where for a few days she again held Court.[112]

The Regent was at Glasgow when, on the 3rd of May, he heard of the Queen's escape. He and the Lords who were with him ' wer sair amazed '; [113] but at once issued proclamations charging the lieges, under the highest penalties, to resort to Glasgow, 'with all diligence possibill, for preservatioun of our Soverane Lordis persoun, his authoritie, and establissing of justice and quietnes within this realme.' [114] Mary was not idle. She had asked two of her lawyers how she might be restored again to honour and power, and when they answered that it could only be by Parliament or by battle, she exclaimed, ' By battle let us try it.' [115] There can be little doubt that she helped to frame the remarkable revocation and proclamation which was prepared in her name, and which for vehemence, vigour, and virulence, is unsurpassed by any document of the period. [116] But while the proclamations in the King's name were well obeyed, hers, it was reported, were riven and her officers punished. [117] Nevertheless, when she marched towards Dumbarton, on the 13th of May, her forces far outnumbered those of the Regent. [118] At Langside, however, Murray won a decisive victory which was greatly due to Grange, ' who that day played his part.' Many prisoners were taken ; but all were not brought in, 'for there was the father against the son, and brother against brother.' [119] At the beginning of the fight, Argyll, who was Mary's Lieutenant-General, swooned, it was said, 'for fault of courage and spirit.' [120]

According to Melville, it was only after the battle was lost that Mary herself ' tint curage,' [121] and fled to Dumfries. That day, by her own account, she covered sixty miles ; and only ventured afterwards to

proceed during the night.[122]   From Dumfries she had
gone to Dundrennan, and on the 16th of May she
crossed the Solway.[123]   From England she wrote to
her uncle, the Cardinal of Lorraine:—' I have endured
injuries, calumnies, imprisonment, famine, cold, heat,
flight, not knowing whither, ninety-two miles across
the country without stopping or alighting, and then I
have had to sleep upon the ground, and drink sour milk,
and eat oatmeal without bread, and have been three
nights like the owls, without a female in this country,
where, to crown all, I am little else than a prisoner.
And in the meanwhile, they demolish all the houses of
my servants, and I cannot aid them; and hang their
owners, and I cannot compensate them: and yet they all
remain faithful to me, abominating these cruel traitors.
. . . When I parted from my people in Scotland, I
promised to send them assistance at the end of August.
For God's sake let them not be both denied and deceived.
. . . It is all one for myself, but let not my subjects be
deceived and ruined; for I have a son, whom it would be
a pity to leave in the hands of these traitors.'[124]

To Cecil, Knollys thus described her:—' This ladie and
pryncess is a notable woman.   She semeth to regard no
ceremonious honor besyde the acknowledging of her estate
regalle.   She sheweth a disposition to speake much, to
be bold, to be pleasant, and to be very famylyar.   She
sheweth a great desyre to be avenged of her enemes; she
sheweth a readines to expose herselfe to all perylls in
hope of victorie; she delyteth much to hear of hardines
and valiancye, commending by name all approved hardy

175

men of her cuntrye, altho they be her enemyes; and she commendeth no cowardnes even in her frendes.   The thyng that most she thirsteth after is victory, and it semeth to be indifferent to her to have her enemies dimynish, either by the sword of her frendes, or by the liberall promises and rewardes of her purse, or by divysion and quarrells raised amongst themselffes; so that for victorie's sake, payne and perryls semeth pleasant unto her, and in respect of victorie, welthe and all thyngs semeth to her contemptuous and vile.'[125]

From her English captivity this royal eagle was only to escape by death.

NOTES AND REFERENCES

CHAPTER I

[1] *Diurnal of Occurrents*, Maitland Club, p. 25; *Foreign Calendar, Elizabeth*, vi. 616; Labanoff's *Recueil des Lettres de Marie Stuart*, i. 1; vi. 68.

[2] Knox, one of Mary's most uncompromising antagonists, gives the correct date (Laing's *Knox*, i. 91); while Bishop Lesley, one of her keenest partisans, places it a day too early (*De Origine Moribus et Rebus Gestis Scotorum*, 1675, p. 437; *History of Scotland*, Bannatyne Club, p. 166); and Adam Blackwood, one of her most unscrupulous champions, post-dates it by five days (Jebb's *De Vita et Rebus Gestis Mariae*, ii. 177). Petit deliberately expresses the opinion that Miss Strickland 'has proved beyond a doubt that Mary can have been born only on the 11th or 12th December' (Flandre's *Petit*, 1873, i. 1 *n.*); but, as the irony of fate would have it, in the same year that the translation of his work was published, Miss Strickland issued a revised edition of hers in which she gives, without comment, the 8th as the true date (Strickland's *Life of Mary*, 1873, i. 2). Bois-Guilbert, who boasts of having drawn his materials from fifteen or sixteen authors, gravely informs his readers, that 'she was born at Edinburgh, the Capital of Scotland' (*Marie Stuart, Reyne d'Écosse*, Paris, 1675, p. 5; Freebairn's *Mary Stewart*, 1725, p. 1).

[3] *Hamilton Papers*, i. 323, 328, 340, 342, 346, 348.

[4] One of Mary's most ardent defenders has charged the greatest of the Scottish Reformers with alleging that Cardinal Beaton was her real father (Chalmers's *Life of Mary*, 1818, ii. 1). Knox, however, only repeats contemporary suspicions (Laing's *Knox*, i. 92)—suspicions which, perhaps, he did not altogether disbelieve (*Ibid.* ii. 72), and which are referred to in the correspondence of the period

M   177

(*Hamilton Papers*, i. 74; ii. 92). The Bishop of Ross testifies, on the other hand, that her mother 'was ane nobill, wyse, and honorable princesse, and chaist ladie, ever weill and verteouslie exerced, keping hir widowit with gret honor' (Lesley's *History*, p. 289).

[5] Lesley's *History*, pp. 155, 156; Calderwood's *History*, i. 114; *Diurnal of Occurrents*, p. 22; Ruddiman's *Buchanan*, i. 277.

[6] In speaking of the disgraceful and disastrous defeat at Solway Moss, Father Stevenson says:—'Knox admits (i. 81) that of the Council which met at Holyrood in November, "some were heretics, some favourers of England, some friends of the Douglases, and so could there be none faithful to the King." Like his daughter Mary, James was surrounded by traitors, and had not a single trustworthy adviser' (Stevenson's *Mary Stuart*, 1886, p. 23 *n.*). Here the quotation from Knox, so far as it goes, is substantially correct; but is misapplied, and so made to completely misrepresent the Reformer's meaning. He was relating the story of the roll of heretics given up to the King by the leaders of the Church for punishment; and, in the words quoted by Father Stevenson, he describes not the Council but the intended victims whose names were in the scroll! The learned Jesuit disarms suspicion by giving volume and page of Knox's *History*, and also by suppressing the three words—'in thaire opinioun'—with which Knox finishes his sentence. But, perhaps, the perversion of Knox's meaning is not the most wonderful thing in Father Stevenson's foot-note. Cardinal Beaton was neither a heretic nor a favourer of England, yet even in him it seems the King had not a trustworthy adviser! Has Beaton ever received a deadlier thrust in the house of his friends?

[7] Laing's *Knox*, i. 91.

[8] Lindsay's *History*, 1728, p. 176.—Pitscottie's version is not improved by a more recent writer, who renders it thus: 'It came with a girl, and it will go with a girl' (Pinkerton's *History*, 1797, ii. 384).

[9] *Hamilton Papers*, i. 339.—For James's death various dates have been assigned ranging from the 8th to the 30th of December. The 14th—the Thursday of the *Hamilton Papers*—is supported by, among others, Bishop Lesley (*History*, p. 166), Buchanan (Ruddiman's *Buchanan*, i. 280, 450), John Smyth, monk of Kinloss (Stuart's *Records of Kinloss*, p. 9), Birrel (*Diary*, p. 3), and Sir James Balfour (*Historical Works*, i. 275). When examined in 1683, the coffin-

plate also bore the date 14th December as the day of his death (Dalyell's *Scotish Poems of the Sixteenth Century*, i. 27 *n.*). Knox, Calderwood, and Hawthornden give the 13th (Laing's *Knox*, i. 92; Calderwood's *History*, i. 152; Drummond's *History*, 1681, p. 345); while David Laing cites the Treasurer's Accounts as giving the 16th (Laing's *Knox*, i. 92 *n.*). Mr. Rawdon Brown is doubly wrong when he says, 'Mary Stuart was born on the 5th December 1542, and her father James v. died on the 8th' (*Venetian Calendar*, v. 116 *n.*).

[10] Within five days, Lisle was informed, by one of his spies, that James had died of poison; and eleven days later he learned from a Scotch priest that 'the Kinge in his sickness did vomytt mervelously moche, and had a great laxe also, and that after he was dedde his bodie did swell very great' (*Hamilton Papers*, i. 342, 349). Lesley records the rumour that he 'wes vexit be some unkindly medicine' (*History*, p. 166). Sir James Melville says that he died 'for displeasour,' as some alleged; while others held that he was poisoned by the prelates who 'had brocht him in that trouble of mynd,' and who had learned the art 'callit ane Italien possat' (Melville's *Memoirs*, Mait. Club, pp. 67, 68); but in Hawthornden's opinion, Beaton was unjustly blamed, as the event proved ruinous to him and his fellow-churchmen (Drummond's *History*, p. 345); and the Jesuit priests, in 1594, say it is very currently reported that he was poisoned by the heretics (Nau's *History of Mary Stewart*, p. 106).

[11] *Hamilton Papers*, i. 342, 350.

[12] Lemon's *State Papers*, *Henry the Eighth*, v. 244.

[13] According to Knox, when James was dying, the Cardinal cried in his ear:—'Tak ordour, schir, with your realme: who shall rewill during the minoritie of your dowghter? Ye have knawin my service: what will ye have done? Shall thare nott be four regentes chosyn? and shall nott I be principall of thame?' Knox adds:—'Whatsoever the King answered, documentis war tackin that so should be, as my Lord Cardinall thought expedient' (Laing's *Knox*, i. 91). According to Buchanan, Beaton 'having bribed Henry Balfour, a mercenary priest, he, with his assistance, forged a false will for the King, in which he himself was nominated head of the government, and three of the most powerful of the nobility joined with him as assessors' (Aikman's *Buchanan*, 1827, ii. 325). These statements, which have been adopted by Calderwood (*History of the Kirk*, i. 152, 153), are partially supported by the contemporary letters of

Lisle (*Hamilton Papers*, i. 348, 358), and wonderfully confirmed by a notarial instrument preserved in Hamilton Palace, and brought to light in 1887 by the Historical Manuscripts Commission.   This instrument, subscribed by 'Henricus Balfour, notarius publicus,' 'tells of the King's illness, alleges his anxiety about his daughter and the kingdom, and narrates how he appointed David Beaton Cardinal and Archbishop of St. Andrews, James Earl of Moray (natural brother of the King), George Earl of Huntly, and Archibald Earl of Argyll, to act as tutors testamentary to his infant daughter, and also as Governors of the Kingdom.'   An indorsation in a different hand bears that Henry Balfour 'never was notar' (*Historical Manuscripts Commission, Eleventh Report*, app. part vi. pp. 205, 219, 220).   Knox gives the names of the four Regents correctly; Buchanan has erroneously included Arran—a mistake which also occurs in the papers of the period (*Maitland Miscellany*, iv. 71; *Hamilton Papers*, i. 342, 345, 346).   Arran himself told Sadleyr that the Cardinal 'did counterfeit the late King's testament; and when the King was even almost dead, he took his hand in his, and so caused him to subscribe a blank paper' (Sadleyr's *State Papers*, i. 138).   This more dramatic version of the charge against Beaton has been more or less fully recorded by Knox (i. 91, 92), Pitscottie (p. 177), Herries (*Historical Memoirs*, pp. 1, 2), Calderwood (i.152), and Hawthornden (p. 345); while Lesley says that the Cardinal alleged 'that the King be his testament nominat four Regentis, bot the same on no wise culd be verefeit nor provin' (*History*, pp. 169, 170).

[14] Spottiswoode states that Beaton caused the will to be published in Edinburgh 'on the Monday after the King's death' (Spottiswoode's *History*, Spottiswoode Society, i. 141); while Lisle places its proclamation a day later, Tuesday, the 19th of December (*Hamilton Papers*, i. 346); but this action was ignored by the nobles in replying to Henry's letter on the 21st (Lemon's *State Papers, Henry the Eighth*, v. 232; *Hamilton Papers*, i. 345).   Lesley (*History*, p. 169) gives the 22nd of December as the date of Arran's proclamation as Governor; and the *Diurnal of Occurrents* (p. 25) places it on the 10th of January; but Lisle within two days of the event states that it occurred on the 3rd of January (*Hamilton Papers*, i. 360).   Arran wrote, as Governor, to Lisle on the 4th, and to Henry on the 6th of January (*Ibid*. i. 355, 361).   His appointment was confirmed by Parliament on the 13th of March (*Acts of Parliament*, ii. 411).

[15] *Hamilton Papers,* i. 346, 352.—Archibald Douglas disclosed these projects to Lisle:—' Some men do sey that she were mete for the second sone of Fraunce, or for a second sone of Denmarke, or for a second sone of Englond if their were one, that one of the second sones might therby be King of Skottes, and dwell among theym keping the estate of Skotland whiche evermore hath byn a realme of yt self, and said that some other do sey that therle of Arren wold have her for his sone and heire, to make hym therby Kynge.' Douglas explained that a second son would be preferred to the first-born because, if the realms were united under one King, everything would be spent in England, whereby Scotland, already poor, ' shulde be utterly beggered and undone' (*Ibid.* i. 358).

[16] *Hamilton Papers,* i. 363-380.—By the open article which was signed by the Solway prisoners, Henry was asked to take Mary into his care and keeping, that he might marry her to his son, and ' by meanes therof to clere all titles and to unyte bothe realmes in oon' ; the subscribers promising to aid and serve Henry. By the secret article—signed only by Cassillis, Glencairn, Maxwell, Fleming, Somerville, Gray, Robert Erskine, Oliver Sinclair, and the Lairds of Craigy and Kerse—the ten subscribers further obliged themselves, in the case of Mary's death, to help Henry to the uttermost in taking upon him the whole rule, dominion, and government of Scotland. Bothwell, who had been long in exile, signed the open article. Angus, who had been much longer in exile (viz. since 1529), signed a separate document which partly embodied both the open and secret articles. There is a list of the Solway prisoners and their respective values in Lemon's *State Papers,* v. 232-235.

[17] Sadleyr's *State Papers,* i. 65.

[18] *Hamilton Papers,* i. 462-467, and p. xliv.

[19] The Ambassadors were Sir William Hamilton of Sanquhar, Sir James Leirmonth of Balcomie, and Henry Balnaves (Lemon's *State Papers, Henry the Eighth,* v. 270 ; *Hamilton Papers,* i. 472). Their Instructions are in the *Acts of the Parliaments of Scotland,* ii. 411-413 ; and in Sadleyr's *State Papers,* i. 59-63. Henry's report of his interview with these Ambassadors, on the 11th of April 1543, is in Lemon's *State Papers,* v. 275-280; his answer to them is in the *Hamilton Papers,* i. pp. ci. cii. ; and the articles, which he thought so reasonable that, if not practically accepted, it should be meet for him to ' folowe his purpose by force,' are in Lemon's *State Papers,* v. 281 *n.* These last are said by Froude to have been

brought to Scotland by the two later Ambassadors, Glencairn and Sir George Douglas (*History of England*, 1887, iii. 565); but the Articles arrived in a letter to Sadleyr, on the 5th of May, before these men had left on their mission to England (Sadleyr's *State Papers*, i. 187), and they are named among those to whom Sadleyr was to open and declare them (Lemon's *State Papers*, v. 282).

²⁰ In Froude's opinion the Scotch Instructions were 'preposterous resolutions.' His summary of them is inaccurate in two points. He says that 'four Scottish noblemen' were to 'reside in England as hostages for the Queen's appearance there when she had arrived at marriageable age' (*History of England*, 1887, iii. 553); but the Ambassadors were at this stage expressly forbidden to yield to a demand for any such pledge. Again, he says, that 'if there should be issue from the marriage, and the crowns of the two kingdoms be united in a single person, the administration should descend by the ordinary laws of inheritance in the Arran family' (*Ibid.* iii. 553). Green makes a similar statement (*History of the English People*, 1878, ii. 210). But this alleged continuance of the Governorship in the Arran family is apparently based on a misprint of *his* for *hir* (compare *Acts of Parliament*, ii. 412, with Sadleyr's *State Papers*, i. 62).

²¹ Sadleyr's *State Papers*, i. 84-88; *Hamilton Papers*, i. 488, 489; Strickland's *Mary Queen of Scots*, 1888, i. 3.

²² Arran's letter to Henry announcing their appointment is dated 4th of May 1543. Sir George Douglas is described as 'brothir germane to the noble and mychti Erle of Angus and Lord Dowglas' (*Hamilton Papers*, i. 532). According to Froude the first Ambassadors—Hamilton, Leirmonth, and Balnaves—had been 'desired to return instantly' to Scotland, 'with an intimation that, if the negotiations were to be renewed, it must be through persons whose insignificance should not in itself be an affront' (*History of England*, 1887, iii. 565). These men—who had not proved pliable in Henry's hands (*Hamilton Papers*, i. 560)—awaited, however, the arrival of Glencairn and Douglas, whose names were joined with theirs in the commissions of 4th May, and all the five signed the treaties at Greenwich, on the 1st of July (*Acts of the Parliaments of Scotland*, xii. 42, 43; Rymer's *Fœdera*, 1712, xiv. 781-783, 792, 796).

²³ This memorial is in Lemon's *State Papers*, v. 302-304.

²⁴ The answer by Arran and the Lords of his Council is in the *Acts of Parliament*, ii. 425, 426; where the 8th of June is given as the date of meeting; but Sadleyr's letter of the 7th speaks of the

assembly as having been held on the previous day. Despite the absence of Murray, Huntly, and Argyll, there was 'great sticking' and 'moche difficultie' among those present concerning Mary's delivery at the age of ten—some insisting that, before she left the realm, Henry should give pledges in Scotland that she should be married to the Prince at twelve (Sadleyr's *State Papers*, i. 212-214; *Hamilton Papers*, i. 535).

[25] *Hamilton Papers*, i. 558, 559.—The treaties of peace and marriage are in Rymer's *Foedera*, xiv. 786-796.

[26] *Hamilton Papers*, i. 655, 660-662; Sadleyr's *State Papers*, i. 270-277.

[27] *Hamilton Papers*, ii. 7.

[28] Father Stevenson says that Arran's 'appointment was undisputed for various reasons'; and alleges, as the first, that 'he stood well with Henry, whose forbearance was of vital importance' (*Mary Stuart*, 1886, p. 33); but the statements in the text are amply borne out by the *Hamilton Papers*, i. 363, 371, 373, 469, 473, 477, 495, 505.

[29] Lisle and Tunstall were informed by a chaplain that Arran was 'a good softe God's man' (Lemon's *State Papers*, v. 238). Knox avers that the hearts of many were bowed unto him in the beginning, partly through 'ane opinioun that men had of his simplicitie' (Laing's *Knox*, i. 94). The Queen Dowager assured Sadleyr that he was 'a simple and the most inconstant man in the world; for whatsoever he determineth to-day, he changeth to-morrow' (Sadleyr's *State Papers*, i. 115). Nineteen years later Randolph reported that he was 'so inconstant, saving in greediness, that in three moments he will take five purposes' (*Foreign Calendar, Elizabeth*, iv. 538, 539).

[30] Before Sadleyr had been many hours in the Scottish capital on this mission, Sir George Douglas explained to him that, by gentle means, Henry might in time 'bring the nobles and others of this realme so farre in love with his Majeste that he shall have the hole dyrection and obedience of the same at his pleasure'—philosophically adding that what love might win should remain for ever, what force had won had engendered hatred. On the other hand, he warned him that should Henry's party try to oust the Governor and attempt the impossible task of subjecting the country to English rule, 'there is not so lytle a boy but he woll hurle stones ayenst it, the wyves woll com out with their distaffes, and the comons

unyversally woll rather dye in it'; yea, as it was, many of the nobles and all the clergy were of the French party (*Hamilton Papers*, i. 477). Douglas soon after told Sadleyr that even the docile Arran, if he knew the King's design, would immediately change sides, and become wholly French; and in that quarrel, 'the hole realme,' said he, 'wooll stand fast with hym, and dye rather all in a daye' than 'be made thrall and subject to England' (*Ibid.* i. 505).

[31] Lord Parr was informed by one of his spies 'that all that whiche the Governour of Scotlande promysethe to the Kingis Majeste is but craft, frawde, and falsitie. . . . His counsaill said to hym that they marvailed that he wolde take upon hym at thende of tenne yeres to make deliverance of the yong Quene of Scottes to the King of Englande. . . . And he aunswered his counsaill againe, "Ye knowe the King of Englande is a mightie prince, and we not able nez of powre to resist his puissance, and for that cause I thinke and take it best by fare wordes and promyses, with the concluding of this peas, to deferre and put over the danger that might otherwise fall upon us; and in the meane tyme the yong Quene maye chance to die or other change maye happene, wherebie Scotlande may be relieved and more able to resist Englande"' (*Hamilton Papers*, i. 554, 555).

[32] *Diurnal of Occurrents*, pp. 26, 27; Laing's *Knox*, i. 97; Lesley's *History*, pp. 171, 172; *Hamilton Papers*, i. 398, 491, 496, 497, 507, 512.

[33] *Hamilton Papers*, i. 409, 410, 419, 486, 510; Herries's *Historical Memoirs*, pp. 5, 6.

[34] Sadleyr's *State Papers*, i. 117, 145; Lesley's *History*, pp. 172, 173; Laing's *Knox*, i. 105, 124.—The Abbot of Paisley had been studying in France.

[35] *Hamilton Papers*, i. 590-593.—On the 22nd of July Sadleyr had written to Henry, telling him of the preparations of the Cardinal's party to surprise the Queen at Linlithgow, and of the Governor's intention to prevent her removal (*Ibid.* i. 584). Now, on the 26th, he writes that there had been a great appearance 'of slaughter and effusion of bloode,' and 'greate preparacions made for the same' both by the Governor's party and Beaton's; but 'by good meanes, all suche inconvenience is clerelie avoyded and a good agreament taken emonges them' (*Ibid.* i. 591). On the 15th of the previous March, Parliament had nominated as Mary's keepers,

the Earls Marischal and Montrose, Lords Erskine, Ruthven, Livingston, Lindsay, and Seton, and the Laird of Calder; 'or ony twa of thaim quarterlie, and ane to be put and marrowit to thaim be my Lord Governour at his plesour' (*Acts of Parliament*, ii. 414, 415).

[36] This 'secret band' is printed in the *Hamilton Papers*, i. 630-632.—The Governor professed to be utterly ignorant of it until Sadleyr showed him a copy. Henry's attention was specially directed by Sadleyr to some of the names appended—names of those supposed to be acting in Henry's interest (Sadleyr's *State Papers*, i. 257, 258). By the 28th of July, Sadleyr had explained to his master that there was so much untruth, jealousy, fear, and suspicion amongst the Scots nobles, towards one another, that he knew not what to write; but he was doubtful of the Cardinal's sincerity (*Hamilton Papers*, i. 602, 606).

[37] Led astray perhaps by poetic feeling, a modern writer says:— 'When the thunder of Hertford's artillery resounded even to the gates of Linlithgow, it was to the Stirlingshire stronghold that the guardians hied with their youthful sovereign' (Thornton's *Stuart Dynasty*, 1890, p. 138); but Mary had been fully nine months in Stirling before Hertford entered Scotland. In writing to Henry from Edinburgh, on the very day of their removal, Sadleyr informs him that, 'This afternone the peax nowe taken with your Majeste was solempnly proclaymed in this towne with herauldes and trompettes; and the Governour himselfe, the Chancelour, Therles of Anguysshe, Cassells, Glencarn, and other, with also soundrie barons of the realme, were present, in the Highe Streate (as they call it here) at the proclamyng of the same; and surelie all kynde and sortes of people, bothe highe and lowe, doo seame greatelie to rejoyse therof, as undoubtedlie they have good cause, for the last warres hathe so impoverisshed them, that they wooll not be able to recover it of a long season. . . . Finallie, the olde Quene and the yong Quene, by common assent of all parties, are this day removed to Sterlyng, in the keping of the iiij barons appoynted, for bicause the house of Lythcoo is so lyttell that they cannott all be well placed and lodged in the same' (*Hamilton Papers*, i. 597). Ten days later Sadleyr assures his royal master that Sir George Douglas was so opposed to Mary's removal to Stirling that he had advised to fight the Cardinal's party rather than consent; and adds—'As I understand, the olde Quene hathe no

mo but her ordinarie officers, and suche as must necessarelie serve
her, to the nomber of xxx or theraboutes, and everie of the saide
lordes hathe xxiiij; but at the next change of the kepers, wheras
nowe there be iiij whiche were at the tyme of this ruffle purposelie
appoynted and indifferentlie named by bothe parties, there shalbe (as
I am infourmed) but twoo at ones from thensfourthe. And so the
hole nombre of the barons appoynted by the Parliament to be kepers
of the said yong Quene shall kepe their course by twoo at oones, with
eyther of them the nombre of xxiiij men, besides suche Englishe
personnes as your Majeste shall appoynte also to be aboute her,
according to the purporte of the treatie' (*Ibid.* i. 625, 626).

[38] Sadleyr's *State Papers,* i. 228; *Hamilton Papers,* i. 551.

[39] Sadleyr's *State Papers,* i. 253, 263; *Hamilton Papers,* i. 629.

[40] The English Ambassador had been warned in the previous
April that this reconciliation was sure to come; but, when it did
come, it came suddenly (Sadleyr's *State Papers,* i. 158, 277, 278;
Hamilton Papers, i. 522, 523, 664). 'The unhappy man,' says
Knox, 'qwyetlie stall away from the lordis that war wyth him in
the Palice of Halyrudhouse, past to Stirling, subjected himself to
the Cardinall and to his counsall, received absolutioun, renunced
the professioun of Christ Jesus his holy Evangell, and violated
his oath that befoir he had maid, for observatioun of the contract
and league with England' (Laing's *Knox,* i. 109). Parr learned
from one of his spies—Sandye Pringill—that Arran met Beaton
at Falkirk on Tuesday the 4th of September; rode with him to
Stirling; there, on the Friday, declared 'all thinges that was
required or laide unto hym on the behalf of the Kinges Majeste';
and, on Saturday, after open penance and a solemn oath, was
absolved and heard mass—Argyll and Bothwell holding 'the
towell over his hede for the tyme he was in receiving of the
sacramente' (*Hamilton Papers,* ii. 38). Herries erroneously places
the recantation after the coronation (*Historical Memoirs,* Abbotsford
Club, p. 5).

[41] The Bishop of Ross, on different pages, assigns the coronation
to two months—August and September (Lesley's *History,* pp. 169,
174); and Sir James Balfour follows his example (*Historical Works,*
i. 275, 279). Lesley relates—and his statement is fully borne out
by Sadleyr (*Hamilton Papers,* ii. 32)—that Angus, Glencairn,
Cassillis, Maxwell, Somerville, Gray, and others who had been
in England, did not countenance the coronation; but Balfour—

to use a Scots legal word—*excambs* the parties, actually saying :
—'All thesse that favored England wer present at the coronatione ;
bot the Earle of Lennox depairted the toune, and wold not be
present, nather yet aney that had breathed the Frenche aire.'
The true date, as proved by the letters of Sadleyr and Parr, is
the 9th of September 1543. Sadleyr says she was crowned 'with
suche solempnitie as they doo use in this countrey, which is not
verie costelie' (*Hamilton Papers*, ii. 33). Parr was informed by
Pringill, who had just returned from Stirling, that the ceremony
took place in the chapel of Stirling Castle, Arran bearing the
crown, Lennox the sceptre, and Argyll the sword (*Ibid.* ii. 38, 39).

42 *Hamilton Papers*, i. 501, 619, 620, 629, 630.

43 *Ibid.* i. 633.

44 *Ibid.* i. 587.

45 *Ibid.* i. 629, 633, 634.—In April, the Queen Dowager had
professed to Sadleyr her desire, that, if the Scots would not
deliver her daughter into Henry's hands, he should take sufficient
pledges for the performance of the marriage, 'and also establish
such a guard of English personages about her person, as would
look well to her surety' (Sadleyr's *State Papers*, i. 114). In July,
Henry had resolved, in exercising the power conferred on him
in the treaty of marriage, to appoint Sadleyr and his wife to wait
on the young Queen—Sadleyr occasionally, his wife constantly—
an honour which Sir Ralph very promptly and very earnestly
declined, giving as one of his reasons that his wife was 'most
unmeet to serve for such a purpose . . . having never been
brought up at Court, nor knowing what appertaineth thereto'
(*Hamilton Papers*, i. 560, 561, 569, 570 ; Sadleyr's *State Papers*, i.
230). Lodge states that Sadleyr 'married a laundress in Cromwell's family, whose first husband, Matthew Barre, a trades-
man of London, was then living' ; and refers to an Act of Mary Tudor's
Parliament legitimating the children she had to Sadleyr (*Illustrations
of British History*, 1838, i. 140). On the other hand, Sir Walter
Scott says that she must have been 'a woman of credit and character
. . . since Lord Cromwell, to whom she was related, not only coun-
tenanced their marriage, but was god-father to two of their children'
(Sadleyr's *State Papers*, i. p. iv.) ; and their descendant, Major
Sadleir Stoney, thinks it probable that she had either been married
or affianced to Barre, who returned home after a long absence to
find that she—believing him to be dead—had married Sir Ralph

(*Sadleyr's Life and Times*, 1877, p. 14 *n.*).   'Mary Stuart underwent many humiliations; but let us be thankful,' exclaims Father
Stevenson,, 'that she escaped the degradation of learning her
morality from an adulteress, and her manners from a washerwoman'
(Stevenson's *Mary Stuart*, 1886, p. 43).

[46] *Hamilton Papers*, i. 638, 656; Sadleyr's *State Papers*, i. 273.

[47] *Hamilton Papers*, i. 513, 515, 651.

[48] *Ibid.* i. 665, 666.

[49] *Ibid.* i. 664.

[50] *Ibid.* ii. 43, 44.

[51] *Ibid.* i. 638, 639; Sadleyr's *State Papers*, i. 274.—Knox is
certainly wrong in saying that it was because of Mary's coronation
and the new promise made to France that Henry arrested 'our
Schotish schippis' (Laing's *Knox*, i. 109).

[52] *Hamilton Papers*, ii. 4.

[53] *Ibid.* ii. 92, 93, 103.

[54] *Ibid.* ii. 56, 61, 82, 151.

[55] *Ibid.* i. 551, 570; ii. 56, 61, 62, 93.—On the 26th of June
1544, Lennox signed and sealed an indenture, by which he bound
himself to hand over Dumbarton Castle and the Isle of Bute to
Henry; and by which Henry became bound to give him Lady
Margaret Douglas in marriage, and lands in England of the yearly
value of 6800 merks Scots or 1700 merks sterling, and by which
Henry further engaged—after he should attain 'the direction and
rule of the realme of Scotland'—to make Lennox 'governour under
him.'   Lennox likewise undertook that he should not only do what
he could that Mary 'be not stollen nor conveyed out of Scotlande,'
but also that he should 'travail to th' uttermoost of his wit and
powre to get hir personne into his oune keping, and so deliver hir
fourthwith into his Heighnes handes with all dilligence possible, to
be nourished and educated at his Majesties ordre' (Rymer's *Fœdera*,
xv. 29-32).

[56] *Hamilton Papers*, ii. 92, 93, 102.—Sadleyr learned that of
money there were a thousand crowns; and of munitions, three
cannons, two double cannons, forty falcons, eighty light pieces for
the field—'whiche they call here quarter faulcons'—three hundred
'haulfe hakes,' with 'shotte according,' and thirty lasts of powder
(*Ibid.* ii. 103).

[57] Sadleyr was instructed to press Glencairn—if Lennox were too
scrupulous—to take the Legate prisoner 'to his oune use, wherby

must nedes growe unto him a greate advantage, for the sayd Legat is very welthie, and woll not fayle to gyve greate sommes of money for his ransom' (*Hamilton Papers*, ii. 99, 100).

[58] *Ibid.* ii. 101.

[59] On the 10th of November, Sadleyr wrote to Suffolk and Tunstall :—'It is sayd that the Cardinall hath devised to divorse the Governour frome his wief, to thentent to make a mariage betwixte him and the Doagier, and then also to make a contracte betwixte the yonge Quene and thErle of Lynoux, who shalbe made Lieutenaunte Generall of Scotlande, and use thauctorite, and the Governor shall bere onely the name of that office, and have a certaine yerely stipende for the same, and so they shalbe frendes, and joyne together on one partie with Fraunce against Englonde' (*Ibid.* ii. 151).

[60] *Acts of the Parliaments of Scotland*, ii. 429.

[61] *Ibid.* ii. 431, 432.—Angus, Lennox, Glencairn, and Marischal, though chosen at the Stirling Convention to be members of the Great Council, would not accept that office, and were not present in this Parliament (*Ibid.* ii. 442). The Scoto-French treaty—dated 15th December 1543—has been printed from the original by Teulet, in his *Papiers D'État*, Bannatyne Club, i. 137-142.

[62] *Hamilton Papers*, ii. 90.

[63] Hertford arrived in the Forth on Saturday the 3rd of May 1544, and landed his army next day (*Ibid.* ii. 360). In his amended Instructions, of 10th April, he is told that his Majesty's pleasure is to 'put all to fyre and swoorde, burne Edinborough towne, so rased and defaced when you have sacked and gotten what ye can of it, as there may remayn forever a perpetual memory of the vengeaunce of God lightened upon [them ?] for their faulsehode and disloyailtye. Do what ye can out of hande, and without long tarying, to beate down and over throwe the castle, sack Holyrod house, and as many townes and villaiges about Edinborough as ye may conveniently, sack Lythe and burne and subverte it and all the rest, putting man, woman, and childe, to fyre and swoorde, without exception where any resistence shalbe made agaynst you ; and this done, passe over to the Fyfelande and extende like extremityes and destructions in all townes and villaiges wherunto ye may reche convenyently, not forgetting among all the rest so to spoyle and turne upset downe the Cardinalles town of St. Andrews, as thupper stone may be the nether, and not one stick stande by an other, sparing no

creature alyve within the same, specially such as either in frendeship or blood be alyed to the Cardinall. And if ye se any likelyhode of wynning the castle, gyve sum stoute assay to the same, and if ye fortune to get it, raised and destroy it pece meale. And after this sorte spending one moneth there' (*Ibid.* ii. 326).

[64] *Hamilton Papers*, ii. 371, 372—The pitiless zest with which Hertford carried out his instructions, as far as he could, is manifest from the contemporary accounts of the expedition (Stevenson's *Selections from Unpublished Manuscripts*, Maitland Club, pp. 3-5; *The Late Expedicion*, in Dalyell's *Fragments of Scotish History*); and from Hertford's own despatches (*Hamilton Papers*, ii. 361-375, 379-382). 'Rejoicings were made in England for this victory' (*Venetian Calendar*, v. 122).

[65] The thoroughness of Hertford's second invasion may be learned from his despatches (Lemon's *State Papers*, v. 513-529); from the contemporary journal of the expedition (*Proceedings of the Society of Antiquaries of Scotland*, i. 272-276); and from the list of 'fortresses, abbeys, frere-houses, market-townes, villages, towres and places brent, raced, and cast downe' (Haynes's *State Papers*, 1740, pp. 52-54).

[66] *Acts of the Parliaments of Scotland*, ii. 460.

[67] In December 1543, the Earl of Montrose and Lord Erskine are referred to as 'chosin to remane continuale with the Quenis Grace in the Castell of Striueling for the suir keiping of hir person' (*Acts of the Parliaments of Scotland*, ii. 442); and in July 1545, Lords Erskine and Livingston are mentioned as having 'the hale cure and keping of our Soverane Ladyis persoun in the Castell of Striveling' (*Register of the Privy Council of Scotland*, i. 11)

[68] *Acts of the Parliaments of Scotland*, ii. 463.

[69] Henry the Eighth died at Westminster early in the morning of the 28th of January 1546-7 (Ellis's *Original Letters*, first series, ii. 137).

[70] Thorpe's *Calendar of Scottish State Papers*, i. 66.

[71] This second Flodden was fought, not on 'Sunday,' as Father Stevenson says (Stevenson's *Mary Stuart*, p. 82), but on Saturday—a day afterwards known as 'Blak Sattirday' (*Diurnal of Occurrents*, p. 44; Calderwood's *History*, i. 249). Mr. Skelton is right with the day of the week, but wrong with the day of the month. He gives the 4th of September (Skelton's *Mary Stuart*, 1893, p. 15); and Miss Strickland gives the 9th (*Life of Mary*, 1888, i. 7). An

English historian, after a long account of the battle and its prelimi-naries, gives the 10th of December as the date, which he says was the thirty-fourth anniversary of Flodden (Hayward's *King Edward the Sixt*, 1636, p. 90). The date in the text—10th September 1547 —is quite certain (Patten's *Expedicion* in Dalyell's *Fragments of Scotish History*, 1798, p. 54; Stuart's *Records of Kinloss*, p. 11; Birrel's *Diary*, p. 4; Lesley's *History*, p. 197). Patten (p. 71) expresses no astonishment when he states that ' the dead bodyes wear stryped out of their garments starke naked ' by his fellow Southrons; but he was surprised at the rapidity with which it was done, and also at 'the personages of the enemies, . . . which for their tallnes of stature, cleanes of skyn, bignes of bone, with due proportion in al partes, I for my part advisedly noted to be such, as but that I well sawe that it was so, I woolde not have beleved sure so many of that sort to have bene in all their cuntree.' The abstract of the expenses of the English army, printed from the original, is in Sadleyr's *State Papers*, i. 353-364.

⁷² Sir James Balfour states that Mary was sent to Inchmahome ' imediatley befor the batell ' (*Historical Works*, i. 288); but Lesley says that it was 'during the tyme of the Inglismennis byding at Leith ' (*History of Scotland*, Bannatyne Club, p. 200), that is between the 11th and 18th of September ; and this is corroborated by the terms of the discharge, under the Privy Seal, to Lords Erskine and Livingston (*The Lennox*, 1874, ii. 431, 432 ; *Red Book of Menteith*, 1880, ii. 331-333 ; *Historical MSS. Commission, Ninth Report*, app. part ii. p. 192).

⁷³ According to Chalmers, Mary remained at Inchmahome until the following February, when she was taken to Dumbarton (Chalmers's *Life of Mary*, 1818, i. 5). Lesley, on the other hand, states that she was only kept with her mother at Inchmahome ' till the Inglismen was departed furth of Scotland, and than returned to Striveling ' (*History*, p. 200) ; and the English army re-crossed the Tweed on the 29th of September (Patten's *Expedicion*, p. 94). She was removed to Dumbarton in February (Laing's *Knox*, i. 219 n.) ; but she was taken there from Stirling, not from Inchmahome (Thorpe's *Calendar*, i. 79). In Hill Burton's opinion, Inchmahome was selected as her abode in this time of special danger, because it was ' deemed less assailable than a fortress on land, or an island approachable by sea ' (*History of Scotland*, 1876, iii. 275).

⁷⁴ Jebb's *Life and Reign of Mary*, 1725, p. 18.

[75] Strickland's *Life of Mary*, 1888, i. 7.

[76] Brown's *Horæ Subsecivæ*, second series, pp. 167-175.—'The original boxwood trees in the bower, like the single one in the garden, had all grown to considerable size'; but the appropriating hands of tourists having 'led to the complete disappearance of nearly the whole' of them, the Duke of Montrose, at the suggestion of Sir William Fraser, in the autumn of 1859, 'gave directions that the bower should be restored with new boxwood plants, and a neat wooden railing placed around the whole.' These young plants from the neighbouring gardens of Cardross have grown so well, that 'when tourists, particularly those from America, obtain a cutting from the boxwood as a relic of Queen Mary, they firmly believe in them as having been planted by her hand' (*Red Book of Menteith*, i. 503, 504).

[77] Bothwell was represented as willing to deliver the Hermitage to the English, if the Protector could obtain for him in marriage the Duchess of Suffolk, the Princess Mary, or the Princess Elizabeth; or permission to see these ladies, 'as though if he liked them they would not mislike him'; or, if allowed a hundred soldiers, he would not only deliver up his house, but become the servant of King Edward (Thorpe's *Calendar*, i. 67). The English Privy Council instructed Lord Grey of Wilton, then at Norham, that Sir George Douglas might be warily trusted, and should be persuaded to deliver the young Queen into England (*Ibid.* i. 69). Patrick, Lord Gray, one of the 'assured Lords,' advised the seizure of Perth and St. Andrews; and the latter town the Laird of Montquhanny offered to deliver (*Ibid.* i. 70, 73). Argyll received a thousand crowns to incline him to the marriage; and the Protector was willing to give him lands or a pension if he brought it to pass (*Ibid.* i. 77-81). Henry Durham was promised a reward for surrendering Broughty Castle (*Ibid.* i. 83); and the Master of Ruthven wished to know what he would get for setting forth the King's purpose and delivering Perth (*Ibid.* i. 82).

[78] By the 20th of October Sir George Douglas—with a view it seems to betray the English (Stevenson's *Selections*, p. 99)— furnished a plan for another invasion (*The Douglas Book*, iv. 164-167), which, however, was then rendered impossible by the great rains (Thorpe's *Calendar*, i. 69). Wyndham, lying in the Tay in December, in asking more men for his ships, informed Somerset that he would not leave a town, village, or fisherboat unburned

from Fifeness to Inchcolm ; and within nine days he had burned
Balmerino Abbey (*Ibid.* i. 72, 73). In January, William Lord
Grey, as Lord Lieutenant, and Wharton and Bowes, the English
Wardens of the West and Middle Marches, consulted as to how
something might be done to scourge Angus and Sir George Douglas ;
but did not see how it was possible at that season of the year (*Ibid.*
i. 76). Before the end of February, Grey had marched to Haddington, and Lennox and Wharton had invaded Dumfries (*Ibid.* i. 79)
—operations not altogether successful.

[79] There is a form of prayer for general peace and prosperity,
and for success of the proposed marriage between Edward and Mary,
which Mr. Lemon thinks was probably used in July 1547 (*Domestic
Calendar*, 1547-1580, p. 4). In the churches of England the *Te
Deum* was sung after Pinkie, in the judgment of the English primate
a victory ' almost above the expectation of man, and such as hath
not been heard of in any part of Christendom this many years :
in which victory above the number of fifteen thousand Scots be
slain, two thousand taken prisoners, and among them many noblemen and others of good reputation ' (Cranmer's *Works*, Parker
Society, ii. 417, 418). Prayers for peace between England and Scotland were also said in 1548, ' every Sunday and holyday.' And
' the most godly and happy marriage of the King's Majesty and the
young Queen of Scotland ' was introduced into the bidding prayer
before the sermon (*Ibid.* ii. 154 and *n.*).

[80] So early as September 1543, it was reported that Francis
wished ' the marriage of the Queen's Grace to the Dauphin's son '
(Lodge's *Illustrations of British History*, 1838, i. 54). On the 1st
of January 1544-5, Lord Eure informed Shrewsbury that he had
learned from one of his spies that the Governor, Cardinal, and
other Lords of the Scots Council, had promised to the French
Ambassador ' that the Frenche Kinge shall have the yonge Quene
to marye where he list,' and that in the spring both Queens should
be sent into France (*Hamilton Papers*, ii. 538).

[81] Lesley's *History*, p. 203.

[82] *Papiers D'État*, Ban. Club, i. 181-184 ; Lesley's *History*, p. 204.

[83] According to Labanoff, the Scottish Lords decided at Stirling,
on the 8th of February 1547-8, to offer Mary in marriage to the
Dauphin, and proposed to send her to France to be educated at
Henry's Court ; and on the same day Arran was created Duke of
Chatelherault by the King of France (*Recueil des Lettres de Marie*

Stuart, i. 3). David Laing has adopted this statement (Laing's *Knox*, i. 217 *n.*). But a council was apparently held at Stirling by the 2nd of the preceding November, at which the removal of Mary to France was discussed, as well as the propriety of placing the principal strongholds in the hands of their allies (Thorpe's *Calendar*, i. 70, 71). Before the end of December, fifty French captains—precursors of the coming army.—arrived in Scotland (*Ibid.* i. 74; Tytler's *Scotland*, 1845, iv. 479, 480). The 27th of January 1547-8 is given as the date of the contract between Arran and Henry the Second, by which Arran obliged himself to assemble the Scots Parliament, in order to obtain its consent to Mary's marriage with the Dauphin, to her deliverance to the King of France, and to the giving up to him some of the chief fortresses ; and by which Henry as a reward for such a great and signal service bound himself, amongst other things, to confer the title of Duke on the Earl of Arran, with a Duchy in France (*Consultation pour Marquis D'Abercorn contre le Duc D'Hamilton*, Paris, 1865, p. 1.). Writing from Edinburgh to D'Aumale, on the 24th of June 1548, D'Oysel mentions that Arran had already given up Dunbar to the French, and that the Queen Dowager had already prevailed on Angus, George Douglas, Cassillis, ' le Cherodaers,' Seton, several other lords and barons, and seven or eight bishops and prelates, to give their written consent, not only to Mary's marriage with the Dauphin, but to her going to France (Teulet's *Papiers D'État*, i. 671, 672). Teulet thought that ' le Cherodaers ' was a name disfigured past recognition, but it stands for ' the Sheriff of Ayr.' This was Sir Hew Campbell of Loudon, referred to by Knox as ' the auld Schiref of Ayr,' and as one of those enemies of the Reformation who acknowledged in 1560 that God was fighting for the Protestants (Laing's *Knox*, ii. 137).

[84] *Papiers D'État*, Ban. Club, i. 666 ; *Hamilton Papers*, ii. 597-604 ; Thorpe's *Calendar*, i. 87 ; Lesley's *History*, pp. 206, 207.— Some interesting details of the Scots preparations for helping the French at Haddington are given in the *Register of Privy Council*, xiv. 3-6.

[85] Mr. Skelton gives the 24th of May as the date of this Parliament (Skelton's *Mary Stuart*, p. 15); Principal Robertson, the 5th of June (Robertson's *Scotland*, 1794, p. 75); and Father Stevenson, ' shortly before the 24th of June ' (Stevenson's *Mary Stuart*, p. 85). The 7th of July is the true date (*Acts of the*

Parliaments of Scotland, ii. 481). Hill Burton says 'the Estates
met at Haddington, just recovered from the English after a hard
struggle' (*History of Scotland,* 1876, iii. 276); but it was not until
September of the following year that the English—reduced by
pest and hunger—evacuated Haddington (*Papiers D'État,* i. 698;
Thorpe's *Calendar,* i. 98; *Diurnal of Occurrents,* p. 48). The
Parliament met not in the town, but in the Abbey 'about a mile
to the eastward' (*Acts of Parliament,* ii. 481; Lesley's *History,*
p. 209; *Archæologia Scotica,* i. 58, 62). By the 2nd of July, part of
the French forces had encamped at the abbey, or 'Nonry' as
Wilford called it (*Hamilton Papers,* ii. 598).

   [86] *Acts of the Parliaments of Scotland,* ii. 481.—Knox explains
their unanimity on the grounds of bribery, flattery, and intimida-
tion (Laing's *Knox,* i. 217). It was at this time, according to
Petit, that 'the Scots resolved to cast aside the English alliance'
(Flandre's *Petit,* i. 15, 16)—a rather superfluous resolution, seeing
that by their Parliament they had nearly five years before cast
aside the English treaties of peace and marriage (*supra,* p. 10).
Hill Burton says :—'There was an understanding and more, that
the royal prize was to be for the Governor's son. Arran, indeed,
held an obligation to this end under the seals of the chief nobles.
In a firmer hand than his it would not have been easy to loosen
such a hold' (*History of Scotland,* iii. 277). But this hold had
been loosened fully two years before, when, on the 11th of June
1546, the Governor, in presence of the Queen Dowager and Lords
of Council, for the good of the Kingdom and healing of divisions,
'dischargit the contract and band, maid to him be quhatsomevir
noble men of the realme, anentis our Soverane Ladyis mariage,
and sall distroy the samyn, and dischargis all noble men, that hes
consentit thairto, of the said band.' On the same day the Queen
Dowager discharged 'all bandis maid to hir be all maner of noble
men incontrair the said contract'; and the assured lords, Angus,
Cassillis, Maxwell, and Sir George Douglas, approved of the Act of
Parliament dissolving the English peace and marriage (*Register of
the Privy Council of Scotland,* i. 27, 29). Notwithstanding Arran's
promise to destroy the 'bands' in his favour, one signed by the
Master of Eglinton is still preserved in Hamilton Palace. The
reason it gives for preferring as Mary's husband a prince 'borne of
the realme', and especially Arran's son, is that princes of other
countries, who might desire her, might, like the King of England,

pursue the same with force and power (*Historical MSS. Commission*, *Eleventh Report*, app. part vi. p. 36).

87 *Domestic Calendar*, 1547-1580, p. 6.

88 *Foreign Calendar, Edward*, p. 21.

89 Thorpe's *Calendar*, i. 83.

90 Tytler's *History of Scotland*, 1845, iv. 477 ; Thorpe's *Calendar*, i. 83.—She had already had small-pox, and was destined to have it again.

91 *Papiers D'État*, i. 662.

92 Hill Burton says that the way in which the English trap to intercept her was escaped 'is one of the cleverest affairs of the kind on record.' He tells how the French squadron sailed down the Firth of Forth in great pomp, and how 'it would have been intercepted and fought in the narrow seas as it crept along to France ; but it turned suddenly northward, and swept round Scotland by the Pentland Firth, then, coasting westwards, it reached Dumbarton' (*History of Scotland*, iii. 277). Nevertheless, the English Government received timely warning as to the port from which Mary was to sail (Thorpe's *Calendar*, i. 89, 91 ; *Hamilton Papers*, ii. 603); and Lesley states that the Protector 'caused prepair ane gret navie of shippes,' which he sent 'to await at the *west* seyis at thaire passage, and to haif taikin thame gif thay could' (Lesley's *History*, p. 210). Froude says that the French commander 'evaded the English cruisers who were watching for him at the mouth of the Forth' (*History of England*, 1887, iv. 321); but apparently the English fleet, on its way north, was still at Berwick on the 2nd of August, when Mary was on board her galley at Dumbarton (Thorpe's *Calendar*, i. 93).

93 According to Sir James Balfour, Mary's retinue consisted of Lords Erskine and Fleming, Lady Fleming, 'with 12 young ladeyes, and 200 gentlemen and servants' (*Historical Works*, i. 292). Bishop Lesley, writing much earlier, is less explicit as to the numbers, but infinitely more interesting in his details. Besides Lords Erskine and Livingston, who had been her keepers, and Lady Fleming, her father's sister, there were, he says, 'sindre gentilwemen and nobill mennis sonnes and dochteris, almoist of hir awin aige.' Of these last, 'thair wes four in speciall, of whome everie one of thame buir the samin name of Marie, being of four syndre honorable houses, to wyt, Fleming, Levingstoun, Setoun, and Betoun of Creich ; quho remanit all

foure with the Quene in France, during her residens thair, and returned agane in Scotlande with her Majestie' (Lesley's *History*, p. 209). It is usually stated that Mary was accompanied to France by her illegitimate brother, the Lord James, then Commendator of St. Andrews Priory, afterwards Earl of Murray and Regent of Scotland. Of the earlier writers who have said so are Buchanan (Ruddiman's *Buchanan*, i. 300), Herries (*Historical Memoirs*, p. 23), and Lindsay (Pitscottie's *History*, 1728, p.196). Among the more modern writers who have perpetuated the statement, are Keith, Chalmers, P. F. Tytler, Mignet, Hosack, Thornton, Walker, and Miss Stewart. Some have waxed eloquent on the influence which the youthful Prior thus early secured over her warm and unsuspecting heart. Yet there is reason to believe that he did not go with her. In support of the usual opinion, Chalmers says that for three of her natural brothers—the respective commendators of Holyrood, Coldingham, and St. Andrews—'licenses to travel are recorded in the Books of Council and Session; and these youthful commendators are said, in the record, to have gone to *the sculis* in France' (Chalmers's *Life of Mary*, 1818, i. 10). But Henry Johnes, writing immediately after her departure, informed the Lord Protector that, while the Abbot of Holyrood and the Prior of Coldingham—'the Kinges two yonger basterde sonnes'—had gone with her; 'thelder brethren'—James, Prior of St. Andrews, and James, Abbot of Kelso—had 'refusid to go, for that they could not have the yong gentylmen of Fyef with theim' (*Hamilton Papers*, ii. 618). Buchanan, Herries, Pitscottie, and Chalmers stultify themselves by assigning to the Prior of St. Andrews a chief part in the repulse of the English on the coast of Fife (Ruddiman's *Buchanan*, i. 300, 301; *Historical Memoirs*, p. 24; Lindsay's *History*, p. 197; Churchyard's *Chips Concerning Scotland*, 1817, p. 7.)—in a skirmish which must have occurred within a few days of Mary's landing in France (*Papiers D'État*, i. 687; Thorpe's *Calendar*, i. 93, 94; Lesley's *History*, pp. 213-215; Churchyard's *Chips Concerning Scotland*, p. 80). If he went to France with her he cannot have remained long there. It is known otherwise that, in September 1549, he drove 'the Frenche from St. Andrews and out of Fyffe' (Stevenson's *Selections*, p. 48); that in November of that year he was present in the Provincial Council which met in Edinburgh (*Concilia Scotiæ*, ii. 83); and that he sat in the Privy Council on the 27th of March 1550 (*Register of the Privy Council of Scotland*, i. 83).

[94] *Diurnal of Occurrents*, p. 47; Thorpe's *Calendar*, i. 93.—Lesley says she embarked in 'the Kingis awin gallay' (*History*, p. 209).

[95] *Hamilton Papers*, ii. 617; Thorpe's *Calendar*, i. 93; Stevenson's *Selections*, Maitland Club, p. 27.—While waiting in the Clyde, Lady Fleming wished to be landed 'to repose her'; but the captain gruffly answered that she should not go on land, but into France or drown by the way (Tytler's *Scotland*, iv. 480). This incident is transposed by Miss Strickland from the beginning to the latter part of the voyage, when the fair passengers had 'suffered severely from sea-sickness' off 'the dangerous coast of Bretagne' (Strickland's *Life of Mary*, 1888, i. 9).

[96] Buchanan merely says that Mary landed in Brittany, a peninsula in France (Ruddiman's *Buchanan*, i. 300); but Lesley, less vague, says the haven of Brest (Lesley's *History*, p. 210); and that port is regarded as the place by such writers as Herries, Conaeus, Jebb, Chalmers, Mignet, Lingard, Labanoff, P. F. Tytler, and Hill Burton; while others, including Dargaud, Francisque-Michel, Petit, Skelton, and Stevenson are satisfied that it was at Roscoff. The latter place it seems can show, in support of its claim, the ruins of a little Gothic chapel, founded by the pious child, in the very year of her arrival, to mark the spot where 'her foot was traced on the rock' (Stevenson's *Mary Stuart*, p. 87 *n.*).

[97] *Diurnal of Occurrents*, p. 47.

[98] Laing's *Knox*, i. 218.—Glassford Bell's chronology of Mary's early years is singularly inaccurate and self-contradictory. He states that she was born on the 7th of December 1542; that 'the two first years of her life' were spent at Linlithgow; that she resided at Stirling Castle 'during the greater part of the years 1545, 46, and 47'; that, when even Stirling Castle became a somewhat dangerous residence, she was removed to Inchmahome, where she 'remained upwards of two years'; and that, 'in the fifth year of her age,' she was taken to Dumbarton, where she was delivered to the French Admiral (Bell's *Life of Mary*, 1828, i. 42-44).

CHAPTER II

[1] *Venetian Calendar*, v. 228; Lesley's *History of Scotland*, Ban. Club, p. 210.

[2] *Register of the Privy Council of Scotland*, i. 88; *National MSS. of Scotland*, Part iii. Nos. xxx, xxxii-xxxiv.

[3] Thorpe's *Scottish Calendar*, i. 97.

[4] Halliwell's *Letters of the Kings*, 1848, ii. 39.

[5] *Foreign Calendar, Edward*, p. 109.

[6] *Foreign Calendar, Edward*, p. 133 ; Tytler's *Edward VI. and Mary*, i. 393–401 ; *Venetian Calendar*, v. 363, 364.

[7] Father Stevenson says she embarked on the 8th of May 1550 (*Mary Stuart*, 1886, p. 106). A contemporary says on the 8th of August (*Diurnal of Occurrents*, p. 50). Considerable alarm was caused at the French Court by her non-arrival—'lest the recent storms should have driven her to the coast of Flanders'—until it was learned that she had not embarked until the 6th of September (*Foreign Calendar, Edward*, p. 55) ; but she could not have sailed even on that day, as she was present at a meeting of Privy Council in Edinburgh on the 7th of September (*Register of Privy Council*, i. 108). 'No sooner had she embarked at Leith for France,' says Father Stevenson, 'than the government of the country passed, for all practical purposes, into the hands of the Lord James Stuart, and the party who acted along with him' (*Mary Stuart*, p. 119). But according to Knox 'all the Kinges sonnes' accompanied the Queen Mother to France (Laing's *Knox*, i. 242) ; the Lord James is specially mentioned as having gone with her (*Diurnal of Occurrents*, p. 50) ; a license to that effect was granted to him on the 6th of September 1550 (Chalmers's *Mary*, 1818, ii. 279) ; and his name does not occur in the sederunt of the Privy Council from 16th July 1550 until the 19th of June 1553.

[8] Lesley's *History*, pp. 234, 235.—Lesley also says that she wished to congratulate and rejoice with the King and her friends there, that Scotland was not only likely to continue on good terms with its old ally, but 'also now it mycht be maide moir subject and bound unto thame, yea as a province joynit unto France be mariage, as Britangze and Normoundie ar subject at this present.'

[9] *Foreign Calendar, Edward*, p. 53.

[10] Lesley's *History*, p. 236 ; *Foreign Calendar, Edward*, p. 57 ; Tytler's *Edward VI. and Mary*, i. 325, 327 ; Tytler's *History of Scotland*, 1845, iv. 482 ; Francisque-Michel's *Les Écossais en France*, 1862, i. 472–474.

[11] Lesley's *History*, pp. 236–239.

[12] Tytler's *Edward VI. and Mary*, i. 327 n.

[13] 'The Queen Dowager having gone to France, taking with her the chief nobility of Scotland, the King bought them completely ;

so that in France there is neither Scottish duke, nor lord, nor prelate, nor lady, nor dame, but who is munificently bribed by the most Christian King' (*Venetian Calendar*, v. 361). Knox says, 'What thei receaved we can nott tell; but few maid ruse [*i.e.* boast] at thare returnyng' (Laing's *Knox*, i. 242). Writing from Amboise on the 18th of April 1551, Sir John Mason informed the English Council that, 'the Scots be here very ill satisfied, having so impoverished themselves as the number of them may for these three years fast, for any profit they are like to have of their lands, having eaten up the same beforehand; which is thought to have been done of purpose, to the intent that, being brought to extreme need, they may be compelled upon hope of relief, like slaves, to hang upon the Queen' (Tytler's *Edward VI. and Mary*, i. 354, 355). In the same letter, Mason refers to the Earl of Huntly having received the promise of the Earldom of Murray. The Bishop of Ross includes that gift among those which he specially mentions, and also refers to 'a gret nombre of utheris giftis and confirmationis maid be the King to syndre uther particuler nobill and gentill men onder his seill and hand wreit, oblishing him *in verbo regio* to caus the Quene of Scotlande, at hir perfyte aige, ratifie and approve the samyn, or ellis he to gif thame as guid within the realme of France' (Lesley's *History*, p. 237).

[14] *Foreign Calendar, Edward*, p. 103.

[15] Edward's *Journal*, Clarendon Historical Society, p. 34; Teulet's *Papiers D'État*, i. 249-260.—While Froude regards the conduct of the English Government in the matter as an illustration of their integrity (*History of England*, 1887, v. 2), Father Stevenson is uncharitable enough to suspect that they 'had a guilty knowledge of this hideous plot from the beginning.' But his reasons for entertaining such a suspicion are rather illogical. 'On January 28th, 1551, the Council,' he says, 'introduced to Sir John Mason, their Ambassador in France, as secret agent, "one that Balneys (Balnaves), the Scot, hath councilled to be in France." They also gave him £10 towards his expenses. The connection of this anonymous Scot with Balnaves—a person so closely associated with the murder of Cardinal Beaton—excites our suspicion, and all the more so when we find that the letter of introduction referred to above—innocent as it looks—was written in cipher' (Stevenson's *Mary Stuart*, p. 109 *n.*). But this secret agent

bearing the Council's letter, who did not arrive until the 24th
of February, 'took not so much leisure in his journey hither-
ward,' says Mason to the Council, 'as he seemed desirous to
make haste to return again.' Afraid for his personal safety, he
next evening brought as his substitute Kirkcaldy of Grange,
who promised to communicate to Mason all that he could learn
(*Foreign Calendar, Edward*, p. 77). Apparently this anonymous
agent had not courage enough to serve as a spy, far less to
undertake the much more hazardous enterprise of poisoning a
queen. His connection with Balnaves need not excite suspicion ;
for, although that senator took refuge in St. Andrews Castle
some months after Beaton's assassination, there is little if anything to show that he was 'closely associated with the murder'
(Laing's *Knox*, iii. 408, 409) ; and even though he had been, it
would not follow that he would approve the murder of an innocent
child. That the project 'was known to the English Ambassador
is proved,' says Father Stevenson, 'by the Calendar of State
Papers, Foreign, 1551, April 29, June 6 and 9' (*Mary Stuart*,
p. 111 *n.*). But the items referred to only show that the
English Ambassador knew of the plot after it was discovered
(*Foreign Calendar, Edward*, pp. 97, 121, 126). Robert Stuart,
the would-be poisoner, passed into the hands of the French
officials, as Stevenson unwillingly admits (*Mary Stuart*, p. 112),
and was lodged by them in the Castle of Angers on the 5th
of June 1551. 'I cannot but observe, however,' he adds, 'that
Mason was at Angers on June 6, the day of Stuart's arrival
there, and that he left on the following day' (*Ibid.* p. 113 *n.*).
But, as he had previously stated (*Ibid.* p. 112), Stuart arrived
at Angers on the 5th of June—not the 6th ; and it was the
French King, not Mason, who left on the following day (*Foreign
Calendar, Edward*, p. 121). If therefore there is anything suspicious in the proximity of the departure, the suspicion attaches
to Henry the Second, not to the English Ambassador, who simply
followed his Majesty to Chateaubriand. Bishop Lesley unhesitatingly says, that, for this plot, Stuart was tortured, hanged and
quartered (*History*, p. 241). But Stevenson—while stating, that,
after the said 5th of June, 'he disappears, how, we know not'—
traces for him a later and murderous career (*Mary Stuart*, pp.
112-115).

[16] Lesley's *History*, p. 239.

[17] Edward's *Journal,* Clarendon Historical Society, p. 48 ; Tytler's *Edward VI. and Mary,* ii. 5, 6; *Foreign Calendar, Edward,* p. 190.—Father Stevenson does not allow her to land at Portsmouth until the 2nd of November (Stevenson's *Mary Stuart,* 1886, p. 118).

[18] Lesley's *History,* p. 240; *De Origine Moribus et Rebus Gestis Scotorum,* 1675, pp. 487*a*, 488*a*.—Collier points out the difficulty of reconciling this alleged proposal with the treaty which Edward had made with France (*Ecclesiastical History of Great Britain,* 1840, v. 444); but Lesley's statement has been followed by Conaeus, who alleges that Edward and the English nobles, after hearing Northampton's attractive account of Mary, resolved to set aside their compact with France and to treat with her mother for her (Jebb's *De Vita et Rebus,* ii. 16). Towards the end of June, Northampton and the other English Ambassadors had met 'the old and the young Scottish Queens,' in the chamber of Catherine de Medici (Tytler's *Edward VI. and Mary,* i. 388). Lesley's statement is also followed by Jebb (*Life and Reign of Mary Queen of Scots,* 1725, pp. 30, 31), by Keith (*History of Affairs,* i. 138), by Chalmers (*Life of Mary,* 1818, i. 14), by Hosack (*Mary and her Accusers,* 1870, i. 16), and by Petit (Flandre's *Petit,* i. 22).

[19] Father Stevenson represents the *Diurnal* as saying that she left France about the 30th of November (*Mary Stuart,* p. 119 *n.*), whereas it clearly means that she arrived in Scotland about that date (*Diurnal of Occurrents,* p. 50); and it is, no doubt, correct, for the Scots were charged to meet her on the Borders on the 24th of November (Tytler's *History of Scotland,* 1845, iv. 487), and she was present at a meeting of Privy Council in Edinburgh on the 7th of December (*Register of Privy Council,* i. 117).

[20] According to Conaeus :—'She devoted great attention to acquiring some of the best languages of Europe, and such was the sweetness of her French that she was considered eloquent in it, in the judgment of the most learned. Nor did she neglect Spanish [see *Reg. of Privy Council,* i. 234 ; *Foreign Calendar, Elizabeth,* vii. 92] or Italian, which she employed more for use than for show or lively talk. She understood Latin better than she could speak it. As for the graces of poetry, she had more from nature than art. She formed her letters well, and, what is rare in a woman, quickly. In the excellence of her singing, she profited greatly by a certain natural—not acquired—modulation of her voice. She played well on the cittern, the harp and the harpsi-

chord (*claircymbalum*) as they call it. She danced excellently to music on account of her wonderful agility of body, but yet gracefully and becomingly, for by quiet and gentle motion of her limbs she could express any harmony of the strings. She learned to mount and control her steed, as far as it was necessary for travelling or hunting, in which she delighted, often saying that further care for that exercise pertained to men, not to women' (Jebb's *De Vita et Rebus*, ii. 15). The last statement is much too commonplace for a more recent biographer, who exclaims :— 'That young lady, so cheerful and playful, whose delicate hand awakes the sweet melodies of Scotland, sometimes breaks in a steed which quivers under her' (Flandre's *Petit*, i. 27). Writing as if Mary had been trained on the division-of-labour principle, Father Stevenson says that her 'moral and religious education' was placed in the hands of her maternal grandmother; that in 'temporal matters' the influence which chiefly served to form her character was exercised by her uncles—the Duke of Guise and Charles, the Cardinal of Lorraine ; that as long as she resided with the royal children in the French Court, 'she was instructed by their masters and shared in their studies'; and that Henry the Second thought himself fortunate in discovering for her and the Dauphin 'an accomplished dancing master' who was also 'a good Christian' (Stevenson's *Mary Stuart*, pp. 94, 96, 103). Much has been said in praise of her poetic gifts ; yet even Mr. Skelton admits that, 'Neither her letters nor her poems are above mediocrity. The style is sufficiently graceful,' he says, 'but the sentiments are faded and common-place' (*Maitland of Lethington*, 1887, i. 297). The imperfections of her *Latin Themes* are enough, in their editor's opinion, to damage her reputation for early learning, and the subject and period of the *Themes* quite sufficient to impair 'the admiration inspired by the praise bestowed by Brantôme on the famous Latin speech delivered in the French Court' (Montaiglon's *Latin Themes of Mary Stuart*, Warton Club, 1855, pp. xvii. xix.). In her attainments, Mary was not unrivalled among her contemporaries. In 1557, Giovanni Michiel reports that Mary Tudor speaks fluently in English, Latin, French, and Spanish, and understands Italian. 'Besides woman's work,' he adds, 'such as embroidery of every sort with the needle, she also practises music, playing especially on the claricorde and on the lute so excellently that, when intent on it (though now she plays rarely), she surprised the best performers, both by the rapidity of her hand and by her style of playing' (*Venetian Calendar*, vi. 1055). In the same report that Ambassador thus speaks of her sister Elizabeth's attainments :—'As a linguist she excels the Queen, for besides Latin she has no slight knowledge of Greek, and speaks Italian more than the Queen does, taking so much pleasure in it that from vanity she will never speak any other language with Italians' (*Ibid.* pp. 1058, 1059). Hooper had previously referred to her proficiency in Greek and Latin (Robinson's *Original Letters*, Parker Society, i. 76); and at a later period Sir James Melville, who had spent two months in Italy, acknowledged that Elizabeth spoke Italian 'raisonable weill'; but her Dutch, he said, 'was not gud' (Melville's *Memoirs*, Maitland Club, p. 125). Charles the Ninth, when in his fifteenth year, spoke no tongue but his own (*Foreign Calendar, Elizabeth*, vii. 337). Two years later, an objectionable phrase in an inscription was excused to the English Ambassador, on the ground that neither Charles nor his mother knew Latin (*Ibid.* viii. 196).

[21] In Mr. Swinburne's opinion, Brantôme's gay and easy pages reveal ' the daily life of a Court compared to which the Court of King Charles II. is as the Court of Queen Victoria to the society described by Grammont' (*Encyclopædia Britannica*, ninth edition, xv. 594, 595). ' The Court of France, in which Mary Stuart was now domesticated, was one of the most refined, and at the same time one of the most dissipated courts in Europe . . . Much of its daily life was a continued school of profligacy' (Stevenson's *Mary Stuart*, 1886, pp. 90, 91). On the other hand, Cardinal Pole refers to the 'great piety' of Henry the Second (*Venetian Calendar*, vi. 3); and Paul IV. called Catherine de Medici 'a little saint' (*Ibid.* p. 951). Six years after Paul's death, orders were taken for the decorum of her Court (*Foreign Calendar, Elizabeth*, vii. 331).

[22] Sir Henry Ellis says that 'after passing a few days at Court, she was conveyed to a nunnery for education, and there remained till the time of her marriage with the Dauphin' (Ellis's *Original Letters*, first series, ii. 252 *n.*). George Chalmers also places her in ' a monastery of virgins ' (*Life of Mary*, 1818, i. 11). Glassford Bell represents her as so pleased with ' the calm and secluded life of a nunnery,' that she thought of separating herself forever from the world, a project which the French King and her ambitious uncles balked by removing her from the convent to the palace (*Life of*

Mary, 1828, i. 45). These allegations and many others concerning
her convent life have probably been drawn, directly or indirectly,
from the statement of Conaeus (Jebb's *De Vita et Rebus Gestis Mariæ*,
1725, ii. 14, 15). Prince Labanoff states that 'she was educated
with the children of Henry II. and Catherine de Medicis' (*Recueil
des Lettres de Marie Stuart*, i. 3). According to an earlier and
equally ardent champion, 'she was . . . nourished in the Court of
Henry the Second and Katharine de Medicis, who did love her
most entirely' (Causin's *Holy Court*, 1678, p. 812 ; Jebb's *De Vita et
Rebus*, ii. 54). Henry himself, in writing to the Scottish Estates,
in October 1557, refers to the upbringing she has received 'with our
very dear and very saintly companion the Queen' (Keith's *History*,
i. 348, 349). Both Causin and Henry are flatly contradicted by one
of Mary's modern apologists : 'Catherine had no share in Mary's
education. During the whole of the reign of Henry the Second, the
influence of his wife in the Court of France was at the lowest; she had
a very special dislike to Mary, whose company she avoided as much as
possible' (Stevenson's *Mary Stuart*, pp. 93, 94). It is rather significant that the learned Jesuit does not state whose influence was highest
in that Court—that of the King's mistress, Diana of Poitiers ; and
that, despite Diana's kindness to the young Queen of Scots (*supra*,
p. 19), he does not deign to notice her, in his elaborate monograph
on the first eighteen years of Mary's life, save by a passing reference
to her presence at a baptism ! Another apologist exclaims :
'It was the child's holiday time only that was spent at Court ;
during the rest of the year she lived in strict seclusion with her
maternal grandmother'; spending 'the most impressionable years
of her youth among devout women who stood severely aloof from
the follies and frivolities of the Court' (Skelton's *Mary Stuart*,
1893, p. 17). Previously he had said : 'By far the greater part of
her life, up to the day when she sailed for Leith, had been passed
in the seclusion of a nunnery' (Skelton's *Impeachment of Mary
Stuart*, 1876, p. 144). She said herself that 'sche was brocht up
in joyusitie' (*infra*, p. 274 n. 80).

　　[23] 'In the refined and voluptuous Court of the Valois, governed
by a favourite, she was brought up rather as an accomplished court
lady than as a future queen ; and her education rather seemed to
fit her for becoming the mistress than the wife of the Dauphin'
(Lamartine's *Mary Stuart*, 1864, p. 8). 'Debauchery of all kinds,
and murder in all forms, were the daily matter of excitement or of

jest to the brilliant circle which revolved around Queen Catherine de Medici. After ten years' training under the tutelage of the woman whose main instrument of policy was the corruption of her own children, the Queen of Scots . . . was married to the eldest and feeblest of the brood' (*Encyclopædia Britannica*, ninth edition, xv. 595).

²⁴ The virtue of Lady Fleming—Mary's 'aunt,' as Sir James Balfour calls her ; 'Mary's Scotch governess,' as Miss Strickland calls her—was irretrievably tarnished by the French King (Tytler's *Edward VI. and Mary*, 1839, i. 361 ; Tytler's *History of Scotland*, 1845, iv. 485 ; Francisque Michel's *Les Écossais en France*, 1862, ii. 2), an event which would not perhaps have surprised her husband had he been alive (*Spalding Miscellany*, v. 309 ; *Analecta Scotica*, ii. 214). 'The family of Guise'—says one not unduly inclined to expose the seamy side of the Papacy—'was now in the ascendant under the auspices of the King's mistress, Diana of Poitiers, with whom they were connected, Claude de Guise having married one of the daughters of Diana' (*Foreign Calendar, Edward*, p. viii. *n.*). As Mary herself testifies, Diana was very kind to her (*supra*, p. 19). Mary's maternal uncle, Charles, Cardinal of Lorraine, bears the reputation of a licentious scoundrel (Mignet's *Mary Queen of Scots*, 1851, i. 39 ; Laing's *Knox*, ii. 318 and *n.*) ; but, it is said that, although avaricious, deceitful, and far from truthful, he has been unjustly blackened, by having attributed to him the viler sins of his uncle John, whom he succeeded as Cardinal of Lorraine in 1550 (Baird's *Rise of the Huguenots*, 1880, i. 270, 271). Before Mary's second marriage, he who was to be her third husband was alleged to have called her 'Cardinal's whore' (*Foreign Calendar, Elizabeth*, vii. 315, 320, 325). Her uncle's enemies depict him as capable of such villainy (*Ibid.* iv. 286 ; Buchanan's *Epigrammatum Liber*, ii. 21). On the other hand, an enthusiastic modern biographer says that 'her youthful godliness enchanted the Cardinal' (Miss A. M. Stewart's *Life of Mary*, p. 12).

²⁵ Labanoff's *Recueil*, i. 9-16.—Father Stevenson quotes a large portion of this letter, but does not give the final sentence (*Mary Stuart*, 1886, pp. 127-130) ; and Mr. Skelton—who unavowedly borrows from Stevenson's translation—also stops short (*Mary Stuart*, 1893, pp. 19, 20). I have followed Miss A. M. Stewart's rendering of that sentence (*Life of Mary*, p. 8).

²⁶ *Foreign Calendar, Mary*, p. 47.

[27] *Venetian Calendar*, v. 517.

[28] Montaiglon's *Latin Themes*, p. xv. ; Stevenson's *Mary Stuart*, p. 134.—There are sixty-four of the themes or letters. The fifth in order is the first that is dated ; the sixty-first, the last. At the end of each of the first four, in the French versions, are the words: 'A Reims.' The other royal residences which are mentioned are Compiègne, Villers-Cotterets, Paris, and Saint-Germain. Barbarigo, the Venetian Ambassador, refers on the 30th of January 1554-5, to Henry having been recently at St. Germain ; next day he was to be at Paris ; and in a few days would go to Fontainebleau with Catherine for her delivery (*Venetian Calendar*, vi. 13). In France, as in England, in those days the removal of the Court, from one palace to another, was at least occasionally rendered necessary by dirt and stench (*Ibid.* vi. pp. xix. and n., 87, 147, 320). The nobles in this respect were apparently in no better case than their sovereigns. One of the reasons why Lord Paget did not wish to go into Staffordshire (*temp.* Edward VI.) was that 'his house of Burton is all plucked down, saving two chambers ; and his house of Bewdesert, though it be pretty is yet so small as after one month it will wax unsavoury for him to continue in, with his wife, children, and family' (Lodge's *Illustrations*, 1838, i. 171).

[29] Hardwicke's *State Papers*, i. 68.

[30] *National MSS. of Scotland*, iii. 34.

[31] Labanoff's *Recueil*, i. 32.

[32] *Ibid.* i. 42.

[33] *Papiers D'État*, i. pp. ix. 261-266.

[34] Lesley's *History*, pp. 249, 250 ; *Venetian Calendar*, v. 540.—'In this Parliament,' says Pitscottie, 'the Governor rode up, from the Abbay to the Tolbooth, with the lords and heralds, having the crown, sword and sceptre born before him. The Queen and *Monsieur d'Ossel* rode up apart by themselves, and stayed till the Parliament was fenced ; wherein the Governor discharged himself of his authority, and the Queen was elected Regent ; who rode down, having the crown, sword and sceptre born before her by the same lords that had carried them up before the Governor, who now rode down as a private nobleman among the rest' (Lindsay's *History*, 1728, p. 199). A summary of the particular articles between the Queen Dowager and the Duke of Chatelherault, dated 19th February 1553-4, is given in the *Eleventh Report of the Historical MSS. Commission*, app. part vi. pp. 40, 41. Mary's own discharge to

the Duke of his intromissions with her money and movable goods, dated the 22nd of March 1553-4, and ratified by Parliament on the 12th of April 1554, is printed in the *Acts of the Parliaments of Scotland,* ii. 600-602. The declaration regarding the Duke's behaviour as Governor, and also the 'band' by the Queen Dowager and the Three Estates warranting him against all actions concerning his intromissions with the Queen's money and jewels, are also printed in the *Acts of Parliament,* ii. 602-604. Mary's congratulation of her mother is in the *National MSS. of Scotland,* iii. 39.

[35] Laing's *Knox,* i. 242.

[36] Melville's *Memoirs,* Mait. Club, pp. 21, 73.

[37] Lesley's *History,* p. 251.

[38] A learned and candid Frenchman has said : 'In all the great affairs of Scotland and France in the sixteenth century, it is evident that the true interests of France were sacrificed to the ambitious views of the House of Guise. Scotland, which was for so many ages the devoted ally of France, the rein, as our ancient Kings said, with which they restrained the encroachments of England, was unwilling to abdicate its nationality and become a French province. Moreover, the unbridled excesses of the French troops in Scotland, no less than the shameless rapacity of the French agents, at last aroused a general spirit of resistance, and England soon found in the rupture of the ancient alliance between France and Scotland an ample indemnification for the loss of Calais ' (Teulet's *Papiers D'État,* i. pp. xii. xiii.).

[39] *Foreign Calendar, Edward,* p. 65.

[40] *Ibid.* p. 103.

[41] *Venetian Calendar,* vi. 532, 690, 1078.

[42] Lesley's *History,* p. 264.

[43] Lesley gives the 20th of April as the date of the handfasting ; but in the contemporary *Discours du Grand et Magnifique Triumphe,* printed both in Paris and Rouen in 1558, the 19th of April is given as the date. The marriage-contract is also dated, at the Louvre, on the 19th of April (*Acts of the Parliaments of Scotland,* ii. 514).

[44] *Venetian Calendar,* vi. 1487.—According to the Bishop of Ross, it was Philip's temporary triumph in arms that moved Henry to hasten the match, 'fearing that by this and sic lyke ourthrowes and accedentis, the Estatis of Scotlande shuld be fundin the moir unwilling to accomplishe the mariage' (Lesley's *History,* p. 261). Giacomo Soranzo, writing from Poissy on the 9th of November

1557, states that 'the causes for hastening this marriage are apparently two; the first to enable them most surely to avail themselves of the forces of Scotland against the kingdom of England for next year, and the other for the gratification of the Duke and Cardinal of Guise, the said Queen's uncles, who by the hastening this marriage chose to secure themselves against any other matrimonial alliance which might be proposed to his most Christian Majesty in some negotiation for peace, the entire establishment of their greatness having to depend on this; for which reason the Constable by all means in his power continually sought to prevent it' (*Venetian Calendar*, vi. 1365, 1366).

[45] Lesley's *History*, pp. 264, 265.—In his Scottish version Lesley gives the true date of the marriage; in his Latin version he assigns it to the 19th of April.

[46] *Venetian Calendar*, vi. 1486, 1487. — Michiel's letter is dated from Paris on the 25th of April. He says that 'the diversions and banquets will continue during the whole of this week, two or three other marriages of the chief personages of the Court having to be concluded. . . . This solemnity has by so much the more gratified and contented the Parisian populace (amongst whom money was thrown on entering the church as a mark of greater rejoicing) as for two hundred years and upwards there is no record of any Dauphin having been married within the realm, all on the contrary marrying abroad.' Lesley also mentions that 'presentlie was gevine to the Dolphine the title of King Dolphine, sua that he and the Quene was called thairefter King and Quene Dolphine' (Lesley's *History*, p. 265). In the marriage-contract, it was stipulated that the Dauphin should bear the name and title of King of Scotland, and have his arms quartered with those of Scotland. This marriage-contract is printed in the *Acts of the Parliaments of Scotland*, ii. 511-514; and in Keith's *History*, i. 353-359. The description of the pompous marriage ceremonies, extracted by Teulet from the *Registers of the Hotel de Ville of Paris*, is printed by him in his *Papiers D'État*, i. 292-303, and in his *Relations Politiques*, i. 302-311. In his opinion, while 'the details of these fêtes may appear rather puerile,' nevertheless 'their unusual splendour had a political signification which should not be overlooked' (*Papiers D'État*, i. p. xii). The *Discours du Triumphe faict au Mariage*, printed at Paris in 1558 by Annet Briere, has been reprinted at Bordeaux by Gounouilhou; and the Rouen edition of the same year was reprinted in 1818 by

O   209

Woodfall, and presented to the Roxburghe Club by William Bentham.

[47] The Commissioners were appointed on the 14th of December 1557, in compliance with the desire expressed in Henry the Second's letter read that day to the Scottish Parliament (Lesley's *History*, p. 262 ; *Acts of the Parliaments of Scotland*, ii. 502, 504, 514). Henry's letter is printed in French by Keith (*History*, i. 348, 349). Lesley gives a translation in Latin (*De Origine Moribus et Rebus Gestis Scotorum*, 1675, pp. 492, 493), and from that translation Father Dalrymple has rendered it into Scots (Dalrymple's *Lesley*, Scottish Text Society, ii. 375-378). Mignet gives the 31st of October as the date of the letter (*History of Mary Stuart*, 1851, i. 44); Keith gives the 30th ; but Lesley and the *Acts of Parliament* give the 29th. The Commission of 14th December 1557 is printed in the *Acts of Parliament*, ii. 514; and in Keith's *History*, i. 359-361. The original, with eighteen seals attached, is preserved in the Archives of the Kingdom of France (Labanoff's *Recueil*, i. 46 *n.*). Nine Commissioners are therein appointed, viz. James Beaton, Archbishop of Glasgow, David Panter, Bishop of Ross, Robert Reid, Bishop of Orkney, the Earls of Rothes and Cassillis, the Lord James, Commendator of St. Andrews, Lords Fleming and Seton, and John Erskine of Dun. In his list (*History*, p. 262; *De Origine*, 1675, p. 494) Lesley omits his own predecessor in the see of Ross. Calderwood (i. 330) and Spottiswoode (i. 187) also omit Panter. Keith says (i. 166 *n.*) that he did not go to France with the others, and that he died at Stirling on the 1st of October 1558. Mary appointed the same Commissioners on the 16th of March 1557-8, adding, however, her maternal grandmother, the Duchess of Guise (*Acts of Parliament*, ii. 513; Labanoff's *Recueil*, i. 48); but, on the 15th of April 1558, in her approbation of the Acts of the Scots Parliaments of 1548 and 1557 concerning her marriage, Panter's name is omitted (*Acts of Parliament*, ii. 518). A tax of £15,000 was imposed to defray the expenses of the Scots Commissioners (*Register of Privy Council*, xiv. 14).

[48] *Acts of the Parliaments of Scotland*, ii. 518.

[49] *Ibid.* ii. 518, 519.

[50] *Ibid.* ii. 519.

[51] *Ibid.* ii. 508-511.

[52] Goodall, while describing these three documents as 'private deeds of a very extraordinary nature,' and as 'illegal, null, and

infamous papers,' that could only serve to 'reflect dishonour on all parties concerned in them,' tried to discredit them (*Examination of the Letters*, 1754, i. 159, 166). Their genuineness, however, cannot now be disputed. Labanoff (*Recueil*, i. 50-56) has printed them—the two deeds of gift from the originals, and the protest from a copy in the Royal Library of Paris.

[53] Even five years before she signed these documents, 'her mother,' says Father Stevenson, 'could so far trust her discretion, as to consult her upon certain private matters, respecting which the young diplomat ventured to express her opinion with mingled candour, good sense and modesty' (Stevenson's *Mary Stuart*, 1886, pp. 126, 127). Perhaps the true explanation of her documentary duplicity is to be found in another passage by the same ingenious writer:—'Mary's long absence from her mother made her turn to her maternal uncles with increased affection, and they found it no difficult task to mould her character according to their own principles. She was an apt pupil; and the lessons which they taught the child were never forgotten by the woman and the Queen' (*Ibid.* p. 97). It is impossible to believe that, in advising Mary on this occasion, the Guises acted either in ignorance or simplicity. 'On the eve of her marriage to the Dauphin,' says Mr. Skelton, 'Diane de Poictiers confirms the impression of Mary's early tact and reasonableness: "She spoke to the Scottish deputies not as an inexperienced child, but as a woman of age and knowledge: they will tell you this when they return"' (Skelton's *Mary Stuart*, 1893, pp. 21, 22). In his account of the marriage, this apologist ignores the three damning documents; but he complacently remarks that 'up to the hour when she left France, Mary, so far as record remains, was honest as the day' (*Ibid.* p. 33); and adds that, 'as a girl at least she was absolutely veracious' (*Ibid.* p. 34); and again that it does not admit of dispute 'that, up to the time of her return to Scotland, Mary's conduct was irreproachable' (*Ibid.* p. 55).

CHAPTER III

[1] Keith's *History*, i. 170, 357 ; *Acts of the Parliaments of Scotland*, ii. 512.—The oath of fidelity which was actually sworn by the Archbishop of Glasgow, the Bishop of Orkney, the Commendator of

St. Andrews, Lords Fleming and Seton, and Erskine of Dun, is in Keith's *History*, i. 363, 364.

² *Papiers D'État*, i. 423, 424; Burnet's *Reformation*, 1715, iii. app. p. 279; *Foreign Calendar, Elizabeth*, ii. 22; Aikman's *Buchanan*, ii. 394, 395; Herries's *Historical Memoirs*, pp. 32, 33; Calderwood's *History*, i. 330, 331; Hill Burton's *Scotland*, 1876, iii. 290.

³ Miss Strickland alleges that Knox attributes the illness of the Commissioners to poison (*Life of Mary*, 1888, i. 36). Knox indeed expresses dubiety as to whether the death of Cassillis, Rothes, Fleming, and the Bishop of Orkney was due to 'ane Italiane posset,' to 'French fegges,' or to 'the potage of thare potingar'—their druggist being a Frenchman (Laing's *Knox*, i. 263, 264); but in his apprehension of foul play, Knox by no means stands alone (Thorpe's *Calendar*, i. 381; Aikman's *Buchanan*, ii. 395; Herries's *Historical Memoirs*, p. 33; Spottiswoode's *History*, i. 188; Balfour's *Historical Works*, i. 311). Even Bishop Lesley states that they suffered 'be evill drogges or onlerned mixtour thairof' (*History*, p. 243). The Lords of the Congregation say that the survivors were 'much amased att the matter' (Burnet's *Reformation*, 1715, iii. app. p. 279). In Hill Burton's opinion, 'their death was as naturally attributed to poison as the disappearance of watches in a London mob is attributed to pocket-picking' (*Scot Abroad*, 1881, p. 135); and 'instead of rejecting the suspicion as ungenerous, one is inclined to be surprised that it was not pressed more strongly, and that no investigations or explanations were demanded regarding the cause of so remarkable a fatality' (*History of Scotland*, 1876, iii. 291). The Manifesto of the Lords of the Congregation says that five died in one night, and only three returned home (*Foreign Calendar, Elizabeth*, ii. 22); but this is an exaggeration (*Ibid.* i. 179; *Acts of the Parliaments of Scotland*, ii. 505).

⁴ *Acts of the Parliaments of Scotland*, ii. 505, 506.—By his procurator—Sir James Hamilton of Crawfordjohn—Chatelherault took care to protest that, should Mary die without issue, his right of succession to the crown should not be prejudged by the coronation of Francis (*Ibid.* ii. 507, 508). According to Herries, the French desire for the matrimonial crown was 'much opposed by those of the Reformed relligion' (*Historical Memoirs*, p. 35); but their consent was won by the Queen Dowager (Laing's *Knox*, i. 292-294, 312; Melville's *Memoirs*, Mait. Club, pp. 73, 81).

⁵ On the 7th of June, 1559, Throckmorton wrote from Paris to

Cecil, that those who were appointed to bring the matrimonial crown to the King Dauphin—the Archbishop of Glasgow, the Prior of St. Andrews, and the Earls of Argyll and Morton—had refused to do it (*Foreign Calendar, Elizabeth*, i. 305). The Cardinal of Lorraine was afterwards reported to have declared that the Scots nobles had agreed to send the very crown—not the matrimonial one—to France that it might be kept at St. Denis; and that they desired that, if there were no issue of the marriage, Scotland should be held for ever, by one Dauphin after another, as a dependency of France. Even Chatelherault, it was alleged, was willing (*Ibid.* ii. 507; iii. 38; Forbes's *Public Transactions*, i. 438).

[6] Lesley's *History*, pp. 268, 269; *Venetian Calendar*, vii. 652, 653.—In 1536, the English Parliament had debarred both Elizabeth and her sister Mary from the succession as illegitimate (Manby's *Statutes*, 1670, pp. 523-525); and the Act, which in 1543-4 restored them to the line of succession, did not remove the stain of bastardy (*Ibid.* pp. 649-652). For references to the assumption of the English title and arms by Mary, see *Foreign Calendar, Elizabeth*, i. 145, 312-314, 324, 328, 329, 416, 559, 561; ii. 145, 147; Murdin's *State Papers*, pp. 748, 749; Laing's *Knox*, vi. 86, 89; Keith's *History*, i. 390.

[7] *Hatfield Calendar*, i. 154; *Foreign Calendar, Elizabeth*, i. 156, 157.

[8] *Foreign Calendar, Elizabeth*, i. 347.

[9] In writing to her mother concerning the sufferings of the newly-widowed Catherine de Medici, Mary says:—'I believe that, if it were not that the King, her son, is so obedient to her, there is nothing that she wishes but to die soon; which would be the greatest misfortune that could happen to this poor country and to us all' (Labanoff's *Recueil*, i. 71, 72).

[10] *Foreign Calendar, Elizabeth*, i. 370.—Francis was crowned at Rheims on the 18th of September 1559, when his mother and all the ladies of the Court, save Mary, were 'apparailled in the dueill' (Forbes's *State Papers*, i. 232; *Foreign Calendar, Elizabeth*, i. 561; *Venetian Calendar*, vii. 124).

[11] Skelton's *Mary Stuart*, 1893, p. 32.—Had Mr. Skelton looked over Brantôme's *Dames Illustres*, he would have found that Mary was there described as one who had always been delicate.

[12] Thorpe's *Scottish Calendar*, i. 96.

[13] *Foreign Calendar, Edward*, p. 54.

[14] *Foreign Calendar, Edward*, p. 181.

[15] Labanoff's *Recueil*, i. 21.

[16] *Latin Themes of Mary Stuart*, Warton Club, letter no. 47.

[17] *Venetian Calendar*, vi. 564, 641.

[18] Lemon's *Domestic Calendar*, i. 88; *Foreign Calendar, Mary*, p. 277.—Next January, the Dauphin, the Queen of Scots, and a great portion of the French Court were at Poissy (*Foreign Calendar, Mary*, p. 282). The Dauphin had also had quartan ague in September 1556 (*Venetian Calendar*, vi. 650), and a relapse in November (*Ibid.* p. 782). On the 3rd of February, 1556-7, the whole Court was to leave Poissy for Paris, 'the Dauphin being rid of his quartan fever' (*Ibid.* p. 938). He had three attacks (*Ibid.* p. 967).

[19] That Mary had small-pox in France is learned from a letter, which, after her return to Scotland, she wrote to Elizabeth, when that Queen was suffering from the same disease (*Recueil*, vii. 304-306; Turnbull's *Letters of Mary Stuart*, 1845, pp. 380-382). On the margin it is marked :—'May 1566. The Q. of Scotts to the Q. Majesty, by de Malvisier.' Notwithstanding this marginal note, and the fact that Mauvissière was in Scotland in May 1566, Stevenson assigns it to November 1562. It is certain that, in October 1562, Elizabeth was dangerously ill of small-pox (*Spanish Calendar, Elizabeth*, i. 262; *Foreign Calendar, Elizabeth*, v. 420). According to Turnbull, Fernel, who saved Mary's beauty, died two days after her marriage with the Dauphin.

[20] *Foreign Calendar, Elizabeth*, i. 179.

[21] Forbes's *Public Transactions*, i. 102; *Foreign Calendar, Elizabeth*, i. 272, 273.

[22] Forbes's *Public Transactions*, i. 144; *Foreign Calendar, Elizabeth*, i. 327.

[23] Forbes's *Public Transactions*, i. 136; *Foreign Calendar, Elizabeth*, i. 329.

[24] *Spanish Calendar, Elizabeth*, i. 79.—The Bishop of Aquila heard that summer that the proposed marriage of Arran and Elizabeth had been favourably discussed in the English Council. Some thought that it should be delayed until he was really King of Scots; but others held that, as Mary's malady was mortal, there was no necessity to wait, that the marriage should take place at once, and he helped to take possession of the kingdom (*Ibid.* i. 90). A year later—July 1560—he said it was believed that if Mary died, Elizabeth would marry Arran (*Ibid.* i. 169). In the following

August the Scots Parliament appointed a commission to move Elizabeth to enter into this marriage (*Acts of the Parliaments of Scotland*, ii. 605, 606; Keith's *History*, ii. 6, 7); and acquainted Francis of the project (*Papiers D'État*, i. 620-622); but Elizabeth declined (Keith's *History*, ii. 9-11; *Foreign Calendar, Elizabeth*, iii. 436).

[25] Forbes's *Public Transactions*, i. 207, 210; *Foreign Calendar, Elizabeth*, i. 495, 496.

[26] Forbes's *Public Transactions*, i. 244; *Foreign Calendar, Elizabeth*, i. 587.

[27] *Foreign Calendar, Elizabeth*, ii. 14.

[28] Forbes's *Public Transactions*, i. 261; *Foreign Calendar, Elizabeth*, ii. 111.

[29] Keen as Mary was to have English geldings—'good to ronne up hill and downe hill'—she did not wish to be indebted to Elizabeth for them (Forbes's *Public Transactions*, i. 268, 269; *Foreign Calendar, Elizabeth*, ii. 146, 147).

[30] Forbes's *Public Transactions*, i. 286; *Foreign Calendar, Elizabeth*, ii. 241.

[31] *Foreign Calendar, Elizabeth*, ii. 243.—The story of this accident in its gradual development furnishes an illustration of the growth of Marian history. As related by Killigrew and Jones, eight days after it occurred, it will be found in Forbes's *Public Transactions*, i. 290. In quoting from Forbes, Whitaker omits the cautious conclusion of the account (*Additions and Corrections*, 1789, p. 144 n.). Glassford Bell, who refers to Whitaker as his only authority, somewhat improves the story (*Life of Mary*, 1828, i. 51, 52); and Petit, who only refers to Bell, improves it still more (Flandre's *Petit*, 1873, i. 27). A few months after Mary returned to Scotland, when she was 'riding between Falkland and Loch Leven, her horse fell with her, and hurt her arm very sore, and somewhat the right side of her face' (*Foreign Calendar, Elizabeth*, v. 31).

[32] *Venetian Calendar*, vii. 198.—Throckmorton heard that Mary blamed her uncles, saying that they had undone her and caused her to lose her realm (*Foreign Calendar, Elizabeth*, ii. 597). At this time the Scots and English were besieging Leith; and Mary of Guise had for safety left Holyrood for Edinburgh Castle. In October 1559, the Lords of the Congregation had ventured, in the name of their Sovereigns, to suspend her commission as Regent (Laing's *Knox*, i. 448-450).

[33] *Foreign Calendar, Elizabeth,* iii. 156, 157 ; *Venetian Calendar,*
vii. 234.—Knox gives the 9th of June as the date of Mary of Guise's
death (Laing's *Knox,* ii. 71) ; Lesley gives the 10th (*De Origine,*
1675, pp. 525, 526 ; *History,* p. 289) ; and Payne heard at Middle-
burgh on the 14th, that she had died on the preceding Monday,
which was the 10th (*Foreign Calendar, Elizabeth,* iii. 116). On the
other hand, Cecil and Wotton, writing from Edinburgh on the 19th,
say that she died on the 11th (Lodge's *Illustrations,* i. 402 ; *Hatfield
Calendar,* i. 235). The statement of Lesley and Payne may be
reconciled with that of Cecil and Wotton by the contemporary
chronicle, which says that she died on the 10th ' at 12 houris at
evin ' (*Diurnal of Occurrents,* p. 59). Perhaps the most reliable statement on the point is to be found in a letter, written to D'Oysel from
Edinburgh Castle a week after the event, in which it is said to have
taken place on the 11th before one o'clock at mid-night (*Foreign
Calendar, Elizabeth,* iii. 125).

[34] *Venetian Calendar,* vii. 227, 228, 234.

[35] The Dauphin was fourteen years old on the 18th of January
1557-8 (*Venetian Calendar,* vi. 1486).

[36] On the 13th of July 1559—three days after Henry's death—
Throckmorton writes, ' the House of Guyse now rulethe ' (Forbes's
Public Transactions, i. 160) ; and a fortnight later he says, ' at this
present th' old French Quene, called *la Royne Mère,* hath, thoughe
not in name, yet in dede and in effect th' authoritie of Regent to
the French King ; . . . the State here presently is governed by the
Cardinal of Lorreyn and the Duke of Guise ; the Duke haveing the
charge onely of the war and the dependances therupon, and the
Cardinal of Lorreyn the ordering of all other affaires, as of fynances
and mater of Estate, and the speciall doing with all Embassadors '
(*Ibid.* i. 179, 180). Montluc, Bishop of Valence, and De Seurre,
the French Ambassador in England, in their Remonstrance (30th
March 1560) against Elizabeth's Proclamation, say that Francis ' is
not under age, and needs no governors or tutors; but of his
obedience to the Queen, his mother, he commits the care of the
realm to her, and such as she has chosen. The House of Guise
comes of so high a race, and has given such faithful tokens, both
in matters of the realm and in feats of arms, and has been so long
used in council and handling the affairs of the realm, that there is
no Prince but would think himself happy to have so great and
worthy ministers ' (*Foreign Calendar, Elizabeth,* ii. 491). Eighteen

days before Francis died, Throckmorton writes, 'the House of Guise practiseth, by all the means they can, to make the Queen Mother Regent of France at this next assembly; so as they are like to have all the authority still in their hands, for she is wholly theirs' (Hardwicke's *State Papers*, i. 140).

[37] Forbes's *Public Transactions*, i. 160.

[38] Forbes's *Public Transactions*, i. 158, 159; *Foreign Calendar, Elizabeth*, i. 378, 379.

[39] Baird's *Rise of the Huguenots*, i. 375-384; *Venetian Calendar*, vii. 160-165, 170-172, 175-177.

[40] 'To the majority of the countrymen, as also to many persons of the Court, the cause of this insurrection is not in itself very displeasing, which also greatly adds to the fear of the Ministry, who know not well in whom to trust, and suspect precisely their chief intimates' (*Venetian Calendar*, vii. 163). 'The Ministers internally have no want of troubled thoughts, most especially the Cardinal and the Duke de Guise, having witnessed so great and universal a commotion of the kingdom on account of religion, coupled with another no less important cause, namely, the discontent of many persons with the present Government, who without the slightest reason conspired against their persons' (*Ibid.* vii. 164). So Giovanni Michiel wrote from Amboise in March 1559-60. Another Venetian Ambassador, Michiel Surian, in writing from Orleans, on the 22nd of November 1560, states that, were extreme measures determined against the Prince of Condé, 'this Guise family, which has the whole government in its hands,' would be 'more detested than ever' (*Ibid.* vii. 273). On the 3rd of December—two days before the death of Francis—Surian writes:— 'It may be hoped, by the will of our Lord God, that the government of the new King may be settled by universal consent and without the din of arms, which is greatly feared from the rivalry of the nobles and the evil humours of the people about religion, and because the present government is not loved. . . . As yet the general opinion is that the House of Guise will do everything possible to unite with the King of Navarre' (*Ibid.* vii. 275). On the day after Francis died, Surian says:—'Although the Duke de Guise is popular, and above all with the nobility, yet everybody so detests the Cardinal of Lorraine that, if the matter depended upon universal suffrage, not only would he have no part in the government, but perhaps not be in this world. It is already reported

that his Right Reverend Lordship has sent his favourite and precious effects into Lorraine for greater safety' (*Ibid.* vii. 276).

[41] Ere Mary had been six months in France, Henry the Second saw, in the Protector's imprisonment of his brother the Admiral, an excellent opportunity for advancing his own affairs in Scotland, and was eager to embroil England in a civil war (*Hatfield Calendar*, i. 64, 102). Three weeks before Henry received his fatal wound, Throckmorton asked Cecil to remember that it was Elizabeth's interest 'to nourish and entertain the garboyle in Scotland as much as may be' (*Foreign Calendar, Elizabeth*, i. 305; Forbes's *Public Transactions*, i. 118). Seventeen days after Henry's death, the same watchful Ambassador further reminded Cecil—for the better conducting of his 'practises' in Scotland—of the great and long-continued enmity between the houses of Hamilton and Lennox (Forbes's *Public Transactions*, i. 180; *Foreign Calendar, Elizabeth*, i. 421). It was 'to nourish the faction betwixt the Scots and the French, so that the French may be better occupied with them, and less busy with England' (Tytler's *Scotland*, 1845, v. 480; *Foreign Calendar, Elizabeth*, i. 460) that Sadleyr was at this time sent to the North. In endeavouring to help on a perpetual concord between Scotland and England he was to distribute the gold entrusted to him with such discretion and secrecy that the recent treaties [of Chateau Cambresis, 2nd April 1559, and of Upsetlington, 31st May 1559] might not be impaired (Sadleyr's *State Papers*, 1809, i. 392). Those Southerns can hardly be blamed who unjustly suspected that the controversy between the French and the Scots was 'a traine to betrappe' the English (*Hatfield Calendar*, i. 174; Haynes's *State Papers*, p. 230). By the Treaty of Berwick (27th February 1559-60) Elizabeth became bound to aid the Lords of the Congregation to utterly expel the French from Scotland (Rymer's *Fœdera*, 1713, xv. 570; *Foreign Calendar, Elizabeth*, ii. 414; *Hatfield Calendar*, i. 188; Haynes's *State Papers*, pp. 253, 254; Laing's *Knox*, ii. 47, 48; Calderwood's *History*, i. 575; Keith's *History*, i. 259).

[42] Rymer's *Fœdera*, xv. 593-597; Keith's *History*, i. 291-308; Haynes's *State Papers*, pp. 349, 351, 352, 355, 356.—The concessions mentioned in the text are not in the Treaty between the English and French, but in the Treaty or 'Accord' between the French and Scots of the same date, which is referred to in the other, and was obtained by means of Cecil and Wotton. On the

9th of July—three days after signing the Treaty of Edinburgh—
Montluc and Randan, the French Ambassadors, explained in a
letter to Catherine de Medici, that they had only agreed to it
because of the disadvantages under which they found themselves ;
that their lives were in the hands of the English ; that, as they
could only have held Leith for a few days longer, they had to
arrange a peace of some sort, or lose four thousand men and
afterwards find it impossible to recover Scotland without ruining
France (Teulet's *Papiers D'État*, i. 605, 606). Francis and Mary
did not ratify this Treaty, although in the commission to their
Ambassadors they had promised to observe and ratify all that they
should do (Rymer's *Fœdera*, xv. 581 ; Keith's *History*, i. 308). In
the opinion of Michiel Surian, the articles were of such a sort ' that
it never could be credited that the King of France would approve
them even had the rope been round his neck.' Surian adds : ' It is
indeed true that the English being then in arms, and the French
almost completely driven out of Scotland, and France being in a
state of confusion everywhere, it was thought fit not to refuse the
proposed conditions, but to procrastinate and give words, taking
advantage of time. This, as seen by the result, was wise policy, for
Queen Elizabeth has already disarmed, and the King of France is
still at liberty to sign or not to sign. The same policy continues at
present [25th November 1560], it being now said designedly that
they will send a person to England to gain more time' (*Venetian
Calendar*, vii. 273).

⁴³ *Acts of the Parliaments of Scotland*, ii. 526-535.—For saying,
hearing, or being present at mass, all the offender's goods were
to be confiscated, and his body punished at the discretion of the
magistrate, for the first offence ; he was to be banished from the
realm for the second ; and justified to the death for the third.
Harsh and excessive as these penalties were, they must be judged
by the standard of that time. Nine years before, the Scots Parliament had enacted anew that shooting ' at' a wild fowl was to be
punished by death (see *infra*, p. 282, note 102). On the eve of
the Reformation, Mary of Guise had issued a Proclamation
threatening death to any who dared to disturb the Church service,
bully the priest, or eat flesh in Lent (Robertson's *Statuta*, vol. i.
p. clvii. *n.*).

⁴⁴ *Venetian Calendar*, vi. 1366 ; *Foreign Calendar, Elizabeth*, i. 85.

⁴⁵ Immediately after Henry's death, Francis was at the Louvre

with his wife and mother (*Foreign Calendar, Elizabeth*, i. 392). When in the following December, he retired to Chambord for hawking and field sports, he was accompanied by them; and there the two Queens daily heard a sermon in the chapel or in their dining chamber (*Venetian Calendar*, vii. 138; Forbes's *Public Transactions*, i. 274; *Foreign Calendar, Elizabeth*, ii. 186). The King returned with them to Blois (Forbes's *Public Transactions*, i. 287; *Foreign Calendar, Elizabeth*, ii. 241). With them, Throckmorton had an interview at Amboise—Mary sitting on Catherine's right hand (Forbes's *Public Transactions*, i. 342, 343; *Foreign Calendar, Elizabeth*, ii. 409, 410). Both were at that castle with the King during the 'tumult' in March (*Venetian Calendar*, vii. 160). When his Majesty—'to show some sign of having taken heart, and that suspicion had subsided'—went with the Duke of Lorraine to the neighbouring heronry, the two Queens went for the afternoon to one of Catherine's palaces two leagues off (*Ibid*. vii. 163). During Passion-week—April 1560—all the three were daily observed listening to the eloquent sermons of the Cardinal of Lorraine in the Abbey-church of Marmoutier in the suburbs of Tours (*Ibid*. vii. 187). A fortnight later, when Mary was depressed by bad news from Scotland, Catherine is found among her would-be comforters (*Ibid*. vii. 198). At the end of June Francis was in the neighbourhood of Chartres, but intended being at Fontaine-bleau by the 12th of July with Catherine and Mary (*Ibid*. vii. 234). At Melun, on the 6th of August, Throckmorton, after seeing the King, had an interview with the two Queens, who came out of an inner chamber to speak with him in Catherine's chamber of presence. He began by addressing Mary, but she requested him to talk first to the Queen-mother, and insisted on his doing so (*Foreign Calendar, Elizabeth*, iii. 224, 225). The first interview which Throckmorton had with her, at which Catherine was not present—19th August—was also at Melun (*Ibid*. iii. 250-253). In a Council held next day in Catherine's Chamber at Fontainebleau, both Queens were present as well as Francis (*Ibid*. iii. 245). Catherine was also present at the interview which Throckmorton had with Francis and Mary on the 15th of September at St. Germain (*Ibid*. iii. 300-302). Mary and Catherine were both with Francis when Condé was arrested on the 31st of October (*Venetian Calendar*, vii. 263). Two Venetian Ambassadors—the old and the new—were graciously received by the two Queens on the 2nd of November (*Ibid.* vii. 265). On the 15th of that month, Throckmorton had, at Orleans, successive interviews with the Cardinal of Lorraine, the Duke of Guise, the King, the Queen-mother, and Mary, concerning the ratification of the Treaty of Edinburgh. It was while he was talking to Catherine that Mary came in, and she in one of her speeches 'uttered some choler and stomach' (Hardwicke's *State Papers*, i. 129-138; *Foreign Calendar, Elizabeth*, iii. 392-394). Francis had determined to go with his wife and mother to Chambord and Chenonceau on Monday the 18th of November; but, on the preceding day, he was seized with that illness which was destined to cut short his career (*Venetian Calendar*, vii. 268). On the 1st of December the gates of the Court were kept closed all day—'no one entered his Majesty's chamber except the Queens and the three Guises' (*Ibid.* vii. 275). It is rather suggestive that in the chapter of his monograph on Mary which deals with her life as Queen of France—a chapter of thirty-nine pages—Father Stevenson does not make the slightest allusion to her mother-in-law.

46 On the 6th of December—the day following the death of Francis—the Venetian Ambassador writes from Orleans :—'This King [*i.e.* Charles the Ninth] will be in ward till he is fourteen years old, during which interval the kingdom will be ruled by others. It is believed that the Queen Mother will still retain her authority, but it cannot yet be known authentically what other persons will have the chief care of the government. . . . Amongst the chief personages there are many old and new enmities, and most especially between the King of Navarre, the House of Guise, and the Constable; and besides this the said Constable is of such a nature that he will admit no one to be equal to himself, nor will the Cardinal of Lorraine tolerate any superior. It is believed that the Queen Mother will favour the House of Guise as much as she can, because from them she has derived the whole or the greater part of the repute enjoyed by her hitherto' (*Venetian Calendar*, vii. 276). Again, on the 18th, he writes :—'The Nuncio, although apparently impartial, favours the House of Guise as much as he can, which renders him very dear to the Queen, who, although she shows herself neutral, cannot in reality bear the Constable from old enmities' (*Ibid.* vii. 280). Thirteen days later, Throckmorton informs Elizabeth that, in France, the management of affairs is now chiefly in the hands of Catherine, of the King of Navarre, and of

the Constable, but adds that he fears the Cardinal of Lorraine's finesse will bring him again into credit, 'because he and the Duke of Guise are in great favour with the Queen Mother' (*Foreign Calendar, Elizabeth,* iii. 470). 'To the Quene Mother,' says Knox, 'was committed regiment: which lifted up asweill the Duck of Gwyse, as the cruell Cardinall for a seassone' (Laing's *Knox,* ii. 136, 137). See *infra,* p. 229, n. 11.

[47] *Venetian Calendar,* vii. 268, 269.—Surian says, 'He had a sudden attack of extreme cold accompanied with some fever, an indisposition to which he is subject, and which he is said to have inherited from his father and grandfather. It is caused by a certain flow of catarrh, which exudes from the right ear, and if the discharge be stopped, he suffers great pain in the teeth and jaws, with a certain inflammation behind the ear, like a large nut, which increases or decreases according to the greater or lesser virulence of the humour.' This was written on the 20th of November. Next day, Throckmorton states, 'This king thought to have removed hence for a fortnight, but the day before his intended journey he felt himself somewhat evil disposed of his body, with a pain in his head and one of his ears' (*Foreign Calendar, Elizabeth,* iii. 408 *n.*). A week later, Throckmorton informs Elizabeth that 'this King's sickness doth so succeed as men do begin to doubt of his long lasting. The constitution of his body is such, as the physicians do say he cannot be long-lived: and thereunto he hath, by his too timely and inordinate exercise now in his youth, added an evil accident' (Hardwicke's *State Papers,* i. 156). After his death it was found that his whole brain was so diseased that no medical treatment could have cured it (*Venetian Calendar,* vii. 278).

[48] On the 24th of November, Surian writes: 'During the last few days, although the fever was very slight, he nevertheless suffered so much that he seemed almost delirious. My informant is a person of importance and one of the few who enter his Majesty's chamber, and he remains there almost constantly; and as this thing is kept very secret he requested me not to divulge it' (*Venetian Calendar,* vii. 274). On the 1st of December, Surian adds—'Although they endeavour to conceal the malady more than ever, the Queen Mother cannot suppress the signs of her sorrow, which is increased by the recollection of the predictions made by many astrologers, who all prognosticated his very short life' (*Ibid.* vii. 274, 275). In

Rouen, it was not believed that the King was actually ill; it was supposed that the alleged illness was a mere device of the Guises, to prevent the supplications of the prisoners being placed before him (*Foreign Calendar, Elizabeth,* iii. 420).

[49] *Venetian Calendar,* vii. 275).

[50] Though the astrologers proved to be right, the Bishop of Viterbo had prophesied, that, after Francis the First and Henry the Second, there should arise another King Francis, who should obtain possession of Venice and Rome, restore peace to Christendom, and reign prosperously for a long time (*Foreign Calendar, Elizabeth,* iii. 420). Two days before his death, Surian says—'The whole Court is now constantly engaged at prayers, and processions are being made in all the churches of the city, which are attended very piously by the brothers and the sister of his most Christian Majesty, by the King of Navarre, and many other personages' (*Venetian Calendar,* vii. 275). Throckmorton and Surian agree that the illness of Francis began on the 17th of November; but they do not agree as to the day of his death. Surian says it occurred on the 5th of December a little before midnight (*Ibid.* vii. 276); whereas Throckmorton places it on the 6th of December at eleven o'clock at night (*Foreign Calendar, Elizabeth,* iii. 421-424). The letters of both are dated the 6th December; but in Throckmorton's drafts blanks were left for the precise time. Cecil states that he was advertised from France that the King died on Thursday (*Ibid.* iii. 424), and Thursday was the 5th; while the contemporary Scottish chronicler places it on the 6th (*Diurnal of Occurrents,* pp. 63, 281). A list of royal jewels handed over by Mary to Charles the Ninth is dated 6th December (*Foreign Calendar, Elizabeth,* iii. 424 *n.*). Considering the hour of the King's death, it is not likely that such a document would be completed on the same day.   On the 6th of December, Mary, by her sole authority, appointed Herbert Maxwell general of the Scottish mint (*Register of Privy Seal,* xxx. 37); whereas a letter granted in the preceding October runs in her name with authority and consent of the King (*Ibid.* xxx. 36). The 15th of the following January was reckoned the fortieth day of Mary's mourning (*Foreign Calendar, Elizabeth,* iii. 500). On Saturday the 6th of December 1561, Mary, then in Edinburgh, 'solemnly celebrated the exequies of her husband' (*Ibid.* iv. 435); but on this first anniversary the 'dirige' was apparently said on Friday the 5th (Keith's *History,* ii. 122).

[51] 'The Reformers, with Knox at their head, were savagely exultant,' says Mr. Skelton, who thus proceeds to quote Knox :— 'Lo ! the potent hand of God from above sends unto us a wonderful and most joyful deliverance ; for unhappy Francis suddenly perisheth of a rotten ear—that deaf ear that never would hear the truth of God' (Skelton's *Mary Stuart*, 1893, p. 23. See also his *Maitland of Lethington*, i. 268). As quoted by Mr. Skelton these words may convey the idea of savage exultation ; but in Knox's own work they do not form a continuous sentence—Mr. Skelton having omitted more than a page. Knox rejoiced not at the death of Francis in itself ; but because the snare was broken, the tyrants disappointed of their cruelty, those appointed to death raised as it were from their graves ; and because the Scots—who by foolishness had made themselves slaves to strangers—were freed from the yoke (Laing's *Knox*, ii. 132-134). It was no wonder that the arrival of the 'new bandis of throte-cuttaris'—as Knox called them—was dreaded in Scotland ; for, when they had formerly come as friends, even the Queen Dowager complained of their fearful excesses by which the Scottish peasantry were often driven to kill themselves in despair (*Papiers D'État*, i. 703). 'Had Francis lived but a week longer, the ruin of the Huguenots might perhaps have been consummated. . . . The Protestants of Paris recognised in the event a direct answer to the petitions which they had offered to Almighty God on the recent days of special humiliation and prayer' (Baird's *Rise of the Huguenots*, i. 449, 450). Writing from Orleans on the 31st of December, Throckmorton says :—'The Estates assembled at this town on the 13th December, but have done little or nothing ; divers of them will not put forth such things as they were instructed in by other provinces now the King is dead. They say that by his death many of the people's doleances are ceased, as the government that they complained about is ceased' (*Foreign Calendar, Elizabeth*, iii. 470). He had previously told Elizabeth that she had cause 'to thank God for so well providing for her surety and quietness by taking away the late King and his father' (*Ibid.* iii. 421). The cautious Calvin expressed his opinion thus :—'Have you ever heard or read anything more seasonable than the death of the King ? There was no remedy for the extreme evils, when suddenly God appeared from heaven, and He, who had pierced the eye of the father, smote the ear of the son. I only fear lest the joy of some by expressing itself too much may overturn the hope of a better state

of things. For you could scarcely believe how inconsiderately many exult and even wax wanton over it' (*Corpus Reformatorum*, xlvi. 270).

[52] Sir James Melville says, 'the Quen Mother was blyeth of the death of K. Francis hir sone, because sche had na gyding of him, bot only the Duc of Guise and Cardinall his brother, be raisoun that the Quen our maistres wes ther sister dochter' (Melville's *Memoirs*, p. 86). 'She was pretty freely accused, indeed, of having shortened her son's life, because she thought she would have more power were he out of the way; and no doubt she was quite capable of the deed' (Hill Burton's *Scot Abroad*, 1881, p. 121).

[53] On the day after the death of Francis, Throckmorton speaks of Mary as being 'as heavy and dolorous a wife, as of right she had good cause to be, who, by long watching with him during his sickness, and painful diligence about him, and specially by the issue thereof, is not in best tune of her body, but without danger' (*Foreign Calendar, Elizabeth*, iii. 421). Two days later, Surian writes :—'The new King has confirmed in his service all the gentlemen and courtiers employed by his predecessor, and this morning the Order of St. Michael was given in public to his most Christian Majesty and to his brother the Duke of Angoulême. So by degrees every one will forget the death of the late King except the young Queen, his widow, who being no less noble minded than beautiful and graceful in appearance, the thoughts of widowhood at so early an age, and of the loss of a consort who was so great a King and who so dearly loved her, and also that she is dispossessed of the crown of France with little hope of recovering that of Scotland, which is her sole patrimony and dower, so afflict her that she will not receive any consolation, but, brooding over her disasters with constant tears and passionate and doleful lamentations, she universally inspires great pity' (*Venetian Calendar*, vii. 278).

[54] Dr. Thomas Wilson informed Cecil, on the 8th of November 1571, that the Bishop of Ross, then in prison, had owned to him that he credibly understood that Mary had poisoned her first husband, the King of France (Murdin's *State Papers*, 1759, p. 57; *Hatfield Calendar*, i. 564). Mr. Skelton unwittingly attributes this statement not to Bishop Lesley, Mary's champion, but to Buchanan, her detractor (*Impeachment of Mary Stuart*, 1876, p. 144).

CHAPTER IV

[1] The phrase 'changed her lodging' does not necessarily imply that she left the palace (*e.g.* see *Foreign Calendar, Elizabeth*, iv. 150; v. 605; vi. 630; viii. 9; *Venetian Calendar*, vii. 263, 513).

[2] Father Stevenson, while professing to follow the letters of the English Ambassador, alleges that 'during this period of her seclusion she admitted no man to come into her chamber but the King and his brethren, the King of Navarre, the old Constable Montmorency, and her uncles' (Stevenson's *Mary Stuart*, p. 201). Throckmorton, however, states distinctly—in a letter calendared by Father Stevenson himself—that this strict seclusion was only observed for fifteen days; bishops, ancient knights and ambassadors being admitted to her presence long before the forty days were ended (*Foreign Calendar, Elizabeth*, iii. 472). On the fortieth day 'she was present at a solemn service for her late husband' in the Grey Friars' church at Orleans (*Ibid.* iii. 500, 501).

[3] See *supra*, p. 225, note 53.

[4] Hosack after citing the affecting passage from Throckmorton's letter of 6th December to Elizabeth—mentioning Mary's watchful care over and grief for her husband (*supra*, p. 225, note 53)—exclaims, 'Notwithstanding this unimpeachable testimony, Mr. Froude asserts that before her husband's body was cold Mary "was speculating on her next choice"' (*Mary Queen of Scots and her Accusers*, 1870, i. 58 *n.*). Had Hosack glanced at the *Foreign Calendar*, he would have found that on the same 6th of December, Throckmorton wrote three letters, one to Elizabeth, another to the Lords of the Council, and a third to Cecil. If the passage cited from the letter to Elizabeth is 'unimpeachable testimony,' so must also this other passage from the letter to the Lords of Council:—'As far as I can learn, she more esteemeth the continuation of her honour, and to marry one that may uphold her to be great, than she passeth to please her fancy by taking one that is accompanied with such small benefit or alliance as thereby her estimation and fame is not increased' (*Foreign Calendar, Elizabeth*, iii. 423). Hosack is not the only one who has unjustly assailed Froude on this point (see *e.g.* Miss A. M. Stewart's *Mary Queen of Scots*, p. 24). When charging Throckmorton with speculating on her second marriage ere 'her husband

had scarce ceased to breathe,' Father Stevenson prudently abstains from noticing his remarks about Mary's own desire; but at a later stage, without giving the date of the letter, he jubilantly quotes them as illustrating the superiority of the widowed Queen of Scots to the unwedded Queen of England (Stevenson's *Mary Stuart*, pp. 199, 213).

[5] A week before Francis died, many in Orleans were speculating on Mary's second husband. 'There is plenty of discourses here,' says Throckmorton, 'of the French Queen's second marriage; some talk of the Prince of Spain, some of the Duke of Austrich, others of the Earl of Arran' (Hardwicke's *State Papers*, i. 156; *Foreign Calendar, Elizabeth*, iii. 410). Fifteen days after the death of Francis, the Duke of Alva expressed the opinion that the French would seek to have the disposal of her again, and suggested to Chamberlain the course which he thought Elizabeth should pursue. In the Spanish Court at Toledo, some believed that the French would, with a dispensation, marry Mary to the new King; others, with one of her uncles, the Prior of St. John; some wished that it might be with the Prince of Spain; while others spoke of the King of Denmark and the new King of Sweden (*Foreign Calendar, Elizabeth*, iii. 459). Some of the Scots were anxious that she should return to her own country and marry there, or, at least, with the consent of the Estates; many, that wherever she married the amity with England should continue (*Ibid.* iii. 462, 463).

[6] *Foreign Calendar, Elizabeth*, iii. 491, 492.

[7] *Foreign Calendar, Elizabeth*, iii. 501.—The clause in the marriage-contract to which Throckmorton refers may be seen in Keith's *History*, i. 357. Mary's Instructions of 12th January to the four deputies contain no reference to her second marriage (Labanoff's *Recueil*, i. 85-88); but Throckmorton explains, on the 22nd and 23rd of January, that Mary had changed her mind as to treating with her subjects on this matter (*Foreign Calendar, Elizabeth*, iii. 512, 514).

[8] *Spanish Calendar, Elizabeth*, i. 183.—This is not the first hint in the State Papers that Darnley had an early eye after that union which was to prove his destruction. Only eighteen days after the death of Francis, Randolph—then at Edinburgh—advised Cecil to call the Earl of Lennox's son 'nearer unto the Court, that all practice to draw him into Scotland, or convey him to any other place, might be taken away' (*Foreign Calendar, Elizabeth*, iii. 460).

In February it was rumoured in Scotland that he had gone to France with Bedford (*Ibid.* iii. 584; iv. 25). The deposition of William Forbes has been cited to show that Darnley met Mary at Orleans (Miss Strickland's *Queens of Scotland*, 1851, ii. 370; *The Lennox*, i. 469); but the proof is not clear (*Foreign Calendar, Elizabeth*, v. 12, 23).

⁹ On the 31st of December Throckmorton writes to the English Council :—' Now that death hath thus disposed of the late French King, whereby the Scottish Queen is left a widow, one of the special things your Lordships have to consider, and to have an eye to, is the marriage of that Queen. During her husband's life there was no great account made of her, for that, being under band of marriage and subjection of her husband (who carried the burden and care of all her matters), there was offered no great occasion to know what was in her. But since her husband's death, she hath showed (and so continueth) that she is both of great wisdom for her years, modesty, and also of great judgment in the wise handling herself and her matters, which, increasing with her years, cannot but turn greatly to her commendation, reputation, honour, and great benefit of her and her country. Already it appears that some, such as made no great account of her, do now, seeing her wisdom, both honour and pity her. . . . For my part, I see her behaviour to be such, and her wisdom and kingly modesty so great, in that she thinketh herself not too wise, but is content to be ruled by good counsel and wise men (which is a great virtue in a Prince or Princess, and which argueth a great judgment and wisdom in her), that by their means she cannot do amiss, and I cannot but fear her proceedings with the time, if any means be left and offered her to take advantage by' (*Foreign Calendar, Elizabeth*, iii. 472, 473). On the same day he wrote to Dudley, who—rid of Amy Robsart and aspiring to the hand of Elizabeth—doubtless perceived the covert rebuke to himself and his royal lover in the following sentences :—' Yet, my lord, this I trust shal be no occasion to make her Majestie [Elizabeth] lesse considerate, or her counsell lesse provident, for assuredlie the Quene of Scotland, her Majestie's cosen, dothe carrye herselfe so honorably, advisidlie, and discretelye, as I cannot but feare her progresse. Me-thinketh it were to be wished of all wyse men and her Majestie's good subjects, that the one of these two Quenes of the Ile of Brittaine were transformed into the shape of a man, to make so happie a marriage, as therbie ther might be

an unitie of the hole Ile and their appendances' (Wright's *Eliza-beth*, i. 58). Father Stevenson gives bits of these two letters as a continuous extract from one document (Stevenson's *Mary Stuart*, 1886, p. 212). As a matter of policy Throckmorton recommends on the 10th of January that the Queen of Scots should be with writing and words kindly handled (*Foreign Calendar, Elizabeth*, iii. 492).

[10] *Foreign Calendar, Elizabeth*, iii. 514. See also *Venetian Calendar*, vii. 290.

[11] To the Scots Estates, in her letters-patent—assigned by Labanoff to January 1560-61—Mary says :—' All the comfort which remains to us in this respect is that he has left a brother as successor to this crown, son . . . of the most worthy and virtuous princess in the world, the Queen, our very honoured lady and mother-in-law, in whom since we came to this country we have found much goodness, love and kindness, and also such and so loving affection from the said lord, her son the King, that we may hope and expect from them all that a daughter might hope for from her own mother, and a sister from a brother' (Labanoff's *Recueil*, i. 81). In December 1562, Randolph refers to the 'unkindness' that had been between Catherine and Mary 'a short time before her departure out of France' (*Foreign Calendar, Elizabeth*, v. 604). A few days before Mary embarked at Calais it was reported in Stras-burg by certain French nobles that Catherine wished to shake off the friendship of the Guises (*Ibid.* iv. 248). In April 1565, Lethington assured De Silva that, while Mary 'was in France, she could not do too much for the Queen Mother, and put her own friends and relatives quite in the background for her, and yet in return for all this she has done her much harm' (*Spanish Calendar, Elizabeth*, i. 421). Nevertheless Mary's conduct in this very matter has been adduced as the cause of the animosity to which Lethington referred. 'The Queen, Catherine de Medicis, . . . as mother-in-law, hated the Queen her daughter, who removed her from the charge of affairs, and transferred the friendship of the King, her son, to the Guises, who entrusted to him no more of the govern-ment than what they knew she could do no prejudice to, giving him the credit and appearance without the effect' (*Mémoires de Tavannes*, cited in Baird's *Rise of the Huguenots*, i. 362 *n.*). In Sir James Melville's opinion, Catherine was a deadly enemy to all who had guided either her husband or her eldest son, and, because of the Guises, had ' a gret mis-lyking of our Quen'; and also had a special

grievance against her, by whom, she alleged, she was despised at the instigation of the House of Guise during the short reign of Francis (Melville's *Memoirs*, Mait. Club, pp. 86-88). Mary, it is said, had imprudently taunted Catherine with being a merchant's daughter (Robertson's *Inventories*, p. xv. *n.*). Buchanan mentions Catherine's estrangement as one of the reasons which induced Mary to return to Scotland (Aikman's *Buchanan*, ii. 437).

[12] *Foreign Calendar, Elizabeth*, iii. 518; *Venetian Calendar*, vii. 297.

[13] *Foreign Calendar, Elizabeth*, iii. 566.

[14] *Foreign Calendar, Elizabeth*, iii. 573-576.—Father Stevenson's account of Bedford's embassy (*Mary Stuart*, 1886, pp. 204-211) is very inaccurate, very misleading, and very unfair. He entirely ignores the interview of condolence on the 16th, though described in a state-paper calendared by himself; but dwells at length on the formal business ones of the 18th and 19th. Not only so, but he states that 'it was not until the 18th of February 1561 that the condolences of Elizabeth, such as they were (for they appear to have been of the curtest and coldest), reached the Queen of Scotland. They were presented by the Earl of Bedford, a strict Puritan. . . . The letters of which he was the bearer express no sorrow for Mary's loss, no sympathy with her grief, no word of kindness or tenderness.' Yet in his own calendar it is expressly stated, that, on the 16th, 'Bedford having done the Queen's commendations unto her, and delivered her letters and condolence to her . . . she thanked the Queen for her gentleness in comforting her woe when she had most need of it' (*Foreign Calendar, Elizabeth*, iii. 566). And Mary's own letter of the 20th of February is very far from implying that Elizabeth expressed no sorrow for her loss, no sympathy with her grief, no word of kindness or tenderness (Labanoff's *Recueil*, i. 92, 93). Father Stevenson further says that Mary was 'asked to believe that all that Elizabeth had done in the affairs of Scotland was "to aid the wardens to reform such lewd outlaws, murderers, and thieves as have remained," forgetting that she herself had supplied these very same persons with men, money, and the aid of the most powerful fleet which England could supply.' Here again he is condemned by his own calendar. Bedford's instructions distinctly recognise the fact that the English army had been in Scotland; while the reference to the wardens and the outlaws respect not the invasion of Mary's realm, but the quieting of the Borders (*Foreign Calendar, Elizabeth*, iii. 507). Father

Stevenson proceeds to say that 'this interview produced a deep
impression upon Throckmorton, who has left upon record the
estimate which he had now formed of the general character of
Mary Stuart. . . . From the date of this remarkable conference,
the despatches of Throckmorton to Elizabeth and Cecil grow more
urgent, his action becomes more prompt and decided; and Mary's
dangers and difficulties assume a more definite character. Let us
see how the English Ambassador works upon the fears and jealousies
of his mistress' (*Mary Stuart*, 1886, pp. 211, 212). He then gives
extracts — more or less correct — from three of Throckmorton's
despatches; but of these he carefully suppresses the dates, for
the very sufficient reason that two of them were written seven
weeks and the other ten weeks before the interview took place!
Notwithstanding this apparently wilful misrepresentation, Father
Stevenson coolly asserts that Elizabeth's despatch is remarkable
for ' its unblushing falsehood.'

[15] Bedford and Throckmorton in taking their leave of the King
of Navarre on the 19th of February interchanged opinions with
him on Mary's marriage. 'Throckmorton said to him that there
was a bruit of a marriage between the Prince of Spain or the Duke
of Austria, and her; if either of which took place, they thought it
might be cumbersome to the Queen [of England], yet it was of
much more importance to France, and most of all to him. The
King replied that there was such a thing in hand, not with the
Prince of Spain, but with the Duke of Austria, which was one of
the chief errands of the Emperor's late Ambassadors coming to
France. . . . He wished to know how they could let [*i.e.* hinder] it, as
she was out of their power. Throckmorton answered that her going
to Joinville in the skirts of Lorraine, fast by Almaine, would greatly
further that matter, for then they may practise as they list; but
she continuing at the Court, there can be no such things done
without knowledge. The King said that there should be no fault
in him to hinder it, as much as in him lay. "But (quoth he) I
told you, M. l'Ambassador, a remedy against this mischief, whereunto you make me none answer; you know what I mean "'
(*Foreign Calendar, Elizabeth*, iii. 576). Writing to Cecil from
Paris, a week afterwards, Bedford informs him that the Court
since it came from Orleans is in many things altered, that the
Scottish Queen is stayed from her purposed journey to Joinville,
and that his being in France had occasioned the same (*Ibid.* iii.

578). The mysterious remedy hinted at by Navarre may have been the marriage of Mary with himself (*Ibid.* vi. 49), a match which she declined on the ground that he already had a wife (Jebb's *De Vita et Rebus Gestis Mariae,* ii. 485).

[16] *Foreign Calendar, Elizabeth,* iv. 27, 34 ; v. 620.

[17] *Foreign Calendar, Elizabeth,* iv. 42.—Besides the office of condolence and congratulation, his coming rested on two points, to propose a league between France and Denmark, and in consideration thereof that his master should marry the Queen of Scots or some one of France meet for such a Prince. The Ambassador is returning—says Throckmorton on the 31st of March—but goes to the Queen of Scotland to talk with her by the way.

[18] It was perhaps at this time that the undated list of one hundred and fifty-nine articles was drawn up, which is printed in Joseph Robertson's *Inventories,* pp. 7-17.

[19] *Foreign Calendar, Elizabeth,* iv. 41.—In this letter of the 31st of March, Throckmorton informs Elizabeth that Mary is to continue all this Easter [Easter day fell on the 6th of April] in Rheims, and then go to Joinville to see her grandmother, and from thence to Nancy in Lorraine, there to remain at least six months. Divers reasons, he says, are pretended for this, such as change of air, and the alleviation of her sorrowful remembrance of her late husband ; but it is thought rather that the recent motion of a marriage with one of the Emperor's sons may be better and more secretly handled there. Throckmorton suggested that, as he was so far off, one of Elizabeth's ministers should look to this matter so greatly followed by the Guises ; and advised the formation of a strong English party in Scotland, which would render puissant foreign princes less anxious to marry the Queen of Scots.

[20] *Foreign Calendar, Elizabeth,* iv. 45. — In Throckmorton's opinion, if this marriage—'a drift of the new Cardinal Granville' —went forward, it would be as little to the profit of England as any yet talked of (*Ibid.* iv. 46). From it might arise some jealousy between Philip and Elizabeth (*Venetian Calendar,* vii. 306). Though Mary remained at Rheims less than three weeks, she has been represented as spending the winter there (Chalmers's *Life of Mary,* 1818, i. 38 ; *Blackwood's Magazine,* clix. 196), a mistake for which Bishop Lesley is partly responsible (*De Rebus Gestis Scotorum,* 1675, p. 531 ; *History,* Ban. Club, p. 293 ; Keith's *History,* ii. 19 *n.*). At Rheims, according to Petit, 'a new vista

now opened up before the kind though persecuted Mary. Heartily welcomed by the holy maidens of the convent, she soon became as one of themselves; the peaceful life and the mystic perfume enveloping the people and the place delighted her extremely. In that gentle solitude she felt happy. There she no longer dreaded the spies of Elizabeth and the Medicis; she was alone with God, nature, and her sisters, surrounded by respect, loved and cherished by all' (Flandre's *Petit*, i. 46). For Miss Benger's opinion of the attractions of Rheims, see *infra*, pp. 238, 239.

[21] *Foreign Calendar, Elizabeth*, iv. 75, 85.

[22] Throckmorton had early suspected and feared this match (*Foreign Calendar, Elizabeth*, iii. 491, 492; *Venetian Calendar*, vii. 290); and although he saw grave objections to it from Philip's point of view, and also from that of the Guises, his suspicions, again aroused, were confirmed by Coligny and Navarre (*Foreign Calendar, Elizabeth*, iv. 76, 82, 83, 97).

[23] Before the Duchess of Ferrara died, on the 21st of April, many in France expressed the opinion that if the Duke were a young widower again he would marry the Queen of Scots; and after the death of the Duchess 'certain persons' at the Spanish Court, 'experienced in French affairs,' did not dissent from this opinion, 'owing to the great affection which the aforesaid Duke and Queen bear to each other' (*Venetian Calendar*, vii. 314; *Foreign Calendar, Elizabeth*, iv. 80).

[24] *Foreign Calendar, Elizabeth*, iii. 475; iv. 41, 50, 60, 65, 115.

[25] Catherine's letter to the Bishop of Rennes sufficiently shows her determination (*Foreign Calendar, Elizabeth*, iv. 65 *n.*); and Bedford's Instructions—although there had been nothing else—are quite enough to show Elizabeth's (*Ibid*. iii. 508).

[26] Lesley's *History*, p. 294. Dalrymple's *Lesley*, Scottish Text Society, ii. 454.—In his letter of 9th April, Throckmorton states that the Lord James had left Paris for Rheims (*Foreign Calendar, Elizabeth*, iv. 55); in his letter of the 20th, that Mary had left Rheims for Lorraine, taking Joinville in the way (*Ibid*. iv. 68); and in his letter of the 23rd that the Lord James, who had accompanied Mary four leagues beyond Joinville, had that day returned to Paris on his way home, and that Mary was now in Nancy (*Ibid*. iv. 75, 76).

[27] *De Rebus Gestis Scotorum*, 1675, pp. 531, 532.

[28] Dalrymple's *Lesley*, ii. 453.

[29] Even from her own point of view there can be little doubt that this was the most prudent policy in the circumstances. Father Stevenson himself admits that Huntly's conduct at this time was 'wavering and suspicious' (*Mary Stuart*, 1886, p. 234). Throckmorton heard that she had been advised by the King of Spain to temporise in matters of religion at first; and, should he succeed with the Turk and the siege of Oran, she might then proceed with rigour against pertinacious heretics (*Foreign Calendar, Elizabeth*, iv. 153). Sir James Melville relates that D'Oysel, Rubbay, and other Frenchmen who had lately returned from Scotland, encouraged her with the hope of the English succession, pressed her to serve the time, and to accommodate herself discreetly and gently to her own subjects, to be most familiar with the Lord James, Argyll, Lethington and Grange, and 'to repoise maist upon them of the Refourmed religion' (*Memoirs*, Mait. Club, pp. 88, 89). According to Randolph, she found this course to be necessary immediately after her arrival in Scotland (Wright's *Elizabeth*, i. 73).

[30] Perhaps no Mariolater in dealing with this point has excelled Father Stevenson in his display of bitterness and rancour (*Mary Stuart*, 1886, pp. 224-236). Blinded by prejudice, he even credits the Lord James with having imposed not only on Mary, but on her astute uncles; and, on the authority of Conaeus, says that he assured her that 'Scotland's allegiance to the Holy See was unshaken' (*Ibid*. p. 226). Mary and the Guises would have been simpletons indeed had they been deceived by any one who could utter such a palpable falsehood, for they knew well the thoroughgoing character of the Scottish Reformation. Lesley was still there to warn her 'not to allow herself to be deceived by the fine phrases of James,' who wished to 'pluck up and completely overturn the Catholic religion which he was assailing in every possible way' (*De Rebus Gestis Scotorum*, 1675, p. 531). But she and the Guises had known the worst before the Lord James arrived, before Lesley arrived, even before Sandilands arrived with his official report of the Parliamentary proceedings. Deception there may have been, but not necessarily on the part of the Lord James. In the Report of the Jesuit Priests to the Pope in 1594—a Report translated and published by Father Stevenson himself—it is said that, on this occasion, 'the Princes of the House of Lorraine thought it was expedient to dissemble' (Nau's *History of Mary Stewart*, 1883, p. 116). Throckmorton attributes Mary's change of purpose, regard-

ing the temporary appointment of her brother as Regent, to his straightforwardness—she could not dissuade him from his devotion to Elizabeth and the observance of the league with England, nor could she and the Cardinal of Lorraine win him from his religion, although they used very great means and persuasions (*Foreign Calendar, Elizabeth,* iv. 91). This steadfastness must have been specially satisfactory to Throckmorton, who had feared that he might be won to France by the offer of a red hat, good abbeys and benefices (*Ibid.* iv. 44). Hence the Ambassador's advice that he—who had 'dealt so plainly with the Queen his Soveraine' on Elizabeth's behalf, 'and shewed himself so constant in religion that neither the feare of his Soveraine's indignacion coude waver him nor great promesses winne him'—should be 'liberally and honorably' considered by the Queen of England (Burnet's *History of the Reformation,* 1715, iii. app. p. 314). On the assumption that Mary had confided her secret intentions to the Lord James, he is charged by Tytler with having 'insidiously betrayed' to Throckmorton everything that had passed between her and himself (*History of Scotland,* 1845, v. 178, 179). Hosack seems disposed to take a similar view (*Mary and her Accusers,* i. 61, 62). This charge is based on Throckmorton's letter to Elizabeth of 29th April, in which he writes that, the Lord James, having returned to Paris, 'came to my lodging *secretly unto me,* and declared unto me at good length all that passed between the Queen, his sister, and him, and between the Cardinal of Lorraine and him' (*Foreign Calendar, Elizabeth,* iv. 84). But Lord James's own letter to Mary informing her that he had had an interview with Throckmorton proves that he was by no means anxious to hide this from her (Philippson's *Marie Stuart,* iii. 438). To make Tytler's charge good, one of two things must be established—either that Mary had revealed her secret intentions to her brother, or that he believed she had. Tytler and Hosack prove neither. It has been asserted by Camden (*Annales Elizabethæ,* 1625, p. 57) and Stranguage (*Historie of Mary Stuart,* reprint 1891, p. 30) that, as he returned through England, he quietly advised Elizabeth to provide for religion and her own safety by intercepting his sister. This grave charge is inconsistent with Lesley's statement that the Lord James hastened home to prepare for her early and honourable reception (*De Rebus Gestis Scotorum,* 1675, p. 533); and is still more inconsistent with the remarkable letter, concerning the English succession, addressed by the maligned

Commendator of St. Andrews to Elizabeth on the 6th of August (*supra*, p. 66). Camden's bare assertion has been implicitly accepted, however, by such writers as Goodall (*Examination*, 1754, i. 172, 173), Chalmers (*Life of Mary*, 1818, i. 40, 44), and Father Stevenson (*Mary Stuart*, 1886, pp. 236, 254 *n.*). Father Forbes-Leith, while quite ready to believe anything against the political leader of the Scottish Reformation, has, with chronic inaccuracy, represented him as giving the alleged advice before instead of after his interview with Mary (*Narratives of Scottish Catholics*, 1885, p. 56).

[31] *Foreign Calendar, Elizabeth*, iv. 91; Lesley's *History*, p. 295.— In his Latin narrative, Lesley includes a fourth uncle, the Marquis D'Elbœuf (*De Origine*, 1675, p. 533).

[32] After narrating how the Lord James and himself waited on Mary, Lesley says :—' Not long eftir, the Erlis Bothwell and Eglintoun, the Bischop of Orknay, and sindre uther nobill men and clarkis, arrivit in France, quha returnit in Scotland with the Quenes Majestie agane' (Lesley's *History*, pp. 294, 295). According to Schiern, 'Bothwell in the spring of 1561 again got an opportunity at Joinville of saluting the Queen, and remained at her Court in France until she herself, in the month of August 1561, was obliged with deep regret to bid farewell to the land of her youth' (Berry's *Schiern*, 1880, pp. 23, 24). A similar statement is made by Miss Strickland (*Life of Mary*, 1888, i. 61). Father Stevenson as emphatically states that she was accompanied from Joinville to Nancy by 'the Earls of Bothwell and Eglinton, and several others of the Scottish nobility' (*Mary Stuart*, 1886, p. 237). Schiern, Strickland, and Stevenson have probably been misled by Lesley's loose phrase, 'not long eftir.' It is certain that Bothwell returned from France to Scotland in the preceding February (*Foreign Calendar, Elizabeth*, iii. 532, 536, 583; *Diurnal of Occurrents*, p. 64); and went back in summer, arriving in Paris on the 5th of July (*Venetian Calendar*, vii. 333; *Foreign Calendar, Elizabeth*, iv. 179). If he was with her at Joinville and Nancy in April, his stay in France at that time must have been short indeed.

[33] Lesley's *History*, p. 295; *Foreign Calendar, Elizabeth*, iv. 91.— Lesley says, that, after spending certain days in Joinville with her grandmother, 'sho tuik her jornay thairfra towart Lorrain in the beginning of May'; but Mary's letter to Throckmorton proves that she was in Nancy on the 22nd of April (Labanoff's *Recueil*, i. 94). The young Duke of Lorraine had, like Mary, been brought up in

the French Court. When, at the diplomatic conference near Cambray, on the 15th of May 1558, his mother saw him, she was from excessive tenderness unable for some time to speak, and almost fainted (*Venetian Calendar*, vi. 1494, 1497). Yet, instead of going with her, he chose to return to the French Court, and had in consequence a most demonstrative reception (*Ibid*. vi. 1498). In the cathedral of Notre Dame, on the 22nd of January, 1558-9, he was married to one of Henry's daughters—the Princess Claude, who had then 'scarcely entered her twelfth year'—with as much ceremony and pomp as had been used, nine months before, at the marriage of Mary and the Dauphin (*Ibid*. vii. 10, 19, 20).

[34] 'Our Quen, then Douagiere of France, retired hir self be litle and litle farther and farther fra the Court of France; that it suld not seam that sche was in any sort compellit therunto, as of a treuth sche was be the Quen Mothers rygorous and vengeable dealing; wha allegit that sche was dispysed be hir gud dochter, during the schort regne of K. Francis 2. hir husband, be the instigation of the House of Guise' (Melville's *Memoirs*, p. 88).

[35] Lesley's *History*, p. 294; *De Rebus Gestis Scotorum*, 1675, p. 531.

[36] While assigning Catherine's dislike of her as the primary reason why 'Mary determined to leave the Court and to spend some time with her own kindred in Lorraine,' Father Stevenson adds :—'It was very natural that she should do so. Rheims was the ordinary residence of her uncle, the Cardinal-Archbishop of that diocese; there too resided her aunt Renée, Abbess of the Convent of St. Pierre in the same city.' This statement is neither logical nor accurate. Rheims is not in Lorraine; and the Cardinal-Archbishop seems, when in power, to have resided as much if not more at the Court than at this archiepiscopal seat. But he proceeds—'She longed for quiet and rest, and she needed them after the agitation and fatigue through which she had passed of late; and the experience of her childhood told her that she would find them nowhere so perfectly as in a community of religious women' (Stevenson's *Mary Stuart*, pp. 216, 217).

[37] *Foreign Calendar, Elizabeth*, iv. 91.—De Vaudemont was uncle to the young Duke of Lorraine (*Ibid*. i. 272; iv. 121; *Venetian Calendar*, vii. 10, 20).

[38] *Blackwood's Magazine*, clix. 196.—This careless popular writer not only makes Mary spend 'the sad winter' at Rheims, but places

her visit to Nancy after instead of before the coronation of Charles
the Ninth.

[39] *Foreign Calendar, Elizabeth,* iii. 576 ; iv. 41 (quoted *supra,*
pp. 231, 232 *nn.* 15, 19).—The Lord James suspected that, as she
would not suffer him to accompany her to Nancy, there was something on hand there which she did not wish him to know of (*Foreign
Calendar, Elizabeth,* iv. 84).

[40] Lesley's *History,* p. 295.

[41] Lesley's *History,* p. 296.—Somer, on arriving at Rheims,
understood that she 'had fallen sick at Joinville' (*Foreign Calendar,
Elizabeth,* iv. 119) ; but the report of her having 'fallen sick of an
ague at Nancy' had reached Paris by the 9th of May (*Ibid.* iv.
106).

[42] She intended being at Rheims on the 8th of May (*Foreign
Calendar, Elizabeth,* iv. 89), where Charles was crowned on the
15th (*Ibid.* iv. 116, 121 ; *Venetian Calendar,* vii. 315); but was
unable to leave Joinville until after the coronation (*Foreign Calendar,
Elizabeth,* iv. 119, 120). Nevertheless, Labanoff asserts that she
assisted at the ceremonial (*Recueil,* i. 95 ; *Portraits de Marie Stuart,*
1860, p. 11), and Miss Benger describes her dress and appearance
on the occasion (*Memoirs of Mary,* 1823, ii. 26). Writing from
Paris on the 25th of May, Throckmorton says that she is yet at
Joinville, that she had been somewhat amended, but was down
again and keeping her bed for the most part, no man saving her
physicians being allowed to speak to her (*Foreign Calendar, Elizabeth,* iv. 125). Lesley alleges that she remained in Joinville till
the beginning of July (*History,* p. 296 ; *De Rebus Gestis Scotorum,*
1675, p. 534); but in this he is clearly in error. As two of her
letters are dated from Rheims on the 28th of May (Labanoff's
Recueil, i. 95-98) she must have been there by that time. The
change from Joinville to Rheims was probably a pleasant one. In
Miss Benger's opinion :—' The austere gravity of the aged Princess
[Mary's grandmother], and the profound reverence she received
from her attendants, gave to every object around her, the sombre
character of funereal pageantry ; no gaieties were here exhibited ;
the most innocent recreations were scarcely allowable. . . . Such
sanctified demeanour was rather calculated to inspire reverence
than love, and Mary was perhaps not unwilling to quit this almost
sacred retreat for the more congenial hospitality of her aunt Renée,
the Abbess of Rheims, an elegant and cultivated woman, whose

luxurious apartments disclaimed all conventual austerity' (*Memoirs of Mary*, 1823, ii. 25). Lesley states that Mary tarried 'certane dayes' at Rheims, 'weill intertenit' by her uncle, the Cardinal-Archbishop, and her aunt the Abbess. Lesley's 'certane dayes' are unwarrantably extended by Miss Strickland into 'several weeks'; and these she says were spent 'in the conventual seclusion of the monastery,' with her aunt. Miss Strickland not only adopts an impossible chronology, but gives rein to her imagination :—'It was with difficulty that the persuasions of her uncles, the Cardinal de Lorraine and the Duke de Guise, could induce the reluctant young Queen to quit this peaceful haven, to launch her lonely bark amidst the same stormy waves which had overwhelmed that of her heart-broken mother' (Miss Strickland's *Life of Mary*, 1888, i. 65).

⁴³ In placing Mary's return to the Court of her brother-in-law at the end of June, Labanoff (*Recueil*, i. 98 ; *Portraits*, p. 11) is undoubtedly in error. Writing on the 23rd of June, Throckmorton says it was on the tenth (*Foreign Calendar, Elizabeth*, iv. 150) ; and Surian, on the 3rd of July, speaks of it as 'a month ago' (*Venetian Calendar*, vii. 333). 'At her coming she was met a league without the town by the Duke of Orleans, the King of Navarre, the Prince of Condé, and all the Princes of the blood who are here [*i.e.* Paris], and most part of the nobility of the Court ; and before she came to her lodgings within the Court the French King and Queen-mother met her, the whole accompanying her honourably to her lodgings' (*Foreign Calendar, Elizabeth*, iv. 150). 'Thair come furth of the town the Kingis brodir Duik of Angeow, the Prince of Condie, Duik of Guise, with mony princis, duikis, erles and noble men, and mett hir, and convoyit hir hichnes verrey honorably throch the toun of Paris, to the Faulxboures of Sanct Germanes, quhair the King was ludged, becaus he had not yet maid his entres in Paris ; and thair remaning in cumpany with the King and Quene modir quhill about the ende of Julij, weill and honorablie intertenyt with all kinde of honest recreatione, aswell be boittis appoun the ryver of Seane, as utherwyis be triumphes and feactis of armes exerced within the abbay of Sanct Germans' (Lesley's *History*, p. 296).

⁴⁴ *Foreign Calendar, Elizabeth*, iv. 68, 89, 90, 110, 119.—Labanoff in his chronological summary—which, during the period of Mary's widowhood in France, is singularly inaccurate—substitutes Mewtas for Somer.

⁴⁵ On the 31st of March, Throckmorton had declared that if he

was not to be allowed to return to England until Mary ratified the
Treaty, he would never return, for she would not ratify it so long
as her council in France could prevent her, and they had more
credit with her than the Lord James or any who could come out
of Scotland (*Foreign Calendar, Elizabeth,* iv. 45, 46). He guessed,
before Somer returned from Nancy, that she would defer the ratification until she arrived in Scotland and consulted her Estates
(*Ibid.* iv. 76); and from Lord James he learned that this was her
intention (*Ibid.* iv. 84). Ere Somer set out on his second attempt,
Throckmorton hinted to Elizabeth that if she received even such
an answer direct from Mary she would the better know how to
proceed afterwards (*Ibid.* iv. 90, 91); but he did not expect an
answer of any kind, thinking rather that Mary was sick, or would
be so, to avoid the difficulty (*Ibid.* iv. 112); and to a certain extent
he was right, for when Somer reached Rheims the Cardinal of
Lorraine and the Duke of Guise informed him that she was sick
at Joinville, and that they 'meddled no more in her matters'
(*Ibid.* iv. 119, 120). It was only at this interview, on the 18th
of June, that Throckmorton was to hear from her own lips that
she was now determined to postpone her definite answer until she
was in Scotland.

[46] Though the Queen of Scots told Throckmorton that she was
to sail from Calais, he hardly seems to have believed her, as he had
been advertised 'that she minds to take shipping at Nantes, and,
passing by the west seas, to land at Dumbarton as it were by
stealth, for that it is put into her head not to trust herself too
much on the coast of England' (*Foreign Calendar, Elizabeth,* iv.
154).

[47] D'Oysel came to Throckmorton to say that he was not to set
out for England for ten days; that he was to request 'a passport,
or safe-conduct, for the Queen of Scotland and her train, in case
through tempest or sickness she should be forced to land in any
part of England'; that after she had conferred with her nobles and
Estates she would satisfy Elizabeth; and that the assumption of
the English arms was entirely due to the Cardinal of Lorraine
(*Foreign Calendar, Elizabeth,* iv. 155). Mary wished to send her
écurie through England (*Ibid.* iv. 183, 190).

[48] *Foreign Calendar, Elizabeth,* iv. 150-152.

[49] D'Oysel was instructed to ask (1) a passport for Mary, with a
clause that if she arrived in any port of England she might tarry

there, purchase provisions, and, if it seemed good to her, pass by land to Scotland; (2) another safe-conduct for her to pass through England with her train, etc. ; and (3) a safe-conduct for himself to go through England to Scotland (*Foreign Calendar, Elizabeth*, iv. 173, 174). Hill Burton—having overlooked these Instructions, and also D'Oysel's statement to Throckmorton (*supra*, p. 240, *n.* 47)—says: 'It seems to be a question whether the passport requested by Queen Mary was for permission to land in England, and travel by land to Scotland' (*History of Scotland*, 1876, iv. 16 *n.*). Elizabeth professed her readiness not only to grant the safe-conducts, but also aid and a personal interview, if Mary would only ratify the Treaty; and she thought it meet that D'Oysel should go back to her with this message, which answer he seemed quietly to receive (*Foreign Calendar, Elizabeth*, iv. 177, 187, 188). At her interview with Throckmorton on the 20th of July, Mary commanded those present to retire further off, saying she knew not well her own infirmity nor how she might be transported with anger, and liked not to have so many witnesses of her passion as Elizabeth had when she talked with D'Oysel (*Ibid.* iv. 200). That Envoy had reported at his return to France that Elizabeth had said she would make provision to keep Mary from passing home (*Ibid.* iv. 206). In Froude's opinion, Elizabeth was, in the circumstances, quite justified in refusing the passport:—'To have allowed a Catholic princess, a rival claimant of her crown, who in defiance of promises was obstinately maintaining her pretensions, to pass three hundred miles through a population the most notoriously Romanist in the realm, and with many of whom the Queen of Scots was already in communication, would have been an act of political suicide' (*History of England*, 1887, vi. 505).

⁵⁰ While Mary was still at Joinville, Throckmorton thought that so long as Elizabeth had so many at her devotion and of her religion in Scotland Mary would not return to her country, and he advised Cecil 'to hold there' in order that she might be kept in France (*Foreign Calendar, Elizabeth*, iv. 122). But after learning Mary's intentions, he reminded the English Privy Council—29th June—that for the maintenance of good amity the Queen of Scots should be in her own country (*Ibid.* iv. 160); and next day urged upon Cecil the expediency of dealing kindly with D'Oysel, lest he should hinder Mary's return (*Ibid.* iv. 163). At the refusal of the passports he marvelled greatly, and all the more so that by all

former writings he understood that Elizabeth wished her to go home and be advised by the counsellors of her own nation, whereby many occasions of unquietness would be taken away. Now—26th July—he was puzzled with Cecil's statement that their friends in Scotland would approve of this refusal, seeing that the Lord James when in France, and ever since, had done what he could to persuade her to return (*Ibid.* iv. 204, 205. See also *infra*, pp. 285, 287, *nn.* 4 and 5). In their Instructions to Lethington—when, next September, he was sent to Elizabeth—the Scots Lords emphatically declare that the refusal of the passport was not due to them, that they were not privy to it, and did not even know of it 'quhil lang eftir' (Keith's *History*, ii. 73).

⁵¹ Elizabeth and her Council, on receiving Throckmorton's letter of the 23rd of June, with the account of his interview with Mary on the 18th (*supra*, pp. 38, 39), had at once resolved to hinder her return if possible. On the 1st of July Elizabeth wrote to the Estates of Scotland (*Foreign Calendar, Elizabeth,* iv. 164-166 ; Laing's *Knox*, ii. 175-178 ; Calderwood's *History*, ii. 137-140 ; Keith's *History*, ii. 35-38), to Chatelherault, to the Lord James, and to Randolph (*Foreign Calendar, Elizabeth,* iv. 166, 167). The Estates were asked, not without a covert threat, to advertise her soon whether they would advise their Queen to ratify the Treaty or not. The argument of the letter to them is founded on Mary's avowal to Throckmorton that she would not give her final answer concerning the ratification without the advice of her realm. For the edification of the friendly Scots there was sent to Randolph a long extract from Throckmorton's letter, which Knox thought important enough to embody in his *History* (ii. 168-174). Elizabeth assured the Lord James that he should find her always ready in his honourable purpose for the cause of religion and the weal of his Queen and country. To Chatelherault and Arran she promised to see that their house should suffer no wrong if Mary died without issue, provided they adjoined themselves to the promotion of religion. In her letter to Randolph, she showed her hand. Mary's coming home, she thought, would alter many things in Scotland, especially the progress of religion and the devotion of many towards herself. A letter should therefore be devised dissuading her return ; or, if she were determined to come, religion and devotion to Elizabeth should be so furthered beforehand that they could not be speedily nor easily altered. If the Estates pressed their Queen to ratify the

Treaty, the French Council might protract rather than hasten her departure. Cecil's letter to Randolph of 30th June (Stevenson's *Selections*, pp. 89, 90; Wright's *Elizabeth*, i. 61, 62) was partly in the same strain, although he did not then seem to be altogether certain as to the wisdom of prolonging Mary's stay in France. In his letter to Throckmorton of 14th July, he says : ' Although in all other things D'Oysel hath been well and gently used, yet so many reasons have induced us to deny the principal request that I think it shall be both of the wise allowed, and of our friends in Scotland most welcome. The very noise of D'Oysel's coming had stirred some maze in sundry heads, and the expectation of the Queen's coming had erected up Huntly, Bothwell, Hume, and others, that it could not be agreeable for us to feed them in their humours ; and by this our denial, our friends in Scotland shall find us to be of their disposition, and so stop them in their humours. I think plainly the longer the Scottish Queen's affairs shall hang in an uncertainty, the longer will it be ere she shall have such a match in marriage as shall offend us' (Hardwicke's *State Papers*, i. 172, 173). Throckmorton does not appear to have been satisfied with these reasons. It was in reply to this letter that he expressed his astonishment at the refusal of the safe-conduct (see preceding note). Cecil had not explicitly said that the Scots Lords wished to hinder Mary's return; and even though he had, there would have been some reason to doubt the assertion. It is questionable whether his letters always reflected his real opinions (see *e.g. infra*, pp. 264, 265); and in connection with the return of Lennox to Scotland, the Lord James and Lethington indignantly repudiated to Cecil himself as untrue the opinion which he had attributed to them (*Foreign Calendar, Elizabeth*, vii. 176, 204, 205). On the 25th of July, Cecil, writing to Sussex, tells him that the safe-conducts had been refused, and adds :—'This proceeding will lyke the Scotts well ' (Wright's *Elizabeth*, i. 67). And on the 12th of August, he again writes to Sussex :—'Nether those in Scotland nor we here doo lyke her going home' (*Ibid.* i. 69). By this time the Lord James, as well as Morton and Lethington, wished, like Cecil, ' that she might be stayed yet for a space' : so Randolph says, writing from Edinburgh on the 9th of August (Robertson's *Scotland*, app. no. 5). As Maitland, on the same day, put it, they had ' looked for a breathing tyme' (Haynes's *State Papers*, p. 369). In his letter of 30th June, Cecil had said :—'Whether it be rightly judged of

here or no I know not, I have uppon theis newes of her coming
wished to have had but one houres conference with my Lord of
Ledyngton' (Wright's *Elizabeth*, i. 62). When Lethington and
the Lord James returned from the north of Scotland to Edinburgh, they were alarmed by Cecil's letter of 1st August to
Randolph, and by St. Colms' to the Lord James. Lethington
was in perplexity (see *infra*, pp. 286, 287); but he at all events
did not hesitate to express approval of D'Oysel's stay, and of
Cecil's opinion 'anent the Queen our Sovereign's journey towards
Scotland, whose coming hither if she be enemy to the religion, and
so affected towards that realm as she yet appeareth, shall not fail
to raise wonderful tragedies' (Keith's *History*, iii. 211).

[52] *Foreign Calendar, Elizabeth*, iv. 172, 173, 180.

[53] *Foreign Calendar, Elizabeth*, iv. 179.—Mary does not appear to
have gone by Fécamp. Lesley, no doubt, says that her route to
Calais was 'throch Normandie and Picardie' (*History*, p. 297); but
he would not have omitted to state that she had gone to her mother's
funeral if she had really done so, especially as he mentions that the
body of the Queen Dowager of Scotland 'was careid to France in
ane ship, to the abbay of Feckin in Normandie' (*Ibid.* p. 289).
Mary's recorded movements make it almost absolutely certain that
she could not have gone to Fécamp at this time, unless she performed even a greater feat than her famous ride to the Hermitage.
It was on the 13th of July that Throckmorton mentioned her
proposal to go by Fécamp to Calais; but she did not leave St.
Germain-en-laye until the 25th of July (*Cabala*, 1691, p. 349); she
had not got beyond Meru by the 28th, the sickness of the Cardinal
of Lorraine and the Duke of Guise having stayed her there (*Foreign
Calendar, Elizabeth*, iv. 209; *Register of Privy Seal*, xxx. 39, 40);
on the 3rd of August she is spoken of as yet in Beauvais (*Foreign
Calendar, Elizabeth*, iv. 229); and Throckmorton found her at
Abbeville on the 7th (*Ibid.* iv. 243 *n*). Chantonnay, moreover, the
Spanish Ambassador in France, writing on the 26th of July, says
that she has changed her route, and goes direct to Calais (Teulet's
Papiers D'État, ii. 6). The obsequies of Mary of Guise had been
celebrated at Paris in the church of Notre Dame on the 12th and
13th of August 1560 (*Venetian Calendar*, vii. 243; Francisque
Michel's *Les Écossais en France*, ii. 21). When she died, the
Scottish preachers boldly opposed the using of 'ony superstitious
rytes . . . within that realme, quhilk God of his mercy had begun

to purge' (Laing's *Knox*, ii. 160). 'Lappit in a cope of leid,' with four ells of white 'taffateis' cord stretched over her in the form of a cross, she was deposited in the chapel of Edinburgh Castle, which was hung with 'blak gray' (Chalmers's *Life of Mary*, 1818, ii. 209 *n.* ; Laing's *Knox*, ii. 590, 591). From thence she was secretly removed at midnight on the 16th of March 1560-61, and placed on board a ship in Leith harbour to be taken to France (*Diurnal of Occurrents*, p. 64). Knox, who was not greatly interested in the matter, gives the 19th of October as the date of her removal from Edinburgh Castle. As for what pomp was used at her funeral in France, 'we nather herd,' he exclaims, 'nor yit regard' (Laing's *Knox*, ii. 160). From Fécamp her body was afterwards taken to the convent of St. Peter at Rheims, where her sister was abbess, and there honourably interred (Lesley's *De Rebus Gestis Scotorum*, 1675, p. 526).

[54] *Foreign Calendar, Elizabeth*, iv. 179, 198, 199, 204.—Dampierre was one of the houses of the Cardinal of Lorraine. He was there with his niece at this time, as were also the Cardinal of Guise and the Duke of Guise. The Duke of Nemours, who arrived there on the 19th, visited Mary before going on to Paris (*Cabala*, 1691, p. 345).

[55] Hosack makes the rather astounding statement, that, during the period of her widowhood in France, Mary was not only openly slighted by Catherine de Medici, but 'even to some extent neglected by her uncles, who were at this time too fully occupied with the affairs of France to give much of their attention to those of Scotland' (*Mary and her Accusers*, i. 63). In reality the Guises were not so fully occupied with the affairs of France during this period as they had previously been ; and had therefore more time to devote to those of Scotland. Unscrupulous and selfish men they may have been, but they cannot be justly charged with at this time neglecting their niece. In my text and relative notes there are casual references enough to vindicate them from this accusation. It is true that the Cardinal of Lorraine and the Duke of Guise told Somer, at Rheims in May, that they meddled no more in Mary's matters (*Foreign Calendar, Elizabeth*, iv. 120) ; that Mary herself told Throckmorton, on the 20th of July, that her uncles being of the affairs of France did not think meet to advise her (*Ibid.* iv. 201) ; and that, at Abbeville on the 7th of August, she assured him that her uncles—why, she knew not—were giving her no advice in the matter of the Treaty

(*Ibid.* iv. 244 *n.*).   But the reason why they professedly stood in
the background at this time is quite apparent.   As it was neither
Mary's interest nor intention to ratify the Treaty, she wished 'to
drive time.'   When pressed by Bedford on the 18th of February,
she urged the plausible plea that she was without counsel, the
Cardinal of Lorraine being absent (*Ibid.* iii. 573).   When this
excuse could no longer be made, the other served as well; and
it was probably her diplomatic uncle who suggested the line of
evasion.   A comparison of the Cardinal's and Mary's answers to
Throckmorton ere she was yet a widow (Hardwicke's *State Papers,*
i. 132-138) shows how her opinions were coloured by his.

[56] Throckmorton sent home two accounts of this interview—one
to Elizabeth, the other to the Council.   The first of these letters is
printed *in extenso* in *Cabala,* 1691, pp. 345-349; and a very full
summary of the other in the *Foreign Calendar, Elizabeth,* iv. 198-
204.   Mary's answer on this point is thus reported in the *Cabala :*—
'I may pass well enough home into my own realm, I think, without
her [*i.e.* Elizabeth's] passport or license; for tho' the late King your
master (said she) used all the impeachment he could both to stay
me, and to catch me when I came hither, yet you know, *Monsieur
le Ambassadour,* I came hither safely, and I may have as good
means to help me home again, as I had to come hither, if I would
imploy my friends.'   The reference to 'the late King your master'
points of course to Edward the Sixth; but in Father Stevenson's
Foreign Calendar, the corresponding passage is thus summarised :—
'She might pass well enough home to her own realm without the
Queen's passport or license, for though King *Henry* used all the
impeachment he could to stay her and catch her when she came
hither, yet she came safely; and she might have as good means to
help her home if she would employ her friends.'   Headstrong and
unscrupulous as was Henry the Eighth, he, poor man, could do
little to hinder Mary's voyage into France, as he was dead eighteen
months before she sailed from Scotland; yet to him Hill Burton
(*History of Scotland,* 1876, iv. 16) also assigns the attempt to kidnap
the innocent infant.

[57] See *supra,* p. 245, *n.* 55.

[58] Sir James Mackintosh characterises this speech as 'one of the
most remarkable specimens of guarded sarcasm and of politely
insinuated menace' (*History of England,* 1853, ii. 297).

[59] *Cabala,* 1691, pp. 348, 349.

[60] Lesley's *History*, p. 297.—The exact date of her departure from St. Germain-en-laye is fixed by Throckmorton's letter (*Cabala*, 1691, p. 349).

[61] *Cabala*, p. 349.

[62] *Foreign Calendar, Elizabeth*, iv. 229.

[63] The passage bearing directly on this point in Throckmorton's letter is thus summarised in the *Foreign Calendar* :—'So he took his leave of the Queen at 5 P.M. at Abbeville, on 8 Aug., where she desired to tarry till the 10th. *That* day she rode five leagues to her bed, to an abbey between this town [Abbeville] and Montreuil, called Forest Monstrier.' That *that* day referred to the 8th, not the 10th, seems to be implied in an earlier passage in the same letter :—' She meant, she said, to go hence to-night.'

[64] *Foreign Calendar, Elizabeth*, iv. 243-245.

[65] *Venetian Calendar*, vii. 334.

[66] Lesley distinctly states that the safe-conduct was granted, but that Mary had landed in Scotland before St. Colms returned to Calais with it (*History*, p. 298). Hayward says the same (*Annals of Elizabeth*, Camden Society, p. 77). Writing from Edinburgh on the 26th of August, Randolph explains :—' Nowe, we stande in better termes then before, in speciall sens the Laird of St. Come's arrivall with hir saulf-conducte four dayes after that she was landed' (Laing's *Knox*, vi. 128 ; *Foreign Calendar, Elizabeth*, iv. 278).

[67] The day before she sailed from Calais, Mary wrote to Lady Throckmorton saying that she had charged D'Esguilly, her maître d'hôtel, to visit her and give her a present as a remembrance of her affection and as a token of the regard in which she held her husband (*Foreign Calendar, Elizabeth*, iv. 248). On the evening of the 3rd of September, D'Esguilly, with many courteous words on Mary's behalf, delivered her letter to Lady Throckmorton, along with two basins, two ewers, two salts, and a standing cup, all gilt, weighing 398 ounces (*Ibid.* iv. 301). Father Stevenson says that D'Esguilly ' had no speech with Throckmorton, who pleaded sickness, although he himself had fixed the hour for the presentation' (*Mary Stuart*, 1886, p. 257). In making such a statement, it was hardly fair to ignore the fact that when in the earlier part of the day, Mary's representative sent to ask when it would be convenient, he asked when he might come and speak, not with Throckmorton but with his wife, and that in recording the incident Throckmorton

tells that he was compelled to keep his bed. In a footnote, however, Father Stevenson adds:—'Throckmorton's avarice tempted him to accept the gift; his dread of the jealousy of his mistress prevented a word of the most ordinary thanks. The English Ambassador saved his dignity by taking to his bed. A pretty picture, and admirably illustrative of the two sides of the same historical medal.' It is difficult to see why Throckmorton should have scrupled to accept a gift, which according to custom he was entitled to expect (see *e.g.* Wright's *Elizabeth*, i. 59); or why, on that account, he should have dreaded his Sovereign's jealousy. The story of the presentation is told by the Ambassador himself in a letter to Elizabeth; and it is from that letter that Father Stevenson—though he does not say so—has drawn his facts in order to pervert them! Throckmorton also sent Elizabeth a copy of Mary's letter to his wife; and at the same time informed her, that the Duke of Guise had told him that his niece had forgot at her departure to use that courtesy towards him which is accustomed to be done to the ministers of other princes (*Foreign Calendar, Elizabeth*, iv. 312). In April 1564, Throckmorton had the further satisfaction of informing Elizabeth that the King of France had presented him with a gold chain, weighing 164 oz., and worth above fourteen hundred French crowns (*Ibid.* vii. 121); and in May 1565 that Mary had given him a chain of gold weighing fifty ounces (*Ibid.* vii. 370). Had he been as avaricious as Stevenson asserts, he would not have refused to do what the French Ambassador did—to accept a present from the Confederate Lords when Mary was a prisoner in Lochleven (*Ibid.* viii. 333; Stevenson's *Selections*, pp. 294, 300).

[68] Brantôme says she spent six days in Calais before sailing (Jebb's *De Vita et Rebus Gestis Mariae*, ii. 483); but in this he cannot be quite accurate. She was certainly there on the 11th of August (Labanoff's *Recueil*, i. 99, 102), though St. Colms' Instructions, which prove this, are misdated the 2nd of August in the *Foreign Calendar*.

[69] Lesley's *History*, p. 297.

[70] *Foreign Calendar, Elizabeth*, iv. 263.—This servant saw two galleys and two great ships leaving Calais. A month before, Throckmorton understood that she was to have four galleys and twelve ships, French and Scottish (*Ibid.* iv. 179). A day after she had sailed, De Seurre, the French Ambassador in England,

informed Cecil that she was to go with two galleys (*Ibid.* iv. 249).
Lesley says two galleys and four great ships (*History,* p. 297). If
the Earl of Rutland was not misinformed, Mary must have had a
much greater convoy. Writing from York on the 17th of August,
he tells Cecil that, at four o'clock on the previous afternoon
(Saturday), eight galleys and sixteen great ships were seen near
Flamborough, that two of the galleys and two of the ships coming
near the coast strake sail, and the rest seemed about to do the
like. He adds :—'It is thought they will draw to the shore, which
if they do and arrive, I have given such order as I nothing doubt
but ye shall hear good news of their stay' (*Foreign Calendar, Elizabeth,* iv. 259). After making inquiry, he writes next day that,
soon after 3 o'clock on Saturday, two great galleys were espied at
Flamborough, within a furlong of the pier ; which letting their
anchors fall, put forth of either galley a naked man to swim, and
then launched two boats to sound the depth. The larger galley
was all white ; the other, coloured red, was well trimmed and
appointed, having two flags—a blue one with the arms of France,
and a white one in her stern glistening like silver. At the same
instant there appeared, at a good distance from the galleys, thirty-
two sail of tall ships, and shortly after further off twenty sail, all
which for lack of wind tried the seas, making no haste away ; thus
they continued in sight till 8 o'clock, and from thence plied
along the coast northwards, the wind being somewhat against them
(*Ibid.* iv. 260, 261). From the letters of Randolph and Cecil (*Ibid.*
iv. 277 and *n.*), as from the statements of Knox (*Works,* ii. 267),
and two contemporary chroniclers (*Diurnal,* p. 66 ; *Extracta,* p. 251),
it may be inferred that Mary arrived in Leith Road with only the
two galleys.

⁷¹ Hayward, like Lesley, speaks as if the mist enveloped them
from the commencement of the voyage :—'The Queene of Scotts,
having the advantage both of a greate callme and thicke mist,
adventured to sea in certayne French gallies' (*Annals of Elizabeth,*
p. 77) ; but Brantôme says that they only encountered the dense fog
on the morning of the day before they landed in Scotland, and his
account of Mary's pathetic farewell to France is inconsistent with
Lesley's and Hayward's statement (Jebb's *De Vita et Rebus Gestis
Mariae,* ii. 483, 484). The Articles, too, against Lady Lennox bear
that she thanked God that 'when the Queen's ships were almost
near taking of the Scottish Queen, there fell down a mist from

heaven that separated them and preserved her' (*Foreign Calendar, Elizabeth*, v. 14). If, as Brantôme tells, some of the voyagers drew from the fog an evil augury concerning the country to which they were bound, there were on the other hand some in that country who saw in the same fog a token that the Queen was bringing with her 'sorow, dolour, darknes, and all impietie' (Laing's *Knox*, ii. 269). While Mary's devout co-religionists may remember that in earlier times it was believed that the corpse and family of the saintly Queen Margaret, as they journeyed by land and sea from Edinburgh Castle to Dunfermline Abbey, had been 'miraculously sheltered' from their foes by 'a cloudy mist' (Skene's *Fordun*, ii. 209), sober Presbyterians may not forget that the aged Peden was more than once delivered from his persecutors by a timely mist (*Biographia Presbyteriana*, i. 66, 67, 70).

[72] It is noteworthy that Lesley—while acknowledging that Elizabeth granted the safe-conduct—represents her ships as waiting to seize the passing prey. Castelnau de Mauvissière, a fellow-voyager, tells too that Mary both saw and had some apprehension of the English fleet, which was at sea either to take her or to hinder her passage—no easy task in his opinion, as the galleys were swifter than the round vessels (Jebb's *De Vita et Rebus Gestis Mariae*, ii. 455). A contemporary, not unduly partial to Mary, says that Elizabeth 'fitted out a large fleet, under pretence of pursuing the pirates, which some supposed was intended to intercept the Queen of Scots, if she endeavoured to pass in opposition to her will' (Aikman's *Buchanan*, ii. 439). Possibly all these fears and rumours owed their origin to Elizabeth's rash speech to D'Oysel (*supra*, p. 241, *n.* 49). Throckmorton thought that instead of threatening to prevent Mary's return, it would have been better to grant the passport; but counselled Cecil that, as the threat had been uttered, there should be at least a rumour of some preparation, that the world might see that they spoke in earnest and did not brag. In a postscript to this letter of 26th July, Throckmorton says that, if they meant to catch the Queen of Scots, their ships must search and see all, for she intends rather to steal away than to pass with force (*Foreign Calendar, Elizabeth*, iv. 206). Two days before Mary left Calais, Cecil wrote to Sussex :—' The Scottish Quene was the 10th of this month at Bulloygn, and meaneth to take shypping at Callise. Nether those in Scotland nor we here doo lyke her going home. The Quene's Majestie hath three ships

in the north seas to preserve the fyshers from pyratts. I thynk they will be sorry to see her pass' (Wright's *Elizabeth*, i. 69). Such a letter implies that no great naval preparations had been made to intercept the Queen of Scots ; but it is certain that arrangements were made to stay her if she entered any North-of-England port (*Historical MSS. Commission, Twelfth Report*, app. iv. pp. 73-77). On the very day that Mary was seen off Flamborough, Elizabeth wrote her from Henyngham in Essex stating, that, although she was dissatisfied with the excuses St. Colms had made in her name, she was content to suspend her conceit of all unkindness ; and emphatically contradicting the rumour that she was attempting to stay her :—' Where it seemeth that report hath been made unto you that we had sent our Admiral to the seas with our navy to impeach your passage, both your servants do well understand how false that is, knowing for a truth that we have not any more than two or three small barks upon the seas to apprehend certain pirates ; being thereto intreated, and almost compelled by the earnest complaint of the Spanish Ambassador made of certain Scotchmen haunting our seas as pirates, under pretence of letters of marque' (*Foreign Calendar, Elizabeth*, iv. 251). Although Bishop Quadra had urgently complained about pirates, he evidently believed that the cruisers were sent out against Mary, and that the suppression of piracy was a mere pretext (*Spanish Calendar, Elizabeth*, i. 209-212 ; *Foreign Calendar, Elizabeth*, v. 68). Writing from Edinburgh to Throckmorton a week after Mary's arrival, Randolph says :—' She nether mette nor sawe shippe upon the sea, for all the bruit [*i.e.* rumour] that was of her staye that shulde have byne' (Laing's *Knox*, vi. 128). Writing to the same Ambassador on the same day, Cecil says :—' The Queen's Majesty's ships, that were upon the seas to cleanse them from pirates, saw her [*i.e.* Mary], and saluted her galleys ; and staying her ships examined them of pirates and dismissed them gently. One Scottish ship they detain, as vehemently suspected of piracy' (Hardwicke's *State Papers*, i. 176). Hosack, not over-fastidious in verifying quotations, has been content to cite part of this letter of Cecil's from Parker Lawson's notes to Keith ; and has in consequence stopped short without giving the sentence concerning the detention of the Scottish ship suspected of piracy. Then, turning upon Cecil, he charges him with being 'silent as to the significant fact that one of the transports belonging to the Queen of Scots, and conveying the Earl of Eglinton and his attendants, was actually taken and detained by the English squadron' (*Mary and her Accusers*, i. 68, 69). Both Buchanan and Hayward refer to the seizure and speedy release of the vessel with Eglinton (Aikman's *Buchanan*, ii. 439; *Annals of Elizabeth*, p. 78). Lesley says:—'In the mein season, the Inglis shippis tuik sum Scottis schippis, quhairin was certane lordis of hir cumpany, sic as the Erle of Eglintoun and utheris, and was stayit in Ingland sume space, albeit thairefter shortlie releved, and suffred to returne in Scotland, the moir easely that the Quenes hienes was alreddye eschapped thair handis' (*History*, p. 298). Chalmers alleges that two Dutch vessels—which were carrying Mary's horses and mules —were seized by the English fleet that had been sent out to intercept her; that these Dutch transports were released, but the horses and mules were detained a month before being allowed to proceed by land to Edinburgh (*Life of Mary*, 1818, ii. 420). Having been assured that her royal stud which was landed at Tynemouth was stayed by the English warden simply because it lacked a passport, the Queen of Scots was satisfied (Keith's *History*, ii. 89, 97).

[73] Lesley's *History*, p. 297.

[74] Robertson's *Inventories*, p. cxvii, *n.* ; Hill Burton's *Scotland*, 1876, iv. 262 *n.* ; *Scot Abroad*, 1881, p. 115 *n.* ; Schiern's *Bothwell*, 1880, p. 411.

[75] Hunter Blair's *Bellesheim*, 1889, iii. 22 *n.*

CHAPTER V

[1] Though the date of Mary's arrival, the 19th of August, is quite certain (see the authorities in note 3), yet Lesley (*History*, p. 297), Spottiswoode (*History*, ii. 6), and Calderwood (*History*, ii. 142) give the 20th of August; Buchanan (Aikman's *Buchanan*, ii. 440) and Pitscottie (*History*, 1728, p. 213) give the 21st; and Sir James Balfour (*Historical Works*, i. 326) retains her at Calais until the 18th of September. Birrel (*Diary*, p. 4) gives the true date, accompanied by the strange statement that she 'wes stollen out of France by certaine lordis.' Lamartine (*Mary Stuart*, 1864, p. 19) is right too in the date, but unaccountably adds, that it was 'the very day on which she completed her nineteenth year,' although

he had previously said (*Ibid.* p. 2) that she was born in December. Mauvissière (Jebb's *De Vita et Rebus Gestis Mariae*, ii. 455) prolongs her voyage to the eighth day; Causin (*Holy Court*, 1678, p. 812; Jebb's *De Vita et Rebus Gestis Mariae*, ii. 55) makes her arrive 'suddenly in her kingdom, as if she had flown through the air.' According to Chalmers (*Life of Mary*, 1818, i. 48), 'she remained on board her galley till the evening'; according to David Laing (Knox's *Works*, ii. 267 *n.*) she 'landed on the following day.' Such are a few of the discrepancies concerning one of the simplest and best attested events in Mary's life.

² According to the *Diurnal of Occurrents* (p. 66), Mary landed at Leith at ten in the forenoon, 'and remanit in Andro Lambis hous be the space of ane hour'; but according to the *Register of Privy Seal* (see following note), she landed at nine; and in the Roslin additions to the *Extracta ex Cronicis Scocie*, Abbotsford Club (p. 251), it is stated that she 'dynit in Andro Lambis howse in Letht.' Knox says that she remained in Leith 'till towardis the evenyng'— Holyrood Palace not being thoroughly in order, as her coming was 'more suddane than many looked for' (Laing's *Knox*, ii. 269). On the 28th of June 1559, the Queen Dowager had asked a safe-conduct for Andrew Lambe of Leith to pass through England and thence beyond the sea for a year (*Foreign Calendar, Elizabeth*, i. 338). When Mary surrendered at Carberry, it was the ensign of 'Capitane Andrew Lammie'—having Darnley's 'creuell murther' painted on it—which was 'layed doune befor her' (Birrel's *Diary*, p. 10).

³ '*Post adventum S.D.N. Regine a partibus Gallie que pervenit ad villam de Leith decimo nono die mensis Augusti anno Domini millesimo quingentesimo sexagesimo primo hora nona ante meridiem*' (*Register of Privy Seal*, xxx. 42). See also *Foreign Calendar, Elizabeth*, iv. 277, 282; Wright's *Elizabeth*, i. 71, 72; Hardwicke's *State Papers*, i. 176; *Diurnal of Occurrents*, p. 66; *Extracta ex Cronicis Scocie*, p. 251; Laing's *Knox*, ii. 267.

⁴ Even on the 26th of July, some in France thought she would not go to Scotland (*Cabala*, 1691, p. 349); Brantôme declares that she herself dreaded the voyage as much as death, and would far rather have remained a simple dowager in France than go to reign in Scotland (Jebb's *De Vita et Rebus Gestis Mariae*, ii. 482); and Randolph, writing from Edinburgh to Cecil ten days before her arrival, says, 'the preparence is very small whensoever that she

arrive, scarcely any man can be persuaded that she has any such thought in her head' (Robertson's *Scotland*, app. no. 5). During the first week of August, the Privy Council warned the nobles, magistrates, and others to be in Edinburgh by the last day of the month, professedly to await upon her coming and attend upon her commands, in reality to answer Elizabeth's letter (*Foreign Calendar, Elizabeth,* iv. 239; Laing's *Knox,* ii. 269 *n.* 4; Keith's *History,* iii. 216); but on the evening of the 14th, Captain Anstruther reached Edinburgh with letters from Mary, and intimated that she would arrive before the 26th (Tytler's *History of Scotland,* 1845, v. 493, 494).

⁵ 'Happie was he and sche,' says Knox, 'that first myght have the presence of the Quene. The Protestantis war not the slowest, and thairintill thai war not to be blamed' (Laing's *Knox,* ii. 269). Lesley states that she was convoyed to Holyrood by the Earl of Argyll, Lord Erskine, the Lord James, by 'sindrie nobill men and the toun of Edinburgh'; and that shortly afterwards Chatelherault, Huntly, Atholl, Marischal, Crawford, and many other nobles—'being rejosed of hir Majesteis returning'—came to her with all possible diligence (Lesley's *History,* pp. 297, 298). Herries also testifies to the 'great signs of joy' with which she was received by the nobility, and to the 'reverence to her persone' inspired in the people by 'her bewtie, youth, and statlie carriage'—interjecting the caveats, however, that the joy of the nobles was mostly counterfeit, and that the affection of the people, 'lyke a cock upon the top of a steeple,' was not long fixed (*Historical Memoirs,* p. 56). Buchanan, too, thought that the nobles were drawn by mixed motives—partly to see the show, partly to congratulate their Sovereign on her return, some to relate their services during her absence and claim her favour or avert the calumnies of their enemies, and not a few to judge of their future prospects (Aikman's *Buchanan,* ii. 440). Mauvissière tells that 'at the outset, such a good opinion of her was given to her subjects, that Scotland esteemed herself happy to have the presence of her Queen' (Jebb's *De Vita et Rebus Gestis Mariae,* ii. 455); but Causin narrows the enthusiasm of her reception by saying that 'she was received by all good Catholics with rejoicings and wondrous plaudits' (*Ibid.* ii. 55; *Holy Court,* 1678, p. 812).

⁶ Laing's *Knox,* ii. 270.

⁷ A rebec was a stringed instrument played with a bow (Nares's

Glossary, 1888, ii. 726, 727); but Mr. Skelton is unable to distinguish between rebecs and bagpipes (*Maitland of Lethington*, i. 62 *n.*).

[8] Jebb's *De Vita et Rebus Gestis Mariae*, ii. 485.—This incident furnishes Father Forbes-Leith with an opportunity of displaying his hyperbolic tendency :—'To close her eyes, during the first three nights of her abode in her own palace, was impossible, in consequence of the diligent zeal with which the unwearied psalmodists continued their nocturnal chorus' (*Narratives oṛ Scottish Catholics*, p. 59).

[9] *Documents relative to the Reception at Edinburgh of the Kings and Queens of Scotland*, 1822, pp. 1-8.—'The banquet, triumphe and propyne to the Quenis Grace' cost about four thousand merks. The deacons of the crafts differed from the magistrates as to how this sum was to be raised. Knox has erroneously placed her public entry into Edinburgh in the beginning of October (Laing's *Knox*, ii. 287); but it was undoubtedly on Tuesday the 2nd of September, exactly a fortnight after her arrival (*Diurnal of Occurrents*, p. 67; Wright's *Elizabeth*, i. 73).

[10] The six-year old 'bony barne'—or 'pretty boy,' as Knox describes him—repeated four stanzas each of eight lines which thus began :—

> 'Welcome, our Souveraine, welcome our natyve Quene,
>   Welcome to us your subjects greate and smalle,
> Welcome, I saye, even from the verie splene,
>   To Edinburghe, your syttie principall'

(*Foreign Calendar, Elizabeth*, iv. 287, 288; Thorpe's *Calendar*, i. 174). 'The verses of hir awin praise,' says Knox, 'sche heard, and smyled. But when the Bible was presented, and the praise thairof declared, sche began to frown : for schame sche could not refuise it. But she did no better, for immediatelie sche gave it to the most pestilent Papist within the realme, to wit, to Arthoure Erskyn' (Laing's *Knox*, ii. 288). If, as Lord Herries alleges, the Psalm Book was in 'Scots vers,' it may have been Wedderburn's version; but his statement that the Bible was in the 'Scots languadge' is altogether incredible (*Historical Memoirs*, p. 56).

[11] Concerning this detail the chronicler, who on all other points of the triumph is most copious, simply says :—'Our Soverane Ladie come to the Salt Trone, quhair thair wes sum spekaris; and

efter ane litell speitche, thai brunt upoun the skaffet maid at the said Trone, the maner of ane sacrifice' (*Diurnal*, p. 68). According to Lord Herries :—' Upon the top of this pageant there was a speech made tending to abolishing of the mass, and in token that it was alreddie banished the kingdome, there was the shape of a priest in his ornaments reddie to say mass, made of wode, which was brought forth in sight of all and presentlie throwen in a fyre made upon the scaffold and burnt' (*Historical Memoirs*, p. 57). Had this really been done, Knox perhaps would not have said of this day's proceedings :—' In ferses, in masking, and in other prodigalities, faine wold fooles have counterfooted France' (Laing's *Knox*, ii. 287, 288). Writing to Cecil, on the following Sabbath, Randolph says, that ' thei were mynded to have had a priest burned at the altar, at the elevation,' but ' the Erle of Huntly stayed that pagient.' He tells, however, that ' for the terrible sygnifications of the vengeance of God upon idolatrie, ther wer burnt Coron, Nathan (*sic*), and Abiron, in the tyme of their sacrifice' (Wright's *Elizabeth*, i. 74). It was probably a compromise that substituted for the mass-priest in canonicals the sons of Izhar and Eliab, for, as Joseph Robertson points out, the Reformers could regard their destruction ' as an example of God's vengeance upon idolatry, the Roman Catholics as an example of God's vengeance upon those who took the priesthood upon themselves without authority' (*Inventories of Mary's Jewels*, p. lxxiii).

[12] She had left Holyrood in the forenoon, riding by ' the lang gait' on the north side of Edinburgh, and through ' ane yet' which had been made for her at the foot of the ' Castle Bank,' and so reached the Castle in time for dinner (*Diurnal*, p. 67). Joseph Robertson identifies ' the lang gait' as ' the terrace on which Princes Street now stands' (*Mary's Inventories*, p. lxxii).

[13] This account of Mary's entry into Edinburgh is mainly drawn from the *Diurnal of Occurrents*, pp. 67-69. Mr. Skelton alleges that Lethington was ' at Westminster on a mission to Elizabeth ; and the civic authorities appear to have taken advantage of his absence to introduce some humorous interludes of which the Secretary of State might possibly have disapproved' (*Maitland of Lethington*, ii. 33). Lethington, however, was not then at Westminster. His letters of credit are dated at Holyrood on the 1st of September (Labanoff's *Recueil*, i. 103), and from his own report it may be inferred that he did not leave until the

2nd (Philippson's *Marie Stuart*, iii. 445), the day of her public entry.

[14] This mass is said to have been celebrated 'in hir Hienes chappell within hir palace of Halyrudhous' (*Diurnal of Occurrents*, p. 66). In Mary's time there were at least two chapels at Holyrood—one the chapel or church of the Abbey, and the other a private chapel in the Palace itself. These two are clearly distinguished, not only in the *Diurnal* (pp. 66, 79, 80, 88), but in the *Kirk Session Records of the Canongate* (Pitcairn's *Criminal Trials*, i. 462*, 489*), and still more clearly by Knox and Randolph (Laing's *Knox*, i. 391; Ellis's *Original Letters*, first series, ii. 198, 199). As David Laing has pointed out, Mary had her mass, not in the church of the Abbey—which was used as the parish church of the Canongate—but in the chapel-royal attached to the Palace (*Proceedings of the Society of Antiquaries of Scotland*, i. 102). It was not until the reign of her great-grandson that the church of the Abbey became the chapel-royal (*Ibid.* i. 114; *Liber Carturum Sancte Crucis*, Bann. Club, p. lxxvii). In Mary's time there was also an apartment in Holyrood known as 'the auld chappell' (*Diurnal of Occurrents*, p. 87). She married Bothwell in this 'auld chappell' (*Ibid.* p. 111), or, as Sir James Melville calls it, 'the gret hall for the consaill uses to sit' (*infra*, p. 455, *n.* 81). She married Darnley in her chapel-royal (*infra*, p. 347, *n.* 113); and Bothwell married Lady Jean Gordon in the church of the Abbey (*Diurnal of Occurrents*, p. 88; Pitcairn's *Criminal Trials*, i. 461*, 462*).

[15] *Diurnal of Occurrents*, p. 66; Laing's *Knox*, ii. 270, 271; Aikman's *Buchanan*, ii. 441; Spottiswoode's *History*, ii. 8; Herries's *Historical Memoirs*, p. 57; *Foreign Calendar, Elizabeth*, iv. 278.—See also Nau's *History of Mary Stewart*, 1883, pp. 307, 326, 327. Father Hunter Blair, who is by no means a slavish translator, has enlivened Bellesheim's (iii. 24) account of this episode. Some of her 'Majesteis maist humble and obedient subjectis' afterwards informed her that they had prayed to God 'with sobbes and teires' that He would so mollify her heart that she 'wald heire the doctryne' publicly taught, and examine all matters by the written Word, whereby she might be inclined to remove from her self and her realm that religion which she found to have 'na ground nor fundation' in the Scriptures (*Register of Privy Council*, xiv. 179).

[16] In his Introduction to the first volume of the *Register of the*

Privy Council of Scotland, pp. xxxvi-xl, Hill Burton has conclusively
shown that this Proclamation is genuine. He is in error, however,
in saying that it is not to be found in Keith's *History*, as it occurs
in both editions—1734, pp. 504, 505 ; 1844, iii. 40, 41 (*cf.* iii. 508,
509). Keith borrowed the Proclamation and Arran's Protest from
Knox's *History*. In Laing's *Knox* it occurs in vol. ii. pp. 272,
273 ; in the *Register of Privy Council*, in vol. i. pp. 266, 267.

[17] Laing's *Knox*, ii. 273-275.

[18] *Register of Privy Council of Scotland*, i. 356, 513.—Bishop Lesley's opinion of this Proclamation was very different from Mary's.
' From this law,' he says, ' as from a spring, has flowed all the evils
in our Scotland, whether of heresy, or of enmities, or of sedition '
(*De Rebus Gestis Scotorum*, 1675, p. 536).

[19] Laing's *Knox*, ii. 275, 276.—Mary of Guise is reported to
have been more afraid of ' Knox's prayers than of an army of ten
thousand men ' (Walker's *Vindication of the Church of Scotland*,
1774, p. 405). In some editions of David Buchanan's *Knox* (*e.g.*
1790, p. 339), the same fear is attributed to her daughter.

[20] *Foreign Calendar, Elizabeth*, iv. 179.

[21] Laing's *Knox*, ii. 277-286.

[22] It had been suggested to Charles the Fifth, and to Philip of
Spain, by their counsellors, that it was fitting to take the knife out
of the hands of the raging father who wishes to kill his son—*al
padre furioso* in their case being Pope Paul the Fourth (*Venetian
Calendar*, vi. 686, 687, 1062).

[23] Laing's *Knox*, ii. 286.—To Cecil a few weeks afterwards he
wrote :—' Her hole proceadinges do declayr, that the Cardinalles
lessons ar so deaplie prented in her hart that the substaunce and
the qualitie ar liek to perrishe together. I wold be glaid to be de-
ceaved, but I fear I shall not ; in communication with her I espyed
such craft as I have not found in such aige ; since hath the Court
bein dead to me and I to it ' (*Hatfield Calendar*, i. 262 ; Laing's
Knox, vi. 132). On the 24th of October, Randolph writes :—' Mr.
Knox cannot be otherwise perswaded but many men are deceived
in this woman ; he feareth yet that *posteriora erunt pejora primis* ;
his severity keepeth us in marvellous order. I commend better the
success of his doings and preachings than the manner thereof, tho'
I acknowledge his doctrine to be sound : his prayer is daily for her
—"That God will turn her obstinate heart, . . . or if the holy will
be otherwise, to strengthen the hearts and hands of His chosen

and elect stoutly to withstand the rage of all tyrants," etc., in words terrible enough' (Keith's *History*, ii. 101, 102). Knox has himself recorded the form of prayer which he afterwards used for the Queen (Laing's *Knox*, ii. 428). On the 16th of December 1562, Randolph reports that Knox has no hope that she will ever come to God or do good in the commonwealth. 'He is so full of mistrust in all her doings, words, and sayings, as though he were either of God's privy council that knew how He had determined of her from the beginning, or that he knew the secrets of her heart so well that neither she did or could have for ever one good thought of God or of his true religion' (*Foreign Calendar, Elizabeth*, v. 560).

[24] For example, a Romanist, as rabid as ill-informed, thus describes Knox's behaviour at his first interview with Mary :—'Knox replied in such a rude and violent manner as to cause the Queen to shed tears. Nothing could surpass the insolence of his invectives and gesticulations—indeed, generally his conduct was more that of a malicious madman, than of a reasonable being' (Wilmot's *Story of the Scottish Reformation*, p. 46). One, who could see how few modern readers could do justice to the Reformer in this, has said :—'Here more than elsewhere Knox proves himself—here more than anywhere bound to do it—the Hebrew Prophet in complete perfection; refuses to soften any expression or to call anything by its milder name, or in short for one moment to forget that the Eternal God and His Word are great, and that all else is little, or is nothing; nay, if it set itself against the Most High and His Word, is the one frightful thing that this world exhibits. He is never in the least ill-tempered with Her Majesty, but she cannot move him from that fixed centre of all his thoughts and actions' (Carlyle's *Portraits of Knox*).

[25] In David Laing's opinion, 'However plain-spoken Knox might be in their conferences, there never was any of that rude insolence on his part which it is so customary to allege' (Knox's *Works*, vi. p. xlvi). 'Considering the actual relations of the two parties,' says Dr. Hume Brown, 'it is absurd to speak of Knox as a coarse man of the people bullying a defenceless queen. The truth is, that if there was any attempt at browbeating it was on Mary's part, and not on that of Knox' (*John Knox: a Biography*, 1895, ii. 195, 196). One gifted authoress, after giving an interesting summary of their first discussion, says :—'Throughout the interview

Knox had been severely plain-spoken, but he had not been churlish'
(Mrs. Maccunn's *John Knox*, 1895, p. 120). Another, who has
been long and widely known, says of Mary :—'She held wonderful
conversations now and then with Knox, which I do not, for my
part, think at all so dreadful as many people have thought. I feel
sure that Mary was much amused by him at first, and that he had
to stand very firm, to "sit tight," as horsemen say, in order not to
be dazzled by her delightful ways' (Mrs. Oliphant's *Child's History
of Scotland*, 1895, p. 139. See also her *Royal Edinburgh*, 1890, pp.
296, 297, 307).

[26] Wright's *Elizabeth*, i. 72.—In his transcript of Randolph's
letter, Keith (ii. 80) reads 'six hundred trumpets.'

[27] Laing's *Knox*, ii. 277.

[28] Haynes's *State Papers*, 1740, p. 372 ; Laing's *Knox*, vi. 131.—
The Protestant Lords were much more tardy in acknowledging
their defection (Calderwood's *History*, ii. 571).

[29] Laing's *Knox*, ii. 277.

[30] From Randolph's letter of the 7th of September, it is certain
that Knox's interview with Mary was either on Tuesday, the 26th
of August, or Tuesday, the 2nd of September (Wright's *Elizabeth*,
i. 72, 73). On the latter of these Tuesdays she had left Holyrood
in the forenoon, dined in the Castle at noon, and then made her
triumphal entry into the capital (*Diurnal of Occurrents*, p. 67);
but at the close of her interview with Knox she 'was called upon
to dennar for it was after-noon' (Laing's *Knox*, ii. 286). The
'long conference,' therefore, must have been on the 26th of
August.

[31] *Foreign Calendar, Elizabeth*, iv. 297.

[32] Laing's *Knox*, ii. 273.—Mr. Skelton thinks that this Proclamation 'was probably drawn by Maitland,' and he credits him with
winning over Murray to his policy, of which this Proclamation
was the official declaration (*Maitland of Lethington*, ii. 17, 23).
'The significance,' of this Proclamation, he says, 'has not been
sufficiently appreciated, and its language deserves careful study'
(*Ibid.* ii. 23, 24). Yet Mr. Skelton has carefully refrained from
referring to the penalties attached to it. Was this because he had
said that Lethington 'certainly did not draw' the Act of 1560
concerning the mass (*Ibid.* i. 265)—an Act whose penalties were
'preposterous' (*Mary Stuart*, 1893, p. 46)? Were the penalties
threatened in this Proclamation less severe or less preposterous?

By the Act of 1560, it was only the third offence which was punishable by death. But the first breach of the Proclamation was to be so punished ; and that penalty was to be inflicted not only on those who attempted privately or openly to innovate on the state or form of the religion standing at Mary's arrival, but on any one who troubled any of her French domestics in word or deed for any cause! Yet apparently in Mr. Skelton's opinion this Proclamation is a notable example of wisdom and moderation !

[33] According to the *Diurnal of Occurrents* (p. 69), she left Edinburgh on the 11th of September; according to Randolph (*Foreign Calendar, Elizabeth,* iv. 296, 297), on the 10th.   One of her letters to Charles the Ninth bears to have been written at Edinburgh on the 11th (Labanoff's *Recueil,* i. 109).

[34] Keith's *History,* ii. 85.—Randolph adds :—'Such as speak much of prophesies say that this is now fulfilled that of old hath been spoken, that a Queen should be burnt at Stirling.' Knox remarks that 'fyre followed hir verray commounlie in that jorney' (Laing's *Knox,* ii. 287).

[35] Keith's *History,* ii. 85, 86.

[36] *Diurnal of Occurrents,* p. 69 ; Keith's *History,* ii. 86.

[37] *Diurnal of Occurrents,* p. 69 ; *Council Register of Aberdeen,* Spalding Club, i. 339 ; Maxwell's *History of Old Dundee,* 1884, p. 187.—Even so late as 1732 an English traveller found that 'Dundee . . . altogether neglects the being tolerably clean ; for needs must I say that many places in this kingdom are nasty enough, but this exceedeth them all' (Loveday's *Diary of a Tour,* Roxburghe Club, p. 135).

[38] Keith's *History,* ii. 86.

[39] Laing's *Knox,* ii. 287.

[40] *Ibid.* vi. 130.

[41] *Diurnal of Occurrents,* p. 69.

[42] *Records of the Burgh of Edinburgh,* Burgh Records Society, 1557-1571, p. 125.—On the 20th of September 1560, the municipal rulers of Edinburgh had ordained that the Act of Parliament— barely a month old—'anent the abolitioun of the messe' should be openly published that no one might pretend ignorance thereof (*Ibid.* pp. 82, 83). The unreformed clergy took occasion from this to spread the rumour that, although willing to hear the Protestant preachers, they durst not resort to Edinburgh. License was therefore freely granted to them, 'without impediment or ony kynde of

injurie, to resorte to the saidis sermonis, and thair place appointit, and all utheris forbidden to occupy the same.' As it was found, after three months' trial, that not only was there 'na signe nor apperance' of amendment, but on the contrary that they were trying 'to hald the sempill pepill in blindnes and errour,' the rigorous Proclamation was adopted on the 24th of March 'in our Soverane Ladeis name, and in name and behalf of the Lordis of Secreit Counsale,' as well as of the Provost and Bailies (*Ibid.* pp. 101, 102). When, on the 2nd of October, it was resolved to publish this Proclamation anew the time for removal was reduced from forty-eight to twenty-four hours. In the beginning of November it was expected that the magistrates would be restored, 'and the selfe same confirmed that theie were put out of their office for' (Wright's *Elizabeth*, i. 83).

[43] Laing's *Knox*, ii. 290.

[44] Wright's *Elizabeth*, i. 77.—This letter is wrongly dated 12th September. As Father Stevenson has pointed out, *September* is a clerical error for *October* (*Selections*, Maitland Club, p. 97). In his *Foreign Calendar*, however (*Elizabeth*, iv. 295 *n.*), it appears under the date of 12th September, without any hint of the clerical slip.

[45] Wright's *Elizabeth*, i. 83.—It was apparently this first highmass which provoked some to raise the question, Whether the Queen, being an idolatress, should be obeyed in civil matters: a proposition so startling to Randolph that he exclaimed :—' I thynke mervilously of the wysdome of God that gave thys unrulye, unconstant, and combersome people no more substance then thei have, for then wolde theie runne wilde' (*Ibid.* i. 82).

[46] Laing's *Knox*, ii. 291, 292, 423-461.—At the meeting in 1561 it was agreed to ask the opinion of the Church of Geneva. Knox offered to obtain this ; but Lethington—'alledging that thair stood mekle in the informatioun'—said that he would write. His offer, it was suspected, was only to gain time, for though Knox on more than one occasion asked him to fulfil his promise, he never did so ; and, in 1564, excused himself by saying that, as the Queen's secretary, he could not presume to seek the solution of a controversy between her and her subjects without her consent. At the close of the second discussion, Knox refused to write to Calvin and the learned men in other churches to obtain their judgment, on the plea that not only was he fully resolved in his own con-

science, but that he had already heard the opinions of 'the moist godlie and moist leirnit that be knawin in Europe.' He suggested, however, that his opponents should write complaining of his public teaching, and so discover the opinions of the Reformers. 'Diverse said the offer wes gude ; bot no man wes founde that wald be the secretour.' It is now known that Knox—though he does not say so in his *History*—did write to Calvin on this very point. His letter of the 24th of October 1561 is printed in Teulet's *Papiers D'État,* ii. 12-14 ; in his *Relations Politiques,* ii. 172, 173 ; and in Laing's *Knox,* vi. 133-135. One of the most impartial of Scottish historical students has said :—'It is not easy to reconcile this letter with what Knox tells us in his *History.* He not only conceals that he had written to Calvin, but he affirms that Secretary Maitland prevented him from writing' (*Inventories of Mary's Jewels,* p. lxxix n.). Here, however, Joseph Robertson has failed to attain his wonted accuracy. Knox does not say that Lethington prevented him from writing, but only that he prevented the others from appointing him to write. At the second discussion the Clerk Register alleged that, at the first, 'it wes concludit, that Mr. Knox sould *in all our names* haif writtin to Mr. Calvin for his jugement in the contraversie.' 'Nay,' was Knox's reply, 'my Lord Secretour wald nocht consent that I sould wrytte, alleging, that the grittest weycht of the ansuer stude in the narrative, and thairfoir he wald wryte, and I sould sey it' (Laing's *Knox,* ii. 292, 459). Knox's account seems to imply that the first discussion was held after the 1st of November 1561, whereas his letter to Calvin was written eight days before that date.

[47] The magistrates of Edinburgh did not confine the expression of their antipathy to the Papacy to proclamations against the mass. Before Mary had been a year in Scotland, they ordered 'the idole Sanct Geyll to be cuttit furth of the townys standert and the thrissil put in place thairof' (*Burgh Records of Edinburgh,* 1557-1571, p. 137).

[48] Several of the old clergy were charged, in 1563, with 'ministrand and abusand on thair pretendit maner, irreverentlie and indecentlie, the Sacramentis of Haly Kirk, namelie, the Sacramentis of the body and blood of our Lord Jesus Christ' (Pitcairn's *Criminal Trials,* i. 428 *). The indictment against the Primate was in similar terms (*Ibid.* i. 429 *).

[49] Laing's *Gude and Godlie Ballates,* p. 184.

[50] Laing's *Knox*, ii. 142, 143.

[51] *Ibid*. vi. 132, 135.

[52] *Ibid*. ii. 272; Calderwood's *History*, ii. 571.

[53] The Lord James hoped that the faithful subjection and good obedience of the Protestants would incline Mary to allow the doctrine of the Gospel and heartily to embrace the same (*Foreign Calendar, Elizabeth*, iv. 353). Lethington professed to see in her a good towardness, and to think that Elizabeth would be able to do much with her in religion if once they were familiar (*Ibid*. iv. 379). Both Randolph and Maitland believed that she would not give up the mass until she had spoken with Elizabeth 'that it might seem rather that she doth it on such reasons and perswasions as the Queen's Majestie will use unto her, than to be forced thereunto by her people' (Keith's *History*, ii. 117, 118). The Scotch Papists, too, believed that the proposed meeting of the Queens boded them no good; and stormed because they feared 'the mass and all' would be overthrown (*Ibid*. ii. 129). It was even reported that the Cardinal of Lorraine had advised his niece to embrace the religion of England—a rumour not particularly gratifying to the Scotch preachers, as they deemed the English Reformation far from perfect (*Foreign Calendar, Elizabeth*, iv. 512, 523). Mr. Skelton's statement, however, is too sweeping, when he asserts that Maitland ' expresses the utmost confidence that were the Queens to meet a religious accord might be brought about,' and that 'the wary Randolph' was 'quite as sanguine of a successful issue' (*Maitland of Lethington*, ii. 27). Mr. Skelton is still further from the mark when he says :—' "The Queen," Throckmorton wrote soon after her arrival, " quietly tolerates the Reformed Religion, who is thought to be no more devout towards Rome than for the contentation of her uncles." This was the common impression, and it appears to have been well grounded' (*Ibid*. ii. 30). Now, the letter here quoted by Mr. Skelton—notwithstanding his previous assertion (*Impeachment of Mary Stuart*, 1876, p. 146) and this reiteration—was not written, as he alleges, by Throckmorton, but by Cecil; and it was written not 'soon after,' but almost ten months ' after her arrival.' It was addressed to Challoner, the English Ambassador at the Spanish Court (*Foreign Calendar, Elizabeth*, v. 82), after Throckmorton, in his dread of the Spanish marriage, had desired Cecil so to work ' that it may appear that the Queen of Scots will become a Protestant' (*Ibid*. iv. 565). In the circumstances it may well be

doubted whether it reflects Cecil's real opinion; but there can be no doubt that it does not convey 'the common impression' of the time. Only nine days later, Randolph writes that he himself, the Lord James (then Earl of Mar) and many others lamented with their hearts that there was so little appearance of her being easily induced to alter her mind in religion (*Ibid.* v. 102). When she thought that she was dying in October 1566, she said :—' O moist mercifull Creator I confess that I have not usit thy giftis to the advancement of thy gloiry and honour and guid exemple of lyif to thi peple that hes been committit onder my charge ass I aucht to have don, bot I rather hes bien transportit be the fragilitie of my nature. . . . I have off dyvers tymis offendit thi devyne guidnes, bot yit have I na wayis declynit fra thy faith, bot still continuit and constantlie perseverit in the Catholique faith, in the quhilk I was instructit, brocht up and nurisit' (Small's *Queen Mary at Jedburgh,* 1881, p. 25).

54 See p. 258, *n.* 23.

65 Froude's *History of England,* 1887, vi. 510, 511.'

66 See Mr. Skelton's *Maitland of Lethington,* i. 304-307.—There one of Mary's most brilliant but most inconsistent apologists displays his usual inaccuracy and lack of judgment. In evidence of Mary's tolerant intentions, her famous statement to Throckmorton, two months before her return, is quoted of course.—' Weill,' quoth she, 'I will be plaine with you. The religione which I professe, I take to be most acceptable to God ; and indeed nather doe I know, or desire to know anie other. Constancie becometh all folks weill, but none better than Princes and such as have rule over realmes, and speciallie in maters of religione. . . . For my part, you may perceive that I am none of these that will change my religione every year; and as I told you in the beginning, I mean to constraine none of my subjects, but would wish that they were all as I am, and I trust they sould have no support to constraine me' (Keith's *History,* ii. 34 ; *Foreign Calendar, Elizabeth,* iv. 151, 152). There is doubtless a noble ring in Mary's words :— 'I mean to constraine none of my subjects'—but even on the supposition that they expressed her intention at the time, there is too much reason to suspect that it was only the intention of unavoidable necessity, not the spontaneous aspiration of the heart. She owned to Throckmorton that she feared her subjects would take in hand to give a law to her in matters of religion, hence her

anxiety that Elizabeth should not aid them in this, hence, too, perhaps, her readiness to promise toleration—a boon which she was too weak to withhold. Neither Lesley's proposal nor Huntly's power was put aside merely for the love of peace. There were other motives as powerful if less magnanimous (*supra*, p. 234, *n.* 29). Mr. Skelton, however, does not confine himself to Throckmorton's letter for quotations on this point. He gives one garbled extract from Knox, another from the *Register of the Privy Council*, and perverts a third from one of Cecil's letters. The last is worth looking at as an example of Mr. Skelton's ingenuity in manipulating State papers. Having given an extract in his text from Cecil's letter to Sussex concerning Mary's return, he appends the footnote :—' Cecil to Sussex, 21st Aug. 1561. He adds, referring to Elizabeth, "I saw small disposition here to be at any new charge, for that there appeared so hard fruit of the former."' Any one would infer from this that Elizabeth's reluctance to incur more expense was connected with Scotland ; and this conclusion would be the more readily arrived at, as, in his text, Mr. Skelton had previously expressed the opinion that ' Elizabeth would hardly have cared to interpose at the moment [of Mary's return]—the French being now fairly out of the country, and her previous venture having been attended, as she thought, with such indifferent success.' Yet the extract from Cecil's letter has no reference whatever to Scotland, but to the troubles in Ireland, where Sussex was deputy. Mr. Skelton, as is his wont, gives no suggestion as to where the letter may be found ; but it is printed in Wright's *Elizabeth*, i. 70, 71.

[57] ' Knox was the foremost of the Reformers ; yet Mary had found that Knox was narrow-minded, superstitious, and fiercely intolerant—so narrow-minded, intolerant, and superstitious that he had no difficulty in believing that the orderly course of nature was interrupted because the Queen dined on wild fowl and danced till midnight. If this was Protestantism, she would have none of it. Nor can we blame her much ' (*Maitland of Lethington*, ii. 49). It is rather amusing to find the narrow-mindedness, the superstition, and the fierce intolerance of Knox singled out as the beacons which kept Mary off from Protestantism. In many respects were not her beloved uncles and her other French connections narrower-minded, more superstitious, and more fiercely intolerant than Knox? What had they ever done for the education of the body

of their people? Did they not believe in signs, in prognostications, in witchcraft? Did they not approve of wholesale slaughters and cruel tortures which Knox would have abhorred and denounced? Was Mary herself so very liberal-minded, so free from superstition, so gently tolerant, that she could afford to point the finger at the Reformer of Scotland? Of two things he was indeed fiercely intolerant—of the mass and of vice. It is needless to say that all her French friends gloried in the first of these, and more than one revelled in the other. Knox's objection to the mass was twofold. He held that it was, in the first place, unscriptural and idolatrous in itself; and, in the second place, an incentive to vice. Mr. Skelton has specially indicated wherein Knox's great faults were most conspicuous and unreasonable—he was ' so narrow-minded, intolerant, and superstitious that he had no difficulty in believing that the orderly course of nature was interrupted because the Queen dined on wild fowl and danced till midnight.' But this is not Knox's presentation of the case—it is only Mr. Skelton's caricature—and not even in any sense a clever caricature. Knox objected to no one—neither prince nor beggar—dining on fowls either wild or tame; but it is true that, although he did not disapprove entirely of dancing, he did object to the indulgence of that pastime on unseemly occasions and at untimely hours. From the extracts, however, which Mr. Skelton has given (ii. 48, 49) in his usual mangled fashion from Knox's *History*, it is plain enough— from Knox's own pages it is still plainer—that in his opinion the frost and famine were sent for sins more serious than dining on wild fowl and dancing at midnight. In dealing with the Reformation, Mr. Skelton does not by any means confine his misrepresentations to Knox. Of the *Confession of Faith*—the *Confession* of 1560, commended by Archdeacon Hardwick, extolled by Edward Irving —he says, 'It hung together with logical tenacity,' and as 'the conclusion' at which its compilers arrived, he quotes the words :— ' And therefore we utterly abhor the blasphemy of them that affirm that men who live according to equity and justice shall be saved' (*Maitland of Lethington*, ii. 20). A startling proposition as thus given, but Mr. Skelton has stopped short without finishing the sentence—'what religion soever they have professed.'

⁵⁸ Anderson's *Collections*, i. 4; *Venetian Calendar*, vii. 653.

⁵⁹ While in France she had with the Dauphin set forth to Paul the Fourth her mother's difficulties in Scotland, and entreated his

Holiness to take the requisite steps for establishing order, restoring the Roman Church, and suppressing false doctrine in a kingdom distracted by religious dissension (*Historical MSS. Commission, Ninth Report*, app. part ii. p. 416). In May 1560, Francis and she, as King and Queen of Scots, made by an Ambassador their allegiance to Pius the Fourth, who, by his Ambassador, on the 17th of the following August, presented with the usual ceremony the Golden Rose to the young Queen of France, whom he regarded as 'a most fair rose among thorns [of heresy], diffusing far and wide the most fragrant odour of faith and good works' (Robertson's *Statuta*, vol. i. pp. clxiv, clxv, and notes; *Foreign Calendar, Elizabeth*, iii. 252). Before she had been five months in Scotland, she wrote to the Pope that she would rather die than abandon her religion (*Spanish Calendar, Elizabeth*, i. 222). When hard pressed she owned her inability to defend the doctrine of the mass; but alleged that she knew what she ought to believe (*Foreign Calendar, Elizabeth*, iv. 152; Laing's *Knox*, ii. 285; Keith's *History*, ii. 96). On the 24th of July 1562—eleven months after her return—Mary had a secret interview with Nicolas de Gouda, a Papal Legate. His report has been edited by Father Forbes-Leith, who confounds his visit with that of Morette, the Ambassador from Savoy, in the previous December. In giving 'the substance of her reply' to his message and to the Pope's brief, De Gouda says :—'She hoped the Supreme Pontiff would have regard to her ready will rather than to anything she had actually done since her return, and much wished that his Holiness could have seen the condition in which she found her kingdom. She herself, and the other adherents of the orthodox religion, had been obliged to do many things which they did not like, in order to preserve the last traces of the Catholic faith and worship in the country. . . . For herself, she would rather forfeit her life than abandon her faith' (*Narratives of Scottish Catholics*, 1885, pp. 66, 67). That De Gouda did not misrepresent her is proved by her own letter to Pius the Fourth, written from Edinburgh on the last day of the following January: —'It being ever our intention, since our return to this kingdom, to employ, as we have done, our studies, thoughts, labour, and manners, such as it has pleased God to give us, in bringing back to the truth our poor subjects, whom we have with the greatest displeasure found to have wandered from the good path, and to be plunged in the new opinions and damnable errors which are now prevalent in many places of Christendom.' She also expressed the hope that all her subjects would yet 'worthily acknowledge the holy Roman Catholic Church, in the obedience of which we desire to live your most devoted daughter. To which end we shall spare no effort in our power, even life itself if need be' (Turnbull's *Mary's Letters*, 1845, pp. 142, 143; Labanoff's *Recueil*, i. 177, 178). Six weeks later she wrote to the Council of Trent lamenting her inability to send representatives to that Synod, and commissioning her uncle, the Cardinal of Lorraine, to explain her helplessness. 'The Queen's letter, the Cardinal's speech, were received with every mark of respect; and the Synod, by the mouth of its prolocutor, declared its conviction that the name of Mary of Scotland would be had in everlasting remembrance as the name of a sovereign prepared to suffer the loss of all, even of life itself, for the faith' (*Ibid.* i. 179, 180; Robertson's *Statuta*, i. pp. clxvi, clxvii). Perhaps the Duke of Parma's standard—'implicit belief cannot be given to all that is said by a great prince' (*Venetian Calendar*, vii. 63)—should be applied to Mary's oral statements and letters; but if the Pope and the Council of Trent held, like Mr. Skelton (*Mary Stuart*, 1893, p. 33), that one of her distinguishing characteristics was a 'fine natural sincerity and directness,' they could hardly fail to understand from her words that she had gone back to Scotland 'with a purpose fixed as the stars' to undo—if not 'to trample down'—the Reformation as best she could. Yet in spite of Mary's own words, and her 'fine natural sincerity and directness,' Mr. Skelton calmly affirms that 'there is no proof whatever that she was devoted to Rome' (*Impeachment of Mary Stuart*, 1876, p. 145).

[60] Laing's *Knox*, ii. 264.—'None within the realme durst more avow the hearing or saying of messe then the theavis of Lyddesdaill durst avow thair stowth in presence of ane upryght judge' (*Ibid.* ii. 265).

[61] *De Rebus Gestis Scotorum*, 1675, p. 537.—As one of the hardships to which Scotch Papists were subjected, Lesley mentions, '*ut pro baptismo salutis aquam nescio quam typicam . . . sufficiant*' (*Ibid.* pp. 536, 537), which Father Dalrymple—mistaking *typicam* for *tepidam*—renders, 'for the baptisme of thair salvatioune to receive water I wat not how lue warme' (Dalrymple's *Lesley*, ii. 462).

[62] Keith's *History*, ii. 118; Laing's *Knox*, ii. 292, 293; Aikman's *Buchanan*, ii. 449.

[63] The first of this series of riots occurred in the previous November, when a flesher—who for adultery had been sentenced to be carted through the town and afterwards banished—was forcibly released from ward, the cart broken, and the officers threatened. 'Certane young fallowis, craftismennis servandis,' were the leaders of this riot; but the deacons and masters of crafts, while disclaiming and condemning the outrage, urged the release of the four offenders who were imprisoned in the Castle (Laing's *Knox*, ii. 155, 156; *Records of the Burgh of Edinburgh*, 1557-1571, pp. 89-95). The second riot occurred on Sabbath, the 11th of May, when, in defiance of the Act of Parliament passed by Mary of Guise and the Estates in 1555 (*Acts of Parliament*, ii. 500), in defiance of the special proclamation of the Edinburgh Town Council (*Records of the Burgh of Edinburgh*, 1557-1571, pp. 107, 108), 'the raschall multitude war stirred up to mak a Robene Hude'; and the third and most serious riot occurred on Monday, the 21st of July (Laing's *Knox*, ii. 157-160, 269, 270; *Diurnal of Occurrents*, pp. 65, 66, 283-285; *Records of the Burgh of Edinburgh*, 1557-1571, pp. 107, 108, 112, 113, 116-119; Pitcairn's *Criminal Trials*, i. 409*, 410*). The first riot seems to have been on the 23rd of November. The third was caused by the attempt to inflict punishment for the second. It has been asserted that the cordiner, who was rescued from the gallows, had been condemned merely for taking part in the prohibited play of Robin Hood (Chambers's *Domestic Annals*, 1874, i. 9; Mrs. Oliphant's *Royal Edinburgh*, 1890, pp. 292, 294), whereas he had taken the chief part in a robbery. It is quite evident that the play of Robin Hood had become rather realistic; and robbery, until recent times, was in Scotland punishable by death.

[64] *Records of the Burgh of Edinburgh*, 1557-1571, p. 114.

[65] After the three noble lords succeeded in breaking open Cuthbert Ramsay's 'yettis and durris,' they searched his house for his daughter-in-law, Alison Craik, 'as appeared to oppresse hyr.' According to Knox, this 'was done in dispyte of the Earle of Arran, whose hoore the said Alison was suspected to have been.' According to Randolph, she was 'a good handsome wench, a merchant's daughter,' with whom Arran was 'known to have had company.' D'Elbœuf, he says, hearing of this woman desired to see her; and, accompanied with Bothwell, and Lord John, 'in a mask,' was admitted into the house the first night; but refused the second—hence the outrage. Mary's sharp condemnation did not

deter Bothwell and the Lord John from threatening to repeat the offence next night in spite of any friend to that house. This being interpreted as a defiance of the Hamiltons, the Duke's servants congregated in the market-place with jack and spear. Bothwell gathered his friends about him. Both parties increased. The townsmen were assembled by the common-bell. D'Elbœuf seized a halberd, and was so eager for the fray that ten men were 'skarse able to hald him'; but he was within the gates of Holyrood, 'and the danger was betwix the Croce and the Salt Trone.' There was every appearance of a fierce contest when Huntly, Argyll, and the Lord James, hastening from the Court, ordered all to depart on pain of death. 'Within half an hour after,' says an eye-witness, 'there was never a man seen, so that of so likely a matter of evil, I never saw less hurt' (Laing's *Knox*, ii. 315-321 ; Keith's *History*, ii. 129, 130 ; *Diurnal of Occurrents*, p. 70 ; *Booke of the Universall Kirk*, i. 11, 12).

[66] Keith's *History*, ii. 115-117, 125 ; *Foreign Calendar, Elizabeth*, iv. 410, 473 ; Laing's *Knox*, ii. 293, 294 ; Aikman's *Buchanan*, ii. 450, 451 ; Calderwood's *History*, ii. 158 ; Spottiswoode's *History*, ii. 15, 16.—David Laing points out that, in two of the MS. copies of Knox's *History*, the passage concerning this episode has been 'amplified in the style of David Buchanan's interpolations.' The extra matter has been drawn from George Buchanan's *History*. By a clerical or typical slip, Hill Burton (iv. 83) says that the sudden alarm of the Court occurred on a 'summer night,' whereas it was on the 16th of November. Trusting entirely to the passage in Randolph's letter of 7th December—bearing that, by appointment, 'every lord that lodgeth within the Court should watch his night about with jack and spear'—Keith says :—'This is far from levying men to serve as a *continual* Body Guard, according as our writers would fain make the world believe.' The native historians, however, were not so very far amiss. A small body-guard was organised, of which James Stewart was captain (*Foreign Calendar, Elizabeth*, iv. 431, 473 ; *Diurnal of Occurrents*, p. 72). The number of Mary's archer-guard was not completed until the 1st of April 1562 (*Maitland Miscellany*, i. 27-36). Buchanan alleges that the alarm was simply a contrivance to excuse the establishment of a body-guard. From one of Randolph's letters, it appears that there was a design very soon after her arrival to have such a guard, with James Stewart as captain (Wright's *Elizabeth*, i. 74).

[67] Laing's *Knox*, ii. 322-330; Aikman's *Buchanan*, ii. 454-456; *Diurnal of Occurrents*, pp. 71, 72; *Foreign Calendar, Elizabeth*, iv. 575, 576, 583-586, 592-594, 628-631.—After revealing the alleged plot by letters from his father's house at Kinneil, Arran escaped by a window, descending 'about thirty fathoms' by cords made of his sheets and blankets, and walked alone, in his doublet and hose, to the Laird of Grange's house in Fife, desiring to be taken to the Queen. When brought to the Court 'he became stark mad,' entering into 'so many vain purposes of devils, of witches, of murder, and the like' that all men judged him to be beside himself. He named the Lord James's mother as one of the witches who had deluded him. It was said that he had twice before been out of his wits, that he took this weakness from his mother, who, with both her sisters, was for 'most part of the year distempered with an unquiet humour.' The tears trickling down the cheeks of his father, as if he had been a beaten child, drew the pity of the Queen and of many others; but as advised he agreed to give up to her the Castle of Dumbarton.

[68] Keith's *History*, ii. 119, 120.

[69] Randolph says that De Foix, the French Ambassador, 'came not unto the dirige or mass upon Friday and Saturday last, to the great mis-liking of the Queen. Moret was there at both. . . . She could not perswade nor get one lord of her own to wear the deule for that day, nor so much as the Earl Bothwell' (Keith's *History*, ii. 122). 'On Saturday last she solemnly celebrated the exequies of her husband, at which M. Moret assisted; of the nobles of Scotland none wore the dueil. The Earl of Huntly came the morrow after the feast' (*Foreign Calendar, Elizabeth*, iv. 435).

[70] Keith's *History*, ii. 123, 125.

[71] Keith's *History*, ii. 121; *Foreign Calendar, Elizabeth*, iv. 435. —Perhaps the mixture of mirth and woe was partly due to the close proximity of the anniversaries of her own birth and her husband's death.

[72] *Records of the Burgh of Edinburgh*, 1557-1571, p. 107.

[73] On the 29th of December 1563, the treasurer of Edinburgh was ordered to buy 'thre tun of the best wyne can be gottin in Leyth, togidder with xx li. [*i.e.* £20] worth of torches to be propynit to the Quenis Grace' (*Records of the Burgh of Edinburgh*, 1557-1571, p. 175). On the 2nd of January 1564-5, the treasurer was ordered 'to pas to Leyth and serche and seik quhair best

wynis may be gottin, and by thre tunnys thairof to be gevin to the Quenys Majestie, quhatevir the samyn cost' (*Ibid.* p. 193). And on the 4th of December 1565, the treasurer was ordered to buy 'for the King and Quenis Majestie, agane Yule, thre tun of the best new wynis with torches and prikettis [*i.e.* wax-tapers] efter the auld ordour' (*Ibid.* p. 210). Her mother had been the recipient of a similar yearly gift (*Ibid.* pp. 26, 60).

[74] *Foreign Calendar, Elizabeth,* iv. 630.

[75] Melville's *Memoirs,* Mait. Club, p. 124; Buchanan's *Detection,* in Anderson's *Collections,* ii. 7; Aikman's *Buchanan,* ii. 465; Forbes-Leith's *Narratives of Scottish Catholics,* p. 92; Laing's *Knox.* ii. 391; Pitcairn's *Criminal Trials,* i. 463*; Robertson's *Inventories,* pp. lxix, lxx; *Foreign Calendar, Elizabeth,* vi. 195, 260.

[76] *Supra,* p. 152.

[77] On the 24th of October 1561, Randolph writes:—'I was sent for into the Council Chamber, where she herself ordinarily sitteth the most part of the time, sowing some work or other' (Keith's *History,* ii. 96). Mary did not do all her own embroidery. On the 24th of March 1565-6, 'oure Soveranis dailie servitoure Pier Veray, thair brodster,' received for all the days of his life 'the office of the clerkschip of thair Majesteis coquet and custumes of Edinburght,' which office pertained to Patrick Bellenden—brother of the Justice-Clerk—then a fugitive for the slaughter of Riccio (*Register of Privy Seal,* xxxiv. 60).

[78] On the 30th of January 1561-2, Randolph informs Cecil that 'there is with the Queen one called Mr. George Buchanan, a Scottish man very well learned, who was schoolmaster to M. De Brisac's son, very godly and honest, whom I have always judged fitter [to be the resident Scots Ambassador at the English Court] than any other that I know' (*Foreign Calendar, Elizabeth,* iv. 513); and on the 7th of the following April he further says:—'She readeth daily after her dinner, instructed by a learned man, Mr. George Buchanan, somewhat of Livy' (*Ibid.* iv. 584). She did not, however, confine her reading to Latin. Sir James Melville told Elizabeth that 'sche red upon gud bukis the histories of dyvers contrees' (Melville's *Memoirs,* Mait. Club, p. 124). The names and nature of her books may be learned from Thomson's *Inventories,* 1815, pp. 242-248; *Maitland Miscellany,* i. 3-12; Robertson's *Inventories,* pp. cii-cxviii, cxliii-cxlvii, 179-183; and Sharman's *Library of Mary Queen of Scots,* published in 1889. Mary's love of learning was

not altogether selfish. On the 21st of July 1564, she granted for life a yearly pension of £100 Scots to 'Maister James Quhyte,' who had 'bestowit the yeiris of his aige bigane to the studie of gude letteres,' and was 'myndit to wair the rest of his liffe thairto.' His pension was designed 'to help his gude purpois in that behalf, to gif occasioun to utheris to gif laubouris to follow knawlege of liberall professioun, and to reporte just reward thairfore of hir Grace's liberalitie' (*Register of Privy Seal*, xxxii. 87).

[79] For the testimony of Conaeus to Mary's musical attainments, see *supra*, p. 202, *n.* 20. Sir James Melville affirmed that she 'somtymes wald play upon lut and virginelis'; and that she played 'raisonably [weill] for a Quen,' but not so well as Elizabeth (Melville's *Memoirs*, pp. 124, 125). In her Inventories stands the entry:—'Thre buikis of Musik.' In the passage quoted in the next note, Knox speaks somewhat disrespectfully of her fiddlers; and as is well known he did not esteem Riccio. Nevertheless, Mary's musicians did not always pander to her desires. They refused—both Scotch and French—'to play and sing at her mass and evensong on Christmas-day,' 1562 (*Foreign Calendar, Elizabeth,* v. 605).

[80] In presence of her Council, says Knox, Mary kept herself very grave, 'but how soon that ever hir Frenche fillockis, fydlaris, and others of that band, gatt the howse allone, thair mycht be sean skipping not verry cumlie for honest wemen.' In private she commonly said that 'sche saw nothing in Scotland but gravitie, which repugned alltogetther to hir nature, for sche was brocht up in joyusitie; so termed sche hir dansing, and other thingis thairto belonging' (Laing's *Knox*, ii. 294). The Queen's 'dansing of the Purpose' was specially distasteful to Knox, being, in his opinion, 'more lyke to the bordell than to the comelynes of honest wemen' (*Ibid.* ii. 368). 'Dancing was in those days,' says Mrs. Oliphant, 'the most decorous of performances: but if Mary had been proved to have danced a stately *pas seul* in a minuet, it was to Knox, who knew no better, as if she had indulged in the wildest bobbing of a country fair—nay, he would probably have thought the high-skipping rural performer by far the more innocent of the two' (*Royal Edinburgh*, 1890, pp. 298, 299). Sir James Melville expressly testifies that Mary 'dancit not sa hich and disposedly' as Elizabeth (*Memoirs*, p. 125); and Conaeus, that she danced 'gracefully and becomingly,' and that the motion of her

limbs was ' quiet and gentle' (*supra*, p. 203). Hill Burton's opinion
of the dancing of that period is somewhat different from Mrs.
Oliphant's:—'It must be remembered that in that age the dance
had often a meaning beyond the mere graceful cadenced exercise.
The forms of the dance were often symbolical of interesting situa-
tions; and of how far these were delicate or decorous, we may
judge by the books, such as those of Brantôme and Margaret of
Navarre, which were the favourite literature of the dancers' (*History
of Scotland*, iv. 57, 58). In Petrus de Witte's *Catechizing upon the
Heidelberg Catechism*, dancing is forbidden as a breach of the seventh
commandment, and the statement made :—' One asked, *What is a
round dance?* and himself answered, *a circle whose center is the devil,
and the circumference his angels.*' But this pastime was not condemned of old merely by rigid Reformers and stern Protestants.
The last Primate of the pre-Reformation Church of Scotland cannot
be justly accused of straitlaced morality or other Protestant fail-
ings, yet he too includes dancing among the breaches of the third
commandment of the second table (Hamilton's *Catechism*, 1884,
p. 91). Never was Knox so displeased with Mary's dancing as in
December 1562, when it was shown to him that she ' had daunced
excessivelie till after mydnycht, becaus that sche had receaved
letteris that persecutioun was begun agane in France, and that hir
uncles war begyning to steir thair taill, and to truble the hoill
realme of France.' It was the sermon which he preached on this
occasion that led to his second interview with the irate Queen.
She received him in her bed-room. Besides her ladies, her servants, and some of her guard, the Lord James, Morton, and
Lethington were present. Knox repeated to her what he had said
in his sermon, that he did not utterly condemn dancing provided
(1) the principal vocation of those using that exercise was not
neglected, and (2) that they danced not as the Philistines did for
the pleasure they took in the displeasure of God's people. If
guilty in either respect, they should, he said, ' receave the reward
of dansaris, and that will be drynk in hell, onless thai spedilie
repent' (Laing's *Knox*, ii. 330–335). The phrase ' drynk in hell'
probably refers to an old custom indicated in a musical MS. :—
'The tune is to be played even through once over every time: so
the first couple has time to take their drink' (Dauney's *Ancient
Scottish Melodies*, Bann. Club, p. 260). Mr. Skelton does not eluci-
date the phrase by making it 'drunk in hell' (*Maitland of Lethington*,

ii. 39). Ere Mary had been imprisoned more than a month in Loch-leven it was reported that she had resumed her dancing (*Foreign Calendar, Elizabeth,* viii. 287).

[81] On the 30th of November 1565, Mary's treasurer, by her special command, handed £50 to 'ane of the virlottis of hir Grace chalmer to gif hir Majestie to play at the cartis' (Robertson's *Inventories,* p. lxxi, *n.* 2). On the 25th of the following December Randolph says that Darnley 'never gave greater token of his religion than that this last night he was at matins, and mass in the morning before day, and heard high mass devoutly upon his knees; though she herself [*i.e.* Mary] the most part of the night sat up at cards, and went to bed when it was almost day' (*Foreign Calendar, Elizabeth,* vii. 541). In justification of his conduct on the evening of Riccio's murder, Darnley accused Mary of usually sitting with the Italian at cards until one or two o'clock in the morning (Ruthven's *Relation,* 1699, p. 30). Her cards helped also to beguile the weary hours in Lochleven (*Foreign Calendar, Elizabeth,* viii. 287).

[82] In the Lent of 1565, Mary and Darnley—then unmarried—played 'biles' against Mary Beaton and Randolph. The latter won. Darnley paid the loss, and gave a ring and a brooch with two agates worth fifty crowns (*Foreign Calendar, Elizabeth,* vii. 329).

[83] On the evening of Sabbath, the 22nd October 1564, Mary 'danced long, and in a mask; and playing at dice lost Lennox a jewel of crystal set in gold' (*Foreign Calendar, Elizabeth,* vii. 230).

[84] Thomson's *Inventories,* 1815, pp. 238, 240, 241.

[85] Thomson's *Inventories,* pp. 238, 240; Robertson's *Inventories,* p. 139.

[86] In his careful and elaborate account of Mary's masques, Joseph Robertson has also referred to a number of her banquets (*Inventories,* pp. lxxii-lxxxix). That Mary enjoyed the banquets is shown by such incidents as the following. On the 1st of March 1564-5, Murray entertained Lennox and Darnley, most of the nobles and the ladies of the Court to dinner. 'The Queen sent word that she wished herself in the company, and was sorry that she was not bid to the banquet. It was answered that she might come undesired. Others said they were merriest when the table was fullest, but princes did ever use to dine alone. She sent word again that she summoned them all against Sunday to be at a banquet at the marriage of her Englishman [*i.e.* Lord Semple's son, who

was to marry Mary Livingstone]. After dinner they all came to her' (*Foreign Calendar, Elizabeth*, vii. 308, 309). It was for a banquet that she took pledges from the men in the streets of Stirling (*Infra*, p. 278, *n.* 89). The motives prompting the banquets were sometimes misunderstood. After recovering from her illness in the winter of 1563-4, 'she determined to pass her time in mirth and such pastimes as were most agreeable for that time approaching unto Shrovetide.' She accordingly sent for most of her nobles, and on Sabbath, the 13th of February, made them such a banquet that no Scotsman could remember anything like it, save at the marriage of a prince; and those of the next two days were little inferior (*Foreign Calendar, Elizabeth*, vii. 48). Nothing was left undone 'that might either fill their bellies, feed their eyes, or content their minds'; yet 'it passes almost the wit of man to think' what devilish devices were suspected. Some feared that while they piped and danced, their enemies would land and cut their throats; others were afraid of what might lurk among the dishes. The rumour that many ships were coming from France confirmed them in the opinion 'that no good was intended to the Protestants, nor amity to be kept with England.' The unjust suspicions were perhaps raised by the remembrance that her mother had given banquets at the same season of the year, 'a little before she went about to suppress God's Word' (*Ibid.* vii. 56).

[87] In his letter to Dudley, on the 15th of January 1563-4, Randolph gives a glowing account of the celebration of the Twelfth Day at the Scotch Court, when Mary Fleming was Queen of the Bean. 'My pen staggereth,' he says, 'my hand faileth, farther to wryt. . . . I never found myselfe so happy, nor never so well treated' (*Maitland Miscellany*, ii. 390-392). He also refers to 'this solemnity' in his letter to Cecil (*Foreign Calendar, Elizabeth*, vii. 13).

[88] 'Such styncken pryde of wemen as was sein at that Parliament'—the Parliament of 1563, at which Huntly's corpse was condemned—'was never sein befoir in Scotland. Thre syndrie dayis the Quene raid to the Tolbuyth. The first day sche maid a paynted orisoun; and thair mycht have bene hard among hir flatteraris, "*Vox Dianæ!* The voce of a goddess (for it could not be *Dei*) and not of a woman! God save that sweat face! Was thair ever oratour spack so properlie and so sweitlie!" All thingis mislyking the Preachearis, thei spack boldlie against the tarejatting

of thair taillies, and against the rest of thair vanitie, which thei
affirmed should provock Goddis vengeance, not onlie against those
foolishe women, but against the hoill realme; and especiallie
against those that manteaned thame in that odiouse abusing of
thingis that mycht have bene better bestowed' (Laing's *Knox*,
ii. 381).   See Additional Note, *infra*, p. 490.

[89] In Stirling, on Easter Monday 1565, ' she [*i.e.* Mary] and divers
of her women apparelled themselves like burgesses' wives, went
upon their feet up and down the town, and of every man they met
they took some pledge for money towards the banquet ; and in the
lodging where the writer [*i.e.* Randolph] was accustomed to lodge
was the dinner prepared, at which she was herself, with the wonder
and gazing of men, women, and children' (*Foreign Calendar*,
Elizabeth, vii. 348).   In Edinburgh, barely three weeks before
their marriage, ' she and my Lord Darlye walked up and downe
the towne disguysed untyll supper time'; and, indulging in a
similar performance next day, made 'men's tonges to chatter faste'
(Stevenson's *Selections*, pp. 119, 120).   A month before Riccio's
murder, the Queen, her Maries, and ladies ' wer all cled in men's
apperrell' at the masque in honour of Rambouillet, who had
brought the Order of the Cockle for Darnley (*Diurnal of Occurrents*,
p. 87).

[90] For an account of these jewels, dresses and furniture, see
Joseph Robertson's *Inventories*, pp. ix-xxii, 3-43.—The Golden
Rose which Robertson was there (p. xvii) inclined to identify as
the one presented by Pope Alexander the Sixth to King James
the Fourth was in reality—as mentioned in his subsequent work
(*Statuta*, vol. i. pp. clxv, clxvi)—the one which Mary herself had
received from Pius the Fourth.   According to Buchanan, when
Mary was arranging in France for her return to Scotland, her
uncle the Cardinal, ' not inattentive to private advantage, advised
the Queen to leave with him her royal furniture and costly wardrobe, as she was about to pass as it were into another world, until
she ascertained the issue of her voyage.   Mary, who well knew the
disposition of the man, understood the hint, and replied, when she
ventured upon danger she did not see why she should take greater
care of her wealth than of her person' (Aikman's *Buchanan*, ii. 439).
Calderwood, who follows Buchanan in this matter, tells, however,
that ' her tapistrie and other stuffe '—or as Keith (ii. 63) calls it,
' the hangings and other furniture of her house '—did not arrive

until October (Calderwood's *History*, ii. 131, 142). And more than two years afterwards there was still 'some stuff of hers . . . to be transported for her own use, which her ministers in France have stayed a long time for fear of danger by sea' (*Foreign Calendar, Elizabeth*, vi. 594; Labanoff's *Recueil*, i. 187, 188, 192-194).

[91] Holyrood was not without its gardens. On the 1st of August 1562, 'Johnñe Morisoun' was appointed 'gardinare and keipar of oure Soverane Ladeis yairdis on the south syde of hir Palice of Halirudhous . . . for all the dayis of his liffe, quhilk office the said Johnne usit and bruikit of before,' his yearly salary being fifty merks Scots and twenty six bolls of meal (*Register of Privy Seal*, xxxi. 32). Mary's father and grandfather had kept a French gardener (Robertson's *Inventories*, p. lxii *n.*).

[92] *Supra*, p. 207, *n.* 28.

[93] More than one of Mary's contemporaries refers to the 'corrupt air' of Paris (*Foreign Calendar, Elizabeth*, iv. 173 ; viii. 413). Bad as Edinburgh and Paris were, they could be eclipsed. England, in Sir Philip Hoby's opinion, possessed 'a stinking city, the filthiest of the world' (*Hatfield Calendar*, i. 139).

[94] Laing's *Dunbar*, 1834, i. 97, 98.

[95] For regulations concerning the 'middens' and offensive trades, see *Burgh Records of Edinburgh*, 1557-1571, pp. 17, 18, 61, 86, 222. In the immediate neighbourhood of St. Giles there was a passage bearing the suggestive name of 'the Stynkand Styll' (*Ibid.* p. 66), and the name, it appears, was only too applicable (Laing's *Dunbar*, ii. 286). One of the entries to the church—the entry known as the Lady Steps—could not be used because it was so 'commonlie abusit with filth, and the samin sa odious' (*Burgh Records of Edinburgh*, 1557-1571, p. 173); and the doors of the church itself had to be kept locked—save at the hours of service— to prevent the seats and benches being polluted by the 'bairnyis and utheris ungodlie pepill' (*Ibid.* p. 97). This open contempt for the church and its precincts was unrestrained even in the presence of the Lords of Session (*Ibid.* p. 189). From the regulations for cleansing the 'scheildis' and 'closettis' (*Ibid.* p. 222), it may be safely inferred that they were the constant causes of intolerable nuisances. With its lofty houses, innumerable gables, and forestairs, the Edinburgh of those days must have been strikingly picturesque ; but the densely packed population must have endured many discomforts.

⁹⁶ 'She has still a great mis-liking to this town' (*Foreign Calendar, Elizabeth*, vii. 73). 'The Quens Majestie remanes at St. Johnston [*i.e.* Perth], as I heare, yit eight dayes, yea, and per-chaunce longar,' writes Knox, on the 3rd of May 1564, 'as for Edinburgh, it lykes the ladeis nothing' (Laing's *Knox*, vi. 541).

⁹⁷ Robertson's *Inventories*, pp. lxvii-lxix, clx.—Robertson was misled (*Ibid.* p. lxvii, *n.* 6) by the abstract of Randolph's letter of 13th June 1563, printed in Keith's *History* (ii. 201). Mary neither made, nor caused to be made, 'her Highland apparel for her journey into Argile.' Hers, which was 'marvellously fair,' was presented to her by James Macconel's wife. Randolph had 'framed himself as near as he could in outer shape to have been like unto the rest'; but was better pleased to return to England than to go to Argyll 'in a saffron shirt or an Highland plaid' (*Foreign Calendar, Elizabeth*, vi. 399). The saffron was 'for avoiding of that evil which cometh by much sweating, and long wearing of linen' (*Lives and Letters of the Devereux*, 1853, i. 23).

⁹⁸ When puzzled by Mary's appointment of Robert Melville as her Ambassador to England, Bedford could only explain it by saying:—'Scottes be and will be Scottes for their owne matters' (Stevenson's *Selections*, p. 158).

⁹⁹ When the Borderers on either side of the March were com-pelled by the Wardens to restore the cattle they had stolen, they frequently so maimed them that they were of little value to the poor owner, who nevertheless by the custom of the March was bound to receive them. Lord Grey alleged that the thieves of Teviotdale used to steal horses and oxen from the English, in ploughing and harrowing time, to labour their ground ; and, when their turn was served, to restore the overlaboured animals by agreement, without consent of the Warden (*Foreign Calendar, Elizabeth*, iv. 12). For a still more unscrupulous practice, see *Ibid.* i. 47.

¹⁰⁰ Hill Burton's *Scot Abroad*, 1881, pp. 23-40.

¹⁰¹ The depredations of the Scotch pirates were not confined to their own seas. In 1558, Thomas Nicholson of Aberdeen and John Hog of Leith seized two English ships—valued at £2800 sterling—in the haven of Westmoney in Iceland, and carried them off, with their cargoes, boats, and anchors (*Foreign Calendar, Elizabeth*, iv. 177, 180, 183). The English agent in Antwerp, in announcing, in April 1559, that he had purchased munition and armour, recom-mended that Elizabeth should send three or four of her best ships

of war which were abroad, to act as a convoy, as three Scots ships of war were yet in Zealand (*Ibid.* i. 201). Among the reasons alleged by D'Assonville on Philip's behalf, why he should not make war between Scotland and his Low Countries, were:—(1) The notorious poverty of the Scots placed the balance of the chances of war in their favour, whereas success would be unproductive to the Low Countries. In proof of this, he instanced the war undertaken by the Emperor at the instigation of Henry VIII., during the progress of which, the Scotch, though frequently defeated, gained upon the whole infinitely more than they lost. (2) The geographical position would enable the small Scotch vessels to intercept without difficulty the ships which trade from the northern seas to the Low Countries, and the trade of the Netherlands would speedily be ruined. (3) The herring fishing off the coast of Scotland—so important for the greater part of Friesland, Holland, Zealand, and Flanders—would be annihilated; or, if carried on, would require the protection of an armed fleet (*Ibid.* i. 215). In April 1561, the Portuguese complained that their ships were seized by the Scots, and taken into English ports (*Ibid.* iv. 54, 55). That very month the *Lion* of Leith, though leaking badly, seized two Portuguese ships in the English Channel (*Ibid.* iv. 145). The crew did not, perhaps, consider themselves pirates, as they had letters of marque. At least one of their number—Edmund Blacater—may be identified as one of the 'famous robberis and pyrates' with whom, Buchanan says, Mary sailed from Newhaven to Alloa shortly after the birth of her son (Anderson's *Collections*, ii. 6). When, in the summer of 1565, the Spanish Ambassador complained to Elizabeth of 'the large number of pirates who still infested the sea, she said she believed many of them were Scotsmen who spoke in English to avoid being known' (*Spanish Calendar, Elizabeth*, i. 440).

[102] The oldest Scots vernacular song plaintively refers to the days

'Off wyne and wax, off gamyn and glé,'

which had prevailed in the time of Alexander the Third (Laing's *Wyntoun*, ii. 266). The wine and wax were not classed together merely for alliteration, but as the emblems of indoor mirth when the light of the shorter days had to be artificially extended (*Records of the Burgh of Edinburgh*, 1557-1571, *cf.* pp. 26, 210). Professor

Aytoun heads a note on the 'fanatical austerity of the Reformers' (*Bothwell: a Poem*, 1857, pp. 224-226), with his own couplet:

> ''Twas sin to smile, 'twas sin to laugh,
> 'Twas sin to sport or play.'

It is a fact, nevertheless, that all the Acts of the Scottish Parliament forbidding foot-ball, golf, and 'uthir sic unproffitable sportis,' were passed long before the Reformation, namely, in 1424, 1457-8, 1471 and 1491. The object of these Acts was to increase the fighting power of the realm by encouraging the more useful sport of archery (*Acts of Parliament*, ii. 5, 48, 100, 226). In one respect the Lords of Parliament were deplorably selfish. Though so anxious to encourage archery and wapinschaws, they sternly forbade the shooting 'at' deer, wild-beasts, or wild-fowl, under pain of death. As this law was so frequently broken that 'the nobill men of the realme can get na pastyme of halking and hunting . . . be ressoun that all sic wylde beistis and wylde foulis ar exilit and banist,' the old statute was revived, eight years before the Reformation, with the provision that not only was the offender to lose his life, but the person who apprehended him was to obtain the escheat of all his goods and be otherwise rewarded (*Ibid.* ii. 483). When Mary and Darnley could 'get na pastyme of hunting' in Peebleshire, in 1566, they ordered the old Acts and their penalties to be proclaimed anew (*Register of Privy Council*, i. 477). The Reformers only opposed such games as foot-ball, golf, and tennis, in so far as they interfered with the due observance of the Lord's day and other preaching days; and in such a town as St. Andrews even the grave elders and staid deacons were allured by golf from their ecclesiastical duties (*Register of St. Andrews Kirk Session*, Scottish History Society, vol. ii. pp. xciv, xcv, 913). In his note, Professor Aytoun cites the Act forbidding the celebrations of Robin Hood and Little John, the Abbot of Unreason and the Queen of May. 'What a genial age it must have been,' he ironically exclaims, 'when poor Maid Marian was liable to "handling" and the pillory for the heinous offence of singing under the summer trees' (*Bothwell*, p. 225). Unluckily for the Professor's theory, this Act is also pre-Reformation, having been passed in June 1555, under the regency of Mary of Guise (*Acts of Parliament*, ii. 500). As time proved, the uproarious celebrations—like the 'unproffitable sportis'—were not easily extinguished by Acts of Parliament (*supra*, p. 270, *n.* 63); and it is exceedingly unfortunate for the Professor that Mary herself, with all her love of pastime, peremptorily forbade the play of Robin Hood a few months after her return to Scotland (*see following note*). It was eleven years after Mary's execution ere the Parliament of Scotland ordained that no man in time coming should work to his master on Monday, that that day should be spent in 'useing and handling of thair armour, and in uther lauchfull gaimes and pastymes procureing habilitie of body, quhairby all personis myndis and bodyis may be recreate' (*Acts of Parliament*, iv. 160).

[103] On the 20th of April 1562, Mary, then in St. Andrews, wrote an urgent letter to the magistrates and town council of Edinburgh, ordering them on their 'utermest perell' to prevent the election in the following month of any Robin Hood or Little John, and to allow no 'uther unleissum gammis' within the burgh 'quhilk may disquiet the communitie thairof' (*Records of the Burgh of Edinburgh*, 1557-1571, p. 134). She was afraid that, as in the preceding year, sedition and tumult would be the outcome.

[104] In a letter to the Lords of Session, concerning a poor woman and her fatherless child, who had suffered sadly through a long lawplea, Mary of Guise added a post-script in her own hand :—'Do justice to this poor woman, for they have done her great wrong. The little flies are taken in the spider's web, and the large ones pass through' (*National MSS. of Scotland*, iii. 28).

[105] For expediting the causes of the poor, which were delayed by the actions of the great, Mary ordered her Lords of Session to sit both forenoon and afternoon three days a week. She not only increased the salaries of the judges, but occasionally, at least, was present herself at the hearing of the cases of the poor (*Foreign Calendar, Elizabeth*, vii. 72, 73; Keith's *History*, ii. 220, 221). When in July 1566, Mary, according to her accusers, was misspending her time in Alloa (*supra*, p. 136), she wrote to the Laird of Abercairnie, urging him to deal mercifully with a poor woman, whom he had violently ejected 'with ane company of puir bairnis furth of hir kyndlie rowme' (*Historical MSS. Commission, Third Report*, p. 418; *The Lennox*, ii. 429).

[106] In the autumn of 1562 she went as far north as Inverness; in the summer of 1563 she was in Argyllshire and Dumfriesshire; in 1564 she was again in the far north; in 1565 she was as far east as St. Andrews, as far west as Glasgow, as far north as

Atholl, and as far south as Dumfries; and in 1566 she was on the Border.

[107] Teulet's *Papiers D'État*, ii. 85.—In 1543 Sadleyr says that the Argyllshire Highlanders were known in Edinburgh as the 'wylde men' (*Hamilton Papers*, i. 597).

[108] 'Singularly enough,' says Hill Burton, 'among the many personal details about Queen Mary, none informs us distinctly of the extent to which she could understand or use the language of her people. It is not likely that she could speak it fluently on her arrival in Scotland' (*History of Scotland*, 1876, iv. 59). There can be little doubt, however, that Mary knew the language of her people before she went to France, and when there she had Scots subjects enough about her to prevent her forgetting it. Throckmorton, moreover, expressly says that at his interview with her on the 6th of August 1560, her talk was all in Scottish (*Foreign Calendar, Elizabeth*, iii. 225); and that she again answered him in that tongue at another interview (*Ibid.* iii. 250). Randolph relates that the oration which she made to her Parliament, in May 1563, was written by her in French, but pronounced in English (*Ibid.* vi. 381).

[109] Aikman's *Buchanan*, ii. 440.

[110] According to Buchanan, James the Fifth was the 106th King of Scots; according to Bishop Lesley, the 105th. At the head of the tenth book of his *De Rebus Gestis Scotorum*, Lesley has the line :—'CVI. MARIA SCOTORUM REGINA.' Father Dalrymple, having mistaken Mary's number for the pronoun *cui*, has thus rendered Lesley's heading :—'To quhilk is appliet Marie Quene of Scotis.'

[111] Keith's *History*, ii. 100; *Foreign Calendar, Elizabeth*, iv. 491, 538, 539; v. 49.—For Chatelherault's inconstancy, see also *supra*, p. 183, *n.* 29.

[112] As Elizabeth's agent, Randolph had been in Scotland for a considerable time before Mary's return. For the Memorial sent to him in the preceding March, see Keith's *History*, ii. 15-18; Haynes's *State Papers*, pp. 366-368; *Foreign Calendar, Elizabeth*, iv. 31-33; *Hatfield Calendar*, i. 258, 259.

[113] Chatelherault had been the first to welcome the Queen on her arrival (*Foreign Calendar, Elizabeth*, iv. 278); but was not present at her public entry into Edinburgh (Wright's *Elizabeth*, i. 74); and for some time he and Arran shunned the Court (*Ibid.* i. 78, 81, 82; *Foreign Calendar, Elizabeth*, iv. 297; Keith's *History*, ii. 99).

[114] Wright's *Elizabeth*, i. 73.

[115] *Foreign Calendar, Elizabeth*, iv. 490.—Huntly occasionally patronised Knox's preaching, but would 'pyck his naillis, and pull down his bonet ower his eyis, when idolatrie, witchecraft, murther, oppressioun, and such vices war rebuked.' He would say, 'When thei knaiffis have railled thair fill, then will thei hald thair peace' (Laing's *Knox*, ii. 362).

[116] Keith's *History*, ii. 98, 99.

[117] *Ibid.* ii. 111.

[118] *Ibid.* ii. 117.

[119] 'This, of all her faults, is the greatest, that she conceives evil where none is thought' (*Foreign Calendar, Elizabeth*, vii. 56).

CHAPTER VI

[1] Lesley's *History*, p. 290.

[2] *Supra*, pp. 37 and 234, *n.* 29.

[3] In Knox's opinion, Elizabeth was 'neather gude Protestant nor yit resolute Papist' (Laing's *Knox*, ii. 174).

[4] As soon as it was known that Francis was dead, many of the Scots wished to have their Queen back in Scotland; some were disposed to follow her inclinations in any way; but the Hamiltons desired to be assured before her return that she would marry Arran (*Foreign Calendar, Elizabeth*, iii. 462, 463, 519, 580). It was hoped that, if the Lord James could persuade her to return without foreign force or counsel—to trust entirely to her native subjects—she might be induced to favour Protestantism (*Ibid.* iii. 533). She herself, from the beginning of her widowhood, felt sure of the Lord James and of all the Stewarts, but mistrusted the Hamiltons (*Ibid.* iii. 473). Lethington, Grange, and Balnaves she afterwards hoped to win, though previously she had no great liking for them (*Ibid.* iv. 92). Lethington indeed professed to know that she would not suffer him to remain long in her realm unless he could do her some good service (*Ibid.* iii. 533). On the 10th of June, he deemed it prudent to write to her. From Paris, she replied to him on the 29th of the same month, in a letter which, according to Mr. Skelton, is pervaded by 'the ring of genuine feeling, of a high and magnanimous nature. She would gladly employ him in her

service, for she had no doubt of his goodwill. She understood the
scruples which he felt; he had been the diplomatic chief of the
disaffected lords; he had been in correspondence with England
and with Elizabeth. But she had forgiven all past offences, and
for the future she would entirely trust him. She had always
appreciated his wisdom and sagacity, and she was now confident of
his affection and fidelity. Hereafter they would deal openly with
each other' (*Maitland of Lethington*, i. 307, 308). Those who have
only read Mr. Skelton's glowing account of Mary's letter may be
surprised to know that even he has to confess that Lethington—
whose 'extraordinary insight' so impresses him (*Ibid.* i. 322)—was
not entirely delivered by it from his ' doubts and scruples.' Those
who have read Mary's letter itself (Tytler's *History of Scotland*, 1845,
v. 492, 493 ; *Foreign Calendar, Elizabeth*, iv. 161) will readily understand why his personal fears were not altogether assuaged, why he of
all the Protestant leaders seemed most to dread her arrival. These
' doubts and scruples,' as they continued to haunt Lethington after
the receipt of Mary's letter, are manifested in three of his letters
to Cecil—his letter of the 9th August (Haynes's *State Papers*, p.
369), his letter of the 10th August (Keith's *History*, iii. 211-216),
and his letter of the 15th August (Tytler's *Scotland*, v. 493-495 ;
Foreign Calendar, Elizabeth, iv. 248, 249). It is in the last of these
that he says:—'If two galleys may quietly pass, I wish the passport had been liberally granted.' From these letters the awkward
position of the Protestant nobles in Scotland may be gleaned. As
Mary had never chosen councillors from those nominated by the
Estates (see *supra*, p. 30) there was no properly authorised ruling
power in her absence ; and consequently it was difficult to enforce
obedience, and to meet the expenses of government. The marvellous peace and quietness which meanwhile prevailed could only
be accounted for by religious influence. If she returned, there
was the fear—in Lethington's opinion the moral certainty—that
attempts would at least be made to suppress Protestantism and
break up the league with England. His letters show, however,
that if—in the event of her return—she refrained from ' following
the wicked advice of God's enemies,' and was content to be at
peace with England, her Protestant subjects would render her all
due obedience. The cautious reply of the Lords (Laing's *Knox*, ii.
178, 179) to Elizabeth's letter (*supra*, p. 242, n. 51), and Randolph's
letter to Cecil of 9th August (Robertson's *History of Scotland*, app.

no. v.) also show that, despite their favour for the English alliance and their distrust of Mary, they were not anxious to cast off their allegiance. In his despair, Lethington suggested to Cecil that a league of the Protestant princes should be formed—a league in which the Scots Protestants would be comprehended (Keith's *History*, iii. 215). Even after Captain Anstruther arrived, five days before her, with the assurance that she was coming, without any forces, to trust herself in the hands of her people, Lethington exclaimed, 'What this message meaneth I cannot judge : . . . it passeth my dull capacity to imagine what this sudden enterprise should mean.' With Mary actually on the way, the 'wonderful tragedies' he had foreseen might be at hand ; and the suggested Protestant league was still a thing of the uncertain future. Elizabeth, he now proposed, should 'keep some ordinary power at Berwick, of good force, so long as we stand in doubtful terms' (Tytler's *Scotland*, v. 494).

⁵ Tytler's *History of Scotland*, 1845, v. 204.—In Mignet's opinion, Murray's letter 'does equally great honour to his head and his heart. It attests, on his part, perfect loyalty, profound judgment, and wise patriotism' (*History of Mary*, 1851, i. 121). His proposal, in Hosack's opinion, 'was clearly the most equitable arrangement that could be devised' (*Mary and her Accusers*, 1870, i. 76, 77). In a footnote, Hosack admits 'that the proposal which he now made seems inconsistent with his alleged complicity in the design of Cecil to intercept the Queen on her voyage to Scotland. But,' he adds, 'the Lord James was so wary a politician that we are often at a loss to make out his real intentions. Even his friend Throgmorton writes about this time that he does not know what the Lord James "meaneth"' (*Ibid.* i. 76 *n.*). Here, however, Hosack has done both Throckmorton and the Lord James injustice. In support of his statement he merely refers to Tytler's quotation from Throckmorton's letter of 26th July to Cecil, concerning the refusal of the passport, a letter in which he only expressed his inability to comprehend what the Lord James 'meaneth,' on the supposition—a supposition it is clear he did not accept—that he had then completely changed his mind as to the desirability of Mary's return (*supra*, pp. 39, 242, 243). Even Randolph's letter of 9th August does not, on this point, imply more than that the Lord James then wished her return 'stayed yet for a space' (Robertson's *Scotland*, app. no. v.).

⁶ *Foreign Calendar, Elizabeth*, iv. 237, 238; Tytler's *Scotland*, 1845, v. 202-204.

⁷ *Foreign Calendar, Elizabeth*, iv. 238.

⁸ This compromise seems to have been first suggested to Cecil by Lethington in London, in December 1560, after unsuccessfully pressing the Arran match on Elizabeth (*Foreign Calendar, Elizabeth*, iii. 533, 581; *Spanish Calendar, Elizabeth*, i. 306). Cecil thus refers to it in his letter to Throckmorton of 14th July 1561 :— 'There hath been a matter secretly thought of which I dare communicate to you, although I mean never to be an author thereof; and that is, if an accord might be made betwixt our Mistress and the Scottish Queen, that this [*i.e.* Mary] should, by Parliament in Scotland, etc., surrender unto the Queen's Majesty all matter of claim, and to the heirs of her body; and in consideration thereof, the Scottish Queen's interest should be acknowledged in default of heirs of the body of the Queen's Majesty. . . . This matter is too big for weak folks, and too deep for simple. The Queen's Majesty knoweth of it' (Hardwicke's *State Papers*, i. 174). In his reply of 26th July, Throckmorton—while regarding the scheme as apparently profitable for both Queens, and honourable without danger—says that when the matter shall be handled some provisions must be considered for Elizabeth's surety, and other circumstances well weighed for the commodity of England (*Foreign Calendar, Elizabeth*, iv. 205).

⁹ *Spanish Calendar, Elizabeth*, i. 306.

¹⁰ Labanoff's *Recueil*, i. 103-105; Keith's *History*, ii. 72-74.— Though the negotiation for the declaration of the English succession is not mentioned in the imperfect copies of Maitland's Instructions printed by Keith, it plainly underlies the whole of Lord James's letter of 1st September to Cecil, which letter was sent with Lethington (*Foreign Calendar, Elizabeth*, iv. 287). It is quite clear from Lethington's own report that he had been asked to negotiate on this point by the Scots nobles (Philippson's *Marie Stuart*, iii. 446-448, 450; *Register of Privy Council*, xiv. 174-176); and his letter of 15th December to Cecil implies that up to that date Mary had not made the proposal to Elizabeth (Haynes's *State Papers*, pp. 375, 376).

¹¹ *Spanish Calendar, Elizabeth*, i. 339.

¹² *Maitland of Lethington*, 1894, ii. 252.—De Foix described Lethington to De Silva as 'a sort of Scotch Cecil' (*Spanish Calendar*,

Elizabeth, i. 412). Sir Thomas Smith informed Cecil that Adam Hume was altogether a Lethington, whom he would find double or rather triple, having pensions of all three princes (*Foreign Calendar, Elizabeth*, vii. 249).

[13] *Maitland of Lethington*, ii. 367.

[14] *Sempill Ballates*, 1872, p. 84.

[15] Keith's *History*, ii. 73, 74.

[16] Keith entertained this suspicion (*History*, ii. 76). Chalmers had no dubiety in the matter :—' Had this offensive proposal come from an Envoy of less talent [than Maitland], it might have been attributed to officious folly : but such a proposal, from such a statesman, must be attributed to the treacherous purpose of villainy ' (*Life of Mary*, 1818, i. 51).

[17] *Foreign Calendar, Elizabeth*, iv. 356-359, 480.—Throckmorton was informed by the Duke of Guise, that no man need doubt, if Mary succeeded to the English throne, that she would reside in England, it being a more commodious realm than Scotland, and the nobles and people more agreeable to her ; that she would be wholly governed by the English Council in all matters of importance wheresoever they occurred ; and that she would also answer with mind and intent to win all hearts, being void of partialities, affectionate to no faction, and free from inveterate malice and desire to revenge (*Ibid.* iv. 358). This was in the autumn of 1561. In the spring of 1563 it was reported that Cecil, in response to Lethington's urgent appeals, had suggested that the Cardinal of Lorraine should devise a plan whereby Elizabeth might be secured for life and Protestantism afterwards maintained ; but Cecil's object, it was suspected, was to divert the Cardinal from any negotiations he might have with Philip or the Emperor (*Spanish Calendar, Elizabeth*, i. 317).

[18] Haynes's *State Papers*, p. 373 ; Philippson's *Marie Stuart*, 1892, iii. 447, 448 ; Aikman's *Buchanan*, ii. 445 ; Camden's *Elizabeth*, 1675, p. 54 ; Spottiswoode's *History*, ii. 10, 11 ; Herries's *Historical Memoirs*, p. 58 ; Hayward's *Annals of Elizabeth*, Camden Society, pp. 82, 84.—The English Parliament in 1536 and again in 1543-4 authorised Henry the Eighth—in case of the failure of his own lawful issue—to nominate the heirs of the crown either by his letters-patent under the great seal or by his last will signed by his own hand (Manby's *Statutes*, 1670, pp. 527, 650, 651). His will—made a month before his death—provided that, in default of lawful issue

of Prince Edward, and of his own by his sixth wife Catherine Parr, or by any other lawful wife he might yet marry, the crown was to descend to his daughters, Mary and Elizabeth, under certain conditions ; and, in default of their lawful issue, to the heirs of his nieces, Lady Frances and Eleanor, the daughters of his younger sister Mary, thus passing over the Queen of Scots and Lady Lennox, the descendants of his elder sister Margaret (Rymer's *Foedera*, xv. 112, 113). Lethington alleged that the will was void, through Henry's signature having been impressed by a stamp—not written (*Egerton Papers*, Camden Society, pp. 45-47). To Lethington Elizabeth said,—' Sa lang as I leiff I salbe Quene of Ingland, quhen I am deid, thai sall succeid that hes maist ryght. Gif the Quene your Soverane be that persone I sall nevir hurt hir, gif ane uther haif beter ryght yt war not ressonable to require me to do a manifest injury. Gif thair be ony law agains hir as I protest to yow I knaw none for I am not curious to inquire of that purpoise, bot gif ony be I am sworne quhen I wes mareit to the realme not to alter the lawis of it' (Philippson's *Marie Stuart*, iii. 448).

[19] *Foreign Calendar, Elizabeth*, iv. 362.

[20] The Commission to Mewtas is dated 17th September 1561 (*Foreign Calendar, Elizabeth*, iv. 308).

[21] The nature of Mary's oral message by Mewtas may be gathered from Elizabeth's letter of 23rd November to Mary (Keith's *History*, ii. 133 ; *Foreign Calendar, Elizabeth*, iv. 410, 411), from Cecil's letter of 4th November to Throckmorton (*Ibid.* iv. 389), and especially from Mary's undated reply to the Ambassadors (Labanoff's *Recueil*, i. 115, 116), and the summary of the same (*Register of Privy Council*, xiv. 178).

[22] Labanoff's *Recueil*, i. 110, 111.

[23] *Foreign Calendar, Elizabeth*, iv. 389.—Both Lethington and the Lord James had written to Cecil on the 7th of October, pressing him to support and carry through the succession proposal (Haynes's *State Papers*, pp. 373, 374 ; *Foreign Calendar, Elizabeth*, iv. 351-353).

[24] *Foreign Calendar, Elizabeth*, iv. 389.—In 1564 the Lord-Keeper was in Elizabeth's displeasure on suspicion of having dealt in the succession (Murdin's *State Papers*, p. 756) ; and two years later, Pembroke and Leicester were excluded from her presence-chamber for furthering the proposal without her allowance (*Ibid.* p. 762).

[25] Keith's *History*, ii. 133 ; *Foreign Calendar, Elizabeth*, iv. 411.

—Even on the 4th of November, Mary was longing greatly to know Elizabeth's resolution (Wright's *Elizabeth*, i. 84).

[26] Haynes's *State Papers*, pp. 375, 376.

[27] Besides his letter of 15th December, of which a brief summary is given in the text, Lethington wrote to Cecil on the 7th of December and also on the 26th, asking his advice for Mary's reply (*Foreign Calendar, Elizabeth*, iv. 429, 455-457); and on the 5th of January, he informed Cecil that, if he would let him know of any point he had neglected, he would reform it accordingly (*Ibid.* iv. 478). Can he have intended that Cecil should return Mary's letter if it did not meet his views? Cecil seems to have resented his pertinacious applications for advice in this matter (*Ibid.* iv. 488).

[28] Labanoff's *Recueil*, i. 123-127 ; Haynes's *State Papers*, pp. 376-378.

[29] On the 28th of February, Randolph tells Cecil that he has been earnestly required by Mary to make means unto him, that she may shortly have her answer (*Foreign Calendar, Elizabeth*, iv. 538). Mr. Skelton alleges that 'Elizabeth did not reply' (*Maitland of Lethington*, ii. 120); but Randolph's letter of the 31st of March proves that she did (*Foreign Calendar, Elizabeth*, iv. 574, 577). Randolph had before stated that, if the reply in any manner of way gives her comfort, she will despatch Lethington to demand an interview (*Ibid.* p. 538); now he trusts that Lethington will shortly be sent with ample commission to demand the same (*Ibid.* p. 574).

[30] Haynes's *State Papers*, p. 380 ; *Foreign Calendar, Elizabeth*, iv. 510, 511 ; v. 161.

[31] 'Thys Quene wished that one of the two were a man, to make an end of all debates. Thys,' says Randolph, ' I trowe was spoken in her merrie moode' (Wright's *Elizabeth*, i. 84). Nearly a year before Throckmorton had expressed a similar wish (*supra*, p. 228, *n.* 9).

[32] 'When any purpose falleth in of marriage, she saith that "she will none other husband but the Queen of England"' (Keith's *History*, ii. 127).

[33] Lethington informed Cecil that the love of the Queen of England had taken such possession of Queen Mary that she wished her as much honour as she desired for herself (*Foreign Calendar, Elizabeth*, iv. 489). She carried one of Elizabeth's letters in her bosom, next her skin, ' and said that if she could put it nearer her heart she would ' (*Ibid.* v. 101).

291

[34] *Foreign Calendar, Elizabeth,* iv. 490, 536, 538.—There was none, Lethington alleged, with whom he dared to confer on this matter save the Lord James (*Ibid.* iv. 488), who also was anxious that Cecil should advise Elizabeth to give Mary a favourable answer (*Ibid.* iv. 538).

[35] 'The worst that they [*i.e.* the Scotch Bishops] like is the accord that they hear is like to be between the Q. Majestie and this Queen; if that be, they think themselves quite overthrown; they say plainly, that she can't then return a true Christian woman. . . . The bruit of her good-will to go into England is far spread abroad in this country, and the purpose well commended of all honest men; but hereof are there diverse judgments' (Keith's *History,* ii. 117, 118). 'The Papists storm; now they think there resteth nothing but the meeting of the two Queens to overthrow the mass and all' (*Ibid.* ii. 129). 'The Papists mistrust greatly the meeting; the Protestants as greatly desire it. The preachers are more vehement than discreet or learned' (*Foreign Calendar, Elizabeth,* iv. 523).

[36] *Ibid.* iv. 538, 571, 572, 575, 631.

[37] Throckmorton learned that the French were trying to alienate Mary from Elizabeth, that they wished to continue the League between France and Scotland, and, failing this, were to try to win the Hamiltons, Huntly, and Hume (*Foreign Calendar, Elizabeth,* iv. 434, 438, 458; v. 155).

[38] *Ibid.* iv. 565, 566, 571, 572, 606; v. 115, 155.

[39] *Ibid.* iv. 565.

[40] *Foreign Calendar, Elizabeth,* v. 82, 93, 101, 144, 191; *Spanish Calendar, Elizabeth,* i. 246, 249.—The English Council, like the Scotch, was not altogether uninfluenced by monetary considerations. It was reckoned that the interview would cost the English nobles and gentlemen at least £40,000 (*Foreign Calendar, Elizabeth,* v. 93) and Elizabeth as much (*Ibid.* v. 108).

[41] Elizabeth speaks of 'the unseasonableness of the yere by the unordinat raynes' (Haynes's *State Papers,* p. 392). Bishop Jewel is still more emphatic :—'There has been here, throughout the whole of this present year, an incredibly bad season both as to the weather and state of the atmosphere. Neither sun, nor moon, nor winter, nor spring, nor summer, nor autumn, have performed their appropriate offices. It has rained so abundantly, and almost without intermission, as if the heavens could hardly do anything

else.' He describes at length the monstrous births which had in consequence taken place (*Zurich Letters*, Parker Society, i. 116, 117).

[42] Haynes's *State Papers*, p. 392.—When Mary heard of Elizabeth's indisposition she 'wished rather to bear half the pain than that it should stay their journey' (*Foreign Calendar, Elizabeth*, v. 161).

[43] *Ibid.* iv. 571.

[44] *Register of the Privy Council of Scotland*, i. 206.

[45] Lethington's Instructions, printed from an imperfect MS., are in Keith's *History*, ii. 142-144 ; and in the *Register of Privy Council*, xiv. 179-182. Mary's letters announcing Lethington's mission are dated 25th May (Labanoff's *Recueil*, i. 137-139 ; *Foreign Calendar, Elizabeth*, v. 48). He left Edinburgh for England that day (*Diurnal of Occurrents*, p. 72) ; and reached the English Court on the 31st (Philippson's *Marie Stuart*, iii. 457).

[46] *Ibid.* iii. 456.

[47] The Articles as agreed on, and Elizabeth's Ratification of the same, are in Haynes's *State Papers*, pp. 388-390, 393.—In the Articles it is agreed that the Queens are to 'mete together at the citie of Yorke, or in default thereof at some convenient place betwixt the sayd citie and the river of Trente, . . . betwixt the twentith of August and the 20th daye of Septembre.' On the 8th of June, Cecil informs Challoner that, if the meeting shall be, it will be at York (*Foreign Calendar, Elizabeth*, v. 82) ; on the 25th of June, Dudley writes to Cecil that Nottingham is to be the place (*Ibid.* v. 129) ; on the 3rd of July, Mason writes to Challoner that it will be at Southwell, and from thence they will repair to Nottingham, where they will remain seven or eight days (*Ibid.* v. 144) ; on the 10th of July, Lady Throckmorton, who was appointed to wait on Elizabeth, says that it will be at Sheffield at Lord Shrewsbury's house (*Ibid.* v. 629) ; and on the 12th of July, Killigrew says it will be at Nottingham (*Ibid.* v. 157).

[48] Haynes's *State Papers*, p. 391 ; *Foreign Calendar, Elizabeth*, v. 61, 72, 103-105, 109, 110, 120, 121, 157, 161.

[49] The interview was only to be held, 'if the controversies in France may be compounded or ended before the last of this moneth of June, without prejudice to the state of the realme of England' (Haynes's *State Papers*, p. 388). In her Instructions to Sir Henry Sydney, Elizabeth states that she was constrained to delay the interview by the Duke of Guise's treachery to the Prince of Condé ;

by the absolute refusal of all religious toleration; by the edict published in Paris, authorising the common people 'to kill and cutt in peecs all such as had broken any church or howses, or that kept them company—an order never herd before! to gyve to the commen people the sword, by meanes wherof many horryble murders were daylie, and yet be committed'; and by many other demonstrations that Guise and his party wished to subvert all nations which differed from them in the rites of religion. Though these things prevented her from leaving the southern part of her realm unprotected at present, she would gladly meet Mary at York, Pomfret, or Nottingham, at any time she chose to name between the 20th of May and the 31st of August 1563 (*Ibid.* pp. 391, 392; Keith's *History*, ii. 148-150).

[50] *Foreign Calendar, Elizabeth*, v. 182.

[51] *Ibid.* iv. 503, 504.

[52] *Zurich Letters*, i. 115, 116; *Foreign Calendar, Elizabeth*, v. 164, 191, 236, 311-314, 358, 362, 367, 368. — In De Quadra's opinion, Elizabeth's indecision in the matter of the interview 'proceeded from the uncertainty as to how affairs in France would turn out. It was her design to make use of the rebel faction if their cause was successful, and, if otherwise, to make friends with the Guises by means of the Queen-mother, and with this object to come to terms with the Queen of Scotland' (*Spanish Calendar, Elizabeth*, i. 249).

[53] *Foreign Calendar, Elizabeth*, v. 59, 304; Labanoff's *Recueil*, i. 155, 163-166.—Though Mary could make merry over the reported victories of her uncles (*Foreign Calendar, Elizabeth*, v. 361, 362), she seemed to retain her goodwill towards Elizabeth (*Ibid.* vi. 60), and professed to lament the state of France, and to fear the success of her uncle's enterprises (*Ibid.* vi. 88).

[54] Wright's *Elizabeth*, i. 73.

[55] *Register of the Privy Council of Scotland*, i. 216, 217.—This meeting of the Scots Council was held on the 15th of August 1562. On the 8th of July, Elizabeth had granted a safe-conduct for Mary and her train, 'although our said sister reposing her hole trust in our honor amytie and natural frendshipp hath not been curious to requyre any assurance of her own person' (Haynes's *State Papers*, p. 390).

[56] *E.g.* for meeting in 1563, see *Spanish Calendar, Elizabeth*, i. 310; for meeting in 1564, see *Foreign Calendar, Elizabeth*, vii. 91,

92, 108, 114, 137, 145, 148; *Spanish Calendar, Elizabeth,* i. 361, 362. In 1565, Cecil thought that 'the two Quenes have satisfyed either themselves with their enterviews, or rather filled the desyres of their traynes' (Wright's *Elizabeth,* i. 197); but, in 1566, Mary again spoke of a meeting (*Foreign Calendar, Elizabeth,* viii. 45; *Spanish Calendar, Elizabeth,* i. 555).

[57] On the 12th of February 1561-2, Randolph intimates that Mary proposes to send to Elizabeth a fair ring with a diamond made like a heart (*Foreign Calendar, Elizabeth,* iv. 523). Labanoff says that this heart-shaped diamond had been sent by the hands of Lethington in the previous September (*Recueil,* i. 102); but it is quite certain that it was not sent until the summer of 1562, and Du Croc seems to have been the bearer (*Foreign Calendar, Elizabeth,* v. 101, 157, 158). Bishop Jewel refers to it as 'a diamond of great value, a most beautiful gem, set in gold, and accompanied by some beautiful and elegant verses'; and again as 'a most splendid and valuable diamond inclosed and fixed in a plate of gold, and set off with some flattering and elegant verses' (*Zurich Letters,* Parker Society, i. 115, 120). Challoner's statement implies that the verses were in French (*Foreign Calendar, Elizabeth,* vi. 249); Killigrew's, that they were in Latin (*Ibid.* v. 157, 158). Causin says that the diamond-heart ' was enriched with a verse of Buchanan's, who had not as yet his spirit infected with treason' (*Holy Court,* 1678, p. 812). In Ruddiman's *Buchanan* there is an epigram, '*De adamante misso a Regina Scotiae ad Reginam Angliae*' (*Epigrammatum,* i. 59), and another, '*Loquitur adamas in cordis effigiem sculptus, quem Maria Elizabethae Anglae misit*' (*Ibid.* iii. 8). The former of these is strangely characterised by Miss Strickland as 'a scoffing epigram' (*Letters of Mary Queen of Scots,* 1843, i. 66). In December 1563, Elizabeth sent by Randolph a ring to Mary, which 'was mar-vellously esteemed, oftentimes looked upon, and many times kissed' (*Foreign Calendar, Elizabeth,* vi. 617; vii. 23). When, at the celebration of Twelfth-day, Mary Fleming was so lavishly decked with jewels as Queen of the Bean, the Queen of Scots wore none save Elizabeth's ring, which was 'hanging at her breast, with a lace of whyt and black about her neck' (*Maitland Miscellany,* ii. 391, 392). Melville refers to a diamond which, in the autumn of 1564, Elizabeth said she would send by him as a token to Mary (*supra,* p. 98); and De Foix speaks of a diamond worth six hundred crowns which she intended to send to her by Lethington

in the summer of 1565 (*Papiers D'État*, ii. 40). The presents which were interchanged are also referred to by Knox's continuator (Laing's *Knox*, ii. 469) and by Bishop Lesley (*Narratives of Scottish Catholics*, 1885, p. 95).

⁵⁸ See *e.g. Spanish Calendar, Elizabeth*, i. 399, 427, 428; and *infra*, pp. 320, 323, 329, 331, 338.

⁵⁹ In November 1564, both Murray and Lethington told Randolph 'that they found Queen Elizabeth's dealing marvellous strange, and that nothing was intended but drift of time' (*Foreign Calendar, Elizabeth*, vii. 248). Mary herself, on the eve of her marriage with Darnley, told Randolph that his Queen had tried 'to abuse' her, and that of this she had been warned 'oute of England, France, and other parts' (Stevenson's *Selections*, p. 122). Elizabeth's latest biographer affirms that 'there was no truth nor honesty in anything she said' (Bishop Creighton's *Queen Elizabeth*, 1896, p. 30); and her reputation for duplicity is not diminished by Major Martin Hume's instructive and entertaining volume on her courtships. In Bishop Quadra's opinion, Cecil wished to exclude the Queen of Scots and Lady Lennox from the English succession, and to 'keep the kingdom in the hands of heretics' (*Spanish Calendar, Elizabeth*, i. 227). Mr. Skelton alleges that of Mary's foreign enemies Cecil was the most powerful, and represents him as relentless in his patient animosity towards the Queen of Scots (*Maitland of Lethington*, ii. 82). On the other hand, a few weeks before the Darnley murder, Maitland assured Cecil that he had constantly regarded him as no enemy of Mary, no hindrance to her preferment, but as a good minister to nourish 'the mutuall intelligence' betwixt her and Elizabeth, though willing to avoid the question of titles (*Egerton Papers*, Camden Society, pp. 41, 42). Still later, Mary professed to regard him as 'na hinderair of the continewance of our amytie, bot rather a weilwillar of all our gude causses' (Labanoff's *Recueil*, vii. 311).

⁶⁰ Camden mentions the suspicion that Mary desired the interview 'that she might either strengthen her title to England, or else give hope and courage to the Papists in England, and to the Guises' (Camden's *Elizabeth*, 1675, p. 60). Bishop Quadra feared that her ambition 'to be declared the heiress of England' might incline her 'to a marriage with a person of lower rank than the Archduke, and one less advantageous to religion' (*Spanish Calendar, Elizabeth*, i. 340, 341). His inability to help her in her claim to

the succession, she afterwards assigned as a reason for not taking the Archduke (Labanoff's *Recueil*, i. 296, 297). Some members of the English Privy Council could see in the Darnley marriage a plain intention to further her title not only to the succession but to the possession of Elizabeth's crown (*Foreign Calendar, Elizabeth*, vii. 384.) On the other hand, Lethington, in December 1564, emphatically denied that Mary only pretended kindness towards Elizabeth in order to hunt a kingdom (*Ibid.* vii. 273). Murray, too, felt sure that nothing prejudicial to Elizabeth's surety had ever entered Mary's mind (*Ibid.* vii. 270); it was the honour and name of heir-apparent that was desired (*Ibid.* vii. 307).

[61] Philippson's *Marie Stuart*, iii. 457 ; *Foreign Calendar, Elizabeth*, iv. 428, 429, 457 ; Haynes's *State Papers*, pp. 376, 380 ; *Spanish Calendar Elizabeth*, i. 307.

[62] On the 24th of October 1561, Randolph writes :—' I receive of her Grace at all times very good words. I am born in hand by such as are nearest about her as the L[ord] James and the L[aird] of Lidington, that they are meant as they are spoken ' (Keith's *History*, ii. 98). Three days later, he says, Whatsoever policy is in all the chief and best practised heads in France, whatsoever craft, falsehood, or deceit there is in all the subtle brains in Scotland, is either fresh in this woman's memory, or she can 'fett' it with a wet finger (*Foreign Calendar, Elizabeth*, iv. 380). In December, he writes :—' So much as I am able myself to conjecture, she meaneth no less than hath been spoke often both by herself and others, to do what she can to unite the two realms in so perfect an amity, as the like hath not been ' (Keith's *History*, ii. 114); ' when I talked with her she was very merry, and spake with such affection as I think came from the heart ' (*Ibid.* ii. 121). On the 30th of January, he thought that Mary's affection to Elizabeth ' was never greater towards any, or else it is the deepest dissembled and covered that ever was ' (*Foreign Calendar, Elizabeth*, iv. 512). In the following November, he trusted that her good mind towards Elizabeth was ' as well meant ' as spoken (Keith's *History*, ii. 181). In February 1563-4, he assures Cecil that he never heard better words, nor ever saw in her better tokens of goodwill, and none of her acts made him suspect the contrary (*Foreign Calendar, Elizabeth*, vii. 49). When he saw, in 1565, that she was determined to take her own way, he was confident that Elizabeth would nevertheless get fair words from her in the meantime (*Ibid.* vii. 381). Long

before, he had suspected that in other matters she could dis-
simulate trimly (*Ibid.* v. 146).

⁶³ By the Articles for the Interview it was provided that Elizabeth
might at her pleasure require the ratification of the Treaty of
Edinburgh ; but Mary was not to be pressed with anything which
she might show herself to mislike before she had returned into her
own realm (Haynes's *State Papers*, p. 389). In her letter of 5th
January, Mary had at last alleged that her real reason for refusing
to ratify that Treaty was its bearing on her right to the English
succession (*supra*, pp. 69, 70). Its obnoxious article, which Cecil
and Wotton had wrung with difficulty from Montluc and Randan
(Lodge's *Illustrations*, 1838, i. 396-400, 405-408 ; Haynes's *State
Papers*, pp. 337, 340), runs thus :—'Seeing the kingdoms of
England and Ireland do by right pertain to the Most Serene Lady
and Princess Elizabeth, upon which account it is not lawful for any
other persons to call, write, name, or entitle themselves, nor yet to
order themselves to be called, written, named, or entitled King
and Queen of England or Ireland, nor to use or take to themselves
the ensigns or arms (commonly called *armoyries*) of the kingdom
of England or Ireland : therefore it is appointed, agreed, and concluded, that the said Most Christian King and Queen Mary, and
both of them, shall thereafter [*deinceps*] abstain from using and
bearing the said title and arms of the kingdom of England or
Ireland, and shall prohibit and forbid their subjects that no one in
the kingdoms of France and Scotland and their provinces, or in any
part of them, shall in any way use the said title or arms ; and
shall likewise prohibit and take care, so far as in them lies, that no
person mix [*i.e.* quarter] the saids ensigns armorial with the arms
of the kingdoms of France or Scotland. And if there be found any
letters or writings which carry in them the title of the kingdoms of
England or Ireland, or be sealed with the seal of the saids kingdoms, or either of them, the same shall be re-made without any
adjection of the saids title and arms of England and Ireland ; and
all letters and writings containing the said title, or sealed with the
seals of the saids arms, which shall not be as above said renewed
and re-made within six months after the publication of this present
Treaty, shall be void and of no avail. Further, they shall see to it
and take care, so far as they can, that in the saids kingdoms of
France and Scotland, the saids arms be no where extant, seen, or
found mixed [*i.e.* quartered] with the arms of the saids King or

Queen Mary; and that the said title be no where extant, seen, or found ascribed to the saids King or Queen Mary' (Rymer's *Foedera*, 1713, xv. 594, 595). The usurpation of the English arms and title by Francis and Mary was, of course, the *raison d'être* of this article, the first clause of which—a clause obtained 'with greate difficultie' (Haynes, p. 337)—would, if ratified, have effectually barred Mary from at any time disputing Elizabeth's right of possession. This may have been Mary's primary objection to the Treaty; but it is not the one to which she alludes. The article was objected to by Mary and Lethington as prejudicial, not to her right of possession, but to her right of succession in the event of Elizabeth dying without lawful issue; and if the words could be construed, 'by any license of diplomacy or verbal ingenuity,' as Mr. Skelton puts it, 'into an absolute renunciation' of her prospective right (*Maitland of Lethington*, ii. 86), she was amply justified in refusing to ratify the Treaty. In Lethington's opinion and in Mary's, it was highly unsatisfactory that a matter of such importance should be 'wrappit up in obscure termis'; but to Mr. Skelton the terms are not obscure. In his judgment, the clause 'provided that Mary "in all times coming" should renounce the right of the English succession' (*Ibid.* ii. 85); and 'Elizabeth required an absolute renunciation of the Scottish right of succession; the Treaty imported as much,—" in all times coming," even in the event of Elizabeth dying without issue, Mary was to refrain from pressing her claim' (*Ibid.* ii. 108). Here there is a double fallacy. Mr. Skelton conveniently assumes that ceasing to use the English arms and title was equivalent to renouncing the right of the English succession; and that the words 'in all times coming' are the English equivalent of '*deinceps*.' If assumptions could be established by mere reiteration, it would be impossible to refute Mr. Skelton. Though in one chapter he quotes the words 'in all times coming' at least four times, they do not occur in this article of the Treaty. As Keith (i. 292) has so rendered '*deinceps*' in his translation, it may perhaps be inferred that Mr. Skelton has simply followed that translation without looking at the original, which is not printed as he says it is in Haynes, but in Rymer. It may be noted that where the word '*deinceps*' occurs in a previous article of the same Treaty, 'Honest' Keith translates it by 'hereafter.' It may also be noted that in Elizabeth's commission to Cecil and Wotton—a commission embodied in the Treaty—the phrase 'in all times coming' is not weakly expressed by '*deinceps*,' but by '*perpetuis temporibus.*' Montluc and Randan in the course of the negotiations used the word '*dorénavant*' (Lodge's *Illustrations*, i. 396); and so little stress did Cecil and Wotton lay on '*deinceps*,' that when, on the 1st of July, they informed Elizabeth that, after threatening, this article had been obtained, they, in quoting it, stopped just before '*deinceps*' (Haynes's *State Papers*, p. 340). Lethington reported that he had, in the autumn of 1561, told Elizabeth plainly that in his opinion the Treaty was so prejudicial to Mary that she would never confirm it, and conceived in such a form that she was not bound to do so. He also reported that Elizabeth was willing even then that in her ratification Mary should state that, although she would neither bear the English arms nor take the English title during the life of Elizabeth or of her lawful issue, she reserved the interest she might thereafter claim (Philippson's *Marie Stuart*, iii. 451; *Register of Privy Council*, xiv. 176, 177). Five years later, Elizabeth was not only willing to accept her ratification, 'omitting anything . . . that may be prejudicial to her title as next heir after us and our children,' but to give her a similar assurance that she would neither do nor suffer to be done anything to the prejudice of her title as next heir (Keith's *History*, ii. 482, 483). This was at the baptism of the Prince. Four years later still, when Mary was a prisoner in Chatsworth, Elizabeth was willing to accept her ratification with the provision 'that therby she shall not be secluded from any right or tytle that she or her children maye hereafter have, yf God shall not give to the Queenis Majestie any yssue of hir bodye to have continuance' (Haynes's *State Papers*, p. 608). Ranke makes the astounding statement that before Mary landed in Scotland she was compelled to renounce her title to the English throne, and to ratify that Act of the Scottish Parliament which forbade the performance of the mass under pain of death (*History of the Popes*, Murray's edition, 1840, i. 321 ; Bohn's edition, 1847, i. 240).

CHAPTER VII

[1] *Foreign Calendar, Elizabeth*, v. 182.

[2] 'The journey of Mary into the north,' says Chalmers, 'was suddenly resolved on, soon after Sir John Gordon's escape [25th

July 1562]; as we see nothing hinted of such an excursion in Randolph's letters to Cecil of the 1st and 4th of August, when the Queen seemed wholly bent on the very different journey of a meeting with her good cousin the English Queen' (Chalmers's *Life of Mary*, 1818, ii. 299, 300). But Mary knew definitely two days before Gordon escaped from prison that she was not to meet Elizabeth that year; and the references in Randolph's letters of 1st and 4th August are to the postponed meeting of the Queens in 1563. It is certain, moreover, that the Provost of Aberdeen had, on the 12th of the previous January, 'exponit to the Consell that he is suirlie informit that the Quenis Grace is to cum to the north partis to vesy the same betuix this and Peace [*i.e.* Easter, 29th March] nixt to cum or thairby'; on hearing which the Town Council at once and unanimously decreed, that two thousand merks should be uplifted, for the decoration of the town and for a present to her Grace (*Burgh Records of Aberdeen*, Spalding Club, i. 339, 340). If, as seems to be the case, the progress to the north had merely been delayed because of the projected and more important journey into England, it was only natural that it should be carried into effect after the meeting of the Queens had been finally abandoned for that year.

³ *Foreign Calendar, Elizabeth*, v. 232.—This was Randolph's opinion of the journey on the eve of setting out. After it was finished and he was again in Edinburgh, he said that it had been more costly than the interview of the Queens would have been; that he had never been in such a dear country before ; that he had buried his best servant, and left another sick behind him ; that his horses were marred ; that he had never been in a worse country; and that the charges were so unreasonable that he never took less pleasure in any journey (*Ibid*. v. 537). While at Old Aberdeen he and Lethington slept in the same bed (Keith's *History*, ii. 176).

⁴ *Register of the Privy Council of Scotland*, i. 216-218.—In the printed *Register* the meeting of 15th August is erroneously said to have been held in Edinburgh.

⁵ Mary's letter to the magistrates and town-council of Edinburgh is dated at Coupar Angus on the 21st of August (*Burgh Records of Edinburgh*, 1557-1571, pp. 148, 149). Her ratification of the Articles, for the interview with Elizabeth in the summer of 1563, is dated at Perth on the 24th of August (Labanoff's *Recueil*, i. 151-156).

[6] A meeting of Privy Council was held at Edzell on the 25th of August (*Register of Privy Council*, i. 218).

[7] The *Register of Privy Seal* (xxxi. 38) indicates that she was at Glammis on the 26th of August.

[8] *Foreign Calendar, Elizabeth*, v. 273.

[9] *Foreign Calendar, Elizabeth*, v. 273.—Randolph and Argyll spent two nights under Huntly's hospitable roof. His house was the fairest and best furnished that Randolph had seen in the country; his cheer was 'marvellous great,' and 'his mind such as it ought to be towards his Sovereign' (*Ibid.* v. 304).

[10] *Foreign Calendar, Elizabeth*, v. 82, 161, 199, 420.

[11] *Acts of the Parliaments of Scotland*, ii. 572.

[12] *Register of Privy Council*, i. 219; *Foreign Calendar, Elizabeth*, v. 303. See also *infra*, p. 310, *n.* 45.

[13] Chalmers alleges that 'the demanding of the possession [of Inverness Castle], by an armed force, in time of peace, was illegal and unwarrantable, even in the Queen herself' (*Life of Mary*, 1818, i. 85). Yet the Castle was hers, though the keepership had long been in the Huntly family (*Foreign Calendar, Elizabeth*, v. 303; *Spalding Miscellany*, iv. 152, 153).

[14] Three years later, Mary, it was said, was provided with 'a "knape scall" for her head' (*Foreign Calendar, Elizabeth*, vii. 489). On the evening of Riccio's murder, Ruthven entered Mary's chamber 'with his knappisca upon his head' (Melville's *Memoirs*, Maitland Club, p. 149). A 'knapschalle,' 'knape-scall,' 'knappisca,' or 'knapscha' was a headpiece, a sort of helmet; but Mr. Skelton, with his wonted carelessness, makes it a *knapsack* (*Maitland of Lethington*, i. 286; *Mary Stuart*, 1893, p. 63).

[15] *Foreign Calendar, Elizabeth*, v. 303, 304.—According to Randolph, she arrived in Inverness on the 9th of September and stayed there five days.

[16] *Foreign Calendar, Elizabeth*, v. 304, 305, 318, 319.—Perhaps 'Laird of *Banke*' should be 'Laird of *Banff*.' The Town Council of Aberdeen experienced considerable difficulty in providing the money to pay for the decoration of their town and for the Queen's present (*Burgh Records of Aberdeen*, Spalding Club, i. 339, 340, 346–349). They had afterwards to recompense Thomas Nicolson, for 'the skayth sustenit be him in braking of certane chalmeris of his arteilyerie, quhilkis the toun borrowit fra him, and wes usit and schot with pulder in volie at the Quenis first entre to this

burght' (*Ibid.* i. 351). The ensign, specially made for the occasion, was still preserved in Aberdeen in 1616, but was 'all lacerat and revin, and nocht seiming to be borne' (*Ibid.* ii. 345).

[17] *Register of the Privy Council,* i. 219.—Randolph tells a curious story as to how Sir John Gordon obtained Findlater (*Foreign Calendar, Elizabeth,* v. 330)—a story which explains why Lady Findlater is, in the Act of Privy Council, termed 'his pretendit spous.'

[18] 'She passed hard by the house of Findlater, which John Gordon has in possession, standing upon the sea, not easy to be taken without cannon. She sent a trumpeter to summon the same, with charge to deliver it up to the captain of the guard, which they denied. There is another house [*i.e.* Auchindoune] summoned and kept against her' (*Foreign Calendar, Elizabeth,* v. 319).

[19] 'It is worth writing how this cannon came into these parts. In the Duke's government [*i.e.* while Chatelherault was Regent] none was so great with him as the Earl of Huntly, then Lieutenant, who to give this people a greater terror obtained to have a cannon to lie in Strathbogie, which stood always in the middle of the court—a terrible sight to as many as entered the house, or who had offended the Earl. This cannon, three days before the Queen should come there, was carried into a cellar' (*Foreign Calendar, Elizabeth,* v. 329).

[20] *Ibid.* v. 329, 330.

[21] *Foreign Calendar, Elizabeth,* v. 360, 361 ; *Records of Aboyne,* New Spalding Club, pp. 465, 466.—The Laird of Grange left Aberdeen early enough in the morning to be at Strathbogie by midday. His visit raised no suspicion, as his men were so few in number. While he questioned the servants, the Tutor of Pitcur rode about the house and gardens, lest any one should escape by the back. Possibly Grange was selected for this work because, by a similar ruse, he had so successfully entered the Cardinal's stronghold at St. Andrews sixteen years before. In this case he failed, through a watchman in the tower seeing the Lord John and his company a mile off. Huntly was warned in time ; and, once in the saddle, they could not overtake him, as their horses were tired with the long journey. Having escaped, there was now little chance of his apprehension, unless he were betrayed. In the *Calendar* there is, however, the suggestive sentence :—'They want in the Highlands no good fellows to be instruments in any such purpose.'

²² *Register of Privy Council*, i. 219, 220.

²³ *Foreign Calendar, Elizabeth*, v. 386 ; *Acts of the Parliaments of Scotland*, ii. 573.—In the teeth of these two authorities, the 21st of October is given as the date of this enterprise (*Records of Aboyne*, p. 466).

²⁴ *Foreign Calendar, Elizabeth*, v. 386.—The present Marquis of Huntly alleges that the Lord Gordon ' was living quietly among his wife's kinsfolk the Hamiltons,' ' when his father and brothers, for their own protection, took up arms' (*Records of Aboyne*, p. 470) ; but this is not implied in Randolph's statement.   Moreover at his trial he was specially charged with being with his father and brother in Aberdeen on the 30th of August ; with being with Sir John near Strathbogie on the 4th of September ; and with being on the 11th of September at Tuwdoun, with eight score horsemen, to aid his brother against the Queen (*Acts of the Parliaments of Scotland*, ii. 576).   According to Knox, Lord Gordon was sent by his father to ask Chatelherault ' to putt to his handis in the south, as he should do in the north ; and so it should not be Knoxis crying nor preaching that should stay that purpose' ; and it was constantly affirmed that Bothwell, who had just escaped from Edinburgh Castle, had been in consultation with Lord Gordon (Laing's *Knox*, ii. 347). One of the charges on which Lord Gordon was condemned was his desiring Bothwell, after breaking ward, to raise men and horses for his service (*Acts of the Parliaments of Scotland*, ii. 577).

²⁵ Rumours were spread that Murray and all his band were slain ; and again that Mary had given herself to the Earl of Huntly (Laing's *Knox*, ii. 351).

²⁶ Knox induced the Master of Maxwell—afterwards Lord Herries—to advise Bothwell ' to behave himself as it became a faythfull subject, and to keape good quyetness in the partis committed to his charge, and so wold his cryme of the breaking of the ward be the more easelie pardoned.'   To Chatelherault, Knox himself wrote, earnestly exhorting him, ' neather to geve eare to the Bischope his bastard brother, nor yit to the persuasions of the Erle of Huntley ; for yf he did, he assured him, that he and his House should come to a suddane ruyn' (Laing's *Knox*, ii. 351).   Eight days after Mary's return to Edinburgh from the North, Knox had an interview with Chatelherault, which is thus described by Randolph :—' Upon Sondaye at nyght the Duke supped with Mr. Knox, wher the Duke desyered that I sholde be.   Thre speciall poyntes

he hathe promised to performe to Mr. Knox before me ; the one is never to goe for any respecte from that that he hathe promised to be a professor of Chrystes worde and setter forth of the same to hys power; the nexte allwayes to shewe hymself an obbedyent subjecte to his Soveregne, as farre as in deutie and conscience he is bounde; the thyrde never to alter from that promes he hathe made for the mayntenance of peace and amytie betwene bothe the realmes' (Stevenson's *Selections*, Maitland Club, p. 106).

[27] *Foreign Calendar, Elizabeth*, v. 386.

[28] *Foreign Calendar, Elizabeth*, v. 399, 421, 422.—Randolph gives the number of Huntly's force as seven hundred, and afterwards as five hundred.   Bishop Lesley avers that he 'assembled a force of twelve hundred brave and trustworthy men, from among his relatives, clansmen, and followers,' but that many deserted when the enemy were beginning to surround him (Forbes-Leith's *Narratives of Scottish Catholics*, pp. 88, 89).   The Jesuit fathers informed the Pope that Huntly 'had collected about five or six thousand men' (Nau's *History of Mary Stewart*, app. p. 119). Goodall hazards the opinion that not one of his men drew a sword (*Examination*, i. 197).   Lesley has carefully recorded the speech with which he encouraged his men to fight; and from that speech it appears that he expected that some of those in arms against him would prove his friends (Forbes-Leith's *Narratives*, p. 89).   This phase of his speech is emphasised by Knox, who, like Buchanan, believed that the vanguard of Huntly's opponents was actuated by treachery (Laing's *Knox*, ii. 355, 356 ; Aikman's *Buchanan*, ii. 463, 464).   Before the battle, Lethington made 'a vehement orisoun,' and willed every man to call upon his God, to remember his duty, and not to fear the multitude ; so says Knox, who has preserved the fervent prayer with which he concluded (Laing's *Knox*, ii. 356). Lesley's statement—that Huntly was 'put to death by Moray's order, with a firelock discharged, as it was said, close into his ear' (Forbes-Leith's *Narratives*, p. 90)—is quite inconsistent with Randolph's account, as given in the text, and with the narrative of a contemporary chronicler, who affirms that, 'in this conflict the said Erle of Huntlie was tane be ane Andro Reidpeth, ane of our Soverane Ladies gaird, quha put him upone his horse to have brocht him to the Quenis Majestie ; bot howsein he was set upoun horsback, incontinent thairefter he bristit and swelt, sua that he spak not one word, bot deceissit' (*Diurnal of Occurrents*, p. 74).   Buchanan

U   305

states that Huntly, 'heavy through age and asthmatic through corpulence, died in the hands of those who took him' (Aikman's *Buchanan*, ii. 464); Knox—who speaks of his spirit failing him before the conflict 'be reassone of his corpolencie'—that he, 'immediatlie after his tacken, departed this lyiff without any wound, or yitt appearance of any strock, whairof death might have enseued' (Laing's *Knox*, ii. 357); and Herries, that 'Huntlie himselfe was taken by one Andro Rippeth, one of the Queen's guard; but being a corpulen man, he died upon horsback, in the throng' (Herries's *Historical Memoirs*, p. 66). According to his present representative, 'he died of apoplexy' (*Records of Aboyne*, p. 467). The battle of Corrichie was fought on the 28th of October 1562.

[29] *Foreign Calendar, Elizabeth*, vi. 399, 421; *Diurnal of Occurrents*, p. 74; *Genealogical History of the Earldom of Sutherland*, p. 141.—Buchanan says that Sir John 'was mangled by an unskilful executioner'; and that 'the Queen beheld his death with many tears' (Aikman's *Buchanan*, ii. 464).

[30] Stevenson's *Selections*, p. 104; Keith's *History*, ii. 180, 181.—Two days after the battle of Corrichie a messenger arrived at Aberdeen, with the assurance that Chatelherault would take no part with Huntly. Lord Gordon had departed from him *re infecta* (*Foreign Calendar, Elizabeth*, v. 422); but, in obedience to Mary's command, was apprehended and kept by him at Kinneil (Keith's *History*, ii. 176).

[31] Stevenson's *Selections*, p. 106; *Diurnal of Occurrents*, pp. 74, 75.

[32] *Acts of the Parliaments of Scotland*, ii. 577.—Lord Gordon was condemned to death by the Justice Court (*Ibid.* ii. 576), not by Parliament, as Lesley erroneously states (Father Forbes-Leith's *Narratives*, p. 91). Three days after being 'put to the knowlege of ane assyiss,' and 'be the samin convictit and declarit tratour,' he was taken from Edinburgh Castle to the Castle of Dunbar, 'and thair put in frie ward' (*Diurnal of Occurrents*, p. 75). By the Parliament which condemned his father, he was 'decernit to pas to Dunbar agane' (*Ibid.* p. 76). Gordonstoun, Straloch, and Father Tyrie tell that Murray surreptitiously obtained Mary's signature to a letter ordering his execution, but that his keeper saved his life by taking the precaution of seeing Mary personally (*Genealogical History of the Earldom of Sutherland*, 1813, p. 143; Gordon's *Scots Affairs*, Spalding Club, i. pp. viii, ix; Forbes-Leith's *Narratives*,

p. 91 *n.*). In the combined revocation and proclamation after her escape from Loch Leven (*supra*, p. 174), Murray is charged with 'falslie steilling our handwrit,' thinking to slay Huntly's 'eldest sone, now Erle, than in Dumbar' (*The Lennox*, 1874, ii. 440; *Memorials of the Earls of Haddington*, 1889, ii. 270). The story, however, would need to be better authenticated; as the present Marquis of Huntly acknowledges, suspicion is thrown upon it by the mere fact of his being in 'free ward' (*Records of Aboyne*, p. 470); and Knox states that, before Chatelherault delivered him up, Murray 'laubored at the Quenis hand for the saiftye of his lyeff, which hardly was granted' (Laing's *Knox*, ii. 360). On the 12th of May 1565, Throckmorton found him still in Dunbar Castle—'a condemned man for high treason' (Keith's *History*, ii. 278, 279); but the time of his deliverance was drawing nigh. On the 3rd of the following August—five days after Mary's marriage with Darnley—he was by open proclamation 'relaxit fra the proces of horn,' and received again into the royal favour (*infra*, p. 358, *n.* 28). Sixteen days after Darnley's murder, Mary granted a precept of remission to Huntly and his friends for Corrichie (*Spalding Miscellany*, iv. 154-156); and—five days before she was carried off by Bothwell to Dunbar—the sentence of death and forfeiture was by Parliament declared null and void on the ground of informality (*Acts of the Parliaments of Scotland*, ii. 576-579).

[33] *Foreign Calendar, Elizabeth*, v. 421; vi. 381; Laing's *Knox*, ii. 359, 380, 381; *Records of Aboyne*, pp. 467, 468; *Diurnal of Occurrents*, p. 76; *Acts of the Parliaments of Scotland*, ii. 573; Forbes-Leith's *Narratives*, pp. 90, 91.

[34] *Acts of the Parliaments of Scotland*, ii. 579-581.—The sentence was reduced on the ground of informality.

[35] According to Chalmers, the Lord James—anxious to secure the Earldom of Murray—saw that a handle might be made of Sir John Gordon's escape from prison; and therefore persuaded Mary to go to the north, where, 'being egregiously imposed upon by a thousand of his fictions and falsehoods, the Queen was at once made the victim of his ambition and the instrument of his murders' (*Life of Mary*, 1818, i. 79, 80, 98; ii. 299, 300). Mary's journey to the north had, however, been planned long before (*supra*, p. 301, *n.* 2). The idea that she was taken there to carry out a premeditated conspiracy of Murray against Huntly is scouted by

Patrick Fraser Tytler as an imagination of those who are 'guided by their prejudices rather than their research' (*History of Scotland*, 1845, v. 225). Hosack, too, holds that Murray 'was in no way responsible' for 'the rebellion of the Gordons, an incident clearly arising from the feudal anarchy which prevailed in Scotland,' and that the expedition to the north 'seems to have been planned, not by Murray, but by the Queen herself' (*Mary and her Accusers*, i. 89).

[36] Even after Knox knew the results of the northern progress, he was dubious about the motives which had impelled Mary to undertake it :—'Whitther thair was any secreat pactioun and confederacye betwix the Papistis in the south, and the Erle of Huntley and his Papistis in the north ; or, to speak more planelie, betwix the Quene hirself and Huntley, we can not certanlie say. But the suspitionis war wounderous vehement, that thair was no good will borne to the Erle of Murray, nor yit to such as depended upoun him at that tyme' (Laing's *Knox*, ii. 346).

[37] It is calmly related by Gordonstoun—the son of Janet, *alias* Jane Gordon, Huntly's daughter, Bothwell's divorced spouse— that Mary went to the north that she might be delivered by Huntly from the power of her bastard brother, and that she might marry 'Sir John Gordon of Findlater, a comly young gentleman, verie personable, and of good expectation, whom she loved intirlie' (*Genealogical History of the Earldom of Sutherland*, 1813, p. 140). According to Buchanan, Sir John 'was a manly youth, extremely handsome, and just in the opening bloom of life' (Aikman's *Buchanan*, ii. 464). Although Sir John had already a 'pretendit spous' (*Register of Privy Council*, i. 219), whom he kept locked up in 'a close chamber' (*Foreign Calendar, Elizabeth*, v. 330), it is quite possible that a royal marriage had been planned for him ; and that the 'great preparations' at Strathbogie were intended for its suitable celebration ; but Gordonstoun's story, that such a marriage had been suggested and approved by the Guises, and desired by the Queen of Scots, is altogether incredible. One of the charges against the dead Huntly was that he had conspired to help Sir John—on the last day of August, the day on which he appeared before the Justiciary Court in the Tolbooth of Aberdeen —to enter the Queen's lodging with a great number of armed men to desire 'sic thingis of hir Hienes as wes nocht lefull,' and in the event of her refusal 'to put violent handis in her persoun, and leid

hir quhair thai plesit' (*Acts of the Parliaments of Scotland*, ii. 572).
And Mary told Randolph 'how detestable a part Huntly thought
to have used against her; as to have married her where he would'
(*Foreign Calendar, Elizabeth*, v. 421).

   38 Mary's northern progress was, as Randolph testifies, 'rather
devised by herself than greatly approved by her Council' (Chalmers's
Mary, ii. 300 *n.*).

   39 *Supra*, pp. 268, 269.

   40 Lists of Huntly's movables which fell to Mary after Corrichie
will be found in Thomson's *Collection of Inventories*, 1815, pp. 153-
158, and in Robertson's *Inventories of Mary's Jewels*, 1863, pp.
49-56; but they did not all belong to Huntly, for, three years
before, the Bishop, Dean, and Chapter of Aberdeen had placed in
his hands for safe-keeping many of their church valuables and
vestments, to be returned on ten days' notice ' under paine of God's
curse' (*Registrum Episcopatus Aberdonensis*, Spalding Club, vol. i.,
pp. lxxxviii-xc). It was no wonder that the Bishop and his chapter
had taken precautions to secure their vestments, seeing that among
them were a number made of cloth of gold captured by Bruce at
Bannockburn (*Ibid.* ii. 189, 190). On the 9th of October 1562—
after Huntly baulked Grange, Lindsay, and the Lord John, by
escaping from Strathbogie—' some searched the house, but found
no suspected person or any kind of stuff in it save a few beds of
the worst sort. Her [*i.e.* the Countess's] chapel remained garnished,
and being demanded why it was not disfurnished, she said she was
sure the Queen would not be offended with it' (*Foreign Calendar,
Elizabeth*, v. 361). It is quite likely—though it cannot be proved—
that the three fair church vestments ' of claith of gold,' which were
delivered by Mary's orders to Bothwell a few weeks after the
murder of Darnley (Robertson's *Inventories*, p. 53), were actually
part of those which had been made of the Bannockburn spoils
(*Ibid.* p. xxvi).

   41 The Lord James had been legitimated on the 4th of February
1561-2, and created Earl of Mar on the 7th of that month (*Register
of Privy Seal*, xxxi. 2). In one passage, Chalmers gives the 10th
of February as the date when he was made Earl of Mar (*Life of
Mary*, 1818, ii. 296); but in another he gives the correct date
(*Ibid.* ii. 432).

   42 Randolph mentions, in his letter from Spynie on the 18th of
September, the gift of the Earldom of Murray to the Lord James

(*Foreign Calendar, Elizabeth*, v. 305); and on the 30th reports:—
'Men have great hope that the Earl of Murray will do much good
in this country. His power of men is great, and the revenue
esteemed 1000 marks a year; the country, pleasant. The place
called Ternawe [*i.e.* Darnaway] is very ruinous, save the halle, very
fair and large. The last Earl was King James the Fifth's bastard
brother, who was much beloved; since that time the whole country
has been under the Earl of Huntly' (*Ibid.* v. 330). The Lord
James had, however, received a gift of the Earldom of Murray on
the 30th of January 1561-2, that is, eight days before he was made
Earl of Mar (*Register of Privy Seal*, xxxi. 45, 46); and, in the
previous November, Randolph had reported that he was 'lyke shortly
to be Erle of Murray' (Wright's *Elizabeth*, i. 83).

[43] Robertson's *Inventories*, p. xxiv, *n.* 2.

[44] *Foreign Calendar, Elizabeth*, v. 334.

[45] Though the keys of Findlater and Auchindoune had been
offered by a horse-boy on the 9th of October, 'it was found that
they had been brought by a brother of Mr. Thomas Ker, who was
committed to ward; suspicious letters were found about him. He
excuses his master, and burdens John Gordon as author of the
whole evil, and yet it is known that he is daily in his father's
company, and does nothing but by his order' (*Foreign Calendar,
Elizabeth*, v. 361). 'Mr. Thomas Ker and his brother being in
custody have confessed that their master determined three several
times to have slain Murray and Lethington, letters were also found
about Mr. Thomas that import no less; but whatsoever was done
by John Gordon, was by his father's counsel' (*Ibid.* v. 386). At
Corrichie, 'there were found about the Earl certain letters, very
suspicious against some' (*Ibid.* v. 399). 'John Gordon has confessed all, and lays the fault on his father. He is not yet [2nd
November 1562] condemned, but doubtless will not escape' (*Ibid.* v.
421). See also Laing's *Knox*, ii. 359; Keith's *History*, ii. 175, 176.

[46] Keith's *History*, ii. 182.

[47] 'She will not yet grant to go to his house, although it is
within three miles of her way, and the fairest in the country.
That purpose of hers will be broken, for so her Council find it
expedient' (*Foreign Calendar, Elizabeth*, v. 273).

[48] Concerning Corrichie, Knox says:—'The Erle of Murray
send message unto the Quene of the mervalouse victorye, and
humblie prayed hir to schaw that obedience to God as publictlie

to convene with thame, to geve thankis unto God for his notable deliverance. Sche glowmed boyth at the messenger and at the requeast, and skarselie wold geve a good worde or blyth countenance to any that sche knew earnest favoraris of the Erle of Murray, whose prosperitie was and yitt is a verray vennoume to hyr boldened harte against him for his godlynes and uprycht plainess. Of many dayes she bair no better countenance; whairby it myght have bene evidentlie espyed, that sche rejosed nott greatlie of the successe of that mater' (Laing's *Knox*, ii. 358). According to Buchanan, Murray ' proceeded to the Court, where, amid the mutual gratulations of the courtiers, the Queen betrayed no symptom of joy, either in her countenance or speech' (Aikman's *Buchanan*, ii. 464).

[49] *Foreign Calendar, Elizabeth*, v. 421.

[50] *Supra*, p. 234, *n*. 29.   See also *Records of Aboyne*, pp. 456-458.

[51] *Spalding Miscellany*, iv. 144-150.—The Indenture between the Duke of Somerset and the Earl of Huntly, of 6th December 1548, declares that the Indenture of the preceding day ' is of none effect, and that we both did not, nor do mane that the said writing shuld binde anie of us or be of anie effect or force, but wes devised onely by the procuirement and desier of me the said Erle to be carried with me the said Erle into Scotland at my going thither, to be shewed to the Governor and others of Scotland for a covert of our proceidingis, and to the intent that by pretence thereof I the said Erle might the better conduce my service to the furtherance of the Kingis Majesteis affaires, and the advancement of such purposes as I have promised to the said Duke to do my best to bring to passe.'

[52] Lesley's *History*, pp. 220-222.—While Sir Ralph Fane's letter to the Protector implies that Huntly's sincerity was suspected, and while it explains how his escape was facilitated, it also sweeps away some of Lesley's details. Fane—or Avane, as Lesley calls him—was not with him in Morpeth ; and his son-in-law had been straitly forbidden by Lord Grey ' to give any semblance of suspicion in thErle, least it might be a meane to alienate his minde when he should perceave that we had no great trust in him.' When benighted at Morpeth, Huntly was allowed—as he had hitherto been on his journey northward—' to have his chamber alone and to use all thingis at his libertie' (*Records of Aboyne*, pp. 449-452). As he had been bound, however, by the second Indenture to give as

hostages—before leaving Berwick—his wife, three of his sons, and his brother, in pledge for his return, the escape at Morpeth cannot be regarded as having been pre-arranged with Somerset. Fane's grief was apparently due to the fear that through the escape he might lose part of the ransom (*Hatfield Calendar*, i. 59). Lesley relates that ere Mary of Guise had long been Regent, she had occasion to punish Huntly (Lesley's *History*, pp. 251, 252; cf. *Register of Privy Council*, xiv. 13). To the present Marquis her conduct in this is inexplicable (*Records of Aboyne*, p. 455).

CHAPTER VIII

[1] Nau's *History of Mary Stewart*, app. p. 119.—In this Report the Jesuit priests show a contemptuous disregard of the most commonplace historical facts. Perhaps they thought that the infallible head of their Church was easily imposed upon.

[2] Causin's *Holy Court*, 1678, p. 812.

[3] *Foreign Calendar, Elizabeth*, vii. 71.—Randolph was not the only one to whom Mary disclaimed all desire for marriage (Forbes-Leith's *Narratives*, pp. 92, 93; Philippson's *Marie Stuart*, iii. 461, 462).

[4] *Foreign Calendar, Elizabeth*, v. 233.

[5] Chatelar—'descended on his mother's side from the Chevalier Bayard'—was 'highly accomplished, a good musician, and an agreeable poet.' As one of the suite of Damville, the Constable's son, he had accompanied Mary on her voyage from France, and had addressed verses to her, to which she had replied (Mignet's *History of Mary*, 1851, i. 128). Drawn, perhaps, by that 'inchantment whereby men ar bewitched,' he again came to Scotland next year, and met the Queen at Montrose, as she returned from her northern progress, in November 1562. He had brought a long letter from his master, and presented her with 'a book of his own making written in meeter.' He was courteously received, kindly entertained, and rode upon 'the soar [*i.e.* sorrel] gelding' that Lord Robert had given to the Queen of Scots (Stevenson's *Selections*, p. 103; Keith's *History*, ii. 177-180). In Randolph's opinion, Mary showed 'over-great familiarity . . . unto so unworthy a creature and abject a varlet'—familiarity which would have been

'too much to have been used to his master himself by any Princess alive' (*Foreign Calendar, Elizabeth*, vi. 133). Knox is quite as plain. 'Chattelett,' as he calls him, 'passed all otheris in credytt with the Quene. In dansing of the Purpose . . . the Quene chosed Chattelett, and Chattelett took the Quene. Chattelett had the best dress. All this wynter Chattelett was so familiare in the Quenis cabinett, ayre and laitt, that scarslye could any of the nobilitie have access unto hir. The Quene wold ly upoun Chatte-lettis shoulder, and sometymes prively she wold steall a kyss of his neck' (Laing's *Knox*, ii. 367, 368). As Lethington was to leave on the 13th of February on his embassy to England and France, he and Murray and other two members of Council had a long meeting with Mary, in her private cabinet, on the evening of the 12th—a meeting which was prolonged until after midnight. The attendants in Mary's chamber having fallen asleep, Chatelar took the opportunity of slipping beneath her bed. There, with his sword and dagger, he was luckily discovered, not, as Mignet alleges, by Mary herself, but by two grooms of the chamber, who 'looked as usual behind the tapestry and the bed.' When next morning she was apprised of what had happened, she ordered him out of her presence. He, notwithstanding, followed her to Dun-fermline, and—finding, as he thought, her wrath appeased—took fresh courage, and boldly entered her chamber at Burnt Island, on the evening of the 14th of February, when only certain of her gentle-women were with her. He desired to clear himself of the crime with which he had been charged, denying that he was found under her bed, and alleging that, being in her chamber late, and over-come for want of sleep, he had retired into her private closet. For this second intrusion he was seized, carried to St. Andrews, where he was tried, and in the market-place of which he was executed on Monday the 22nd, being the market day (*Foreign Calendar, Elizabeth*, vi. 133, 166, 167; *Spanish Calendar, Elizabeth*, i. 314). According to Brantôme, he recited on the scaffold Ronsard's hymn to death; and, turning to the place where he supposed the Queen to be, cried aloud, 'Adieu, the most beautiful and the most cruel Princess of the world' (Jebb's *De Vita et Rebus Gestis Mariæ*, ii. 497). According to Knox, 'At the place of executioun, when he saw that thair was no remeady but death, he maid a godly confessioun, and granted that his declyning from the treuth of God, and following of vanitie and impietie, was justly recompensed upoun him. But in the end he concluded, looking unto the heavenis, with these words, "O cruelle dame"' (Laing's *Knox*, ii. 369 and *n.*). According to Randolph, he died with repentance, and confessed privately more than he spake openly. His purpose was, that night he was found under her bed, to have tried her constancy, and by force to have attempted what by no persuasions he could attain unto (*Foreign Calendar, Elizabeth*, vi. 167). Long afterwards, Randolph referred to this incident in terms which seem to imply that he believed her honour was compromised (Raumer's *Queen Elizabeth and Mary Queen of Scots*, 1836, p. 121); but, as Raumer has pointed out, if Mary 'had intended a meeting, she might easily have arranged it in a more convenient and safe manner' (*Ibid.* p. 23). Chatelar's rash and wicked conduct was, of course, exaggerated at the time in the rumours that found currency. Randolph reports, in his first communication after the Burnt Island episode, that when Mary was going to bed, and only two of her gentlewomen present, Chatelar, coming out of a secret corner, set upon her with such force, and in such impudent sort, that she herself had to cry for help ; that the matter was so manifest 'that no colour could be found to hide the shame and dishonour'; and that 'the Earl of Murray was sent for out of his lodging, whom the Queen incontinent commanded to put his dagger into him, which incontinent had been done if God had not put into his mind to have him reserved, and to be justified according to order of law' (*Foreign Calendar, Elizabeth*, vi. 133). The only material difference between Mary's own account and Randolph's seems to have been in the alleged reiterated command for immediate punishment (Philippson's *Marie Stuart*, iii. 464). The conversation between her and Murray on this point as reported by Knox (Laing's *Knox*, ii. 368) may be apocryphal ; but Mr. Skelton does not prove it to be so by alleging that Knox and Murray were then on bad terms (*Maitland of Lethington*, i. p. xxvii *n.*), for they did not quarrel until the following summer (Laing's *Knox*, ii. 382, 461). In England, Lady Throckmorton was informed that Chatelar had been left at the Scots Court by the Duke of Guise (*sic*), for whose sake he received much courtesy at Mary's hands (*Foreign Calendar, Elizabeth*, vi. 154). Henry Cobham not only confounded the two intrusions and intensified the excitement of the situation—as did Lady Throckmorton and others—but averred that Chatelar at first spoke for his master (*Ibid.* vi. 337, 338). The culprit himself, in passing through London, had said 'that he was going to Scotland to see his lady love' (*Spanish Calendar, Elizabeth*, i. 314). When the story of the Holyrood incident reached Paris, Chatelar was said to have been discovered below Mary's bed, not only with sword and dagger, but booted and spurred (*Venetian Calendar*, vii. 355). A month after the 'little Frenchman'—'who was always joking amongst the ladies'—had been executed, Lethington informed Bishop Quadra that, on being discovered, he tried hard to pass it all off as a joke; but afterwards 'said that he had been sent from France by persons of distinguished position' to 'try to make himself so familiar' with Mary and her ladies 'that he could seize an opportunity of obtaining some appearance of proof sufficient to sully the honour of the Queen;' that he intended, therefore, 'to remain that night underneath the bed, and go out in the morning, so that he could escape after being seen.' She who had given the principal instructions to him was 'Madame de Curosot'; but Mary had written to Lethington that the other names could not be intrusted to letters (*Spanish Calendar, Elizabeth*, i. 314). Madame de Guise told the Venetian Ambassador in Paris that Chatelar had 'confessed to having been sent by Madame de Cursolles,' a lady in great favour in the French Court, 'and supposed to be of this new religion, so that by this means she might defame that Queen, in order to thwart any marriage that might be treated for her' (*Venetian Calendar*, vii. 356. *Cf.* Teulet's *Papiers D'État*, iii. 4, 5). After Chatelar's intrusions, Mary Fleming slept with the Queen of Scots (*Foreign Calendar, Elizabeth*, v. 195).

⁶ *Supra*, pp. 33, 34, 226, 227.

⁷ *Spanish Calendar, Elizabeth*, i. 222.

⁸ Besides those mentioned in the text, the King of Sweden, his brother, the King of Denmark, the King of Navarre, the Duke of Ferrara, the Prince of Condé, the Duke of Orleans (afterwards Henry the Third), the young Duke of Guise, the Cardinal of Bourbon, Don John, Ferdinand, a son of Geoffrey Pole's, and the Duke of Norfolk, were suggested or spoken of at various times as suitors for the hand of the Queen of Scots.

⁹ Laing's *Knox*, ii. 360, 361.

¹⁰ *Spanish Calendar, Elizabeth*, i. 309, 310.—Next summer, in discussing with Bishop Quadra the prospects of the Archduke Charles, Lethington stated plainly that Mary's revenues were hardly enough for herself (*Ibid.* i. 340). At a later period one of

her agents was instructed to 'enter,' as of himself, with De Quadra's successor concerning the Don Carlos match, marvelling that he seeks not the Queen, 'considdering sche is the greatest mariage this day in Europe,' by reason of what she presently possesses, has title unto, 'and is *in potentia propinqua* to obtene' (Philippson's *Marie Stuart*, iii. 476). See also Mauvissière's *Memoirs*, 1724, p. 290.

¹¹ *Spanish Calendar, Elizabeth*, i. 312, 332 ; *Foreign Calendar, Elizabeth*, vi. 207, 302.

¹² *Foreign Calendar, Elizabeth*, vi. 302.

¹³ *Foreign Calendar, Elizabeth*, vi. 339, 417.—Sir James Melville says that he also was employed to make inquiries concerning the Archduke Charles—'to knaw of his religion, of his rentis, and of his qualites, and to send hame word to the Quen ; as also of his age and stature, and his pictour to send therewith, gif it culd be possible' (*Memoirs*, Maitland Club, p. 92). In the spring of 1565, Lethington told De Silva that although the Cardinal of Lorraine had entered into negotiations for this match without Mary's consent, yet 'as the Archduke was a son and relative of such powerful monarchs, she could not refuse him hastily, but in a respectful way said that she would lay the matter before her subjects, and in the meanwhile could learn what the Emperor was going to do for his son ; the idea being to drop the business politely on one or other of these points' (*Spanish Calendar, Elizabeth*, i. 422).

¹⁴ *Spanish Calendar, Elizabeth*, i. 308, 312.—It was reported at the French Court 'that so long as the Earl of Marr and Lethington rule in that realm [*i.e.* Scotland], they will never suffer the Archduke of Austria to have the Queen of Scotland, nor to come there ; and therefore means must be found to make them away' (*Foreign Calendar, Elizabeth*, vi. 418).

¹⁵ Labanoff's *Recueil*, i. 296, 297 ; Turnbull's *Mary's Letters*, p. 148.

¹⁶ *Spanish Calendar, Elizabeth*, i. 340, 341.

¹⁷ Mary was 'loth to have it thought that the Cardinal of Lorraine was a suitor for her in marriage to the Emperor's son.' The Cardinal wrote to her protesting that 'he was never suitor to the Emperor'; which Lethington said was true enough, for the Emperor was ever suitor to the Cardinal. Lethington was willing that Randolph should tell Elizabeth, 'as a great secret and a thing unfeignably true,' that the Emperor was offering '2,000,000 francs by year during his life, and 3,000,000 after his death to live with

her in Scotland'; and that he looked 'for a resolute answer by the end of May' 1564 (*Foreign Calendar, Elizabeth*, vii. 84, 89). As a dowry he had previously offered the country of the Tyrol, worth 30,000 francs a year (*Ibid.* vi. 339). The bigger sum would need to be better vouched.

[18] *Spanish Calendar, Elizabeth*, i. 307, 308.—Knox says that Lethington had been sent 'with large commissioun both to the Quene of England and unto the Guisianes'; but owns that what his 'credyte was, we know not' (Laing's *Knox*, ii. 360, 361). Another contemporary states that Maitland left Edinburgh on the 13th of February 1562-3, 'to quhat effect non knowis' (*Diurnal of Occurrents*, p. 75). The Instructions for his English embassy are printed in Keith's *History*, ii. 188-192; in Labanoff's *Recueil*, i. 161-169; and in the *Register of Privy Council*, xiv. 185-188.

[19] Philippson's *Marie Stuart*, iii. 459, 460, 463.—*Sark* is, by M. Philippson, misprinted *sarle*. Lethington's report is dated 9th March 1562-3. The Rhinegrave alleged on the 28th of that month that the Prince of Spain wished to marry the Queen of Scots (*Foreign Calendar, Elizabeth*, vi. 241).

[20] *Spanish Calendar, Elizabeth*, i. 309, 318.—It was at this time suspected that there was 'some practice of marriage,' though no man then in Scotland knew her mind. The preachers prayed daily that God would keep them from the bondage of strangers; and for her, that He would either turn her heart or send her short life (*Foreign Calendar, Elizabeth*, vi. 167, 168). Murray and Lethington were not then on the best of terms. 'Would that he [*i.e.* Lethington] had been plainer with Murray than he has been,' was Randolph's prayer. 'In his absence he never wrote to Murray. It was so determined between the Queen and him before his departure' (*Ibid.* vi. 382). On the 30th of April 1564, a well-informed Scot thus wrote :—'The Quene Mother [of France] hathe writin to our Quene, that Lid[dington] said to hir, that all that was spoken of the mariage with Spaine was done to caus England grant to our desyris' (Laing's *Knox*, vi. 540). Throckmorton was afterwards led to believe that the Spanish match 'was chiefly overthrown by Murray and Lethington' (*Foreign Calendar, Elizabeth*, vii. 371).

[21] Labanoff's *Recueil*, i. 296; Turnbull's *Mary's Letters*, pp. 147, 148.

[22] *Spanish Calendar, Elizabeth*, i. 332.

[23] To Philip, Guzman de Silva thus writes on the 21st of April 1565 :—' In addition to the Queen of Scotland's great claims to this kingdom [*i.e.* England], she certainly has here a very strong party, and it is highly desirable in many respects that she should be reckoned with in the consideration of affairs here which deeply concern us. The ports of this kingdom are necessary for the success of trade between Spain and the Netherlands and for other interests of the States ; but, besides this, these people are beginning to navigate largely, and may hinder us greatly in the Indies, upon which they look greedily, unless they are prevented in some way from going to those parts' (*Spanish Calendar, Elizabeth,* i. 419).

[24] *Spanish Calendar, Elizabeth,* i. 332, 333.—In this letter of 15th June 1563, Philip writes to his ambassador in London :—' If I saw any appearance of the Archduke's match being carried through, and of the possibility of getting from it the same advantages as at present appear derivable from the marriage with my son, I would embrace and promote it to the full extent of my power in preference to the latter, for the affection I bear to the Emperor my uncle and his sons. What has moved me to take this business up, and not to wait until the Emperor has been undeceived about it, has been the information you send me respecting the objections entertained by the Queen and her Ministers to the match with the Archduke, and the small benefit they think they will derive from it ; but, above all, your advice that they were about to enter into negotiations for the marriage of their Queen with the King of France. I well bear in mind the trouble and anxiety I underwent from King Francis when he was married to this Queen, and I am sure that if he had lived we could not have avoided plunging into war ere this on the ground of my protection of the Queen of England, whose country he would have invaded as he intended to do.'

[25] *Spanish Calendar, Elizabeth,* i. 334.

[26] *Spanish Calendar, Elizabeth,* i. 345.

[27] *Spanish Calendar, Elizabeth,* i. 346, 347.—In Bishop Jewel's opinion the Bishop of Aquila was 'a clever and crafty old fox, and formed for intrigue' (*Zurich Letters,* Parker Society, i. 102).

[28] *Foreign Calendar, Elizabeth,* vi. 510.—Two days before, Throckmorton had reported that the House of Guise was in no great credit in the French Court, but was regarded with jealousy for

'the practice' of this marriage, notwithstanding the rumour of the
Prince of Austria (*Ibid.* vi. 506). By the 12th of October, Smith
understood that 'without doubt the Queen of Scots had agreed to
take King Philip's son' (*Ibid.* vi. 551). In the beginning of
November Throckmorton perceived that the French still greatly
feared this marriage (*Ibid.* vi. 579). They were soon afterwards
relieved by the illness of Don Carlos and the expectation that he
would not live long (*Ibid.* vi. 590).

[29] *Spanish Calendar, Elizabeth,* i. 311, 321.

[30] *Spanish Calendar, Elizabeth,* i. 338.—Lethington told the same
story to the French Ambassador, adding, however, that Elizabeth
also objected to Mary's marriage with the French king. 'I asked
Lethington,' says De Quadra, 'whom he thought the Queen wished
her to marry, and he said he imagined it was some private gentleman, and as a last resort she would agree to the King of Denmark,
or another Protestant Prince, or even with the Duke of Ferrara,
or a person of similar position in France.'

[31] Laing's *Knox,* ii. 384-390.—The Reformer states that this
sermon and interview took place 'befoir the Parliament dissolved.'
They must therefore have been at the end of May or beginning of
June, the Queen having opened Parliament on the 26th of the one
month and closed it on the 6th of the other (*Foreign Calendar,
Elizabeth,* vi. 381, 399). According to Knox, 'The Quene wold
have had the censement of the Lordis of Articles, yf that such
maner of speaking deserved not punishement; but she was con-
sailled to desist: and so that storm quiettit in appearance, but
never in the hearte.'

[32] 'The rest of that sommer [1563] the Quene spent in hir
progresse through the West Countrey, whair in all tounes and
gentil-mennes places she had her messe. . . . From the West
Countrey, the Quene past in Ergyll to the hunting, and after
returned to Striveling' (Laing's *Knox,* ii. 391). 'The Queen after
this [*i.e.* the rising of Parliament] went to Argyllshire for relaxation,' says Bishop Lesley, 'and spent all the summer in hunting and other royal diversions' (Forbes-Leith's *Narratives,* p.
92). Buchanan represents her as hunting 'in Athole' (Aikman's
Buchanan, ii. 465; Ruddiman's *Buchanan,* i. 339); and William
Barclay describes a stag-hunt, which, he says, she witnessed there
that year, and of which he himself was a spectator (Robertson's
Inventories, p. lxx, *n.*; Chambers's *Domestic Annals,* 1874, i. 30, 31).

So early as the preceding Easter Eve, Randolph had reported that this year Mary purposed to take her progress into Argyll (*Foreign Calendar, Elizabeth*, vi. 280); and on the 13th of June he mentioned the preparations that were being made for her journey thither (*Ibid.* vi. 399).

[33] *Foreign Calendar, Elizabeth*, vi. 518.—Randolph's Instructions, dated the 20th of August 1563, are printed, from the original, in Keith's *History*, ii. 205-208.   For summaries of an earlier and of a corrected draft, see *Foreign Calendar, Elizabeth*, vi. 509, 510.   For the form in which they were given in to Mary by Randolph, see Melville's *Memoirs*, Mait. Club ed. pp. 105-107.   It was only if Mary made light of mere advice, and if Randolph saw no other means to satisfy her, that he was to say:—'We are well content, if our sister will in her marriage have regard to these things, and content us and this our nation in her marriage, upon assured knowledge thereof, to proceed to the inquisition of her right and title to be our next cousin and heir, and to further that which shall appear advantageous for her, and to hinder and impeach that which shall seem to the contrary ; using also therein such means as may be to the contentation of our realm, both nobility and commons.'

[34] Melville's *Memoirs*, Mait. Club, p. 107.

[35] *Spanish Calendar, Elizabeth*, i. 313.—Lethington said to De Quadra that he ' was anxious to escape from this colloquy by bringing on the subject of the succession, which he knew would shut her mouth directly, and therefore told her that the Queen his mistress was very young yet, and what this Queen might do for her was to marry Lord Robert herself first and have children by him, which was so important for the welfare of the country, and then when it should please God to call her to Himself, she could leave the Queen of Scots heiress both to her kingdom and her husband.   In this way it would be impossible for Lord Robert to fail to have children by one or other of them, who would in time become Kings of these two countries, and so turning it to a joke, he put an end to the conversation.'

[36] *Spanish Calendar, Elizabeth*, i. 395, 396, 407.

[37] Melville's *Memoirs*, Mait. Club, pp. 107, 108.

[38] *Spanish Calendar, Elizabeth*, i. 294, 307, 315, 318; *Foreign Calendar, Elizabeth*, v. 424; vi. 144.—The result of his wound proved fatal on Ash Wednesday, 24th of February 1562-3 (*Ibid.* vi. 169, 180).   When Mary received the news in St. Andrews, on the

15th of March, she was 'marvellously sad, and her ladies shed
tears like showers of rain' (*Ibid.* vi. 211). A fortnight afterwards,
Randolph delivered a letter from Elizabeth to her as she was on
the fields hunting. She said:—'I have now received no small
comfort, and the greatest that I can, coming from such one as my
dear sister, so tender a cousin and friend as she is to me; and
though I can neither speak nor read but with tears, yet think you
not but that I have received more comfort of this letter' (and
incontinent putteth it into her bosom next her skin) 'than I have
of all that hath been said unto me since I heard first word of my
uncle's death. Now I trust God will not leave me destitute; and,
for my part, I will show myself as loving and as kind unto my sister,
your mistress, as if God had given us both one father and mother.
It is most needful for us both, and I perceive it to be God's will it
should so be; for I see now that the world is not that that we do
make of it, nor yet are they most happy that continue longest in
it.' At dinner, after taking out the letter and re-reading it, she
said to those about her:—'God will not leave me destitute. I
have received the best letter from the Queen, my good sister of
England, that ever I had, and I do assure you it comforteth me.'
She needed all the comfort she could get, for immediately afterwards the death of the Grand Prior was broken to her (*Ibid.* vi.
260, 261).

[39] *Spanish Calendar, Elizabeth,* i. 223, 369, 422; *Foreign Calendar,
Elizabeth,* iv. 65 *n.*; vi. 553, 555, 579, 600; Philippson's *Marie
Stuart,* iii. 476.—Philippson says that Catherine opposed Mary's
match with Don Carlos, because she foresaw terrible dangers for
her own sons in the support which the policy of the Guises would
derive from the combined power of Spain, Scotland, England, and
Ireland, and therefore she wished to marry her daughter Margaret
to Philip's heir, and so bind Spain to France for ever, and thus
thwart the hostile intrigues of the Guises (*Ibid.* i. 277).

[40] *Foreign Calendar, Elizabeth,* vi. 616, 617, 636, 637, 649, 650.
—On the 15th of January, Randolph reported that Mary was well
again (*Ibid.* vii. 14). In the end of February the Cardinal of
Lorraine asked Throckmorton to procure a safe-conduct for Lugerie,
her physician, as she desired his advice for the recovery of her
health. He seems to have left Paris towards the close of April
1564, and to have remained in Scotland until the following March.
In Randolph's opinion, he was the Cardinal of Lorraine's spy

X   321

(*Ibid.* vii. 66, 67, 118, 308, 318). He, at all events, told the Cardinal of Mary's regard for Darnley (*Papiers D'État*, ii. 42).

[41] *Spanish Calendar, Elizabeth*, i. 371.—In the previous January, Randolph could see that Mary's heart was in Spain; but he thought that in the end she would be content with some one nearer home (*Foreign Calendar, Elizabeth*, vii. 23). Only eight days before Philip intimated to De Silva that the negotiations must cease, Challoner wrote from Madrid that the Prince had been very inquisitive regarding her estate, and that his affection appeared to bend most that way (*Ibid.* vii. 183).

[42] *Foreign Calendar, Elizabeth*, vii. 193, 196.

[43] *Spanish Calendar, Elizabeth*, i. 22, 23.—It was said that Philip befriended Elizabeth, during the reign of her sister Mary, in the hope of afterwards marrying her (Mauvissière's *Memoirs*, 1724, p. 59).

[44] *Spanish Calendar, Elizabeth*, i. 308; *Foreign Calendar, Elizabeth*, vii. 217.

[45] Of 'the children of France,' the Duke of Orleans, as well as Charles the Ninth, was thought of as a possible husband for the Queen of Scots. The description of the brothers written in April 1565 for the edification of Elizabeth, not of Mary, is thus calendared:—'The King was born on 17th of June 1550, and the Duke of Orleans on the 19th of September 1551. This winter the King shot up two fingers almost three higher than the Duke. The King is longer faced than he, and slender. The Duke looks more like King Edward. The Duke was christened Edward Alexander; now he signs Henry, having changed his name at his confirmation at Toulouse. The King is likely to grow taller, for he is slender, and has great knees and ancles, and his legs are not proportioned to them. The Duke is better proportioned of his legs and body, which shows he will not be very high. They are both pale, and not greatly timbered. They were in their youth sickly, and subject to many physicians and medicines. The King is amiable in countenance, and of more gentle nature than the Duke. This is the opinion of the courtiers. Howbeit he cannot perceive but that they are both gentle. The King seems tractable and wise for his years, and understands more of his affairs and gives wittier answers than a man would easily think. If the answer is to be given in few words, he gives it, and sometimes out of hand. He speaks somewhat fast and thick, which is a token that he is hot of

nature, a greater doer than speaker. But he neither lisps nor
stammers; he has not been much brought up in learning, and
speaks no tongue but his own' (*Foreign Calendar, Elizabeth*, vii.
336, 337).

[46] Randolph's Instructions of 17th November 1563 are printed in
Keith's *History*, ii. 213-217.—He was to tell Mary that she might
'most readily judge what sort of persons are not meet by the
example of her past marriage with the French King'; that none
who should 'practise in like sort to make any marriage betwixt her
and the children of France, Spain, or Austria, can have any other
intention, if not worse, than was in that of France'; and that
Elizabeth desired God 'to direct her heart' to such an one either
abroad or nearer home—'if it so be even in our own country'— as
might be 'affected to the perpetual concord and weal of these two
kingdoms.' If she gave just cause to think that she would so
choose, then the inquisition of her right to the succession would be
proceeded with; and if the matter fell out in her behalf, the declaration of her right would be gone on with 'upon plain knowledge had with whom she shall match in marriage.'

[47] Instigated by the Queen Mother of France, the Cardinal of
Guise had written to Mary warning her that Elizabeth meant no
good faith, and that her honour would not be advanced by marrying
any one so base as either Lord Robert or the Earl of Warwick.
Randolph perceived that the French were now beginning 'to make
fair weather' to Mary, 'which makes her think nothing less of
herself than ever she did' (*Foreign Calendar, Elizabeth*, vii. 22, 23).
On the eve of her marriage to Darnley, the French Ambassador in
England assured De Silva that Elizabeth had through him begged
the King and Queen-Mother of France to intercede with Mary for
Leicester; that they had done so; and that the Cardinal of Lorraine
had promised to Leicester 'to marry him to his niece—not saying
that he would try, but that he would do it' (*Spanish Calendar,
Elizabeth*, i. 444). The reasons urged in Scotland against Mary
marrying an English noble were that she could 'never imbase
herself so low' as to marry an inferior; of all who were in England,
it was known who was most worthy, but it was also known how
'evil-willing' Elizabeth would be to give him up, and 'how hardly
his mind could be diverted or drawn from that crown where it is
placed'; and even though Mary did marry to please Elizabeth, and
her right and title to the English succession were thereupon pub-

lished, her estate might not be advanced, as Elizabeth was 'as apt to marry and to have succession as this Queen herself.' On the 17th of February, Mary told Randolph (and Lethington confirmed the same) that the last message he brought was to less effect than the former, and that nothing was answered to what was chiefly desired. He was pressed to show his private Instructions, but he simply adhered to his oral statements. 'They gather that his Sovereign desires much that this Queen should marry in England. He acknowledges it to be her mind. They desire to know the person. He says that the Queen will not take from her that charge. They cast in "the Lord Darlie," though of him they mean nothing, nor find in him any great thing. He disallows no man. Has gone thus far with them, that they nothing doubt of the Queen's mind, nor can they perceive but there is good liking enough in this Queen, both of the person and his qualities. Sometimes she likes to hear of marriage. Many times the widow's life is best; sometimes she may marry where she will; sometimes she is sought of nobody. He pities many times unto her her state and case, and moves her that at the least she will take compassion upon her four Marys, that for her sake have vowed never to marry if she be not the first. . . . This people greatly desire that she were married. Divers suspect that overtures have been made by him in behalf of some Englishmen. Many believe it to be for "Lord Darlie." Few think upon the other, for the reasons he wrote before, but they would be content with either, and rather with this than the other [i.e. Leicester rather than Darnley], for the great "combers" he shall bring with him by both his father's and mother's titles here. . . . Lethington once was of mind that she might have her choice of Christendom, and liberty to bring in whom she would, but now he says he finds no man in the world so fit as he whom they desire. Has pressed him thereupon to work stoutly, but he alleges the dangers and difficulties. Murray is plain and faithful; his desire with Lethington is one. Argyll finds it good, and wishes that it were plainly so said unto her. The Duke [of Chatelherault] may suspect more than he can know by anything that has yet been said unto him. . . . For the rest, the writer [i.e. Randolph] cares not what they think, for these are they that will rule the roast when it comes to stirring the coals' (Foreign Calendar, Elizabeth, vii. 54, 55). On the 2nd of March, Murray, Argyll, and Lethington let Randolph understand that they thought their Sovereign

' could but give as uncertain an answer as he came with a doubtful message'; yet ' she desired nothing more than the Queen's contentment, with her own honour and weal of her country.' The response then given to Randolph's message was confirmed orally by Mary on the 4th of March (*Ibid.* vii. 72); and is printed by Philippson (*Marie Stuart*, iii. 468-472), who erroneously dates it November 1563.

⁴⁸ *Foreign Calendar, Elizabeth*, vii. 88-92.—In Mary's conversation with Randolph, her doubts and difficulties were practically the same as those given in the preceding note.

⁴⁹ *Foreign Calendar, Elizabeth*, vii. 91, 92, 108, 137, 148.

⁵⁰ Laing's *Knox*, vi. 541.

⁵¹ Knox's letter was written on the 3rd of May 1564. Four days before, Kirkcaldy of Grange had written from Perth :—' The Erll of Lenox will obtene licence to cum home and speak the Quene. Hir meanyng therin is not knawing, bot sum suspectis scho sall at lentht be perswadit to favour his *sonne*' (Laing's *Knox*, vi. 539, 540). In the *Foreign Calendar, Elizabeth*, vii. 122, this letter—the signature of which has been carefully obliterated—is attributed to Knox, and *sonne* is read *suit*. Bishop Jewel had suspected the Darnley match long before (*Zurich Letters*, Parker Society, i. 102); but Randolph thought it unlikely (*Foreign Calendar, Elizabeth*, iv. 512, 575 ; vi. 650).

⁵² *Foreign Calendar, Elizabeth*, vii. 108.

⁵³ Melville's *Memoirs*, p. 108.

⁵⁴ *Foreign Calendar, Elizabeth*, vi. 415; vii. 176, 177, 204, 205 ; Melville's *Memoirs*, pp. 108, 113; Wright's *Elizabeth*, i. 193; Philippson's *Marie Stuart*, iii. 474.—In the return of Lennox to Scotland, Sir Thomas Smith thought that Elizabeth had been overreached (*Foreign Calendar, Elizabeth*, vii. 404).

⁵⁵ *Foreign Calendar, Elizabeth*, vii. 207.

⁵⁶ *Foreign Calendar, Elizabeth*, vii. 204, 205.—Kirkcaldy of Grange feared that she would not accept Lord Robert, because he came not of a great old house, and that his blood had been spotted (*Ibid.* vii. 207) ; but she afterwards owned that she never bore better goodwill to any man, until she despaired through Elizabeth's irresolution (*Ibid.* vii. 372).

⁵⁷ Tytler's *Scotland*, 1845, v. 257 ; *Foreign Calendar, Elizabeth*, vii. 210.

⁵⁸ Melville's Instructions, which are incorporated in his *Memoirs* (pp. 112-115), are dated 28th September 1564; but 28th is probably

a mistake for 18th (*Foreign Calendar, Elizabeth*, vii. 204, 205, 211 ; Keith's *History*, ii. 228, *n.* 2).

[59] 'I had na will that sche suld think that I lyked of him, or had any ey or deling that way,' says Melville, ' albeit I had a secret charge to deall with his mother my Lady Lenox, to purches leave for him to pass in Scotland, wher his father was alredy, that he mycht se the contre, and convoy the Erle his father bak again to England' (Melville's *Memoirs*, p. 120).

[60] Melville thought that Elizabeth had a special reason for wishing to remain unmarried. 'I knaw your staitly stomak,' he said to her, ' ye think gene ye wer maried, ye wald be bot Quen of England, and now ye ar King and Quen baith ; ye may not suffer a commander' (Melville's *Memoirs*, p. 122).

[61] The frontispiece to Turnbull's *Letters of Mary Stuart* is a spirited engraving of Kirkpatrick Sharpe's clever and amusing drawing of Elizabeth dancing before Sir Roger Aston, who, when he delivered letters to her from James the Sixth, was always so placed in the lobby that ' he might see the Queen dancing to a little fiddle ; which was to no other end than that he should tell his master, by her youthful disposition, how likely he was to come to the possession of the crown he so much thirsted after.'

[62] Melville's *Memoirs*, pp. 122-126.

[63] Melville's *Memoirs*, p. 126.

[64] ' Hir Majeste was very glaid that matters wer brocht again in sa gud termes, as that famylier dealing mycht continew betwen hir and the Quen of England ; wherby sche mycht have acces to get intelligence fra a gret nomber of noble men and uthers, hir frendis and factioners in England ; and because sche fearit also to get the wyet [*i.e.* blame] of ther discord, gif it had continowed' (Melville's *Memoirs*, p. 129). On the evening of Melville's arrival in London, Throckmorton had supped with him. They were old friends ; and Melville says that Throckmorton 'was also a devot frend to the Quen my mestres, and to hir richt and title to the succession of the crown of England. Be him I had ample and famylier infourmation, and sur intelligence and frendly advise, how to procead with the Quen and every courteour in particulair. . . . Albeit he had na lyking for the tym, nother of my L[ord] Robert, nor of Mester Cicill, yet he knew that then nathing culd be done without them. Amang uther thingis he gaif me advyse to use gret famylarite with the Ambassadour of Spain, in caice I fand the Quen his maistres

our hard and difficill ; alleging that it wald be a gret spure to move
the Quen of England to geve our Quen a greter contentement in
hir desyres then sche had yet done' (*Ibid.* pp. 115, 116). Melville
had received oral instructions from Mary to deal, not only with
Elizabeth, but ' with the Spanisch Ambassadour, and with my Lady
Margret Douglas, and with sindre frendis sche had in England of
dyvers oppinions' (*Ibid.* p. 111).   Ere he left London, Lady
Lennox and Throckmorton sent ' many gud advyces to the Quen,
to be folowed fourth according to the tym and occasions.' Lady
Lennox sent also valuable presents to Mary, to her own husband,
to Murray, to Lethington, and to Melville's brother, Sir Robert,
' for sche was still in gud hope that hir sone my Lord Darley suld
com better speid then the Erle of Leycester, anent the mariage
with the Quen.   Sche was a very wyse and discret matroun, and
had many favorers in England for the tym' (*Ibid.* p. 127).   On his
return, Melville had given Mary ' the oppinions and advertismentis
of dyvers of hir frendis in England, as weill Catholikis as Protestantis ; and from the Ambassadour of Spain, of the K[ing] his
masters gud will towardis hir Majeste ; and lyk wayes of Don Carle
the Prince, albeit that he was for the tym in some suspition with
his father ; wherby the purpose of mariage wald apperantly tak
some delay, untill matters mycht fram better betwen the father
and the sonne ; assuring hir Majeste of his awen perticulair service
and furtherance at his power, and suld from tym to tym mak hir
intelligence' (*Ibid.* pp. 128, 129).

⁶⁵ Mary's 'princely qualites' are thus set forth by Melville :—
' Sche was sa effable, sa gratious and discret, that sche wan gret
estymation, and the hartis of many baith in England and Scotland,
and myn amang the rest ; sa that I thocht her mair worthy to be
servit for litle proffet then any uther Prence in Europe for gret
commodite.   Then sche was naturally liberall mair than sche had
moyen' (Melville's *Memoirs,* p. 111).   After her return from
France, she ' behaved hir self sa princely, sa honourably and dis-
cretly, that hir reputation spred in all contrees ; and was deter-
mynit and also inclynit to continow in that kynd of comelynes
unto the end of hir lyf ; desyring to hald nane in hir company bot
sic as wer of the best qualitez and conversation, abhorring all vices
and vitious personnes, whither they wer men or wemen. . . . Sche
was of a quyk spirit, and curious to knaw and to get intelligence of
the estait of uther contrees ; and wald be sometymes sad when sche

was solitary, and glaid of the company of them that had travelit in uther partis' (*Ibid.* pp. 130, 131).

⁶⁶ Melville's *Memoirs*, p. 129.

⁶⁷ The Memorial for Randolph, dated 4th October 1564, is printed, from the original, in Keith's *History*, ii. 234-239. Read in the light of Elizabeth's urgent letter to Cecil (*supra*, p. 97), the excuses for her delay are rather amusing. Mary and her advisers had little difficulty in repelling the attempt to throw the blame upon them (*Foreign Calendar, Elizabeth*, vii. 227-230).

⁶⁸ It was rather a lively time at the Scottish Court. Lord Seton had wronged Douglas of Longniddry, and over this Seton and Lethington—formerly great friends—had become mortal enemies. Five hundred horsemen, with spear, sword, and jack, assembled to debate this action on the day—Thursday—of Randolph's arrival. The conflict was averted by Mary at the last moment. On Friday, 'at the sermon,' Randolph met such of the Lords as he had most to do with. On Saturday the Lords were in the Tolbooth until five in the afternoon, occupied 'about a murder committed by some of the Eliots upon certain Scots.' Of the five condemned, three were beheaded on the Castlehill, after eight o'clock in the evening, under the weird glare of flaming torches. On Sabbath, a daughter of the Lord Justice Clerk's was married. Most of the ladies were there, and after dinner the Queen and her four Maries went thither —three miles from Edinburgh—to honour the bride. The Queen returned at night to Edinburgh in time to sup with Lennox and Randolph. In the midst of her supper she drank to Elizabeth, adding the words, ' *De bon cœur.*' That night she danced long and in a mask ; and 'playing at dice lost Lennox a jewel of crystal set in gold.' Chatelherault was expected on Monday, well accompanied ; and Argyll, on Tuesday. The Queen was 'determined to accord the Earl of Lennox and the Duke' ; and there was much talk as 'to what end all this favour showed to Lennox tends' (*Foreign Calendar, Elizabeth*, vii. 227-231). After three days' hot discussion about their lands, they were reconciled by Mary's efforts, formally shook hands, and drank to each other (*Ibid.* vii. 235 ; *Diurnal of Occurrents*, p. 78).

⁶⁹ *Foreign Calendar, Elizabeth*, vii. 234, 235 ; Keith's *History*, ii. 243-250.—Randolph had many reasons for doubting Mary's inclination to, and Lethington's approval of, the Darnley match ; but could assure Cecil of nothing, 'men's minds are so uncertain.'

[70] By the 3rd of November, Murray and Lethington had been appointed (*Foreign Calendar, Elizabeth*, vii. 236, 237). That the matter might be the more covertly handled, it was arranged that Mary should go to Dunbar for six or seven days; that Murray and Lethington should 'have leave to ride into the Merse ahawking, and also to visit some lands of theirs'; and that, while there, Bedford should send a gentleman to them, desiring them to rest one night in Berwick, 'forasmuch as there are divers matters in controversy upon the Borders' (*Ibid.* vii. 242, 243). Lest they might see the garrison's lack, Elizabeth sent pressing orders to her Lord Treasurer to forward the money of which it stood in need (*Ibid.* vii. 244). Mary's two representatives arrived at Berwick on the 18th of November; and next day entered into conference (*Ibid.* vii. 248). In their Instructions, Bedford and Randolph were directed to express Elizabeth's earnest desire that Mary should content herself with Leicester; if pressed by the Scotch to know what Elizabeth would do concerning the establishing of Mary's title, they might well say that they saw no way in her power more likely to further it than this; and that if Mary would live with her in England, she would 'gladly bear the charges of the family, both of the Earl of Leceister and her, as shall be meet for one sister to do for another.' They were in anywise to obtain of Mary's Commissioners 'as many requests as they will make, and by reasoning with them reduce them to as few as they can, and to the meanest estate and conditions that they may' (*Ibid.* vii. 219, 220). It is no wonder that Murray and Lethington told Randolph 'that they found Queen Elizabeth's dealing marvellous strange, and that nothing was intended but drift of time.' They were loath, however, to break off negotiations, and promised to let him know Mary's mind on the subject when he returned to Edinburgh (*Ibid.* vii. 248). Elizabeth was not altogether satisfied with the management of Bedford and Randolph (*Ibid.* vii. 264, 265); although they told her in their report that they had not exceeded their Instructions (Keith's *History*, ii. 250-256).

[71] On the 31st of October, Randolph reported that he had had many conversations with Mary, who was much inclined to think well of Elizabeth, and, as she said, to please her in all things reasonable, and in her marriage to follow more of her advice than that of any other. What made Murray and Lethington so loath to give

her counsel she knew not, except it was the fear that she should
be deceived, or the thought that the match was not honourable
for her. These things, she said, moved her to stay, and made
her the longer to take resolution, yet would she by no ways offend
Elizabeth, but honour her as an elder sister and follow her counsel
as that of a mother (*Foreign Calendar, Elizabeth*, vii. 235). On the
2nd of December, he reported that she had taken no great mis-
liking of the conference at Berwick, thinking that things were
now more earnestly meant than before. Murray and Lethington
found her 'daily more and more appliable' to Elizabeth's will
(*Ibid.* vii. 253).

[72] In their letter of 3rd December 1564, Murray and Lethington
informed Cecil that, though perilous to themselves, they were
ready to 'fall roundly to work' in trying to induce their Queen 'to
embrace such friendship and alliance as in reason ought to content'
Elizabeth, provided they knew that his Queen would so deal with
theirs that she would not be forced to have recourse to foreign
friendship. While pointing out that the foreign practices 'already
set abroach' rendered it imperative that no time should be lost, .
they stated that they would only deal with him in this matter if he
meant 'to deal frankly and friendly with their mistress, having
good respect to her honour and surety'; and they warned him
that if—after being encouraged, either by Elizabeth's letters or by
his, to take up this enterprise—they should find themselves frustrated through default of his or her friendly dealing, he must not
find it strange should they change their deliberations and seek to
save themselves as best they could (*Foreign Calendar, Elizabeth*,
vii. 255, 256). On the 14th of December, Randolph wrote to
Cecil that Murray and Lethington were expecting a full and decisive answer to their letter with frank dealing; that Mary's
friends were pressing her to marry; that the offers were such as
without good cause could not be refused; that no man would be
more acceptable to the Scotch people than Lord Robert; that
Darnley was less thought of since his father came; that his mother
was more feared than beloved; and that Lennox had told Lesley
(afterwards Bishop of Ross) that his son should marry the Queen
of Scots (*Ibid.* vii. 258, 259). In his letter of 16th December to
Murray and Lethington, Cecil enlarged on the virtues, prospects,
and suitability of him whom Elizabeth had named 'as best for all
respects.' He thought that she would never willingly consent to

so much of their request, either in form or substance, as with the
Lord Robert; and with him—finding other respects answerable—
would cause inquisition to be made of their Sovereign's right, and
as far as should stand with justice and her own surety would abase
such titles as should be proved unjust and prejudicial to Mary's
interest, and so leave to her entirely her whole right whatsoever it
might be. This was cautious enough, but Cecil had never spoken
so plainly before; and now, lest he had not been sufficiently
guarded, he reminded them that in all Elizabeth intended to do
she must be ruled by her laws and the consent of her Parliament,
and so could make no absolute promise. Before finishing his
letter he had had another interview with her, the sum thereof
being that 'she is bent to proceed wholly herein in conditions meet
for friendship, and is disposed to do more of good will than upon
any pressing or request.' He asked them not to let this their
negotiation, so full of terms of friendship, 'be converted to a
matter of bargain or purchase'; and, in this device for conciliating
these two Queens and countries by perpetual amity, to exclude
'any intention to compass at his Sovereign's hand a kingdom and
crown, which, if it be sought for, may be sooner lost than got, and
not being craved may be as soon offered as reason can require'
(*Ibid.* vii. 263, 264). Murray and Lethington received this letter
on the 24th of December, and wrote a spirited reply the same day.
They complained that while his general terms were satisfactory,
his exposition was the reverse. They complained, too, of his
'many obscure words and dark sentences.' They protested that
in this matter 'they never meant anything prejudicial to the
safety of Queen Elizabeth,' and were certain 'that nothing sound-
ing thereunto ever entered their mistress's mind.' They asserted
that to have the succession orderly established was 'no less surety
for his Sovereign than for theirs.' They declared that 'whatsoever their mistress is minded to perform, she will not stick to
promise it, and herself make for it what surety is convenient.'
They explained that if Elizabeth would 'nowise establish the succession of her crown,' then he might conclude absolutely that they
could never induce Mary to marry an Englishman, and they
would not 'speak one word more of it.' Nevertheless, they did
not see 'why the amity should be dissolved,' although their
Queen married where her heart should be best inclined, in whatsoever country that might be. They suggested that Cecil should

come to Scotland to treat with Mary, or at least to Berwick, to meet them (*Ibid.* vii. 268-271). Next day Lethington wrote another letter to Cecil, telling him that nothing did so much harm with Mary as Elizabeth's baseless opinion that she 'looks for her death, and that all this kindness is pretended only to hunt a kingdom.' To Randolph, also, Murray and Lethington showed their dissatisfaction with Cecil's letter (*Ibid.* vii. 273, 274). Well did Cecil know that his letter would not content them. In writing to Sir Thomas Smith on the 30th of December, he said in reference to these negotiations :—' At this present no full answer is yet gyven ; but to saye the truth of my knowledg in these fyckle matters, I can affirm nothyng that I can assure to contynue' (Wright's *Elizabeth,* i. 187).

⁷³ Writing on Sabbath the 24th of December, Randolph says that on the previous Wednesday Mary kept her chamber, as she has done ever since, not for any sickness, but for the cold which proceeded of the great storm of snow and wind, such as for many years has not been seen (*Foreign Calendar, Elizabeth,* vii. 271). On the 29th of December, the frost was so intense that Cecil thought the shipping would be affected (Wright's *Elizabeth,* i. 184). The statement in the text about the severity of the winter was written on the 5th of February (*Foreign Calendar, Elizabeth,* vii. 293). On the 4th of March, Randolph refers to a great storm of snow ; no one daring to ride to Berwick (*Ibid.* vii. 308). 'The Thames was so frozen over that men might goe over it' (Camden's *Elizabeth,* 1675, p. 76).

⁷⁴ *Foreign Calendar, Elizabeth,* vii. 293.

⁷⁵ On the 13th of January, Randolph informs Cecil that Mary within four days departs over the water with four in company to pass her time from place to place for twenty days (*Foreign Calendar, Elizabeth,* vii. 283).

⁷⁶ Randolph found her in St. Andrews lodged with her small train in a merchant's house. He dined and supped at her table during the four days he remained there. She passed her time very merrily, and rode abroad after dinner. After being there three days, ' he desired to know her resolution touching the matters propounded at Berwick by the Earl of Bedford and himself to Murray and Lethington. She said that she sent for him to be merry and see how like a bourgeois wife she lived with her little troop, and he would spoil their pastime with his grave matters. If he was weary, he might return to Edinburgh and keep his

gravity and great embassade until the Queen came, for he would not get her there.' 'She spoke much of France for the honour and friendship shown her, for which she is bound to love the nation. To lose such friends without assurance of as good no one would advise her. If his mistress would use her as her natural-born sister, she would show no less readiness to oblige and honour her than her mother or elder sister ; but if she always repute her as her neighbour Queen of Scots, how willing soever she be to live in amity, yet must she not look for that which otherwise she would. Until they have further proceeded she must apply her mind to the advice of those who seem to tender most her profit' (*Foreign Calendar, Elizabeth*, vii. 292).

[77] Randolph's letter of 12th February plainly implies that it was by means of Leicester and Cecil that Darnley obtained license to come to Scotland. Poor Randolph was ever anxious to obey his Sovereign ; 'but how to fashion this that it may be both to her honour and contentment he must be supported by Cecil's advice, for he knows not what to think or how to behave himself' (*Foreign Calendar, Elizabeth*, vii. 299). On the 21st of February, Darnley sent a grateful note to Leicester from Dunkeld (Ellis's *Original Letters*, second series, ii. 294 n.).

[78] In his despatches Bedford states that Darnley arrived at Berwick on the 10th of February and left next day (*Foreign Calendar, Elizabeth*, vii. 298). In his letter to Cecil (19th February), Randolph says that he arrived at Dunbar on the evening of the day on which he left Berwick, rode next day to Haddington, tarried three nights in Edinburgh, and on Friday passed over the water to the Laird of Wemyss, where he was well received of the Queen and lodged in the same house (*Ibid.* vii. 301). Friday was the 16th, and it was no doubt this letter which led Cecil to enter in his *Diary* that Darnley 'cam to the Quene' on the 16th of February (Murdin's *State Papers*, p. 758 ; Wright's *Elizabeth*, i. 186 n.). But in his letter to Leicester—also written on the 19th—Randolph, while again affirming that he spent one night at Dunbar, one at Haddington, three in Edinburgh, and passed over the water on Friday, adds that upon Saturday he met with the Queen, where he hears that he was welcomed and honourably used, lodging in the same house that she did, and this day repairs towards his father (*Foreign Calendar, Elizabeth*, vii. 301). Mr. Skelton alleges that Darnley's first night in Scotland was 'spent at Lethington' ; and

therefore presumes that Maitland 'was still anxious to be friendly' (*Maitland of Lethington*, ii. 144).

[79] Melville's *Memoirs*, p. 134.

[80] *Foreign Calendar, Elizabeth*, vii. 304, 305.—When Darnley left Edinburgh on the 16th of February to see the Queen, Randolph lent him a couple of horses, because his own were not yet come (*Ibid.* vii. 301).

[81] The Guises had thought of many husbands for their royal niece both in France and out of it. In January 1562-3, Smith says that they had offered her to the King of Spain's son, the Kings of Navarre and Sweden, the Emperor's son Ferdinand, and the Cardinal of Bourbon, who is no priest: 'Fain would they have one to have her that should break the amity betwixt England and Scotland, and enhance the House of Guise, which is now so great that the King and Queen here [*i.e.* France] rather fear than love them' (*Foreign Calendar, Elizabeth*, vi. 49). In October 1563, Eric xiv. of Sweden explained to Elizabeth that he had never asked the Queen of Scots for himself, but only for his brother (*Ibid.* vi. 559). Before the end of December it was reported that the Cardinal of Lorraine had almost completed the settlement of a marriage between Mary and a son of the King of the Romans (*Ibid.* vi. 616). In November 1564 he was believed to be working for the Prince of Condé (*Ibid.* vii. 239). He had previously commended the Duke of Orleans (*Ibid.* vii. 242), and a few months later wished her either to have him or Charles the Ninth (*Ibid.* vii. 307); but the Duke of Orleans was, by her and those about her, 'so despited as nothing can be' (*Ibid.* vii. 321). In October 1564, Smith reported from Avignon that the two Cardinals and all their kind were most earnest for the young Duke of Guise, and most in fear for the Darnley match (*Ibid.* vii. 217, 218); and next January he again reported that the House of Guise was 'marvellous eager' for the Duke of Guise (*Ibid.* vii. 280).

[82] On the 15th of March 1564-5, Randolph says that Mary was daily in hand with him to know how soon Elizabeth would resolve what way she intended to conclude (*Foreign Calendar, Elizabeth*, vii. 314).

[83] Elizabeth at the same time, however, promised that if Mary married Leicester she would advance him to all the honour she could, and also favour her title as far as she could, although she would not proceed to the examination or declaration of the same,

until she herself had married or notified her intention of never marrying, one or other of which she meant shortly to do. The substance of Elizabeth's resolution may be gleaned from Stevenson's *Selections*, pp. 134, 135; Keith's *History*, ii. 266; iii. 330; Murdin's *State Papers*, p. 758; Nares's *Burghley*, ii. 234. Mr. Skelton's grotesque summary of Elizabeth's message is more characteristic of himself than of the English Queen :—'She had not yet made up her mind, she said, whether she would marry or not. She must decline to recognise the Queen of Scots as second person, or to take any measures to settle the succession; meantime she could only say that if Mary would marry Leicester and listen to Knox, something might be done for her by and by' (*Maitland of Lethington*, ii. 143). The idea of Elizabeth wishing to subject Mary to the teaching of Knox is so delicious that it must have originated with Mr. Skelton, who, of course, gives no authority.

[84] *Foreign Calendar, Elizabeth*, vii. 315, 316.

[85] On the 20th of March, Randolph writes to Cecil :—'Of thys Quene's mynde hytherto towards hym [*i.e.* Darnley], I am voide of suspicion, but what affections may be stirred up in her, or whether she will be at anye tyme moved that waye, seeing she is a woman, and in all thynges desyreth to have her wyll, I cannot saye' (Wright's *Elizabeth*, i. 194; Keith's *History*, ii. 273). Sir James Melville alleges that after Darnley 'had hanted a quhill in Court, he proponit mariage to hir Majeste; quhilk sche tok in ane evell part at the first, as sche tald me that same day hir self; and how sche had refused the ring quhilk he then offerit unto hir. Wher I tok occasion, as I had begun, to speak in his favour, that ther mariage wald put out of dout ther title to the succession. I can not tell how he fell in acquantance with Seignieur David [Riccio], bot he also was his gret frend at the Quenis hand; sa that hir Majeste tok ay the langer the better lyking of him, and at lenth determinit to mary him' (Melville's *Memoirs*, p. 134).

[86] *Foreign Calendar, Elizabeth*, vii. 338.—At Berwick, Randolph had been told to his face, that Elizabeth had sent Darnley to Scotland in order to match Mary meanly, and for another end than amity (*Ibid.* vii. 334).

[87] *Foreign Calendar, Elizabeth*, vii. 334, 338, 347, 353, 372, 373, 381, 382.

[88] Lethington, according to his biographer, 'went to England in May' (Skelton's *Maitland*, ii. 147); but his appointment for this

embassy is dated March (*Register of Privy Council*, xiv. 213, 214), and it is certain that he arrived at Westminster by the 18th of April (*Foreign Calendar, Elizabeth*, vii. 334; *Spanish Calendar, Elizabeth*, i. 418; Keith's *History*, iii. 332; Stevenson's *Selections*, p. 136; Teulet's *Papiers D'État*, ii. 35). To Elizabeth he professed that Mary had, for her sake, 'forboren to harken to the matching with any foren Prince'; and that 'she could enclyne hir self' to marry Darnley, if she had her 'good will and assent therto' (Stevenson's *Selections*, p. 115). To this message Elizabeth found that Lethington was tied (*Foreign Calendar, Elizabeth*, vii. 349, 350); and he 'found great offence' (Ellis's *Original Letters*, second series, ii. 296). To De Silva he alleged that it was only after waiting more than two years on Philip's decision that Mary had listened to Darnley's proposals; and if he—De Silva—would give her any hope of the negotiation with Don Carlos proceeding, 'her own wishes and intentions on the subject were unchanged' (*Spanish Calendar, Elizabeth*, i. 421). On this occasion Lethington treated for Mary's marriage with Leicester, and also suggested Norfolk as a more worthy candidate, but the Duke at that time modestly declined (Murdin's *State Papers*, p. 759; Camden's *Elizabeth*, 1675, p. 77). De Foix, who was then in London, alleges that Throckmorton was empowered to offer her the choice of Norfolk, Arundel, or Leicester (Teulet's *Papiers D'État*, ii. 39); but Norfolk and Arundel are not mentioned in the corrected draft of Throckmorton's instructions (*infra*, p. 338, *n.* 92). In the same letter, De Foix says that Elizabeth sent to Mary by Lethington a diamond worth six hundred crowns.

[89] In the beginning of April, Darnley was 'very evil at ease,' and, while trying to drive out the supposed cold by perspiration, 'the measles came out upon him.' He was lodged in Stirling Castle, and was served with 'a mess of meat' at his own charge; but occasionally 'a reversion' came to him from the Queen's table. When he and the Queen lost, in playing at 'biles' against Randolph and Mary Beaton, he gave a ring and a brooch with two agates worth fifty crowns (*Foreign Calendar, Elizabeth*, vii. 328, 329). By the middle of April, it was said that she had already 'such good liking of him' that she could forsake all other offers and be content with her own choice (*Ibid.* vii. 334). In a few days, Bedford learned from Lennox's man that while Darnley was ill and since, he had been almost continually visited by the Queen, and at

almost all hours. 'It appeareth by her tenderness over him that
she feared not whether the sickness were infective' (*Ibid.* vii. 338).
By the 22nd, he was somewhat convalescent; but the Queen, who
had intended to ride to Perth, was not to go without him (*Ibid.* vii.
340). He was now troubled with an ague, and the Queen commonly stayed with him till midnight, sometimes later (*Ibid.* vii.
342). Her care had been 'marvellous great and tender over him.'
There were 'such tales spread abroad of her doings,' that it was
wonderful to hear what discontentment there was among the wisest
of her people. Her marvellous doings, however, were not restricted
to the care of Darnley. 'Greater triumphs there were never in
time of Popery than were this Easter at the resurrection and at her
high mass. Organs were wont to be the common music. She
wanted now neither trumpet, drum, nor fife, bagpipe, nor tabor'
(*Ibid.* vii. 347, 348). Her exploits on Easter Monday were not
religious (*supra*, p. 278, *n.* 89). On the 21st of May, Darnley was
still confined to his room, having only left it on one occasion
(*Foreign Calendar, Elizabeth,* vii. 373).

90 'The Quen of England began to fear and suspect that the said
mariage [of Mary and Leicester] mycht perchance tak effect. And
therefore my L[ord] Darley obteanit the rather licence to com in
Scotland, wha was a lusty youth, in hope that he suld prevaill
being present, before Leycester that was absent. Quhilk licence
was obteanit be the meanis of the Secretary Cicill; not that he was
myndit that any of the mariages suld tak effect, bot with sic schiftis
and pratikes to hald the Quen onmaried sa lang as he culd. For
he persuadit him self, that my L[ord] Darley durst not pass fordwart without the consent of the Quen of England to the said
mariage; his land lying in England, and his mother remanyng ther'
(Melville's *Memoirs*, pp. 129, 130). In this matter, at least, Melville's memory does not seem to have altogether played him false.
Leicester and Cecil not only approved of but recommended the visit
of Darnley to Scotland (*supra*, p. 333, *n.* 77), and Melville was not
the only one who suspected that Darnley was sent to Scotland to
further Elizabeth's designs (*supra*, p. 335, *n.* 86). Before Mary left
France, Cecil had thus expounded his policy to Throckmorton:—
'I think plainly the longer the Scottish Queen's affairs shall hang
in an uncertainty, the longer will it be ere she shall have such a
match in marriage as shall offend us' (Hardwicke's *State Papers*, i.
173). On the 30th of December 1564, Cecil had written to Sir

Thomas Smith:—'The Erle of Lennox frends wish that the L[ord] Darly might marry with the Scottish Quene; and I see some devise to bryng the Quenes Majesty [*i.e.* Elizabeth] not only to allow therof, but also to move it to the Quene hir sistur: but I see no disposition therto in hir Majesty; but she rather contynueth hir desyre to have my L[ord] of Leicester preferred that way. . . . I see the Qu[enes] Majesty very desyrooss to have my L[ord] of Lecester placed in this high degree to be the Scottish Queen's husband, but whan it commeth to the conditions which ar demanded, I see her than remiss of hir ernestnes' (Ellis's *Original Letters*, second series, ii. 293, 294). On the 21st of May 1565, Throckmorton wrote from Edinburgh to Cecil:—'I should be sorry' if Mauvissière, or any others coming to Scotland, 'should be able to give this Queen intelligence that her proceedings with L[ord] Darnly are not so ill taken there by her Majestie [*i.e.* Elizabeth] and her Council as I pretended in all my negociations; for that would much hinder the purpose the Queen would be at' (Keith's *History*, ii. 287; *Foreign Calendar, Elizabeth*, vii. 371). Notwithstanding this attempt to hoodwink Mauvissière, he has recorded the opinion that while Elizabeth 'seemed to disapprove of the match,' she only 'disguised the pleasure which she really had at heart to see it go on' (Mauvissière's *Memoirs*, 1724, p. 296). On the 2nd of July, Randolph wrote to Cecil:—'The lesse comforte that thys Queen be put in, that the Queen's Majestie [*i.e.* Elizabeth] will allowe of her doyngs, the souner shall her Majestie brynge that to passe here [*i.e.* in Scotland] that she moste desyrethe' (Keith's *History*, ii. 307).

91 *Foreign Calendar, Elizabeth*, vii. 345, 347, 360, 394, 398; Keith's *History*, ii. 297-299, 336, 337.

92 One set of Instructions for Throckmorton is dated 24th April 1565 (*Foreign Calendar, Elizabeth*, vii. 344); another set, 2nd May (*Ibid.* vii. 349, 350). In the latter he was directed to tell Mary that Elizabeth simply mislikes this marriage as dangerous to the amity of the two kingdoms; that she would permit her to choose any other of her nobles, but would only yield to the public declaration of the succession if she took Leicester. Furnished also with the adverse opinion of certain members of the English Privy Council against the Darnley match (Stevenson's *Selections*, pp. 115-117; Keith's *History*, ii. 276-278), Throckmorton left for Scotland early in May (*Spanish Calendar, Elizabeth*, i. 430, 431; Teulet's *Papiers*

D'État, ii. 39; Stevenson's *Selections*, p. 137).   He arrived at
Stirling on the 15th, and with some difficulty got access to Mary
on the same day.   He set forth to her Elizabeth's 'disliking and
disallowance of her hasty proceeding with my Lord Darnly, as
well for the matter as for the manner.'   Mary, of course, justified
herself; and over this she and Throckmorton 'spent long time and
had many and sundry disputes.'   He found that she was 'so far
past in this matter with my Lord Darnly as it is irrevocable, and
no place left to dissolve the same by perswasion and reasonable
means, otherwise than by violence.'   That day Darnley was
knighted, made a baron, and belted Earl of Ross; but she promised to defer the creating him Duke of Albany until she heard
how Elizabeth accepted 'the proceedings and answer' to Throckmorton's legation.   He could see, however, that she was 'so
captived, either by love or cunning (or rather, to say truly, by
boasting or folly),' that she was 'not able to keep promise with
herself, and therefore not most able to keep promise' with Elizabeth
in these matters.   She further promised that the marriage would
not be celebrated for three months, 'in which mean time she
meaneth all the best means she can devise to procure your
Majestie's [*i.e.* Elizabeth's] acceptation and allowance of the
matter, offering in general words to leave nothing undone that
she may honourably, safely, and conveniently do, to win your
Majestie's favour to this matter.'   Before Throckmorton left, on
the 19th of May, she sent him a chain of gold weighing fifty ounces.
'I do well perceive,' he wrote to Elizabeth, 'that it is in your
Majestie's power either to dissolve this matter betwixt my L[ord]
Darnly and the Queen of Scotland (if you shall like to use your
power), as at my coming I shall declare particularly unto your
Majestie; or it resteth in your pleasure to end the matter more
amicably, with such conditions as may be (in my simple judgment)
to your honour, surety, and felicity' (Keith's *History*, ii. 279-289;
Foreign Calendar, Elizabeth, vii. 369-371).

    93 In May, Randolph said that his credit was lost at Court (*Foreign
Calendar, Elizabeth*, vii. 358); and in June his men were fought
with at its gates (*Ibid.* vii. 395).   On the 2nd of July, he writes that
he had been received by Mary 'in straynger sorte' than ever he was
before, 'as a man newe and fyrste come into her presence whome
she had never seene' (Keith's *History*, ii. 298).   It was no wonder,
for he had just delivered Elizabeth's letters recalling Lennox and

Darnley—letters which marvellously abashed them, as appeared by Mary's tears and the sad countenance of Lennox (*Ibid.* ii. 299). A fortnight later he had to report that she would not send Lennox and Darnley back to England at the request of Elizabeth, who—as she had been warned from England, France, and other parts—had tried to deceive her. Having discovered the truth of this, she would no longer trust her fair words, but would stand to her own choice. ' Let not her be offended with my mariage, no more than I am with hers, and for the reste I will abyde suche fortune as God will sende me' (Stevenson's *Selections*, pp. 121-123).

[94] *Supra*, p. 107.—Mauvissière represents Murray—as well as Lethington—as in favour of the Darnley match (*Memoirs*, 1724, p. 294); while Mary says that he only approved of it until he saw that she was inclined to it in good earnest (Turnbull's *Letters of Mary*, pp. 149, 150; Labanoff's *Recueil*, i. 298, 299).

[95] On the 3rd of May, Randolph reported from Edinburgh that Lethington was suspected to favour Darnley more than he would seem, though despiteful words were spoken against him because he had written to Murray to advise Mary to make no haste in the matter (*Foreign Calendar, Elizabeth*, vii. 353). At this time Maitland was in London, and there professing to De Silva that if Mary could not marry a powerful foreign Prince, it certainly seemed that Darnley was the best match for her, although Elizabeth's opposition might prove a serious objection (*Spanish Calendar, Elizabeth*, i. 423). When De Silva warned him that Throckmorton was going to Scotland to try to prevent the marriage, Lethington replied that he ' had nothing to fear in that respect,' and ' was certain nothing could be done now to prevent the match' (*Ibid.* i. 429). On his way back to Scotland he was met betwixt Newark and Grantham by John Beaton, who brought him a commission from Mary, ordering him to return to Elizabeth, and to declare to her that, having been so long beguiled with her fair speech, she now intended to choose a husband with the advice of her own Estates. The commission had been penned by Mary, and, according to Throckmorton, who saw it, ' there wanted neither eloquence, despite, anger, love, nor passion.' She also commissioned Lethington to go into France, and there make the French King and that State agree to her choice; and to induce him to go, she sent him a bill of credit, authorising the receivers of her dowry in France to disburse unto him what money he should ask, and to spare no cost.

She also sent him a holograph letter, 'the most favourable and gentle . . . that ever Queen did write to her servant,' making him 'large promises for his benefit and greatness in time to come.' Instead of obeying the Instructions of his Sovereign, Lethington hurried after Throckmorton, overtook him at Alnwick, and accompanied him to Scotland. While at Berwick, he wrote to Leicester, explaining that he had not turned back, as the Instructions were not agreeable to his own opinion, and he purposed rather to speak his mind than commit it to a letter. At Berwick, too, he was shown Randolph's letter concerning the haste that Mary was making in her marriage. Never had Throckmorton seen him 'in so great perplexity, nor passion, and would have little believed that for any matter he could have been so moved.' He even wished for power to threaten his Queen with war, 'as the last refuge to stay her from this unadvised act' (*Foreign Calendar, Elizabeth*, vii. 361, 362). Mr. Skelton does not, of course, record this kindly wish of Lethington's, nor does he tell of his perplexity and passion, but merely says :—'He was unusually moved. Elizabeth had told him in effect that the Lennox marriage would be taken as a declaration of war' (*Maitland of Lethington*, ii. 149). In the commission which Beaton had brought to him, Lethington was enjoined to stay Throckmorton's coming into Scotland (*Foreign Calendar, Elizabeth*, vii. 361); and at Edinburgh he received a new command to use means to stay him there for two or three days; but instead he hastily departed for Stirling, after 'making him privy to his charge, and leaving him to his own liking' (*Ibid.* vii. 370). Throckmorton found that Lethington no longer stood 'in the best terms' with Mary, and that she meant to send some one else to Elizabeth (Keith's *History*, ii. 283). Maitland's 'stoutness and good conduct,' from Randolph's point of view, were more than many looked for (*Foreign Calendar, Elizabeth*, vii. 273). Nevertheless, Throckmorton advised that it should be brought to the knowledge of Lady Lennox that Elizabeth, Leicester, and Cecil did 'all marvel how Lidington, being a man of knowledge and judgment, can be so blinded to further and prosecute this marriage, whereof besides your certain intelligence from hence, you did too well espy it in his last legation' (Keith's *History*, ii. 291; *Foreign Calendar, Elizabeth*, vii. 372).

[96] *Foreign Calendar, Elizabeth*, vii. 361, 494; Stevenson's *Selections*, p. 122; Wright's *Elizabeth*, i. 197.

[97] 'This Queen is so much altered from what she was that who beholds does not think her the same. Her majesty is laid aside ; her wits not such as they were ; her beauty another than it was ; her cheer and countenance changed. . . . The saying is that she is bewitched, the parties named to be the doers ; the tokens the rings and bracelets are found and daily worn that contain the sacred mysteries' (*Foreign Calendar, Elizabeth*, vii. 381). More than once Randolph refers to Ruthven as one of her most trusted advisers at this time, as one who 'stirs coals as hot as fire to have these matters take effect' (*Ibid.* vii. 353, 373). Could he be one of those who had bewitched her ? He was believed to deal in sorcery (*Ibid.* vi. 169 ; Nau's *Mary Stewart*, 1883, p. 23); and Mary herself had said that she could not love him, for she knew him 'to use enchantment' (Laing's *Knox*, ii. 373). He had indeed given her a ring with a pointed diamond, saying that it had the virtue to save her from poison ; but he afterwards explained that he merely wished to rid her of the fear of being poisoned by the Protestants (Ruthven's *Relation*, 1699, pp. 35, 36). His counsel, however, was suspected three weeks before the Darnley marriage took place ; but at that time even the four Maries were 'cleane owte of credite' (Keith's *History*, ii. 301) ; and soon few retained her confidence save Lennox and Riccio (Stevenson's *Selections*, p. 125 ; Keith's *History*, ii. 333).

[98] Labanoff's *Recueil*, i. 296, 297 ; Turnbull's *Mary's Letters*, pp. 147-149.—See also *Foreign Calendar, Elizabeth*, v. 12-14.

[99] *Foreign Calendar, Elizabeth*, vii. 380, 381, 406.—Even when bedfast in Stirling, Darnley had threatened that when whole he would knock the Duke's pate (*Ibid.* vii. 353); when confined to his chamber he was stout in words, and threatened the Justice-Clerk with his dagger for conveying to him the unwelcome tidings that his creation as a Duke was deferred (*Ibid.* vii. 372, 373); and in token of his manhood he did not spare to let some blows fly where he knew they would be taken (*Ibid.* vii. 380). On the 2nd of July, Randolph writes :—'Hys behavior is suche that he is runne in open contempte of all men, even of those that wer hys cheif freinds. Whate shall become of hym, I knowe not, but yt is greatly to be feared that he cane have no longe lyfe amongste thys people. The Queen herself, beinge of better understandinge, seekethe to frame and fashion hym to the nateur of her subjects. No perswation can alter that which custome hath made old in hym : he

is counted prowde, disdaynefull, and suspicious, which kynde of men this sayle [*i.e.* soil] of any other cane worse bear' (Keith's *History*, ii. 299, 300). At the time of his marriage, the tale is still the same :—' His words to all men agaynste whom he conceaveth anye dyspleasure, howe unjuste soever yt be, so prowde and spytefull, that rather he seemethe a monarche of the worlde, then he that not long since we have seen and knowne, the Lord Darlye. He lookethe nowe for reverence of maynie that have lytle will to gyve it hym, and some ther are that do gyve yt that thynke hym lyttle worthye of yt' (Ellis's *Original Letters*, first series, ii. 201).

[100] Randolph's opinion on the 3rd of May is thus summed up :—' A greater plague to her there cannot be, a greater benefit to the Queen's Majesty [*i.e.* Elizabeth] could not have chanced than to see this dishonour fall upon her, and to have her so match where she shall be assured that it shall pass her power to attain to that which hitherto so earnestly she looked for, and without that would accord to nothing' (*Foreign Calendar, Elizabeth*, vii. 351).

[101] One of the reasons which troubled the Queen of England and her Council is thus set forth :—' By the marriage of the Queen of Scots with the English Lord Darnley—both of them being next heirs to the crown of England, and descended from Margaret, sister of King Henry VIII.—their respective claims are thus consolidated. The rivalry between them therefore ceases, and the Queen of England had always looked for her security to the maintenance of this rivalry by delaying the nomination of her successor' (*Spanish Calendar, Elizabeth*, i. 434).

[102] This was one of the chief dangers which the English Privy Council professed to see lurking in the Darnley match (Keith's *History*, iii. 222 ; *Foreign Calendar, Elizabeth*, vii. 385 ; Robertson's *Scotland*, app. no. 10). Lennox said that he was sure of the greatest part of England (*Foreign Calendar, Elizabeth*, vii. 353) ; and Darnley alleged that if there were war, Mary would find more friends in England than Elizabeth (*Ibid.* vii. 381).

[103] Teulet's *Papiers D'État*, ii. 42.—The Cardinal of Lorraine's description of Darnley as ' *ung gentil hutaudeau*' is rendered by Joseph Robertson ' a great girlish nincompoop' (*Inventories*, p. xxxvi. *n.*). Yet the Cardinal, it was said, preferred Darnley to any other Scotch or English noble (*Foreign Calendar, Elizabeth*, vii.

371); and procured the Papal dispensation for their marriage (*Ibid.* vii. 401, 435).

[104] Before the end of March, Lady Lennox informed De Silva that the French Ambassador in London had 'sent to her in great secrecy to offer and promise all his support for the marriage of her son, and anything he might require. She says she knows the French way of dealing, and thinks this is for the purpose of discovering whether there is anything afoot, and perhaps even on the advice of this Queen' [*i.e.* Elizabeth] (*Spanish Calendar, Elizabeth,* i. 413). On the 2nd of July, De Silva reported to Philip that the French Ambassador—who at first 'was not at all pleased with the marriage of the Queen of Scotland, and spoke strongly against it' —had now turned completely round, asserting that 'she has done very rightly,' and that, if Elizabeth attacks her, 'his King could not refrain from helping her for the sake of old friendship' (*Ibid.* i. 444). Eleven days later, he says :—'Lady Margaret tells me that the French Ambassador makes her many offers of service on behalf of his master, and makes similar offers to the Queen of Scotland. I tell her to thank him and beware' (*Ibid.* i. 449). On the very day of the marriage De Silva confirms the truth of what he had previously heard, that the French Ambassador had spoken to Elizabeth officially concerning Mary's affairs, and urged her in his master's name to be reconciled to the Darnley match (*Ibid.* i. 458). On the last of June, Charles the Ninth had written to Elizabeth stating that he approved of Mary's marriage, and hoped that she did the same (*Foreign Calendar, Elizabeth,* vii. 399). Perhaps he had been quickened by Mary's offer of the old amity of alliance and more, and by Darnley's offer of service (*Ibid.* vii. 401).

[105] *Spanish Calendar, Elizabeth,* i. 432-434.

[106] In April, after presenting De Silva with his credentials, Lethington spoke to him on Mary's behalf, saying how great was the desire she had always had, even in France, to be guided by Philip's will, and to place herself in his hands. 'I can affirm positively,' he said, 'that she will follow in every respect the wishes of your master' (*Spanish Calendar, Elizabeth,* i. 421, 423). On the 25th of June, John Hay, Mary's Master of Requests and Commendator of Balmerino, asked De Silva whether he had received a reply from Philip to the matter discussed with Lethington. 'I gave it to him,' says De Silva, 'in accordance with your Majesty's

commands. He appeared highly delighted with it, and said that his Queen desired nothing so much as that your Majesty should take her under your protection, and that she should follow your Majesty's orders in all things without swerving a hair's-breadth from them. I urged him to endeavour to get his Queen to manage her affairs prudently, and not to strike until a good opportunity presented itself' (*Ibid.* i. 442). On the day before her marriage, one of her gentlemen handed De Silva a letter from her, expressing the greatest gratitude for what he had told her Ambassador in the name of Philip, in whom she placed all her confidence (*Ibid.* i. 457).

[107] *Supra*, p. 243, n. 51.

[108] In her Instructions to the Commendator of Balmerino, Mary avers that it was due to 'the greiter regaird' she had for Elizabeth's advice than for that of any of her 'uther nerrest freindis'—whose counsel, out of respect to her, she had 'passit over and disdaynit to use'—that she had resolved 'to matche with ane of this Ile, hir awin subject and neir cousyne, thinkand thairby to haif fullie applesit hir'; and could not 'winder aneuch' that a meaning so sincere was so mistaken. Though fully determined to marry Darnley, yet, having consideration to the amity and regard to her message delivered by Throckmorton, she had delayed the final accomplishment, that Elizabeth might perceive how desirous she was to follow her advice, and that commissioners might be appointed for the removal of doubt, suspicion, and misliking. These Instructions, dated the 14th of June, are printed in Keith's *History*, ii. 293-296; and in Labanoff's *Recueil*, i. 267-271. Though Mary sent two letters—one of them holograph—to the English Queen, commending the Commendator and his message (Labanoff's *Recueil*, i. 271-274), Elizabeth 'flew into a rage' whenever he mentioned the marriage (*Spanish Calendar, Elizabeth,* i. 441).

[109] On the 26th of April, De Foix, then French Ambassador in London, wrote to Catherine de Medici that Elizabeth had received letters from Randolph, saying that Mary had married Darnley, and that only the ceremonies of the Church were required to complete the match (Teulet's *Papiers D'État*, ii. 35, 36). On the 2nd of May, De Foix further wrote that Lethington assured Elizabeth that Mary was not bound to the marriage with Darnley ; though, on the other hand, Lady Lennox had been informed that the marriage was accomplished, and that Mary was fulfilling the offices of a wife,

having during his illness watched a whole night in his chamber (*Ibid.* ii. 37, 38). Two days after Lethington's departure, he again wrote, saying that that Ambassador had averred that his mistress had not gone so far in the matter that she could not withdraw from it, if her own nobles and the Queen of England so wished ; but that Lady Lennox was continually telling her friends that the marriage was concluded (*Ibid.* ii. 39). As De Silva was closing his letter of the 26th of April, Lady Lennox sent to say that she considered her son's affair ' an accomplished fact that admits of no doubt' (*Spanish Calendar, Elizabeth,* i. 425). De Silva had previously heard that one of her servants had been to Scotland to sign a deed on this subject as a witness (*Ibid.* i. 424). When asked by Elizabeth whether the Darnley match had been carried through, Lethington replied that he had no instructions to make any communication on that subject, and knew no more (*Ibid.* i. 427) ; but De Silva inferred—from his saying to him that it could not now be prevented—that it had actually taken place (*Ibid.* i. 429) ; and Leicester—in spite of Lethington's denial—believed in its reality (*Ibid.* i. 430). Miss Strickland—who, on the faith of an anonymous document printed by Labanoff (*Recueil,* vii. 67) fixes on Riccio's apartment in Stirling Castle as the place where, and on the second week of April as the time when, the marriage took place— explains that it was only after Mary was united to Darnley ' by the holy ties which sanctioned such demonstrations, that she took upon herself the tender office of his nurse, that she kept her wakeful vigils by his restless pillow' (Strickland's *Life of Mary,* 1888, i. 200, 201). Dr. John Stuart suggests that at that time they were merely espoused or handfasted (*Lost Chapter,* 1874, pp. 26-28).

[110] So Randolph tells Elizabeth (M'Neel-Caird's *Mary Stuart,* 1866, p. 233; *Foreign Calendar, Elizabeth,* vii. 407). From his letter to Cecil of the same date (16th July) it is apparent that he knew there was something unusual going on at Holyrood. 'That whole daye was solemnised, as I do believe, to some divine God, for suche quietnes was in Courte that fewe coulde be seen and as fewe sufferde to enter.' Her horses having been secretly prepared, at eight o'clock that night she and Darnley with a handful of attendants rode to Seton. 'Hereupon rose maynie fowle tales, whear libertie inoughe is geven for men to speake what theie wyll. . . . Two nightes she tarried ther and the next daye came to her dinner to the castle of Edenboroughe ; then was it saide that she

wolde remayne ther. That afternone she and my Lord Darlye walked up and downe the towne dysguysed untyll suppertyme, and retorned thyther agayne, but laye that nighte in the Abbaye; thys manner of passinge to and fro gave agayne occasion to maynie men to muse what might be her meaninge. The nexte daye in lyke sorte she comethe after dyner upon her feete from the Abbaye, the Lord Darlye ledinge her by the one arme and Fowler by thother. In that troupe ther were the Ladie Ersken and old Ladie Seton, the Erle of Lenox and Seignor David with 2 or 3 other. These vagares mayke mens tonges to chatter faste' (Stevenson's *Selections*, pp. 119, 120). Though Randolph does not appear to have given the story of this secret marriage full credit, Lingard accepts it as at once true and as an adequate explanation of their 'supposed harlotry' (Lingard's *History of England*, 1855, vi. 53); but, from his standpoint, it should hardly be satisfactory, as the Papal dispensation did not arrive in Edinburgh until the 22nd of July, the day on which the banns were proclaimed (Robertson's *Statuta*, vol. i. p. clxix, *n.*).

[111] *Diurnal of Occurrents*, p. 79; *Foreign Calendar, Elizabeth*, vii. 359, 363, 366, 369, 378, 383, 410; Keith's *History*, ii. 289, 337; Ellis's *Original Letters*, first series, ii. 198, 199; Pitcairn's *Criminal Trials*, i. 488*, 489*; *Register of Privy Council*, xiv. 226.

[112] Ellis's *Original Letters*, first series, ii. 202.—The warrant for the Proclamation is printed in the *Register of Privy Council*, i. 345, 346; in Anderson's *Collections*, 1727, i. 33, 34; in Keith's *History*, ii. 342, 343; in Labanoff's *Recueil*, i. 277, 278; and in the *National MSS. of Scotland*, iii. 48.

[113] *Diurnal of Occurrents*, p. 80.—By 'the chapell of Halyrudhous' this chronicler evidently means Mary's private chapel, and not the church of the Abbey; the latter is termed by him 'the Abbay Kirk of Halyrudhous' (*Ibid.* p. 88). Spottiswoode also says that the marriage took place 'in the chapel of Halyrudhouse' (*History*, ii. 31). Birrel says 'in the palaice of Holyroudhous' (*Diary*, p. 5); and Sir James Melville, 'in the palice of Halyrodhouse, within the Quenis chapell' (*Memoirs*, p. 136). Cosmo Innes is certainly wrong in assigning it to 'the church of the Abbey' (*Liber Cartarum Sancte Crucis*, p. lxxiv). He has himself printed the Act of Privy Council, of 1672, appointing the Abbey Church to be used in future as the Chapel Royal (*Ibid.* p. lxxvii); but the chapel in which Mary was married to Darnley was known at the

time as the Chapel Royal (Laing's *Knox*, ii. 495 ; Herries's *Historical Memoirs*, p. 70). The *Kirk-Session Records of the Canongate* also point decisively to Mary's own chapel (*cf.* Pitcairn's *Criminal Trials*, i. 462 * and 489*).

[114] Laing's *Knox*, ii. 495.—Randolph, who was not an eye-witness though in Edinburgh, at once sent an account of the proceedings to Leicester :—'Theie wer married with all the solemnities of the Popyshe tyme, saving that he hearde not the masse. . . . Upon Sondaye, in the morninge, betwene five and six, she was conveide by divers of her nobles to the chappell. She had upon her backe the greate mourninge gowne of blacke, with the greate wyde mourninge hoode, not unlyke unto that which she wore the dolefull day of the buriall of her housbande [*i.e.* Francis]. She was ledde unto the chappell by the Earles Lenox and Athol, and there she was lefte untyll her housband came, who also was conveide by the same lords. . . . The words were spoken, the rings, which were three, the middle a riche diamonde, were put upon her finger, theie kneel together, and manie prayers saide over them. She tarrieth owte the masse, and he taketh a kysse and leaveth her there and wente to her chamber, whither in a space she followeth, and there being required, accordinge to the solemnitie to cast off her care, and lay asyde those sorrowfull garments, and give herself to a pleasanter lyfe, after some prettie refusall, more I believe for manner sake than greef of harte, she suffreth them that stood by, everie man that coulde approche to take owte a pyn, and so being commytted unto her ladies changed her garments. . . . After the marriage followeth commonly cheere and dancinge. To their dynner theie were conveide by the whole nobles. The trompets sounde, a larges cried, and monie thrown abowte the howse in greate abundance to suche as were happie to gete anye parte. . . . After dyner theie dance awhyle, and retire themselves tyll the hower of supper, and as thei dyned so do theie suppe. Some dancing ther was, and so theie go to bedd' (Wright's *Elizabeth*, i. 202, 203). This letter is also printed by Robertson (*History of Scotland*, app. no. xi.) ; and fully the half of it by Ellis (*Original Letters*, first series, ii. 200-204). Though quoting Wright, I have adopted the readings of Ellis where they seem to be better. Calderwood erroneously gives the 27th of July as the date of the marriage (*History*, ii. 292) ; and Bishop Lesley is as far astray in giving the 1st of August (Forbes-Leith's *Narratives*, p. 104).

[115] Wright's *Elizabeth*, i. 202 ; Ellis's *Original Letters*, first series, ii. 202.—There, Randolph also tells that a doubt had risen amongst the lawyers, as to ' whether she beinge clade with a housbande, and her housbande not twenty-one yeres, anythynge withowte Parlemente can be of strengthe that is done betwene them.' According to Buchanan, the Proclamation 'greatly offended not only the nobility, but likewise also the common people, and some indignantly pronounced it a precedent of the worst description. Of what use is it, asked they, to assemble the Estates for creating a King, if their advice be never asked, or their authority required ? if an herald can answer the purpose of a meeting, and a proclamation be as effectual as an Act of Parliament ? ' Nevertheless, this same historian affirms that the announcement of the marriage was ' received by the multitude with loud shouts of God save our Sovereigns, King Henry and Queen Mary' (Aikman's *Buchanan*, ii. 471). The ablest of all Mary's modern apologists, and a barrister-at-law to boot, candidly says :—' It cannot be doubted that this step was alike imprudent and illegal, for Mary had no power to confer this title without the sanction of her Parliament' (Hosack's *Mary*, 1870, i. 111). The same opinion had been previously expressed by a Scottish Historiographer (Robertson's *Scotland*, 1794, p. 201) and challenged by at least one eminent Scottish lawyer (Riddell's *Law and Practice in Scottish Peerages*, 1842, i. 112, 113). The warrant for this second proclamation is printed in the *Register of Privy Council*, i. 346 ; in Anderson's *Collections*, i. 34, 35 ; and in Keith's *History*, ii. 347). While the warrant for the proclamation of the 28th of July was signed by Mary alone, this of the 30th was subscribed by Darnley as well.

CHAPTER IX

[1] *Foreign Calendar, Elizabeth*, vii. 328.—According to Randolph, Murray had left the Court that he might not countenance the ' ungodly ceremonies' preceding Easter. He had been dealing with the Queen ' for redress of things to be reformed in the country.'

[2] *Foreign Calendar, Elizabeth*, vii. 341, 347.

[3] *Foreign Calendar, Elizabeth*, vii. 357, 358.—It is not possible, in Mr. Skelton's opinion, ' to hold that Moray was in earnest, when he opposed the Lennox marriage on the plea that religion was in

peril.' On this point Mr. Skelton is very emphatic. 'There is,' he says, 'the best evidence—evidence under his own hand—that until won over by Elizabeth he ridiculed the notion that either father or son could be a danger to the state.' Yet all he can produce is an irrelevant extract from Murray's letter to Cecil, of 13th July, concerning Elizabeth's dishonourable suggestion for preventing Lennox returning to Scotland. The extract has no reference whatever to Darnley, and its climax is that there was no reason on religious grounds to fear his father's return to Scotland, even 'if he had the greatest *subject* of this realm joined to him' (*Mary Stuart*, 1893, p. 69). The same argument and the same proof are presented by Mr. Skelton in his *Maitland of Lethington*, where (ii. 147) he says, 'I am, for my part, constrained to believe that the pretence of religion was a mask.' It was perhaps the opinion of Patrick Fraser Tytler (*History of Scotland*, 1845, v. 303, 304) which led Mr. Skelton astray in this matter; but in his apparent desire to blacken Murray he runs the risk of being deemed as unscrupulous as the English Queen whom he so heartily despises (see *infra*, p. 385).

[4] *Foreign Calendar, Elizabeth*, vii. 352.

[5] *Ibid.* vii. 388.

[6] Keith's *History*, ii. 294.—Hay's Instructions are also in Labanoff's *Recueil*, i. 267-271; and in the *Register of Privy Council*, xiv. 221-224.

[7] Stirred up by the more ardent brethren of the West, the Edinburgh Protestants had warned Mary that the Papists, 'of obstinate malice,' intended to 'set up their idolatry and superstition' at the coming Easter, 'which the brethren and professors of the Evangel could not suffer.' Though the Queen, it was said, gave special orders that the mass should not be used, a priest was bold enough to celebrate it in the Cowgate. While riding hard to escape he was seized, re-attired in his ecclesiastical garments, bound to the Market Cross with the chalice in his hand, and for an hour served by the boys with Easter eggs. Next day he was tried, confessed, condemned to stand three hours at the Market Cross, and to be afterwards imprisoned. During this second public exposure, 'there were 10,000 eggs spent upon him, and at his down taking, because the people were not so satisfied with that punishment, there were 300 or 400 men ready with batons to have killed him, and the Provost was for the safety of the priest compelled to come to the

Market Cross and bring him down, and make proclamation that no man should stone him under pain of death, and so returned him to the Tolbooth and made him fast in irons.' The two hearers—who had also confessed and been found guilty by a jury, 'half Papists and half Protestants'—had their goods confiscated, and their bodies made fast with irons in prison, there to abide the Provost's will. By the Queen's command—she was then at Stirling—the two hearers were set at liberty, and their goods restored, ' but not without great offence to the whole people.' Her extreme wrath was only modified when she learned that the priest was not dead (Laing's *Knox*, ii. 474-478 ; *Burgh Records of Edinburgh*, 1557-1571, pp. 195, 196 ; *Foreign Calendar, Elizabeth*, vii. 340, 341, 346). In the contemporary letter his exposure on the Market Cross before being formally tried is not mentioned ; but is described by the continuator of Knox, who also relates that, by the Queen's orders, the priest too was set at liberty instead of being ' handled according to his demerite, being not only a Papist idolater, but a manifest whoremaster, and a common fighter and blasphemer.'

⁸ *Register of Privy Council*, i. 338.—Opposite Murray's name, in the sederunt of Privy Council of 19th May, there is written in a small hand :—' Last tyme he sits.' In the printed *Register* (i. 335) *half* is substituted for *last*.

⁹ *Register of Privy Council*, i. 339.—On the 22nd of July, it was resolved to issue the same proclamation with a few alterations. The special promise assuring all her good subjects that they should not be 'inquietit' in the using of their religion and conscience in time to come was omitted ; and the penalty to be incurred by those who did not resort to her standard with all possible haste was declared to be 'tinsall of lyff, landis, and gudis' (*Ibid.* i. 343). For raising help, Mary did not trust entirely to her proclamations, but also sent out pressing letters (Laing's *Knox*, ii. 493 ; Keith's *History*, ii. 326-328 ; Labanoff's *Recueil*, i. 275-277 ; *Foreign Calendar, Elizabeth*, iv. 407).

¹⁰ *Booke of the Universall Kirk*, Ban. Club, i. 59, 60.—It was desired that the heads of the first article should be ratified by the Queen in Parliament. The other articles related to the 'sustentation of the ministers,' the admission of teachers, the 'sustentation of the poore,' the punishment of abounding crimes, and 'the ease of the poore labourers of the ground' from the unreasonable payment of their teinds. Parker Lawson says that Argyll and Knox

'appointed the " General Assembly " of the Reforming preachers to be held at Edinburgh on the 25th of June,' in opposition to the Convention of the nobles which Mary had summoned to be held at Perth on the 22nd (Keith's *History*, ii. 312 *n.*). He cannot have known that the General Assembly met on the 25th of June in 1563, 1564, 1565, 1566, and 1567. Mary herself explained that by Lethington's advice she delayed the Convention lest any matter offensive to her conscience or dignity should have been discussed (Labanoff's *Recueil*, i. 302 ; Turnbull's *Letters of Mary*, p. 151).

[11] Keith's *History*, ii. 329, 331.—The Lords had intended to assemble partly in Perth, partly in Glasgow, but were forbidden (Stevenson's *Selections*, p. 125). In standing up for the demands of the Kirk, they were only fulfilling the promise they had made two years before. In 1563 they had said :—' Lett that Parliament pas ower, and when the Quene asked any thing of the nobilitie, as sche most do befoir hir mariage, then should the Religioun be the first thing that should be establessed' (Laing's *Knox*, ii. 382). Tytler supposed that Mary at once gave her answers to the commissioners of the General Assembly (*History of Scotland*, 1845, v. 307); M'Neel-Caird, that she answered on the same day (*Mary Stuart*, 1866, p. 227); Knox's continuator makes her delay until the 21st of August (Laing's *Knox*, ii. 487); but a copy of her answers is endorsed by Cecil, 29th July 1565 (*Foreign Calendar, Elizabeth*, vii. 414). Her answers bear that she was neither persuaded of the truth of their religion, nor of any impiety in the mass ; that she would not leave the religion in which she had been 'nourishit and upbrocht,' as she would thereby wound her own conscience and ' tyne the freindship of the King of France, . . . and of other great princes her friends and confederates' ; that she prayed all her loving subjects, that, as she intended, in the future as in the past, to ' prease the conscience' of no man, they would not ' prease her to offend her awin conscience' ; that she would establish religion throughout the realm when the three Estates of Parliament were agreed ; and that she would ' allwayes make them sure that no man salbe troublit for using themselves in religioun according to ther conscience, so that no man sall have cause to doubt that for religiouns sake men's lyves or heiritages salbe in hazard' (*Booke of the Universall Kirk*, i. 67, 68). These answers ' satisfied not fullie the Kirk,' when laid before the General Assembly on the 25th of December, and therefore answers to them were drawn up (*Ibid.* i. 66, 68-71).

[12] Keith's *History*, ii. 329, 330.—In the previous March, Chatelherault, Murray, and Argyll had entered into a band 'to defende each other's quarrel, that is not agaynste God and theire Soverayne' (Wright's *Elizabeth*, i. 193); and the Queen was not overjoyed when she heard of it (Keith's *History*, ii. 312).

[13] *Register of Privy Council*, i. 340.—The Commendator of Balmerino was sent to Murray, to declare the goodwill of Lennox and Darnley towards him, to deny that they had consented to slay him, and to state that Lennox was willing to fight any who would avow the report. The plot was said to have become known through Lord Gray (Keith's *History*, ii. 333). The plan of this enterprise against Murray as related by Buchanan (Aikman's *Buchanan*, ii. 468, 469) and Calderwood (*History*, ii. 286) is somewhat different from that given by Randolph (Keith's *History*, ii. 300).

[14] *Register of Privy Council*, i. 341, 342.

[15] In Randolph's opinion, Mary was determined on Murray's overthrow (Keith's *History*, ii. 337). Besides eleven members of the Privy Council there were nineteen nobles and others at the meeting at which Murray's assurance was granted. 'To prevent all possibility of cavil,' says Tytler, 'it was signed not by the Queen alone but by all her Privy Council' (*History of Scotland*, v. 311). The minute and also the assurance bear indeed that:—'In fayth and securitie heirof, the Quenis Majestie hes subscrivit thir presentis with hir hand; lykeas alswa the Lordis of hir Secreit Counsall, and utheris of hir nobilitie present at hir Hienes commandment, hes likewyise subscrivit the samyn.' But the assurance, nevertheless, only bears the signatures of Mary, Darnley, Lennox, and Morton (*National MSS. of Scotland*, iii. 47). Judging, however, from the appearance of the original, which is in the Register House, part of it may have been torn off. Darnley signs as Earl of Ross. In presence of Queen Elizabeth, her Council, and two French Ambassadors, Murray afterwards declared that he had answered, 'that for his life's sake he would not place in trouble and peril the good friends who had given him the warning, as he undoubtedly should do if he named them at present, but that he humbly begged her to give him a term of six months during which he would undertake to say who had given him the information'; and 'if he failed to divulge their names during that period he would willingly submit to the punishment she thought fit' (*Spanish Calendar, Elizabeth*, i. 501).

[16] On Monday evening, the 25th of June, Mary left Perth for Ruthven and Dunkeld, and by Saturday was back in Perth (Keith's *History*, ii. 301-304, 309), where she was alarmed by the tidings that Argyll and Murray had assembled their friends and followers, intending to seize her and Darnley—as they rode next day to Lord Livingston's house of Callendar, near Falkirk—to carry her to St. Andrews, and the man of her choice to Castle Campbell. Deeming it unsafe to remain in Perth, and determined to keep her promise to Livingston, she caused Atholl and Ruthven to collect immediately three hundred men ; and, taking horse by five o'clock on Sabbath morning, she rode with great speed until she came to Queensferry and arrived safely at Callendar seeing ' in her whole waye not six persons mo then those whiche she broughte wyth her for her defence' (*Ibid.* ii. 309-312). Within three days the story of the Queen's ' greate haste and feare' had ' runne throughe the whole countrie' in ' divers brutes and tales' (*Ibid.* ii. 314). One of these rumours was that some were 'lying in wait at the Path of Dron,' at the foot of the Ochils (Laing's *Knox*, ii. 490). Melville's story is that Chatelherault, Argyll, Murray, Glencairn, Rothes, and others ' maid a mynt to tak the Lord Darley in the Quenis company, at the raid of Baith, and to have send him in England as they allegit' (*Memoirs*, p. 135). And Pitscottie says that ' Rothes, with certain gentlemen, came to Parrat-Well beside Dowhill, thinking to have taken my Lord Darnley from the Queen, as they rode from St. Johnstoun to the Queensferry' (Lindsay's *History*, 1728, p. 216). Buchanan (Aikman's *Buchanan*, ii. 469) and Calderwood (*History*, ii. 286, 287) treat the alleged plot as an idle tale. In Hill Burton's judgment ' it would not be difficult to believe in such a conspiracy, if tolerably well vouched ; but there is scarcely a vestige of evidence in its support' (*History of Scotland*, 1876, iv. 121). Patrick Fraser Tytler, however, unhesitatingly accepts it as genuine (*Scotland*, 1845, v. 307-309) and has been cheerfully followed by Parker Lawson (Keith's *History*, ii. 312, *n.* 3) and by others. On the 1st of July, Argyll and Murray wrote to Randolph from Loch Leven, saying that they had that day convened with Lord Boyd ' to dettermyn apon some matters of consequence' ; and, being willing to communicate the same to him, had sent the bearer to declare their mind at length (Stevenson's *Selections*, p. 118). Putting this alongside a passage in Randolph's letter, of the following day, to Cecil, Tytler had no difficulty in discovering

that the 'matters of consequence' related to Darnley's capture.
The passage in Randolph's letter runs thus :—'Some that allreddie
have hearde of my Ladie's Grace [*i.e.* Lady Lennox's] imprisonment, lyke verre well thereof, and wyshe bothe father and sonne to
keape her compagnie. The question hath byne asked me, Whether,
yf theie were delyvered us into Barwick, we wolde receave them?
I answerde, That we coulde nor wolde not refuse our owne, in
what sorte soever theie came unto us' (Keith's *History*, ii. 307).
That this was not the burden of Argyll and Murray's confidential
message seems quite clear.   In the first place, although Randolph's
letter is dated 'the seconde of Julye at nyghte,' there is internal
evidence to prove that most of it—and in special the first part at
least of the paragraph containing the above passage—was written
before the end of June.   In the next place, Tytler has overlooked
the very important fact that it was on the 1st of July that the
Queen rode from Perth to Callendar House—the very day on which
Argyll and Murray wrote the letter to Randolph.   As Mary passed
Loch Leven that morning, Lord Erskine, who was in her train,
sent in a bantering message to Murray, to know what he 'was
doynge, and howe yt came to passe that the Queen had taken so
greate feare of hym.'   By the messenger, who 'founde hym scarce
owte of hys bedde,' Murray returned answer 'that he marvelled
muche of her Grace's haste and feare, whear no daynger was,
or anie matter intended' (Keith's *History*, ii. 313, 314).   Even
although there had been such a plot, why should Murray and
Argyll—after learning that the prey had escaped—ask Randolph
whether the English would receive Darnley and his father at
Berwick?   Four months afterwards, Mary professed to be able to
prove by a hundred gentlemen, who were in Murray's company
and whom she had since pardoned, that he had conspired on that
occasion the death of Darnley and Lennox, and her imprisonment
(Labanoff's *Recueil*, i. 304, 305).   And—as Tytler has pointed out
with the caution, 'if we may believe the assertion of a brother
conspirator'—when Mary was in England, and Argyll and Murray
were on fiercely opposing sides, Argyll set his hand to a document,
in which it was alleged that Murray had then planned the slaughter
of Darnley, Lennox, and divers other nobles, the perpetual imprisonment of the Queen in Loch Leven, and the usurpation of the
government by himself.   In this document, however, there is no
confession that Argyll was one of the 'mony quha wer in counsal

355

with him' (Goodall's *Examination*, ii. 358, 359). Had Tytler
carefully read Randolph's letter of 4th July—a letter to which he
thrice refers—he might have perceived that Argyll and Murray's
confidential messenger was not the bearer of a question as to
Darnley's reception at Berwick, but of an urgent request that
Elizabeth should advance them £3000 sterling 'for thys year,' with
which they thought they would be quite able to bring Scotland into
rest and quietness (Keith's *History*, ii. 317, 318). Chalmers had,
of course, no doubt as to the reality of the plot to intercept the
Queen (*Life of Mary*, 1818, i. 140, 141). In his opinion this has
been most satisfactorily proved ; and the evidence, he says, is to be
found 'in Randolph's dispatch to Cecil of the 2nd of July 1565,
which speaks of a concert, between the Duke, Argyle, Murray,
and Glencairn " *to coerce the Queen* " ' (*Ibid.* ii. 323 *n.*). Strange as
it may seem, the words which Chalmers thought important enough
to be italicised and enclosed within inverted commas are not to be
found in the despatch to which he refers. Had he detected such a
misrepresentation in the pages of Buchanan or Knox, he would
have unhesitatingly denounced it as a falsehood ; but a milder
epithet may nevertheless be applied to such a lapse on the part of
the author of *Caledonia*.

[17] 'The Queen's marriage with the Lord Darnley was prepared
and propounded in Councell, and the chief of the nobilitie, such as
the Duke, the Earles of Argyle, Murray, Glencarne, with the rest,
granted freely to the same, providing that they might have the
Religion established in Parliament by the Queene, and the idolatrous masse and superstition abolished' (Laing's *Knox*, ii. 481 ; *cf.*
Aikman's *Buchanan*, ii. 469 ; Calderwood's *History*, ii. 291 ; and
Spottiswoode's *History*, ii. 27). On the 12th of May, Throckmorton wrote to Leicester and Cecil :—Murray will in no wise yet
be conformable. He will have the Queen leave the mass and quit
all Popery, or he will never agree. She and Darnley will in nowise
agree thereto (*Foreign Calendar, Elizabeth*, vii. 363). Early in June
rumours were spread that in the next Parliament she would
establish a law for religion, thinking that she might marry whom
she chose if her people had their conscience free (*Ibid.* vii. 381).
Mary herself informed Paul De Foix, in the following November,
that Murray, when he perceived that she wished to marry Darnley,
offered so to contrive that all her nobles and subjects would approve
the match, provided that he alone might manage the business, that

all should know that he was the leader, and that the Roman Catholic religion should be banished from the kingdom (Turnbull's *Mary's Letters*, 1845, pp. 150, 151; Labanoff's *Recueil*, i. 301). In his interview with her on the 13th of July, Randolph had suggested, '"What yf your Majestie woulde alter your religion." "What wolde that do?" saythe she. "Paradventure," saide I, "somewhat move her Majestie [*i.e.* Elizabeth] to allowe the souner of your marriage." "What! wolde you," saythe she, "that I sholde mayke marchandize of my religion, or frame myself to your menestors willes? yt cane not be so." I tolde her thāt to knowe her deutie to God and by that meane to be called was no makinge of merchandes, and to frame her will to Godes will was but the humble desyer and prayer of her Grace's subjectes and mynesters of Godes trewe worde. I procede no farther with her Grace in thys kynde of tawlke,' says the somewhat discomfited Ambassador, 'but desyred her Grace to consyder her estate in tyme, that the Queen, my mestres, were not forced by her unkinde dealinge towardes her to do that for honor's cawse that agaynste her she wolde be loothe to attempte' (Stevenson's *Selections*, p. 124).

[18] Laing's *Knox*, ii. 482.

[19] *Ibid.* ii. 490.

[20] *Foreign Calendar, Elizabeth*, vii. 409–413.

[21] Thomworth's Instructions are dated 30th July (*Foreign Calendar, Elizabeth*, vii. 415–417).

[22] By this new assurance—of 28th July—Murray and 'four scoir utheris personis with him' were promised protection (*Register of Privy Council*, i. 345). According to Thomworth's Instructions, it was commonly reported that the malice of certain persons, having credit with Mary, has been such towards Murray as of late it was fully determined to have slain him at his coming to the Court when sent for (*Foreign Calendar, Elizabeth*, vii. 416).

[23] Unless the clerk of the Privy Council has by mistake written 'first' for 'fift,' this summons was so peremptory that Murray was commanded to present himself before their Majesties 'at Edinburgh, or quhair it sal happin thame to be for the tyme,' on the first of August, the same day that the summons had been resolved on (*Register of Privy Council*, i. 347). That the clerk has made a mistake may be inferred from the fact that Murray was not outlawed until the 6th of August (see following note), and also from the statement of Randolph (*Foreign Calendar, Elizabeth*, vii. 421).

[24] *Foreign Calendar, Elizabeth,* vii. 423.—It was on the 6th of August that Murray was 'ordourlie denuncit thair Hienessis rebell'; and next day the Privy Council—finding that he 'nevirtheles resortis and frequentis in the cuntre, resset and suppliit as gif he wer thair fre liege'—ordained that the said denunciation should be intimated to Chatelherault and Argyll, personally, or at their dwelling-places, and proclaimed to all the other lieges at the market-crosses of the head burghs, with the charge that any who presumed 'to resset, supple, or intercommoun' with him, 'in thair houssis cuntreis or utherwyise,' should be held as partakers with him in his rebellion, and be pursued 'with all extremitie in exempill of utheris' (*Register of Privy Council,* i. 349, 350; *Diurnal of Occurrents,* p. 81).

[25] *Foreign Calendar, Elizabeth,* vii. 425, 426, 431.—Thomworth's speech to Mary and her spirited answer are in Keith's *History,* iii. 223-232; and in the *Register of Privy Council,* xiv. 224-232. Camden is clearly in error in stating (*Elizabeth,* 1675, p. 79) that Thomworth was not admitted into Mary's presence; and so is Spottiswoode (ii. 32), Balfour (i. 334), Chalmers (i. 148), and Petit (i. 99). Cecil's statement—'refused to be heard'—can only mean that she would not follow his suggestions (Murdin's *State Papers,* 1759, p. 760).

[26] Keith's *History,* iii. 232-234; *Register of Privy Council,* xiv. 232-234; *Foreign Calendar, Elizabeth,* vii. 428, 429. These apparently were the offers presented to Thomworth in writing which he would not accept (Murdin's *State Papers,* p. 760).

[27] *Register of Privy Council,* i. 348; *Diurnal of Occurrents,* p. 81. —Archbishop Hamilton, as Lord of the Regality of St. Andrews, claimed 'the right of uplifting the escheats of all landowners within the same lawfully put to the horn,' and in particular of Rothes, Balcomy, Halyburton, and Monypenny, which were being uplifted for their Majesties, who, on the 7th of November, referred his claim to the Lords of Session (*Register of Privy Council,* xiv. 307, 308). It may perhaps be inferred from the imperfect entry that he also claimed—but claimed in vain—the fruits of the Priory of St. Andrews, of which Murray was Commendator.

[28] Lord Gordon—having found half-a-dozen cautioners that he would re-enter into ward when commanded by the King and Queen —was released on the 3rd of August (*Register of Privy Council,* i. 348). That day he was by proclamation at the market-cross of

Edinburgh 'relaxit fra the proces of horn and ressavit to peace,' receiving 'licence and tollerance to resort, pas and repas quhair he pleissis, in any pairt of this realme,' and two days later, he 'gaif presens to the King and Quene in the Palice of Halyrudhous, quhair he was gentilly intertenyit be thame' (*Diurnal of Occurrents*, p. 80). By another proclamation, he was, on the 25th of August, restored 'to his fame, honour, and dignitie, and to the lordschipe of Gordoun' (*Ibid.* p. 81; *Foreign Calendar, Elizabeth*, vii. 437). By the 10th of October he appears in the sederunt of Privy Council as Earl of Huntly (*Register of Privy Council*, i. 379), having been restored to that honour a few days before (*Diurnal of Occurrents*, p. 84; *Foreign Calendar, Elizabeth*, vii. 484).

[29] Before the end of July, the Laird of Riccarton fell into Bedford's hands. According to Randolph he was then the bearer of Mary's letter to fetch Bothwell home (*Foreign Calendar, Elizabeth*, vii. 413). Before the end of August, Sir Thomas Smith had learned in France that Bothwell had been privily sent for ; and that he had gone from Paris, 'no man knows whither' (*lbid.* vii. 438). Mary had sent for him and Seton (*Ibid.* vii. 440). So recently as the 2nd of May, Bothwell had been denounced as a rebel and put to the horn (Pitcairn's *Criminal Trials*, i. 462 *).

[30] In this proclamation of 22nd August 1565, it is mentioned that although the proclamation of 25th August 1561—forbidding the alteration or innovation of 'the estait of religioun,' which she 'fand publictlie and universalie standing at hir first arryvall'—had been divers times duly published, 'swa that nane can pretend ignorance thairof,' yet it is murmured that some forgetting their duty 'haif contravenit and purposlie intendis to contravene the samyn' ; and that those who were now their Majesties' rebels were trying to cover their rebellion, by persuading the good subjects that she and the King were attempting 'the plane subversion of the estait of religioun,' and 'be sic untrew reportis to alienate the hartis of the guid subjectis fra the obedience of thair Hienessis.' It was for the eschewing of this 'untrew brute and fals rumour' that the lieges were again charged to keep the former proclamation (*Register of Privy Council*, i. 356).

[31] According to Spottiswoode (ii. 31) and the continuator of Knox's *History* (ii. 497), Darnley had gone to hear Knox, to make himself more popular, and to take from the Lords the pretext of religion. He considered the sermon rather personal, as well as

much too long, and was so angry that he would not dine, but passed in the afternoon to the hawking. As the *Diurnal* (p. 81) puts it, 'he was crabbit.' 'At that sermon,' says Knox, 'wer auditours unto me not onely professors of the truth, and such as favor me, but rancke Papistes, dissembled hipocrites, and no small number of covetous clawbaks of the new Court' (Laing's *Knox*, vi. 231). And for this sermon, he says, 'from my bed I was called before the Councell; and, after long reasoning, I was by some forbidden to preach in Edingbrough so long as the King and Queene were in the towne' (*Ibid.* vi. 230). He answered, 'That he had spoken nothing but according to his text; and if the Church would command him either to speak or abstain, he would obey, so far as the Word of God would permit him' (*Ibid.* ii. 498). Both Spottiswoode and Knox's continuator state that in his defence before the Council the Reformer spoke even more plainly than he had done in his pulpit, alleging that as the King had gone to mass and dishonoured God, to please the Queen, so God in His justice would make her an instrument of his ruin. The Queen apparently was present, for they add that, being incensed at these words, she burst into tears. The sermon had been preached on Sabbath the 19th of August. Next Thursday, the magistrates and town council of Edinburgh sent a deputation to the King and Queen, 'desiring to be hard of thame tuiching the dischargeing of Johne Knox, minister, of forder preiching,' and to Knox himself they sent their unanimous deliverance, 'that thai will na maner of way consent or grant that his mouth be closit or he dischargeit in preiching the trew word, and thairfoir willit him at his plesour, as God sould move his hart, to proceid fordwart in trew doctrine as he hes bene of befoir, quhilk doctrine thai wald approve and abide at to thair lifis end' (*Records of the Burgh of Edinburgh*, 1557-1571, p. 200). It was to let such 'as Sathan hath not altogether blinded' see how great offence might be easily given that Knox afterwards wrote this sermon—the only one he ever published—from memory and committed it to the press.

[32] *Register of Privy Council*, i. 355.—The charge was, 'to pas furthwart and depend upoun thair Majesteis as thai salbe commandit, for the space of xv dayis.' It is an evidence, perhaps, of the haste in which the minute was prepared, that not one of the five days—Settirday, Sonday, Mononday, Twysday, Weddnusday—on which the lieges were commanded to appear corresponds with the

day of the month. Had they been a little less loyal, or a little
more quirky, they might have tried to evade the charge because of
the technical error. At the request of the magistrates and town
council, the inhabitants of Edinburgh were, on payment of £1000,
permitted to 'remane and bide at hame fra this hoist and armie,
ordanit . . . to pass fordwart for the persute of the Erle of
Murray' (*Records of the Burgh of Edinburgh*, 1557-1571, pp. 200-
203). This town, says Randolph, has now given £200 sterling,
and none of them goes with her, for she knows how they favour
the other part (*Foreign Calendar, Elizabeth*, vii. 437).

[33] *Register of Privy Council*, i. 357, 358.

[34] *Foreign Calendar, Elizabeth*, vii. 437 ; *Diurnal of Occurrents*,
p. 82.—Randolph states that, on the previous Friday, proclamation
was made that any who left the Lords would be pardoned.

[35] *Foreign Calendar, Elizabeth*, vii. 441, 443, 446, 447; Laing's
Knox, ii. 498, 500 ; *Diurnal of Occurrents*, p. 82.—Before Mary left
Edinburgh, strict injunctions were given that a continual watch
should be kept in town, so that nothing should be permitted to
pass furth to the rebels, and that no suspected person should
resort there 'without apprehensioun.' To meet this command, the
magistrates and town council ordained, that there should be a
night-watch of thirty-two men and a day-watch of eight (*Records
of the Burgh of Edinburgh*, 1557-1571, pp. 203, 204). When the
captain of the Castle was showing that he was more faithful to the
Queen than were the magistrates, Knox was just finishing his
obnoxious sermon for the press; and so in the colophon he in-
serted : — 'Lord ! in thy hands I commend my spirit ; for the
terrible roring of gunnes, and the noyce of armour, doe so pierce
my heart, that my soule thirstith to depart' (Laing's *Knox*, vi.
273). The day before the Lords left Edinburgh, they issued a
proclamation, summoning all, who loved the Lord Jesus or the
commonwealth, to assist them with all diligence by their presence
and counsel. To their Queen they sent the message, that they
were enclosed in the capital, and could flee no further ; that they
sought nothing but the maintenance of the true religion ; that they
begged her to leave off her rigorous pursuit, and suffer their cause
to be tried by her Council ; and that, if still pursued, their blood
should be sold as dear as any ever shed in the realm (*Foreign
Calendar, Elizabeth*, vii. 442).

[36] Randolph writes, that the Lords were on the 3rd of September

at Hamilton, on the 4th at the Laird of Drumlanrick's house, who now takes open part with them, that the Master of Maxwell was come to them, purposing to convoy them to Dumfries, and either to defend them against all her power or to put them in safety into their friends' hands at Carlisle (*Foreign Calendar, Elizabeth*, vii. 448). They arrived at Dumfries with the Master of Maxwell on the 5th of September (*Ibid.* vii. 452).

[37] *Foreign Calendar, Elizabeth*, vii. 448.—She returned, Randolph says, to Stirling, and from thence to Glasgow, where she was on Tuesday when he wrote.

[38] *Foreign Calendar, Elizabeth*, vii. 446.

[39] Laing's *Knox*, ii. 500, 501.

[40] *Register of Privy Council*, i. 361.

[41] It had been the same at Pinkie, where the universal use of the jack occasioned the slaughter of many Scots gentlemen—'Their armour among theim so little differing and their apparail so base and beggerly, whearin the lurdein was in a maner all one wyth the Lorde, and the lounde with the larde : all clad alyke in jackes cooverd wyth whyte leather, dooblettes of the same or of fustian, and most commonly al white hosen. Not one with either cheine, brooch, ryng, or garment of silke that I coold see, onles cheynes of latten drawen four or fyve tymes along the thighs of their hosen and dooblet sleves for cuttyng ; and of that sort I sawe many' (Patten's *Expedicion*, in Dalyell's *Fragments*, p. 69). The perplexed Englishmen did not know who were worth saving for ransom.

[42] *Foreign Calendar, Elizabeth*, vii. 448.

[43] *Ibid.* vii. 452, 453.

[44] *Ibid.* vii. 449.

[45] *Register of Privy Council*, i. 362.

[46] 'Palyeonis' were pavilions or tents. The common Scotch ones of the period were so simple in construction, and so modest in size, that it was no great hardship for the forces to provide their own. Even those of the nobles were neither very great nor very grand. Both kinds were minutely described by an observant Englishman who saw them at Pinkie. Few of the larger ones reached—none exceeded—twenty feet in length. The common ones were made by stretching a canvas sheet over four sticks, each about an ell in length, which were set up in pairs like inverted V's, one pair at the head, and another at the feet. These small tents

were 'skant shut at both endes, and not very close beneath on the sydes, onles their stiks wear the shorter, or their wives the more liberal to lend them larger naperie : howbeit, within they had lyned them and stuft them so thick with strawe, that, the weather as it was not very cold, when they wear ones couched, thei wear as warme as thei had bene wrapt in horsdung' (Patten's *Expedicion*, in Dalyell's *Fragments of Scotish History*, pp. 70, 71).

[47] *Register of Privy Council,* i. 362, 363.

[48] *Ibid.* i. 364, 365.

[49] *Register of Privy Council,* i. 365-367.—On the previous day, twenty-one of the Lords and Barons of the West Country bound themselves, in presence of their Majesties, truly and faithfully to 'serve the King and Quenis Majesteis, and the rycht nobill and mychty Lord Mathow Erle of Lennox, Lord Dernle, etc., thair Hienessis lieutennent,' in whatever 'he sall command tending to the furthsetting of thair Majesteis autoritie, and resisting of thair Hienessis rebellis' (*Ibid.* p. 363).

[50] *Register of Privy Council,* i. 365.—On the 27th of September, Chatelherault, Glencairn, and the Abbot of Kilwinning 'wer denuncit our Soveranis rebellis, and put to thair horne, and all thair movabill guidis decernit to be escheit' (*Diurnal of Occurrents*, p. 83; *Foreign Calendar, Elizabeth*, vii. 475).

[51] Labanoff's *Recueil,* i. 281-283.

[52] *Register of Privy Council,* i. 359, 360.—The lieges of several of the northern shires were commanded to meet Atholl in Lorne, with provisions for twenty days, and 'weill bodin in feir of weir'; which muster was afterwards merged in another (*Ibid.* i. 363).

[53] Bothwell brought with him six or eight men, certain pistolets, and some armour. With his two small boats, by dint of oar and sail, he escaped the shot of Wilson the pirate. He did not tarry a quarter of an hour at Eyemouth (*Foreign Calendar, Elizabeth*, vii. 463, 465); and on the 20th of September 'gat presens of our Soveranis in Halyrudhous and was thankfullie ressavit of thame' (*Diurnal of Occurrents*, p. 83). On the 1st of September, Bedford had reported the capture of Sutherland, and that Yaxley would also have been caught by the same adventurer had not his ship been furred with long lying abroad. Bedford had then pled with Elizabeth that, as this pirate—who had a letter of marque from the King of Sweden—might be of service in impeaching Bothwell, she should not think of such things as might be brought against him

(*Foreign Calendar, Elizabeth*, vii. 443, 444). Elizabeth quite approved of Sutherland's capture by Wilson and detention by Bedford ; but gave instructions that Wilson was 'not to be used directly,' as he had spoiled the English, as well as the French and Flemish, and as she was more pressed, by the French and Spanish Ambassadors, for his apprehension than for that of any other pirate (*Ibid.* vii. 453). It was not expected that he would be able to encounter Seton, who was coming home with armour and a very well-furnished ship (*Ibid.* vii. 464) ; but Bedford gave him temporary letters of protection, that he might transport Lady Murray from Fife to Berwick (*Ibid.* vii. 471, 473, 502) ; nevertheless, he and his ship were seized by Jenkinson of the 'Aid,' greatly to Bedford's mortification, who had never been ' so touched in honour and credit or so traitorously sought upon to be defaced as by that vile man' (*Ibid.* vii. 492, 495, 516, 517).

[54] *Register of Privy Council*, i. 378, 383, 509.—Eleven days after Bothwell landed at Eyemouth, Bedford reported that he was already one of Mary's Council, and besides Atholl and Ruthven the chiefest man, and looking daily to be advanced higher (*Foreign Calendar, Elizabeth*, vii. 473). By the 10th of October, his name occurs in the sederunt of Privy Council.

[55] *National MSS. of Scotland*, iii. 49.—In the *Register of Privy Council* (i. 371), the date is erroneously given as the *third* of September.

[56] *Register of Privy Council*, i. 371-373.

[57] *Foreign Calendar, Elizabeth*, vii. 455, 464, 467.—In the middle of October, Randolph is more explicit about the pledging of her jewels. Part of them he says had been laid to gage for 2000 merks sterling (*Ibid.* vii. 489). For lack of money too, she had given Yaxley at his departure some plate and two jewels (*Ibid.* vii. 462). For her monetary transactions with Edinburgh, see *Ibid.* vii. 437, 477, 478 ; *Diurnal of Occurrents*, pp. 83, 84 ; *Records of the Burgh of Edinburgh*, 1557-1571, pp. 200-203, 207, 208, 229.

[58] *Foreign Calendar, Elizabeth*, vii. 459.

[59] 'If the Queen [*i.e.* Elizabeth] so countenance this matter with aid as it is hoped, many that stand to look how things should pass will wholly come to this side, and that in great number' (*Foreign Calendar, Elizabeth*, vii. 460). 'If the Queen grants this aid, the Earl of Morton, Lord Ruthven, and Lethington will come to the Lords, and also many other great personages' (*Ibid.* vii. 464).

' Many that are willing to take their parts doubt so much of the issue, that before they know what succour they shall receive of the Queen they join not with the others ' (*Ibid.* vii. 466). ' Some wise men are enemies to this government, as the Lord of Lethington. Of the same band are Morton and Ruthven, who only espy their time, and make fair weather until it come to the pinch ' (*Ibid.* vii. 486).

[60] Robert Melville was instructed to ask from Elizabeth three thousand men—of these a thousand to be arquebusiers, a thousand pikemen, five hundred bowmen, and five hundred archers—and that money for their pay should be sent with haste to Lord Scrope, her Warden of the West Marches. He was also to ask some field-pieces and siege guns, and that certain ships be sent to keep the Firth and East Coast (*Foreign Calendar, Elizabeth,* vii. 457). At the same time (10th September), the Lords wrote to Elizabeth and to Cecil (*Ibid.* vii. 456). Bedford, too, sent a pressing letter to Cecil by Melville (*Ibid.* vii. 459, 460).

[61] *Foreign Calendar, Elizabeth,* vii. 476.

[62] On the 10th of August, Thomworth, then at Edinburgh, informed Cecil that he was so earnestly pressed by Murray and the others with Elizabeth's promise for their relief that he must send to Berwick for the money he had left there, which he now meant to deliver to such as by Murray are appointed to receive it (*Foreign Calendar, Elizabeth,* vii. 426). This was probably the 3000 crowns handed to Lady Murray, on account of which Randolph was dismissed from the Scotch Court (*supra,* p. 130). Murray also received £1000 from Elizabeth, through Bedford, ' to be employed in the common cause and action in Scotland, enterprised by the nobility thereof, for maintenance of the true religion and commonwealth of this realm ' (*Foreign Calendar, Elizabeth,* vii. 458, 463, 473, 476, 477). The Elwoods—or Elliots—received £50, ' in such secret manner as in this case behoves' (*Ibid.* vii. 451); and Bedford lent £500 of his own to Murray (*Ibid.* vii. 473). Knox's continuator alleges that Nicholas Elphinston, when sent to England for support, returned with £10,000 sterling (Laing's *Knox,* ii. 496).

[63] *Foreign Calendar, Elizabeth,* vii. 459, 478, 481, 487, 488.

[64] *Ibid.* vii. 468.

[65] *Foreign Calendar, Elizabeth,* vii. 465 ; Calderwood's *History,* ii. 569-576. — They denied that they had been guilty of sedition, rebellion, or treason, having neither done nor intended to do

more than became 'the faithfull of God and true subjects to doe to their Prince, native countrie, and commoun weal of the same.'

[66] *Foreign Calendar, Elizabeth*, vii. 480; Stevenson's *Selections*, p. 145.

[67] Teulet's *Papiers D'État*, ii. 96-110; *Relations Politiques*, ii. 245-258; *Foreign Calendar, Elizabeth*, vii. 477.

[68] *Diurnal of Occurrents*, p. 84; *Foreign Calendar, Elizabeth*, vii. 479, 480, 484, 485, 488; Laing's *Knox*, ii. 512.

[69] Mary's disaffected Lords were at Carlisle with Lord Scrope on the 6th of October (*Foreign Calendar, Elizabeth*, vii. 483); and arrived at Newcastle on the 16th (*Ibid.* vii. 493). Although they were in Carlisle two days before Mary left Edinburgh with her army, Mr. Skelton declares that 'she herself in steel jacket at the head of her troopers swept them away out of Edinburgh, over the Pentlands to Dumfries, and at last—such of them as remained together—clean across the English border' (*Mary Stuart*, 1893, p. 71). And Mr. T. F. Henderson says:—'In hope of Elizabeth's aid Moray ultimately marched south to Dumfries, but on the appearance of Mary on 10 Oct., at the head of eighteen thousand men, he took refuge in England' (*Dictionary of National Biography*, xxxvi. 381).

[70] *Foreign Calendar, Elizabeth*, vii. 488, 489, 492.—Perhaps some of the disorderliness was due to the fact that 'the whole force of the North,' under Huntly, had accompanied her (*Ibid.* vii. 484), and that those formed the greatest part of her army (*Ibid.* vii. 485).

[71] Mary was at Dumfries by the 13th of October (*Foreign Calendar, Elizabeth*, vii. 488), and left it for Lochmaben on the 14th, intending to proceed next day to Moffat and so to Edinburgh (*Ibid.* vii. 492). In his letter of the 19th, Scrope says that Bothwell is at Dumfries with 1600 men (*Ibid.* vii. 497). Six days later he puts down the number at 300 horse and 300 arquebusiers (*Ibid.* vii. 500). Bothwell, it was alleged, was lying at Dumfries to watch the Master of Maxwell, who had made his peace with Mary and was trying to negotiate for the restoration of Chatelherault and the others on similar terms (*Ibid.* vii. 499). On the 2nd of November, Scrope reported that Bothwell had departed and that the Master of Maxwell had obtained from Mary 300 horsemen and some footmen (*Ibid.* vii. 508).

[72] *Diurnal of Occurrents*, p. 85; *Foreign Calendar, Elizabeth*, vii. 496.

[73] 'That Queen [*i.e.* Mary] increases her displeasure towards them because they have entered this realm' (*Foreign Calendar, Elizabeth*, vii. 493). Four days before, Bedford had written :—' That Queen hath plainly affirmed in open and manifest sort that whosoever of these Lords and others now with them shall by any means enjoy her pardon and so be received, that the same shall become thenceforward a professed and sworn enemy to this realm and the peace and amity of the same' (*Ibid.* vii. 487, 488).

[74] On the 14th of October, Murray wrote to Cecil from Carlisle, thanking him for his aid ; and stating that neither he nor the other Lords would have enterprised this action, if they had not been moved to it by the handwriting of Elizabeth, and her Council, directed to them thereupon ; and praying that the promised support might be hastened with all expedition. On the same day Murray wrote to Leicester, expressing the hope that Elizabeth would make an end of those troubles, and intimating that they would send some gentleman to her to expedite the support, and that they were not inclined to accept any agreement with Mary of which Elizabeth was not the 'dresser' (*Foreign Calendar, Elizabeth*, vii. 491).

[75] *Foreign Calendar, Elizabeth*, vii. 493, 494.—Chatelherault wrote to Cecil asking his favour for the Abbot of Kilwinning who was to accompany Murray (*Ibid.* vii. 494). By this time Cecil had informed Sir Thomas Smith that, in the English Council, 'arguments have bene made contrarywyse, some to ayd the Lordes of Scotland playnly and oppenly, some but covertly, some not at all ; but in the end the Quene's Majesty hath resolved to use all good meanes by mediation, by outward countenance, to relieve them, but to do nothyng that may break peace' (Wright's *Elizabeth*, i. 208).

[76] The English Council wrote to Murray that it was not meet for him to come at this time, and that he should forbear from such open dealing with her Majesty until it may be considered what shall be meet for him to do. The Queen wrote to Bedford to stay him (*Foreign Calendar, Elizabeth*, vii. 497). Bedford afterwards explained to Leicester that he had no order from the Queen to stay him when he left, and neither persuasions nor dissuasions would serve (Wright's *Elizabeth*, i. 215).

[77] *Foreign Calendar, Elizabeth*, vii. 498, 499, 504.

[78] The dramatic story of Murray's interview with Elizabeth on the 23rd of October 1565, as related by Sir James Melville

(*Memoirs*, pp. 135, 136) is well known ; but as told by De Silva to Philip (*Spanish Calendar, Elizabeth*, i. 499-502), and by the English Privy Council to their Ambassador at the French Court (*Foreign Calendar, Elizabeth*, vii. 499, 500), it is far less humiliating for Murray. Melville's version having had a long start in type—the first edition of his *Memoirs* was published in 1683—retains its hold, even where it is clearly in error. His assertion that the Spanish as well as the French Ambassador was present, has not only been repeated by Keith, Robertson, Chalmers, Lingard, Bell, Strickland, Caird, Petit, and Hill Burton, but even by Mignet and Hosack, who refer to De Silva's letter—a letter in which he states that he received his account from Elizabeth. So far as Murray's reputation is concerned, De Silva's report of the interview is none the less valuable that it was derived from Elizabeth, who was not the one to minimise her supposed exculpation. Yet it contains nothing implying that Murray formally confessed that she had not encouraged the enterprise of the Scots Lords ; nor does the report sent by the English Privy Council to Sir Thomas Smith. Sinfully silent Murray seems to have been under Elizabeth's denunciation, staggered perhaps by her shameless audacity, and depressed by the bad fortune of his party ; but according to the continuator of Knox, after the French Ambassador withdrew, he told her plainly enough, that, whatever she had intended in her heart, her Ambassador and familiar servants had promised in her name to assist them, and they had also her own handwriting in confirmation (Laing's *Knox*, ii. 513). Chalmers alleges that Sir James Melville received his 'circumstantial account' of the interview 'from his brother Robert, who was then present in the Court of Elizabeth as the Scotish resident' (*Life of Mary*, 1818, i. 159 *n.*). Robert Melville had been sent to the Queen of England in the preceding September, not by Mary, but by the Protestant Lords (*Foreign Calendar, Elizabeth*, vii. 457, 459) ; and had returned to them with her answer before the 12th of October (*Ibid.* vii. 485), when Murray and the other Lords were at Carlisle (*Ibid.* vii. 483, 491), and before Murray had set out for Newcastle or London. If he did not actually return to London with Murray, he was certainly left there by him as his agent, at the end of October (*National MSS. of Scotland*, iii. 56 ; *Foreign Calendar, Elizabeth*, vii. 525, 526). Though not a witness perhaps of the interview, he may have told his brother of it ; but Sir James does not say so. Robert Melville did not obtain his formal remission until the 20th of January (*Register of Privy Seal,* xxxiv. 42); and it was not until the 12th of the following February —sixteen weeks after the famous interview—that Mary despatched him to the English Court (*Foreign Calendar, Elizabeth,* viii. 17).

[79] In Mary's Instructions to the Bishop of Dunblane, when she sent him to France to explain why she had married Bothwell, there is the following passage :—' At quhilk tyme, be oure commandment being callit hame, and immediatlie restorit to his former charge of Lieutenent-Generall, oure authoritie prospered sa weill in his handis, that suddanlie oure haill rebellis wer constranit to depart the realme, and remane in Ingland, quhill sum of thame upoun submissioun and humill sute wer reconceylit to us' (Labanoff's *Recueil,* ii. 35).

[80] *Foreign Calendar, Elizabeth,* vii. 428, 436, 453.

[81] *Ibid.* vii. 417, 457.

[82] *Ibid.* vii. 483; Labanoff's *Recueil,* i. 293, 294.

[83] De Foix, writing from London to Catherine de Medici, on the 29th of September 1565, informed her that Shan O'Neil was fightin Mary's name in Ireland, and that she had sent over to him as envoys 'deux gentilshommes du païs des sauvaiges d'Escosse, qui usent de mesme langaige' (Teulet's *Papiers D'État,* ii. 85).

[84] In the autograph fragment concerning her second marriage, Mary says that Leicester wrote to her, explaining how she might induce Elizabeth to consent to their marriage, by means of the disturbances in Ireland, 'where,' adds Mary, 'I had power at that time, of which she was much afraid' (Labanoff's *Recueil,* i. 297, 298; Turnbull's *Mary's Letters,* p. 149). It was no new plan for the Scots to foment trouble in Ireland (*Foreign Calendar, Elizabeth,* iv. 321; Haynes's *State Papers,* p. 353).

[85] *Hamilton Manuscripts,* Hist. MSS. Com., p. 43; *Foreign Calendar, Elizabeth,* vii. 530-532; *Spanish Calendar, Elizabeth,* i. 524, 527.— Darnley was apparently displeased at Chatelherault's pardon (Ruthven's *Relation,* 1699, pp. 34, 35), though it runs in his name as well as Mary's. In the license to go abroad, granted on the 3rd of January to Chatelherault and three of his sons, and also to the Commendator of Kilwinning and James Hamilton of Rouchbank, they are permitted 'to depairt and pas furth of this realme to the pairtis of France or uthiris beyond sey for doing of thair lefull erandis and besines and to remane and abyde furth of the same at thair plesouris for the space of fyve yeiris' (*Register*

of Privy Seal, xxxiv. 30, 31).   Chatelherault's passport bears that
he is to travel abroad for his health (*Register of Privy Council,* xiv.
241).   Mary had applied to Elizabeth, a month before, for a passport to Chatelherault to go through her realm (Labanoff's *Recueil,*
i. 309, 310).   His remission is dated 2nd January; the letter to
Elizabeth, 1st December.

   [86] *Foreign Calendar, Elizabeth,* vii. 511, 530.—By the 25th of
December it was said that Murray had not 200 crowns in the
world; and that Melville's pleading for him was ineffectual, but
this was understood to be due more to Darnley than to Mary (*Ibid.*
vii. 541).   On the 16th of January it seemed still impossible by
any means to find favour for him at her hands (Stevenson's *Selections,* p. 146); but in another eight days Randolph was able to
report 'that some parte of her extremitie is asswaged she nether
usethe so greveus wordes as she hathe done, nor so unpatient to
here hym spoken of as she was' (*Ibid.* p. 151).   Soon after the
arrival of Clerneau and Thornton from France, however, it became evident that no good was intended towards Murray and the
other exiled Lords, unless they could persuade Elizabeth to make
Mary 'her heir apparent to the crowne of England' (*Ibid.* p. 152).
On the 8th of February, Bedford reported that 'Murray's landes
be gyven awaye, and he having nowe but a litell place leafte must
sell the same for the further maintenance of him selfe' (*Ibid.* p.
155).   It is certain that Bothwell—fifteen days after his arrival at
Eyemouth—obtained a gift of the teind sheaves, etc., of the parish
church of Haddington, for the crop of that year, which belonged
to Murray (*Register of Privy Seal,* xxxiii. 105); and that the Earl
of Mar got a gift of the escheat of the teind sheaves of Eglisgreg,
which pertained to Murray (*Ibid.* xxxiii. 112, 113).

   [87] *Register of Privy Council,* i. 409; *Diurnal of Occurrents,* pp.
85, 86; *Foreign Calendar, Elizabeth,* vii. 540; *Master of Gray's
Papers,* Ban. Club, app. p. ix.

CHAPTER X

   [1] Calderwood's *History,* ii. 572, 573.—See also Information for
Melville (*Foreign Calendar, Elizabeth,* vii. 469).

   [2] Calderwood's *History,* ii. 285; Spottiswoode's *History,* ii. 27.

3 Melville's *Memoirs*, pp. 131, 132.—Birrel says that Riccio was
'verey skilfull in music and poetry' (*Diary*, p. 5).

4 Francisque-Michel's *Critical Inquiry into the Scottish Language*,
1882, p. 219.

5 Blackwood affirms that Mary did not esteem him 'for any
beauty or grace that was in him, being a man sufficiently old, ugly,
gloomy, and unpleasant' (Jebb's *De Vita et Rebus Gestis Mariae*,
ii. 202); or, as the sixteenth century translator renders it, 'he
was a man of no beautie or outwarde shape, for he was mishapen,
evil-favoured, and in visage verie blacke' (Blackwood's *Mary Queen
of Scots*, Mait. Club, p. 9). Herries speaks of him as 'neither
handsome nor well-faced' (Herries's *Memoirs*, p. 75). Causin describes him as 'an old and discreet man . . . but of a deformed
(*disgracié*) body' (*Holy Court*, 1678, p. 813; Jebb's *De Vita et Rebus
Gestis Mariae*, ii. 57). Buchanan also refers to the deformity of
his body—'*corporis vitia*'—as well as to the meanness of his
birth (Ruddiman's *Buchanan*, i. 344; Aikman's *Buchanan*, ii. 477).
According to Bishop Lesley he was 'a man of fifty years of age'
(Forbes-Leith's *Narratives of Scottish Catholics*, p. 109); but, according to a despatch drawn up shortly after his murder, he was only
about twenty-eight (Labanoff's *Recueil*, vii. 86).

6 Jebb's *De Vita et Rebus Gestis Mariae*, ii. 202; Labanoff's
Recueil, vii. 65, 86, 87; Forbes-Leith's *Narratives*, p. 109; Ruddiman's *Buchanan*, i. 340; *Foreign Calendar, Elizabeth*, vii. 308.

7 'Here, however, he remained, and finally determined to try
his fortune. To this he was chiefly induced by learning that the
Queen delighted greatly in musicians, and was herself no despicable
performer. He therefore, in order to procure access to her
Majesty, bargained with her musicians, the majority of whom were
Frenchmen, that he might be allowed to perform among them.
After being heard once or twice, he succeeded in pleasing the
Queen, and was immediately enrolled as one of the band' (Aikman's *Buchanan*, ii. 466, 467). 'Hir Majeste,' says Melville, 'had
thre varletis of hir chamber that sang thre partis, and wanted a
beiss to sing the fourt part; therfor they tald hir Majeste of this
man to be ther fourt marrow, in sort that he was drawen in to
sing somtymes with the rest; and eftirwart when the Ambassadour
his maister retournit [*i.e.* to Savoy], he stayed in this contre, and
wes retiret [? retenit or recivet] in hir Majestes service as ane varlet
of hir chamber' (Melville's *Memoirs*, p. 132).

371

[8] *Foreign Calendar, Elizabeth*, vii. 262, 308.—Goodall (*Examination*, i. 260) was so misled by the abstract of Randolph's letter printed by Keith (folio editions, p. 268 ; Spot. Soc. ed. ii. 259) as to infer that Raulet was dismissed for immorality, whereas the rumour was that he had been too familiar with the English Ambassador. 'A lyttill befoir the trubles quhich Sathan raised in the bodie of the Kirk, began Davie to grow grit in Courte. The Quene usit him for Secretarie in thingis that appertenit to hir secreit effaires in France or ellis quhair' (Laing's *Knox*, ii. 421, 422). Melville was disposed to think that the jealousy between Elizabeth and Mary was partly due to Riccio who was 'not very skilfull in dyting of French lettres' (Melville *Memoirs*, p. 109).

[9] Melville's *Memoirs*, p. 132.—'Grit men maid in Courte unto him, and thair sutes wer the better heard' (Laing's *Knox*, ii. 422). According to Buchanan, 'in household furniture, dress, the number and breed of his horses, and rank of his attendants, he far exceeded the King himself' (Aikman's *Buchanan*, ii. 476). This statement is indorsed by Spottiswoode (*History*, ii. 35), and also by Calderwood (*History*, ii. 311). For notes concerning his income, see Laing's *Knox*, ii. 596, 597 ; and for an account of 'the greate substance' he left, see Wright's *Elizabeth*, i. 233, 234 ; Ellis's *Original Letters*, first series, ii. 218.

[10] Aikman's *Buchanan*, ii. 467.

[11] Melville's *Memoirs*, pp. 134, 136 ; Spottiswoode's *History*, ii. 27 ; *Foreign Calendar, Elizabeth*, vii. 353 ; Labanoff's *Recueil*, vii. 88.

[12] 'The chief dealers in these matters are David Riccio, the Italian, Mingo, valet de chambre, Athole and Ruthven' (*Foreign Calendar, Elizabeth*, vii. 353). 'David is he that now works all, chief secretary to the Queen, and governor to her goodman' (*Ibid.* vii. 380). 'These matters are thus guydid by my Lord of Lenox, Lord Roberte, and David. Other counsell she takethe lyttle of anye subjecte she hathe' (Keith's *History*, ii. 333).

[13] 'What countenance that Queen [*i.e.* Mary] shows to David, an Italian, he will not write for the honour due to the person of a Queen' (*Foreign Calendar, Elizabeth*, vii. 464). 'Mr. James Balfoure [parson of Flisk, afterwards Sir James of Pittendreich, and clerk-register] once rowed in a galley ; and now, except David, no man is so great with her' (*Ibid.* vii. 480). 'The parson of Flyske flings at all men "as he were wode."' As for David, 'he that may attain unto it is worthy to wear it' (*Ibid.* vii. 506).

[14] Melville's *Memoirs*, p. 138.

[15] 'Inventions and bruits wer raised how that the said Seigneur David had a pension of the Paip; and, having baith Quen and K[ing] of his oppinion, mycht the rather and easeyler attempt, with tym, to plant again in Scotland the Roman Catholik religion' (Melville's *Memoirs*, pp. 136, 137; see also p. 147). Bishop Lesley alleges that 'the motive of the conspirators for their particular animosity against Rizzio was the constancy and firmness with which he had acted throughout these transactions in support of the ancient religion and the Queen's authority, and the great ability and acquaintance with Scottish politics which enabled him ever to suggest fresh means of defeating their machinations' (*Narratives of Scottish Catholics*, p. 109). The importance of Riccio's murder, 'as a political blow,' says Hill Burton, could only be known to a few. 'In the traces of the Queen's intercourse with the Court of Rome and the Papal powers we now see its significance more clearly than even the leading statesmen of the day in England and Scotland' (*History of Scotland*, 1876, iv. 158).

[16] Calderwood's *History*, ii. 572.

[17] Ten days before the marriage Randolph writes :—'My Lord Darlye wolde seeme to be indifferente, sometyme he goeth wyth the Queen to the masse, and these two laste dayes hathe byne at the sermonds' (Keith's *History*, ii. 332); two days after the marriage :—'He wolde nowe seeme to be indifferente to bothe the religions, she to use her masse, and he to come sometymes to the preachyng' (Wright's *Elizabeth*, i. 201). Even on his marriage day, he had retired from the chapel before the celebration of mass (see *supra*, p. 348, *n.* 114); and, after taking grievous offence at Knox's preaching, he had gone to hear Craig (*Foreign Calendar, Elizabeth*, vii. 475). In 1562, it had been deponed that Lady Lennox had not only grafted him into 'that devilish Papistry,' but that the curtains of his bed were pinned round with idols (*Ibid.* v. 15, 24). Yet it was alleged that in England he had plainly professed the Reformed religion (Melville's *Memoirs*, pp. 134, 136). It was asserted by his son that he was a Protestant (*The Workes of the Most High and Mighty Prince James*, 1616, p. 301).

[18] In the Dumfries Declaration, the Lords say :—'That ungodlie and wicked religioun, wherin her Grace hath beene brought up, beganne hastilie, after her arrivall, to crave one quiett masse to her owne household onlie. And we, hoping that the mercie of

God by processe of time sould have converted her therefra, alas !
(to the great dishonour of God, as His heavie displeasure powred
out upon us this day testifieth) past over with silence, and, to the
great greefe of our conscience, oversaw the same.   For, from
thence it proceeded plainlie to all that resorted to her Chappell
Royall unpunished, from saying to singing ; and from her Chappell
to all the corners of the country that listed.   And when we craved
punishment of the transgressors, according to the Act of Parliament
and her Highnesse' owne proclamations, even when we would
obteane them convicted in judgement, and the partie offending
confesse the crime, and coming in will therefore, we could have no
execution of the lawes against them' (Calderwood's *History*, ii.
571).

    [19] The open and defiant celebration of mass in the West of Scot-
land by priests and dignitaries at Easter, 1563, so roused the zealous
Protestants that they resolved to take the law into their own hands
by punishing what was at once a breach of the Act of Parliament
and of the Queen's Proclamation.   Mary sent for Knox to Loch
Leven, where he boldly avowed and defended the right of the
people to carry out the law when their rulers neglected to do so.
Having afterwards consulted two of her judges—Henry Sinclair and
the elder Lethington—they advised her to punish the offenders ; and
accordingly forty-nine of them were brought to trial in Edinburgh
on the 19th of May.   Of these, five by a jury were convicted of
'ministrand and abusand on thair pretendit maner, irreverentlie
and indecentlie, the Sacramentis of Haly Kirk,' and were committed
to ward—three in Dumbarton Castle, two in Edinburgh Castle, the
latter having been attended, at their celebration of mass at Kirk-
oswald and Maybole, by 'twa hundreth personis, bodin in feir of
weir, with jakkis, speris, gunnis, and utheris wapins invasive.'
The other forty-four culprits put themselves in the Queen's will ;
and of these thirteen were warded, eight discharged on finding
caution that they would not again contravene, and twenty-three
remitted.   At Paisley the illegal proceedings had been singularly
patent, auricular confession having been taken in the 'kirk, toune,
kirk-yaird, chalmeris, barnis, *middingis*, and killogeis thairof.'
The Archbishop of St. Andrews was one of those who put themselves in the Queen's will, and was warded in the Castle of Edinburgh (Laing's *Knox*, ii. 370-380 ; Pitcairn's *Criminal Trials*, i.
427*-430*).   It was then regarded as a strange tragedy that the

Primate of the Kingdom should be committed to prison 'for
Papistry, in the time of a Queen of his own religion.' To declare
that it was with her will, she 'came to a house not far from
the place where the Lords sat in judgment, supped, and remained there till all was ended, near unto 8 p.m.' (*Foreign Calendar, Elizabeth*, vi. 355). 'All this was, done,' says Knox, 'of a
most deape craft, to abuse the simplicitie of the Protestantis, that
thei should not prease the Quene with any other thing concernyng
materis of religioun at that Parliament. . . . Sche obteined of the
Protestantis whatsoever sche desyred; for this was the reassone of
many, "We see what the Quene has done; the lyek of this was
never heard of within the realme: we will bear with the Quene;
we doubt not but all shalbe weill." Otheris war of a contrarie
judgement, and foirspak thingis, as after thei cam to pas, to wit,
that nothing was meant but deceat; and that the Quene, how soon
that ever Parliament was past, should set the Papistis at freedome:
and thairfoir willed the nobilitie not [to] be abused. But becaus
many had thair privat commoditie to be handilled at that Parliament, the commoun cause was the less regarded' (Laing's *Knox*, ii.
380). On the other hand, Bishop Lesley alleges that the true
reason why the Primate was imprisoned during the sitting of
Parliament was to prevent him from opposing the deprivation of
Huntley's heirs (Forbes-Leith's *Narratives*, p. 92). The Parliament thus referred to was opened by the Queen on the 26th of
May and closed by her upon the 6th of June (*Foreign Calendar,
Elizabeth*, vi. 381, 399; *Diurnal of Occurrents*, p. 76). On the
19th of June, Randolph writes to Cecil:—'Our pestilent prelate,
put in the Castle, made great means unto the Queen for his de-
liverance, so far that he won her consent. It came so far that the
Lords were fain to resist her will so far as that the tears burst out,
but nothing able to prevail' (*Foreign Calendar, Elizabeth*, vi. 420).
Lethington informed De Quadra that the prosecution had been
undertaken on the advice of the Archbishop himself, not to condemn his religion but to preserve the Queen's peace (*Spanish
Calendar, Elizabeth*, i. 339). Nine weeks after his committal to the
Castle, he was set at liberty, caution having been found that he
should 'nocht controvene the Ordinance and Proclamatione maid be
hir Grace anent the Religione quhilk hir Majestie fand publiclie and
universalie standing at hir arryvall within this realme, . . . and
on na wyis publiclie nor privatlie mak innovatione or alteratione

thairof, or attempt ony thing aganis the samin, under the pane of thre thowsand pundis' (Pitcairn's *Criminal Trials*, i. 429* *n*.).

[20] Laing's *Knox*, ii. 393, 394 ; Calderwood's *History*, ii. 571.

[21] Calderwood's *History*, ii. 570 ; *Register of Privy Council*, i. 372.

[22] Robertson's *Statuta*, vol. i. p. clxix.

[23] *Register of Privy Council*, i. 338, 339, 343.

[24] *Ibid.* i. 356.

[25] Labanoff's *Recueil*, i. 282.—It is in this letter that Mary accredits and commends Yaxley as her Envoy.

[26] *Register of Privy Council*, i. 372.—In this proclamation, Scottish Protestantism is not described as 'the Reformed religion of Scotland,' but as the 'religioun quhilk thair Majesteis fand publictlie and universallie standing at thair arryval.' In the original *Register*, the clerk has by mistake written 'abolissit,' which has been subsequently changed into 'stabblissit.' In the printed *Register* only the original reading is given. In the French copy the word is 'establie' (Teulet's *Papiers D'État*, ii. 67).

[27] To Beaton, Mary wrote :—'We, accompanied with our nobility for the time, past to the Tolbuith of Edinburgh, for holding of our Parliament upon the 7th day of this instant [March], elected the Lords Articulars ; the Spirituall Estate being placed therein in the ancient maner, tending to have done some good anent restoring the auld religion, and to have proceeded against our rebels according to their demerits' (Keith's *History*, ii. 412, 413). Bishop Lesley says : — 'The Parliament was opened and two measures submitted for discussion, one allowing the bishops and rectors of the churches the full exercise of their ancient religion, and the other punishing the leaders of the conspiracy, who had more than once broken their faith, and had taken up arms against the Queen' (Forbes-Leith's *Narratives*, p. 108). As Rambouillet returned from Scotland, about the end of February, De Silva learned from him that Mary and Darnley were 'treating matters connected with the Catholic religion with great solicitude, they themselves offering a good example to the people' (*Spanish Calendar, Elizabeth*, i. 527). Rooksby alleged that, in his secret interview with Mary, she informed him that when time served she expected to win the friendship of certain English nobles the more readily as she believed they were of the Old Religion, which she meant to restore with all possible expedition, and thereby win the hearts of the common people (Haynes's *State Papers*, p. 446 ; *Hatfield Calendar*, i. 339).

[28] Nau's *Mary Stewart*, app. p. 203.

[29] Father Stevenson quoted *supra*, p. 211, *n.* 53.

[30] *Supra*, pp. 268, 269.

[31] Mary's letter, commending Francis Yaxley and his mission to Philip, is dated 10th September 1565 (Labanoff's *Recueil*, i. 281-283). He embarked at Dumbarton on the 17th of that month (*Foreign Calendar, Elizabeth*, vii. 467, 484), sailed apparently on the 26th (*Spanish Calendar, Elizabeth*, i. 499), and reached Philip on the 20th of October, at the Wood of Segovia, where he tarried five days with him 'so secretly that none knew of his coming till ten days after his departure' (*Foreign Calendar, Elizabeth*, vii. 519). On the 24th of October, Philip wrote to De Silva that this Englishman—'who was in the service of Queen Mary, my wife, now in glory'—had arrived. 'He brought us letters from the King and Queen of Scotland accrediting him, and spoke at great length in virtue thereof. . . . The first thing was to inform us in very fair words of the great hope and confidence they reposed in me, desiring to govern themselves by my direction, and to do nothing whatever without my consent and pleasure, and for this reason they wished to inform me of the state of need in which they were, and assure us generally of their zealous desire to establish and reform their kingdom under the Christian religion, and join other Christian princes with that end. Not having sufficient forces of their own, they begged me to aid them as a Christian monarch, and, to induce me to do so, set forth the danger in which the Sovereigns of Scotland were, by reason of the heretics, stimulated and favoured by Englishmen and English money, so that the said Sovereigns might easily be conveyed by the rebels out of the country, and the state left unprotected, *unless* [? if] I, in whom after God they put their trust, did not aid them with money and troops. If I would consent to do this it would not only be the way to destroy the rebels, but would confirm the King and Queen in their hope of succeeding to the English throne, and would banish their fear that the heretics with their innovations and artfulness would oust them, the real heirs, and elect some heretic of their own faction. They promised that if they obtained the succession to the crown by our means, they would renew more closely the league and alliance between England and our house against all Christendom, and leave all their other friends. . . . He begged in the name of his Sovereigns that we would counsel them how they should proceed

in all things, and as I was so far off that I should nominate some person to whom they could address themselves for such advice without so much delay' (*Spanish Calendar, Elizabeth*, i. 497). Philip advised them in the meantime to punish the rebels, and pacify their kingdom, adding that, when they had smoothed things down, they could look further ahead. He wrote a holograph letter to Mary, and one by another hand to Darnley, 'encouraging them to persevere in their good purpose,' and assuring them that he would not fail them. He also gave instructions that 20,000 crowns should be paid over secretly to Yaxley outside Antwerp, for their behoof (*Ibid.* i. 498). The instructions were followed, and Yaxley embarked in good weather. A storm which arose, however, drove the vessel on the English coast, and the money which was found on Yaxley's corpse was claimed by the Earl of Northumberland because found in his territory. He was 'considered very Catholic,' and, as De Silva believed, 'an affectionate servant' of Philip's, and besides, secretly professed to be one of Mary's friends; but he would not disgorge the treasure (*Ibid.* i. 508, 509, 516, 523, 546, 557, 558; Melville's *Memoirs*, p. 137). Mary wrote to Northumberland and also to Bedford, claiming the money (Labanoff's *Recueil*, i. 321-323); Bedford forwarded his letter to Cecil (Stevenson's *Selections*, p. 158); and Elizabeth instructed Northumberland to tell the Queen of Scots that he had no crowns or ducats save what were found with Yaxley, an Englishman, who was drowned (*Foreign Calendar, Elizabeth*, viii. 40).

[32] In her letter of 31st January 1565-6, to Pius the Fifth, announcing the appointment of the Bishop of Dunblane as her Ambassador, Orator, and Proctor, at the Holy See, Mary informs the Pope that 'the most pious and holy requests' of his predecessor —who compassionated the 'poor scattered sheep' of Scotland 'a prey to the ravening wolves'—would have been carried into force but for the many enemies of her religion who had hitherto thwarted her efforts; that now, however, some of her enemies are in exile, some in her hands; and that although 'their fury, and the great necessity in which they are placed, urges them on to attempt extreme measures,' nevertheless, 'if God and your Holiness be with us (whose cause we are fighting), by your help we will leap over the wall' (Nau's *Mary Stewart*, app. pp. 191, 192; Labanoff's *Recueil*, vii. 9, 10). The Bishop of Dunblane assured the Pope that Mary and Darnley, since their marriage, had been kept in perpetual agitation,

'for no cause whatever save this, that they would not deviate one
single hair's-breadth from their obedience to the See of Rome';
that the obedience which they now offered to him could only be
kept at the greatest personal risk; that, unless he helped them,
there was no hope of the preservation of religion for their kingdom;
and that the same danger threatened England, 'which, as all the
world knows, belongs by the right of inheritance to Scotland'
(Nau's *Mary Stewart*, app. pp. 195, 196).   De Silva learned from
Mary's messenger that the Pope had received him very well, and had
sent 20,000 crowns for her present aid, and promised 4000 crowns a
month to pay a thousand soldiers for her defence (*Spanish Calendar,
Elizabeth*, i. 559).   The rumour was already current in Scotland
that Philip and the Pope were helping her (*Ibid.* i. 535).

    [33] That Mary joined the Catholic League before the murder of
Riccio has been affirmed by Principal Robertson, Patrick Fraser
Tytler, Mignet, Froude, and others; and questioned by writers of
such various schools as Lingard, Hill Burton, and Hosack.   Hill
Burton holds, however, that, 'whether in the form of a bond or not,
beyond doubt Mary was the close ally of the King of Spain in all
his formidable views and projects for crushing the new religion'
(*History of Scotland*, 1876, iv. 136).   The charge is explicitly made
by Randolph to Cecil in a letter of 7th February 1565-6.   Randolph
was then in Edinburgh, and wrote as if absolutely certain that
Mary had subscribed the League, and that she was to return the
principal and retain a copy (Stevenson's *Selections*, pp. 152, 153;
Wright's *Elizabeth*, i. 219, 220).   Tytler regarded this action 'as
one of the most fatal errors of her life,' and as 'the source of all
her future misfortunes' (*History of Scotland*, 1845, v. 331, 332).
But Bedford, who wrote to Cecil from Berwick on the 14th of
February, refers to the League 'for the overthrowe of religion . . .
which is come to this Quen's [*i.e.* Mary's] hand, but not yet
confirmed' (Stevenson's *Selections*, p. 159).   It is inferred that in
the week which had elapsed since Randolph wrote, Bedford had
received fuller and more correct information on the matter.
Hosack concludes, from 'the absence of all further testimony on
the subject,' that although Philip at this time tried to induce Mary
to join the Catholic League, 'she declined to do so' (Hosack's
Mary and Her Accusers, i. 129).   The recently printed *Calendar of
Spanish State Papers* shows, however, that, in the previous October,
the unfortunate Yaxley had assured Philip, in her name and in

379

Darnley's, of their desire to join other Christian princes in such a league (*supra*, p. 377, *n.* 31). Hosack's further argument—that, having now completely suppressed Murray's rebellion, she did not require Philip's help—is overturned by the fact that it was only eight days before the date of Randolph's letter that she wrote to Pius the Fifth, pleading for help (*supra*, p. 378, *n.* 32). The Bishop of Dunblane, whom she then sent to Rome, was well fitted to urge her claims on His Holiness; for, only a few months before, he had borne to her the earnest requests and promises of Pius the Fourth, which were of no dubious nature (Nau's *Mary Stewart*, app. p. 123). It is only fair to her to state that, according to the report of the Jesuit priests—written nearly thirty years afterwards—part of her answer was to the effect 'that she could not stain her hands with the blood of her subjects' (*Ibid.* p. 123); and Sir James Melville says that she was naturally more inclined to mercy than to rigour (*Memoirs*, p. 146). Of much more importance is the statement of the Papal Nuncio, that, despite the advice of the Bishop of Dunblane and of Father Edmond, she would not embrace the league (Labanoff's *Recueil*, vii. 107). It is impossible to say, however, what Mary might have been induced to do had the Nuncio gone to Scotland, instead of timorously returning to his bishopric of Mondovi, after lingering nine months in France (*Ibid.* ii. 20; *Venetian Calendar*, vii. 383, 385, 390).

[34] On the 10th of August, Thomworth reported to Leicester that there was some greater matter in it than is fit to be written, as he perceived by the talk he had with her (*Foreign Calendar, Elizabeth,* vii. 426).

[35] In his letter of 13th October, Randolph thus refers to the real cause of Mary's hatred of Murray :—' She knoweth that he understandeth some such secret *part* (not to be named for reverence sake) that standeth not with her honour, which he so much detesteth, being her brother, that neither can he show himself as he hath done, nor she think of him but as one of whom she mortally hateth. Here is the mischief, this is the grief, and how this may be salved and repaired, it passeth I trow man's wit to consider' (*Foreign Calendar, Elizabeth,* vii. 489). Von Raumer has suggested an explanation of this passage which would at once blacken Murray, and make Mary morally worse than her enemies have represented her to be (*Queen Elizabeth and Mary Queen of Scots*, 1836, pp. 68-70). The key to the true explanation, however, is to be

found in the word *part*, which Randolph here uses in the sense of action or conduct. Had he used *port*, the meaning would have been quite obvious. In his letter of 27th August, Randolph had said :—' I may conjecture that there is some heavier matter at her heart against him [*i.e.* Murray] than she will utter to any. I told Mr. Tamworth my opinion of that I think to be her grief. He will give an account by word of mouth' (Raumer's *Elizabeth and Mary*, p. 66). The nature of Thomworth's oral report may perhaps be inferred from what Elizabeth told De Foix, namely, that Mary hated Murray because she had been informed that he ' wished to hang an Italian named David, whom she loved and favoured, giving him more credit and authority than was consistent with her affairs and honour' (Teulet's *Papiers D'État*, ii. 93). De Foix's letter is dated from London, on the 16th of October. Nearly a month before, Bedford had told Cecil that Riccio, Fowler, and Balfour, ruled all in the Scotch Court ; but of the countenance which Mary showed to David, he would not write, for the honour due to the person of a Queen (*Foreign Calendar, Elizabeth*, vii. 464). On the 18th of October, Randolph laments to Leicester that Mary has been ' brought to that extremity, that the fame she had gotten through virtue and worthiness is now clean fallen from her, as though neither the one nor the other had been known unto her. Her country so evil guided that justice lies dead in all places, and her noblemen chased out of the country, and such others placed nearest her that are most unworthy. What most men complain of (and in his judgment has been the chief cause of this mischief) in this place shall not be spoken of. He may well think what the matter means when so many mislike that a stranger, a varlet, shall have the whole guiding of this Queen and country' (*Ibid.* vii. 495).

[36] Melville's *Memoirs*, pp. 139-146.—As it was, Randolph feared that Elizabeth would now lose all the goodwill she had in Scotland (*Foreign Calendar, Elizabeth*, vii. 512, 513); and Bedford thought that the Scots Lords who had hitherto been friendly to England would now become its enemies (*Ibid.* vii. 509, 510).

[37] Melville's *Memoirs*, pp. 146, 147.

[38] Melville's *Memoirs*, p. 147.—Melville's story loses nothing in Mr. Skelton's hands. In his opinion, Murray, while in England, ' behaved like a beaten hound,' and ' the depth of baseness to which he fell almost exceeds belief' (*Mary Stuart*, 1893, p. 74); for ' not

content with writing to Elizabeth to intercede for him with Mary, not content with writing to Mary herself, he actually addressed a letter to Rizzio, imploring him to exert his good offices with the Queen on his behalf, and promising that he would always be his friend' (*Ibid.* p. 75). This Riccio episode is thus retailed by Mr. Skelton as an undoubted fact; although previously, in his first edition of *Maitland of Lethington*, he had—and subsequently in his second edition he has—heralded the same charge with the words, 'if we are to believe Melville' (ii. 161), and also declared that 'every statement' of Melville's 'must when necessary or practicable be traced back to its source' (i. p. xxv). As Mr. Skelton can produce no corroboration of Melville's statement on this point, he might at least have paralleled it by Spottiswoode's (*History of the Church of Scotland*, ii. 27), that 'of all others' Lethington 'most fawned on this Italian'; or by Buchanan's (Aikman's *Buchanan*, ii. 467), that of all the nobles, 'Moray alone . . . did not flatter him.' Better still, he might have shown that Murray did not altogether behave 'like a beaten hound' when he warned Randolph not to incur further suspicion, for his sake, at the Scotch Court (*Foreign Calendar, Elizabeth*, vii. 513); or when he stated to Cecil that the grief of his heart was for the other Scots Lords at Newcastle, especially for Rothes (*Ibid.* vii. 525). He might even have pointed out that Melville's disparaging statement as to Murray's conduct a few months later is somewhat discredited by contemporary documents (see *infra*, pp. 394, 395). Though it cannot be proved that Murray addressed either an abject or an imploring letter to Riccio, it is known that, with or without his sanction, Douglas of Loch Leven indirectly offered Seigneur Davie five thousand pounds Scots if he would stay Murray's forfeiture; and that he answered, 'twenty thowsand and that wer all alik : it wald not be' (*Loch Leven Papers*, quoted by M'Crie, *Life of Knox*, 1861, p. 293 n.), an answer which does not altogether harmonise with Melville's statement that he 'apperit to be also wone to the same effect,' but it illustrates his other statement as to the way in which 'he becam very rich' (*supra*, p. 121), and at the same time indicates the inordinate power he was believed to possess.

[39] Mary's antenuptial love of, and devotion to, Darnley were manifest enough during his illness at Stirling (*supra*, p. 337, n. 89), her regard for him immediately after marriage is thus referred to by Randolph :—'All honor that maye be attributed unto any man by

a wyfe, he hathe yt wholly and fully, all prayse that maye be spoken
of hym he lacketh not from herselfe, all dignities that she can
indue hym with are alreadie given and granted.   No man pleaseth
her that contenteth not hym, and what maye I saye more, she
hathe given over unto hym her whole wyll, to be ruled and guyded
as hymself beste lyketh.   She can as muche prevayle with hym in
anye thynge that is agaynst his wyll, as your Lordship [*i.e.*
Leicester] maye with me to perswade that I sholde hange myself'
(Wright's *Elizabeth*, i. 201 ; Ellis's *Original Letters*, first series, ii.
201).

[40] Nine weeks after their marriage Mary and Darnley were 'at
great strife'; and the noble who was to play such a prominent part in
their tragic story was already the bone of contention.   In the army
raised to crush the Protestant Lords, Darnley wished his father to
be Lieutenant-General ; but she preferred Bothwell, because of 'his
evil will against Murray,' and his promise 'to have him die as an
alien' (*Foreign Calendar, Elizabeth*, vii. 477, 489).   Lennox was
appointed to lead the vanguard ; Huntly, Atholl, and Crawford
the rear-guard ; and the King's Majesty to lead ' the battell '—in
which he was to be accompanied by Morton, Bothwell, Mar, and
others (*Register of Privy Council*, i. 379).   This may have been a mere
temporary explosion leaving no bad effects.   William Tytler holds
that until Riccio was murdered, Mary's affection towards Darnley
was unbounded (Tytler's *Enquiry*, 1790, ii. 15); but by the beginning of the previous December the relations between her and
Lennox were becoming strained (*Foreign Calendar, Elizabeth*, vii.
532); it was noticed, too, that Darnley followed his pastime more
than the Queen wished, and that there was 'some misliking
between them' (*Ibid.* vii. 539); and, by Christmas, Randolph was
struck by the numerous alterations in the Government.   'Awhile
there was nothing but King and Queen, His Majesty and Hers ;
now the Queen's husband is the most common word.   He was wont
in all writings to be first named, but now he is placed second.
Lately pieces of money were coined with both their faces, "Hen. et
Maria"; these are called in and others framed . . . Some private
disorders there are among themselves' (*Ibid.* vii. 541).   The Act
of Privy Council authorising the new coinage runs in the names of
the 'Quene and Kingis Majesteis,' etc. (*Register of Privy Council*,
i. 413).   This is not the only document of the period in which
Mary takes precedence of Darnley (Nau's *History*, app. p. 190);

but the usual form—after as well as before the date of Randolph's letter—is for the King to be mentioned first. It is now acknowledged that the ryals, which were called in, were not mere pattern pieces, but were in actual circulation for a short time (Cochran-Patrick's *Records of the Coinage of Scotland*, 1876, i. p. cxlii ; Burns's *Coinage of Scotland*, 1887, ii. 338). It was apparently in reference to the new coinage that Drury wrote, 'The grey mare is the better horse' (*Foreign Calendar, Elizabeth*, viii. 5). Burns points out that on the one-third ryal there is a large rose on the back of the 'schell padocke' climbing the palm-tree.

[41] Immediately after Riccio's murder, Darnley thus excused himself to the Queen :—'Since yon fellow Davie fell in credit and familiarity with your Majesty, ye regarded me not, neither treated me nor entertained me after your wonted fashion ; for every day before dinner, and after dinner, ye would come to my chamber and pass time with me, and thus long time ye have not done so ; and when I come to your Majesty's chamber, ye bear me little company, except Davie had been the third marrow : and after supper your Majesty hath a use to set at the cards with the said Davie till one or two of the clock after mid-night ; and this is the entertainment that I have had of you this long time' (Ruthven's *Relation*, 1699, p. 30).

[42] The Lord Robert showed Darnley 'in the Scotche mappe, what lands my Lord of Murraye had, and in what bounds, the Lord Darlie saide that it was too muche. Thys came to my Lord of Murraye's eare, and so to the Quene, who advised my Lord of Darlie to excuse hymself to my Lord of Murraye' (Wright's *Elizabeth*, i. 195).

[43] Tytler's *History of Scotland*, v. 334.—It was even said that Darnley had consented to Mary's death (Labanoff's *Recueil*, vii. 60).

[44] *Foreign Calendar, Elizabeth*, viii. 23.—The Protestant Lords had complained, in their Dumfries Declaration, that Mary had, so far as she could, made and proclaimed a King over them without consulting the nobles, and that this King 'nather hath the title therof by anie lineall descent of blood and nature, nather by consent of the Estats' (Calderwood's *History*, ii. 573). At that time, in Randolph's opinion, while they thought it their duty to endure under her, they deemed it intolerable to suffer under him (*Foreign Calendar, Elizabeth*, vii. 469). Yet now they were to return to take part with him in all his actions, causes, and quarrels, to the uttermost of their power, to be friends to his friends, and enemies

to his enemies, and not to spare lives, lands, or goods in doing him service. In special, they were in Parliament to give him the crown-matrimonial, for all the days of his life; and, failing succession by the Queen, were to fortify and maintain his ' just titell to the croun of Scotland,' even to the extirpation or slaughter of those who might usurp the same (*Maitland Miscellany*, iii. 188, 189). The inconsistency of this engagement of the Lords was exceeded by its injustice to Chatelherault, who had been declared next in succession; and hardly deserved such treatment for offering to desert them in their recent unequal struggle against Mary and Darnley. This was bad enough; but Mr. Skelton has charged Murray with ' laborious hypocrisy ' for telling Mary that he could not consent to her marriage with one ' who he could not assure himself would set forth Christ's true religion' (*Mary Stuart*, 1893, p. 70); and again, ' I have *said* already that his pretended zeal for Protestantism was a mask; if further *proof* were needed it is supplied by what now took place ' (*Ibid.* p. 78). As Mr. Skelton's bare assertion cannot be taken as evidence in such a matter, it may be well to look at the ' further proof' which he apparently considers almost unnecessary. Murray, he says, ' had risen in arms against his sister because she had elected to marry Darnley; he now returned to make Darnley King, and that there might be no mistake, either then or afterwards, the shameful bargain was reduced to writing. These are the articles to which Moray set his hand:—"The Earl of Moray shall,"' etc. (*Ibid.* p. 78). The articles, as misquoted by Mr. Skelton, need not be reproduced here; they are also to be found in his *Maitland of Lethington*, ii. 164, 165: and in neither work does he give, as his language implies, the articles themselves, but merely a summary—an imperfect, a misleading, a dishonest summary! In the articles signed at Newcastle on the 2nd of March 1565-6 by Murray and the other Lords acting with him, and also in those signed by Darnley, the safety of the Protestant religion was specially provided for; but Mr. Skelton does not give the slightest hint of this. Had he done so, where would have been the proof of Murray's ' laborious hypocrisy '? The articles signed by the Lords at Newcastle are printed, from the original, in the *Maitland Miscellany*, iii. 188-191; and in Sir William Fraser's *Melvilles and Leslies*, 1890, iii. 110-112. The articles signed by Darnley are printed, from the original, in the *Sixth Report of the Historical MSS. Commission*, app. p. 641. Both sets of articles are

in Goodall's *Examination*, 1754, i. 227-233; in Ruthven's *Relation*,
1699, pp. 20-22; and—in an abridged form—in Keith's *History*,
iii. 261-263. There is good reason to believe that Murray and
the other Protestant Lords had offered to consent to the marriage,
on condition that the Queen would in Parliament establish Protestantism and abolish the mass (see Laing's *Knox*, ii. 481; Aikman's
Buchanan, ii. 469; Calderwood's *History*, ii. 291; Spottiswoode's
History, ii. 27; *Foreign Calendar, Elizabeth*, vii. 356, 363; Labanoff's
Recueil, i. 301); but this is ignored—not emphasised—by Mr.
Skelton.

⁴⁵ In their letter, Bedford and Randolph say that Darnley ' hath
assured knowledge of such usage of herself as altogether is intolerable to be borne, which if it were not overwell known, we would
both be very loath to think that it could be true. To take away
this occasion of slander, he is himself determined to be at the
apprehension and execution of him whom he is able manifestly to
charge with the crime, and to have done him the most dishonour
that can be to any man, much more being as he is. We need not
more plainly to describe the person : you have heard of the man
whom we mean of' (Tytler's *Scotland*, v. 340; *Foreign Calendar,
Elizabeth*, viii. 28).

⁴⁶ *Diurnal of Occurrents*, pp. 85, 86; *Register of Privy Council*, i.
409.

⁴⁷ Though Morton took care not to commit himself during the
Chase-about Raid (*supra*, p. 364, *n.* 59) he had not escaped suspicion. On the 31st of October, Randolph tells that Mary—who
had ' laid still since her return from Dumfries'—had on the
previous day ridden to Dalkeith, where she would remain for a
day or two to enrich the Lord of Morton, who was not altogether
delighted to receive her (*Foreign Calendar, Elizabeth*, vii. 505). It
was deemed likely that he would soon be in Edinburgh Castle
(*Ibid.* vii. 507). In the beginning of December it is mentioned
that he and Lethington could by no means purge themselves of
suspicion (*Ibid.* vii. 530). Hosack takes Froude to task for saying
that Mary had deprived Morton of the chancellorship with the
intention of bestowing it upon Riccio; and exclaims, ' So far as I
am aware the possibility of a friendless adventurer like Riccio
being raised to that high office has never been alluded to by any
one before Mr. Froude' (*Mary Queen of Scots and her Accusers*, i.
145 *n.*). Here Hosack, however, only exposes his own ignorance;

for the matter is referred to by Knox (Laing's *Knox*, i. 446), by his continuator (*Ibid.* ii. 521), by Spottiswoode (*History*, ii. 35), and by Calderwood (*History*, ii. 311). It is also mentioned—and of course, contradicted—by Chalmers (*Life of Mary*, 1818, ii. 9), as it had previously been by Goodall, who contended that the story had arisen from 'a gross blunder in translating one of George Buchanan's sentences' (*Examination of the Letters*, 1754, i. 271, 272). But Goodall—like Hosack—was mistaken, for this transference of the great seal is mentioned in the contemporary state papers. Three days before Riccio's murder, Randolph, who had recently left Edinburgh, writes from Berwick that displeasure is grown towards Morton, from whom the seal is taken, and as some say given to David ; and that the cause of this displeasure is that he will not give over a piece of land to Lord Fleming, so that Riccio may come by the house and lands of Melvin (*Foreign Calendar, Elizabeth*, viii. 28). Three weeks after the murder, De Silva says, 'another of the conspirators was the former holder of the Great Seal there, which had been handed over to the secretary David' (*Spanish Calendar, Elizabeth*, i. 537). It is quite certain, therefore, that the story—whether true or false—was neither invented by Froude, nor based on a mistranslation of Buchanan's *History*. Bedford and Randolph, in their letter of 6th March, include Morton among those who were privy to the conspiracy (*Foreign Calendar, Elizabeth*, viii. 27) ; and now on the day before the murder he is reported as present in Edinburgh (*Ibid.* viii. 29).

⁴⁸ *Foreign Calendar, Elizabeth*, viii. 29, 30.—Besides the articles mentioned on p. 385, and the bond mentioned on p. 389, Darnley—as King of Scots and as 'husband to the Quenis Majestie'—signed a formal remission to Murray and the others, for all their actions, quarrels, and crimes, permitting them also to repair to him, and charging the lieges to convoy them safely. This remission, dated 6th March, is printed, from the original, in the *Sixth Report of the Historical MSS. Commission*, app. p. 641. On the day before Riccio's murder Cecil informed Lady Lennox of it as of an event that had occurred (*Spanish Calendar, Elizabeth*, i. 540).

⁴⁹ Accounts of the Riccio murder are given in Laing's *Knox*, ii. 521, 522 ; Aikman's *Buchanan*, ii. 480-482 ; Calderwood's *History*, ii. 313-315 ; Spottiswoode's *History*, ii. 36-38 ; Melville's *Memoirs*, pp. 147-149 ; Herries's *Memoirs*, pp. 76, 77 ; *Diurnal of Occurrents*, pp. 89-91 ; Forbes-Leith's *Narratives of Scottish Catholics*, pp.

108-110. The account drawn up by Bedford and Randolph, for the English Privy Council, is printed in Ellis's *Original Letters*, first series, ii. 207-222; in Wright's *Elizabeth*, i. 226-235; and an abstract in the *Hatfield Calendar*, i. 333-336. 'This interesting and circumstantial letter,' says Wright, 'redounds very little to the credit of the Queen of Scots, and therefore, apparently, it was not printed by Keith.' Mary's own account of the tragedy, sent to Beaton, her Ambassador in France, is printed in Keith's *History*, ii. 411-423; and in Labanoff's *Recueil*, i. 341-350. Her account to the King and Queen-mother of France is in the *Venetian Calendar*, vii. 375-378. Bothwell's version of the 'wicked and horrible trans-action' is in *Les Affaires du Conte de Boduel* (Ban. Club, p. 10; Hosack's *Mary*, ii. 581). Ruthven's *Relation* has been reprinted in *Scotia Rediviva*, 1826, pp. 327-360; and by E. and G. Goldsmid in 1890 and 1891. It is also given in Keith's *History*, iii. 260-278; but in an abridged form, and with one or two rather important variations. In the Spottiswoode Society edition of Keith, nothing is said as to the source from which this version was drawn; but in both the folio editions—1734 and 1748—there is the marginal note, 'Julius, F. 90 a copy.' On the other hand, the version in *Scotia Rediviva* is a reprint of the London edition of 1699, which professes to be 'printed from an original manuscript.' For other contemporary accounts see Labanoff's *Recueil*, vii. 60-62, 70-80; Teulet's *Papiers D'État*, ii. 112-120. The statement that Riccio was slain in Mary's presence cannot be accepted as strictly accurate, although it occurs in Darnley's declaration (Ellis's *Original Letters*, first series, ii. 222), in an entry in the *Register of Privy Council* (i. 463), and in Mary's own letters to Elizabeth (Labanoff's *Recueil*, i. 336; ii. 74). Mary, of course, ought to have known; but, like too many of her apologists, she cannot be implicitly trusted in details. From Ruthven's *Relation*, and from the letter which Bedford and Randolph wrote after making careful inquiry, it appears that he was dragged out of the Queen's cabinet, hustled through her bed-chamber, and slain at the furthest door of the outer room (the chamber of presence), or on the stairs leading down from it. Sir James Melville states that the slaughter was in Mary's presence, although he had previously said that, 'geving gret skirlis and cryes,' Riccio was 'rudly reft from the Quen, . . . drawen fourth of the cabinet, and slain in the utter hall.' In her letter to Beaton, Mary herself says that he was invaded in her presence, taken forth of her cabinet, and despatched with fifty-six wounds at the entry of her chamber. According to Ruthven, it was Darnley's device and desire—a desire which he would not relinquish—that Riccio should be seized in Mary's presence. Morton and Ruthven 'were loth to grant thereto'; and—considering that Darnley 'was a young Prince and having a lusty Princess to lie in his arms afterwards, who might perswade him to deny all that was done for his cause, and to alledg that others perswaded him to the same'—they deemed it necessary that he should grant a bond taking all the responsibility upon himself, and undertaking to keep them skaithless for the same. In this bond, provision is made for the safety of the actors, in case 'it may chance to be done in presence of the Queen's Majesty or within her Palace of Holyrood House' (*Relation*, 1699, pp. 24-27 ; Goodall's *Examination*, i. 268). In her letter to Beaton, Mary says that the conspirators struck Riccio 'over our shoulders with whinzeards, one part of them standing before our face with bended daggs' (*i.e.* pistols). This was atrocious enough, but much wilder stories were being circulated in Mary's name; and so in the close of his *Relation*, Ruthven declares :—' Where her Majesty alledgeth, that night that Davie was slain some held pistols to her Majesties womb, some stroke whiniards so near her crag [*i.e.* throat] that she felt the coldness of the iron, with many other such like sayings, which we take God to record was never meant nor done; for the said Davie received never a stroke in her Majesty's presence, nor was not stricken till he was at the farthest door of her Majesty's utter chamber.' Robert Chambers was inclined to believe, and thought Sir Walter Scott did not disbelieve, in the genuineness of the Riccio blood-stains shown on the floor of Holyrood (*Book of Days*, 1886, i. 235). It is Ruthven who relates that, at Darnley's command, 'Davie was hurled down the steps of the stairs from the place where he was slain, and brought to the porter's lodg ; where the porter's servant taking off his clothes, said, This hath been his destiny ; for upon this chest was his first bed when he entred into this place, and now here he lieth again, a very ingrate and misknowing knave' (*Relation*, 1699, p. 39). One of Mary's more reckless champions has not scrupled to allege that the English Privy Council advised that Riccio should be murdered in her presence (Blackwood's *Mary*, Mait. Club, p. 14). Goodall asserts that it was also intended to murder in Mary's presence the Earls of

Huntly, Bothwell, and Atholl, the Lords Fleming and Livingston, and Sir James Balfour (*Examination of the Letters*, i. 244, 252, 254, 268). These were all in the Palace on the evening of the 9th of March ; but Ruthven's *Relation* and the letters of Bedford and Randolph show that the plot was not directed against them. Even the Bishop of Dunblane, in delivering Mary's message to the Pope, does not say that there was any conspiracy against their lives, but states that the three Earls—Huntly, Bothwell, and Atholl, whom he feelingly describes as 'men of piety and faithful to the poor Queen'—finding themselves 'unable to help her,' and being 'prevented from leaving the Palace,' escaped by the windows (Nau's *Mary Stewart*, app. p. 204).

[50] 'No hint of the outrage,' says Mr. Skelton, 'appears to have reached the magistrates of the city until the following morning' (*Mary Stuart*, 1893, p. 79); but this is only a harmless specimen of that writer's utter contempt for the best known and most thoroughly vouched facts. That evening the common bell was rung—struck with hammers, as one account has it—the Provost and townsmen in armour rushed to the Palace, desiring to see the Queen, anxious to speak with her, and only retiring when ordered to do so by Darnley, who assured them that she was well. It was hardly worth Mr. Skelton's while, on such a point, to discredit Lord Ruthven (*Relation*, p. 35), and Mary herself (Keith's *History*, ii. 418; *Venetian Calendar*, vii. 377), not to speak of Buchanan, the author of the *Diurnal of Occurrents*, and the continuator of Knox. In her letter to Beaton, Mary says that she was not allowed to answer the Provost and citizens, and was told by the Lords that, if she wished to speak to them, they would cut her 'in collops,' and cast her over the walls. In her letter to the King and Queen-mother of France—as translated from French into Italian, and from Italian into English—she is made to say that they threatened to throw her 'over the wall in pieces, in order to make steaks' of her. The citizens did not march to Holyrood in the dark. The Town Council afterwards paid £4, 7s. 6d. to Alexander Purves, wax-maker, for thirty-five torches 'furneist be him to the gude toun' on 'the ix day of Marche . . . to pas to the Abbay to vise the Quenis Grace immediatle efter the slauchter of umquhile Seinyeour Dauid Ricio' (*Burgh Records of Edinburgh*, 1557-1571, p. 214).

[51] Spottiswoode's *History*, ii. 37, 38.—In Hill Burton's opinion, this account, 'if better vouched,' would be 'formidable evidence'

of Mary's 'intention to work for what afterwards came to pass' (*History of Scotland*, 1876, iv. 152 n.). As he remarks, the Herries *Memoirs*—which fully corroborate Spottiswoode on this point—are of dubious authority, having been recast; but, if any part of them can be taken as genuine, the passage on this point (p. 77) may, for it begins:—'The originall sayes.' Besides these two, and the threat to which Hill Burton also refers, as preserved by Bedford and Randolph (Wright's *Elizabeth*, i. 229)—'It shall be deare blude to some of you, if hys be spylte'; there are, at least, other three passages to the same effect. The continuator of Knox's *History* says:—'The Queen, when she heard he was dead, left weeping, and declared she would study revenge, which she did' (Laing's *Knox*, ii. 522). Ruthven represents Mary as thus addressing Darnley:—'I shall never . . . like well, till I gar you have as sore a heart as I have presently' (*Relation*, p. 31). And Nau avers that next morning after Darnley had expressed his penitence, she said to him, 'You have done me such a wrong, that neither the recollection of our early friendship, nor all the hope you can give me of the future, can ever make me forget it' (Nau's *Mary Stewart*, pp. 7, 8).

[52] In her letter to her Ambassador in France, Mary explains that on the 7th of March, when she and her nobles went to the Tolbooth to elect the Lords of the Articles, her husband refused to go with her (Keith's *History*, ii. 411, 412). That day, Huntly bore the crown, Bothwell the sceptre, and Crawford the sword—'the Kingis Majestie past nocht to the Tolbuith' (*Diurnal of Occurrents*, p. 89). At nine o'clock on Sabbath morning—the morning after Riccio's murder—'thair wes ane proclamatioun maid at the mercat croce of Edinburgh, in the Kingis name, chargeing all and sindrie the Erllis, Lordis, Barronis, and Bischopis, that come of befoir to Edinburgh to the Parliament, to depairt of the samin within thre houris, under the pane of tressoun' (*Ibid.* p. 91; Ruthven's *Relation*, pp. 38, 39; Keith's *History*, ii. 418). The proclamation was most effective (Laing's *Knox*, ii. 522; Nau's *Mary Stewart*, p. 3).

[53] By eight o'clock on Sabbath evening, Murray, Rothes, and 'their complices,' as Ruthven calls them, arrived at Holyrood, and were thankfully received by the King. Murray having afterwards gone to Morton's for supper, Mary immediately sent one of her ushers to bring him back, and received him pleasantly. 'She sayde that he was welcome, and layde the faulte upon other that

he was owte of the countrye, requyred of hym to be a good subjecte, and she wold be to hym as he oughte.' Seeing her 'state and intertainment,' he was moved, Mary says, 'with natural affection' towards her. Next day 'her Majesty took the King by the one hand and the Earl of Murrey by the other, and walked in her said utter chamber the space of one hour' (Ruthven's *Relation*, pp. 41, 45; Wright's *Elizabeth*, i. 230; Keith's *History*, ii. 419; *Diurnal of Occurrents*, p. 91). Melville describes the meeting as a touching one. Mary 'embracit him and kissit him, alleging that incaice he had bene at hame, he wald not have sufferit hir to have bene sa uncourtesly handlit; quhilk movit him sa, that the teares fell from his eyn' (Melville's *Memoirs*, p. 150). Nau says that Murray excused 'himself of the murder of the late David,' and 'swore by his God that he knew nothing of it before his return' (Nau's *Mary Stewart*, p. 13).

⁵⁴ On Monday morning, 'the King fell in reasoning with her Majesty towards the returning of the said Lords that were banished, and forgiving of them all offences, and likewise for the slaughter of Davie; and as appeared to him her Majesty was content.' Morton and Ruthven were not so easily satisfied, and told him that 'all was but words that they heard.' They feared that she would persuade him 'to follow her will and desire, by reason she hath been trained up from her youth in the Court of France.' Darnley again 'reasoned of many things with her Majesty: and at his returning to his dinner at eleven [A.M.], he declared to the Earls of Murrey and Morton, Lords Ruthen and Lindzay, that he had dressed the Queen's Majesty; that the said two Earls and Lord Ruthen should come to the presence of the Queen's Majesty, and she would forgive, and put in oblivion all things by-past, and bury them out of her Majesty's mind, as they had never been. The said Earls and Lords answered, that all that speaking was but policy; and suppose it were promised, little or nothing would be kept. Always the King took freely in hand, and bad them make such security as they pleased, and the Queen's Majesty and he should subscribe the same.' In the afternoon, Darnley took Morton, Murray, and Ruthven to the Queen. 'The said Earls and Lords, sitting down upon their knees, made their general oration by the Earl of Morton, chancellor, and after, their particular orations by themselves.' Mary reminded them that she had never been blood-thirsty, nor greedy of their lands and goods, and promised that

she 'would remit the whole number that was banished, or were at the last dead [*i.e.* at Riccio's slaughter]; and bury and put all things in oblivion as if they had never been'; and 'desired them to make their own security in that sort they pleased best, and she should subscribe the same.' Articles were accordingly framed which Darnley took to her for signature, and which, he said, she found very good, and would subscribe in the morning. The Lords left the Palace ; and after midnight, with a handful of followers, she did the same (Ruthven's *Relation*, pp. 42–46). According to Bedford and Randolph, she had sent for Lethington, and 'in gentle words' devised with him 'that he wolde persuade that she might have her libertie, and the garde that was about her removed, seeing that she had graunted their requests' (Wright's *Elizabeth*, i. 230). According to Claud Nau's rather dubious narrative, Mary and Darnley had been reconciled on the Sabbath morning, when he had assured her that he would not rest until he avenged her 'upon those wretched traitors,' whom he advised her to pardon in order to mollify them. 'My conscience,' she said, 'will never allow me to promise what I do not mean to perform, nor can I bring myself to tell a falsehood even to those men who have betrayed me so villanously. You, however, have already gone as far as I have ; if you think it good, you can promise them whatever you please in my name. But as for me, I will never pledge them my faith' (Nau's *Mary Stewart*, pp. 6–9). A contemporary not only says that Mary promised to pardon the Lords, but that she 'drank to every ane of thame in speciall' save Ruthven (*Diurnal of Occurrents*, p. 92). After riding to Dunbar—twenty-five miles as the crow flies—'in five houris of the nycht,' she felt 'tyrit and evill at ease' (Labanoff's *Recueil*, i. 337). She alleged that evil had been intended against her (Keith's *History*, ii. 419).

[55] The protestation of the Lords—that they had appeared on the day to which they had been summoned, 'and na persone nor personis said or proponit any thing aganis thame'—was formally objected to by Crichton, 'advocat to our Soveranes,' as of no avail, because the Lords of the Articles had been compelled by Darnley's proclamation to leave the town (*Diurnal of Occurrents*, p. 93).

[56] *Register of Privy Council*, i. 436 ; *Diurnal of Occurrents*, pp. 93, 94.

[57] 'Upon the xvij day of Merche, quhilk wes Sonday, the haill Lordis, committaris of the slauchter and crymes, abonewrittin,

with the Lordis that was banist in Ingland of befoir (except Alexander, Erle of Glencairne, quha red to Dunbar to speak with our Soveranis), with all thair complices and men of weir, with dollorous hartis departit of Edinburgh towart Lynlithgow, at sevin houris in the mornyng' (*Diurnal of Occurrents*, p. 94). On the previous Tuesday Lord Semple had been sent to Dunbar to ask Mary to fulfill her promise by signing the document for their security. He was put off for two or three days until she had pardoned and fully restored Glencairn and Rothes, and so detached them from their party. Ruthven and Morton were dismayed to find that they had not only been deserted by Darnley ; but that the banished Lords—for whom they had ventured so much—were thus dropping from them. Two days after they left Edinburgh, Mary sent Balfour, the parson of Flisk, to Linlithgow, offering terms to Murray, Argyll, and the other leaders of the Chase-about Raid, with the provision that for some time they would not approach the Court, nor sue for those who had slain Riccio (Wright's *Elizabeth*, i. 231, 232; Keith's *History*, ii. 420, 421; Labanoff's *Recueil*, i. 348, 349). Sir James Melville is no doubt correct when he says that Mary pardoned Murray and his associates, because she 'thocht not meit to have sa many Lordis in hir contraire,' and 'that sche mycht the easelier be revengit upon the last maist detestable dede'; but Melville's memory seems to have failed him when he wrote :— ' Murray and his defenders desyred me to cary his humble thankis and consent unto hir Majesteis desyre, and how that he had dischargit himself unto them that had committed the lait odious crym ; and wald promyse hir Majeste never to have to do with them, nor travell for them' (Melville's *Memoirs*, p. 152). Joseph Robertson has not exhibited his wonted impartiality and acumen, when, on the strength of this statement, he alleges that Murray lies under the 'imputation of deserting his fellow-conspirators, when the success of the common enterprise, achieved at the hazard of their lives, had restored him to prosperity and power' (*Inventories of Mary's Jewels*, p. cxxxi n.). From Ruthven's *Relation* (p. 47), and from Randolph's letter of 21st March, it is known that, before making terms for himself, Murray consulted the Lords of the Riccio conspiracy, who advised him 'not to forbear for their cause to agree with the Queen'; and that, while the others were content to leave them, Murray, Pittarrow, and Grange, were more consistent (*Foreign Calendar, Elizabeth*, viii. 35). On the 30th of March, De Silva writes :—'Murray has seen her and asked her pardon. The Queen received him well, and said she would pardon him if he would swear to oppose those who had taken part in the second conspiracy, which is that for the murder of the Secretary. The Earl replied that he would swear always to serve her loyally, but he could not undertake to oppose those the Queen mentioned, as his conscience would not allow him to do it' (*Spanish Calendar, Elizabeth*, i. 537). Joseph Robertson was hardly entitled to adopt Melville's statement on the one hand, and to ignore his counter-statement on the other, that Murray knew 'that it was not for his cause, bot for ther awen particulairs, that the maist part of them maid that enterpryse' (Melville's *Memoirs*, p. 150). Nor was it left to Father Stevenson to discover that Murray used his influence for their kindly reception in England (Nau's *Mary Stewart*, p. xcix; Ellis's *Original Letters*, first series, ii. 220; Wright's *Elizabeth*, i. 235; *Foreign Calendar, Elizabeth*, viii. 40, 43).

[58] *Diurnal of Occurrents*, p. 94.—Knox retired into Ayrshire, and afterwards expressed his cordial approval of the murder; but it cannot be shown that he knew of it beforehand, though P. F. Tytler has done his best to inculpate him. Tytler's 'Historical Remarks' on this point are in his *History of Scotland*, 1845, v. 498-507. Replies may be found in the appendix to M'Crie's *Sketches of Scottish Church History*; in Crichton's edition of M'Crie's *Knox*, 1847, pp. 451-470; in Hetherington's *History of the Church of Scotland*, 1848, i. 402-406; in *Tytler's History of Scotland Examined*, 1848, pp. 186-214; and in Hume Brown's *Knox*, ii. 304-310. The evidence against Knox—if evidence it can be called—is infinitesimal as compared with that against Lethington; yet Mr. Skelton, with characteristic perversity, repeatedly charges the one with complicity (*Maitland of Lethington*, ii. 53, 165, 167), and tries to clear the other. Three days before the assassination, Bedford and Randolph sent to Cecil the names of those who were privy to it (*Foreign Calendar, Elizabeth*, viii. 27); twelve days after the murder, Randolph sent a fuller list of the doers and their associates (*Ibid.* viii. 35); six days later still, Bedford and Randolph sent a much longer list to the English Council (Ellis's *Original Letters*, first series, ii. 220-222). In each of these lists stands the name of Lethington, but not of Knox. The only list in which the Reformer's name is found is the one first brought to light by Tytler, which is imperfectly dated and unsigned, which embraces John

Craig as well as Knox, and which bears the palpable error that they were present at the murder. This list is the only shred of evidence against Knox, and it also includes Lethington. It is true that Lethington's name is not found at the 'articles,' or in the two long lists of names in the *Register of Privy Council* (i. 437, 462, 463); but, as even Mr. Skelton is constrained to admit, neither is Knox's. Darnley never incriminated Knox, but persisted that Lethington was a prime mover, Mr. Skelton easily gets rid of this difficulty by saying that 'Darnley's testimony is absolutely worthless.' The fourfold line of defence he advances for Maitland is—the nature of the incidental references to him in Ruthven's *Relation*; Buchanan's statement that he was not 'advertisit be the Lordis of thair enterprise'; Robert Melville's, that Mary had 'takin tryal,' and found him 'not giltie thairin'; and Sir James Melville's, that he was permitted to leave the palace with Atholl and Tullibardine in fear of his life (*Maitland of Lethington*, ii. 171-177). He might have added that De Silva was assured that Lethington was not in the plot, and that the only evidence against him was Darnley's word (*Spanish Calendar, Elizabeth*, i. 547, 550). On the other hand, Mr. Skelton does not attempt to explain what Maitland meant, when he wrote to Cecil, on the 9th of February, that he could 'see no certain way, unless we chop at the very root.' It is not enough to say that this letter is 'enigmatical and ambiguous' (*Maitland of Lethington*, ii. 158, 171). Had it been written by Knox it is not at all likely that he would have found any enigma or ambiguity in it. Claude Nau asserts that 'Lethington was secretly of Moray's party—not so openly, however, that he could be charged therewith' (Nau's *Mary Stewart*, p. 19). Another contemporary alleges that it was Lethington who cunningly instilled the spirit of jealousy into Darnley (*Historie of James the Sext*, Ban. Club, p. 4); and Calderwood not only declares that Maitland laboured to persuade Morton and Herries 'to cutt off this base stranger,' but explains his politic behaviour on the fatal evening (*History*, ii. 311, 314). In Sir Ludovick Stewart's MS. Collections (Pitcairn's *Criminal Trials*, i. 479*), Lethington is included among the conspirators; and, in the *Diurnal of Occurrents* (p. 90), he is 'judgit' to be one of the party. But, on this point, Mr. Skelton has discreetly ignored Nau and Calderwood, the *Historie of James the Sext*, Stewart's MS. Collections, and the *Diurnal of Occurrents*. Goodall tried to show that there was an intimate connection between Riccio's death and the fast appointed by the General Assembly in the previous December; and that appropriate lessons were accordingly selected for each day of the fast (*Examination of the Letters*, i. 247-251, 257, 258, 272, 273). Hosack (i. 135), Petit (i. 103), and others, have been readily caught by this bait. But Goodall's distorted account of the fast was much too tame, as well as too inartistic, for Mr. Skelton, who has thus improved it :—' The tragedy took place in the early twilight of an evening in March. It had been a day of fasting; the zealots of the congregation had gathered into the great church in the High Street to hear how Oreb and Zeeb had been slain, how the Benjamites had been cut off, how Haman had been hanged. There was a hush of expectation throughout the city; the not altogether obscure intimations which Knox had ventured to make from the pulpit had prepared the "professors" for the coming judgment' (*Mary Stuart*, 1893, p. 79). Even on the supposition, however, that the fast had been postponed for a week, the lessons prescribed for that day contain nothing about Oreb or Zeeb, the slaughter of the Benjamites, or Haman; and Mr. Skelton can neither produce Knox's text nor a single sentence from his sermon. But this was not enough. Mr. Skelton asserts that 'in the form of prayer prepared by Knox' for the fast, 'his knowledge of the plot enabled him to exercise his prophetic gifts with marked advantage' (*Maitland of Lethington*, ii. 53). Strange as it may seem, that form of prayer (Laing's *Knox*, vi. 418, 419, 422; Sprott and Leishman's *Book of Common Order*, 1868, pp. 180-183, 187), though examined microscopically, does not yield the slightest reference to the Riccio tragedy or prophetic hint of any kind! Has Mr. Skelton been drawing on a disordered imagination? The story that the fast was appointed with reference to, and delayed that it might coincide with, the Riccio murder is as ill-founded as it is monstrous and absurd. It is quite certain that, in the previous December, the General Assembly fixed the time as 'the last Sunday of February and the first Sunday of Marche,' with services on the six intervening days (Laing's *Knox*, vi. 393, 421). In the continuation of Knox's *History*, and in the *Diurnal of Occurrents*, it is placed a week later, but without the slightest hint of its having been postponed. Indeed, the *Diurnal* (p. 88) distinctly bears that 'the ministeris exhortaris and reidaris of this realme' ordained that it should begin on Saturday evening the 2nd of March and end on Sabbath the 10th. Although some portions of the *Diurnal* are extremely accurate chronologically, yet as a whole it is by no means immaculate, and this entry concerning the appointment of the fast must be regarded as one of its blemishes. Knox's continuator simply says that 'upon Sunday the third day of March began the fasting at Edinburgh,' and speaks of the 10th of March as 'the second Sunday of our fast in Edinburgh' (Laing's *Knox*, ii. 520, 522). Possibly this writer—who had not even been born at that time—may have had access to a MS. copy of the *Diurnal*, and by it been misled. Calderwood, whose usual sources of information were quite as good, places it in May (*History*, ii. 317), that is two months after Riccio's murder. The *Register of the Kirk Session of the Canongate* indisputably shows that in that parish—the parish in which the murder was committed—the fast was held on the days appointed by the Assembly, the last Sabbath of February and the first Sabbath of March, and that the ordinary business of the Kirk Session was in consequence held over for a week (*infra*, p. 495).

[59] According to Randolph, Mary entered Edinburgh on the 18th of March, accompanied by 'aboute three thousand persons,' and took up her abode in the High Street (Wright's *Elizabeth*, i. 232). According to the *Diurnal of Occurrents* (p. 94), there were two thousand horsemen with her, and she 'lugeit in my Lord Home's lugeing, callit the auld Bischope of Dunkell his lugeing, anent the salt trone.' Knox's continuator makes her horse and foot number eight thousand (Laing's *Knox*, ii. 525); and Bishop Lesley, a thousand more (Forbes-Leith's *Narratives*, p. 113).

[60] Two incidents are enough to show how thoroughly Mary kept her wits about her during the terrible ordeal through which she passed. After Riccio had been torn from her and hustled out of her chamber, and before she knew whether he had been actually killed, Morton was sent to the victim's chamber 'to fetch a black coffer with writings and cyphers' (Ruthven's *Relation*, p. 30). After asking Ruthven what had 'become of Davie,' she inquired what 'great kindness' was between Murray and him, that to save him from forfeiture he was running the risk of being forfeited with him; and bade him remember what Murray had wished her to do to him for giving her a magical ring (*Ibid.* p. 35).

[61] Mariolaters of course scout the Riccio scandal as baseless and preposterous. Principal Robertson, who was not biassed in Mary's favour, believed that Darnley's suspicion was groundless, and that Randolph's silence was 'in itself a sufficient vindication of her

innocence' (*History of Scotland*, 1794, p. 212 *n.*); the same argument had been used by Keith (*History*, ii. 396 *n.*); but it cannot be used now. The covert allusions in Randolph's letters (*supra*, p. 380, *n.* 35) gave place to statements plain and direct. In his letter of 13th February, he says, 'I know that he [*i.e.* Darnley] knoweth himself that he hath a partaker in play and game with him' (Tytler's *Scotland*, 1845, v. 334); and the language of Bedford and Randolph's letter of 6th March is still more plain (*supra*, p. 386, *n.* 45). On the evening of the Riccio tragedy, Darnley charged her to her face with unfaithfulness, and her reply has been regarded— perhaps unjustly—as an avowal and defence of her criminal connection with the hated foreigner (Ruthven's *Relation*, pp. 30, 31; Wright's *Elizabeth*, i. 228). After the Riccio murder the stories that were current were scandalous enough (Aikman's *Buchanan*, ii. 477, 478; Teulet's *Papiers D'État*, ii. 120; Von Raumer's *Elizabeth and Mary*, p. 79; *Foreign Calendar, Elizabeth*, viii. 37). Randolph had emphatically refused to believe the ante-nuptial slanders concerning Mary and Darnley (Wright's *Elizabeth*, i. 203); but that he believed in Mary's guilt with Riccio is evident from a marginal note, which he added to a paper written in her defence (Von Raumer's *Elizabeth and Mary*, p. 121). Hill Burton remarks that at the birth of James the Sixth, it was noticed 'as a memorable fact that Darnley acknowledged the infant as his own, and that this should have been deemed a fact of importance is curiously suggestive of the unsatisfied and suspicious feelings which had become prevalent' (*History of Scotland*, 1876, iv. 160). Not less remarkable are the words attributed to Mary a few hours after the birth of the prince: —'My lord, God hes given you and me a sone, begotten by none but you . . . My lord, heer I protest to God, and as I shall answer to Him at the great day of judgment, this is your sone, and no other man's sone. And I am desyrous that all heer, both ladies and others, bear witness; for he is so much your owen sone, that I fear it be the worse for him heerafter' (Herries's *Memoirs*, p. 79). Writing to Leicester almost six weeks before Riccio's slaughter, Randolph had said :—'Woe is me for you when David sone shalbe a kynge of England' (*Foreign Calendar, Elizabeth*, viii. 13). As Hill Burton suggests, the ugliness of James the Sixth gave emphasis to the common taunt of those who disliked him (*History of Scotland*, v. 372) —a taunt which was hurled at him on a memorable occasion in Gowrie House by Alexander Ruthven, who, hearing that the Earl was slain, cried up, 'Come down, thou son of Signeur Davie ! thou hast slain an honester man nor thyself' (*Bruce's Life*, Wodrow Society, p. 193). To Henry the Fourth is attributed the saying, that James's title to be called the Modern Solomon was, that he was the son of David, who played upon the harp (Hill Burton's *Scotland*, iv. 141). Towards the close of the reign of James the Seventh, a persecuted Covenanter declared that it was still the surviving suspicion of most men that the father of Mary's son was 'her darling Davie Rizio, the Italian Fidler,' and that some thought it 'not unlikely that his successors have derived from this stock the Italian complexion and constitution, both of body and mind, spare and swarthy, cruel and crafty' (Shiel's *Hind Let Loose*, 1687, p. 24). According to Sir James Balfour, Riccio 'was interred in the churchyard of Holyrudhousse Abbey' (Balfour's *Historical Works*, i. 334). According to Nau, when Mary and Darnley escaped from Holyrood, 'they crossed the cemetery in which lay buried the body of the late David, and almost over the grave itself' (Nau's *Mary Stewart*, p. 16). Buchanan tells that Mary after her return to Edinburgh caused 'David's body, which had been buried before the neighbouring church door, to be removed in the night, and placed in the tomb of the late king and his children, which alone, with a few unaccountable transactions, gave rise to strange observations; for what stronger confession of adultery could she make, than that she should equal to her father and brothers in his last honours a baseborn reptile, neither liberally educated, nor distinguished by any public service; and what was still more detestable, that she should place the miscreant almost in the very embrace of Magdalene of Vallois, the late Queen' (Aikman's *Buchanan*, ii. 483). Keith thought fit to question this statement as 'unsupported by any body else' (*History*, ii. 410 n.). Buchanan's own belief in the story is proved by the curious conversation recorded by James Melville (*Autobiography and Diary*, Wodrow Society, p. 121); and the story itself is corroborated not only by Calderwood (*History*, ii. 316), but by Paul de Foix (Teulet's *Papiers D'État*, ii. 119). De Silva says that she 'had him disinterred and placed in a fair tomb inside the church' (*Spanish Calendar, Elizabeth*, i. 546). From Drury's letters of 20th April, it appears that, in deference to public opinion, she departed from her intention of laying him in the tomb of her father, and placed him in another part of the church (*Foreign Calendar, Elizabeth*, viii. 51, 52). When the vault, to which James

the Fifth's body had been removed by his grandson (Drummond's
History, 1681, pp. 349, 350), was opened, in 1683, some doubted
whether the occupant of one of the lead coffins—' a very tall proper
man '—was Darnley or Riccio (Fountainhall's *Historical Observes*,
Ban. Club, pp. 89, 90). As to the question of Mary's guilt with
Riccio, Mr. M'Neel-Caird alleges with seeming triumph that
' Darnley himself, a few days after the murder, declared to the
conspirators that he would stake his life on Mary's honour' (*Mary
Stuart*: *Her Guilt or Innocence*, 1866, p. 56). Unfortunately for
Mr. Caird's own honour, the passage to which he refers (Keith's
History, folio editions, app. p. 128 ; Spottiswoode Society, ed. iii.
276) has no bearing whatever on the matter—relating, as it does,
not to Mary's chastity but to her truthfulness.

[62] Ruthven's *Relation*, 1699, pp. 31, 41, 42.—The ' circumstances
form such a picture of savage cruelty and falsehood, of criminal
lust and brutish stupidity—such a mixture of vicious and disgusting matters and facts—that few scenes in the history of the world
can be compared with it' (Von Raumer's *Elizabeth and Mary*, p.
85).

[63] Nau's *Mary Stewart*, p. 17.

[64] Ellis's *Original Letters*, first series, ii. 222 ; Goodall's *Examination*, i. 280, 281 ; *Diurnal of Occurrents*, p. 96.—De Silva was told
by Henrison—Archbishop Beaton's secretary—that it was because
Riccio's murder had been so much condemned by the Scotch people
that it was necessary to proclaim very emphatically that Darnley
had no hand in it (*Spanish Calendar, Elizabeth*, i. 541). According
to one contemporary the proclamation ' excited considerable merri-
ment' (Aikman's *Buchanan*, ii. 484). According to Mary, it was
published at Darnley's desire (Labanoff's *Recueil*, i. 349).

[65] *Spanish Calendar, Elizabeth*, i. 544.—This letter of De Silva's
is dated 22nd April. The bond referred to is apparently that mentioned on p. 389.

[66] *Foreign Calendar, Elizabeth*, viii. 45.—In this letter of Randolph's, dated 4th April, he not only states that Mary had now
seen all the covenants and bonds between Darnley and the Lords,
but that she now found that his declaration before her and the
Council was false. If, however, Claude Nau and Bishop Lesley are
to be believed, she knew the substance of that declaration to be
false before it was either made or proclaimed ; and so was a party
to Darnley's deliberate lie. Lesley states that before she escaped

from Holyrood, Darnley 'related to her the whole course of the conspiracy and his own share in it' (Forbes-Leith's *Narratives*, p. 111); and Nau says that on the very morning after Riccio's murder, Darnley 'handed to her the Articles drawn up and signed between himself and the conspirators' (Nau's *Mary Stewart*, p. 7), and that she at once read them (*Ibid.* p. 9). But implicit trust ought not to be placed—not even by Mary's admirers—in the narratives of Lesley and Nau. In her letter of 2nd April to Archbishop Beaton, she enclosed Darnley's declaration without giving the slightest hint of its untruthfulness (Keith's *History*, ii. 422).

[67] *Spanish Calendar, Elizabeth,* i. 544.

[68] Nau's *Mary Stewart,* p. 18; *Spanish Calendar, Elizabeth,* i. 547; Laing's *Knox,* ii. 526; *Foreign Calendar, Elizabeth,* viii. 35, 60.

[69] *Spanish Calendar, Elizabeth,* i. 550.

CHAPTER XI

[1] *Diurnal of Occurrents,* pp. 81, 87, 88; *Foreign Calendar, Elizabeth,* vii. 419, 420; viii. 19, 20; Labanoff's *Recueil,* i. 317-320, 326-330. —The sum has also been reported as 4000 crowns (*Register of Privy Council,* xiv. 248). Mary wished, in August, to exclude Randolph from the interview which Thomworth had with her Council; but Thomworth declined to meet them without him. By Mary's command, Lethington required Randolph to promise on his honour that he would in no way have to do with her rebels. He replied that he would promise nothing; and he would neither submit to have guards placed upon him, nor agree to live at Berwick (*Foreign Calendar, Elizabeth,* vii. 431, 432). In September, Mary told him that she knew that Elizabeth had given her rebels money; which, of course, he denied (*Ibid.* vii. 469). Thomworth, having been instructed not to recognise Darnley as Mary's husband (*Ibid.* vii. 417), refused to take her passport because it was signed by Darnley as King, and was in consequence seized on his way home and lodged for a few days in Hume Castle (*Ibid.* vii. 430, 432-436, 445). Undeterred by Thomworth's temporary imprisonment, Randolph now refused to accept a passport because it also was signed by Darnley (*Ibid.* viii. 23); and as he seemed to be in no hurry to leave, the Privy Council sent to inquire on Thursday the 28th of February, why he had not departed. On Friday the Provost ordered him to

leave on his peril by ten o'clock next day. A few friendly Scots convoyed him to Dunbar, and on Sabbath he reached Berwick (*Ibid.* viii. 28).

² Labanoff's *Recueil*, i. 319, 320.—It was known that even in the matter of aiding her rebels, Mary could hide her suspicions and dissemble her feelings when it was prudent to do so (*Spanish Calendar, Elizabeth*, i. 549).

³ *Foreign Calendar, Elizabeth*, viii. 23, 26 ; Ellis' *Original Letters*, first series, ii. 205, 206.—In Melville's credit Mary had said :— ' Quhome, in respect of his humill submissioun maid to us, and of the sute of diverse nobill men and utheris oure trustie servandis his freindis, we haif pardonit of his formar offenceis, in hope of his honest behaviour and faythfull service in tyme cumming' (Labanoff's *Recueil*, i. 315).   It may have been good policy on Mary's part to send one to the English Court who had been there so shortly before pleading for help to the disaffected Lords against herself.   Bedford could not fathom the motives which had prompted his appointment (Stevenson's *Selections*, pp. 158, 159).   As Elizabeth's letter threatening to send him back is dated the 3rd of March, he could not then have been more than a fortnight at her Court.   De Silva speaks as if he had not been received (*Spanish Calendar, Elizabeth*, i. 528).   By the middle of March he was dismissed (*Foreign Calendar, Elizabeth*, viii. 33), and by the beginning of April was again in Scotland (*Ibid.* viii. 42, 44).

⁴ For the reasons which prompted their pardon, see *supra*, p. 394.

⁵ Ellis's *Original Letters*, first series, ii. 232 ; Labanoff's *Recueil*, ii. 73.

⁶ *Register of Privy Council*, i. 436, 437 ; *Diurnal of Occurrents*, p. 95.—On the 29th of March, Morton and several others were, at the Market Cross of Edinburgh, denounced as rebels, put to the horn, and their moveable goods escheated ; and on the 2nd of April, Lord Ruthven and others were also denounced and outlawed (*Diurnal of Occurrents*, pp. 97, 98).   Six weeks later Ruthven died at Newcastle (*Ibid.* p. 99), his departure, according to Morton, being 'so godly that all men who saw it did rejoice' (*Foreign Calendar, Elizabeth*, viii. 66).   According to Nau, some alleged 'that he died like a madman, exclaiming that he saw Paradise opened, and a great company of angels coming to take him.'   Nau suggests 'that these were diabolical illusions, wrought by evil spirits, who wished to

delude him as he was passing away, that he might not escape them, for during his life they had possessed him with the art of magic' (Nau's *Mary Stewart*, pp. 22, 23).

[7] Pitcairn's *Criminal Trials*, i. 480*–482* ; Arnot's *Criminal Trials*, pp. 376–381; *Diurnal of Occurrents*, pp. 97, 98 ; *Foreign Calendar*, *Elizabeth*, viii. 45.—Elizabeth told De Silva that one had been hanged and another beheaded (*Spanish Calendar*, *Elizabeth*, i. 540). Henry Yair was not executed until the 10th of August (*infra*, p. 412, *n*. 48). Because Scott's children were innocent of his crime, they were restored to their honours and right of succession by Mary and Darnley (*Register of Privy Seal*, xxxv. 48) ; and Yair's sister obtained the gift of his escheat (*Ibid.* xxxvi. 3, 4).

[8] *Foreign Calendar*, *Elizabeth*, viii. 43.

[9] On the 16th of January, Randolph had written :—'I cane not tell what mislykinges of late ther hathe byne betwene her Grace and her howsbonde; he presseth ernestlye for the matrimonial croune, which she is loothe hastilye to graunte, but willinge to keape somewhat in store untyll she knowe howe well he is worthye to injoye such a sovereigntie, and therfore yt is thoughte that the Parliament for a tyme shalbe dyfferred' (Stevenson's *Selections*, p. 147). And eight days later he wrote :—'Wheather the Parlement yet holde or not yt is uncertayne; her howsbonde pressethe so ernestlye for the Crown matrimoniall that she repentethe to have done so myche for him as is paste' (*Ibid.* pp. 151, 152).

[10] According to the continuator of Knox's *History*, Darnley passed his time 'in hunting and hawking, and such other pleasures as were agreeable to his appetite, having in his company gentlemen willing to satisfy his will and affections' (Laing's *Knox*, ii. 514). His letter to the Laird of Loch Leven shows that he was keenly interested in fowling (*Registrum Honoris de Morton*, i. 14). According to Buchanan, Mary encouraged him in his pastime to weaken his influence; and in the depth of winter (1565-6) despatched him to Peebles with a mean train that he might be out of the way (Aikman's *Buchanan*, ii. 475, 476). Chalmers appeals to his father's letter to prove that this excursion 'was sought for by the king himself as an amusement, and not imposed upon him as a task' (*Life of Mary*, 1818, i. 161 *n*.). Miss Strickland also regards Lennox's letter as a satisfactory refutation of Buchanan's charge (*Life of Mary*, 1888, i. 256); and William Chambers has adopted her statement (*History of Peeblesshire*, 1864, pp. 100, 101). The

letter, however, which was first printed by Keith (*History*, i. pp. xcviii, xcix), does not show whether Darnley went to Peebles at that time willingly or unwillingly—at his wife's suggestion or his own—but it confirms Buchanan's statement about the inclemency of the weather.

[11] Two months after Riccio's murder, De Silva writes that Darnley is well treated, but 'as regards business he does nothing' (*Spanish Calendar, Elizabeth*, i. 548). 'He passed his time . . . mostly in warlike exercises' (*Ibid.* i. 549).

[12] See *supra*, p. 370, *n.* 86, also p. 382, *n.* 33; and *Foreign Calendar, Elizabeth*, viii. 21.

[13] Bothwell blamed Murray for his prosecution and exile; and Huntly regarded him as the overthrower of his house, and as the cause of his imprisonment. On the 3rd of April, Robert Melville, writing from Edinburgh, speaks of them as already agreed (*Foreign Calendar, Elizabeth*, viii. 44). The reconciliation, however, was accomplished apparently by degrees and required the personal influence of the Queen to complete it (*Ibid.* viii. 53, 54; *Diurnal of Occurrents*, p. 99). According to Nau, it was to strengthen the position of her child, in the event of her dying in childbed, and because 'she could not entirely trust that child to the keeping of her husband,' that she tried to reconcile the feuds of her nobles (*History of Mary Stewart*, p. 23).

[14] Atholl had special reason for his bitterness towards Argyll, who, during the Chase-about Raid, had not joyned his forces to those of Murray; but had spoiled Lennox and Atholl (*Foreign Calendar, Elizabeth*, vii. 455, 467, 509, 510, 522). So early as the 6th of July, Argyll had gathered his whole force to invade Atholl's territory (*Ibid.* vii. 405). In his account of the reconciliation, De Silva, by mistake, brackets Murray instead of Argyll with Atholl (*Spanish Calendar, Elizabeth*, i. 548).

[15] It was apparently on Good Friday, the 12th of April, that Darnley left the Court to meet Murray and Argyll, and on the 17th that he returned (*Foreign Calendar, Elizabeth*, viii. 52; *Spanish Calendar, Elizabeth*, i. 545). They arrived in Edinburgh on the 21st (*Diurnal of Occurrents*, p. 99); and on the 29th are in the sederunt of Privy Council (*Register of Privy Council*, i. 454).

[16] *Spanish Calendar, Elizabeth*, i. 545, 549.—For the conditions of Arran's release, see *Register of Privy Council*, i. 452, 453; *Diurnal of Occurrents*, p. 99.

¹⁷ Melville's *Memoirs*, p. 153.—Melville's statement is amply borne out by the substance of Randolph's on the 25th of April:—
'It is commonly believed that Thornton has gone to Rome to sue for a divorce between them. He [*i.e.* Darnley] is neither accompanied or looked upon of any nobleman, at liberty to do and go where and what he will' (*Foreign Calendar, Elizabeth*, viii. 53).

¹⁸ *Foreign Calendar, Elizabeth*, viii. 51.

¹⁹ *Ibid.* viii. 59.—For the watching and warding of the King and Queen in Holyrood at the time of Riccio's murder, remissions were granted in June (*Register of Privy Seal*, xxxv. 30), in July (*Ibid.* xxxv. 38, 39), in September (*Ibid.* xxxv. 82), and in October (*Ibid.* xxxv. 84).

²⁰ Labanoff's *Recueil*, vii. 301.

²¹ *Foreign Calendar, Elizabeth*, viii. 62, 66.

²² In her letter of 31st March, Mary had written to Argyll:—
'In this meyntyme, we pray you interteny familiaritie with Oneill in the best manner ye can' (Labanoff's *Recueil*, i. 339, 340). In the middle of the preceding January, Randolph had perceived that the league between Argyll and Shan was to take immediate effect (Stevenson's *Selections*, p. 148); and by the 7th of February he had been able to report that 'my Lord of Argile and Shan Oneil have mett and accorded to take each others parte' (*Ibid.* p. 154). Mary was advised to allow Argyll to entertain O'Neil as of himself, she not seeming to know thereof (Melville's *Memoirs*, p. 162). On the 16th of April, Mary wrote to the Pope on behalf of O'Neil, whom she describes as 'a nobleman of the Irish nation united to us by familiarity, friendship, and the bond of religion,' and urging, 'on account of his constancy in the Catholic religion,' that a dispensation should be granted to him 'concerning certain impediments of marriage between himself and a certain [lady] sprung from a noble stock and family of our kingdom' (*Register of Privy Council*, xiv. 250, 251). Shan had put away O'Donnell's wife, Argyll's step-mother; and now wished to marry M'Donnell's wife, Argyll's illegitimate sister (Hamilton's *Irish Calendar*, i. 172, 296; *Foreign Calendar, Elizabeth*, iv. 522; vii. 272).

²³ *Foreign Calendar, Elizabeth*, viii. 60, 64, 72, 86.

²⁴ *Ibid.* viii. 43, 45, 62.

²⁵ 'Argyll and Murray . . . have such misliking of their King as never was more of man' (*Foreign Calendar, Elizabeth*, viii. 64).

²⁶ *Foreign Calendar, Elizabeth*, viii. 81.—On the 2nd of June, Mary and Darnley signed an order forbidding the Magistrates and Town Council of Edinburgh to pursue, trouble, or molest, in any way, David Hoppringill, apothecary, or his wife. Hoppringill had been imprisoned 'at the instance of the Kirk for mareing of his spous Katheren Creychtoun efter the Papis fassoun, he being of befoir adjonit to the Kirk of God and thair disciplyne.' He was set at liberty two days after the birth of the Prince (*Burgh Records of Edinburgh*, 1557-1571, pp. 215-216).

²⁷ On the 5th of April, the Lords of Privy Council thought 'it maist commodious for the commoun weill of this cuntre, gif it may stand with the Quenis Majesteis plesour, and with the helth of hir body, that hir Majestie remane in the Castell of Edinburgh till hir Grace be deliverit of hir birth' (*Register of Privy Council*, i. 445). As their 'Soveranis hous wes empty and desolat of wynis, quhilkis necessarlie behuvit to be provydit,' the Lords ordered eleven and a half tuns at fifty pounds Scots the tun (*Ibid.* i. 451). Mary had entered the Castle of Edinburgh before the 3rd of April (*Foreign Calendar, Elizabeth*, viii. 44). 'Upon Monday [3rd of June] she took her chamber. . . . Argyll and Murray lodge in the Castle. Huntley and Bothwell were refused' (*Ibid.* viii. 81).

²⁸ Melville calls her 'the Lady Boyn.' She had just been married to Alexander Ogilvie of Boyne (*Maitland Miscellany*, i. 37-49).

²⁹ Melville's *Memoirs*, p. 158; *Foreign Calendar, Elizabeth*, viii. 91; *Spanish Calendar, Elizabeth*, i. 561.—In the days of stage-coaching, a reverend writer complacently noted that Melville accomplished his journey 'with speed now equalled every day, but then mentioned as remarkable' (Cook's *History of the Reformation*, 1811, iii. 231). Randolph had made special arrangements to forestall Melville, if possible (*Foreign Calendar, Elizabeth*, viii. 86, 87); but Cecil heard first of the birth of the Prince from Robert Melville, on the evening of his brother's arrival in London, and, though enjoined to temporary secrecy, informed Elizabeth the same night. 'Hir Majeste was in gret merines and dancing efter supper; but sa schone as the Secretary Cicill roundit the newes in hir ear of the Prince birth all merines was layed asyd for that nycht; every ane that wer present marveling what mycht move sa sodane a chengement; for the Quen sat down with hir hand upon hir haffet [*i.e.* cheek], and boursting out to some of hir ladies, how that the Quen of Scot-

landis was leichter of a faire sonne, and that sche was bot a barren stok.' When Melville obtained audience next day, she told him that the joyful news 'had recoverit hir out of a heavy seaknes quhilk had halden hir xv dayes.' Having heard that Elizabeth was again threatening to marry, Melville took care to tell her that the Queen of Scots 'was sa sair handled in the mean tym, that sche wissit never to have bene maried' (Melville's *Memoirs*, pp. 158, 159).

[30] *Diurnal of Occurrents*, p. 100; *Foreign Calendar, Elizabeth*, viii. 93.—According to Claude Nau, through a premature report the bonfires were lighted four days too soon. 'Immediately upon the birth of the Prince, all the artillery of the Castle was discharged, and the lords, the nobles, and the people gathered in St. Giles' Church to thank God for the honour of having an heir to their kingdom' (Nau's *Mary Stewart*, p. 27).

[31] *Foreign Calendar, Elizabeth*, viii. 93.—Melville states that Bothwell, Huntly, and Bishop Lesley envied the favour which Mary now showed to Murray, and tried to persuade her to put him in ward until the birth of the Prince, alleging that they were assured that he and his dependants intended to bring home the banished Lords at the critical moment of her distress. 'They thocht, gif anes he wer wardit, that they suld get devyces anew to cause him be kepit, and disgracit ay the langer the mair, when he suld not be present nor have plaice to answer and resist their callomnies' (Melville's *Memoirs*, pp. 154, 155). Goodall has unsuccessfully attempted to prove that there was such a plot to bring home the banished Lords, and that Melville was involved in it (*Examination*, i. 286-288). George Chalmers, boldly improving Goodall's theory, gives details of the plot, and calmly asserts that its object was 'the transfer of the Queen's sceptre to Murray's guilty hand' (*Life of Mary*, 1818, i. 170, 171); but, in spite of the formidable list of authorities given in a footnote, Chalmers also fails to prove his charge.

[32] *Foreign Calendar, Elizabeth*, viii. 94.

[33] Nau's *Mary Stewart*, p. 25; *Foreign Calendar, Elizabeth*, viii. 81.—Of the three copies, she is said to have retained one in her own hands, left one under seal to those who were to have the chief trust in her realm, and sent the third to her friends in France.

[34] The Testamentary Inventory was discovered, in August 1854,

among some unassorted law papers in the Register House, Edinburgh, and has been carefully printed, with elaborate and valuable notes, by Joseph Robertson in his *Inventories of Mary's Jewels*, pp. xxx-lix, 93-124.

[35] 'This hir ruitit disdayn [to Darnley] still continewing, a little before hir deliverance of hir byrth, in Maij or Junij 1566, in making of hir later will and testament, she named and appointed Boithuile amangis utheris to the tutele of hir birth and yssue and governament of the realm in cais of her deceis, and unnaturaly secludit the father from all kind of cure and regiment ower his awin childe, avancing Boithuile above all uthers to be Lieutenent Generall, gif warres suld happin in the Princes less aige. She disponit also her haill movables to uthers beside hir husband. And least reasoun suld have overthrawin this hir later will amangis the nobilitie eftir hir deceis, she caused thame gif thair solempnit aith for observance of the haill contentis thairof without inspectioun of ony thing contenit thairin' (*The Book of Articles*, in Hosack's *Mary*, i. 525). The statement that 'sche disponit also hir haill movables to uthers beside hir husband' is inconsistent with the bequests to Darnley in the testamentary inventory. In the absence of the will itself, it might, however, be argued that it may have set aside or superseded this testamentary inventory. The number of bequests to Darnley in the latter is perhaps a little uncertain. There are only fifteen marginal references to him; but Joseph Robertson, by making these include the next lots, opposite which nothing has been written, raises the number to twenty-six. When Mary was ill at Jedburgh, the Lords promised to execute her testament 'gif it may stand with the lawis of the realme' (Keith's *History*, iii. 288; Small's *Mary at Jedburgh*, 1881, p. 24).

[36] *Water-stained* was too commonplace a term in the eyes of Mary's sentimental apologists to be applied to such a document; and so Petit says, 'the writing is blurred with tears' (Flandre's *Petit*, i. 112); and Miss Strickland alleges that Mary's handwriting is 'now scarcely intelligible in consequence of the tears, which have apparently fallen upon it while the ink was wet, having run the words one into another' (*Life of Mary*, 1888, i. 309). This is much more touching than truthful, as may be readily seen by the admirable facsimiles in Robertson's *Inventories*, p. xxxii, and in the *National MSS. of Scotland*, iii. 50.

[37] The testamentary inventory is in two gatherings—one of ten leaves and one of six. It is on the last page of the larger gathering that there is written in the Queen's hand :—' *Jentands que cestuissi soyt execute au cas que lanfant ne me survive mays si il vit ie le foys heritier de tout* MARIE R̃.'

[38] Joseph Riccio arrived at the Scotch Court with Mauvissière on the 14th of April, and within eleven days was appointed to that post of secretary from which his brother had been so violently extruded (*Foreign Calendar, Elizabeth*, viii. 51, 53, 54). To him Mary bequeathed a jewel containing ten rubies and a pearl, which she had accepted as a gift from his murdered brother (Robertson's *Inventories*, p. 123).

[39] Mary bequeathed an emerald ring enamelled in white to Joseph to be delivered by him to one whose name he knew (Robertson's *Inventories*, p. 113) ; and also a jewel, containing twenty-one diamonds, the name of the ultimate recipient being also secret (*Ibid.* p. 122).

[40] To the University of St. Andrews the Queen left her Greek and Latin books to form the nucleus of a library (Robertson's *Inventories*, p. 124; *National MSS. of Scotland*, iii. 50). Lethington's name does not occur in the Testamentary Inventory, although Mr. Skelton says that it does, and even tells what was bequeathed to him : ' a piece of the same silver or gold edged stuff which she had left to Bothwell' (*Maitland of Lethington*, ii. 181 *n.*). As a matter of fact, no 'silver or gold edged stuff' was left to Bothwell. Elsewhere, Mr. Skelton boldly alleges that Bothwell's name does not appear among the beneficiaries (*Impeachment of Mary Stuart*, 1876, p. 164), although it occurs twice (Robertson's *Inventories*, pp. 113, 122).

[41] *The Book of Articles* in Hosack's *Mary*, i. 525, 526 ; Buchanan's *Detection* in Anderson's *Collections*, ii. 5, 6.—Chalmers says that Mary went by water to Alloa, as she had no wheeled carriage, and was not strong enough to go on horseback (*Life of Mary*, 1818, i. 180 ; ii. 18) ; but it is quite certain that she had both a litter and a coach (*Diurnal of Occurrents*, p. 72 ; Robertson's *Inventories*, p. xxi ; *Foreign Calendar, Elizabeth*, vii. 532) ; and that she rode in her coach when she had few geldings (*Ibid.* vii. 57). Perhaps the true reason of her going by water was that she liked sailing. The author at least of the *Oration*, appended to the *Detection*, says (p. 44) that she could abide at the pump, and 'joyit to handill the boysterous cabilis.'

[42] Stevenson's *Selections*, p. 165.

[43] Nau's *History of Mary*, p. 29.—Keith (*History*, ii. 445), Goodall (*Examination*, i. 294) and Chalmers (*Life of Mary*, i. 181) assert that Darnley remained two nights with Mary at Alloa ; but these writers were misled by an imperfect abstract of Bedford's letter of 9th August (*cf.* Keith's *History*, iii. 349, and Thorpe's *Calendar*, ii. 839). A minute of a meeting of the Privy Council, dated at 'Alloway,' on the 28th of July, begins thus :—' Forsamekill as the King and Quenis Majesteis considdering,' etc. (*Register of Privy Council*, i. 475). Hosack is in error in supposing that the *Register* proves that Murray was with her at Alloa (Hosack's *Mary*, i. 153). For the kindly interest she took in a poor woman while in Alloa see *supra*, p. 283 *n*. 105 ; and while there she also showed kindness to the inhabitants of Kelso (*Historical MSS. Commission, Fourteenth Report*, app. iii. pp. 39, 40).

[44] *Foreign Calendar, Elizabeth*, viii. 110.

[45] Stevenson's *Selections*, pp. 164, 165.—Bedford gives in this letter an illustration of Mary's feeling toward Darnley. 'One Hickeman, an Englishe merchaunt there, having a water spanyell that was verie good gave him to James Melvyn [*i.e.* Sir James Melville], who, afterward for the pleasure that he sawe that the King had in suche kind of dogges, gave him to the King. The Quene therupon fell mervelously out with Melvyn, and called him dissembler and flatterer, and sayed she could not trust him who wold gyve any thing to such one as she loved not.'

[46] *Foreign Calendar, Elizabeth*, viii. 114.

[47] Thorpe's *Calendar*, ii. 839.—See also *Spanish Calendar, Elizabeth*, i. 573.

[48] Raumer's *Elizabeth and Mary*, pp. 88, 89.—Darnley had told Mary that he meant to kill Murray ; and she not only informed him of that threat, but willed him to charge her husband with it, which he did   She then ' affirmed that the King had spoken such words unto her, and confessed before the whole house that she would not be content that either he or any other should be unfriendly to Murray.' Raumer, who does not give the date of this report of Bedford's, places it before his letter of 8th August ; but the report is apparently based on, if not identical with, the ' advertisements out of Scotland,' forwarded by him to Cecil on the 15th of August (*Foreign Calendar, Elizabeth*, viii. 118 ; Thorpe's *Scottish Calendar*, ii. 839). In the ' advertisements,' reference is made to

the execution of Ruthven's servant on the preceding Saturday ; and Henry Yair was executed on Saturday the 10th of August (Birrel's *Diary*, p. 5).

[49] *Foreign Calendar, Elizabeth*, viii. 117.—The district or parish of Megget or Rodono—afterwards, if not then, annexed to Lyne, though at a considerable distance from it—is in the southern extremity of Peeblesshire. The Water of Megget, after running through the whole length of it, falls into St. Mary's Loch. 'At Cramalt, about half-way up the valley, there is said to have been a royal hunting seat, and certainly there was here a tower of considerable size' (Chambers's *Peeblesshire*, 1864, pp. 409-412 ; *Old Statistical Account*, xii. 556-558, 564 ; *Acts of the Parliaments of Scotland*, iv. 607). On the occasion of this visit, Mary and Darnley found that, notwithstanding the Acts of Parliament (*supra*, p. 282), they could get 'na pastyme of hunting,' and therefore ordained that the lieges be warned by proclamation 'that nane of thame tak upoun hand, in tyme cuming, to schute at deir with culverings, half-haggis, or bowis' (*Register of Privy Council*, i. 477). This Act is dated at Rodono on the 16th of August. On the same day she wrote from 'Crammald' to Lord Gray, requesting his presence at the approaching baptism of the Prince, 'in sic honest maner as the tyme and occasioun cravis . . .'. Ye will not agane in many yeiris have the like thyng in hand ' (*Master of Gray's Papers*, Ban. Club, app. p. x.).

[50] *Detection*, in Anderson's *Collections*, ii. 7.

[51] Goodall's *Examination*, i. 296.

[52] Nau's *Mary Stewart*, p. 30.—They were apparently at Traquair on the 19th of August (*Register of Privy Seal*, xxxv. 63).

[53] Nau's *Mary Stewart*, p. 30.—The 22nd of August is the date assigned for the Prince's journey (Birrel's *Diary*, p. 5). For the furnishings of his nursery, see *infra*, pp. 499, 500.

[54] *Detection* in Anderson's *Collections*, ii. 7.

[55] Lethington had been denounced by Darnley as one of the Riccio conspirators (*supra*, p. 396) ; but Darnley was not his only opponent at Court. On the 2nd of April Randolph reported that there had been a controversy between Bothwell and Atholl concerning him (*Foreign Calendar, Elizabeth*, viii. 43). He had leave to go 'to the laich cuntreis of Germany' for a year (*Ibid.* viii. 53 ; *Register of Privy Seal*, xxxiv. 71, 72), but went not, because, when ready, he learned that Bothwell intended to intercept him on the

sea (*Foreign Calendar, Elizabeth,* viii. 94), and, as was supposed, put him to death (*Ibid.* viii. 91). Bedford heard that Lethington was to speak with Mary at Alloa on the 2nd of August, and that it was expected that this would lead to reconciliation (Stevenson's *Selections,* p. 163). Bothwell and Murray were next 'at evil words' about him (*Foreign Calendar, Elizabeth,* viii. 117, 118), and Atholl was still befriending him (*Ibid.* viii. 124). He arrived at Stirling on the 4th of September, and next day, at William Bett's house, the Queen 'dined with him, and liked him very well.' With Murray and Argyll, she went to her capital on the 6th, leaving the Prince temporarily in charge of Lady Murray at Stirling, and appointing Lethington to be at Edinburgh by the 11th (*Ibid.* viii. 128). A few days afterwards, accompanied by Murray and Bothwell, she reconciled the latter to Lethington, at a friend's house, when all differences were accorded (*Ibid.* viii. 132).

[56] *Book of Articles,* in Hosack's *Mary,* i. 526, 529, 530 ; *Detection,* in Anderson's *Collections,* ii. 7-9.—In the Paper, sometimes described as Cecil's *Journal,* sometimes as Murray's *Journal,* there is the entry :—'September 24. She ludgit in the Chekker Hous and met with Bothwell. The King cumming frome Striviling wes repulsit with chyding' (Anderson's *Collections,* ii. 269 ; Laing's *Scotland,* 1804, ii. 85). Chalmers points out that the letter of the Lords of Privy Council shows that when Darnley came to Edinburgh, Mary was not in the 'Chekker Hous' but in Holyrood ; and therefore brands the statement of the *Journal* as a falsehood (*Life of Mary,* 1818, i. 185 *n.*). The *Detection* was not an amplification of the *Journal,* as Chalmers supposed, but a compression rather of the *Book of Articles* ; and that *Book* reconciles the statement of the *Journal* and of the *Detection* with the Privy Council statement; for it says that, when she knew he was coming, she 'purposelie fled out of the chekker-hous and past to the Palace of Halyrudehous' (Hosack's *Mary,* i. 526). This is by no means the only instance where Buchanan has laid himself open by being less precise than the *Book of Articles.* Writing on the 8th of September, Forster says that Mary was to return from Stirling to Edinburgh on the 11th to sit in her Exchequer, to understand her revenues, and to appoint what shall be for the keeping of her house and the young Prince's (*Foreign Calendar, Elizabeth,* viii. 128). Lamartine accepts the story of Mary's adventures in the Exchequer House as true (*Mary Stuart,* 1864, pp. 54, 55). If true, her guilt was not lessened by

the writ which she had issued from Stirling on the 31st of August, commanding the magistrates of Edinburgh to search out and punish without exception those who committed 'adultre, furnecatioun, oppin harlatrie, and utheris sic filthe lustis of the flesche' (*Burgh Records of Edinburgh*, 1557-1571, p. 217).

[57] Keith's *History*, ii. 457.

[58] *Ibid.* ii. 451.—In her letter, of 30th September, to Lennox, Mary says that Darnley 'mysknawis that he has ony sic purpos in hede, or ony caus of miscontentatioun. Bot his speking is conditionall, sua that we can understand na thing of his purpos in that behalf' (*Hist. MSS. Com., Third Report*, p. 395 ; *The Lennox*, ii. 351).

[59] Du Croc's letter was addressed to Archbishop Beaton, Mary's Ambassador in France. Keith printed a translation from the original (*History*, ii. 448-452). The letter of the Privy Council was addressed from Edinburgh, on the 8th of October, to Catherine de Medici. Keith printed a translation of it from a copy (*Ibid.* ii. 453-459)—perhaps the copy which Lethington sent to Beaton (Malcolm Laing's *Scotland*, 1804, ii. 72, 73)—and intended to print both it and Du Croc's letter in French as well (*History*, ii. 448, *n.* 2), but was obliged to omit them for want of room (*Ibid.* iii. 284). Teulet has, however, supplied the omission so far as the letter of the Privy Council is concerned (*Papiers D'État*, ii. 139-146 ; *Relations Politiques*, ii. 282-289); but, like Keith, was unable to give the names of the subscribers. There is a restricted sense in which these letters do not confute Buchanan's statement about Darnley's reception in Edinburgh. And while they do not warrant the counter-statement of an apologist, that 'she received him with all the old tenderness' (Walker's *Mary*, 1889, p. 26), the letter of the Privy Council tends to confirm Buchanan's allegation, that the King could not 'get sa mekle as to mantene his daylie necessarie expensis to find his few servandis and his horsis.'

[60] *Register of Privy Council*, i. 480, 481.

[61] One contemporary chronicler gives the 7th of October as the day of her departure (*Diurnal of Occurrents*, p. 100), and another gives the 8th (Birrel's *Diary*, p. 5). Father Stevenson says she left Edinburgh on the 8th, and reached Jedburgh on the same day (Nau's *Mary Stewart*, p. cxxix). Mary herself dated a letter to the Pope from Edinburgh on the 9th (Labanoff's *Recueil*, i. 369-372) ; and a letter of Forster's—which Father Stevenson, in his *Calendar*,

has misplaced by a year—bears that she arrived in Jedburgh on Wednesday, which was the 9th (*Foreign Calendar, Elizabeth,* vii. 490). The *Register of Privy Council* (i. 448) shows that she was there by the 10th.

[62] Keith's *History,* ii. 451.

[63] Knox's continuator says that it was 'by the advice of foolish cagots' that Darnley wrote to the Pope, the King of Spain, and the King of France; and that 'by some knave this poore Prince was betrayed and the Queen got a copie of these letters into her hands, and therefore threatened him sore; and there was never after that any appearance of love betwixt them' (Laing's *Knox,* ii. 533, 534). Chalmers was inclined to cast doubt on this statement as unsupported (*Life of Mary,* 1818, i. 185); but Darnley's complaining to the Pope and other Catholic princes of his wife's religious indifference is admitted in Hunter Blair's *Bellesheim,* iii. 110, and by Father Stevenson in his preface to *Claude Nau,* p. cxxxiv. Indeed, lest the King of Spain should believe Darnley, Mary asked De Silva to assure Philip 'that, as regards religion, she will never with God's help fail to uphold it with all the fervour and constancy which the Roman Catholic Christian religion demands. That in the religion in which she was born and bred she will remain forever, even though it may entail the loss of her crown and life, and she will postpone all things for its benefit' (*Spanish Calendar, Elizabeth,* i. 597). Darnley's letters do not seem to have reached Philip (*Ibid.* i. 613, 618).

[64] It was at first rumoured that Bothwell was slain (*Foreign Calendar, Elizabeth,* viii. 137). 'Happy had it been for Mary,' says Sir Walter Scott, 'had the dagger of the moss-trooper struck more home' (*Minstrelsy of the Scottish Border,* 1869, p. 21). Bothwell received three wounds, 'ane in the bodie, ane in the heid, and ane in the hand' (*Diurnal of Occurrents,* p. 101). The 7th of October is given by Lord Scrope, and the author of the *Diurnal,* as the date of his misadventure. He had been at a meeting of Privy Council in Edinburgh on the previous day (*Register of Privy Council,* i. 485).

[65] According to Lord Scrope's letter, Mary did not ride to the Hermitage until the 15th of October (*Foreign Calendar, Elizabeth,* viii. 139); and the same date is given by a contemporary chronicler (*Diurnal of Occurrents,* p. 101). An entry in the *Register of Privy Seal* (xxxv. 77) implies that it was on the 16th. In writing from

Jedburgh to Catherine de Medici on the 17th, Du Croc does not mention Mary's ride to the Hermitage, but states that Bothwell 'is out of danger, with which the Queen is well pleased; it had been no little loss to her to lose him' (*Papiers D'État*, ii. 150). Her ride from Edinburgh to Jedburgh was apparently rapid as well as long; but was quite eclipsed by the ride to and from the Hermitage. On the authority of Sir Walter Elliot, the distance from Jedburgh to Hermitage by the most likely route is said to be 'more than thirty miles.' As she returned to Jedburgh on the same day, this estimate makes the ride upwards of sixty miles (Small's *Mary at Jedburgh*, 1881, pp. 8, 9). Lamartine, who—unlike Sir Walter Elliot—does not know the district, represents Mary as riding to the Hermitage 'without resting by the way,' and returning 'the same day to Holyrood' (*Mary Stuart*, 1864, p. 55). So far as the Justice Court was concerned she might have gone to the Hermitage on the 10th or 11th of October, as no cause or complaint had been lodged (*Register of Privy Council*, i. pp. xliii, 489); but Nau tells that that week she was troubled with the spleen (*History of Mary Stewart*, p. 31). Impelled by guilty love she may have been; but Buchanan's exaggerated narrative implies a sustained, headlong haste all the way from Borthwick [1]—her affection, 'impatient of delay,' urging her towards the object of 'hir outragious lust' (*Detection*, in Anderson's *Collections*, ii. 10). It is rather curious that even Nau should say, 'she went very speedily' to the Hermitage; but instead of adopting Buchanan's language—that she went 'with ane company as na man of ony honest degre wald have adventurit his life and his gudes amang'—he is careful to state that she was accompanied by Murray and some other lords, in whose presence she conversed with Bothwell. The *Book of Articles* says, that, after hearing at Borthwick of Bothwell's injury, she took no 'kyndlie rest' until she saw him; and that she was heedless of the weather, the length and difficulty of the way, and 'the danger of hir persoun amangis the handis of notorious theifis and traitouris' (Hosack's *Mary*, i. 530). This statement is very different from Buchanan's, and is quite reconcilable with Nau's.

[66] Keith's *History*, ii. 451.

[67] *Diurnal of Occurrents*, p. 101; *Historie of James the Sext*, Ban. Club, p. 2; Forbes-Leith's *Narratives*, p. 115 n.; Nau's *Mary*

[1] In the 1572 edition of the *Detectioun*, reprinted by Anderson, *Jedburgh* erroneously appears in this passage instead of *Borthwick*.

Stewart, pp. cxxx, cxxxi, cxliii, 31 ; *Venetian Calendar*, vii. 383, 384 ; Hunter Blair's *Bellesheim*, iii. 104; Keith's *History*, ii. 465. It was on Thursday the 17th of October that Mary took ill. Huntly, Atholl, Murray, and Maitland, writing to Archbishop Beaton on the morning of the 23rd, say 'hir Majestie hes bene sick thir sex dayis bypast' (Keith's *History*, iii. 284) ; and Bishop Lesley speaks of the 25th as 'the nynt day' of her sickness (*Ibid.* iii. 286).

[68] Small's *Queen Mary at Jedburgh*, 1881, p. 18.

[69] Malcolm Laing's *History of Scotland*, 1804, ii. 72 ; 1819, ii. 74. In the same letter to Archbishop Beaton, Lethington says :—'I write freely to your L[ordship] as to a man that, being employit in the chairge ye beir, suld not be ignorant in quhat estait things stands at hayme, and yit as to a frend with quhom I may safely communicat my opinion. I see betwixt tham [*i.e.* Mary and Darnley] na agreement nor na appeirance that they sall agree weill theirefter. At leist I am assurit that it hes bene hir mynd this gude quhile, and yit is as I write. How sone or in quhat maner it may change God knawis.'

[70] Keith's *History*, iii. 286.—According to Claude Nau, 'all present, especially her domestic servants, thought she was dead, and they caused the windows to be opened. The Earl of Moray began to lay hands on the most precious articles, such as her silver plate and rings. The mourning dresses were ordered and arrangements were made for the funeral' (Nau's *Mary Stewart*, p. 32). This statement is probably very much over-coloured. Lethington, writing next day to Cecil, says they all for half an hour despaired of her life (*Foreign Calendar, Elizabeth*, viii. 141). For accounts of the curious method of the cure, see Keith's *History*, iii. 286 ; Nau's *Mary*, p. 32 ; Laing's *Knox*, ii. 534.

[71] 'The 25 of October, word came to the toune of Edinburghe, frome the Queine, that her Majestie wes deadly seike, and desyrit the bells to be runge, and all the peopell to resort to the kirk to pray for her, for she wes so seike that none lipned her life' (Birrel's *Diary*, p. 6). 'Publict prayaris' were made 'in all pairtis' (*Diurnal of Occurrents*, p. 101). 'There was continually prayers publikely made at the Church of Edinburgh, and divers other places, for her conversion towards God and amendment' (Laing's *Knox*, ii. 535). In the 1574 edition of the *Order and Doctrine of the General Fast*, there is a list of the 'chapters and partes of the

Scriptures used be the ministers of Edinburgh and Halyrudhous
. . . in the tyme when in the Court rang all impietie, as murther,
huredome, and contempt of God's word, bot especially in the tyme
when the Quene wes strikken be God's hand in Jedburgh' (Laing's
Knox, vi. 427; Sprott and Leishman's *Book of Common Order*, 1868,
pp. 187, 188).

[72] Small's *Queen Mary at Jedburgh*, 1881, p. 26.—Lesley thus
records her words, 'My Lordis, ye knaw the goodnes that I have
usit towardis sum quhilkis I have avancit to ane gret degre of
honneur and preeminence above otheris, quha notwithstandyng
has usit mair nor ingratitude towardis me, quhilk hes ingendrit
the displesour that presentlie maist grieves me, and also is the
cause of my syknes. I pray God mend them' (*Ibid.* p. 23). By
the 6th of November the Venetian Ambassador in Paris had heard
that her 'illness was caused by her dissatisfaction at a decision
made by the King, her husband, to go to a place twenty-five or
thirty miles distant, without assigning any cause for it, which
departure so afflicted this unfortunate Princess, not so much for
the love she bears him, as from the consequences of his absence'
(*Venetian Calendar*, vii. 384).

[73] 'That illness,' says Petit, 'which was to show to the world the
Queen's magnanimity, revealed at the same time Darnley's meanness and ingratitude. Informed on an early day of his wife's
danger, he felt no uneasiness, but went on hawking, and did not
trouble himself to visit her . . . Darnley, who would not leave
his dogs and falcons to visit his wife, stood forth self-accused.
The mystery of their separation was being unravelled . . . On
the 28th Darnley, tired of hunting, or no longer able to withstand
the entreaties of his friends, went to Jedburgh to see the Queen.
She endeavoured to win him back to his duty and to more seemly
ways, but it was in vain. He left on the morrow. The nobles
were wounded by his heartlessness' (Flandre's *Petit*, i. 120-122).
'Neither during the period of Mary's severe illness, nor that of her
lingering recovery,' says Father Stevenson, 'did her husband ex-
hibit either concern or affection. He visited her once, remaining
one night at Jedburgh, and on the following day he returned to
Glasgow' (Nau's *Mary Stewart*, pp. cxxxi, cxxxii). Chalmers,
with his usual vigour, denounces both Buchanan and Knox for
saying that Darnley hastened to Jedburgh on hearing of his wife's
illness (*Life of Mary*, 1818, i. 192 *n.*). On this point, too, Hosack

refers to 'the slanderous narrative of Buchanan' (*Mary and her Accusers*, i. 162). Buchanan and the continuator of Knox, however, do not stand alone; and their assailants—like Darnley's— have apparently nothing better to stand upon than Keith's mistranslation of a somewhat ambiguous passage in Du Croc's letter of 24th October, which he renders thus :—'The King is at Glasgow, and has not come to this place, although he has both received advertisement, and has had time enough to come had he been willing. This is such a fault as I know not how to apologise for it' (Keith's *History*, ii. 467). The crucial clause is thus translated by Dr. John Small :—'It is certain he has been informed of it by some one, and has had time enough if he had been willing' (*Queen Mary at Jedburgh*, 1881, p. 17). The passage in the original is :— 'Le Roy est à Glasco, et n'est point venu icy. Si est ce qu'il a eté adverty par quelqu'un, et a eu du temps assez pour venir s'il eust voullu; c'est une faulte que je ne puis excuser' (Keith's *History*, iii. 285). From the expression 'some one' (*quelqu'un*), it may be inferred that no special messenger was sent from Jedburgh to the distant Darnley. Writing two days later, Bishop Lesley says nothing about Darnley being advertised, but merely states that 'the King all this time remaneis in Glasgow, and yit is nocht cum towart the Quenis Majestie' (*Ibid.* iii. 288). According to a contemporary chronicler, Darnley was then hawking and hunting with his father in 'the west pairtis of this realme'; and 'so sone as he wes adverteist of hir infirmitie, he come to Edinburgh upon the twantie sevint day at evin, and raid to the Quenis Grace to Jedburgh upoun the twantie aucht day in the mornyng. And efter his cuming to the said burgh, he was not so weill intertynijt as neid suld have bene; and upoun the twantie nyne day he returnit thairfra without tarying to Edinburgh, and thairefter past to Striueling' (*Diurnal of Occurrents*, pp. 101, 102). 'During this seiknes King Henrie hir husband was in cumpanie of Matho Erle of Lennox his father in the wast part of Scotland : and howsone he understude of this sudden visitatioun, he addressit himself with expeditioun towart hir, altho he was not welcome as appertenit; wharefore he addrest his jorney back to Sterling, whare he remaynit till the Prince was baptesit' (*Historie of James the Sext*, Ban. Club, p. 4).

74 *Foreign Calendar*, *Elizabeth*, viii. 141; Keith's *History*, iii. 289.

[75] *Book of Articles*, in Hosack's *Mary*, i. 530.—This statement— serious enough in itself—becomes infinitely worse in the hands of Buchanan, who describes in suggestive language their alleged guilty intercourse, and declares that they misconducted themselves 'sa oppinlie as thay semit to feir nathing mair, than leist thair wickitnes suld be unknawin' (*Detection*, in Anderson's *Collections*, ii. 10-12).

[76] 'Although this misfortune is of itself greatly to be deplored, other evils greater and more general will follow, as it may now be said that the Catholic religion will become extinct in that Kingdom, both because those who govern and have authority with the King are its open enemies, and also because the King himself is disaffected towards it. The Queen leaves a son just born, who will now imbibe this poison with his milk, and there can be no doubt but that he will rather resemble his father than his most virtuous and religious mother' (*Venetian Calendar*, vii. 383, 384).

[77] Small's *Queen Mary at Jedburgh*, p. 26 n.

[78] *Foreign Calendar, Elizabeth*, viii. 143.

[79] In reference to the letters which Mary received at Kelso from Darnley, Froude quotes Calderwood as saying that she exclaimed, in the presence of Murray and Maitland, 'that unless she was freed of him in some way she had no pleasure to live, and if she could find no other remedy she would *put hand to it herself*' (*History of England*, 1887, vii. 491). But the threat, as given by Calderwood, was suicidal, not murderous—she would 'putt hand *into* herself' (Calderwood's *History*, ii. 326). Froude has, doubtless, been misled by the idiom. Calderwood had the *Detectio* before him ; and the expression there used—'*sese sibi manum illaturam*' —is rendered in the Scotch version 'scho wald slay hirself' (Jebb's *De Vita et Rebus Gestis Mariae*, i. 241 ; *Detection*, in Anderson's *Collections*, ii. 13). Buchanan in turn was simply following the *Book of Articles*—'to be the instrument of hir awin death' (Hosack's *Mary*, i. 533).

[80] With a view to the declaration of the English succession in her favour, Mary wrote from Dunbar, on the 18th of November, to Elizabeth's Privy Council, expressing her affection for their Queen, and her resolution to keep through life on such terms with their Sovereign and realm that she would withstand to the utmost of her power any Prince who would offend them. As a proof of her affection she said :—'When we lookt not to have bruiked this

life twelve hours in our late sickness, . . . our meaning was that
the special care of the protection of our son should rest upon our
said good sister' (Keith's *History*, ii. 472). It is rather curious
that in the four accounts of Mary's speeches at that critical time
neither England nor Elizabeth is even mentioned; that, on the
contrary, in each of them it is stated that she commended her son
to the Scots nobles, and to the King and Queen-mother of France;
that one of them represents her as expressing her goodwill to the
French alliance, and another as saying, 'I desyre that alliance mai
still continue' (*Ibid.* iii. 286-288; Small's *Mary at Jedburgh*, pp.
22-25; Nau's *Mary Stewart*, pp. 32, 33; *Historie of James the Sext*,
Ban. Club, pp. 2-4).

[81] Keith's *History*, ii. 469-471; *Foreign Calendar, Elizabeth*, viii.
147; *Diurnal of Occurrents*, p. 102.—Sir James Melville says that
when Sir John Forster ' was speaking with hir Majeste upon hors-
bak, his cursour raise up with his forther legges, to tak the Quenis
horse be the nek with his teeth, bot his forder feet hurt hir
Majesteis thy [*i.e.* thigh] very evell. Incontinent the Warden
leichted aff his horse, and sat down upon his knees, craving
pardone at hir Grace; for then all England bure hir Majeste
gret reverance. Hir Majeste maid him to ryse, and said that
sche was not hurt; yet it compellit hir Majeste to tary twa dayes
at the castell of Hum, untill sche was weill again' (Melville's
Memoirs, p. 173). Unfortunately for the credibility of this story,
it was after Mary had left Hume that Forster met her on the 15th
of November; but this part of Melville's *Memoirs* is badly mixed—
the visit to Jedburgh being placed after, instead of before, the
baptism of the Prince. Forster, however, seems to have previously
met Mary near the Borders, a day or two before her ride to the
Hermitage (*Foreign Calendar, Elizabeth*, viii. 138, 139).

[82] From Home, or Hume, Lethington had written to Cecil, on
the 11th of November, that Mary was restored perfectly to health
(*Foreign Calendar, Elizabeth*, viii. 145). The statement in the text
is from Du Croc's letter of 2nd December (Keith's *History*, i. p.
xcvi).

[83] 'Grant me mercy, for I seik not lang lyif in this world, bot
only that thy will may be fulfillit in me. O my God thow hes
apointit me above the peple of this realme to reule and gouverne
them, gif theirfor yt be thi plessour that I remain with them in
this mortell lyiff, albiet that yt be painfull to my body, so that yt

pleas thi devyne guidnes I will gif myself to thi keiping.' Gif thi
plessour and purpose be to call me frome hence to thi mercy, with
guid will I remitt miself to thi plessour, and is alss weill deliberat
to die ass to lyive, desyryng that thi will be fulfillit, and as the
guid Kyng Ezechios (afflictit with seyknes and other infirmites)
turnit him to thi devyne will and plessour, so do I the lyk' (Small's
Queen Mary at Jedburgh, 1881, p. 25). See also Keith's *History,*
iii. 287.

[84] Keith's *History,* i. pp. xcvi, xcvii.

[85] 'Sair gretand and tormentand hir selff miserablie,' to Murray,
Huntly, and Lethington she said that unless 'she war quyt of the
King be ane meane or uther, she culd nevir have a gude day
in hir lyff, and rather or she fallit thairin, to be the instrument
of hir awin death' (Hosack's *Mary,* i. 533). See *supra,* p. 420, *n.*
79.

[86] Hosack's *Mary,* i. 533.

[87] The *Protestation* is in Anderson's *Collections,* iv. part ii. pp.
188-193; in Keith's *History,* iii. 290-294; and in Goodall's *Examination,* ii. 316-321.

[88] Though commonly known as the Protestation of Huntly and
Argyll, it is not at all probable that either the one or the other of
these nobles ever saw it. It was drawn up by Lord Boyd's advice,
'conforme to the Declaratioun' Huntly had made to Bishop Lesley,
and was sent by Mary from Bolton, on the 5th of January 1568-9,
to Huntly, with a letter directing him and Argyll to subscribe;
but leaving it to their discretion 'to eik and pair' as they thought
best, and to extend 'in sic forme' as they thought most necessary,
before returning it to her signed and sealed (Anderson's *Collections,*
iv. part ii. p. 186). Lord Hunsdon, however, seized Mary's
messenger—Thomas Karr—as he neared the Border, and her letter
to Huntly and the draft Protestation were taken from him on the
9th of January, and despatched to Cecil next day (*Hatfield Calendar,*
i. 390). As to Camden's statement (*Elizabeth,* 1675, p. 93) and
Stranguage's (*Historie of Mary,* reprint, p. 81), that they had
seen the original Protestation sent by Huntly and Argyll to
Elizabeth, *cf.* Tytler's *Inquiry,* 1790, ii. 31, 32, and Malcolm Laing's
Scotland, 1804, i. 182 *n.*

[89] Assuming that the narrative of the Protestation is trustworthy,
it is difficult to know what Lethington meant by the expression
that Mary would 'sie nathing bot gud, and approvit be Parlia-

ment.' If, as Professor Aytoun argues, the reference to the approval of Parliament utterly negatives the idea of violent means being hinted at (Aytoun's *Bothwell*, 1857, p. 252), why should Lethington have spoken of Murray looking through his fingers? or why should Mary have objected to any spot being laid on her honour or conscience? In another document, which was signed by Huntly and Argyll, and by more than a dozen of Mary's other nobles, there is the more explicit statement:—'Thay causit mak offeris to our said Soverane Lady, gif hir Grace wald give remissioun to thame that wer banishit at that time, to find causis of divorce, outher for consanguinitie, in respect thay alledgit the dispensatioun was not publishit, or else for adulterie; or then to get him convict of tressoun, because he consentit to hir Grace's retentioun in ward; or *quhat uther wayis to despeche him*; quhilk altogidder hir Grace refusit, as is manifestlie knawin' (Goodall's *Examination*, ii. 359). Lesley also alleges that although they offered, if she pardoned Morton, to procure a divorce between her and Darnley, yet she would not agree (*Defence of Queen Mary's Honour*, in Anderson's *Collections*, i. 14, 15).

[90] Keith (*History*, ii. 510 *n.*) and Goodall (*Examination*, i. 318) deem Murray's denial of having signed any 'band' at Craigmillar irrelevant; but in the light of Ormiston's confession—that Huntly and Argyll had about that time signed a 'band' for the destruction of the 'young fooll and proud tirrane'—it was a telling home-thrust (Arnot's *Criminal Trials*, pp. 385, 386; Pitcairn's *Criminal Trials*, i. 512*). According to Ormiston, this 'band' was also signed by Lethington and Sir James Balfour. Hay of Tallo confessed on the scaffold that he, too, had seen this 'band,' and that it was subscribed by Bothwell, Huntly, Argyll, Lethington, and Balfour (*Diurnal of Occurrents*, pp. 127, 128). If Claude Nau is to be believed, when Bothwell parted with Mary at Carberry he handed her the 'band'—after pointing to the signatures of Morton, Lethington, Balfour, and some others—and bade her take good care of it (Nau's *Mary Stewart*, p. 48). Hosack misrepresents Murray's denial on two points, and then unwarrantably charges him with alleging what is known to be untrue (*Mary and her Accusers*, i. 165). He asserts that Murray 'only expressly denies what was not alleged—namely, that he had signed any bond at Craigmillar'; but, in the quotation he had just given, Murray expressly denies that in his presence there was any proposal 'tending

to any unlawful or dishonourable end.' Murray's statement about the bond which he had signed in the beginning of October, in token of his reconciliation with Bothwell and Huntly, is not known to be untrue. He does not say—as Hosack unaccountably supposes—that he signed the bond before he was restored to the Queen's favour, but only that he had then promised to do so.

[91] *Foreign Calendar, Elizabeth*, viii. 130.

[92] Labanoff's *Recueil*, vii. 97-100; iv. 4; Stevenson's *Selections*, pp. 167, 168; *Spanish Calendar, Elizabeth*, i. 601; *Hatfield Calendar*, i. 341; Thorpe's *Calendar*, i. 239, 240, 379.—Twenty years later the same Scot, as Tulchan, Archbishop of St. Andrews, was sent by King James to desire the minister and reader of St. Andrews 'to pray publiclie for his Hienes' mother, for hir conversioun and amendment of lyfe, and, if it be Godis plesour to preserve hir from this present danger quhairin sche is now, that sche may heirefter be ane profitabill member in Christis kirk' (*Register of St. Andrews Kirk Session*, Scottish History Society, ii. 583, 584). In this case Patrick Adamson did not, as in the other, cut before the point, for Mary was led forth to execution six hours before he made the tardy request.

[93] The true date of the Prince's baptism—17th December 1566—is given in the *Diurnal of Occurrents*, p. 103; Birrel's *Diary*, p. 6; Laing's *Knox*, ii. 536; *Venetian Calendar*, vii. 387; Keith's *History*, i. p. xcvii. The 15th of December is given by Spottiswoode (*History*, ii. 41); the 18th of December by Pitscottie (*History*, 1728, p. 219), and by De Silva (*Spanish Calendar, Elizabeth*, i. 606); the 15th of November by David Laing (Laing's *Knox*, ii. 536 *n.*); and the 22nd of August by Sir James Balfour (*Historical Works*, i. 335). For assigning the baptism to the month of December, the *Historie of James the Sext* has been challenged by a presumptuous writer, who alleges that 'all other accounts agree in fixing the date to be the 22d of August' (*Notices of the Bannatyne Club*, 1836, p. 24).

[94] *Venetian Calendar*, vii. 387.

[95] *Workes of the Most High and Mighty Prince James*, 1616, p. 301. —Mary did not stand alone in objecting to the use of the spittle in baptism. In the spring of 1562, a remonstrance was sent from France to the Pope, bearing that many who will not leave the church are nevertheless troubled in conscience over several points. One of these was—'They cannot well bear that a diseased priest, and many times of the pockes, should put his spittle in the child's

mouth, and think that thereof comes many inconveniences (*Foreign Calendar, Elizabeth,* v. 624).

[96] *Diurnal of Occurrents,* p. 104.

[97] *Foreign Calendar, Elizabeth,* viii. 110.

[98] Mary warmly acknowledged Elizabeth's kindness on this occasion (Labanoff's *Recueil,* i. 389-391). But Father Stevenson sees, in the choice of 'the Puritanical Earl of Bedford' as Ambassador, the fruit of Elizabeth's ingenuity in discovering 'a cheap and easy method of mortifying her rival through this very interchange of civilities' (Nau's *Mary Stewart,* p. cxxxiii). It is true that, in the previous January, Mary had 'no good lykinge' of Bedford (Stevenson's *Selections,* pp. 149, 151); but, two years before, she thought better of no man (*Foreign Calendar, Elizabeth,* vii. 91); and in the August preceding the baptism, Murray had informed Cecil that Mary hoped that Leicester, or Bedford, and Throckmorton, would come to the ceremony (Thorpe's *Calendar,* i. 238). Sir James Melville, too, who was sent to meet Bedford at Coldingham, and who again accompanied him to the Borders, describes him as 'ane of the surest and maist loving frendis' Mary then had in England (Melville's *Memoirs,* p. 170). While Father Stevenson adds, that 'so little' did Elizabeth 'care to make his visit acceptable, that he was instructed to press Mary for the ratification of the obnoxious Treaty of Leith' (Claude Nau's *Mary,* p. cxxxiii), he refrains from mentioning the fact that Bedford's Instructions bore that now the Treaty was to be purged of the obnoxious words to which the Queen of Scots had objected (Keith's *History,* ii. 482). Even Hosack declares that 'nothing could be more equitable than this proposal on the part of Elizabeth,' being, 'in fact, substantially the same as that which Mary herself had formerly made' (Hosack's *Mary and her Accusers,* i. 175). Father Stevenson further says that, 'as her proxy in the baptismal office,' Elizabeth 'selected a lady whose opinions were so pronounced that when her services were required at the font, she refused to assist at a Catholic function or even to enter a Catholic church' (Nau's *Mary Stewart,* p. cxxxiii). The lady so selected was the Countess of Argyll (*Foreign Calendar, Elizabeth,* viii. 142), Mary's illegitimate sister, her companion during the Riccio tragedy, and who was now so far from refusing to assist at a Catholic function, that she was afterwards enjoined by the General Assembly 'to make public repentance' for 'giving her assistance and presence to the baptizeing of

the King in a Papisticall maner'; and this repentance was to be
made in that chapel which Father Stevenson's words imply she as
a Protestant would not enter (*Booke of the Universall Kirk*, i. 117;
Calderwood's *History*, ii. 397). For acting at the baptism, Bedford
gave the Countess a ruby worth five hundred crowns (*Venetian
Calendar*, vii. 387).

[99] Pitscottie's *History*, 1728, p. 219.—The *Historie of James the
Sext* (p. 5) also gives the weight of the font as 'thre hundreth
threttie thrie unces.' The *Diurnal of Occurrents* (p. 103) says
that it was of fine gold, and 'twa stane wecht.' The Count de
Brienne had presented Mary, in the name of the King of France,
with a necklace of pearls and rubies, and two most beautiful ear-
rings; but 'much greater,' says the Venetian Ambassador, 'was
the present from England, as it was a font of massive gold, of
sufficient proportions to immerse the infant Prince, and of exquisite
workmanship, with many precious stones, so designed that the
whole effect combined elegance with value.' Morette carried to
her, from the Duke of Savoy, a large fan with jewelled feathers,
worth four thousand crowns (*Venetian Calendar*, vii. 387).

[100] *Foreign Calendar, Elizabeth*, viii. 151.

[101] Keith's *History*, ii. 479.

[102] *Foreign Calendar, Elizabeth*, viii. 226, 240.—The Lords were
reported to have afterwards got part of it at the mint unmelted
(*Ibid.* viii. 249, 256; Malcolm Laing's *Scotland*, 1804, ii. 108).

[103] *Diurnal of Occurrents*, p. 105.—This chronicler says that
from a fort, beside the kirk-yaird, were shot 'fyre ballis, fyre
speris, and all utheris thingis plesand for the sicht of man.'
Forty days were spent in preparing the fireworks, and the cost
was £190, 17s. 5d. (Robertson's *Inventories*, p. lxxxviii, *n.* 1).

[104] Buchanan has been often and fiercely assailed for the utter
incongruity of his *Detectio* with his Latin verses, especially those
prepared for the baptism of the Prince. Dr. Hume Brown, in his
eloquent vindication of the great Scottish Humanist from this
charge, remarks that 'it would be absurd to take as genuine
expressions of opinion the panegyrics of the Latin poets of the
Renaissance' (*George Buchanan, Humanist and Reformer*, 1890,
p. 203). Had Buchanan thought it worth while to clear himself
from the imputation of inconsistency, he might perhaps have stated
that, as the baptism had been long delayed, the Latin lines in
question were written before he knew of the Queen's guilty love

for Bothwell, which, even according to the *Detection*, she had not openly shown till October.

[105] Melville's *Memoirs*, p. 171.

[106] 'Nather did King Henrie cum ther, albeit he was in Sterling all that tyme, nather was he requyrit or permitted to cum oppinlie' (*Historie of James the Sext*, p. 5). · Relying on Camden's statement that Elizabeth expressly forbade Bedford and his companions to give Darnley the title of King (Camden's *Elizabeth*, 1675, p. 87), several of Mary's apologists have thrown the blame on the Queen of England. Many will question the soundness of Hosack's opinion, that, 'if the statement of Camden . . . is true,' Darnley's 'absence from the baptism is sufficiently accounted for' (Hosack's *Mary*, i. 168). Instead of pressing the counter-opinion that the excuse at the best is 'frivolous and unsatisfactory' (Keith's *History*, ii. 489 *n.*), it may be affirmed that there are good reasons for doubting Camden on this point, although corroborated by Nau, and by the writer of an anonymous *Life of Mary* (*History of Mary*, pp. cxlvii, 33). Not only is there nothing in Elizabeth's Instructions to Bedford forbidding him to honour Darnley, but the English Ambassador and his associates, in parting with their Scots convoy on the Borders, 'lamented that they saw so little accompt maid of the King,' and Bedford asked Melville to urge Mary to entertain him as at the first, 'for hir awen honnour, and advancement of hir affaires' (Melville's *Memoirs*, p. 172). When, on the day of the baptism, Du Croc flatly declined Darnley's thrice-repeated request for an interview, he did so, not because of Elizabeth's or Bedford's supposed scruples, but on the ground that, as Darnley was 'in no good correspondence' with Mary, his own King had charged him 'to have no conference with him' (Keith's *History*, i. p. xcvii). Morette, who arrived too late for the baptism, was anxious to see Darnley, and he also wished to see Morette; but Mary prevented them from meeting, by telling the Ambassador that she did not think Darnley would be pleased to see him, in consequence of the murder of Riccio; and by telling Darnley that Morette declined to meet him because of that murder (*Spanish Calendar, Elizabeth*, i. 622).

[107] *Foreign Calendar, Elizabeth*, viii. 155.—In the *Book of Articles* it is said that at the baptism 'it wes mervelous to behald the Quenis care and solicitude taken for preparatioun of apparell and riche garmentis to Boithuile, of hir awin stuff, be hir awin devise,

and commanding of the craftismen, quhen as na kynd of thing wes
appointed for the King in apparell furniture or utherwise'; and
at that time 'she causit begin to mak a passaige betuix hir chalmer
in the New Work or Palace, within the Castell of Streuiling and
the Great Hall thairof, thinking to have had access at all tymes be
that meane to Boithuile, quhome purpoislie she causit be ludgit at
the north end of the said Greit Hall' (Hosack's *Mary and her
Accusers*, i. 530, 531). Bothwell was not the only one who received
robes from the Queen in the month of the Prince's baptism
(Robertson's *Inventories*, pp. 61, 63, 69); and Forster reported in
September that, for the baptism, she had given Murray a suit of
green; Argyll, a suit of red; and Bothwell, a suit of blue (*Foreign
Calendar, Elizabeth*, viii. 131).

[108] Blackwood's *Mary*, Mait. Club, pp. 24, 28.—Lesley alleges
that 'for a time she did dissemble and forbeare outwardly to shew
and utter her most inwart hart and affectionate love, . . . for
the better reclaiming of the wandering mind and wavering wil of
the youthful unadvised gentleman' (*Defence of Mary's Honour*, in
Anderson's *Collections*, ii. 11).

[109] Hunter Blair's *Bellesheim*, iii. 108 ; Joseph Robertson's *Statuta*,
i. p. clxxx.—Hosack admits that, 'if there was the slightest evidence
to show that Mary was cognisant of the schemes of Bothwell, the
restoration of the consistorial jurisdiction at this time would be a
circumstance of strong suspicion' (*Mary and her Accusers*, i. 176,
177). The signature—which is printed in Malcolm Laing's *Scotland*,
ii. 75, 76—is dated 23rd December 1566; and four days later the
General Assembly petitioned the Privy Council to 'stay the same,'
as 'that conjured enemie of Jesus Chryst, and cruell murtherer of
our brethren, most falslie stylit Archbischop of St. Androes,' might
under 'that colourit comission' again usurp his former authority,
and by its means 'oppresse the haill kirk be his corrupt judgement'
(*Booke of the Universall Kirk*, i. 88-90). Knox wrote, too, a stirring
and uncompromising letter to the same effect (Laing's *Knox*, ii.
542-544). According to Knox's continuator, Hamilton had procured the signature from the Queen, 'by means of the Earl Bothwell,' and was coming to Edinburgh with a hundred horse to take
possession, but at Murray's instigation the Provost, 'for fear of
trouble and sedition,' prevailed on him to desist for the time (*Ibid.*
ii. 548, 549). Bedford, who had now returned to Berwick, reported
on the 9th of January that Mary had, at Murray's suit, revoked the

authority which she had so recently granted to the Archbishop (*Foreign Calendar, Elizabeth*, viii. 164 ; Thorpe's *Calendar*, i. 241 ; Robertson's *Statuta*, i. p. clxxx, *n.* 1). This revocation, unless merely temporary, favours Riddell's and Hill Burton's theory that the Queen issued, on the 27th of April 1567, a special commission to the Archbishop and several other clergy to decide in Bothwell's action for divorce (*Peerage and Consistorial Law*, 1842, i. 433 ; *History of Scotland*, 1876, iv. 221) ; and their theory is favoured by the print of the Falconar manuscript (Stuart's *Lost Chapter*, p. 91).

[110] Mauvissière had done his best for the Lords, when he saw Mary in August, and even Du Croc had pled for Morton (*Foreign Calendar, Elizabeth*, viii. 114 ; Stevenson's *Selections*, p. 165). With death staring her in the face at Jedburgh she said :—' Their is sum that hes greivouslie offendit me and of quhom I desyre na gret vengeance, bot committis them to the will of God, for I am sure that he will have regarde to my juste cause, yit for all aventures I pray yow that gif that cum to pass that eftir my decess thai returne to this realme, ye suffer them not to have any access nier my sonne, nor gouvernment or authorite nier his persone' (Small's *Mary at Jedburgh*, p. 23). For their pardon, Bedford and Murray did what they could with Mary at the baptism ; but if Bothwell, Atholl, and the other Lords had not helped, they would not have succeeded so soon (*Foreign Calendar, Elizabeth*, viii. 158, 159). Melville says that Bothwell spoke for them, 'to mak them his frendis, and to fortifie his faction be them ; for apperantly he had then alredy in his mynd, to perfourm the foull mourthour of the King . . . that he mycht marry the Queen' (*Memoirs*, p. 170). In the revocation of her abdication (*infra*, p. 486, *n.* 116), she is made to say that Bothwell, 'having court, was thair consiliatour and purchessar of thair remissiones' (*Memorials of the Earls of Haddington*, 1889, ii. 271). Chalmers, P. F. Tytler, Hosack, and Hill Burton allege that George Douglas and Andrew Ker, having by their violence given gross offence to the Queen at Riccio's murder, were specially excepted from the remission (*Life of Mary*, 1818, i. 197 ; *History*, 1845, v. 372 ; *Mary and her Accusers*, i. 169 ; *History*, 1876, iv. 181) ; but Ker got a separate remission on the same day as the others (*infra*, pp. 502-504).

[111] Tytler's *Inquiry*, 1790, ii. 78.—Catherine de Medici 'appeirit to be verie content' that Mary 'had sa graciouslie treatit thame' (Keith's *History*, i. p. ciii).

[112] Malcolm Laing's *History of Scotland*, 1804, i. 23 ; Hill Burton's *Scotland*, 1876, iv. 182.

[113] Anderson's *Collections*, ii. 271.—In the *Book of Articles* it is said that Mary and Bothwell ' departit togidder towart Drymmen the Lord Drummondis hous, abyding there five or sex dayis, and fra that come to Tullybardin. In quhat ordour they wer chalmerit during thair remaining in thay twa houssis mony fand fault with it that durst not reprove it. How lascivius alsua thair behaviour was it wes verie strange to behald notwithstanding of the newis of the Kingis grevous infirmety, quha wes departed to Glasgow and thair fallin in deidlie seiknes' (Hosack's *Mary and Her Accusers*, i. 531).

[114] Hosack's *Mary and Her Accusers*, i. 527, 528, 533, 534.—A month after the baptism, De Silva wrote to Philip that he heard that Mary had tried to take away some of Darnley's servitors, and for some time had given him no money for his ordinary expenditure (*Spanish Calendar, Elizabeth*, i. 612). According to the *Book of Articles*, ' that it was poysoun that grevit him apperit be the breking out of his body and mony uther circumstances, quhilk alswa James Abirnethy chyrurgian at the sycht of him playnelie jugeit and spak' (Hosack's *Mary*, i. 534). Alexander Hay, a ' physitian who ministred unto him,' is also said to have ascribed his illness to poison (Blackwood's *Mary*, Mait. Club, p. 28), Buchanan, both in his *Detection* (pp. 15, 16) and in his *History* (Aikman's *Buchanan*, ii. 488, 489), alleges that he had been poisoned ; and his statement—including James Abernethy's opinion, and the Queen's forbidding her physician to attend him—is adopted by Calderwood (*History*, ii. 328). Knox's continuator (Laing's *Knox*, ii. 537) and Spottiswoode (*History*, ii. 43) do not follow Buchanan's narrative so closely, but both affirm that Darnley received poison. Melville says that ' he fell seak for displeasour, as was allegit, not without some bruit of ane il drink be some of his servandis' (Melville's *Memoirs*, p. 173). Another says, ' he becam extreyme seik, so as his haill bodie brak out in evill favourit pustullis, be the force of yong eage that potentlie expellit the poyson, whilk was supposit to have bene gevin him to end his trublit dayis' (*Historie of James the Sext*, pp. 5, 6).

[115] Birrel notes that Darnley ' wes layand seike in Glasgow of the small poks, bot some sayed he had gottene poysone' (Birrel's *Diary*, p. 6) ; Nau says that at Glasgow ' he was seized with the small pox' (Nau's *Mary Stewart*, p. 33) ; and Bedford reported that he was

full of the small-pox (*Foreign Calendar, Elizabeth*, viii. 164), which Drury said was spreading in Glasgow (Tytler's *Scotland*, v. 510). In the *Diurnal of Occurrents* (p. 105) it is said that he had 'the polkis'—a name now given in Scotland to small-pox; but then, occasionally at least, as in Mary's reference to the 'pockie priest,' to a disease still more loathsome. Bothwell said he had the itch (Hosack's *Mary*, ii. 583). From the appearance of 'the reputed skull of Darnley'—which, in the museum of the Royal College of Surgeons at London, has found a 'strange resting-place among the illustrative crania of barbarous tribes from every quarter of the globe'—Sir Daniel Wilson surmised that he had suffered from 'virulent syphilitic disease' (*Proceedings of Antiquaries of Scotland*, xxiv. 423, 425). Sir Daniel was not the first to suspect this (Keith's *History*, ii. 497 n.; Malcolm Laing's *Scotland*, 1804, i. 24 n.).

[116] *Foreign Calendar, Elizabeth*, viii. 164.

[117] Nau says that Darnley 'sent several times for the Queen, who was very ill, having been injured by a fall from her horse at Seton. At last she went' (Nau's *Mary Stewart*, p. 33). Du Croc reported that she had an accident with her horse on the day she left Edinburgh for Stirling (Keith's *History*, i. p. xcviii), which was the 10th of December (*Diurnal of Occurrents*, p. 102). This, at Seton, must have been later.

[118] *Foreign Calendar, Elizabeth*, viii. 163.

[119] Keith's *History*, i. pp. xcix-ci.—During her illness at Jedburgh she earnestly recommended her son to the care of her nobles. Nau says that she did this, 'not doubting that the King his father would wrong him as to the succession to the Crown, to which he laid claim in his own right, and might probably take a second wife' (Nau's *Mary Stewart*, pp. 32, 33).

[120] Keith's *History*, i. pp. ciii, civ.—Catherine de Medici thought that a reconciliation with Darnley would greatly help Mary to compass her designs; and, in special, would cause Lady Lennox—who was favoured by many of the English nobles—to concur with her.

[121] Labanoff's *Recueil*, ii. 3, 6.

[122] Stevenson's *Selections*, pp. 173, 175; *Foreign Calendar, Elizabeth*, viii. 179.—Du Croc had reached Calais, when he was overtaken by a messenger from the French Ambassador in England, acquainting him with the dread news, and entreating him to hasten on with it to the most Christian King (*Venetian Calendar*, vii. 388).

CHAPTER XII

[1] Lesley's *Defence of Queen Mary's Honour*, in Anderson's *Collections*, i. 7, 8, 11, 12.

[2] *Diurnal of Occurrents*, p. 105 ; Birrel's *Diary*, p. 6.—According to Drury, Mary reached Darnley on the 22nd (Tytler's *Scotland*, v. 510).

[3] Crawford deponed that Darnley told her that he had heard 'that a lettre was presented to her in Cragmiller, made bye her owne divise and subscribed bye certeine others who desired her to subscribe the same, which she refused to doe. And he said that he woulde never thinke that she, who was hys owne propre fleshe, would do him anie hurte, and if anie other woulde do it theye shuld bye it dere, unlesse theye tooke him slepinge' (Hosack's *Mary*, i. 581).

[4] Crawford had said to Darnley that the Queen was taking him away more like a prisoner than a husband. ' He aunswred that he thowght little lesse himsellfe, and feared himsellfe indede save the confidence he had in her promise onelye, notwithstandinge he woulde goe with her, and put himsellfe in her handes, thowghe she showlde cutte hys throate' (Hosack's *Mary*, i. 583).

[5] Cecil's *Diary* gives the 30th of January as the day on which Mary and Darnley arrived in Edinburgh (Anderson's *Collections*, ii. 272) ; Birrel, the 31st (*Diary*, p. 6) ; and the *Diurnal of Occurrents* (p. 105), the 1st of February.

[6] Nelson, who had long been a servant to Darnley, who was with him when ' the Quene convoyit him to Edinburgh,' and who was extracted from the ruins of Kirk of Field, deponed that 'it wes devysit in Glasgow that the King suld haif lyne first at Craigmyllare; bot becaus he had na will thairof the purpois wes alterit, and conclusioun takin that he suld ly beside the Kirk of Feild' (Anderson's *Collections*, iv. part ii. p. 165). That the Queen intended to take him to Craigmillar is also mentioned by Crawford (Hosack's *Mary*, i. 582, 583) and by Nau (*History of Mary Stewart*, p. 33). Unless, therefore, the Kirk of Field had been thought of, in case Darnley objected to Craigmillar, the *Book of Articles* must be wrong in saying, 'it apperis weill thay had divisit the fatall hous for him before she raid to Glasgow' (Hosack's *Mary*, i. 534).

Robert Melville told De Silva that Darnley had chosen the house, because it had gardens and was 'in a good and healthy position' (*Spanish Calendar, Elizabeth,* i. 619). Nau not only states that he chose Kirk of Field against Mary's wishes, but that he did not want any one to see him until he had gone through a course of baths, and that 'he always wore a piece of taffeta drawn down over his face' (*History of Mary Stewart,* pp. 33, 34). Nelson, however, had understood that he was to occupy the Duke's house, and only learned his mistake when he arrived there.

[7] Forbes-Leith's *Narratives,* p. 117.—Lesley adds that it 'was considered by the doctors the most healthy spot in the whole town.'

[8] *Detection,* in Anderson's *Collections,* ii. 18.—The house 'contained a hall, two chambers or bedrooms, a cabinet, a wardrobe, and a cellar, besides a kitchen, apparently under another roof. Of these rooms, only three or four seem to have been furnished from Holyrood. The rest either stood empty, or more probably were left with the furniture which was found n them. The hall was hung with five pieces of tapestry. . . . The walls of the King's chamber, on the upper floor, were hung with six pieces of tapestry, which, like the hangings of the hall, had been spoiled from the Gordons after Corrichie. The floor had a little Turkey carpet. There were two or three cushions of red velvet, a high chair covered with purple velvet, and a little table with a board-cloth or cover of green velvet brought from Strathbogie. The bed, which had belonged to the Queen's mother, was given to the King in August 1566. . . . A bath stood beside the bed, having for its lid one of the doors of the house taken from its hinges for the purpose. It was in this room that the Queen sat talking with the King, on the Sunday night before his murder, while Bothwell, having seen the sacks of gunpowder emptied on the floor of the chamber below, played at dice with Argyll, Huntly, and Cassilis. . . . In a chamber on the ground floor, directly under the King's chamber, there was a little bed of yellow and green damask, with a furred coverlet, in which the Queen slept on the nights of Wednesday and Friday, and intended to sleep on the very night on which the King was murdered. It was in this room, which had a window looking into the close, and a door opening into the passage to the garden, that the murderers placed the gunpowder by which the building was hurled into the air; the

Queen's bed, it was said, being moved to one side of the chamber, so that the powder might be heaped up right under the King's bed' (Robertson's *Inventories*, pp. xcviii-c).

[9] No one, who accepts as true the statements in the Instructions and Articles signed by so many of Mary's Lords on the 12th of September 1568, can deny that she knew that some of her nobles were willing to despatch Darnley (see the passage quoted *supra*, p. 423, *n.* 89). Before Mary had set out for Glasgow to visit him in his affliction, De Silva had heard that 'the displeasure of the Queen of Scotland with her husband is carried so far, that she was approached by some who wanted to induce her to allow a plot to be formed against him, which she refused; but she nevertheless shows him no affection' (*Spanish Calendar, Elizabeth*, i. 612).

[10] Nelson's deposition in Anderson's *Collections*, iv. part ii. p. 166; in Malcolm Laing's *Scotland*, 1804, ii. 266, 267; and in Pitcairn's *Criminal Trials*, i. 501*.

[11] Nelson's deposition as in foregoing note.—In the *Book of Articles* it is said :—'Becaus thair wes a bed and some tapestrie of valour in that ludging sett up for the King befoir his cuming thairto, she causit remove the samin be the kepaires of hir gardrob to Halyrudhous on the Fryday preceding the murther, and ane uther wors wes sett up in the place thairof quhilk she thocht guid anewch to be wairit in sic use, seing it was destinat for the same' (Hosack's *Mary*, i. 537). Joseph Robertson has pointed out that in the inventory of the furniture lost by the explosion—an inventory authenticated by the Queen's subscription—there is no mention of one bed having been exchanged for another (*Inventories of Mary's Jewels*, p. ci). As that inventory was not drawn up until five days after Mary had married Bothwell (*Ibid.* p. 178), it would have been very surprising if it had contained any reference to such a suggestive exchange. Nelson's statement is to a slight extent borne out by the inventories. He says that the bed which was brought in place of the first was 'ane auld purple bed that wes accustomat to be carit.' The bed which 'wes tint' by the explosion was 'ane bed of violett broun velvot,' and had belonged to Mary of Guise (Thomson's *Inventories*, p. 124; Robertson's *Inventories*, pp. 19, 31, 177). The one which was removed was, says Nelson, 'ane new bed of blak figurat velvet.' The Queen had such a 'bed of blak figurit velvot' among the spoils of Strathbogie, and it was sent to her at Hamilton after she escaped from Loch Leven (Thomson's

Inventories, p. 153; Robertson's *Inventories*, p. 49). Buchanan, with his usual carelessness in details, says that it was the Queen's bed — not Darnley's — which was changed for a worse (Aikman's *Buchanan*, ii. 493). Nicholas Hubert, better known as French Paris, confessed that he had been sent by Margaret Carwod on the Saturday before the murder to fetch a furred coverlet from the Queen's chamber; and that next day Mary asked him if he had done so (Teulet's *Lettres de Marie Stuart*, 1859, pp. 87-89).

[12] Nelson's deposition, as in note 10.

[13] For Robert Melville's opinion of the salubrity of Kirk of Field see *supra*, p. 433, *n*. 6; for Leslie's statement on the same point, p. 433, *n*. 7; and for the opinion which Blackwood attributes to Murray, see Jebb's *De Vita et Rebus Gestis Mariae*, ii. 214.

[14] Melville's *Memoirs*, pp. 173. 174.—According to the *Book of Articles*, Mary tried to provoke a quarrel between Darnley and the Lord Robert, in connection with this warning and denial, 'thinking it mair semelie to have hir husband cuttit of be sic an accident proceding in contentioun then be the pulder and raising of the hous' (Hosack's *Mary*, i. 536). Buchanan represents her as trying also to involve Murray in the strife (*Detection*, in Anderson's *Collections*, ii. 18, 19).

[15] Richard Bannatyne's *Memoriales*, Ban. Club, p. 319.—Melville and Morton were not the only contemporaries of Darnley who referred to this trait of his character. He 'was sa facile as he could concele no secreit altho it mycht tend to his awin weill' (*Historie of James the Sext*, p. 7).

[16] Nelson's deposition as in note 10; Hosack's *Mary*, i. 536, 537; Forbes-Leith's *Narratives*, p. 118; *Spanish Calendar, Elizabeth*, i. 619; Aikman's *Buchanan*, ii. 492, 493; Calderwood's *History*, ii. 344.—In the following July, Murray told De Silva that the Queen of Scots 'had done an extraordinary and unexampled thing on the night of the murder in giving her husband a ring, petting and fondling him after plotting his murder, and this had been the worst thing in connection with it' (*Spanish Calendar, Elizabeth*, i. 665). Morette, who was in Scotland at the time of the murder, said that Mary had 'promised her husband that on the following night she would sleep with him, and in faith and as security for this promise she gave him a ring in pledge' (*Venetian Calendar*, vii. 389). The gift of the ring is mentioned in the contemporary ballad on Darnley's murder (Maidment's *Scotish Ballads and Songs*,

1868, ii. 12; Froude's *England*, 1887, viii. 163). Buchanan states that after Mary had left him, Darnley was somewhat disturbed by a remark she had made that 'it was about this time last year, that David Rizzio was slain' (Aikman's *Buchanan*, ii. 493). Calderwood (ii. 344) has borrowed this from Buchanan. Drury was informed that he went over the 55th Psalm a few hours before his death. He had said to some that he would be slain, and complained of his harsh treatment (Tytler's *Scotland*, v. 520; *Foreign Calendar, Elizabeth*, viii. 229).

[17] Hay confessed that the powder was placed in her room while she was upstairs with Darnley; Hepburn, that it was put directly under Darnley's bed; and both said that they were locked in beside the powder (Pitcairn's *Criminal Trials*, i. 497*-499*). Paris confessed that purposely he did not place Mary's bed where Bothwell bade him, and she ordered him to alter it. Perceiving that she knew what was intended, he said to her that Bothwell wished the key of the room that he might put powder there to blow up the King (*Ibid.* i. 508*). Nau says when Mary was leaving the King she met Paris, 'and noticing that his face was all blackened with gunpowder, she exclaimed in the hearing of many of the Lords, just as she was mounting her horse, "Jesu, Paris, how begrimed you are"' (*Mary Stewart*, p. 34). *Cf.* Jebb's *De Vita*, ii. 215.

[18] Keith's *History*, i. p. cii; Labanoff's *Recueil*, ii. 3. Cf. *Register of Privy Council*, i. 498.— 'The noise did awake those that were sleeping in the farthest parts of the town' (Spottiswoode's *History*, ii. 47). 'Great staynis, of the leuth of ten fut and of breadth of four futtis, war fundin blawin from that hous a far way' (*Historie of James the Sext*, p. 6). A facsimile of the contemporary drawing of the ruins is in the *Registrum Domus de Soltre*. Chalmers gave it with instructive variations.

[19] Buchanan says that Darnley and the servant who slept in the same room were strangled and carried into the garden before the house was blown up; that 'no fracture, contusion, or livid mark appeared on his body'; and that 'his clothes, which were lying near, were not only not singed with the flames, nor sprinkled with the powder, but were so regularly placed that they appeared to have been carefully put there, and not either thrown by violence or left by chance' (Aikman's *Buchanan*, ii. 494). This statement is more or less followed or corroborated by Calderwood (ii. 344, 345; iii. 58, 59), by Spottiswoode (ii. 47, 48), by Herries (p. 84), by Bishop Lesley

(*Narratives of Scottish Catholics*, pp. 118, 119), by Birrel (p. 7), by the
authors of the *Diurnal of Occurrents* (pp. 105, 106), and the *Historie
of James the Sext* (p. 6), and by the contemporary correspondence
(*Foreign Calendar, Elizabeth*, viii. 175, 177 ; *Spanish Calendar, Elizabeth*, i. 617, 619 ; *Venetian Calendar*, vii. 389). Bothwell told Sir
James Melville that he 'saw the strangest accident that ever
chancit, to wit the powder cam out of the luft [*i.e.* the sky], and
had brunt the Kingis house, and himself found lying dead a
litle distance from the house under a tre ; and willit me to ga up
and se hym, how that ther was not a hurt nor a mark in all his
body.' Melville also records the story of a page, that 'the K[ing]
was first tane fourth, and brocht down to a laich stable, wher a
sarvyet was stopped in his mouth, and smored be halding in of his
end, and efterwart laid under a tre, and blew up the house'
(*Memoirs*, p. 174). When Morette reached Paris he gave the
following circumstantial account :—'Towards midnight the King
heard a great disturbance, at least so certain women who live in the
neighbourhood declare, and from a window they perceived many
armed men round about the house ; so he, suspecting what might
befall him, let himself down from another window looking on the
garden, but he had not proceeded far before he was surrounded by
certain persons who strangled him with the sleeves of his own shirt
under the very window from which he had descended. One of his
chamberlains followed him, and was heard to say, "The King is
dead, oh, luckless night"; nor was the wretched man deceived,
for he and the father of the King both lost their lives' (*Venetian
Calendar*, vii. 389). 'His father was first said to have been
slain,' wrote Cecil on the 20th of February, 'but it is not true,
for he was at Glasco at that time : it is constantly affirmed that
there were thirty at the killing of him' (*Cabala*, 1691, p. 125).
Bowton and Talla alleged that, so far as they knew, only nine were
at the deed, and that he was blown into the air (Pitcairn's *Criminal
Trials*, i. 500*).

[20] Sir James Melville says that Darnley 'failed rather for lak of
gud consaill and experience, then of evell will. It apperit to be his
desteny to lyk better of flatterers and evell company then of plane
speakers and of gud men' (*Memoirs*, p. 153). 'He was,' says
another contemporary, 'a cumlie Prince of a fayre and large
stature of bodie, pleasant in countenance, affable to all men, and
devote, weill exercesit in martiall pastymis upoun horsback as ony

Prince of that eage, bot was sa facile as he could concele no secreit altho it mycht tend to his awin weill' (*Historie of James the Sext*, p. 7). In the spring of 1560, De Quadra understood that he was ' very promising and of good parts' (*Spanish Calendar, Elizabeth*, i. 135); and, in the summer of 1566, De Silva learned from Mauvissière that he mostly passed his time in warlike exercises, and was a good horseman (*Ibid.* i. 549). Drury tells that he was ' too much addicted to drinking,' and that he induced at least one Frenchman to partake too freely of *aqua composita* (Keith's *History*, ii. 403). Causin speaks of him as being ' accomplished with all excellent endowments both of body and mind' (*The Holy Court*, 1678, p. 812). He wrote a very neat hand when he was eight years old (*National MSS. of Scotland*, iii. 36). In Maidment's opinion, the ballad which he composed ' indicates no mean poetic power' (Maidment's *Scotish Ballads and Songs*, 1868, ii. 9-11). Knox's continuator thus describes him :—' He was of a comely stature, and none was like unto him within this island; he died under the age of one and twenty years; prompt and ready for all games and sports; much given to hawking and hunting, and running of horses, and likewise to playing on the lute, and also to Venus chamber : he was liberal enough : he could write and dictate well ; but he was somewhat given to wine, and much feeding, and likewise to inconstancy ; and proud beyond measure, and therefore contemned all others ; he had learned to dissemble well enough, being from his youth misled up in Popery' (Laing's *Knox*, ii. 551). Eleven months before his murder Darnley was said to be nineteen (*Papiers D'État*, ii. 112). Miss Strickland gives the 7th of December 1545 as the exact date of his birth, but owns that her only authority for the day is Mademoiselle Keralio (*Queens of Scotland*, 1851, ii. 325 ; *Life of Mary*, 1888, i. 56). Maidment follows Miss Strickland in the date of Darnley's birth, and yet says that he was murdered ' before he had attained majority' (*Scotish Ballads and Songs*, ii. 1, 8). Sir William Fraser falls into the same inconsistency (*The Lennox*, 1874, i. 467, 529).

[21] Keith's *History*, i. pp. ci, cii ; Labanoff's *Recueil*, ii. 3, 4.— Both Keith and Labanoff date this letter the 11th of February ; but it is clear from the letter itself, and also from her letter of the 18th February (Labanoff, ii. 6), that it was written on the 10th.

[22] Melville's *Memoirs*, p. 174.

[23] Labanoff's *Recueil*, ii. 6-10 ; Stevenson's *Selections*, pp. 170-172. —·In this letter Mary asks Beaton diligently to maintain the good

offices of friendship with the Queen-mother of France, whose
counsels and admonitions from time to time are so profitable to the
Queen of Scots that she intends ' to be governit be thame befoir all
uthers.' She also thanks him for that message of warning which
had arrived too late; but about the murder she will at present 'be
na mair tedious.'

[24] Stevenson's *Selections*, pp. 173-176.—The feeling in Paris
against Mary was none the less remarkable that Du Croc had left
Scotland less than three weeks before Darnley's murder (*Foreign
Calendar, Elizabeth*, viii. 169; *Venetian Calendar*, vii. 388). From
Stirling, on the 23rd of December, he had written, ' I can't pretend to foretell how all may turn ; but I will say, that matters can't
subsist long as they are, without being accompanied with sundry bad
consequences' (Keith's *History*, i. p. xcviii). He suspected that
Darnley's death was drawing nigh (*Spanish Calendar. Elizabeth*,
i. 630; *Foreign Calendar, Elizabeth*, viii. 176); and though
friendly to Mary, he may have injudiciously repeated in Paris what
he knew of the bad feeling between her and her husband. The
bare information that Darnley had been murdered was not enough
in the French capital to inculpate her. 'Until further advices
are received'—wrote Giovanni Correr, from Paris, on the 21st of
February—' this assassination is considered to be the work of the
heretics, who desire to do the same by the Queen, in order to
bring up the Prince in their doctrines, and thus more firmly to
establish their own religion to the total exclusion of ours ' (*Venetian
Calendar*, vii. 388, 389).

[25] *Foreign Calendar, Elizabeth*, viii. 194.

[26] In the *Book of Articles* it is said that there was ' mair travell
for the inquisition of certane money' stolen from Margaret Carwod,
than there was for the King's murder ; although it is admitted that
' thair wes a proclamatioun sett furth promitting a thousand pund
to ony that wald reveill the murtherars' (Hosack's *Mary*, i. 539,
540). This is an under-statement of the reward, for the minute of
Privy Council of 12th February runs thus :—' Quhilk horrible and
mischevious deid, as Almychty God will nevir suffer it to ly hid, sa
or it sould remane untryit, the Quenis Majestie, oure Soverane,
quhome unto of all utheris levand the caise is maist grevous, had
rather losse lyff and all ; and the nobilitie and Counsall likewyise
will leif na thing possibille undone quhairthrow the authoris of sa
ungodlie and strange ane interpryise may be revelit and regorouslie

puneist, as the offence justlie dois requeir. Quhairfoir hir Majestie, with avyise of hir Secreit Counsall, hes statute, ordanit, and decreed, that quhasaevir will first reveill the personis devysaris counsalouris or actuall committaris of the said mischevious aud tressonabill murthour, to the effect that thai may be dewlie puneist thairfoir—the first revelar, as said is, althoch he be ane culpabill and participant of the same cryme—sal haif fre pardoun and remit, quhairunto this present act and ordinance salbe sufficient warrand to him ; and, besydis that, salbe honestlie rewardit and recompansit to the lestand weill of him and his posteritie ; at leist sal haif twa thowsand pundis money, and be provydit of ane honest yeirlie rent at the sycht of hir Majestie and hir Counsall' (*Register of Privy Council*, i. 498). In the circumstances, Her Majesty could hardly have done less than this to discover the murderers of her husband ; and, however her conduct is to be explained, she did little more.

[27] 'The Queen-mother wrote very severely to the Queen affirming that if she performed not her promise to have the death of the King revenged to clear herself, they would not only think her dishonoured, but would be her enemies' (*Foreign Calendar, Elizabeth*, viii. 198).

[28] The letters which passed between Lennox and Mary concerning the trial of the murderers are in Anderson's *Collections*, i. 40-54 ; ii. 109-112.—In the first accounts of Darnley's death, Lennox was also said to have been murdered (*supra*, p. 437, *n.* 19). Drury heard on the following day that evil was intended against Lennox (*Foreign Calendar, Elizabeth*, viii. 175). A month after the murder he was safe among his friends at Glasgow (*National MSS. of England*, iii. 58).

[29] Elizabeth's letter, of 24th February, to Mary is thus summarised :—' Is horrified at the abominable murder of her husband. Most people say that she has not looked to the revenge of this deed, nor to touch those who have done it. Exhorts her to show to the world what a noble princess and loyal wife she is. Desires her to ratify the Treaty made six or seven years ago ' (*Foreign Calendar, Elizabeth*, viii. 180). Elizabeth afterwards said that Bothwell's power was so great Mary could not take action (*Spanish Calendar, Elizabeth*, i. 628).

[30] *Foreign Calendar, Elizabeth*, viii. 209.

[31] *Spanish Calendar, Elizabeth*, i. 619.

[32] *Foreign Calendar, Elizabeth*, viii. 185; *National MSS. of England*, iii. 58.—The story that Killigrew found the feigned mourning

arrangements out of order at the Court is told in the *Book of Articles*
(Hosack's *Mary*, i. 542), and more dramatically in the *Detection*
(Anderson's *Collections*, ii. 28), but both are wrong in the date indicated for Killigrew's interview, which was not within ten or twelve
days of the murder, but six-and-twenty after it. The *Diurnal of
Occurrents* (p. 107) is also wrong in saying that he arrived at Holyrood on the 19th of February, and next day 'gat presens of our
Soverane ladie.' He himself states plainly that he had no audience
before the 8th of March.

³³ Hosack's *Mary*, i. 538, 539; Robertson's *Inventories*, p. lvii.
n. 4.—To Bastien's wife, Mary gave a marriage dress which cost
£115, 11s.; to Margaret Carwod, one which cost £125, 15s.
(*National MSS. of Scotland*, iii. 53).

³⁴ According to the *Book of Articles*, Darnley's corpse was left
lying for three hours in the garden where it was found, before it
was carried by some of 'the irascall people' into a neighbouring
house, and there it remained for forty-eight hours—the door being
kept lest the multitude moved by the sight should have made
an uproar—before 'she causit the same be brocht' to the chapel
of Holyrood House by ' certane soldiours, pynouris, and utheris
vile personis, upoun ane auld blok of forme or tre '; and after
' the corps had lyne certane dayis in the chapell, quhair alswa
she beheld it, the same corps without ony decent ordour wes cast
in the erth on the nycht without ony ceremony or cumpany of
honest men,' although it had been proposed in Council that honourable preparation should be made for his burial (Hosack's *Mary*,
i. 539). Sir James Melville was not allowed to see the corpse at
Kirk of Field (*Memoirs*, p. 175); nor were Clairvaulx and Morette
(Birrel's *Diary*, p. 7). Sir James Balfour is plainly in error in
saying that the funeral was the day after the murder (*Historical
Works*, i. 336). One contemporary says :—' Upoun the fyft day
therefter his bodie was bureit in the tombe of the Kings at Halyruidhous, quyetlie in the night, without any kynd of solemnitie
or murnyng hard amang all the persounis at Court' (*Historie of
James the Sext*, p. 7). Another says that he was buried on the 14th
of February 'besyid King James the Fyft, in his sepulture, quietlie
(*Diurnal of Occurrents*, p. 106). Still another says that he was
buried on the 15th ' verey secretly in the night at Holyruidhous'
(Birrel's *Diary*, p. 7). In Lord Grey's Instructions, reference is
made to the ' contempt, or at least neglect, used in the burial of

the King,' which had 'caused great indignation' (*Foreign Calendar, Elizabeth*, viii. 214). The Queen paid £42, 6s. for embalming him; and for her 'duille,' which she ordered on the 15th, £142, 15s. (Chalmers's *Mary*, i. 207; *Archæologia Scotica*, iii. 80-82; *National MSS. of Scotland*, iii. 51, 53). Bishop Lesley denied that the Council had taken any order for the honourable interment of the King; and alleged that 'the ceremonies indeede were the fewer, bycause that the greatest parte of the Counsaile were Protestantes,' who 'had before enterred their owne parentes without accustomed solennities of ceremonies' (*Defence of Queen Mary's Honour*, in Anderson's *Collections*, i. 23; see also Forbes-Leith's *Narratives*, p. 119). In his *History*, Buchanan says that Mary looked earnestly upon Darnley's corpse, 'but gave no sign by which the secret emotions of her heart could be discovered' (Aikman's *Buchanan*, ii. 495); but in the *Detection* he ventures to assert that 'scho lang beheld, not only without greif, bot alswa with gredy eyis, his deid corps' (Anderson's *Collections*, ii. 27). In both, he alleges that Darnley was buried beside Riccio; but he had previously said that the Italian favourite was placed in the tomb of James the Fifth (*supra*, p. 400). Birrel records that on the 23rd of March 'ther wes ane solemne saule mass with a dergie soung after noone, and done in the Chapell Royal of Holyroudhous, for the said Henrey Steuarte and hes saule, by the Papists, at her Majestie's command' (*Diary*, p. 7). Drury also refers to this mass and dirge (*Foreign Calendar, Elizabeth*, viii. 198).

[35] *Diurnal of Occurrents*, p. 106.—That Mary was at Seton on the 16th of February is also implied by an entry in the *Register of Privy Seal*, xxxvi. 99. Cecil's *Diary* is therefore wrong in saying that she remained with Bothwell in Edinburgh from the murder until the 21st of February (Anderson's *Collections*, ii. 273). Bishop Lesley alleges that Mary would have continued 'enjoying and using none other then candle light' for a longer time, had not her Privy Council, moved by the advice of her physicians, pressed her to 'leave that kind of close and solitarie life, and repaire to some good open and holsome air' (*Defence of Queen Mary's Honour*, in Anderson's *Collections*, i. 24, 25). Drury mentions her sickness in his letters of the 29th and 30th of March (*Foreign Calendar, Elizabeth*, viii. 198).

[36] *Foreign Calendar, Elizabeth*, viii. 182; Tytler's *Scotland*, v. 516. —Hosack and Mr. Skelton imagine that Drury's statement about

the shooting-match is completely disproved by the entry in the *Diurnal of Occurrents* (p. 106), which bears that when Mary went to Seton, on the 16th of February, she 'left the Erlis of Huntlie and Bothwill in the Palice of Halyrudhous to keip the Prince unto hir returning' (*Mary and her Accusers*, i. 281 ; *Impeachment*, 1876, p. 179). They might have noticed, however, that, on the same page of the *Diurnal*, it is said that she returned from Seton to Holyrood on the 19th of February, while the alleged shooting-match did not apparently take place until the 26th, that being the day on which the losers paid for the dinner at Tranent.

[37] Hosack's *Mary and her Accusers*, i. 542.

[38] Concerning Bothwell even Father Stevenson says : — 'The evidence against him was so abundant and so conclusive that his guilt was unquestionable from the night of the murder' (Nau's *History of Mary Stewart*, p. clii).

[39] See *supra*, p. 439, n. 26.

[40] *Foreign Calendar, Elizabeth*, viii. 178, 181, 198 ; Birrel's *Diary*, p. 8 ; Spottiswoode's *History*, ii. 48 ; Anderson's *Collections*, i. 43–47 ; ii. 156, 157 ; *Cabala*, 1691, p. 126.

[41] *Foreign Calendar, Elizabeth*, viii. 182 ; *Cabala*, 1691, p. 126.

[42] *Register of Privy Council*, i. 500 ; *Foreign Calendar, Elizabeth*, viii. 194.

[43] *Foreign Calendar, Elizabeth*, viii. 198.—In this letter of 29th March, Drury tells that Mary had sent for David Ferguson, the minister of Dunfermline, and asked him if he knew not the deviser of the Mermaid. He said, No. 'Bothwell asked him whether James Murray had not said evil of him ; and he said that he had never heard him say well of him.' There is a facsimile of the rude drawing of the Mermaid and the Hare—Mary and Bothwell—in the *National Manuscripts of England*, iii. 63.

[44] 'Bothwell does all in the Court' (*Foreign Calendar, Elizabeth*, viii. 198).

[45] When Mary went to Seton six days after the murder she left her child at Holyrood under the charge of Huntly and Both-well (*supra*, n. 36). At Seton, on the first of March, she made over to Bothwell the bygone casualties of the sheriffdoms of Edinburgh principal, of Edinburgh within the constabulary of Haddington, of Berwick, and of the bailiary of Lauderdale (*Register of Privy Seal*, xxxvi. 24, 25). It was alleged that she gave Edin-burgh Castle and the superiority of Leith to Bothwell (*Foreign*

Calendar, Elizabeth, viii. 214). Mar was indeed persuaded to give up Edinburgh Castle, the discharge to him by the Queen and Privy Council being dated 19th March (*Acts of the Parliaments of Scotland,* ii. 547); and the discharge by Cockburn of Skirling who was made captain is dated two days later (Thomson's *Inventories,* p. 176). Cockburn was probably regarded as merely a tool of Bothwell's. As security for 10,000 merks, the superiority of Leith had, on the 4th of October 1565, been made over by Mary and Darnley to the burgh of Edinburgh (*Register of Privy Seal,* xxxiii. 110; *Burgh Records of Edinburgh,* 1557-1571, pp. 207, 229); but possession was not taken until the Queen was in Loch Leven (*Ibid.* pp. 213, 224, 227, 233).

[46] Anderson's *Collections,* i. 49; Labanoff's *Recueil,* ii. 18.

[47] Anderson's *Collections,* i. 48.

[48] Robertson's *Inventories,* pp. cxxv, 53.—Servay de Conde, in his note to the Inventory, does not give the exact date of this present to Bothwell; but the words, 'in Merche 1567,' imply that it was between the 25th and 31st of March. As Robertson points out, ' not long afterwards he had a gift of some of her mother's Spanish furs, and, if her adversaries can be trusted, she bestowed upon him the horses, armour, clothes, and furniture of her murdered husband.' Buchanan indeed alleges that Darnley's effects were so openly divided among his murderers and his father's enemies, that a tailor, who was altering the King's dress to suit Bothwell, was bold enough to remark, 'that it was but right, and according to the custom of the country, for the clothes of the deceased to be given to the executioner' (Aikman's *Buchanan,* ii. 499).

[49] *Register of Privy Council,* i. 504.

[50] It was on the 29th of March that Drury informed Cecil that ' the judgment of the people is that the Queen will marry Bothwell' (*Foreign Calendar, Elizabeth,* viii. 198).

[51] *Foreign Calendar, Elizabeth,* viii. 199, 200, 202, 207, 214; *Spanish Calendar, Elizabeth,* i. 636; Anderson's *Collections,* i. 52-54; ii. 106, 107.—Writing from Alnwick, on the 15th of April, Forster says that Lennox had come to Linlithgow accompanied by three thousand friends; but, receiving intimation that he must not have more than six in his company, refused to proceed (*Foreign Calendar, Elizabeth,* viii. 206). A few days before the trial Drury was assured that a man went nightly about the streets of Edinburgh crying lamentably, ' Vengeance on those who caused me to shed innocent

blood, O Lord open the heavens and pour down vengeance on me and those that have destroyed the innocent' (*Ibid.* viii. 203). This man was apprehended and shut up in a prison called for its loathsomeness the 'foul thief's pit.' It was also reported that a servant of Sir James Balfour's was secretly killed and buried, lest—having been touched by 'remorse of conscience or other folly'—his utterance might tend to the whole discovery of the King's death (*Ibid.* viii. 211).

[52] Tytler's *Scotland*, 1845, v. 518-521 ; *Foreign Calendar, Elizabeth*, viii. 207.

[53] *Register of Privy Council*, i. 522.—In the same document—the bond signed on the day after Mary's surrender at Carberry Hill—it is said :—'Wes nocht the triall be him impedit and delayit ; and the speciall authouris of the murthour being requirit to be wardit quhill the tryall of thair caus—howbeit the petitioun wes maist ressonabill and nocht repugnant to the lawis—yit could na part thairof be grantit, becaus the cheif murtherare being present maid the stay ; and than what ane inordinat proces wes deduceit to clenge and acquite him of that horrible deid all men persavit, quhen nowther the accustumat circumstances in caussis of tressoun nor the ordinar forme of justice wes observit, bot quhatsoevir the fader and freindis of the innocent Prince saikleslie [*i.e.* innocently] murtherit justlie desyrit, the contrair wes alwayis done. The said Erll, the day that he chosit to thoill law, being accumpaneit with a greit power, alsweill of wageit men of weir as utheris, that nane sould compeir to persew him' (*Ibid.* i. 521). The court sat for more than eight hours (Tytler's *Scotland*, v. 519). A copy of the proceedings, attested by Sir John Bellenden, the Justice-Clerk, is in Anderson's *Collections*, ii. 97-114. Hill Burton points out that 'the established practice was, when a criminal prosecution was determined on, for the crown to take the office of accuser,' whereas in this case 'Lennox is brought up as the accuser, and the tenor of the procedure looks like an arbitration in a dispute in which he and Bothwell hold opposite sides' ; and that, as nothing whatever was put before the jury except the indictment, they had no alternative but to acquit (*History of Scotland*, 1876, iv. 208, 211). . On the 20th of the following December, the Earl of Caithness, as foreman of the jury which had tried Bothwell, protested in his own name, and on behalf of his fellow-jurymen, that they should 'incur na scayth nor danger therthrow,' in respect of the protestation they had then made

when 'thair was na dittay sworn,' when 'thai knew him nawise culpable therof, and na sufficient verification nor testificatioun wes than producit befor tham that he wes gilte of the samin' (*Acts of Parliament*, iii. 10). On the 15th of March, the Justice-Clerk had bidden Sir John Forster 'never give him trust in time coming if the Earl Bothwell and his complices gave not their lives ere midsummer for the King's death' (*Foreign Calendar, Elizabeth*, viii. 192).

[54] Melville's *Memoirs*, p. 174.

[55] *Detection*, in Anderson's *Collections*, ii. 32.

[56] *Diurnal of Occurrents*, p. 108.

[57] Goodall's *Examination*, ii. 163, 342, 361; Forbes-Leith's *Narratives*, p. 121; Nau's *Mary*, p. 36; *Foreign Calendar, Elizabeth*, viii. 212; *Spanish Calendar, Elizabeth*, i. 637.—Lingard says that 'there cannot be a doubt of the fact' (*History of England*, 1855, vi. 73); but, in the opinion of such a Mariolater as Chalmers, the silence of the Parliamentary record shows that the 'assumption must be false' (*Life of Mary*, 1818, i. 215).

[58] *Acts of the Parliaments of Scotland*, ii. 550-552.

[59] *Diurnal of Occurrents*, p. 109.

[60] Hosack's *Mary and her Accusers*, i. 543, 545; Forbes-Leith's *Narratives of Scottish Catholics*, p. 121; Anderson's *Collections*, i. pp. lxiii, 107-112; iv. part ii. pp. 59, 60; Goodall's *Examination*, ii. 140, 141; Calderwood's *History*, ii. 351-355; Keith's *History*, ii. 562-569; Miss Strickland's *Letters of Mary*, 1843, i. 45-48; Labanoff's *Recueil*, ii. 37.—The copy printed by Anderson, by Keith, and by Miss Strickland, is dated the 19th of April; but Keith mentions that an attested copy in the Scotch College at Paris is dated the 20th. Calderwood does not say whether he followed a copy or the original; but his document is dated the 20th; and, in giving the subscriptions, he notes that Archbishop Hamilton's 'is counterfoote in the principall,' a fact which is not noted in the Scotch College attested copy. Mary's advocates have alleged that Murray was among those who signed. Hosack examines the point at some length; and—despite the facts that Murray was not then in the country, and that there is nothing to inculpate him save the memory of John Read—he holds that, although the evidence is not conclusive, the balance is strong against him (*Mary and her Accusers*, i. 301-304). Murray's name, however, is not in Calderwood's list; moreover, in the Instructions given by Mary's lords on the 12th

of September 1568, he is not included among those who consented to the marriage (Goodall's *Examination*, ii. 361); and Mary's confessor owned that he did not sign (*Spanish Calendar, Elizabeth*, i. 662). These facts were unknown to Hosack.

⁶¹ *Foreign Calendar, Elizabeth*, viii. 212; Tytler's *Scotland*, 1845, v. 403.—This statement of Kirkcaldy's is regarded as merely hearsay by Hosack, who declares, however, that:—'If Kirkcaldy had said that he himself had heard this notable speech of the Queen, we should have believed him, for he appears to have been a man incapable of wilful falsehood' (Hosack's *Mary and her Accusers*, i. 305, 306). According to this estimate of Kirkcaldy's character it may at least be held that he believed the Queen had said so. And it must be remembered that he was a shrewd statesman as well as a brave soldier. Nearly eighteen months before, Bedford had spoken of him as being as able a man in war or peace as any in Scotland or France (*Foreign Calendar, Elizabeth*, vii. 508, 509). Mr. Skelton does not believe that Mary ever said she would follow Bothwell round the world in a white petticoat, but, if she did, the occasion he thinks deprives it of importance. She was then, he says, 'being ignominiously carried into Edinburgh' from Carberry, and her nature 'prevented her from deserting those who, to use a vulgar phrase, were in the same boat with her.' Though she 'had never loved Bothwell in his prosperous days,' she 'may have clung courageously to him in his adversity' (*Impeachment of Mary Stuart*, 1876, pp. 192, 193). Alas for Mr. Skelton's ingenuity, Kirkcaldy's letter was written eight weeks before Carberry, and when Bothwell was not in adversity.

⁶² Four weeks after his baptism, the Prince—accompanied by the Queen and the nobles—had been carried from Stirling to Edinburgh (*Diurnal of Occurrents*, p. 105; Birrel's *Diary*, p. 6). Buchanan alleges that it was on the pretence, that the Stirling house 'stude in ane cauld and moyst place, dangerous for bringing the chylde to ane reum,' that she thus took him 'in the deip of a schairp wynter' to Holyrood, which was 'set in ane law place and a verray marische' (*Detection*, in Anderson's *Collections*, ii. 17). After two months, he had been taken back to Stirling to be placed, on the 20th of March, in the hands of the Earl of Mar (*Diurnal of Occurrents*, p. 107; Birrel's *Diary*, p. 7). 'On Monday [21st April] the Queen took her journey to Stirling to see the Prince' (*Foreign Calendar, Elizabeth*, viii. 213; *Diurnal*

of Occurrents, p. 109). Both before and after this visit, Kirkcaldy of Grange affirmed that she intended to take her child out of Mar's keeping, and place him into that of the man who had murdered his father (*Foreign Calendar, Elizabeth*, viii. 212, 215). It was even reported to Drury that she and Bothwell had brought the Prince back to Edinburgh and placed him in the Castle (*Ibid.* viii. 215)— a report which he was soon able to contradict as untrue, Mar having defeated their intention (*Ibid.* viii. 216). Nearly a month afterwards, Drury reported the much more incredible story that, at this time, Mary had tried to poison her child—then ten months old—with an apple, which was potent enough to cause the death of a grey-hound bitch and her whelps (*Ibid.* viii. 235). Bothwell, after his marriage with the Queen, says Sir James Melville, ' was very ernest to get the Prince in his hands ; bot my L[ord] of Mar, wha was a trew nobleman wald not delyver him out of his custody, . . . preing me to help to saif the Prince out of ther handis wha had slain his father, and had maid his vant alredy amang his famyliers, that gif he culd get him anes in his handis, he suld warrant him fra revenging of his father's death ' (Melville's *Memoirs*, p. 179). Melville further states that Mar did not intend to deliver the child into Mary's hands ' sa lang as he mycht resist ' (*Ibid.* p. 181).

[63] It was on the ninth anniversary of her marriage with the Dauphin that Mary was seized by Bothwell. Keith sought to identify, as the place of her capture, the bridge over ' Avon-water, a short mile to the west of the town of Linlithgow ' (*History*, ii. 570). Goodall (*Examination*, i. 367), Lingard (*History*, vi. 74), Miss Strickland (*Life of Mary*, 1888, i. 442, 443), and Hill Burton (*Scotland*, iv. 216) put it quite as near Edinburgh Castle—at Fountain Bridge. Malcolm Laing contends that it was at Cramond Bridge (*History of Scotland*, 1804, i. 79, 80). Robert Chambers, after minutely investigating the point, decides that it was where the Gogar burn joins the Almond river—an excellent place to surprise an unsuspecting victim, but quite as suitable for keeping up the show of an unwilling capture (*Proceedings of the Society of Antiquaries of Scotland*, ii. 331-336 ; *Domestic Annals of Scotland*, i. 42 and *n.*). De Silva said that it happened six miles from Edinburgh (*Spanish Calendar, Elizabeth*, i. 638); but Cuthbert Ramsay, brother of Lord Dalhousie, testified that it was at Calder Castle (Philippson's *Marie Stuart*, iii. 494).

[64] Melville's *Memoirs*, p. 177.—Melville says, however, that 'the Quen culd not bot mary him, seing he had ravissit hir and lyen with hir against hir will'; and that Bothwell boasted he would marry her 'wha wald or wha wald not; yea, whither sche wald hirself or not.' Sir James was allowed to leave Dunbar the day after the capture. His brother, Sir Robert, writing from Cairnie in Fife, on the 7th of May, to Cecil, says :—' Boduell did karye the Quenes Majestie violentlie to Dunbare, quhare sche is judgit to be detenit withoute her awyne lybertie. Dyvers noblemene—ye ! the moist part of the hoill sudjectis of the realme—is verraye miscontent therwith, and apperis will not beare with it. . . . And because of the Erle Boduel's presumptiuis attemptats in detenyng the Quenes Majestie against her will, in pressing her to mariage (quhilk he has persuadit her to grant unto), inlykmaner the ernist suting he makis to haif the Prynce in his custodie, with the pryncipals strenthis within this land, makis all mene to judge him pryncipall awtoure of this detestable murder. . . . I haif lernit, the said Lordis will in nowis think the Quenes Majestie at lybertie so lòng is sche beis in the said Erls cumpane, albeit he maye persuad Her Majestie to saye utherwise. The treughe is, quhaue sche wes first karyit to Dunbarre be him,' she ' commandit sum of her cumpane to pas to Edinbroughe, and charge the towne to be in armour for her reskew. Quhilk theye incontinent obeyit, and past withoute there portis apone fut, bot culd not helpe ; quhilk schame done be a sudject to our Soverane offendis the haill realme.' Sir Robert seems to have had his own doubts as to how the Queen herself regarded her captivity, or the plans which were being laid for her release, for he adds :—' Traisting ye will ryve my letter ; fore beyng in the cuntre is I am, dois not knaw quhither my Soverane wald allow of it' (*National MSS. of England*, iii. 60). Robert Melville is not the only one who refers to the attempt of the Edinburgh citizens to rescue her (*Diurnal*, p. 110 ; Philippson's *Marie Stuart*, iii. 492, 494). When the rumour that Mary had been ravished by Bothwell against her will reached Aberdeen, her loyal nobles and subjects there immediately sent (27th April) a message, desiring to know her pleasure, and what they should do ' towards the reparation of that matter' (Nau's *Mary*, p. clxxii). Father Stevenson absurdly regards their offer of help as a proof that they were willing to fight under her banners after she married Bothwell (*Ibid.* p. clvii). Among the score of documents which passed

2 F   449

the Privy Seal while she was supposed to be a prisoner in Dunbar, there is a respite to three men, for slaughter and all other crimes, 'tressoun in our Soverane Ladyis persoun, fyir, revesing of wemen, thift, and resset of thift allanerlie except' (*Register of Privy Seal*, xxxvi. 75). At Dunbar she also held, on the 29th of April, a meeting of Privy Council, but the sederunt is not given (*Register of Privy Council*, i. 507).

⁶⁵ *Foreign Calendar, Elizabeth*, viii. 217.

⁶⁶ See Birrel's *Diary*, p. 9; *Diurnal of Occurrents*, p. 110; *Historie of James the Sext*, p. 9; Laing's *Knox*, ii. 553; Aikman's *Buchanan*, ii. 504, 505; Calderwood's *History*, ii. 356; Spottiswoode's *History*, ii. 51.—Bothwell's intention to seize her leaked out before the purpose was accomplished (*Foreign Calendar, Elizabeth*, viii. 213, 214). Two days afterwards, Kirkcaldy of Grange wrote:—'She was minded to cause Bothwell ravish her, to the end that she may the sooner end the marriage whilk she promised before she caused Bothwell murder her husband' (Tytler's *Scotland*, v. 405; *Foreign Calendar, Elizabeth*, viii. 215). Tytler points out that the word 'ravish' is, in this letter, used 'in the sense of forcibly to seize: *rapio*'; and in some other contemporary documents it is used in the same sense, as for example in the 'band' entered into on the day after Carberry Hill, where it is said that 'he umbeset hir Majesteis way, tuke and reveist hir maist nobill persoun, and led the samyn with him to Dunbar Castell, thair detening hir presonar and captive' (*Register of Privy Council*, i. 522). The *Book of Articles* seems to distinguish between this ravishing or seizing her by the way, and the actual ravishing which followed at Dunbar (Hosack's *Mary*, i. 543). This plan of seizing the Queen was not new to Bothwell. He was charged with having fully five years before suggested to Arran a very similar scheme:—'We sall provyde and keip in cumpany sa mony freindis, servandis, and parttakaris, as salbe abill, quhenne hir Majestie is at the hunting upone the feildis, or utherwayis passand hir time mirralie, to execute this purpoise: that is to say, we sall cutt in pecis sa mony of hir counsalouris, servandis, or utheris that will mak us resistance, and sall tak hirself with us captive, and haif hir to the Castell of Dumbertane, and thair keip hir surelie, or uthirwyise demayne hir persoun at your plesour, quhill scho aggre to quhatsumevir thing ye sall desyre' (Pitcairn's *Criminal Trials*, i. 463*). Buchanan alleges that there were several reasons for the ravishing. The

Queen could not enjoy her intercourse with Bothwell, so openly
as she wished, without losing her honour; but by this plan his
egregious criminality would wipe away her infamy; and when he
obtained a formal pardon for this offence, its general terms would
also cover the murder of the King. Buchanan also asserts that the
last reason was the chief, and that for this ulterior object the plan
was believed to have been recommended by the Bishop of Ross
(Aikman's *Buchanan*, ii. 504). In her Instructions to the Bishop
of Dunblane, whom she sent to France to excuse her hasty marriage,
Mary refers to 'the plane attempting of force [by Bothwell] to haif
us in his puissance,' to his having 'awayted us be the way, accumpaneit with a greit force, and led us with all diligence to Dunbar,'
and there 'albeit we fand his doingis rude, yit wer his answer and
wordis bot gentill,' and when 'we saw na esperance to be red of
him, nevir man in Scotland anis makand ane mynt to procure oure
delivrance, . . . we wer compellit to mitigat oure displeasour, and
began to think upoun that he propoundit.' Not content with the
promise he had 'partlie extorted,' he would not agree 'to have
the consummatioun of the mariage delayit; . . . bot as be a
bravade in the begynning he had win the fyrst point, sa ceased he
nevir till be persuasionis and importune sute, accumpaneit nottheles
with force, he hes finalie drevin us to end the work begun at sic
tyme and in sic forme as he thocht mycht best serve his turne'
(Labanoff's *Recueil*, ii. 36, 38-41). Her mandate for prosecuting a
divorce from him in 1569 never hints that she was forced into the
marriage (*National MSS. of Scotland*, iii. 59); but in 1571 her
Instructions to Ridolfi do (Labanoff's *Recueil*, iii. 231, 232).

⁶⁷ *Spanish Calendar, Elizabeth*, i. 633.

⁶⁸ *Ibid.* i. 635.

⁶⁹ *Spanish Calendar, Elizabeth*, i. 638.—Froude quotes this statement almost *verbatim* (*History of England*, 1887, viii. 142). Hosack
perceiving its importance, and ignorant of the source whence it was
derived, boldly says:—'This is the speech not of the Queen of
Scots, but of Mr. Froude, who has put it into her mouth for the
obvious purpose of leading his readers to conclude that she was an
accomplice in the designs of Bothwell' (Hosack's *Mary*, i. 308).

⁷⁰ *Spanish Calendar, Elizabeth*, i. 639.—As 'the fullest, the most
satisfactory and explicit testimony of the forcible nature of the
royal victim's abduction,' Miss Strickland triumphantly cites an
Act of Parliament as stating that she was 'suspecting no evil,' and

was taken to Dunbar 'against her will' (*Life of Mary*, 1888, i. 442); but unfortunately the quotation is taken not from the Act proper, but from the summons of treason embodied in it (*Acts of the Parliaments of Scotland*, iii. 6, 8); and the writer of that summons apparently drew that part of it from Mary's post-nuptial Instructions to the Bishop of Dunblane (Labanoff's *Recueil*, ii. 38). In several of their documents preceding her abdication, the confederate Lords, however, undoubtedly refer to her capture and captivity as if she had not been a free agent. On the 11th of June they say :—'The Quenis Majesteis maist nobill persoun is and hes bene detenit in captivitie and thraldome be a lang space bigane' (*Register of Privy Council*, i. 519). On the 12th of June they say :—'Bothuile put violent handis in our Soverane Ladiis maist nobill persoun upoun the xxiiii day of Apprile last bipast, and thaireftir wardit hir Hienes in the Castell of Dunbar . . . and be a lang space thaireftir convoyit hir Majestie invironned with men of weir . . . quhair he had maist dominioun and power, hir Grace beand destitute of all counsale and servandis ; into the quhilk tyme the said Erll seducit be unlesum wayis oure said Soverane to ane unhonest mariage with himself' (*Ibid*. i. 520). The treasonable ravishing is mentioned by them on the 26th of June (*Ibid*. i. 524); and again on the 9th and 21st of July, along with the bondage, thraldom, and constrained marriage (*Ibid*. i. 527, 530). On the latter date they say :—'Our Soveraigne wes led captive ; and by feare, force, and, as by mony conjectures may be weill suspected, other extraordinary and mair unlauchfull meanys, compelled to become bed-fallow to another wyves husband' (Stevenson's *Selections*, p. 233).

[71] The process at the instance of Lady Bothwell was begun on the 29th of April; and on the 3rd of May the Commissaries declared 'the said noble lord to be separate, cut off and divorced *simpliciter* from the said noble lady, and she to be free to marry in the Lord where she pleases, as freely as she might have done before the contract and solemnisation of marriage with the said noble lord.' A summary of this process is printed by Father Stevenson in Nau's *History of Mary Stewart*, pp. clxiii-clxvi. Though the libel was dated 26th April, the procuratory for Lady Bothwell was dated 20th March. The approaching divorce was referred to by Drury on the 29th of March (*Foreign Calendar, Elizabeth*, viii. 198).

[72] The commission to the Papal clergy was dated 27th April

(Robertson's *History of Scotland*, app. no. xx.); but it has been questioned whether it was issued by Mary herself or by Archbishop Hamilton (*supra*, p. 429, *n.* 109).

[73] *Supra*, p. 452, *n.* 71.

[74] Robertson's *History of Scotland*, app. no. xx.

[75] Stuart's *Lost Chapter*, 1874, 21-23, 32; *Foreign Calendar, Elizabeth*, viii. 199, 221, 224; *Spanish Calendar, Elizabeth*, i. 635; *Venetian Calendar*, vii. 395.—Lady Bothwell's acquiescence was hastened, says Lesley, by her husband giving her the option of quaffing a cup of poisoned wine or setting her hand to the necessary document (Forbes-Leith's *Narratives*, p. 122). Before the end of March it had been reported in France by the English Ambassador, that, soon after Darnley's murder, 'the wife of one of the principal personages of the kingdom died by poison,' and that 'a marriage between this personage and the Queen would follow' (*Venetian Calendar*, vii. 390).

[76] The dispensation had been granted by Hamilton as Legate, on the 17th of February 1565-6. This long-lost document is given in facsimile in Dr. John Stuart's *Lost Chapter in the History of Mary Queen of Scots Recovered*; in the first vol. of *The Lennox*; and in the third vol. of *The Sutherland Book*. The dispensation has been characterised as 'a ridiculous forgery,' because it is dated in the pontificate of Pius the Fourth, who had died on the 9th of the preceding December (Walker's *Mary Queen of Scots*, 1889, p. 86); and this objection to its authenticity appears to carry considerable weight with Father Hunter Blair (Blair's *Bellesheim*, iii. 128 *n.*); but such an error by a Papal notary was by no means unprecedented (Renwick's *Glasgow Protocols*, 1547-1555, p. xiii). The Hon. Colin Lindsay has, to his own satisfaction, demonstrated its spuriousness. 'Murray,' he says, 'was evidently ignorant of this dispensation. It would have been a trump card in his hands . . . especially when he accused' Mary 'of immorality before the Commissioners at York and Westminster' (*Mary Queen of Scots and her Marriage with Bothwell*, 1883, p. 28). This is Mr. Lindsay's most striking argument; but it only proves that he has not taken the trouble to read the *Book of Articles* which was laid before these Commissioners. There it is plainly stated that the divorce for consanguinity 'procedit onelie becaus the dispensatioun wes abstracted' (Hosack's *Mary*, i. 544). Nor does Mr. Lindsay display an intimate knowledge of his subject when he says, 'I believe I am correct that

no contemporary writer alluded to this dispensation' (*Mary and her Marriage with Bothwell*, p. 28). He would hardly have ventured to make such a statement had he ever looked through such a well-known tract as the *Detectio*. Mr. Lindsay labours also to prove that the dispensation, even though genuine, was rendered inoperative because the Protestant rite was observed at the marriage of Bothwell and Lady Jean Gordon (*Ibid.* pp. 8-16). Unluckily for this contention, when two years later the captive Mary was thinking of a fourth husband, she granted a commission for prosecuting a divorce from Bothwell; and in that commission she relates that she has asked counsel 'of the gretast clarkis, best learned and expert doctouris in divine and humane lawis, as we could haif in dyvers cuntreys,' by whom she is informed that her 'pretendit maryage' with Bothwell was in 'na wayis lauchfull,' because, among other reasons, 'he wes befoir contractit to ane uther wyf, and he nocht lauchtfullie divorcet fra hir' (*National MSS. of Scotland*, iii. 59).

[77] *Diurnal of Occurrents*, pp. 110, 111; *Foreign Calendar, Elizabeth*, viii. 223-226.—Cecil's *Diary* gives the 3rd of May as the day on which Mary was convoyed by Bothwell and his friends to Edinburgh Castle; and it adds that they 'for fear of accusation kast thair speres from thame be the way' (Anderson's *Collections*, ii. 276).

[78] *Booke of the Universall Kirk*, i. 115, 116.—Craig not only washed his hands of this iniquitous marriage in presence of the church, but, on the 9th of May, faithfully admonished Bothwell in presence of the Privy Council. 'I laid to his charge,' he says, 'the law of adulterie, the ordinance of the Kirk, the law of ravisching, the suspicion of collusioun betwixt him and his wyfe, the sudden divorcement, and proclaiming within the space of foure dayes, and last, the suspitioun of the King's death, quhilk her mariage wald confirme. Bot he ansuerit nothing to my satisfactioun.' For his free speech on Sabbath, Craig was called before the Privy Council on the 13th of May, and accused of having passed the bounds of his commission in calling the marriage 'odious and slanderous befor the world.' He answered:—'The bounds of my commission, quhilk was the Word of God, guide lawes and naturall reason, was able to prove quhatsoever I spake; yea that their awn conscience could not but beare witnes that sick a mariage wald be odious and scandalous to all that sould heir of it, if all the circumstances therof were rightlie considderit; bot quhill,' he adds, 'I was

coming to my probatioun, my lord put me to silence and send me away' (*Ibid.*). It is not surprising that Bothwell threatened to hang Craig (*Foreign Calendar, Elizabeth*, viii. 230).

[79] *Diurnal of Occurrents*, p. 111; *Foreign Calendar, Elizabeth,* viii. 231; Tytler's *Scotland*, 1845, v. 413.

[80] The marriage-contract, dated the 14th of May 1567, is in Goodall's *Examination*, ii. 57-61; and Labanoff's *Recueil*, ii. 23-30.— Among the witnesses are Huntly, Lindsay, Rothes, Herries, Archbishop Hamilton, Bishop Lesley, and Lethington.

[81] *Diurnal of Occurrents*, pp. 111, 112.—'The mariage was maid in the palice of Halyrudhouse, at a preaching be Adam Bodowell, Bischop of Orkeney, in the Gret Hall for the Consaill uses to sit, according to the ordour of the Refourmed religion; and not in the chapell at the mess, as was the Kingis mariage' (Melville's *Memoirs*, pp. 178, 179). Drury reports that they were married at four in the morning, in the chamber of presence, before few witnesses, and not with the mass (*Foreign Calendar, Elizabeth*, viii. 232). One of Bishop Lesley's servants bears witness that they were married in a hall of the palace (Philippson's *Marie Stuart*, iii. 493). All these are contradicted by Birrel, who alleges that the marriage was 'in the Chapel Royall of Holyrudhous' (*Diary*, p. 9). To Catherine de Medici, Du Croc reported that they were married according to the Protestant rite (*Papiers D'État*, ii. 154). Perhaps, as Keith supposed, Mary meant to apologise for marrying a Protestant, and for marrying him after the Protestant form, when she instructed the Bishop of Dunblane to explain at the French Court that she did not intend to leave the religion in which she had been nourished, 'for him or ony man upoun earth' (Keith's *History*, ii. 599). When the Bishop got to Paris, he assured Don Frances de Alava that the marriage was celebrated in the Great Hall, and according to the Calvinistic manner by a most heretical bishop (*Papiers D'État*, iii. 31); and wound up his long speech to Charles ix. and his mother by remarking 'that even this marriage, celebrated according to the Huguenot rite, was brought about rather by destiny and necessity than by her free choice.' 'This excuse,' says the Venetian Ambassador, 'was listened to by their Majesties, who are well informed of the circumstances, but was not accepted by them, upon the ground that it was wrong to attribute any results to force which were openly brought about by free will and premeditated determination' (*Venetian Calendar*, vii. 396, 397). For Calderwood's account of the

Bishop's reception, see his *History*, ii. 366, 367. An early Mariolater describes the Bishop of Orkney as 'a camelion, a sorcerar
and execrable magitian, a perfect athiest' (Blackwood's *Mary*, Mait.
Club, p. 49). In the General Assembly he was charged with having 'solemnized the marriage of the Queen and the Earl of Bothuell, which was altogither wicked, and contrair to God's law and
statutes of the Kirk' (*Booke of the Universall Kirk*, i. 112); and
for having thus 'transgrest the Act of the Kirk in marrying the
divorcit adulterer,' he was suspended 'fra all function of the
ministrie,' until he promised to publicly confess his offence (*Ibid.*
i. 114, 131).

[82] *Venetian Calendar*, vii. 395; *Spanish Calendar, Elizabeth*, i.
646; *Papers D'État*, iii 31.

[83] *Register of Privy Council*, i. 522; Cecil's *Diary*, in Anderson's
Collections, ii. 276; *Book of Articles*, in Hosack's *Mary*, i. 545;
Calderwood's *History*, ii. 358.

[84] Stuart's *Lost Chapter*, pp. 95, 100; Robertson's *Inventories*, pp.
xciii, xciv; Pitscottie's *History*, 1728, p. 217; *Diurnal of Occurrents*,
p. 88.

CHAPTER XIII

[1] Sir James Melville affirms that Lord Herries entreated Mary
on his knees not to marry Bothwell, that he himself gave her
Thomas Bishop's letter to the same effect, and also intimated his
own opinion (Melville's *Memoirs*, Maitland Club, pp. 175-177).
Grange states that Du Croc also urged her to desist from Bothwell,
and warned her that if she married him she should neither have the
friendship nor favour of France (*Foreign Calendar, Elizabeth*, viii.
225).

[2] Skelton's *Maitland of Lethington*, ii. 205.—In his earlier work,
Mr. Skelton has not only owned that 'it is in vain to contend . . .
that Mary was utterly ignorant of the dangers which threatened
Darnley'; but has admitted that 'knowing in a general way that
the nobility of Scotland were leagued against him, she gave him no
warning, and did not lift her hand to save him' (*Impeachment of
Mary Stuart*, 1876, pp. 171, 172); and has avowed that 'when the
deed was done, it is not surprising that she should have acquiesced

in the action of the nobility' (*Ibid.* p. 195). These admissions are
all the more significant that they are freely made by one who,
among Mary's modern apologists, is unsurpassed in adapting facts
and manipulating documents. Morette, who according to Hosack
(*Mary and her Accusers,* i. 270) was 'an intelligent and impartial
observer,' was in Scotland at the time of the Darnley murder, and
had apparently little doubt that Mary was an accessory (*Spanish
Calendar, Elizabeth,* i. 621). De Silva, who was shrewd, well
informed in Scotch affairs, and, as became the Ambassador of Spain,
suspicious of information derived from heretics, seems to have had
less doubt than Morette.

³ Mary's chief champion argued that, even though she had been
guilty, her subjects had no right to lay hands upon her. 'King
David,' he said, 'was both an adulterer and also a murtherer. I
finde that God was highly displeased with him therfore ; yet find I
not that he was therefore by his subjects deposed' (Lesley's *Defence
of Mary's Honour,* 1571, in Anderson's *Collections,* i. 56). But the
Bishop of Galloway, in his famous sermon in her behalf, compared
the Queen of Scots to the Psalmist King of Israel in no hypothetical
way. 'All synneris,' he said, 'aught to be prayed for. Gif we
shuld not pray for sinneris, for whome suld we pray? seing that
God come not to call the rychteous, but synneris to repentance.
Sant Dauid was a synner, and so was shoe : Sant Dauid was an
adulterer, and so is shoe : Sant Dauid committed murther in slay-
ing Vrias for his wyfe, and so did shoe. But what is this to the
mater ? The more wicked that shoe be, hir subjectis sould pray for
hir, to bring hir to the spreit of repentance . . . Na inferiour subject hes power to depryve or depose their lawchfull magistrat, hie
or sho whatsumever, albeit thai committ whordome, murther, incest,
or ony uther cryme' (Richard Bannatyne's *Memorials,* Ban. Club,
pp. 139, 140). Brunton and Haig allege that this sermon 'bears
evident marks of forgery' (*Senators of the College of Justice,* 1832, p.
131). Mr. Skelton suggests that it was 'a *jeu d'esprit,* a satirical
effusion directed against the Bishop as much as against Mary'; and
thinks that this view is supported by another passage in which the
preacher confessed his own offences (*Maitland of Lethington,* i. p.
xxxi. *n.*). The other passage runs thus :—'I confes myself, yea,
this foule carkage of myne to be most vyle carioun, and altogether
gevin to the lustis of the flesche ! Ye, and I am not eschamet to
say the grittest trumper in all Europe, until sic tyme as it pleasit

God to call upoun me, and make me ane of his chossen vashelis, in whome he hes powret the Spreit of his Evangle.' It is by no means incredible that a sixteenth century preacher should have made such a confession in the pulpit of St. Giles. On the 9th of February 1896, one of the most cultured and popular preachers of the present day thus addressed an appreciative Edinburgh audience:—'He who watches the workings of self in his own mind and heart, he will not be forward to throw a stone at David; he will not be surprised at anything he reads about David or any other man. He will not wonder either at David's fall or at his subsequent self-deceit. I can fully, and down to the bottom, study the curse and shame and pain of self in no other heart but in my own; not even in David's heart . . . If my heart is worse than I know it to be, then God Almighty, with all the blood of His Son, and with all the patience and power of His Spirit, help me! Me, and all men like me; if there is another man like me in this matter on earth or in hell' (*British Weekly* of 13th February 1896). Terrible as are the charges brought against Mary in the *Book of Articles* and in the *Detection*, they are exceeded by those of Lesley, who, when in danger, lost heart, and avowed his belief that she had poisoned her first husband, the King of France; that she consented to the murder of Darnley; that she matched with the murderer, and brought him to the field to be murdered; and pretended marriage with Norfolk, with whom she would not long have kept faith (Murdin's *State Papers*, 1759, p. 57; *Hatfield Calendar*, i. 564). Mary's willingness to pension Bothwellhaugh shows that she did not disapprove of assassination (Labanoff's *Recueil*, iii. 354; Turnbull's *Mary's Letters*, p. 216); although to Murray's widow she professed to be sorry for the Regent's death (*Hist. MSS. Commission's Sixth Report*, p. 638).

⁴ Blackwood's *Mary*, Mait. Club, p. 35; Jebb's *De Vita et Rebus Gestis Mariae*, ii. 218.

⁵ Labanoff's *Recueil*, ii. 42, 49.

⁶ 'The only reason assigned by Bothwell for a divorce,' says Bishop Lesley, 'openly proclaimed his baseness and utter disregard of all decency, for it was the confession of his own adultery, committed with a woman of low rank, whom he produced in presence of the Calvinist ministers. He was in consequence proclaimed by them free from the bond of matrimony, and announcement was made from the pulpit, in particular by John Craig, a

preacher of Edinburgh, that Bothwell was now at liberty to marry any woman he pleased' (Forbes-Leith's *Narratives of Scottish Catholics*, p. 122). There are nearly as many lies as lines in this short quotation. Bothwell did not assign his own adultery as a reason for divorce ; he did not confess that adultery in the process for divorce ; he did not produce the woman in presence of the Calvinist ministers, nor in presence of the Commissaries ; he was not proclaimed free from the bond of matrimony by the Calvinist ministers ; he was not declared, either by the Calvinist ministers or the Commissaries, to be at liberty to marry whom he pleased ; and John Craig was so far from announcing any such liberty that he incurred Bothwell's violent displeasure for publicly proclaiming the contrary (*supra*, p. 454, n. 78). If Lesley had merely been Bishop of Ross, it might have been charitably supposed that he was ignorant of the constitution of the Commissary Court ; but he was also a member of Privy Council and a Lord of Session. Well did he know that the trial for adultery was not before Calvinist ministers ; that in that trial Lady Bothwell, and not her husband, was the professed pursuer ; and that the trial in which Bothwell was the avowed suitor was before a Papal Court. To vindicate his co-religionists and to clear himself, Lesley was un-scrupulous enough to add falsehood to falsehood. Concerning Mary's marriage with Bothwell he says :—'All the ecclesiastics and the greater part of the secular nobility, who made open pro-fession of Catholicism, publicly opposed such nuptials. Above all, the Archbishop of St. Andrews, the Bishops of Ross and Dun-blane, the Earl of Montgomery, and the Lord Seton, all of whom had ever been foremost supporters of the Queen, used on this occasion their utmost efforts to oppose a proceeding which was illicit, and likely to bring great harm and shame upon her' (Forbes-Leith's *Narratives*, p. 123). How, it may be asked, did Archbishop Hamilton oppose the impolitic and sinful marriage ? If, at Mary's expense, he is to be exculpated from the guilt of appointing his Papal delegates to try the validity of Bothwell's marriage with Lady Jean Gordon (*supra*, p. 429), that does not excuse his silence as to the dispensation. Or did he act as a witness to the marriage-contract between Mary and Bothwell to show his detestation of their nuptials ? Was Bishop Lesley himself less guilty than the head of the Scottish hierarchy ? How did he use his 'utmost efforts to oppose a proceeding which was illicit, and likely to bring great harm and shame upon her'? He signed the bond recommending Bothwell to her as a husband, before the capture and before the divorce (Keith's *History,* ii. 569; Calderwood's *History,* ii. 354); recommending as a husband—to the Queen he professed to esteem so highly—a married man, a profligate, a murderer! Lesley as well as Hamilton was a witness to the marriage-contract (*supra,* p. 455, *n.* 80); and according to at least one contemporary, he and the Archbishop, and the Bishop of Dunblane, were present at the infamous marriage itself (*Diurnal of Occurrents,* p. 111). Had these three Popish Prelates been half as faithful as John Craig, Mary might have been saved from the disgrace of the Bothwell marriage.

[7] Forbes-Leith's *Narratives,* p. 123.—When the Confederate Lords spoke of the Queen having been 'seducit be unlesum wayis' and by 'unlauchfull meanys' to marry Bothwell (*supra,* p. 452, *n.* 70) they intended probably to include witchcraft. It was said that she was bewitched before she married Darnley (*supra,* p. 342, *n.* 97), and on one of the placards posted on the Tolbooth door, a few days after the tragedy of Kirk-of-Field, it was alleged that she had assented to the murder 'throw the perswasioun of the Erle Bothwell, and the witchecraft of the Lady Buckcleugh' (Anderson's *Collections,* ii. 156). Drury makes a covert allusion to the means by which Lady Buccleuch bred Bothwell's greatness with the Queen (*Foreign Calendar, Elizabeth,* viii. 229).

[8] Nau's *History of Mary Stewart,* p. 124.

[9] For the statements of the Confederate Lords on this point, see *supra,* p. 452, *n.* 70; and for Sir Robert Melville's, p. 449. Malcolm Laing holds that 'the gloss put upon her marriage by a part of the lords was necessary from their situation; especially before the rest had determined whether to conceal or to expose her guilt and deprive her of the crown' (*Scotland,* 1804, ii. 120). The language was used to within a few days of her abdication.

[10] *Supra,* p. 158.

[11] Anderson's *Collections,* i. 88.

[12] Lindsay's *Mary and her Marriage with Bothwell,* 1883, p. 47.

[13] *Supra,* pp. 105, 348.

[14] *Spanish Calendar, Elizabeth,* i. 662. Her confessor said she had no knowledge of the murder (*Ibid.* i. 665).

[15] 'No entreaties,' says Joseph Robertson, 'could overcome Bothwell's tender regard for the Protestant religion; the conscience

which smiled at murder and adultery was appalled by the forms of a heterodox belief' (*Inventories of Mary's Jewels*, p. xciv). It is true that, from November 1565 to the summer of 1567, Bothwell showed an unconquerable aversion to the mass (Laing's *Knox*, ii. 514, 520 ; Wright's *Elizabeth*, i. 220 ; Stevenson's *Selections*, pp. 153, 157 ; *Diurnal of Occurrents*, p. 104) ; but it does not appear that in this scrupulosity he was credited with sincerity of principle or Protestant zeal. Randolph, in naming those who had refused to go to mass, says :— ' Of them all Bothwell is stowtest but worst thought of ' (Stevenson's *Selections*, p. 153). Bedford, in telling that Mary's entreaties in this matter were ineffectual with Bothwell and Huntly, adds :—' that th'one so did, I mervell not a litell' (*Ibid.* p. 157). Only six days before he had said that Bothwell neither feared God nor loved justice (*Ibid.* p. 155). In the summer of 1561 Bothwell had been regarded as an uncompromising Papist (*Venetian Calendar*, vii. 333) ; and down at least to April 1564 as an adversary of the Protestants (*Foreign Calendar, Elizabeth*, vii. 122 ; Laing's *Knox*, vi. 540). Calderwood alleges that, at his marriage with Mary, the Bishop of Orkney not only declared the bridegroom's ' repentance for his former offensive life ' ; but ' how he had joyned himself to the Kirk, and embraced the Reformed religioun ' (Calderwood's *History*, ii. 358).

¹⁶ *Venetian Calendar*, vii. 393.—As in the same despatch Murray is said to be ' about thirty years of age,' although he must have been quite six-and-thirty, implicit trust cannot be given to the statement that Bothwell was only five-and-twenty when he married the Queen. Mary herself speaks of him as in ' his verie youth ' at his father's death (Labanoff's *Recueil*, ii. 33) ; and it is certain that his father died in the autumn of 1556 (Hailes's *Remarks on the History of Scotland*, 1773, pp. 173-175). In November 1560, Throckmorton describes him as ' a glorious, rash, and hazardous young man ' (Hardwick's *State Papers*, i. 149) ; and, fully three years later, Sir Henry Percy still speaks of him as being young (*Foreign Calendar, Elizabeth*, vii. 83). If he had attained thirty, it is not at all likely that he was far beyond it, when he won Mary's hand in 1567 ; and she was then in her twenty-fifth year. William Tytler held that at that time he could not have been less than sixty (*Inquiry into the Evidence against Mary*, third ed., p. 280) ; bu when he issued the next edition of his work he reduced the estimate to forty-four (*Inquiry*, 1790, ii. 155) ; Chalmers

reduced it still further to thirty-six (*Life of Mary*, 1818. ii. 206) ; and Schiern, to thirty or thirty-one (*Life of Bothwell*, translated by Berry, p. 3). But Mr. Skelton still asserts that he was old enough to be her father (*Maitland of Lethington*, ii. 187). It has been supposed that Bothwell's father divorced his wife, Agnes Sinclair, that he might marry Mary of Guise (*Bannatyne Miscellany*, iii. 279), who, he alleged, 'promest faithfullie, be hir hand writ, at twa sindre tymis' to marry him (*Ibid.* iii. 414). He had also been willing to marry more than one presumptive heiress to the English throne (*supra*, p. 192, *n.* 77). Bloody Mackenzie remarks :—'It was hereditary to the House of Hales to be kinde to the widow Queens, as Patrick to Queen Jean, widow to King James 1st ; his son to Queen Mary of Gelderland ; Patrick Earl of Bothwell to Queen Mary of Lorain, widow to King James 5th ; his sone to Queen Mary' (*Bannatyne Miscellany*, iii. 279 *n.*).

[17] Forbes-Leith's *Narratives*, p. 117.—The question of Bothwell's beauty has been discussed by Lord Hailes (*Remarks on the History of Scotland*, 1773, pp. 167-172), and by Joseph Robertson (*Inventories*, pp. xxvi, xxvii, xcv, xcvi). His language was so filthy that Melville left his company (Melville's *Memoirs*, Mait. Club. p. 179) ; but the conversation which so disgusted Melville was not addressed to 'the gentlewomen,' as the early editions of Sir James's *Memoirs* (1683, p. 80 ; 1735, p. 160 ; 1751, p. 157) erroneously bear, and as Froude has repeated (*History of England*, 1887, viii. 153). His vicious life is not infrequently alluded to in the contemporary correspondence (*Foreign Calendar, Elizabeth*, vi. 383 ; vii. 327 ; viii. 229, 285).

[18] Forbes-Leith's *Narratives*, p. 123.—Lesley says that this reception of the Eucharist was 'on the Feast of Pentecost,' which was on the 18th of May. But even on this matter it may be doubted whether he was speaking the truth. Don Frances de Alava was assured by Archbishop Beaton that, on the day after her marriage with Bothwell, Mary publicly attended mass with a thousand persons ; but, on the other hand, he was assured by the Bishop of Dunblane, who had arrived in Paris on the 12th of June, that, so far as he knew, she had had no mass said since her marriage (Teulet's *Papiers D'État*, iii. 31, 32). About the same time, one of Mary's French servants told De Silva that she 'maintained the Catholic service in her chapel, to which many went as formerly' (*Spanish Calendar, Elizabeth*, i. 646).

[19] *Foreign Calendar, Elizabeth*, viii. 237, 240.

[20] 'The Duke openly uses great reverence to the Queen, ordinarily bare-headed, which she seems she would have otherwise, and will sometimes take his cap and put it on' (*Foreign Calendar, Elizabeth*, viii. 237).

[21] 'He was sa beastly and suspitious, that he sufferit hir not to pass ouer a day in patience,' and 'making hir cause to sched aboundance of salt teares' (Melville's *Memoirs*, p. 182). 'Lethington also told me,' writes Du Croc, 'that from the day of the marriage there had been no end of Mary's tears and lamentations; for Bothwell would not allow her to look at or be looked on by anybody, for he knew very well that she loved her pleasure and passed her time like any other devoted to the world' (Raumer's *Elizabeth and Mary*, p. 102; Teulet's *Papiers D'État*, ii. 170). Before the marriage there had been a great unkindness between her and Bothwell for half a day. He had the reputation of being the most jealous man alive; and it was believed that they would not long agree after they were married (*Foreign Calendar, Elizabeth*, viii. 229).

[22] *Spanish Calendar, Elizabeth*, i. 648; *Papiers D'État*, ii. 170; Raumer's *Elizabeth and Mary*, p. 102; *Foreign Calendar, Elizabeth*, viii. 229, 292; Stevenson's *Selections*, p. 234.

[23] *Papiers D'État*, ii. 155; Raumer's *Elizabeth and Mary*, p. 99.

[24] *Spanish Calendar, Elizabeth*, i. 648.

[25] An offer of help had been sent to Mary from Aberdeen, on the 27th of April (*supra*, p. 449). On the 2nd of May Drury relates that divers of the nobles had convened at Stirling, and sent to the Queen to know her pleasure and mind (*Foreign Calendar, Elizabeth*, viii. 221). In the draft bond, dated at Stirling on the 1st of May, they bind themselves to strive, to the utmost of their power, and by all possible means, to set their Queen at liberty; and to defend her, the Prince, and his keepers (*Register of Privy Council*, xiv. 315). In the bond of 16th June it is stated that 'the fame' of Darnley's murder 'wes in sic sort blawin abrede and dispersit in all realmis, and amangis all Cristiane nationis, that this cuntre wes abhorrit and vilipendit, the nobilitie and haill people na uther wayis estemit bot as thai had bene all participant of sa unworthie and horribill a murthour, that nane of ony of the Scottis natioun, thoch he wer nevir sa innocent, wes abill for schame, in ony foreyn cuntre, to schaw his face' (*Ibid.* i. 521; Cf. *Booke of the Kirk*, i. 108). Sir James Melville alleges that it was this foreign

feeling which drove the Scots to revenge the murder (*Memoirs*, p. 181).

[26] Birrel says this was on the 11th of June (*Diary*, p. 9); but the *Diurnal* (p. 112) says the 10th; and Drury says Tuesday (*Foreign Calendar, Elizabeth*, viii. 248) which was the 10th. Her proclamation is dated at Borthwick on the 11th (*British Museum, Add. MSS.*, 23, 241).

[27] *Foreign Calendar, Elizabeth*, viii. 246.—'The Lords finding he was escaped, cried out of him, bidding him come out, traitor, murderer, and butcher, and maintain his challenge, *with divers undutiful and unseemly speeches used against their Queen and Sovereign, too evil and unseemly to be told, which poor Princess she did with her speech defend, wanting other means for her revenge*' (*Ibid.* viii. 248, 249). The passage in italics has been erased in the despatch. Birrel says: 'They desyred the Earll Bothuell might be delivered to them; but the Lord Borthuick ansuered, that he wes fled to Dumbar. Therafter, they desyred the Queine to come and assist them in perseute of her husband's murther, and she altogether refusit' (*Diary*, p. 9). 'It apperit weill,' the Lords afterwards said, 'quhen at the first enterprise we came about Borthuik, we ment nathing to the Quenes person; in sa far as, hearing that he was escaped out of the hous, we insisted na farther to persew the same, it being maist easie to have bene taken, but cam bak to Edinburgh, there to consult how farther we suld proceid for his apprehension' (Stevenson's *Selections*, p. 235).

[28] *Diurnal of Occurrents*, p. 113; Malcolm Laing's *Scotland*, 1804, ii. 107, 108; *Foreign Calendar, Elizabeth*, viii. 249, 250.

[29] *Diurnal of Occurrents*, pp. 112, 113; Malcolm Laing's *Scotland*, ii. 108; *Register of Privy Council*, i. 519.

[30] *Foreign Calendar, Elizabeth*, viii. 254, 256; Teulet's *Papiers D'État*, ii. 162-166; Malcolm Laing's *Scotland*, ii. 110-113; *Diurnal of Occurrents*, pp. 114, 115; *Historie of James the Sext*, pp. 12, 13; Melville's *Memoirs*, pp. 183-185; Aikman's *Buchanan*, ii. 519-522; Nau's *History*, pp. 44-49.—In her appeal to foreign princes, Mary alleges that the Lords promised that, if she put herself into their hands, they would disperse their men, and serve, recognise, and honour her as their natural Princess (Teulet's *Papiers D'État*, ii. 244). But Melville says that the promise was on condition that she would abandon Bothwell (*Memoirs*, p. 183). And when Lethington was afterwards taking her part openly, he said :—'That same

nycht the Queine was brocht to Edinburgh, I made the offer to hir, gif shoe wold abandon my Lord Bothuel, sho shuld have as thankfull obedience as ever sho had sen sho come in Scotland. Bot noewayis wald schoe consent to leive my Lord Bothuell ; and sua shoe was put into Lochlevin' (Richard Bannatyne's *Memoriales*, p. 126).

[31] Melville's *Memoirs*, p. 185.—Melville states that some suspected this letter to be invented.

[32] *Foreign Calendar, Elizabeth*, viii. 254 ; Birrel's *Diary*, p. 10.— De Silva, no doubt, mistook the name of the place, when he said that this banner had been displayed on Edinburgh Castle (*Spanish Calendar, Elizabeth*, i. 648).

[33] *Historie of James the Sext*, p. 13 ; *Foreign Calendar, Elizabeth*, viii. 254 ; Aikman's *Buchanan*, ii. 523.

[34] Malcolm Laing's *Scotland*, 1804, ii. 114.—'The people of the toun convenit unto hir in great nomber, and persaving hir so afflicted in mynd, had pitie and compassioun of hir estait. The Lords persaving that, came unto hir with dissimulat countenance, with reverence and faire speachis, and said that ther intentioun was nawayis to thrall hir ; and therfore immediatlie wald repone hir with freedome to hir awin Palace of Halyruidhous, to do as she list ; wherby she was so pacifeit as the people willinglie depairtit' (*Historie of James the Sext*, p. 13).

[35] 'Though her body be restrained, yet her heart is not dismayed ; she has given to divers very bitter words' (*Foreign Calendar, Elizabeth*, viii. 254).

[36] Sir James Balfour had been made Captain of Edinburgh Castle on the 8th of May (*Diurnal of Occurrents*, p. 111). He declared that Mary had told him that she was determined to have Darnley killed, and had requested him to take charge of the business, and had, on his refusal, upbraided him as a coward (*Spanish Calendar, Elizabeth*, i. 673). In Knox's opinion Balfour was not distinguished for truthfulness (Laing's *Knox*, i. 202) ; in Richard Bannatyne's, 'he could wagge as the busse wagged' (*Memoriales*, p. 302). For an opinion quite as candid see *infra*, p. 488.

[37] Malcolm Laing's *Scotland*, ii. 113, 114.—Claude Nau gives an account of her treatment during the short time she was allowed to remain in Holyrood, and of her journey by night to Loch Leven. 'The hardest heart among the most cruel barbarians,' he says, 'would have been moved to pity at the departure of this poor princess,' who 'was permitted to take no other clothes than her

night-dress, nor any linen.' 'At the edge of the lake she was met by the laird and his brothers, who conducted her into a room on the ground floor, furnished only with the laird's furniture' (Nau's *History of Mary*, pp. 54-56). Nau assigns as the reason for the midnight journey, the fear 'that if her departure should be in the sight of the people, some insurrection would follow.' Drury alleges that it was to avoid the reproachful words of the people, 'burn her, burn her, she is not worthy to live, kill her, drown her' (*Foreign Calendar, Elizabeth*, viii. 256). Nau says that, 'partly from distress of mind, partly from the fear of being poisoned,' she ate nothing. The relentless Drury explains that she made a vow that she would eat no flesh till she saw Bothwell again, and that she kept her vow until she reached Loch Leven. The ignominy of her journey, as pictured by Nau, is quite eclipsed by the account given in the anonymous *Life* quoted by Father Stevenson (Nau's *Mary*, p. clx, *n.*); but that account has been drawn apparently from Adam Blackwood (Jebb's *De Vita et Rebus Gestis Mariae*, ii. 219, 220; Blackwood's *History of Mary*, Maitland Club, p. 40). Lesley says :—
' In the night privily she was conveyed, and with haste, in disguised apparel, to the strong forte of Lochleven, and after a few daies, being stripped out and spoyled of al her princely attirement, was clothed with a course broune cassoke' (*Defence of Mary's Honour*, in Anderson's *Collections*, i. 36). While Mary was in Loch Leven there ' wes assignit to ane part of the furnessing and provisioun of her house' the sum of £172, 'of the fewmales of the lands of Vrquhart, Glenmoreistoun, and utheris'; but it was still due to the Laird of Loch Leven long after her escape (*The Chiefs of Grant*, 1883, ii. 11). Eleven weeks after her arrival in Loch Leven, she urged Robert Melville to send her certain dresses, and also her 'madynis clais, for thai ar naikit' (*Maitland Miscellany*, iii. 186, 187; Labanoff's *Recueil*, ii. 61, 62). For a list of the clothing sent to her from Loch Leven three days after her escape, see *infra*, pp. 511, 512. When in Carlisle she wished more of her apparel from Loch Leven, but offered nothing to the English messengers for their trouble or expense (Wright's *Elizabeth*, i. 288). When at Bolton, she gave Robert Melville a formal receipt for the jewels, clothing, and horses she had committed to his charge while in Loch Leven (*Maitland Miscellany*, iii. 187, 188; Labanoff's *Recueil*, ii. 218).

[38] Burns-Begg's *History of Loch Leven Castle*, 1887, pp. 33, 34, 37-40.

[39] Knox has given an account of this double interview (Laing's *Knox*, ii. 371-376). 'Mary,' says Mr. Skelton, 'after a few more Old Testament precedents illustrative of Jewish justice had been produced, adroitly contrived to turn the conversation to other subjects—Alexander Gordon, Ruthven, Lethington, the Argylls' (*Maitland of Lethington*, ii. 40). Mary's adroitness on this occasion was by no means conspicuous, as she only imparted a turn to the conversation after a whole night had elapsed.

[40] The warrant charging Lord Lindsay, Lord Ruthven, and the Laird of Loch Leven to convey her to the house of the latter, and there to keep her surely, is signed by Atholl, Morton, Glencairn, Mar, Grahame, Hume, Sanquhar, Semple, and Ochiltree. Mr. Burns-Begg, in his *History of Loch Leven Castle*, p. 49, has omitted Hume and Sanquhar.

[41] The warrant for sequestrating her Majesty's person is in Malcolm Laing's *Scotland*, 1804, ii. 116-118; in the *Registrum Honoris de Morton*, Ban. Club, i, 24-26; in the *Maitland Miscellany*, i. 250-252; and in the *National MSS. of Scotland*, iii. 55.—The same reasons for imprisoning the Queen are given in more ample form in 'The Answer of the Lords of Scotland,' handed to Throckmorton, on the 20th of July, by Lethington (Stevenson's *Selections*, pp. 232-237).

[42] *Spanish Calendar, Elizabeth*, i. 618, 619, 623, 641.—Though the suspicions raised by Darnley's murder alienated many of Mary's English supporters, De Silva tells, a month after that event, that she had still many friends, who could not believe that she had any hand in it, and who would not believe even although they had more proof (*Ibid.* i. 626). Towards the end of April he reports that certain Catholics were sure that Bothwell could not be culpable, but they greatly feared that she would marry him and were anxious to prevent it (*Ibid.* i. 637, 638).

[43] In Teulet's opinion the documents, which he edited for the Bannatyne Club, 'prove beyond doubt the violent and mad passion of Mary Stuart for the Earl of Bothwell' (*Papiers D'État*, i. p. xxi). Patrick Fraser Tytler, who was certainly not biassed against Mary, had been previously forced to the conclusion that, on the eve of her marriage to Bothwell, she was 'swept forward by the current of a blind and infatuated passion' (*History of Scotland*, 1845, v. 405, 406).

[44] On the 21st of June, Du Croc reported that Mary's party—

including the Hamiltons, Argyll, and Huntly—was the strongest in the field, but the others had the Queen, the Prince, horses, and artillery (*Foreign Calendar, Elizabeth*, viii. 258). By the 1st of July, Drury knew that 'though the Hamiltons pretend the liberty of the Queen, yet is the same not for her good, for neither likes she of them or they of her. Already it is, What is he, a Hamilton or a Stewart?' (*Ibid.* viii. 269). 'I doe fynde,' says Throckmorton on the 14th of July, 'amonges the Hamyltons, Argyell, and that companye, twoo straunge and soundrye humors. The Hamyltons doe make show of the lybertye of the Queen, and prosecute that with great earnestnes, because they woulde have theys lordes destroye her rather than she shoulde be recovered from them by violence. An other whyle theye seme to desyre her lybertye and Bodwells destructyon, because they woulde compasse a marryage betwixte the Queen and the Lord of Arbrothe. Thearle of Argyell dothe affecte her lybertye and Bodwells destructyon, because he woulde marye the Queen to hys brother, and yet neyther of them, notwithstandynge thyre open concurrence, as appearethe by theyre bande, dothe dyscover theyre myndes to eache other, nor mynde one end' (Stevenson's *Selections*. p. 208).

[45] *Infra*, p. 471, *n.* 63.

[46] *Foreign Calendar, Elizabeth*, viii. 232, 265, 267, 282, 293; *Spanish Calendar, Elizabeth*, i. 641, 645.

[47] *Spanish Calendar, Elizabeth*, i. 420, 441, 442.

[48] *Foreign Calendar, Elizabeth*, viii. 252, 269, 270, 271; Stevenson's *Selections*, p. 184.

[49] Teulet's *Papiers D'État*, iii. 33, 35; *Spanish Calendar, Elizabeth*, i. 643.—'The Hamiltons can in no way digest that the Prince should be at the devotion of England' (*Foreign Calendar, Elizabeth*, viii. 264). Throckmorton found by Lethington that it was not a time to speak of handing over their Prince (*Ibid.* viii. 284); but the principal point that would make the Lords consent would be to declare his right of succession to the English crown (*Ibid.* viii. 296).

[50] Nau's *Mary Stewart*, p. 56.

[51] *Foreign Calendar, Elizabeth*, viii. 269, 270.

[52] Stevenson's *Selections*, p. 205.—Throckmorton reached Edinburgh on the 12th of July and wrote this letter on the 14th. On the 17th of July Bedford reported that 'the Queen of Scots is calmed and better quieted than of late and takes both rest and

meat, and also some pastime as dancing and play at the cards, much better than she was wont, so as (it is said) she is become fat' (*Foreign Calendar, Elizabeth*, viii. 287).

[53] In the same letter Throckmorton says :—'She is waited on with five or six ladyes, four or five gentlewomen, and two chamberers, whereof one is a Frenche woman. The Earle of Boughan [*i.e.* Buchan], thearle of Murrey's brother, hathe also libertye to come to her at hys pleasure' (Stevenson's *Selections*, p. 205).

[54] At Carberry, Lindsay had made himself specially obnoxious to Mary by challenging Bothwell to single combat; and on the way to Edinburgh she had passionately declared that she would have his head (Melville's *Memoirs*, p. 184 ; *Foreign Calendar, Elizabeth*, viii. 252 ; Tytler's *History of Scotland*, 1845, v. 424, 427 ; *Lives of the Lindsays*, 1849, i. 284).

[55] When, a few weeks later, Throckmorton asked Murray what Mary's condition and estate would be after Bothwell had been apprehended and justified, he received the cautious answer that they could not merchandise for the bear's skin before they had him (Stevenson's *Selections*, pp. 298, 299 ; *Foreign Calendar, Elizabeth*, viii. 333).

[56] The Queen was in great danger, Throckmorton said, 'by reason of the great rage and furye of the people against her' (Stevenson's *Selections*, p. 228). He had previously said to Cecil that he had never seen greater confusion amongst men, 'for they chainge theyr opinions very often.' Though ever 'resolute to use all severitye to the Quene' they could not agree about the form of it. The preachers, with a great number who depended on them, were of one mind, but the lords were divided amongst themselves, and, to avoid the fury of the people, the wisest would not speak (*Ibid.* p. 224).

[57] Stevenson's *Selections*, pp. 205, 206 ; *Foreign Calendar, Elizabeth*, viii. 282, 283.—Claude Nau states that Ruthven was removed —at the instance of the Laird of Loch Leven—because he had promised to set the Queen free if she would love him (Nau's *Mary*, p. 59). Ruthven appears to have again been one of her keepers in August (Keith's *History*, ii. 738).

[58] Stevenson's *Selections*, p. 228.

[59] *Foreign Calendar, Elizabeth*, viii. 280 ; Stevenson's *Selections*, p. 267 ; also *infra* p. 471, *n.* 61.

[60] Stevenson's *Selections*, p. 221.—On the 15th of June Bedford had reported that the Prince was in greater danger than before as Mary was with child (*Foreign Calendar, Elizabeth*, viii. 252). It was then alleged that she was 'five months gone' (*Spanish Calendar, Elizabeth*, i. 649). Throckmorton's letter, quoted in the text, is dated 18th July. Nau says that, when Lord Lindsay prevailed on Mary—three months after her abduction—to sign her abdication, 'she was lying on her bed in a state of very great weakness, . . . partly in consequence of a great flux, the result of a miscarriage of twins, her issue by Bothwell' (Nau's *Mary*, p. 60). On the 26th of July Throckmorton writes :—'I doe understand the Quene of Scot- lande hathe had twoe fyttes of an ague, so as she dothe keape her bed' (Stevenson's *Selections*, p. 250). On the 28th Drury mentions that she is sick of a fever (*Foreign Calendar, Elizabeth*, viii. 303); and on the 31st Throckmorton reports that she doth still 'keape her bed' (Stevenson's *Selections*, p. 260); but says nothing about a miscarriage, although, on the 5th of August, he did not altogether despair of her relinquishing Bothwell (*Foreign Calendar, Elizabeth*, viii. 309, 310). If Nau's story is true it would completely dispose of the other which Labanoff believed and thus formulated :—'1568. In February, Mary Stuart is at Lochleven delivered of a daughter, who is carried into France where she afterwards becomes a nun in the convent of our Lady of Soissons' (*Recueil*, ii. 63). On the other hand, Nau's story would clear the way for the possibility of that other, which represents Mary as having borne a son to George Douglas of Loch Leven (Burnet's *History of His Own Time*, 1823, i. 58; Wodrow's *Analecta*, Maitland Club, i. 166)—a legend which has been partly discredited by the acceptance of the story of the nun (Keith's *History*, ii. pp. ix-xiv ; Hill Burton's *Scotland*, 1876, iv. 364, 365). The relative passage of Drury's letter to Cecil, of 28th October, is thus calendared :—'The suspicion of the over great familiarity between the Queen here and Mr. Douglas, brother to the Laird of Lochleven, increases more and more, and worse spoken of than he may write' (*Foreign Calendar, Elizabeth*, viii. 363). The alleged son was the reputed father of Robert Douglas, the famous Covenanter, who preached at the coronation of Charles the Second at Scone in 1651.

[61] To Leicester, Throckmorton writes on the 31st of July :— 'Whether yt were feare, fury, or zeale, wych caried these men to thende they be come to, I know not ; but I dare boldly affyrme

to your Lordship, albeyt I cowld neyther obteyne accesse to thys Quene nor procuer hyr lybertie with restytution off hyr to hyr estate, yet I have at thys tyme preservyd hyr lyffe, to what contynuance I am uncertayn; suer I am theyr ys nothyng shall so soone hastyn hyr deathe as the dowte that these lords may conceave of hyr redemption to lybertie and aucthoritye by the Quenes Majesties [*i.e.* Elizabeth's] ayde or by anye other foreyne succor' (Stevenson's *Selections*, p. 261).

⁶² Stevenson's *Selections*, pp. 253, 255.

⁶³ On the 27th of July Elizabeth wrote to Throckmorton :— 'You shall plainly declare unto them, that if they shall determine any thing to the deprivation of the Queen their Sovereign Lady of her royal estate, . . . we will make ourselves a plain party against them, to the revenge of their Sovereign for example to all posterity. And therein we doubt not but God will assist us, and confound them and their devices, considering they have no warrant nor authority by the law of God or man to be as superiors, judges or vindicators over their Prince and Sovereign, howsoever they do gather or conceive matter of disorder against her' (Keith's *History*, ii. 703, 704). That Elizabeth was really opposed to the action of the Confederate Lords is proved by Leicester's letter to Throckmorton (*Foreign Calendar, Elizabeth*, viii. 311), and by Cecil's to Norris (*Cabala*, 1691, p. 129). When Throckmorton partly acquainted Lethington with Elizabeth's Instructions of the 27th July, he was promptly informed that, if he had said as much to the Lords, all the world could not have saved Mary's life for three days (*Foreign Calendar, Elizabeth*, viii. 314). As Lethington put it, they could not gratify Elizabeth's wishes, unless they cast away their infant King, their country, and themselves. Throckmorton saw that they were determined to take their own way, more especially as they knew that no party was to be made in Scotland against them—such as lay aloof now seeking to concur with them. Lethington told him plainly that he had better return to England, for, if he were over busy with the Scots, he would drive them faster to France than they desired to run (Stevenson's *Selections*, p. 267; *Foreign Calendar, Elizabeth*, viii. 314).

⁶⁴ The Hamiltons, Throckmorton informed Elizabeth on the 18th of July, would concur with the Confederate Lords in all things, 'yea in anye extremytie agaynst the Quene,' if they were assured that Darnley's brother would not inherit the Crown

should the infant Prince die without issue (Stevenson's *Selections*, p. 222; *Foreign Calendar, Elizabeth*, viii. 288). The Lords were reported to favour this transfer of the succession to the Lennox family (*Ibid.* viii. 261). Tullibardine told Throckmorton, on the 7th of August, that the Hamiltons, Argyll, Huntly, and that faction, refrained from joining the Confederate Lords only because they suffered the Queen to live; and Lethington said that, if they took her life, all the Lords who held out would join them in two days—that the Archbishop of St. Andrews, the Abbot of Kilwinning, and Huntly had sent to conclude with them on these terms (*Ibid.* viii. 313, 314). Twelve days later, Throckmorton received a letter from the Archbishop, Arbroath, Fleming, and Boyd, bearing that they—and, as they assuredly believed, the other Lords of their party, Huntly, Argyll, and Herries—intended by all honest means to seek the liberty of their Sovereign, her restoration to power, the preservation of the Prince, the punishment of the horrible murder, and the safety of the Confederate Lords who had acted against their Queen (Stevenson's *Selections*, pp. 278-280; *Foreign Calendar, Elizabeth*, viii. 323). Next day Throckmorton wrote to Cecil :—'As for the Hamyltons and theyre faction, theyre condicions be suche, theyre behavyor so inordynate, the moost of them so unhable, theyre lyvynge so vycyous, theyre fydelytye so tyckle, theyre partye so weake, as I counte yt loste whatsoever ys bestowed apon them. . . . The Lord Herryes ys the connynge horsleache and the wysest of the wholle faction ; but as the Quene of Scotland sayethe of hym, there ys nobodye can be sure of hym' (Stevenson's *Selections*, p. 282 ; *Foreign Calendar, Elizabeth*, viii. 324). Throckmorton was probably convinced that there was too much truth in what Lethington had said, that among the Scots there were some who could entertain 'practize' with any foreign prince, to get money, though they had no intention of shedding one another's blood for the same (Stevenson's *Selections*, pp. 267, 268). Buchanan alleges that when Lethington failed to get 'the Quene slane be Act of Parliament,' he solicited private men 'to gar hang hir on hir bed with hir awin belt'; and that when he could not thus rid himself, and his partners in the Darnley murder, of a dangerous witness, he sent to her while still in Loch Leven 'ane picture of the deliverance of the lyoun by the mouse' (*Chamæleon*). Nau says that it was before her abdication that Lethington sent her a gold ornament on which was enamelled the fable of the lion and the mouse (Nau's *Mary*, p. 59). Sir John Scott represents him as using this fable after she was in England (*Staggering State*, 1754, p. 54.)

[65] On the eve of Carberry, De Silva wrote to Philip :—' Lady Margaret [*i.e.* Darnley's mother] thinks the French will not help the Queen of Scots, and that the Queen-mother will consider this a good opportunity to be revenged on her. I do not know whether she is deceived in this, as it is to be expected that the French will always go with the stronger party in Scotch affairs to serve their own ends' (*Spanish Calendar, Elizabeth,* i. 645). After Mary had been a month in Loch Leven, Charles the Ninth professed to Chatelherault, then in Paris, that he would spare neither cost nor anything else to set her at liberty, and restore her to absolute authority, if he and others who had power and credit in Scotland would join with him. On receiving Chatelherault's assurance that he would hazard his life to redress his Sovereign's cause, the King advised him to hasten home, and promised to aid them to the uttermost of his power. Martigues said that if he had three thousand harquebusiers for three months he would set the Queen at liberty ; but the Queen-mother said that they had irons enough in the fire already. 'The Quene Mother, I knowe,' writes Sir Henry Norris to Elizabeth, 'loves not the Quene of Scotland ; and but that she feareth to be prevented by your Majestie, either in curtesye or otherwise, nowe in this tyme of her neede, she woulde lette her trye it by the teethe, for any greate devotion she hathe to procure her libertye' (Wright's *Elizabeth,* i. 259-261 ; Stevenson's *Selections,* pp. 242, 243). Lignerolles arrived in Edinburgh with Murray on the 11th of August. Next day Throckmorton wrote to Cecil : —' The French do in theyr negotiations as they do in theyr drynke, put water to theyr wyne. As I am able to see into theyr doings, they take it not greatlye to the heart, how the Quene spede ; whether she lyve or dye, whether she be at lyberty or in prison. The marke they shote at is to renewe theyr old league ; and can be as well contented to take of this lyttel Kinge (howsoever his tytle be) and the same by the order of these Lords as otherwise' (Wright's *Elizabeth,* i. 263, 264). See also Throckmorton's letters of 12th and 13th August to Elizabeth in Stevenson's *Selections,* pp. 268-274.

[66] 'The Quene,' writes Throckmorton on the 18th of July, 'is in verye greate peryll of her lyffe, by reason that the people

473

assembled at thys conventyon doe mynde vehementlye the destructyon of her. It is a publyke speache amongest all the people and
amongest all estates, saving the counsellors, that theyre Quene
hathe no more lybertye nor pryveledge to comyt murder nor
adulterye than anye other pryvat person, neyther by God's lawe,
nor by the lawes of the realme' (Stevenson's *Selections*, p. 222).

[67] Stevenson's *Selections*, p. 240.—Throckmorton had advised
Knox and Craig 'to preache and perswade lenytie'; but he had
found them very austere (*Ibid.* p. 221).

[68] Each of these three deeds signed by Mary at Loch Leven is
dated 24th of July; and all are printed in the *Acts of the Parliaments of Scotland*, iii. 11-14; in the *Register of Privy Council*, i.
531-533, 539-541; in Anderson's *Collections*, ii. 208-214, 216-220;
and in Keith's *History*, ii. 706-712.—Claude Nau gives ample
details of the manner in which Lord Lindsay extorted Mary's
signature (Nau's *Mary*, pp. 59-61). Bishop Lesley also alleges
that Lindsay 'most grevously, with fearefull wordes and very cruel
and sterne countenance, thretned her, that unlesse she would therto
subscribe, she should lose her life' (*Defence of Mary's Honour*, in
Anderson's *Collections*, i. 37, 38). The Bishop had already stated
that Atholl and Lethington, 'with other principals of their factious
band,' had sent Robert Melville to Loch Leven to advise her for the
safety of her life to sign all the writings which should be brought to
her, as, in the circumstances, they could not be prejudicial to her;
and that Throckmorton gave her the same advice (*Ibid.* p. 37).
Elsewhere, the Bishop tells a similar story, but naming Tullibardine
as one of the three who sent Robert Melville to Loch Leven with
secret advice, and adding that Melville carried Throckmorton's
letters in the scabbard of his sword. In this other account, Lesley
says that she, 'with manie tares and weepinge,' set her hand to all
the letters presented to her by Lindsay without reading them, but
protesting that 'whensoever God should putt her to libertie shee
would not abide thereat for it was done against her will' (Lesley's
Negotiations, in Anderson's *Collections*, iii. 19, 20). Sir James
Melville names Atholl, Mar, Lethington, and Grange, as those who
asked his brother to advise her to sign the documents; but he says
she refused utterly to follow the advice, until she heard that
Lindsay had arrived and was in a threatening humour, then she
showed Robert Melville 'that sche wald not stryve with them,
seing it culd do hir na harm when sche was at libertie' (Melville's

Memoirs, Mait. Club, pp. 189, 190). Yet Throckmorton reported that a week before she had offered to commit the government wholly to Murray, or to certain of the Lords (Stevenson's *Selections,* p. 220). In the supplication presented in the Queen's name, on the 12th of June 1571, to the Parliament held by her party, it is stated that 'it behoved hir to yeild to force, whairunto shoe was not able to resist, for sic threatninges and feirfull languages was used to hir, accompanied with a vehemencie and awfull countenance of them who had the charge to deall in the matter'; and reference is also made to the secret advice to comply sent to her by 'sum noblemen and trusty persones,' and also by Throckmorton (Richard Bannatyne's *Memoriales,* Ban. Club, p. 166). Throckmorton understood that if Mary could not be induced by fair means to do as the Lords wished, they intended to charge her with tyranny, incontinence, and the murder of her husband (Keith's *History,* ii. 699). At the coronation of the infant Prince a few days later, Lindsay and Ruthven swore that she resigned willingly without compulsion (Stevenson's *Selections,* p. 257; Richard Bannatyne's *Memoriales,* p. 131). But, unless Keith's copyist has misread one of Throckmorton's letters, it seems to imply that Ruthven could not have been present when Mary signed the documents (Keith's *History,* ii. 699). And Lethington afterwards asserted that, when the Regent wished Lindsay to go with him to England to testify that she had demitted willingly, he refused; and when pressed 'swore ane grit oathe, and said, my Lord, and ye caus me to goe to England with you, I will spill the whole mater, for, and thei accuse me, of my conscience I cannot but confess the treuth' (Bannatyne's *Memoriales,* p. 131). In the document presented to the Queen's Parliament, on the 12th of June 1571, it is stated that the Privy Seal was 'violentlie and be force reft out of the keiparis handis' that it might be appended to her demission (*Ibid.* p. 167). Between the exterior binding of an old Protocol Book and the backs of the leaves, John Riddell discovered 'a thinly folded scrap of paper' which proved to be the Minute of a Protest taken on the 25th of July 1567. It embodies the copy of a fourth document signed by Mary on the previous day—the warrant charging the Keeper of the Privy Seal to seal the other three. The Minute of Protest also bears that Lindsay required Thomas Sinclair—the deputy-keeper—to seal the said letters, and offered him the said warrant; that Sinclair answered, 'that sa lang as the Quenis

Majeste is in warde, he wald seall na sic lettres that ar extre-ordinare'; and that Lindsay 'preissit him therto, and tuke fra him the Privy Seill, and wyth cumpany of folkis compellit him to seill the same' (*Ibid.* pp. xxii, xxiii). This minute is now in the Register House, and among the other traces of haste which it bears, the year date is 1566 instead of 1567. The Laird of Loch Leven was careful to have a notarial protest taken in the Queen's presence on the 28th of July, to the effect, that he was absent on the 24th, and in no way responsible for the demission; that he now offered to convoy her to Stirling, there to declare freely 'hir awin plesour and will'; that she desired instead to remain in Loch Leven 'and use hir self at hir eas and quietnes as sche has done heirtofore'; that she affirmed the letters of demission 'to be of propir motive'; and that 'in respect therof the said Williame [Douglas] protestit that hir Majestie suld not be comptit heireftir as captive or in preson with hym, quhilk protestation hir Majestie allowit and admittit' (*Registrum Honoris de Morton*, i. 26, 27). His conduct was approved by Parliament next December (*Acts of Parliament*, iii. 28, 29).

[69] Stevenson's *Selections*, p. 257; *Register of Privy Council*, i. 537-542; *Diurnal of Occurrents*, pp. 118, 119; Laing's *Knox*, ii. 566; Dalyell's *Fragments*, pp. 82, 83; *Historie of James the Sext*, p. 17; Pitscottie's *History*, 1728, p. 220; Spottiswoode's *History*, ii. 68; Calderwood's *History*, ii. 384; Ruddiman's *Buchanan*, i. 366.—Buchanan's translators have rendered his '*quarto calendas Augusti*' by the 29th of August (1690 ed. ii. 214; 1762 ed. ii. 398; Aikman's ed. ii. 527).

[70] Stevenson's *Selections*, p. 258.—The great number of the bon-fires—twice as many as had been at the birth of the Prince—was perhaps partly due to the fear of the 'unlaw' of £10 which the magistrates exacted from those inhabitants of the burgh 'that set nocht out thair fyris upoun the tuenty nyne day of Julij' (*Burgh Records of Edinburgh*, 1557-1571, p. 238). Throckmorton would not countenance the coronation of the Prince, but sent his cousin Henry Middlemore to see the proceedings (Stevenson's *Selections*, pp. 251, 252); and Robert Melville, unwilling to assist at the ceremony, remained with Throckmorton in Edinburgh (*Ibid.* pp. 259, 260). Sir James Melville had been sent to invite the Hamil-tons to attend the coronation. The result of his mission was recorded at the time by Throckmorton (*Ibid.* p. 258), and long

afterwards by Melville himself (*Memoirs,* pp. 190-192). In one point at least Melville is clearly wrong. He says that some of the Lords 'had particulairs against the Hammiltons, and supponit to get them wraked therby to won vantages be fisching in dromly watters. Sa that the Hammiltouns wer evell used then ; for they wald fayn have agreed with the rest, bot ther frendschip and societe was planly refused at this tym, and wer not admitted to com unto the corownation, nor yet to tak instrumentis that they suld not be prejuged in any sort.' This last statement is not only explicitly contradicted by Throckmorton, who tells that Arthur Hamilton was allowed at Stirling to protest for the preservation of Chatelherault's interest; but the substance of the protest is entered in the *Register of Privy Council.* This protest had been probably confounded in Melville's memory with the one which Chatelherault wished to make four and a half months later in Parliament.

[71] Two days after the coronation Throckmorton writes to Elizabeth :—'Thys Quene dothe, as I understande, keape her bed, and is notwithstandinge thys her sonnes coronation garded in the same place as strayetlye as she was; the Lorde Lynseye beinge retorned from Sterlynge to Loughleven immedyately after the ceremonye was ended' (Stevenson's *Selections,* p. 260).

[72] On the 2nd of August—four days after the coronation— Throckmorton writes to Cecil :—'The Quene of Scotlande is straytlyer kept at Loughleven then she was yet, for now she ys shot up in a tower and can have non admytted to speake with her but suche as be shut up with her' (Stevenson's *Selections,* pp. 263, 264). On the 9th Throckmorton informs Elizabeth that Mary has her health better, and that she is lodged in the tower as a place more sure to guard her in the night (*Foreign Calendar, Elizabeth,* viii. 314). Until the eve of her release Mary bitterly complained of her hard treatment (Labanoff's *Recueil,* ii. 64-69).

[73] *Foreign Calendar, Elizabeth,* viii. 309, 310.—Yet, after her escape from Loch Leven, it was said that she not only clave to the absent Bothwell as her husband, but sent for him to return (*Ibid.* viii. 467, 469).

[74] Murray seems to have left Edinburgh on the 7th of April (*Diurnal of Occurrents,* p. 107); he was at Whittinghame on the 9th, and at Berwick on the 10th (*Historical MSS. Commission, Sixth Report,* app. p. 643 ; *Foreign Calendar, Elizabeth,* viii. 203); and by the end of the month he was at Dieppe (*Ibid.* viii. 220). Bothwell

and his faction, it was said, were glad at his departure (*Ibid.* viii. 218); but Mary wept, wishing he were not so precise in religion (*Ibid.* viii. 229). He was received into Edinburgh on his return—11th August—with great joy of all the people (*Ibid.* viii. 317).

[75] Murray was accompanied to Loch Leven by Atholl, Morton, and Lindsay. Before supper Murray talked with her alone for two hours, and after supper until one o'clock in the morning. 'The said Earl did plainly, without disguising, discover unto the Queen all his opinion of her misgovernment, and laid before her all such disorders as either might touch her conscience, her honour, or surety . . . He behaved himself rather like a ghostly father unto her than like a counsellor. Sometimes the Queen wept bitterly, sometimes she acknowledged her unadvisedness and misgovernment, some things she did confess plainly, some things she did excuse, some things she did extenuate. In conclusion, the Earl of Moray left her that night in hope of nothing but of God's mercy, willing her to seek that as her chiefest refuge . . . The next morning betime she desired to speak with her brother; he repaired unto her. They began where they left over night, and after these his reprehensions he used some words of consolation unto her.' Now he told her 'that for his own part, according to his many obligations, he had a desire to spend his own life to save her life, and would employ all that was in him for that purpose.' He cautioned her, however, that in this he had not the sole power, as the Lords and others had an interest in the matter. He also warned her that it would be perilous for her to disturb by her practices the quiet of her realm and the reign of her son, to attempt to escape, to animate any of her subjects to disobedience, to induce the Queen of England or the King of France to trouble the realm, or to persist in her inordinate affection for Bothwell. On the other hand, he said that, for her preservation, she ought to acknowledge her faults to God, with lamentation for her past sins, so that it might appear that she detested her former life, intended a better conversation and more modest behaviour, abhorred the murder of her husband, and misliked her former life with Bothwell. Nor did he forget to tell her that she ought to show clearly that she harboured no thoughts of revenge towards those who had sought her reformation and preservation. 'Whereupon she took him in her arms and kissed him, and shewed herself very well satisfied, requiring him in any ways not to refuse the Regency of the realm, but to accept it

at her desire . . . The Earl declared many reasons why he should refuse it. The Queen again replied with earnest intercession, and prayed him to prefer her reasons and requests before his own. . . . At length he accorded unto her the acceptation of the Regency' (Keith's *History*, ii. 736-739). So Throckmorton learned from Murray himself. One of the reasons which Murray gave Herries for accepting the Regency was the Queen's oral desire (*Historical MSS. Commission, Sixth Report*, app. p. 641). Mary's own account, which is very brief, bears that when Murray saw that she would not press him to accept, he owned that he had already promised to do so, and could spare no more time excusing himself to her (Teulet's *Papiers D'État*, ii. 246, 247). According to Nau she begged him not to accept, and cautioned him of the danger he would thereby incur (*History of Mary Stewart*, pp. 66-71). 'Moray seems to have been in no haste to enter the presence of his captive sovereign and sister,' says Mr. Burns-Begg, who alleges that his first visit to her took place 'nearly a fortnight after his return from France' (*History of Loch Leven Castle*, pp. 65, 66). As a matter of fact he visited her on the fourth day after his arrival in Edinburgh; and Throckmorton tells that the Lords would not allow him to go 'untill they had consulted of the matter' (Stevenson's *Selections*, pp. 273, 275, 277).

76 *Diurnal of Occurrents*, p. 119; *Foreign Calendar, Elizabeth*, viii. 325; Stevenson's *Selections*, p. 289; Birrel's *Diary*, p. 11.—Murray's oath and proclamation as Regent are in Keith's *History*, ii. 751-754; and in the *Register of Privy Council*, i. 548-550. The articles between Murray and the Privy Council, as well as his oath, are in Stevenson's *Selections*, pp. 283-287. By the articles he was bound not to speak to the Queen without the advice of the Privy Council.

77 Keith's *History*, ii. 744.—See also Stevenson's *Selections*, pp. 282, 290, 291.

78 Huntly sent his offers by his uncle, the Bishop of Galloway. Fleming, Boyd, and Livingston wrote to Murray himself (Keith's *History*, ii. 741).

79 In the *Diurnal of Occurrents* (p. 115) it is stated that, on the 16th of June, 'Sebastiane Frencheman, suspectit for the art and pairt of the slauchter' of Darnley, 'wes takin and put in captivitie within the Tolbuith of Edinburgh'; and that on the 17th, 'Williame Blacader, Capitane, suspectit in lykwise for the said slauchter, wes takin be Capitane Johne Clerk, servand to the King

of Denmark, . . . and brocht to the burgh of Edinburgh, and put
in the Tolbuyth thairof.' Another contemporary gives, as the
Frenchman's name, 'Sabastion de Villour,' and states that he
escaped (*Historie of James the Sext*, p. 15). Beaton says those
arrested were Bastien Pages and Captain Culain (Laing's *History of
Scotland*, ii. 115). On the 18th of June, Drury mentions that the
Lords had caused Signor Francois and Bastien to be apprehended;
and also refers to the capture of Captain Blacater and his brother
(*Foreign Calendar, Elizabeth*, viii. 253, 254).

[80] *Diurnal of Occurrents*, p. 116; Birrel's *Diary*, pp. 10, 11;
Foreign Calendar, Elizabeth, viii. 256, 261, 262; Pitcairn's *Criminal
Trials*, i. 490*.—For his escheat, see *infra*, p. 484, n. 102.

[81] *Register of Privy Council*, i. 525.—The proclamation was duly
made at Edinburgh on the 27th of June (*Diurnal of Occurrents*, p.
116). William Powrie, one of Bothwell's servitors, had been examined before the Lords of Privy Council on the 23rd of June;
and George Dalgleish, his page, before Morton, Atholl, Grange,
and the Provost of Dundee, on the 26th of June (Anderson's *Collections*, ii. 165-177; Malcolm Laing's *Scotland*, 1804, ii. 243-251;
Pitcairn's *Criminal Trials*, i. 493*-496*; *Foreign Calendar, Elizabeth*,
viii. 262, 288; Stevenson's *Selections*, pp. 222, 223). The resolution
of the Privy Council to offer a reward for Bothwell's capture is
followed in the *Register* by the significant entry:—'Forsamekill
as Williame Blacater, James Edmonstoun, Johnne Blacater, and
Mynart Freis, all suspectit of the Kingis murthour, ar takin and
apprehendit, the Lordis of Secreit Counsall thairfoir ordanis the
saidis personis to be put in the irnis and turmentis, for furthering
of the tryall of the veritie, provyding that this caus—being for the
trying of a Prince's murthour—induce na preparative to utheris
personis suspectit of utheris crymes.'

[82] *Diurnal of Occurrents*, p. 117; Stevenson's *Selections*, p. 222.—
Among those denounced at this time were the Ormistons, Adam
Murray, Hepburn of Bolton, John Hay, younger of Tallo, Patrick
Wilson, and French Paris.

[83] *Register of Privy Council*, i. 531.—From Spynie, on the 16th of
July, Bothwell wrote to the Laird of Langton exhorting him to be
ready to rise for the Queen's deliverance (*Historical MSS. Commission, Sixth Report*, app. p. 640).

[84] Stevenson's *Selections*, pp. 255-259.—Throckmorton's information concerning the plot against Bothwell and the Bishop of

Moray was derived from Anthony Rokesby, or Rooksby, whose brother Christopher as an English spy had long been a prisoner in Spynie Castle.

[85] Stevenson's *Selections*, p. 240.

[86] *Register of Privy Council*, i. 544-546; Stevenson's *Selections*, pp. 277, 294.

[87] *Foreign Calendar, Elizabeth*, viii. 318.

[88] Tullibardine and Grange sailed with four ships on the 19th of August, and returned on the 13th or 14th of September (*Diurnal of Occurrents*, pp. 119, 122, 123; Birrel's *Diary*, p. 11; *Foreign Calendar, Elizabeth*, viii. 340-342). Sir James Melville credits Grange with having captured Hay of Tallo, Hepburn of Bolton, and Dalgleish, 'quhilkis wer the first that gaif maist knawlege of the maner of the mourthour' of Darnley (*Memoirs*, pp. 186, 187). But George Dalgleish had been apprehended in Edinburgh on the 20th of June (*Register of Privy Council*, i. 641), and examined on the 26th (*supra*, p. 480, *n.* 81); and although John Hay, younger of Tallo, had gone to Orkney with Bothwell, he hired a fishing-boat which brought him to Pittenweem, where the fishermen handed him over to Lord Lindsay, who lodged him in Edinburgh Castle on the 11th of September (*Diurnal of Occurrents*, p. 121). It was evidently to the fishermen that Hay referred, when, before his execution, he asked John Brand to tell Lord Lindsay that he heartily forgave him and also those who betrayed him (Pitcairn's *Criminal Trials*, i. 500*). He was examined before Murray, Morton, Atholl, Douglas of Loch Leven, Wishart of Pittarrow, Macgill, and the Justice-Clerk, on the 13th of September (Anderson's *Collections*, ii. 177-183; Laing's *Scotland*, 1804, ii. 252-255; Pitcairn's *Criminal Trials*, i. 496*-498*; *Foreign Calendar, Elizabeth*, viii. 342).

[89] On the 12th of September, the Regent with the rest of the Lords dined in the castle which was delivered to him (*Foreign Calendar, Elizabeth*, viii. 340). Sir James Melville states that Balfour resigned the castle on condition that Grange, on whose constant friendship he most reposed, should be made captain (*Memoirs*, p. 198). Another contemporary represents Balfour as requiring and receiving a remission for his part in the Darnley murder, a gift of the Priory of Pittenweem, a large sum of money in hand, and a pension to his son from the Priory of St. Andrews (*Historie of James the Sext*, p. 18). The sum in hand is said to have been £5000 (*Diurnal of Occurrents*, p. 120). Grange received

the keys on the 24th of September (*Ibid.* p. 124). In the bond of maintenance which Murray granted to Balfour, it is said that the latter is 'baith willing and reddie to the furth setting of the tryell and executioun for the said murthure' (*Historical MSS. Commission, Sixth Report,* app. p. 642).

[90] *Foreign Calendar, Elizabeth,* viii. 350, 351 ; *Diurnal of Occurrents,* pp. 122-125 ; Birrel's *Diary,* p. 12.

[91] *Acts of the Parliaments of Scotland,* iii. 5-10.

[92] *Ibid.* iii. 11.

[93] *Ibid.* iii. 11.

[94] *Ibid.* iii. 13.

[95] *Ibid.* iii. 27, 28.

[96] *Foreign Calendar, Elizabeth,* viii. 367.

[97] *Acts of Parliament,* iii. 34.

[98] Chatelherault's protest was directed against all attempts which the Regent might make to divert the title and succession to the Scottish crown. His proxy reported that Murray, knowing his errand, denied him a place in Parliament, and added : 'Gyff the Duke will not come heir and join himself with us, let him luk for nathing heir ; and gyff he proposes (as we understand) our destructioun and to cutt our throwtes, ye sal be assurit that we sal find remeid and cut his and all thame that wald so do, rather nor our own sould be cuttit' (*Maitland Miscellany,* iv. 118 ; *Historical MSS. Commission, Eleventh Report,* app. vi. pp. 43. 44).

[99] *Acts of Parliament,* iii. 38.

[100] *Diurnal of Occurrents,* pp. 127, 128.—On Lethington's share in the Darnley murder, Mr. Skelton has blown both hot and cold : —'The subtle wit of Lethington must have sketched at least the outline of the plot. "Kill him by all means," we can hear him suggesting ; "but what think you of this plan of mine? He has grossly outraged the Queen : let us take her along with us—a mere hint of connivance will compromise her. . . . A whisper to Bothwell that Darnley has abused her, and I would not give a straw for the boy's life. Nay, hold ; can we not teach him to look for something more than gratitude? . . . The saint whom he worships is a woman who may be won, and she will not press too hardly on the ever-bold wooer. And behind this irrational brute violence—what? James the Sixth, by the grace of God and of Lethington, King of Scotland, and—England"' (*Impeachment of Mary Stewart,* p. 176). 'It may be said with some confidence that

the clumsy catastrophe that ensued was directed neither by the keen brain of Maitland, nor by the deft hand of Mary' (*Maitland of Lethington*, ii. 19€). While Mary was in Carlisle Castle, she affirmed to Scrope and Knollys, 'that bothe Lyddyngton and the Lord Morton were assentyng to the murder of her husband, as it could wel be proved, altho nowe they wold seem to persecute the same' (Wright's *Elizabeth*, i. 278).

[101] Nau alleges that, shortly after Mary signed her abdication, an attempt was made to poison her, but he explains that 'the vigour of her youth contributed much to expel this poison and hinder its effects' (*History of Mary Stewart*, pp. 62, 63), unconsciously reminding one of the phrase concerning Darnley's illness in Glasgow, 'the force of yong eage that potentlie expellit the poyson' (*supra*, p. 430, *n.* 114). This illness in Loch Leven may have been that referred to by Drury and Throckmorton in the end of July (*supra*, p. 470, *n.* 60). After Murray's first visit to her as a prisoner, he declared 'that he never saw the Queen in better health nor in better point' (Keith's *History*, ii. 740); and a month later he informed Bedford that she was in good health, and to outward appearance as merrily disposed as at any time since her arrival in the realm (*Foreign Calendar, Elizabeth*, viii. 345). At the end of September Drury reports that Robert Melville has often recourse to her, that she waxes fat, and instead of choler makes show of mirth (*Ibid.* viii. 349). Towards the end of October, Bedford mentions that the Regent has gone to see her, and that she is as merry and wanton as at any time since she was detained (*Ibid.* viii. 359). In February Drury refers to a disease in her side and a swelling in her arm with which she had been troubled (*Ibid.* viii. 413); but she was soon better again (*Spanish Calendar, Elizabeth*, ii. 11).

[102] Throckmorton's letter of 5th August (*supra*, p. 169) is supplemented by Drury's of the 30th of September. In the latter it is said that Mary has already drawn divers to pity her, who before envied her and wished her evil, the Regent's mother for one (*Foreign Calendar, Elizabeth*, viii. 349, 350). Even Drysdale—the prototype of Dryfesdale in *The Abbot*; and, in Mr. Burns-Begg's opinion, the Queen's inveterate enemy — carried letters and messages between her and George Douglas (*Registrum Honoris de Morton*, i. 29; Wright's *Elizabeth*, i. 269). Possibly it was with the view of securing his services that, ere she had been five full weeks

in Loch Leven, she gave him the escheat of 'Capitane William Blacater,' convicted 'for art and pairt of the crewell tressonabill and abhominabill slauchter and murthour of umquhile hir Majesteis derrest spous the King' (*Register of Privy Seal*, xxxvi. 108).

[103] *Supra*, p. 469, *n*. 52; *Venetian Calendar*, vii. 408.

[104] 'Some affirm that the Earl of Morton sought the matching with the Queen, whereunto she could no way like' (*Foreign Calendar, Elizabeth*, viii. 431).

[105] 'It seems that the Earl of Murray waxes weary of his office of Regency. . . . Therefore, he has the rather yeilded to such a request of the Queen's, or device of himself, as breeds great comfort unto her Grace, and yet furtherance and countenance to the Earl's side, viz. a husband for the Queen, the young Lord Meffeyne, a gentleman of twenty or twenty-one years of age, being a Stewart. It is holden [20th March] very secret, and about Easter it is thought that it will be more apparent, and her Grace so set at liberty as the Earl, by further confirmation, shall still use the office he does till the King comes of age' (*Foreign Calendar, Elizabeth*, viii. 431). De Silva calls this prospective husband Lord Moffat (*Spanish Calendar, Elizabeth*, ii. 22-26).

[106] For Throckmorton's reference to this see *supra*, p. 468, *n*. 44. 'It is said that the Frenchman [De Beaumont] who has come into Scotland has to move a marriage between the Queen and the Abbot of Arbroath' (*Foreign Calendar, Elizabeth*, viii. 448). Buchanan says that 'with merie luikis and gentill countenance (as sche could weill do) sche had enterid' this son of Chatelherault's 'in the pastyme of the glaikis, and causit the rest of the Hamiltounis to fond for fainness' (*Admonition to the Trew Lordis*). It was suspected that she would have been driven into this marriage if she had won Langside (Melville's *Memoirs*, p. 200).

[107] *Supra*, p. 468, *n*. 44.

[108] On the 2nd of April, Drury writes to Cecil that, when Murray was last at Loch Leven, Mary 'entered into another purpose, being marriage, praying she might have a husband, and named one to her lykinge, George Dowglas, brother to the Lord of Lowghlewyn. Unto the which th'erle replied, that he was over meane a marriage for her Grace, and sayd furder that he with the rest of the nobilitie would take advice thereupon' (Wright's *Elizabeth*, i. 266). In another letter to Cecil of the same date, Drury alleges that she had declared unto George Douglas's mother that she

had spoken to the Regent of marrying George, and that the Regent was unwilling (*Foreign Calendar, Elizabeth,* viii. 437). For earlier gossip concerning the Queen's regard for George Douglas, see *supra,* p. 470, *n.* 60. On the 22nd of July—five weeks after the beginning of her imprisonment—she granted to him, 'for gude and thankfull service done to hir,' ' all and sindrie the mailis, fermes, custumes, profittis, and dewiteis quhatsumevir, of hir Majesteis landis of Tulycultre, in yeirlie pensioun for all the dayis of his lyfe' (*Register of Privy Seal,* xxxvi. 107, 108).

109 On the eve of Mary's escape De Beaumont arrived in Scotland, to demand an interview with—if not the release of—the captive Queen (Teulet's *Papiers D'État,* ii. 202, 203 ; *Historie of James the Sext,* pp. 22, 23 ; *Diurnal of Occurrents,* pp. 128, 129 ; Aikman's *Buchanan,* ii. 532) ; and up to the very day of the escape, Elizabeth was professing her willingness to agree with the French King in anything that should be thought fit for her aid and relief (*Foreign Calendar, Elizabeth,* viii. 449). She had nevertheless bought secretly twelve thousand crowns' worth of Mary's jewels (*Papiers D'État,* ii. 214), the Regent being very bare of money (*Foreign Calendar, Elizabeth,* viii. 349).

110 For Mary's attempted escape on the 25th of March, when she was betrayed by her 'very fayre and white' hands, see Wright's *Elizabeth,* i. 266, 267. De Silva places this attempt on the 14th of April (*Spanish Calendar, Elizabeth,* ii. 26). For other unsuccessful schemes and her final deliverance, see *Ibid.,* i. 661, 662 ; *Registrum Honoris de Morton,* i. 29, 30 ; Nau's *Mary Stewart,* pp. 78-91 ; *Foreign Calendar, Elizabeth,* viii. 451, 452 ; *Diurnal,* p. 129 ; *Venetian Calendar,* vii. 413-415 ; Labanoff's *Recueil,* vii. 135-138 ; *Papiers D'État,* iii. 41 ; *Historie of James the Sext,* pp. 23, 24. For notes on the keys of Loch Leven, see *Proceedings of Society of Antiquaries of Scotland,* iii. 375-382. Sir James Melville affirms that the escape was not only carried out by George Douglas, but that 'the auld lady his mother wes also thocht to be upon the consaill' (*Memoirs,* p. 199). The fact that the Queen's baggage was sent after her on the 5th of May, and a formal receipt taken for it from her master-cook (*infra,* pp. 511, 512), seems to imply either that her escape was connived at, or that her late keepers wished to secure her favour. Tytler alleges that when Mary despatched Hepburn of Riccarton from Niddrie to Dunbar, with the hope of securing that Castle, she also ' commanded him to proceed afterwards to Denmark, and carry

to his master, Bothwell, the news of her deliverance' (*History of Scotland*, 1845, vi. 37).

[111] De Beaumont, who was at Glasgow with the Regent on the 29th of April, and with the Queen at Hamilton by the 4th of May, told Sir James Melville that 'he never saw sa mony men convenit sa sodainly' (*Memoirs*, p. 200). The bond entered into by her supporters at Hamilton, on the 8th of May, was signed by nine earls, nine bishops, eighteen lords, and others (Keith's *History*, ii. 807-810 ; *Foreign Calendar, Elizabeth*, viii. 451).

[112] The various accounts of Mary's escape represent her as going from Niddrie to Hamilton, and Nau says distinctly that she remained at Hamilton until the 13th of May ; but Drury, on the 6th of May, speaks of her as 'still at Draffen among the Hamiltons' (Keith's *History*, ii. 802), and, on the 12th of May, he says, 'she is now gone to Draffen' (Wright's *Elizabeth*, i. 270). A document corrected by Cecil says she came to Hamilton about the 4th (Anderson's *Collections*, iv. part i. p. 1). See also *infra, n.* 115 and p. 543.

[113] *Diurnal of Occurrents*, p. 129.

[114] *Foreign Calendar, Elizabeth*, viii. 450 ; *Register of Privy Council*, i. 622.

[115] So Drury wrote to Cecil on the 31st of May (*Foreign Calendar, Elizabeth*, viii. 469). On the other hand, Sir James Melville says : —'Hir Majeste was not myndit to feicht, nor hazard battaille, bot to pass unto the castell of Dombertan, and draw hame again to hir obedience, be litle and litle, the haill subjectis. Bot the Bischop of St. Androwes and the house of Hammiltoun, with the rest of the lordis that wer ther convenit, finding themselves in nomber far beyond the other party, wald nedis hazard the battaill ; wherby they mycht ouercom the Regent ther gret ennemy, and be also maister of the Quen, to command and reull all at ther plesour' (Melville's *Memoirs*, p. 200). Her letter of 5th May to the Laird of Nether Pollok (*The Maxwells of Pollok*, 1863, ii. 1, 2), and her letters of 6th May to the Laird of Adamtoun (*infra*, p. 514) and to the Laird of Rowallan (*Scottish National Memorials*, 1890, p. 71) show that she was anxious to increase her force with the utmost speed. These three letters are dated from Hamilton.

[116] This remarkable document has been printed by Sir William Fraser—from what he describes as 'a contemporary copy, if not the original draft'—in *The Lennox*, 1874, ii, 437-447 ; and also in his *Memorials of the Earls of Haddington*, 1889, ii. 268-277. It

begins:—'Marie be the grace of God undoutit and richteous Quene heretrix of the realme of Scotland'; and is addressed 'to all and sindrie kingis, princes, duikis, dominatouris and magistratis, our freindis, alyantis,' etc.; and also 'to all and sindrie our lauchfull and weill advysit subjectis.' She refers to the rebellion lately perpetrated against her, by those whom she had so often pardoned for previous conspiracies; she describes the grievous condition of the country, and the hardships of her subjects during her imprisonment; she blames Murray for Huntly's overthrow, the Darnley match, and regal ambition. He is described as 'James, callit Erle Morray, quhome we of ane spurious bastard (althocht nameit our brother) promovit fra ane religious monk to Erle and Lord.' He is referred to as 'that beistlie traitour,' as the 'bastard traitour,' and as 'ane bastard gottin in schamefull adulterie.' He and his faction are charged with sowing jealousy between her and Darnley, murdering the latter, and inciting Bothwell to ravish her. On the other hand, she speaks of 'our darrest father adoptive, the guid Duik of Chestellarault'; and of his house as 'that guid hous of Hammiltoun.' Being now at liberty, she revokes—in presence of the subscribing lords, barons, and members of Privy Council—'the pretendit commissiones' extorted from her when 'in strait presoun' and 'amangis these dispairit bludie tyrantis handis.' By this deed, which she wills to have the force of an Act of Parliament, she creates and nominates Chatelherault and his heirs the protectors and regents of her realm, and tutor to her son during his minority and her own absence in foreign countries, and also in future minorities when it shall please God to call her or her successors 'furth of this fatal lyfe.' In the event of her own death without further lawful issue, and of her son's dying childless, she transfers the regal power, crown, and sceptre of Scotland to Chatelherault and the House of Hamilton, their heirs and successors perpetually. Meanwhile, she requires all kings, princes, dukes, etc., to help her to recover her just authority; and charges all her faithful lieges to assist her in establishing the same and in punishing the usurpers; and orders her heralds to make proclamation hereof at the market crosses of her burghs and other public places. The following extract will serve as a specimen of the language which is used and also reveal the writer's estimate of Murray's supporters:— 'Bot suld we keip silence of the mischent unworthie traitour Williame

Maitland, quhome, from ane simple unworthie page, our darrest mother and we did nurische and bring up to perfectioun, and thaireftir not onlie promovit to the office of Secretar, bot richlie rewardit him and all his freindis with benefites, giftis, and promositiones: the ingrait traitour. Mr. James Balfour, and Gilbert his brother, quhome fra slaverie and indigence we erectit to the estait of counsallour and Clark of Register, and gave that mensworne ethnik [*i.e.* heathen] the keiping of our cheif strenth and haill jouellis, the Castell of Edinburgh, and maid his brothir our maistir houshald: the cowart traitour, the Laird of Craigmiller, quhome we had in sic credeit as our awin hairt, and nevir denyit his ressonabill sute: the dowbill flattering traytour, Maistir Johne Hay, quhome we promoveit fra ane puir simple clerk to ane abot and pryour: the Bischope of Orknay, quhome we promovit thairto fra ane puir clerk: the hell houndis, bludy tyrantis, without saullis or feir of God, yung Cesfurd, Andro Ker of Faldounsyde, Drumlangrig, yunger and elder: the fibill tyrant Mynto: the schameles boutschour, George Dowglas,[1] with ane greit number of godles traitouris, commoun murtheraris and throt cutteris, quhome na prince, ye not the barbarus ethnik, the Turk, for thir perpetrat murthouris culd pardoun or spair: and thay craftie, perjureit foxis and oppin traitouris, quhais branes dois nevir ceis fra tressonabill inventiones, airis to Judas, sones of Sathane and of the progenie of cruell Cayin, Johnne Wischart of Pittarra, Maistiris Hendrie Balknawis, James M'Gill, James Haliburtoun, Robert Richesone, Johne Wod, and the rest of that pestiferous factioun, quhome fra mair indigence, schamefull slaverie, and base estait, we promovit, and oft pardonit thair offences.' The day, month, and place are left blank, and it may be doubted whether this galling document was ever signed or issued. As the writer was neither ignorant of legal phraseology nor of the language of ecclesiastical cursing, but in evident sympathy with the House of Hamilton, and no admirer of the reformed clergy, it may perhaps be inferred that he was none other than the Archbishop of St. Andrews. There are passages, however, which seem to savour of feminine rancour, and others which recall Throckmorton's description of Mary's commission to Lethington (*supra*,

---

[1] This George Douglas, an illegitimate son of the Earl of Angus, must not be confounded with the hero of Mary's escape from Loch Leven.

p. 340, n. 95), which 'wanted neither eloquence, despite, anger, love, nor passion.'

[117] *Foreign Calendar, Elizabeth*, viii. 452 ; Keith's *History*, ii. 805 ; Nau's *History*, p. cciv.—For her proclamation of 5th May see *infra*, pp. 512-514.

[118] One account estimates her army at 6000 and Murray's at 4000 (*Foreign Calendar, Elizabeth*, viii. 457) ; another at 5000 and 3000 respectively (*Diurnal of Occurrents*, p. 130). Mary herself says that her people were twice as many as her enemies (Labanoff's *Recueil*, ii. 76).

[119] Melville's *Memoirs*, pp. 200-202 ; *Diurnal of Occurrents*, pp. 130, 131 ; *Foreign Calendar, Elizabeth*, viii. 457, 458. Aikman's *Buchanan*, ii. 535-537 ; Calderwood's *History*, ii. 414-416. To the King of France, Mary's lords tried to explain and palliate their defeat (*Registrum Honoris de Morton*, i. 30, 31).—For a careful account of the battle and the battlefield, see Mr. A. M. Scott's *Battle of Langside*.

[120] *Foreign Calendar, Elizabeth*, viii. 457.—Another account represents Argyll as taking a 'fitt of the epilepsy' (*The Earls of Cromartie*, 1871, ii. 496), Mary's commission appointing him Lieutenant of Scotland, and dated at Hamilton 13th May, is printed in *The Lennox*, ii. 437. The act and warrant 'for the transport of the Queen's Majesty's most noble person from Hamilton to Dumbarton,' signed by her at Hamilton on the 12th of May, is printed by Father Stevenson (Nau's *History*, p. ccii.).

[121] Melville's *Memoirs*, p. 202.—Birrel says that, despairing of victory, she fled in the middle of the battle (*Diary*, p. 15).

[122] Labanoff's *Recueil*, ii. 77 ; Ellis's *Original Letters*, first series, ii. 236, 237.

[123] Herries's *Historical Memoirs*, p. 103 ; Labanoff's *Recueil*, ii. 76 ; *Foreign Calendar, Elizabeth*, viii. 460 ; Sir Herbert Maxwell's *History of Dumfries and Galloway*, 1896, p. 197.

[124] Labanoff's *Recueil*, ii. 117-119 ; Turnbull's *Letters of Mary Stuart*, pp. 163, 164.—This letter was written at Carlisle on the 21st of June.

[125] Wright's *Elizabeth*, i. 280, 281.—This letter is dated 11th June. Mr. Skelton gives fragments of it, and part of another letter of 8th August, as a continuous extract from one document (*Mary Stuart*, 1893, pp. 34, 35).

ADDITIONAL NOTES AND REFERENCES

For Knox's denunciation of the 'styncken pryde of wemen,' see *supra*, p. 277, n. 88. The display of grandeur which called forth that denunciation is thus described by Randolph:—'The xxvi of May, her Grace roode unto the Parlemente Howse in thys order—Gentlemen, barons, lordes and erles in their arraye and place. After them the trompettes and suche other musike as theie had. Next the herauldes, then the Erle of Murraye that caried the sworde, the Erle of Argile the septer, and the Duke the crowne regall. Then followed herself in her Parlement roobes and a verie fayer riche crowne upon her heade. Ther followed her Grace fyrste the noblemen's wyves as theie were in dignitie, 12 in number, after them the four virgins, maydes, Maries, damoyselles of honor, or the Quen's mignions, cawle them as please your honor, but a fayerrer syghte was never seen. These beinge nowe of the principals 16, ther followed them as maynie more so wonderfull in beautie that I knowe not what courte maye be compared unto them. The choyce, I assure your Lordship, that daye was ther of the whole realme. Havinge receaved her plase in Parliment, silence beinge commaunded unto th'assistance, she pronouncethe with a singular good grace an oration shorte, and verie prettie, whearof I sende your honor the coppie, as I am sure she made yt herself and diserved great prayse in utteringe of the same. I had that daye the honor to convoye her Grace to the Parlemente Howse, and to be presente at the whole solemnities and tyme of her beinge ther' (*Historical MSS. Commission, Twelfth Report*, app. iv. pp. 84, 85).

The process of forfeiture against Lennox, in 1545, is printed in Ruddiman's *Epistolae Regum Scotorum*, ii. 333-341; and in the *Acts of Parliament*, ii. 456-458. The doom was revoked by Parliament in December 1564 (*Diurnal of Occurrents*, pp. 78, 79).

For Rokesby's attempt to act as a spy on the Queen of Scots see Haynes's *State Papers*, pp. 445-448; *Hatfield Calendar*, i. 337-339; *Foreign Calendar, Elizabeth*, viii. 64, 65, 71, 76, 85, 86, 87, 91, 94, 101, 104, 109, 237; Melville's *Memoirs*, Mait. Club, pp. 155-157; Nau's *Mary*, pp. 25-27.

DOCUMENTS HITHERTO UNPUBLISHED [1]

[MARY TO HER MOTHER. 24TH APRIL 1558.] [2]

Ma Dame, messieurs mes oncles m'ont adverti qu'ils de-
peschoit devers vous dequoy je este fort aise pour avoir trove
le moyen de vous faire ce petit mot pour tous jours me
ramantevoir en votre bonne grace, ce que je suis bien marrye
ne puis faire p[lu]s souvent, mays madame vous excuses bien
le peu de moien que depuis quelque temps je eu, et reseves
la bonne voulonte et obeisante pour le fait.   Quant a vous
dire ce que je fait aveques mes Écosois je espere que vous
vous contenteres de moy, car comme je pance que monsieur
le Cardinal mon oncle vous aura fait entendre, et monsieur *de*
Rube aussi, j'en ay a peu pres fait tout ce que je voul[ois]
. . . a ceste heure et pour ce que en serais advertie je ne
p . . . ons . . . . . . d'une si longue naration pour vous

[1] It is possible that, in one or other of the almost innumerable works
bearing on the history of Mary Stuart, some of the following documents may
have been previously published; but I do not remember seeing any of them
in type.   Here they are arranged chronologically.   Two are taken from
the *Register of the Privy Seal*, and two from the *Register of the Canongate
Kirk Session*, the others are printed from the original documents; and
all, save the letter on p. 514, are in the Register House.   Except in proper
names, I have followed the modern usage in dealing with *u* and *v*, and with
i and *j*.

[2] This letter, in Mary's autograph, written on the day she married the
Dauphin, bears many traces of haste and excitement.   It is now considerably
discoloured; and the strips of tracing paper, which have been pasted over its
margins, somewhat obscure the ends of the lines.   In this transcript, words
which are illegible are represented by dots, parts of words torn out are supplied in brackets, and those which are rather doubtful are italicised.   In the
original there is neither punctuation nor apostrophes.

parler du de me . . . . . *ant.* Et premier, madame, je diray
que si Dieu *ma* r . . . fait la grace de connoytre l'obligation
que je vous dois, ce n'est rien ce me samble au pris de ce que
par experiance j'en connois a sette heure, voiant la poine
que je eue si peu de temps pour les ranger, au[1] pris de vous
madame qui en prens sans fois plus, et si long temps, et ne
pouvant autrement vous en rendre satisfaite que prier Dieu
qu'il me face tant de grace de ne permetre me tant aveugler
que je ne vous sois toute ma vie tres obeisante file, et ne
vous fois autre requeste si non tous jours commender sur
moy et tout ce qui me tousche, sans que je aie ni opinion ni
voulonte, car madame, je ne veus avoir voulonte que la votre.
Au reste, madame, il[2] faut que je vous face partisipante de
l'onneur que le Roy et la Royne me font de m'aymer propre
fille, comme il m'ont fait paroitre ce xxiiii d'Avril de m'avoir
resceue pour leur belle fille, et pour ce, madame, que vous
saures asses comme tout c'est passe, je ne vous en diray rien
plus si non que je m'estime l'une de plus heureuses fames
du monde pour avoir et le Roy et la Royne et madame et
messieurs et mesdames *tients* que je les sauroys souhaiter, et
le Roy mon m[ary] qui me *faynie* estime comme telle que je
veus vi[vre] et mourir.   Le Roy la Royne et messieurs
m'ont donne ch[acun] un [b]rodure de piarrerie, et la Roine
encore une a . . . . cote et boutons outre les cinq ac-
coustremens que le Roy *ma* donne et ma chambre garnie
de vesselles.   Quant a messieurs mes oncles il ne posible de
me plus faire d'onneur et d'amitie qu'ils ont tous fait tant
aises et contents que rien plus, et sur tout monsieur le Cardinal mon oncle qui a eu la poine de tout et tout avance si
onestement que on ne parle d'autre chosse.   Il n'eut seu
faire plus pour personne du monde.   Je reseu vos dernieres
letres, je fairays votre commandement : qui sera l'endroit ou

[1] In the original *qu.* Throughout the letter the writer has made a good
many slight corrections and alterations. Had she made a few more, her
meaning might have been more apparent.
[2] In the original *is.*

je vous presenterays mes tres humbles recommandations a votre bonne grace, priant Dieu, madame, qui me donne la grace de vous faire cervise selon ce que je dois. Vous excuseres si j'ecris si mal car les nocces de lunde des filles de la Royne ne m'ont donne loysir.

Votre tres humble et tres obeisante fille,

MARIE.

Je vous envoye des lettres que je peur avoir guarde trop long temps mais sa este faute de moien.

[Indorsed :—] A la Royne ma mere.

[THE QUEEN'S LETTER TO THE SCOTTISH ESTATES ANNOUNCING HER MARRIAGE WITH THE DAUPHIN. 26TH JUNE 1558.]

Marie, be the grace of God Quene of Scottis and Dolphines of Viennois, to the nobillitie and rest of the estaitis of our realme, greting. Forsamekill as ye will undirstand be thir Lordis youre Ambassatouris and Deputis, beraris of this present, how it hes pleissit God that the foir spokin mariage, betuix oure maist deir and best belovit husband, the King of Scotland, Dolphin of Viennois, and us, hes tane effect eftir the avice and consent of oure maist honorabill and derrest moder, the Quene Dowriare, Regent of oure realme, and youris; of the quhilk we haif greit occasioun to thank God and stand content, beand sa heichlie and honorabillie alliat and associat with so worthy and vertuus ane Prince, sua effectionat to the weill of yow and oure realme, that we could nocht haif wissit nor askit at God ane greitar thing in this warld. And becaus we knaw the greit contentment that his grace hes of yow, throw the demonstratioun of youre faithfull love and obedience towart him, we pray yow maist deir and weilbelovit to continew and perseveir in that will, and be youre gude and affectionat service to manteine yow in his gude favoure, and in the deliberatioun that

493

his Hienes hes to thankfullie intreit yow and do for yow all that sall appertene to the weill honour proffeit and avancement of yow and our realme. The quhilk doand, we will haif the greitar occasioun and myance to amploy us for yow, as ye will do us thankfull and aggreabill service, sik as youre forisaid Ambassatouris will geif yow mair amply to undirstand, referand forder of oure mynd to thame;[1] and prayis God almychting to haif yow in his blissit keiping. Of Villiers Costeretz the xxvj^t day of Junii the yeir of God j^m fyve hundreth and fyfty aucht yeiris.

MARIE.

Be the Quenes Grace
Degrantrye.

[WARRANT FOR EXTRACTING THE PROCESS OF FORFEITURE LED AGAINST THE EARL OF LENNOX. 27TH SEPTEMBER 1564.]

Regina.

Clerk of oure Registre we greit yow weill. Forsamekill as thair wes ane proces of forfaltoure[2] led aganis Mathew sumtyme Erle of Leuenax, at the instance of oure advocattis for the tyme, OURE will is, and for certane considderationis moving us, that ye extract draw furth and deliver the said proces of forfaltoure to the said Erle with expeditioun, as ye will ansuer to us upoun the executioun of youre office, kepand thir presentis for your warrand. Subscrivit with oure hand at Edinburgh the xxvij day of September and of our regnne the xxij yeir.

MARIE R̃.

[TREASURY WARRANT CONCERNING THE CASTLE OF ST. ANDREWS. 31ST JULY 1565.]

Thesaurer, forsamekill as Robert Leslye of Arthourseir haid charge of us to keipe the Castell of Sanctandrois in thir

---

[1] This allusion is no doubt to the request for the matrimonial crown to the Dauphin (*supra*, pp. 25, 26).   [2] See *supra*, p. 490.

lait trublis, quharbye we onderstand that he onderlyis charge
and expensis for the keping of the said Castell according
to our command; quhairfoir we command yowe to heir his
comptis and allowe him resonabill expensis, and mak him
payment incontinent of the foirsaid expensis meid be him;
and this ye feill nocht to do, all excusis being byput, as
ye will ansuer to us therupone, quhilk salbe sufficientlye
allowit to yowe in your comptis, ye keipand this wryt for
your warrand. Subscryvit with our hand at Halyrudhous the
last daye of Julij the yeir of God j^m v^c lxv, and of our regnis
the first and xxiii yeris.

MARIE R̃.   HENRY R.[1]

[EXTRACTS[2] CONCERNING THE FAST OBSERVED ON THE 24TH
OF FEBRUARY AND THE 3RD OF MARCH 1565-6.]

The 23 of Februer 1565 . . . . The quhilk day, the
ordinance of the Generall[3] Kirk of Scotland for fasting
biand knawand to be apone the morn to be exersisit with
all hummilite, the kirk,[4] knawand the same to be varie
godlie and necessar, promissis, with the essastanss of Godis
Holie Spreit, to fulfill it to thair uttermost of thair power,
bothe for thame selfis and also in gud exampell of the pepill
of quhome thay ar chosine to be oursiaris; requiring and
commandand the minister to exhort the pepill for the observatioun of the same, and also to hant priching and prayers
nocht onlie the twa Sondayis bot also the hole rest of the
olk,[5] according to the ordinance.

The secound of Marche 1565. The quhilk day, be resone
of the exortatioun and sermone for fasting in the tyme mad[6]

[1] When Darnley signed this warrant he had only been king for two days.
[2] From the *Register of the Canongate Kirk Session*. See *supra*, p. 398,
n 58.
[3] That is the General Assembly.
[4] That is the Kirk Session of the Canongate.
[5] Week.   [6] Made.

DOCUMENTS HITHERTO UNPUBLISHED

that the brether suld essemblat, it wes thocht necessar to defer all matteris quhill the nixt Satterday.

The Quenis graces precept to the Baillies of Abirden to ansuer Hew Lawder of xxiiij li.[1] [28th March 1566.]

Baillies off Aberdeine, fforsamekill as thair was wount to be pait owtt off the few malis off the said burgh to the Blak and Quhytt Freris off the said towne the sowme off twenty four pundis in almous yeirlie, quhilk was allowit in your comptis in the chekkeris bypast; and now it hes plesit the Kyng and Quenis Majesteis to dispone the haill rentis and proffittis off the saidis Freris to Capitane Hew Lawder in assedatione, as thair lettres under the Previe Seill grantit to hyme therapon proportis; quharfor ye sall nocht faill to content and pay the said sowme off xxiiij lib. to the said Capitane Hew, quhilk was pait to the said Freris off befoir, off this instant yeir, and siclyk yeirlie in tyme cuming during the yeris contenit in his tak. And keip this precept with his acquittance to your warrand, and the samyn salbe thankfullie allowit to you in your comptis. Subscryvit with our hand att Edinburgh, the xxviij day of Marche, in the yeir off God j m v⁰ lxvj yeiris.

Marie R̃. fiat.[2]

[Order for procuring hawks. 27th April 1566.]

Comptrollar we greit you weill. It hes bene the ancient custume observit of langtyme bigane, that yeirlie our falconaris resortis to the boundis of Orknay, Zetland, and

---

[1] This is the indorsation.

[2] In the *Book of Articles*, it is said that Mary invented a new device, and, in place of Darnley's subscription, 'writt *Fiat* efter hir awin name for warrand to the signet and seales, secludand him thairby utterlie fra the knawlege of the state of the realme' (Hosack's *Mary*, i. 525). At Linlithgow, on 29th of January 1566-7, when convoying Darnley to the Kirk-of-Field, she wrote *fiat* after her name (*Pitcairn's Criminal Trials*, i. 486*).

utheris the north cuntreis, for hambringing of the haulkis thairof to us. And sua we have send thir beraris this instant yeir. Thair expenssis is accustomat to be pait furth of your office. And sen ye ar in the cuntre your self we pray yow not onlie to ansuer thame thankfullie of thair accustomat dewitie and expenssis; bot als tak ordour how thai salbe reddelie and thankfullie ansuerit of the halkis within the saidis boundis, quhilkis ar als necessair for us as ony uther the like thing, alsweill for our awin pastyme as for the gratificatioun of our freindis. This we doubt not bot ye will do. Subscrivit with our hand at Edinburgh the xxvij day of Aprile 1566.

MARIE R̃.   HENRY R.[1]

[ORDER FOR PROCURING HAWKS.   27TH APRIL 1566.]

Comptroller, clerk, or argentier of our hous. It is our will and we charge yow, or ony of yow to quhome this our precept salbe presentit, to ansuer our servitouris Johnne Fraser, [*blank*,] falconaris, of the sowme of twenty pundis equale betuix thame, in part of pament of thair dewitie and expenssis, to pas to Orknay and Zetland for hambringing of our haulkis; and the samyn salbe thankfullie allowit to yow in your comptis, kepand this write for your warrand. Subscrivit with our hand at Edinburgh the xxvij day of Aprle the yeir of God j^m v^c lx six yeris.

MARIE R̃.   HENRY R.[1]

[PRECEPT FOR REGISTERING MARY BEATON'S MARRIAGE-CONTRACT.   16TH MAY 1566.]

Rex et Regina.

Advocatis, it is our will and we charge yow that ye compeir incontinent efter the sicht heirof befoir the Lordis of

---

[1] Mary's signature is in the same ink as the body of the document. Darnley's is not.

our Counsall and Sessioun, and, in our name and behalf, consent to the regestring of ane contract[1] of mariage—betuix us, takand the burding on us with consent of the Kingis grace our spous, with Robert Betoun of Creich, for our servitrix Marie Betoun, on that ane part; and Alexander Ogilby of Boyne, with consent of his frendis on the uther part—of the dait the thrid day of Maij the yer of God j^m v^c lxvj yeris; and to promis, in our name, befoir the saidis Lordis *verbo regio*, to releif the cautioneris contenit in the said contract for thair partis, sa far as we ar oblist to do, conforme to the tennour heirof; and that the saidis Lordis interpone thair authorite therto, *promittentes de rato*; as ye will ansuer to us therupoun; kepand thir presentis for your warrand. Subscrivit with our hand, at Edinburght, the sextene day of Maij, and of our regnis the first and xxiiij yeiris.

MARIE R̃.   HENRY R.

Regina.

Thesaurar we grete yow weill. This precept sene ye sal no[cht][2] faill to ansuer and deliver to oure foure capitanes[3] of futemen of weir, now being present in oure service, the sowme of ellevin hundre[d][4] fourtie aucht pundis, for the fourt monethis pay, beginning[5] at the tuelf day of Junij and endand the ellevint day of Julij, quhilk salbe thankfullie allowit to yow in your comptis, takand thair acquittance therupoun as ye did of befoir. We will and als chargeis yow

---

[1] The contract itself is printed, from the original, in the *Maitland Miscellany*, i. 43-49.—See *Register of Privy Council*, iii. 207, 208.

[2] Cut off.

[3] The acquittance on the back is signed by Captain Alexander Stewart.

[4] Cut off.

[5] In original *being*, with no mark of contraction.

to do, as ye will ansuer to us therupoun, without ony delay. Subscrivit with our hand, at our castell of Edinburcht, the xv day of Julij anno 1566 yeiris.

MARIE R̃.

ANE MEMORIALL OF SIK NECESSARIS AS ARE NEIDFULL AND REQUESEIT FOR MY LOIRDE PRINCE CHALMER.[1] [5TH SEPT. 1566.]

First tuay cofferis.

Ten hankis off gold and ten hankis of silver the fynest that can be gottin. Threttie elnis of fyne camberage.

Four pound of fyne suyng threide.

Sax pound of secundar threid in divers sortis.

Fourtie tuay elne of blew ostage to be ane cuvering of ane bed and ane cannabie to the Laidie Reres.

Sax elnis of plaiding to lyne the cuvering with.

Tuelf ellis of fustean to be ane matt and bowster with ane codde.

Tuay stane of woll to put in the matt.

Ane stane of fedderis to put in the bowster.

Auchtein elnis of camves to be the pavilyeas and the cuvering of the pavilyeas.

Five elnis of blankattis. And the trees of ane bedde.

Tuay skenyeis of girdis to bind up the bedde.

Thre scoir elnis of small linnyng to be schetis to the Ladie Reres and the maistres nureis.

Fyftein elne of blew plading for to mak ane cannabie to the rokaris.

Twentie four elnis of fustean to mak tuay mattis and tuay bowsteris.

Nyn elne of camves to dowbill thame.

[1] This is apparently the order for the furnishing of the first nursery of the infant Prince at Stirling. Four of the lines are partially scored out. This was probably done when the items were checked off.

Four stane of woll to the tuay mattis.

Tuay stane of fedderis to the bowsteris.

Threttie sax elnis of camves to be the tuay pavilyeasis and the tuay cuveringis.

Four skenye of girdis to bind thame with.

Tuay cuveringis of tapestrie.

Tuelf elnis of blankattis.

Sax scoir elnis of linnyng for to serve in my Loirde prince chalmer and to be schetis to the rokaris.

Tuelf elne of rownd cleith to be schetis to the servandis that lyis on my Loirde prince uter chalmer.

Ane cuvering.

Aucht elnis of camves to be ane pavilyeas.

Thesaurire, forsamekle as this memoriall being sein be yow, we chairge yow thatt sik necessaris as ar contenit in this former memoriall ye caus the sammyn be ansourit incontinent, becaus the sammyn is requesit and verray neidfull to be had. And this ye feill nocht to do, but ony delay as ye will mak us thankfull service. Subscrivit with our hand, at Striuiling Castell, the fyft of September 1566.

MARIE R̃.

MEMORANDUM FOR THE QUENS GRACES CHALMAR.
[4 NOVEMBER 1566.]

Item of fyne smalle lynine claiht iiij^{xx} elle.

Item of holene claiht xx elle.

Item of yallow silk quyht silk and blak silk vj unce.

Item of treid tua pund weicht.

Item of velvat iij elle.

Item of quyht fustiane xvi elle.

Mr Robert Richartsoune, thesaurer, ye salle nocht faeille to ansour Mr Jhone Balfour of alle this aboune wretine, quilk salle be allouit to yow in your comptis, keipand this

our precepe for your warrand. Subscrivit wyth our hand,
Tantalloune, the 4 of November 1566.[1]

Inscript.

MARIE Ř.

[WARRANT FOR SOME PREPARATION FOR THE BAPTISM OF THE PRINCE. 3RD DECEMBER 1566.]

Thesaurar, faill nocht incontinent efter the sycht heiroff
to furnis to this bearar fourty elnes off taffetas off the cord,
to be some prepartatefs for the baptesme, as ye will ansuer
to us. Subscrivit with our hand at Cragmellor the iij day
off December 1566.

MARIE Ř.

Je soubs signe confesse avoyr receu de Maistre Robert
Richarson tresaurier de la Royne d'Escosse xl aulnes de
tafetas a corde de troys coleurs, et tout par le comandement
de la Royne comme il est contenu audessus, le vj^{me} jour de
Decembre 1566.

BASTIEN PAGEZ.[2]

Inscript.

[WARRANT FOR THE PAYMENT OF LUTE-STRINGS. 9TH DECEMBER 1566.]

Maister Robert Rychardson thesaurer that ye incontinent
efter the sycht heirof ansueir to our servant Jhon Hume[3] ten
poundis, usual mony of Scotland, for luit stryngis that he hes

---

[1] Mary was not at Tantallon, but at Jedburgh, on the 4th of November
1566. Balfour's acquittance is dated, at Edinburgh, the 6th of *December*;
but the first three letters of the month have been altered. The indorsation
bears the date '4 Novembris, 1566.' In the *Diary* known as Cecil's, it is
said that Mary and Bothwell came to Tantallon on the 16th of November
(Anderson's *Collections*, ii. 270).

[2] Bastien writes a bold, clear, firm hand. The material of which he acknowledges the receipt was probably intended for the masque at the Prince's
baptism.

[3] Hume's acquittance is on the back.

DOCUMENTS HITHERTO UNPUBLISHED

bocht, and for to by otheris alsua, and for to pay for the caryage of the luitis and raparyng of thaym; and it salbe weill allouit to yow, ye schawand this our precept at your comptis for your warrand. Subscrivit wyth our hand, at our Paly[ce] of Halyroudhous, the ix day of December, the yeir of God a m . v° lxvj yeris.

Marie R̃,

Inscript.

[Remission to the Earl of Morton and seventy-five others for the murder of Riccio, granted 24th December 1566.][1]

Henricus et Maria, etc., quia ex nostris gratia et favore specialibus remisimus dilectis et predilecto nostris consanguineo et consiliario Jacobo comiti de Mortoun Domino de Dalkeith etc., quondam Patricio Domino Ruthuen, Willelmo nunc Domino Ruthuen ejus filio, Patricio Domino Lindsay, Magistro Archibaldo Douglas rectori de Douglas, Patricio Murray de Tybbermure, Patricio Bellenden de Stenhous, Joanni Balfour ejus servo, [*blank*] Cuninghame juniori de Cuninghameheid, [*blank*] Mure de Rowallane, Jacobo Douglas de Knychtisrig, Magistro Thome Dowglas in Clappertoun, Jacobo Douglas ejus filio, Hectori Dowglas in Spittelhauch, Jacobo Douglas ibidem, Jacobo Douglas in Todhoillis, Joanni Dowglas de Scheill, Willelmo Douglas in Lintoun, Roberto Douglas fratri Willelmi Douglas de Caveris, Roberto Douglas de Coschogill, Jacobo Dowglas coquo, Jacobo Douglas servo *lie paige,* Archibaldo Douglas filio quondam Georgii Douglas de Wattersyde, Willelmo Douglas ejus fratri, Joanni Douglas in Howden, Willelmo Douglas vocato de Panitre, Alexandro

[1] From the *Register of Privy Seal,* xxxv. 101, 102. Had Hosack compared the names in this document with the lists in the *Register of Privy Council* (i. 437, 462, 463), he would not have said that George Douglas and Ker of Fawdounside were 'the only two persons exempted from the general amnesty' (*Mary and Her Accusers,* i. 169).

Douglas, Georgio Auchinlek, Alexandro Jardane, Archibaldo Carmichaell, Willelmo Bruce, Andree Cristie, Georgio Symsoun, Georgio Neisbit, Johanni Harvy, Johanni Hwme, Andree Hume, Joanni Reid, Patricio Ruthuen de Ardonaquhy, Alexandro Lindesay de Culterany, Dauidi Lindesay in Craigingaw, Luce Brice de West Mylntoun, Georgio Ruthuen in Arlywicht, Willelmo Ruthuen filio Nicholai Ruthuen, Domino Roberto Oistlar, Willelmo Moncreiff de Tibbermalloch, Bartholomeo Arnot, Willelmo Stewart filio Andree Stewart de Fossoquhy, Edwardo Youngar, Alexandro Brounfeild, Ricardo Cranstoun de Skatisbus, Georgio Cranstoun, Thome Cowy, Willelmo Levingstoun de Kilsyth, Jacobo Striueling de Keir, Willelmo Striuiling de Ardocht, Alexandro Forestar de Carden, Jacobo Witherspvne de Brighous, Jacobo Giffert de Schirrefhall, Jacobo Someruile in Humby, Hugoni Anderstoun in Pumfraystoun, Alexandro Guthrie, Alexandro Clerk, Andree Armestrang, burgensibus de Edinburgh, Jacobo Millar ibidem, Alexandro Creichtoun fratri Joannis Creichtoun de Bruntstoun, Willelmo Creichtoun in Fawlawis, Stephano Dowglas in Bankend, Joanni Giffert in Lintoun, Thome Richartsoun ibidem, Joanni Mowbray ibidem, Jacobo Millar in Brighous, Patricio Purdy servo dicti Hectoris Douglas, Magistro Andree Hay rectori de Renfrew, Joanni Craufurd in Schaw, Roberto Hendersoun chirurgo in Edinburgh, ac omnibus aliis suis complicibus hominibus domesticis servitoribus et tenentibus, cum ipsis presentibus et participibus criminum subscriptorum rancorem etc.; pro eorum proditoriis captione detentione et incarceratione nobilissime persone nostre dicte regine intra Palacium nostrum de Haliruidhous, nono, decimo, et undecimo diebus mensis Marcii ultime elapsis; et pro arte et parte interfectionis quondam Dauidis Riccio nostri familiaris servitoris dicto nono die commisse; et pro omnibus actione et crimine, que dictis personis aut earum alicui inde quovismodo imputari aut desuper sequi poterint; necnon pro omnibus aliis actionibus criminibus proditionibus transgressionibus et offensis quibuscunque per

dictas personas aut earum aliquam aliquibus temporibus
elapsis datam presentium precedentibus commissis seu quomodolibet perpetratis. INSUPER volumus et concedimus ac
pro nobis et successoribus nostris decernimus et ordinamus,
quod dictus Willelmus nunc Dominus Ruthuen per brevia
capelle nostre ad omnes terras annuos redditus et officia que
dicto quondam suo patri pertinuerunt intrare poterit, non
obstantibus aliquibus criminibus aut offensis per ipsum in
vita sua commissis, pro quibus nunquam actionem move-
bimus, et non obstante quod extra hoc regnum nostrum et
non ad pacem et fidem nostram obiit, penes quos tam
cum dicto Willelmo quam cum judicibus et personis inquisi-
tionis ejus brevia servituris dispensamus. Vobis etc. Apud
Striuiling vicesimo quarto die mensis Decembris anno Domini
j^m v^c lxvj^o et regnorum nostrorum annis secundo et vicesimo
quinto.

Per signetum.

[REMISSION TO ANDREW KER OF FAWDOUNSYDE FOR THE
MURDER OF RICCIO, GRANTED 24TH DECEMBER 1566.][1]

Preceptum remissionis Andre Ker de Fawdounsyde pro
ejus proditoriis captione detentione et incarceratione nobilissime persone S.D.N. Regine, intra Palacium suum de Haliruidhous, nono, decimo, et undecimo diebus mensis Martij
ultimo elapsis; et pro arte et parte interfectionis quondam
Dauidis Riccio sui familiaris servitoris, dicto nono die commisse; et pro omnibus actione et crimine etc.; necnon pro
omnibus aliis actionibus criminibus proditionibus transgressionibus et offensis quibuscunque per ipsum aliquibus temporibus retroactis datam presentium precedentibus commissis
seu quomodolibet perpetratis etc. Apud Striuiling vicesimo
quarto die mensis Decembris anno etc. lxvj^o.

Per signetum.

---

[1] From the *Register of Privy Seal*, xxxvi. 50.—See *supra*, p. 429, *n.* 110.

504

DOCUMENTS HITHERTO UNPUBLISHED

Item to lyne tua gounis of satine and velvat of reid taffatis of the sax treid xiiij elle.

Item of reid frisse iij elle and half.

Item of schiuine[1] gold iiij doubil hankis.

Item of canvass iij elle.

Item to be rufis to the Kyngis sarkis of camarage viij elle.

Item of pasmentis of silver xx elle.

Mr Robert Richartsoune, thesaurer, ye salle nocht faeille to ansour Jhane de Compiegne[2] alle this aboun wretine, quilk salbe allouit in your comptis, keipand this our precepe for your warrand. Subscr[i][3]vit with our hand at Stirlyng the 4 of Januar 1566.

MARIE R̃.

MEMORANDUM TO BE ANE GARMOUND TO BE ANE GARMUND (*sic*) TO JEANE DE COMPIEGNE. [9TH JANUARY 1566-7.]

Item to be hyme ane Almine cloiche of blak iiij elle.

Item of velvat iiij elle.

Item of satine gray vj elle.

Item of frisse iiij elle.

Item to be hoyss and collette of sarge of Florence iii elle.

Item of blak sylk viii unce.

Item of fustiane iii elle.

Item ane hatte and ane belte.

Item of ormasi taffatis vj elle.

Maister Robert Richartsoune, thesaurer, ye salle nocht faeille to ansour alle this aboune wretine to Jhane de Com-

---

[1] Sewing.

[2] The acquittance is signed by Mr Jhone Balfour, at Stirling, on the 8th of January.

[3] Apparently cut off.

DOCUMENTS HITHERTO UNPUBLISHED

pienge,[1] quilk salle be allouit to yow in your comptis, keipand this our precepe for your warrand. Subscrivit wyth our hand at Styrlyn the 9 of Januar 1566.

MARIE R̃.

Inscript.

[TREASURY WARRANT. 16TH JANUARY 1566-7.]

Maister Robert Richartsoune, thesaurer, ye salle nocht faeill to ansour our sarvitor, Mr Jhone Balfour, of iiij hankis of gold and silver at xxxii s. the hank, *summa*, sax pund aucht s.; and ane elle of quyht satine at trei pund; quilk salbe alluitte to yow in your comptis, ye keipand this our precepe for your warrand. Subscrivit wyth our hand at Kallander the xvj of Januar 1566.

MARIE R̃.

Inscript.

MEMORANDUM TO BE ANE GARMOUND TO ANE FUILLE CALLIT GEORDE STYNE.[2] [17TH FEBRUARY 1566-7.]

Item to be cotte and hoyss of blew carsis vj elle.
Item of lynyne to be sarkis viij elle.
Item of cannvas to be ane doublette x quarters.
Item of lynyng ane elle.
Item of lyncum tuyne to schew the Quens curges tua unce.
Item for schiuine and the fassoune and pontis——xxv s.

Maister Robert Richartsoune, thesaurer, ye salle nocht faeille to ansour alle this abounwretine, quilk salle be allouitte to yow in your comptis, keipand this our precepe for your warrand. Subscrivit wyth our hand, at Cetoune, the xvij of Fabruar 1566.

MARIE R̃.

Inscript.

---

[1] Compiegne's acquittance is dated at Edinburgh the 12th of January.
[2] The indorsation is:—'Stewin the fule, 17 Februar 1566.' The acquittance is signed by Mr. Jhone Balfour on 18th February. Darnley was murdered on the 10th of the same month.

DOCUMENTS HITHERTO UNPUBLISHED

[TREASURY WARRANT. 28TH FEBRUARY 1566-7.]

Maistre Robert Richasson, notre tresorier, ne faillez de delivrer a Balthazar Hullin, ung de mes valetz de chambre, premierement,

Cinquante aulne de futaine blanche pour garnir plusieurs accoutrement.

Deux coffres de baher[1] pour mon service.

Deux paire de vergette.

Deux paire de decroutoire.

Six aulnes destamynes.

Six once de soye noire.

MARIE R̃.

Je confesse avoir receu de Maistre Robert Richarson, notre tresorier, le contenu, qui est cy dessus pour le service de la Royne.

BALTAZAR HULLIN.

Inscript.

[Indorsed:] Baltazar Hullin to the garderobe, 28 February 1566.

MEMORANDUM FOR THE QUENS GRACE.   [7TH MARCH 1566-7.]

Item ane steik of blak themine[2] to be ane goune.

Item of ormasi taffatis to lyne the goune ij elle.

Item to me lord prince of frenyeis v unce.

Item of bucchasi vi elle.

Item to Nicola the fuille to be sarkis and uder gaeir of lynyne xxx elle.

Mr. Robert Richartsoune, thesaurer, ye salle nocht faeill to ansour our sarvitor, Mr. Jhone Balfour, of alle this aboune wretine, quilk salle be allouit to yow in yowr comptis,

---

1 Perhaps *bahee*.   2 Probably meant for *stamine* or *estamine*.

keipand this our precepe for your warrand.   Subscrivit wyth
our hand at Edinburg the vij of Marche 1566.

MARIE R̃.

Inscript.

MEMORANDUM FOR MY LORD PRINCE.   [23RD MARCH 1566-7.]

Item of Hoilland claith lx elnis.   *Inscript.*[1]
Item of quhyte Spanyie taffiteis x elnis.
Item of quhyte hals[2] armosie taffiteis vj elnis.
Item of quhyte Florens ribbennis lxxx elnis.
Item of quhyte knettingis lx elnis.
Item of small lyncum twyne xvj unce.
Item ane steik of quhyte bukkase.
Item ane steik of fyne camrage.
Item xxiiij papir of prenis to the Quenis dule.[3]   *Inscript.*
Item xij elne of small lynning to be fuit sokkis to the
Quenis grace and uther necessaris.   *Inscript.*
   Maister Robert Richertsoun, thesaurar, ye sall nocht faill
to ansuer Madame de Mar of this foirsaid geir, ye keipand
this precept for youre warrand.   Subscrivit with our hand at
Edinburght the xxiij day of Marche 1566.

MARIE R̃.

MEMORANDUM FOR THE QUENS GRACE.   [25TH MARCH 1567.]

Item of blak ormasi taffatis to lyne tua gounis vij elle.
Item of cammarage to be ruffis iiij elle.
Item of Florence ribbens xliiij elle.

---

[1] The thrice-repeated *Inscript.* in the margin, the Queen's signature, and
the date *xxiij*, are not in the same ink as the body of the document.
[2] Perhaps *half.*
[3] Mourning.   For the precept ordering her 'duille' for Darnley, 15th February, see *Archæologia Scotica*, iii. 82; *National MSS. of Scotland*, iii. 51.

DOCUMENTS HITHERTO UNPUBLISHED

Item of blak sylk viii unce.

Item of smalle lyncum tuyne xvj unce.

Item of sylk to be hoyss to the Quens grace viij unce.

Mr. Robert Richartsoune, thesaurer, ye salle nocht faeille to ansour Mr. Jhone Balfour of alle this aboune wretine, quilk salbe allouit to yow in your comptis, keipand this our precepe for your warrand. Subscrivit with our hand at Edinburg, the xxv of Marche 1567.

MARIE Ř.

Inscript.

[TREASURY WARRANT FOR PAYING SIXTY CROWNS OF THE SUN TO CORMAC O'CONOR. 4TH APRIL 1567.]

Thesaurer we grete yow wele. It is our will and we command yow that, incontinent eftir sycht heirof, ye thankfulie content pay and deliver to our lovit Cormac Oconquhair, gentilman of Ireland,[1] the sowme of thre scoir crownis of the sone, or thane the just avale and pryce thairof quhilk the samin crownis now presentlie gevis within oure realme, swa that this berare have na forther occasioun of complaynt to us be youre delay in payment thairof; quhilk salbe thankfulie allowit to yow in your comptis, kepand this our precept for youre warrand. Subscrivit with our hand at Seittoun the fourt day of Aprile the yeir of God jᵐ vᶜ thre scoir sevin yeiris.

MARIE Ř.

Inscript.

---

[1] This 'gentilman of Ireland' was not one of Elizabeth's most loyal subjects; but he had written to her from Edinburgh, three weeks before the date of this warrant, thanking her for his pardon, and promising to repair to her Court with speed. Shan O'Neil wrote to him a few days later, telling him of his success against the English, advising him not to seek Elizabeth's pardon, inviting him to return to Ireland, and promising to help him to win his country (Hamilton's *Irish Calendar*, i. 328).

DOCUMENTS HITHERTO UNPUBLISHED

[TREASURY WARRANT. 4TH APRIL 1567.]

Maister Robert Richartsoune, thesaurer, ye sal nocht faeille to ansour Ganat Cohuyne[1] trei elle of France blak, quylk salbe allouit to yow in your comptis, keipand this our precepe for your warrand. Subscrivit wyth our hand at Edinburg the fourt of Aprille 1567.

MARIE R̃.

Inscript.

MEMORANDUM FOR THE QUENS GRACE. [8TH MAY 1567.]

Item of blak velvat vj elle the [elle][2] vij lib. . xlij lib.[3]
Item of blak satine vj elle . . . xix lib. x s.
Item of blak ormasi taffatis vj elle . . . xij lib.
Item vj hankis of gold . . . . x lib. iiij s.
Item send to Dumbar of blak sylk v unce . . xlv s.
Item tua paeir of oghani glavis . . . . viij s.
Item for the Quens grace bainyei of lynyne x elle . xl s.

Mr. Robert Richartsoune, thesaurer, ye salle nocht faeille to ansour alle this aboune wretine, quilk salbe allouit to yow in your comptis, keipand this our precepe for your warrand. Subscrivit with our hand, at Edinburg, the viij of Maij 1567.

MARIE R̃.

Inscript.

I, Mr. Jhone Balfour, grantis me to have ressevit alle this wythin wretine. Subscrivit wyth my hand at Edinburg the x of Maij 1567.

Mr. JHONE BALFOUR.

MEMORANDUM FOR THE QUENS GRACE. [15TH MAY 1567.]

Item to lyne ane goune of yallow sylk of quyht taffatis of the four treid xij elle . . . . . . xij lib.

---

[1] The acquittance is in the name of Mr. Jhone Balfour, and is signed by him at Edinburgh on the 10th of April. The document is indorsed:—'Jonat Colquhonzo 4 Aprilis 1567.'

[2] Omitted.   [3] The prices have been filled in afterwards.

Item to lyne the bodeis of the sammine i elle of ormasi . . . . xl s.

Item to lyne ane vasquine of blak taffatis of the four treid v elle . . . . v lib.

Item to lyne ane goune of blak figurat velvat of blak taffatis of the four treid xij elle . . . . xij lib.

Item to lyne the bodeis of blak ormasi i elle . xl s.

Item of pasmentis of gold to bordour the said goune xxij elle x s. . . . . xj lib.

Item for broderine of the said goune of schiuine gold and silver xxij hankis . . . . . xxxvij lib. viij s.

Item of fyne lyncum tuyne iiij unce . . . xl s.

Item of blak satine ij elle . . . . vj lib. x s.

Mr. Robert Richartsoune, thesaurer, ye sal nocht faeille to ansour alle this aboun wretine, quilk salbe allouit to yow in your comptis, keipand this our precepe for your warrand. Subscrivit wyth our hand, at Edinburg, the xv of May 1567.[1]

MARIE R̃.

I, Mr. Jhone Balfour, grantis me to have ressevit alle this wythin wretine. Subscrivit wyth my hand, at Edinburg, the xx of Maij 1567.

Mr. JHONE BALFOUR.

THE INVENTAR OF THE QUENIS GRACES CLEITHING AND UTHER BAGGADGE, send to hir grace furth of Loch Leuin, and ressavid be the Quenis graces master cuik and Elles Boug his spous at Loch Leuin, the v of Maij anno 1568, and put wythin a coffer.

Item in primis foure silk gounnis. Thre weylicoittis. Ane blew purpoure goun. Ane pair of scheittis. Item twa[2] thre pair of hois. Item ane broun goun. Item ane saiting pait-cleyth.

---

[1] The prices have been filled in afterwards. It will be noticed that the Queen signs this precept on the very day that she married Bothwell.

[2] *Twa* is perhaps intended to be deleted.

Item ane goun of chamnet of silk.

Item aucht sarkis. Item twa neipkynnis. Item ane curchshe.

Item ane pair of kelsounis.

Item ane littill silver stoupe.

Je confesse avoir receu le conteneu cy dessus lequel je mis deans ung cofre pour le mener et condure a la Royne la part ou elle sera. En tesmoiys je seigne la presente ce jourdhuy vme jour de May 1568.

ESTIENNE HAUET.

Plus je receu une coupe doree et une esceulles a boullon ung cadenay et six veselles d'argent lesquel je prins pour me condure. En seigne comme dessus.

ESTIENNE HAUET.

[Indorsed :—] Ane dischairge of sum littill geir perteining to the Queinis Majestei quhilk hir servitour resaivit.

[THE QUEEN'S PROCLAMATION OF 5TH MAY 1568.]

Marie, be the grace of God Quene of Scottis, to our lovittis Johne Ingles, [blank] messingeris, our schireffis in that part, conjunctlie and severalie, specialie constitut greting. Forsamekle as it is nocht unknawn to all our luffing liegeis and subjectis within this our realm, how we have bene retenit captive in the maist strait presoun thir ten monethis bygane or therby, and from tym to tym maist grevouslie manneschit and boistit to have takin our lyif, and to have causit us to gif over our authorite and powar reginall to sum particular personis, quha allegeis thame to have the samyn, and hes usurpit the use therof, in name of our derrest sone ; and in the meyntym hes causit divers of our liegeis, part be mannesching and boisting, and uthiris be persuasioun and tyisting, to consent and authores the samyn, and alswa to gif voit in Parlament to that effect ; and now sen it hes plesit almychtie God to place us in that authorite induring our lyiftym, as our maist noble progenitouris of gude memorie hes usit the samyn of befor, we intend, be our selff and Lordis of our Consall, to tak sick gude ordour anentis the commoun wele of this realme, and for tranquillitie and rest to be haid to the liegeis and subjectis of the samyn according to the anceant lawis and libertie therof. OURE will is heirfor and we charge yow straitlie and commandis that incontinent thir our lettres sene ye pas to the mercat croces of our burrowis of Edinburgh, Haddingtoun, Dunbar, Jedburght,[1] Selkirk, Peblis, Laudar; and thair be oppin proclamatioun command and charge all and sindry our liegeis and subjectis, that nane of thame tak upoun hand to ansuer nor obey the forsaid pretendit authorite, usurpit in maner forsaid, in tym cuming, for na maner of charge nor command to be direct sett furtht be thame for obeying therof; bot that all our saidis liegeis reddelie ansuer and obey us and our authorite, thir our lettres and proclamacionis, and all uthiris our lettres, proclamacionis, wirttingis, to be direct be us thair native Soverane, in all tym cuming, under the pane of tressoun; and siclyk makis it knawin and patent be thir our lettres, to all our liegeis that wes persuadit, be the principall conspiratouris, to be upoun the ground quhair our maist noble persoun wes detenit, tyistit and seducit for that effect ignorantlie, gif thai or ony of thame cum to us betuix the dait heirof and the xv day of Maij now instant, declarand tham penitent therof, and causing us knaw thair faithfull obedience in tym cuming as trew and deutefull subjectis aucht to do to thair native Soverane, and in the meyntym nocht assistand nor joining thame selffis with the saidis conspiratouris, we ar myndit to extend our clemencie and mercie upoun thame as the native Soverane aucht to do to thair faithtfull subjectis; accordinglie as ye will ansuer to us therupoun. The quhilk to do we commit to yow, conjunctlie and severalie, our full powar be thir our lettres; delivering thame, be yow deulie execut and indorsat, agane

---

[1] *Jedburght* has been altered.

to the berar. Subscrivit with our hand, at Hammiltoun, the v of Maij, and of our regne the xxvj yeir.

MARIE Ř.

[Indorsed:—] Ane charge and proclamatioun commanding that nane obey the Kingis auctorite.[1]

[MARY TO THE LAIRD OF ADAMTOUN. 6TH MAY 1568.][2]

Regina.

Traist freind we greit yow weill. We beleve it is nocht unknawin to yow the greit mercie and kyndnes that Allmychtie God, of his infinit gudnes, hes furthschewin towart us at this tyme, in the deliverance of us fra the maist straittest presoun, in the quhilk we war captiv[at], of the quhilk mercie and kyndnes we can nocht thank him eneuch. And therfor we will desire yow, as ye will do us acceptable service, to be at us with all possible diligence upoun Settirday[3] nixt, be aucht houris afor none, or sonar gif ye mai, weill accumpanyit with your honorable freindis and servandis bodin in feir of weir, to do us service as ye salbe appointit. Becaus we knaw your constance at all tymes we neid nocht to mak langar lettres for the present bot will bid yow fair weill. Off Hammiltoun the vj of May 1568.

And that ye with your hale folkis be heir upon Sonday nixt at the fordest baith on fute and hors.

MARIE Ř.

[1] The indorsement must have been added by one of the Regent's officials or supporters.

[2] The original is in the Antiquarian Museum, Edinburgh.

[3] That is the 8th of May.

ITINERARY

In the headlines of the columns the letter P stands for *Register of Privy Seal*; G, for *Register of Great Seal*; C, for *Register of Privy Council*; and L, for Letters, etc. The number of documents signed on each day is shown by the figures. There are a few entries in the *Register of Privy Council* which possibly do not refer to formal meetings of the Council, but these are distinguished by an asterisk. The meetings of Council seem to have been usually, if not always, held in the town or place where the Queen was for the time being. Implicit reliance must not be placed on any one column, as the royal clerks were not always immaculate in their dates. In the notes at the foot of the pages, B stands for Birrel's *Diary*; D, for *Diurnal of Occurrents*; F. C. E., for *Foreign Calendar, Elizabeth*; K, for Keith's *History*; S, for Stevenson's *Selections*; and W, for Wright's *Elizabeth*. Easter is distinguished by a Gothic 𝕾.

19th Aug. 1561-   20th Sept. 1561

		P	G	C	L			P	G	C	L
Aug.						Sept.					
Tu. 19						6	Holyrood	1	...	1	1
20						S. 7					
21						8	Edinburgh	2	1		
22							Holyrood	...	...	1	
23							Edinburgh	6			
S. 24						9	Holyrood	...	...	1	
25	Edinburgh	...	...	1			Dundee	1			
26						10	Holyrood	1	...	1	
27	Edinburgh	1					Edinburgh	1			
28						11	Holyrood	2			
29							Edinburgh	...	...	...	1
30						12					
S. 31	Edinburgh	4				13	Linlithgow	2			
						S. 14					
Sept.						15					
						16					
M. 1	Edinburgh	1	1			17	Perth	1			
	Holyrood	...	...	...	1	18					
2	Edinburgh	1				19	Perth	...	...	1	
3							Dundee	3			.
4	Holyrood	...	...	1		20					
5											

Mary lands at Leith on 19th Aug. (F. C. E. iv. 277), makes her public entry into Edinburgh on 2nd Sept. (W. i. 73), leaves Edinburgh for Linlithgow on 10th (F. C. E. iv. 296), or 11th Sept. (D. p. 69), remains two days at Linlithgow, two at Stirling, two nights at Kincardine, arrives in Perth on the 17th, at Dundee on the 19th (D. p. 69), is in St. Andrews on the 21st Sept. (K. ii. 86), and gives audience to Mewtas at Edinburgh on 2nd Oct. (S. p. 92).

One of the two documents in the *Register of Privy Seal*, dated 8th September 1561, is dated in the Queen's twenty-first regnal year, which would place it in 1563.

21st Sept. 1561-   5th Dec. 1561

Date	Place	P	G	C	L
Sept.					
S. 21					
22	Edinburgh	3			
23					
24					
25	Edinburgh	1			
26					
27					
S. 28					
29					
30					
Oct.					
W. 1					
2	Edinburgh	1			
3	Edinburgh	1			
4	{ Edinburgh	1			
	{ Holyrood	...	...	...	1
S. 5	Edinburgh	1			
6	Edinburgh	2			
7	Holyrood	...	...	...	1
8	Edinburgh	...	...	...	1
9					
10	Edinburgh	1			
11					
S. 12	{ Edinburgh	2	1		
	{ Holyrood	...	...	...	1
13	{ Edinburgh	1			
	{ Holyrood	...	...	1	
14	Edinburgh	2			
15					
16	{ Edinburgh	1			
	{ Holyrood	...	...	1	
17	{ Edinburgh	1			
	{ Holyrood	...	...	1	
18	{ Holyrood	1	...	1	
	{ Edinburgh	2	1		
S. 19					
20	Edinburgh	1			
21					
22	Edinburgh	4			
23	Edinburgh	2	1		
24	{ Edinburgh	1			
	{ Holyrood	...	...	...	1
25	Holyrood	...	...	1	
S. 26	Edinburgh	1			
27	{ Holyrood	1	1		
	{ Edinburgh	3	1		
28					
29					

Date	Place	P	G	C	L
Oct.					
30	Edinburgh	2			
31	{ Holyrood	1			
	{ Edinburgh	1			
Nov.					
S. 1					
S. 2					
3					
4	Edinburgh	1			
5	Edinburgh	1			
6	Edinburgh	1			
7	Holyrood	1			
8	{ Holyrood	2			
	{ Edinburgh	5			
S. 9	{ Edinburgh	1			
	{ Holyrood	1	1		
10	{ Edinburgh	3	...	...	1
	{ Holyrood	1			
11	{ Edinburgh	2			
	{ Holyrood	...	...	1	
12	{ Edinburgh	1			
	{ Holyrood	...	...	1	
13	Holyrood	...	...	1	
14	{ Edinburgh	2			
	{ Holyrood	...	...	1	
15	Holyrood	...	...	1	
S. 16	Holyrood	...	...	...	1
17	Edinburgh	1			
18					
19					
20					
21					
22					
S. 23					
24					
25					
26	Edinburgh	1	1		
27	Edinburgh	1			
28	Holyrood	1	1		
29					
S. 30	Holyrood	2			
Dec.					
M. 1					
2	{ Holyrood	1	...	1	
	{ Edinburgh	4			
3					
4	Holyrood	...	...	1	
5					

In the printed *Register of Privy Council* (i. 190), the meeting of 15th November is misdated *decimo quarto*.

6th Dec. 1561.   1st Mar. 1561-2

Date	Place	P	G	C	L
Dec.					
6	Edinburgh	3	2		
S. 7					
8	Edinburgh	1			
9	Edinburgh	1			
10	{ Edinburgh	1			
	Holyrood	1			
11	{ Holyrood	2			
	Edinburgh	...	...	1	
12	{ Edinburgh	1			
	Holyrood	...	...	...	1
13					
S. 14					
15	Holyrood	1			
16					
17					
18	Edinburgh	1			
19					
20					
S. 21	Edinburgh	2	1		
22	Edinburgh	...	...	1	
23	Edinburgh	2			
24					
25					
26					
27					
S. 28	Edinburgh	2			
29	Edinburgh	1	1		
30	{ Holyrood	1			
	Edinburgh	1			
31	Edinburgh	5			
1561-2					
Jan.					
Th. 1	Edinburgh	5			
2	Edinburgh	3	1		
3					
S. 4	Seton	...	...	...	1
5	Seton	...	...	...	2
6					
7	Edinburgh	...	...	1	
8					
9					
10					
S. 11					
12					
13	Edinburgh	1			
14	Edinburgh	1			
15	Edinburgh	2			
16	Edinburgh	...	1		

Date	Place	P	G	C	L
Jan.					
17					
S. 18	Linlithgow	1			
19	Linlithgow	1			
20					
21	Edinburgh	1			
22					
23	Linlithgow	1			
24	Linlithgow	...	...	1	
S. 25					
26	Linlithgow	...	...	...	1
27					
28					
29					
30	Edinburgh	1			
31	{ Holyrood	1	1		
	Edinburgh	3			
Feb.					
S. 1					
2	Edinburgh	3			
3					
4	Edinburgh	2			
5					
6	Edinburgh	...	...	1	1
7	Edinburgh	3			
S. 8					
9					
10					
11					
12	Edinburgh	2	1	1	
13	Edinburgh	1	...	1	
14	Edinburgh	8	1	...	1
S. 15	Edinburgh	...	...	1	
16	{ Holyrood	1			
	Edinburgh	1			
17					
18					
19					
20	Edinburgh	...	...	1	
21	Edinburgh	1	...	1	
S. 22					
23	Edinburgh	2			
24	Edinburgh	1			
25					
26					
27					
28	Edinburgh	1	1	1	
Mar.					
S. 1	{ Edinburgh	5	1		
	Holyrood	1			

On the 11th of January she is at Crichton, next day at Borthwick, purposes going for eight days to Linlithgow (F. C. E. iv. 489), where she arrives by the 14th or 15th (*Ibid.* p. 512), and returns to Edinburgh on 30th Jan. (*Ibid.* p. 513).

ITINERARY

		P	G	C	L			P	G	C	L
Mar.						**April**					
2	Holyrood	...	...	...	1	13	St. Andrews	...	...	...	1
3						14					
4						15	St. Andrews	1			
5						16					
6						17					
7						18					
S. 8						S. 19					
9						20	St. Andrews	...	...	...	1
10	St. Andrews	2				21					
11						22					
12						23					
13						24	St. Andrews	1	...	...	1
14						25					
S. 15						S. 26	St. Andrews	1	1		
16	St. Andrews	1				27					
17	St. Andrews	1				28	St. Andrews	5			
18	St. Andrews	2				29	St. Andrews	1			
19						30	St. Andrews	2			
20	St. Andrews	2									
21						**May**					
S. 22						F. 1	St. Andrews	1			
23						2					
24	Falkland	1				S. 3					
						4					
1562						5					
25						6					
26						7					
27						8					
28						9					
S. 29						S. 10					
30						11					
31						12	Edinburgh	1			
						13	Edinburgh	1			
April						14					
W. 1						15					
2	St. Andrews	2				16	Edinburgh	2			
3						S. 17					
4						18	Edinburgh	2	1		
S. 5						19	Edinburgh	...	...	1	
6						20	Edinburgh	1			
7						21	Edinburgh	5	...	1	
8						22					
9	St. Andrews	1	1			23	Holyrood	1	...	...	1
10						S. 24	Edinburgh	1	...	...	1
11	St. Andrews	...	...	...	1	25	Holyrood	...	...	...	3
S. 12						26	Edinburgh	5	...	1	

On the 28th of March she is at Falkland (F. C. E. iv. 576, 586), which she leaves for St. Andrews on 1st April (*Ibid.* iv. 584).

On 18th April she is in St. Andrews (D. p. 72), and is there on the 20th, 21st, and 22nd April (F. C. E. iv. 629). By the 11th of May she had been eight days in Loch Leven, and intended being at Edinburgh on 12th or 13th (*Ibid.* v. 25, 31).

ITINERARY

Date	Place	P	G	C	L
May 27	Edinburgh	1			
28					
29	Edinburgh	...	...	...	1
30	Edinburgh	...	...	1	1
S. 31	Edinburgh	1	...	1	
June M. 1	Edinburgh	...	...	1	
	Holyrood	...	...	...	1
2	Edinburgh	1			
3					
4	Edinburgh	2	1		
5					
6	Edinburgh	2			
S. 7					
8	Holyrood	1	1	...	1
	Edinburgh	4	...	1	
9	Edinburgh	1			
10	Edinburgh	1	1		
	Dunfermline	...	...	...	1
11					
12					
13					
S. 14					
15					
16					
17					
18					
19					
20					
S. 21					
22	Stirling		1		
23					
24	Stirling		2		
25					
26	Stirling		2		
27	Stirling		1		
S. 28	Stirling	...	...	...	1
29					
30	Stirling		1		
July W. 1					
2	Stirling		1		
3	Edinburgh		1	1	
4					
July S. 5					
6					
7					
8	Stirling	1	1		
9	Stirling	1			
10					
11					
S. 12					
13					
14	Stirling	1	1		
15					
16					
17					
18	Stirling	1			
S. 19					
20	Edinburgh	1			
21	Edinburgh	1			
22	Edinburgh	1			
23	Edinburgh	3			
24					
25	Edinburgh	2	1		
S. 26					
27					
28					
29	Edinburgh	1			
30	Edinburgh	...	...	1	1
31	Edinburgh	3			
Aug. S. 1	Holyrood	3	2		
	Edinburgh	2			
S. 2					
3	Edinburgh	2			
4					
5					
6	Edinburgh	1			
	Holyrood	...	1		
7					
8	Edinburgh	2			
S. 9					
10	Edinburgh	5	...	1	1
11					
12	Linlithgow	...	...	...	1
13					
14	Stirling	2	...	1	
15	Stirling	...	...	1	

On 9th June she leaves Edinburgh for Dunfermline (F. C. E. v. 89), and by the 17th had left Dunfermline for Alloa, and from thence had gone to Stirling (*Ibid.* v. 100, 101).

On the 15th of July the Queen is still at Stirling, but is to leave next day for Edinburgh (*Ibid.* v. 161). She is in Edinburgh on 25th July (*Ibid.* v. 199), and is to go to Stirling on 11th August (*Ibid.* v. 232). See *supra*, p. 301, *n.* 4.

16th Aug. 1562-   31st Oct. 1562

Date	Place	P	G	C	L
Aug.					
S. 16					
17	Stirling	3	1	...	1
18					
19					
20					
21	Cupar-Angus	...	...	...	1
22					
S. 23					
24	Perth	...	...	...	1
25	Edzell	...	...	1	
26	Glamis	1			
27					
28	Aberdeen	1			
29					
S. 30	Aberdeen	1			
31					
Sept.					
Tu. 1					
2	Aberdeen	...	...	...	1
3					
4					
5					
S. 6					
7					
8					
9					
10	Darnaway	...	...	1	
11					
12					
S. 13					
14					
15					
16	Inverness	1	1		
17	Inverness	1	1		
18	Spynie	1			
19					
S. 20					
21					
22					
23					

Date	Place	P	G	C	L
Sept.					
24	Aberdeen	3	1		
25					
26					
S. 27					
28					
29					
30					
Oct.					
Th. 1					
2					
3	Aberdeen	1			
S. 4					
5	Aberdeen	1			
6	Aberdeen	1			
7					
8					
9	Aberdeen	2			
10					
S. 11					
12	Aberdeen	1			
13	Aberdeen	3	2	1	1
14					
15	Aberdeen	4	...	1	
16					
17					
S. 18					
19	Aberdeen	4			
20					
21					
22					
23	Aberdeen	1			
24	Aberdeen	1			
S. 25	Aberdeen	1	1		
26	Aberdeen	1	...	1	
27	Aberdeen	...	...	1	
28					
29	Aberdeen	1			
30	Aberdeen	1	1		
31	Aberdeen	5			

On 31st August she is in Old Aberdeen (F. C. E. v. 273), on 9th September arrives at Inverness (*Ibid.* v. 303), remains there for five days, and is at Spynie on 18th (*Ibid.* v. 304). On 20th September she comes to the Laird of Bank's [? Banff's] house, and on 22nd arrives again in Old Aberdeen (*Ibid.* v. 319).

In the printed *Register of Privy Council* (i. 220), *Edinburgh* is given instead of *Abirdene* as the place of meeting on 26th October.

On 30th October she is still in Aberdeen (F. C. E. v. 421).

Chalmers owned Ogilvy's *Diary* of Mary's first northern progress. For the substance of that *Diary* and of other household-books bearing on her movements, see his *Life of Mary*, 1818, i. 81-88, 96, 97, 101-104, 107, 108, 139, 152-154.

ITINERARY

Date	Place	P	G	C	L	Date	Place	P	G	C	L
Nov.						Dec.					
S. 1	Aberdeen	3				11					
2						12	Edinburgh	1			
3	Aberdeen	1	1	...	1	S. 13					
4	Aberdeen	...	...	...	1	14	Edinburgh	2			
5	Aberdeen	2				15	Edinburgh	3	1		
6	Aberdeen	2				16	Edinburgh	3	1		
7						17					
S. 8						18	Edinburgh	2			
9						19	Edinburgh	2			
10	Aberdeen	2				S. 20	Edinburgh	2			
11						21					
12	Aberdeen	1				22	Edinburgh	1	1		
13						23	Edinburgh	...	...	1	
14						24	Edinburgh	1			
S. 15						25					
16						26					
17						S. 27	Edinburgh	1			
18						28	Edinburgh	1			
19	Aberdeen	2				29					
20	Stirling	1				30					
21						31					
S. 22	Aberdeen	1				1562-3 Janry.					
23	Edinburgh	1				F. 1					
24	Edinburgh	1				2	Edinburgh	3			
25						S. 3	Edinburgh	1	1		
26						4	Edinburgh	1			
27						5	Holyrood	...	...	...	1
28						6	Edinburgh	1	...	1	
S. 29						7	Edinburgh	3			
30	Edinburgh	1				8	Edinburgh	4	4		
Dec.						9					
Tu. 1						S. 10					
2						11					
3	Edinburgh	...	...	1		12	Castle Camp-bell	1			
4						13					
5						14	Edinburgh	1			
S. 6	Edinburgh	1	...	1		15	Edinburgh	1			
7	Edinburgh	1				16					
8						S. 17	Edinburgh	1			
9						18	Edinburgh	2	...	1	
10											

She leaves Aberdeen on 3rd November (D. p. 74), returning to the South by Dunnottar, Montrose, and Dundee, where she was on the 15th November, and purposing to go by Stirling to Edinburgh (K. ii. 181 ; S. pp. 102-105), she reaches Holyrood on 21st November (D. p. 74), and, immediately taking the disease called ' the Newe Acquaintance,' keeps her bed for six days (S. p. 105).

On 30th Dec. she is in Dunbar, and intends to be in Edinburgh again on 1st Janry., and at Castle Campbell on the 10th (F. C. E. v. 605). By the 12th of Janry. she had left Castle Campbell for Stirling, and Stirling for Edinburgh (*Ibid.* vi. 59).

ITINERARY

		P	G	C	L
Janry.					
19					
20	Edinburgh	3	1		
21	{ Edinburgh	1			
	{ Holyrood	1			
22	{ Edinburgh	4	...	1	
	{ Holyrood	...	...	...	1
23	Edinburgh	1	...	1	
S. 24					
25					
26	Edinburgh	1			
27	Edinburgh	2	...	...	1
28	Edinburgh	2	1	1	
29	Edinburgh	...	...	...	1
30	Edinburgh	1	...	...	1
S. 31	Edinburgh	4	...	...	1
Feb.					
M. 1	Edinburgh	1	...	1	
2	Edinburgh	2			
3	Edinburgh	1			
4	Edinburgh	1			
5	Edinburgh	4			
6	Edinburgh	1	...	1	
S. 7	Edinburgh	3	1		
8					
9	Edinburgh	1			
10	Edinburgh	1			
11	Edinburgh	1	...	1	
12	Edinburgh	25	4		
13	Edinburgh	1			
S. 14					
15					
16	Edinburgh	1			
17	Edinburgh	...	...	...	1
18					
19					
20	{ Edinburgh	1			
	{ St. Andrews	...	...	...	1
S. 21	St. Andrews	1	1		
22	St. Andrews	1	1		
23					

		P	G	C	L
Feb.					
24	St. Andrews	1	1		
25					
26					
27					
S. 28	{ Edinburgh	1			
	{ St. Andrews	1			
March					
M. 1	St. Andrews	1	1		
2	St. Andrews	1	1		
3					
4	St. Andrews	1			
5					
6	St. Andrews	2			
S. 7					
8					
9	St. Andrews	1			
10					
11					
12					
13					
S. 14					
15					
16	St. Andrews	3	1		
17	St. Andrews	...	...	1	
18	St. Andrews	...	...	...	1
19					
20	Edinburgh	1			
S. 21					
22					
23					
24					
1563					
25					
26	St. Andrews	1			
27					
S. 28	St. Andrews	1			
29					
30	St. Andrews	1			
31	St. Andrews	2	1		

By the 22nd of Jan. she had been in Edinburgh for several days (F. C. E. vi. 59, 60).

On the 14th Feb., three days after leaving Edinburgh, she is in Burnt Island on her way to St. Andrews (F. C. E. vi. 133, 167). On 11th March she leaves St. Andrews [? for Pitlethie] for three days (F. C. E. vi. 196), and on 18th leaves St. Andrews for Falkland for eight or ten days (*Ibid.* vi. 212). She returns to Pitlethie on 25th March (*Ibid.* vi. 260), and on the 29th to St. Andrews, from which she is in six days to go to Falkland (*Ibid.* vi. 262).

The document in the *Register of Privy Seal*, dated 16th Febry., is placed here according to the A.D., the regnal year is given as the twenty-second.

ITINERARY

1st April 1563-   24th June 1563

Date	Place	P	G	C	L	Date	Place	P	G	C	L
Apr.						May					
Th. 1						12	St. Andrews	2	1		
2	Edinburgh	1				13	St. Andrews	3			
	St. Andrews	3				14	St. Andrews	2	1		
3	St. Andrews	1	1			15					
S. 4						S. 16	St. Andrews	1			
5						17					
6	St. Andrews	2	1			18	Edinburgh	2			
	Falkland	4				19	Edinburgh	1			
7	Falkland	1				20					
8	Falkland	1				21					
9						22					
10	Falkland	1				S. 23					
S. 11						24	Edinburgh	1			
12						25	Edinburgh	1	...	...	1
13						26					
14						27	Holyrood	1	1		
15						28	Edinburgh	...	...	...	1
16						29	Edinburgh	1			
17						S. 30					
S. 18	St. Andrews	1				31					
19						June					
20	St. Andrews	...	...	1		Tu. 1	Edinburgh	1			
21						2	Edinburgh	1	...	...	1
22						3	Edinburgh	1			
23	St. Andrews	...	...	...	1	4	Edinburgh	3			
24						5	Edinburgh	2			
S. 25	St. Andrews	1	...	...	1	S. 6	Edinburgh	1			
26	St. Andrews	1	...	...	1	7					
27						8	Edinburgh	4			
28	St. Andrews	1				9					
29	St. Andrews	1				10					
30	St Andrews	1				11					
						12	Edinburgh	3			
May S. 1						S. 13					
S. 2	Edinburgh	1				14	Edinburgh	3			
	St. Andrews	1				15	Edinburgh	5	1		
3						16	Edinburgh	10	1		
4						17					
5						18	Edinburgh	3	...		1
6	St. Andrews	3				19	Edinburgh	5	1		
7						S. 20	Edinburgh	10	3		
8	St. Andrews	1				21	Edinburgh	1			
S. 9						22	Edinburgh	15	1		
10	St. Andrews	1				23	Edinburgh	2			
11						24	Edinburgh	10	2		

On 7th April she is at Falkland (F. C. E. vi. 278), which she is to leave by the 13th, and is to be at St. Andrews by the 18th (*Ibid*. vi. 280). She has been in St. Andrews since Easter (*Ibid*. vi. 311), and on 16th May leaves it for Edinburgh (*Ibid*. vi. 340). On 26th of May she opens Parliament in Edinburgh (*Ibid*. vi. 381), and closes it on the 6th of June (*Ibid*. vi. 399).

523

ITINERARY

25th June 1563-   27th Aug. 1563

Date	Place	P	G	C	L	Date	Place	P	G	C	L
June						July					
25	Edinburgh	1				28	Dunoon	5	3		
26	Edinburgh	1				29					
S. 27	Edinburgh	3				30	{ Dunoon	2	2		
28	Edinburgh	1					{ Edinburgh	1			
29	Edinburgh	1				31	Southannan	1			
30	Edinburgh	1	1	...	1	Aug.					
						S. 1					
July						2					
Th. 1	Edinburgh	1				3					
2	Dunipace	1	1			4					
3	Glasgow	2				5					
S. 4	Hamilton	2				6					
5						7					
6						S. 8	Edinburgh	2			
7						9					
8	{ Dumbarton	1				10					
	{ Glasgow	1	...	1		11					
9						12					
10						13					
S. 11						14					
12	Glasgow	1	1			S. 15	{ Dunure	1			
13	Glasgow	2	1	1			{ St. Mary's				
14	Glasgow	2					Isle	1			
15						16					
16						17					
17						18	St. Mary's				
S. 18							Isle	2			
19						19	Dumfries	...	...	1	
20						20	Dumfries	...	...	1	
21						21					
22						S. 22					
23	Inveraray	1				23					
24	Inveraray	...	...	...	1	24					
S. 25	Glasgow	1				25					
26	Inverary	...	...	...	1	26					
27						27					

26th June. She is to leave Edinburgh for Stirling within four days (F. C. E. vi. 426). On the 1st of August she is with Lord Eglinton ; on the 2nd and 3rd at St. John's, Ayr ; on the 4th, 5th, and 6th at Dunure Castle ; on the 7th at Ardmillan ; on the 8th at Ardstinchar ; on the 9th at Glenluce ; on the 10th at Whithorn ; on the 11th and 12th at Clary ; on 13th and 14th at Quin [? Kenmure] with Laird of Lochinvar ; on 15th, 16th, and 17th at St. Mary's Isle ; on 18th goes to Dumfries ; from thence goes on 21st to Drumlanrick ; from thence goes on 23rd to Crawfordjohn ; on 24th goes to Cowdailly, which she leaves on 26th for Skirling ; on 27th goes to Peebles ; reaches Borthwick on the 28th, leaves it on the 30th for Daousy [? Dalhousie] where she sleeps, and goes to Roslyn on the 31st August and sleeps there (*Roll of Expenses of the Queen's Equerries* in Register House).

One of the documents of 14th July in the *Register of Privy Seal* bears the regnal year 22.

ITINERARY

28th Aug. 1563.   22nd Nov. 1563.

		P	G	C	L			P	G	C	L
Aug.						Oct.					
28						9					
S. 29	Borthwick	...	...	...	I	S. 10					
30						11					
31	Edinburgh	I	...	...	I	12					
						13					
Sept.						14	Stirling	I			
W. 1	Stirling	I				15	Stirling	I			
2	Edinburgh	I	I			16					
3						S. 17	Stirling	2			
4	Edinburgh	...	...	I		18					
S. 5						19					
6	Craigmillar	I				20					
7	Edinburgh	I				21					
8	{ Edinburgh	II	3			22					
	{ Holyrood	...	...	...	I	23					
9	Stirling	I				S. 24	Stirling	2	I		
10						25					
11						26					
S. 12						27					
13	Stirling	...	...	I		28	Stirling	I			
14						29	Stirling	I			
15						30					
16	Stirling	I				S. 31	Stirling	2			
17						Nov.					
18						M. 1					
S. 19						2	{ Edinburgh	I	I		
20	Stirling	I					{ Stirling	3			
21	Stirling	I				3					
22	{ Stirling	2	...	I	I	4					
	{ Edinburgh	I				5					
23	Stirling	I				6					
24	Stirling	I	I			S. 7					
25						8					
S. 26	Stirling	2	...	...	I	9					
27						10					
28	Stirling	I				11					
29						12	Stirling	I			
30	Stirling	I	I			13					
Oct.						S. 14	Stirling	I			
F. 1						15	Stirling	I			
2	Stirling	I	...	...	2	16					
S. 3						17	Stirling	...	...	...	I
4	Stirling	I				18	Stirling	I			
5						19	Aberdeen	I			
6						20	Stirling	I			
7						S. 21					
8	Edinburgh	I				22					

On 1st Sept. she is at Craigmillar (F. C. E. vi. 518). On 18th Sept. she is at Stirling (*Burgh Records of Edinburgh*, 1557-1571, p. 170). Her letter to the Rhinegrave from Stirling is dated 22nd Sept. by Labanoff; the 21st in *Hist. MSS. Com. Rep.*

525

23rd Nov. 1563-   12th Feb. 1563-4

Date	Place	P	G	C	L
Nov.					
23					
24	Linlithgow	2			
25	Linlithgow	1			
26					
27					
S. 28					
29					
30					
Dec.					
W. 1					
2					
3					
4	Edinburgh	1			
S. 5					
6					
7					
8	Edinburgh	9	1		
9					
10					
11	Edinburgh	1			
S. 12					
13					
14	Edinburgh	...	...	2	
15					
16					
17					
18					
S. 19					
20	Edinburgh	2			
21					
22					
23					
24					
25					
S. 26	Edinburgh	2	1		
27					
28	Edinburgh	1	...	1	
29					
30	Edinburgh	...	...	1.	
31					
1563-4					
Janr.					
S. 1	Edinburgh	1	...	1	

Date	Place	P	G	C	L
Janr.					
S. 2	Edinburgh	8	2		
3	Edinburgh	1			
4	Edinburgh	1			
5					
6					
7					
8	Edinburgh	13	6	1	
S. 9					
10	Edinburgh	...	...	1	
11	Edinburgh	1			
12	Edinburgh	...	...	1	
13					
14	Edinburgh	...	...	...	1
15	Edinburgh	1			
S. 16	Edinburgh	1			
17	Edinburgh	2			
18					
19					
20	{ Edinburgh	1			
	{ Holyrood	...	...	...	1
21					
22	Edinburgh	4			
S. 23	Edinburgh	1			
24	Edinburgh	1	1		
25	Edinburgh	...	...	...	2
26					
27					
28	Edinburgh	2			
29					
S. 30	Edinburgh	1			
31	Edinburgh	...	...	1	
Feb.					
Tu. 1	Edinburgh	2			
2	Edinburgh	1			
3					
4	Edinburgh	3			
5	Holyrood	...	...	...	1
S. 6	Edinburgh	4			
7					
8	Edinburgh	4	2	...	1
9					
10	Edinburgh	3	1		
11					
12	Edinburgh	4			

On 10th Dec. she is in Edinburgh (F. C. E. vi. 616), on the 12th she is there (*Ibid.* vi. 617), and on the 21st (*Ibid.* vi. 636) and 26th she is still there (*Ibid.* vi. 649).

In the *Register of Privy Council* two meetings with different sederunts are dated 14th December. Probably one of them should be the 24th.

On 16th Janry. she is in Edinburgh (F. C. E. vii. 24).

ITINERARY

Date	Place	P	G	C	L		Date	Place	P	G	C	L
Feb.							Mar.					
S. 13							22	Perth	1	...	1	
14							23	{ Perth	3	1		
15								{ Falkland	2	1		
16	Edinburgh	3	1				24	Perth	1	1		
17	Edinburgh	1					1564					
18							25	Falkland	1			
19	Edinburgh	...	...	1			S. 26	{ Falkland	1			
S. 20	{ Holyrood	...	...	...	1			{ Edinburgh	1			
	{ Edinburgh	18	3	...	3		27					
21	Edinburgh	1					28	Falkland	1			
22	Dunbar	1					29					
23	Edinburgh	...	...	1			30					
24	Edinburgh	...	...	...	1		31	Edinburgh	1			
25	Edinburgh	1					April					
26	Edinburgh	6	1				S. 1	{ Falkland	...	...	...	1
S. 27	Edinburgh	1	...	...	1			{ Perth	...	1		
28	Edinburgh	1	1	...	1		S. 2					
29	Edinburgh	3	1				3					
							4	St. Andrews	1			
Mar.							5					
W. 1	Edinburgh	3	...	1			6					
2	Edinburgh	...	...	1			7					
3	Edinburgh	2					8	Perth	1			
4	Edinburgh	2					S. 9					
S. 5	{ Edinburgh	2	1	...	2		10					
	{ Holyrood	...	...	...	1		11	Falkland	3	1		
6	Edinburgh	15	4				12	Edinburgh	1			
7	Edinburgh	1					13					
8	Loch Leven	...	...	...	2		14	Falkland	1	1		
9							15	Falkland	1	1		
10							S. 16	Falkland	1			
11	Perth	...	...	...	1		17					
S. 12	St. Andrews	1					18	Falkland	1			
13	Perth	1					19	Perth	...	...	1	
14	Perth	1					20	Perth	...	...	1	
15	Edinburgh	1					21	Perth	4	1		
16	Perth	1					22					
17							S. 23					
18	Perth	1	...	1			24					
S. 19	{ Perth	1					25					
	{ Edinburgh	1					26	Perth	2	...	1	
20	{ Edinburgh	1	1				27	Perth	...	...	1	
	{ Perth	2	1				28	Perth	...	...	1	
21	Perth	3										

She is in Edinburgh on 13th Feb. (F. C. E. vii. 48). On 21st Feb. she goes to Dunbar (*Ibid.* vii. 57). On the 1st of March she is in Edinburgh (*Ibid.* vii. 72), which on the 7th she leaves for Perth (*Ibid.* vii. 73).

On 18th March she is at Perth (*Ibid.* vii. 83, 89), which before the end of the month she left for Falkland (*Ibid.* vii. 91). This Easter she has been at Falkland, saving two days at St. Andrews, and will go to Perth and Stirling before returning to Edinburgh (*Ibid.* vii. 107).

Date		P	G	C	L	Date		P	G	C	L
April						June					
29	Edinburgh	1				6					
S. 30						7					
May						8					
M. 1						9					
2	Edinburgh	1				10					
3	Perth	1				S. 11					
4	Perth	2	1			12					
5	Perth	3	1			13					
6	Perth	1				14					
S. 7						15					
8	Perth	4	2	1		16					
9						17					
10	Perth	1				S. 18	Edinburgh	1			
11						19					
12	Perth	4	1			20	Edinburgh	1			
13	Perth	1				21					
S. 14	Perth	2	2			22					
15						23					
16						24	Edinburgh	4	2		
17						S. 25					
18						26	Edinburgh	3	1		
19	Stirling	1				27					
20						28	Edinburgh	2			
S. 21						29	{ Edinburgh	1			
							{ Holyrood	...	...	1	
22	Edinburgh	2	1			30	Edinburgh	1			
23						July					
24	Edinburgh	1				S. 1					
25	Edinburgh	1				S. 2	Edinburgh	3			
26						3					
27	Edinburgh	2				4	Stirling	1			
S. 28						5					
29	Edinburgh	1				6	Edinburgh	3			
30						7					
31	{ Holyrood	...	...	1		8	Edinburgh	2			
	{ Edinburgh	...	...	...	3						
June						S. 9					
Th. 1	Edinburgh	4	2	...	2	10					
2	{ Edinburgh	1	1			11					
	{ Holyrood	...	...	...	1	12	Edinburgh	1			
3	{ Edinburgh	2	1			13					
	{ Holyrood	...	...	1		14	Edinburgh	1			
S. 4	Edinburgh	1				15	Edinburgh	...	...	...	1
5						S. 16					

On 22nd May she is apparently in Edinburgh (F. C. E. vii. 137, 138), which she leaves on the 5th June to visit Lady Murray [? at Loch Leven], for a few days (*Ibid.* vii. 148, 149).

In the MS. *Register of Privy Council* the year date of the meeting of 29th June has faded out. The printed *Register* (i. 268) gives 1564; and Keith (iii. 508) gives 1563.

ITINERARY

July		P	G	C	L
17	Edinburgh	1	1		
18	⎧ Perth	1			
	⎨ Edinburgh	5	1		
	⎩ Holyrood	1			
19					
20	Edinburgh	4	1		
21	Edinburgh	2	1		
22	Linlithgow	3	3		
S. 23					
24					
25	⎰ Kincardine	1			
	⎱ Perth	1	1		
26					
27					
28	Perth	3			
29	Perth	2			
S. 30	Perth	1	1		
31	Perth	5			
Aug.					
Tu. 1					
2					
3	⎱ Lunkartis	...	...	...	1
4	⎰ in Glentilt	...	...	...	1
5					
S. 6					
7					
8	Edinburgh	...	2		
9					
10					
11	Inverness	...	...	1	
12					
S. 13					
14					
15					
16					
17					
18					
19					
S. 20					
21					
22					
23					
24	Gartly	...	...	...	1
25					

Aug.		P	G	C	L
26					
S. 27					
28	Edinburgh	1			
29					
30	Aberdeen	...	...	1*	
31					
Sept.					
F. 1					
2					
S. 3					
4					
5	Dunnottar	1	1		
6					
7					
8	Dundee	1			
9	Dundee	...	...	...	1
S. 10					
11					
12					
13					
14					
15					
16					
S. 17	⎧ Edinburgh	1			
18	⎩ Holyrood	...	...	...	1
19					
20					
21	Edinburgh	1			
22					
23	Edinburgh	1	...	1	
S. 24	Edinburgh	1			
25	Edinburgh	...	...	...	1
26	Holyrood	...	...	...	1
27	Edinburgh	1	...	...	1
28	⎧ Edinburgh	...	...	1	1
	⎩ Holyrood	...	...	...	1
29	Edinburgh	1	...	...	1
30	Edinburgh	...	...	1	
Oct.					
S. 1					
2	Edinburgh	1			
3					
4					

On 27th July, her secretary writes from Perth (F. C. E. vii. 182).

The two documents in the *Register of Great Seal*, dated 8th Aug., both bear the year date 1564, but one of them is 'an. reg. 21,' which was 1563.

On 15th Sept. she arrives in Edinburgh (F. C. E. vii. 207, 208). She is in Edinburgh on 25th Sept. (*Ibid.* vii. 213).

ITINERARY

Date	Place	P	G	C	L
Oct.					
5	Edinburgh	2	2		
6	{ Edinburgh	1	1		
	{ Holyrood	...	...	...	1
7	Edinburgh	...	...	1	
S. 8					
9	Holyrood	1			
10	{ Edinburgh	1	...	1	
	{ Holyrood	2	...	...	1
11	Edinburgh	...	...	...	1
12	Edinburgh	1			
13	Edinburgh	2			
14	Edinburgh	1	...	...	1
S. 15	Edinburgh	1			
16	Edinburgh	4	1	1	
17	Edinburgh	1			
18	Edinburgh	1	...	1	1
19	Edinburgh	2	2	1	
20	Edinburgh	...	...	1*	1
21	Edinburgh	4	1		
S. 22	Edinburgh	1			
23					
24					
25	Dunbar	1			
26					
27	Edinburgh	1	1	1	
28					
S. 29					
30	Edinburgh	2	1		
31	Edinburgh	2			
Nov.					
W. 1	Edinburgh	...	...	1	1
2	Edinburgh	3	1	...	1
3	Edinburgh	...	...	1	
4	Edinburgh	1	1		
S. 5					
6	Edinburgh	...	...	...	1
7	Edinburgh	1			
8	Edinburgh	4			
9	Holyrood	...	...	...	1
10	Edinburgh	1			
11	Edinburgh	4	1		
S. 12	Edinburgh	3			
Nov.					
13	{ Edinburgh	1	1		
	{ Holyrood	1	.		
14					
15					
16	Edinburgh	2			
17					
18					
S. 19	Dunbar	2			
20					
21					
22					
23					
24					
25					
S. 26	Edinburgh	1			
27	Edinburgh	2	1	1	
28					
29					
30	Edinburgh	1	1		
Dec.					
F. 1	Edinburgh	6	3	...	1
2					
S. 3	Edinburgh	1	1	1	
4	Edinburgh	5	1		
5					
6	Edinburgh	1	1	...	1
7	Edinburgh	1			
8	Edinburgh	3			
9	Edinburgh	2	1		
S. 10	Edinburgh	1			
11	Edinburgh	1	...	1	
12	Edinburgh	2	...	1	
13	Edinburgh	...	...	1	
14					
15					
16	Edinburgh	7			
S. 17					
18	Edinburgh	5	1		
19	Edinburgh	...	...	1	
20	Edinburgh	...	...	1*	2
21	{ Edinburgh	1	...	1	
	{ Holyrood	1			

On 20th Oct. she is in Edinburgh (F. C. E. vii. 229). On 22nd Oct. she goes to the Justice-Clerk's, and returns that night to Edinburgh (*Ibid.* vii. 230).

In the printed *Register of Privy Council* (i. 290) the meeting of 27th October is misdated the 28th.

In November she intends going to Dunbar for six or seven days (F. C. E. vii. 242). She is present at Parliament in Edinburgh, which is opened on 4th December and closed on the 9th (*Ibid.* vii. 261). From 20th to 24th December she keeps her chamber because of the cold (*Ibid.* vii. 271).

ITINERARY

		P	G	C	L			P	G	C	L
Dec.						**Janry.**					
22	{ Edinburgh	3	1			26	Ballinbreich	1			
	{ Holyrood	1				27					
23	Edinburgh	2				S. 28	{ Balmerino	...	...	...	1
S. 24							{ St.Andrews	...	...	...	1
25	Edinburgh	...	...	1		29					
26						30					
27						31					
28						**Feb.**					
29						Th. 1	St. Andrews	2	1		
30	Edinburgh	1	...	1		2	St. Andrews	1			
S. 31						3	St. Andrews	1			
1564-5						S. 4					
Janry.						5					
M. 1						6					
2	Edinburgh	1	1			7	The Struther	...	...	...	1
3	Edinburgh	1	1	1	1	8					
4	Edinburgh	1				9					
5	Edinburgh	...	...	1		10	St. Andrews	...	...	...	1
6						S. 11	Lundie	1			
S. 7						12	{ Lundie	1			
8							{ Edinburgh	1			
9						13	Edinburgh	1			
10						14					
11						15					
12	Edinburgh	2				16	{ Durie	2			
13	Edinburgh	1	...	1			{ Wemyss	1			
S. 14						17					
15	{ Edinburgh	6	...	1		S. 18					
	{ Holyrood	1				19					
16	{ Edinburgh	4				20					
	{ Holyrood	2	1			21					
17	Edinburgh	6	...	1		22					
18	{ Edinburgh	1	...	1		23					
	{ Holyrood	1				24					
19	Edinburgh	...	...	1*		S. 25					
20	{ Edinburgh	2				26	Edinburgh	4	1		
	{ Holyrood	1				27					
S. 21						28	Edinburgh	2			
22	{ Edinburgh	...	...	1*		**Mar.**					
	{ Falkland	1	1			Th. 1	{ Edinburgh	3	1		
23	{ Falkland	1					{ Holyrood	2			
	{ Edinburgh	1				2	Edinburgh	3	1		
24	Collairnie	2	1			3	Edinburgh	1			
25											

On 11th January, and again on the 16th, she dines in Edinburgh Castle (F. C. E. vii. 283, 285), by the 18th she has crossed the Forth (*Ibid.* vii. 285) to pass from place to place for twenty days (*Ibid.* vii. 283), and reaches St. Andrews on the evening of the 28th (*Ibid.* vii. 289). On the 9th Feb. her secretary writes from St. Monans (*Ibid.* vii. 296), on the 17th she meets Darnley at Wemyss (*Ibid.* vii. 301), and crosses the Queensferry on the 24th (*Ibid.* vii. 305).

4th March 1564-5-   22nd May 1565

		P	G	C	L			P	G	C	L
Mar.						April					
S. 4	Edinburgh	1	1			9	Stirling	1			
5						10	Stirling	2			
6	Edinburgh	1	1			11	Stirling	1	1		
7	Edinburgh	3	1	1		12	Holyrood	1			
8	Edinburgh	4	1	1		13					
9	{ Edinburgh	1	...	1		14					
	{ Holyrood	1				S. 15	Stirling	1			
10	{ Edinburgh	4	1			16	Stirling	...	...	1	
	{ Holyrood	1				17					
S. 11						18	{ Edinburgh	1			
12	Edinburgh	4	...	...	1		{ Stirling	1			
13	Edinburgh	...	...	1		19					
14						20	Stirling	1	1		
15	{ Edinburgh	1				21	Stirling	1			
	{ Holyrood	2				S. 22					
16						23					
17	Edinburgh	1	1	1		24	Stirling	6	4	...	1
S. 18	Edinburgh	2	2			25	Stirling	1			
19	Edinburgh	4	1			26					
20	{ Edinburgh	8	1			27					
	{ Stirling	1				28	Stirling	2	2		
21	Edinburgh	...	...	1		S. 29					
22	{ Edinburgh	7	1	1	1	30	Stirling	1			
	{ Perth	1				May					
23	Edinburgh	3	1			Tu. 1	Stirling	2			
24	Edinburgh	1	...	1		2					
1565						3	Stirling	...	...	...	1
S. 25	Edinburgh	2	1			4	Stirling	...	...	...	1
26	{ Edinburgh	1				5	Stirling	...	...	...	2
	{ Holyrood	1				S. 6	Stirling	2			
27						7	Stirling	2	1	...	4
28						8	Stirling	2	1		
29	{ Linlithgow	...	...	...	1	9	Stirling	1	...	1	
	{ Edinburgh	...	...	1		10					
30	Holyrood	...	...	...	2	11					
31	{ Edinburgh	1				12	Stirling	...	...	...	1
	{ Linlithgow	7	4			S. 13					
April						14	Stirling	1			
S. 1	Stirling	1				15	Stirling	2	1	1	
2	{ Edinburgh	1	1			16	{ Perth	...	...	...	1
	{ Stirling	3	1				{ Stirling	2			
3						17	Stirling	1			
4	Stirling	2	1			18	Stirling	5	1	...	1
5						19	Stirling	2	1	1	
6	Stirling	1	1			S. 20	Stirling	3	1	1	1
7	Stirling	1	1			21	Stirling	4			
S. 8	Stirling	5	1			22	Stirling	2			

On the 4th and 17th of March she is apparently in Edinburgh (F. C. E. vii. 309, 315). On the 7th of April she is at Stirling (*Ibid.* vii. 328), and is still there on 22nd April (*Ibid.* vii. 340), and on 4th, 15th, and 18th May (*Ibid.* vii. 357, 369, 370).

23rd May 1565-   30th July 1565

Date	Place	P	G	C	L	Date	Place	P	G	C	L
May						June					
23	Perth	1				28					
	Stirling	1				29	Perth	1			
24	Stirling	1					Dunkeld	...	...	1*	1
25	Stirling	2	2			30	Dunkeld	1	1		
26	Stirling	2					Perth	3			
S. 27	Stirling	...	...	...	2	July.					
28	Stirling	2				S. 1					
29	Edinburgh	10	7			2	Edinburgh	1			
30	Stirling	...	...	...	1	3					
	Edinburgh	1				4					
31	Edinburgh	13	3			5	Edinburgh	1			
	Stirling	2	1			6	Edinburgh	1			
June						7	Edinburgh	1			
F. 1	Perth	1				S. 8	Edinburgh	2	1		
2						9					
S. 3	Stirling	1				10	Edinburgh	20	1		
4	Perth	1				11	Edinburgh	1			
5	Perth	1				12	Edinburgh	1	...	1	
6	Perth	1					Holyrood	1			
7						13	Edinburgh	...	...	1	
8	Perth	1				14					
9						S. 15	Edinburgh	3	...	1	
S. 10	Perth	1				16	Edinburgh	2	...	...	2
11						17	Edinburgh	...	...	1	2
12	Ruthven	...	...	...	1	18	Edinburgh	2			
	Perth	1				19	Edinburgh	1	...	1	
13	Perth	1					Holyrood	...	...	...	1
14	Perth	1	...	...	2	20	Edinburgh	10	2	1	
15	Perth	...	...	...	1	21					
16	Perth	1				S. 22	Edinburgh	2	...	1	
S. 17						23	Edinburgh	1			
18	Perth	2	1			24	Edinburgh	6	1	1	1
19							Holyrood	1			
20						25	Edinburgh	1			
21						26	Edinburgh	6	1		
22	Perth	2				27	Edinburgh	4	1		
23	Perth	20	7				Holyrood	1			
S. 24	Perth	1				28	Edinburgh	8	3	1	
25	Perth	1					Holyrood	...	...	...	1
26						S. 29					
27	Ruthven	2				30	Holyrood	...	...	...	1

On the 4th June she reaches Perth (F. C. E. vi. 388), on the 25th she rides from Perth to Ruthven, and next day to Dunkeld (K. ii. 301-304), and returns to Perth on the 30th (K. ii. 309). On the 1st of July she rides from Perth to Callendar House (K. ii. 310), and on the 4th arrives in Edinburgh (K. ii. 321).

On the 9th of July she rides to Seton, on the 11th returns to Edinburgh (S. p. 119), and on the 29th marries Darnley in Holyrood (B. p. 5).

The warrant of 12th June is dated 1565, and *an. reg.* xxii.

ITINERARY

July 31 – Aug. 30

Date	Place	P	G	C	L
July					
31	Edinburgh	2	...	...	
	Holyrood	...	...	...	1
Aug.					
W. 1	Edinburgh	1	...	1	
2	Edinburgh	2	...	1	
3	Edinburgh	2	...	1	
4	Edinburgh	5	...	1	
	Holyrood	1			
S. 5	Edinburgh	5	1		
6	Edinburgh	2			
7	Edinburgh	1	...	1	
	Holyrood	1			
8	Edinburgh	4	1		
9	Edinburgh	...	...	1	
10	Edinburgh	...	1	1	
11	Edinburgh	1			
S. 12	Edinburgh	10			
13	Edinburgh	...	...	1	
14	Edinburgh	...	...	1	
15	Edinburgh	...	...	1	
	Holyrood	2			
16	Edinburgh	...	...	...	1
17	Holyrood	1			
18	Edinburgh	2	...	...	1
S. 19					
20	Edinburgh	3			
21	Edinburgh	4	1		
	Holyrood	1			
22	Edinburgh	5	2	1	3
23	Edinburgh	...	...	1	1
24	Edinburgh	6	2	1	
25	Edinburgh	1			
	Holyrood	...	...	...	1
S. 26	Edinburgh	8	3	1	1
	Holyrood	...	...	...	2
27	Edinburgh	1	1		
28	Edinburgh	3			
	Stirling	...	...	...	2
29					
30	Glasgow	1			

Aug. 31 – Sept. 28

Date	Place	P	G	C	L
Aug.					
31	Edinburgh	1			
	Stirling	1			
Sept.					
S. 1	Glasgow	1			
S. 2	Callendar	...	...	1	
3					
4					
5	Glasgow	1	...	1	
6	Glasgow	2	...	1	
	Kilsyth	...	...	...	1
7	Glasgow	1			
	Stirling	...	...	...	1
	Edinburgh	1			
8	Glasgow	...	...	...	2
	Edinburgh	1			
	Dunfermline	1			
S. 9	Edinburgh	1			
10	Glasgow	...	...	...	1
11					
12	St. Andrews	...	...	1	
13	St. Andrews	1	...	...	1
	Dundee	...	...	...	1
14	Dundee	...	...	1	3
15	Dundee	...	...	1	
S. 16	Dundee	1			
17	Perth				
	Dunfermline	3			
	Holyrood	1			
18					
19	Edinburgh	1			
20	Edinburgh	2			
21	Edinburgh	3	...	1	
22	Edinburgh	1	...	...	1
S. 23					
24	Edinburgh	2	...	...	1
	Holyrood	...	...	...	1
25	Edinburgh	2			
26	Edinburgh	1	...	...	2
27					
28	Edinburgh	13	1		
	Holyrood	1			

She leaves Edinburgh on 26th Aug. (F. C. E. vii. 437). She was to leave Callendar for Stirling on 2nd Sept., and was to be at Kilsyth next day (*Register of Privy Council*, i. 361). On the 4th of Sept. she is at Glasgow (F. C. E. vii. 448).

On the 9th of Sept. she leaves Stirling for St. Andrews, purposing to take Castle Campbell and Loch Leven by the way, and from St. Andrews will go to Dundee, and so to Perth (F. C. E. vii. 455). By the 19th she has been in St. Andrews, Dundee, and Perth (*Ibid.* vii. 467), and on that day arrives in Edinburgh from Stirling (D. p. 83).

ITINERARY

29th Sept. 1565-   8th Dec. 1565

		P	G	C	L				P	G	C	L
Sept.							Nov.					
29	Edinburgh	4					S. 4	Edinburgh	4			
S. 30	Edinburgh	2					5	Edinburgh	...	...	1	
							6	Edinburgh	2	...	1	
Oct.							7	Edinburgh	2	...	1	
M. 1	Edinburgh	3	1	...	3		8	Edinburgh	5	1	1	1
2	{ Edinburgh	2					9	Edinburgh	1			
	{ Holyrood	1					10	Edinburgh	3	1		
3							S. 11	Edinburgh	4			
4	{ Edinburgh	5	1				12	{ Edinburgh	2	...	1	
	{ Holyrood	...	...	...	1			{ Linlithgow	1			
5	Edinburgh	...	...	1*			13	Edinburgh	...	...	1	1
6	Edinburgh	3					14	Edinburgh	1			
S. 7	Edinburgh	4	1	1			15	Edinburgh	1	...	1	
8	Edinburgh	7	...	...	1		16	Edinburgh	1			
9	{ Edinburgh	1					17	Edinburgh	...	...	...	1
	{ Lamington	...	...	...	1		S. 18	{ Edinburgh	3	1	1	
	{ Crawfurd	1						{ Holyrood	1			
10	Castlehill	...	...	1			19	Edinburgh	3	3	1*	.
11							20	Edinburgh	1			
12							21	Edinburgh	...	...	1	
13	Dumfries	...	...	1			22					
S. 14							23	Holyrood	...	...	...	1
15	Lochmaben	1					24	{ Edinburgh	2	1		
16								{ Holyrood	1	...	...	1
17							S. 25	Edinburgh	1	...	1*	
18	Edinburgh	1					26	Edinburgh	3	...	1	
19	Edinburgh	1	...	1			27					
20	Edinburgh	1	...	...	1		28	Edinburgh	5			
S. 21	Edinburgh	...	...	1			29	{ Edinburgh	8	1	1	
22	{ Edinburgh	5	...	1				{ Holyrood	1			
	{ Holyrood	1					30	{ Holyrood	1			
23								{ Edinburgh	1			
24	Edinburgh	4						{ Linlithgow	1			
25							Dec.					
26	Edinburgh	4	...	1			S. 1	{ Edinburgh	1	1	1	
27	{ Edinburgh	...	...	1				{ Holyrood	...	...	...	1
	{ Holyrood	1					S. 2	Edinburgh	1	...	1*	1
S. 28	Edinburgh	5	1	1			3					
29	Edinburgh	2	...	1			4	Linlithgow	2			
30	Edinburgh	1	...	1*	1		5					
31	{ Edinburgh	1	...	1	1		6	{ Linlithgow	1			
	{ Dalkeith	2	2					{ Holyrood	1			
Nov.							7	{ Linlithgow	1			
Th. 1	Edinburgh	...	...	1				{ Edinburgh	...	...	1	
2	Edinburgh	1	...	1			8					
3	Edinburgh	...	...	1								

On 8th Oct. she leaves Edinburgh for Biggar (D. p. 84), meets her forces at Crawford-moor (F. C. E. vii. 485), is at Dumfries on 13th (*Ibid.* vii. 488, 489), leaves it on the 14th for Lochmaben, intending to go next day to Moffat, and so to Edinburgh (*Ibid.* vii. 492), which she reaches on the 18th (D. p. 85). On 30th Oct. she rides to Dalkeith, where she remains for a day or two (F. C. E. vii. 505).
On the 3rd of Dec. she goes to Linlithgow (F. C. E. vii. 531, 532).

ITINERARY

Date	Place	P	G	C	L
Dec.					
S. 9	Linlithgow	2	1		
10	{Linlithgow	1			
	{Edinburgh	...	...	1*	
11	Linlithgow	2			
12	Linlithgow	1			
13	Linlithgow	4	1		
14	{Linlithgow	3	1		
	{Edinburgh	1			
15	Edinburgh	1			
S. 16	{Edinburgh	1			
	{Linlithgow	3			
17	{Linlithgow	1			
	{Edinburgh	...	...	1	
18	Edinburgh	6	3		
19					
20	Edinburgh	2			
21	Edinburgh	...	...	...	1
22	Edinburgh	2	...	1	
S. 23	Edinburgh	3			
24	Edinburgh	3			
25					
26					
27	Edinburgh	2	1		
28	Edinburgh	1			
29					
S. 30					
31	{Edinburgh	2	1		
	{Holyrood	...	...	...	1
1565-6					
Janry.					
Tu. 1	{Edinburgh	1			
	{Holyrood	...	...	...	1
2	Edinburgh	5	1		
3	{Edinburgh	2			
	{Holyrood	1			
4	Edinburgh	...	...	1	
5					
S. 6	Edinburgh	2			
7	Edinburgh	2	...	1	
8					
9	Edinburgh	1			
10	Edinburgh	1			
11					
12	Edinburgh	4	1	1	
S. 13					
14	Edinburgh	1			
15	Edinburgh	2			
16	Edinburgh	2			

Date	Place	P	G	C	L
Janry.					
17	Edinburgh	1	...	1	
18	Edinburgh	2			
19					
S. 20	Edinburgh	8	1		
21					
22	Edinburgh	5	1		
23	Edinburgh	5			
24	Edinburgh	7	5	1	
25	Edinburgh	1	...	1	
26	Edinburgh	4	1		
S. 27					
28	{Edinburgh	3			
	{Holyrood	1			
29	Edinburgh	...	...	1	
30	Edinburgh	2	...	1*	
31	{Edinburgh	6	2	1	
	{Holyrood	...	...	...	2
Feb.					
F. 1	Edinburgh	5	1		
2	Edinburgh	11	2		
S. 3					
4	Edinburgh	1			
5					
6	Edinburgh	4			
7	Edinburgh	2			
8	Edinburgh	4	1		
9	Edinburgh	2	...	1	
S. 10					
11	Edinburgh	...	...	...	2
12	{Edinburgh	5	1	1	1
	{Holyrood	...	...	...	1
13	Edinburgh	1	1		
14	Edinburgh	1			
15	Edinburgh	5	1		
16	Edinburgh	6			
S. 17	Edinburgh	1	...	...	1
18	Edinburgh	5	2		
19	Edinburgh	1			
20	Edinburgh	4			
21	Edinburgh	1			
22	Edinburgh	2			
23	{Edinburgh	...	...	1	
	{Holyrood	...	...	...	1
S. 24	Edinburgh	7			
25	Edinburgh	1			
26	{Edinburgh	1	1		
	{Holyrood	...	...	...	1

She is to return from Linlithgow to Edinburgh on 17th Dec. (F. C. E. vii. 538).
The letter from Edinburgh on 12th February is dated the 2nd by Labanoff.
In Thorpe's *Calendar*, and in the *Foreign Calendar*, the 12th is given.

ITINERARY

Date	Place	P	G	C	L
Feb.					
27	Edinburgh	4			
28	Edinburgh	1			
	Holyrood	...	...	...	1
Mar.					
F. 1	Holyrood	1			
	Edinburgh	1			
	Seton	1			
2	Seton	1			
	Edinburgh	1			
S. 3	Edinburgh	2			
4	Edinburgh	2			
5	Edinburgh	1			
6	Edinburgh	2	1		
7	Edinburgh	1	1		
8	Edinburgh	4	2		
9	Edinburgh	1			
S. 10					
11					
12					
13					
14	Edinburgh	1			
15	Dunbar	...	...	...	1
16	Dunbar	1	...	1	
	Edinburgh	...	...	...	1
S. 17	Dunbar	1			
	Edinburgh	...	1		
18					
19	Edinburgh	4	...	1	2
20	Edinburgh	6	1		
21	Edinburgh	7	1	1	
22	Edinburgh	6	...	1	
23	Edinburgh	1			
S. 24	Edinburgh	7			
1566					
25	Edinburgh	1	...	1	
26	Edinburgh	3	...	1	
27	Edinburgh	3	2		
28	Edinburgh	...	...	...	1
29	Edinburgh	2			
30	Edinburgh	1	...	1*	
S. 31	Edinburgh	2	1	...	1
April					
M. 1	Edinburgh	5	...	1	2
2	Edinburgh	1	...	...	1
3	Edinburgh	2	1	1*	

Date	Place	P	G	C	L
April					
4	Edinburgh	1	...	1*	1
5	Edinburgh	1	...	1	
6	Edinburgh	1			
S. 7	Edinburgh	2	...	1*	
8	Edinburgh	3	1		
9	Edinburgh	1			
10	Edinburgh	10	...	1*	1
11	Edinburgh	2	...	1	
12	Edinburgh	4	...	1	
13	Edinburgh	5	...	1*	1
S. 14	Edinburgh	7	1		
15	Edinburgh	...	...	1	
16	Edinburgh	5	...	...	1
17	Edinburgh	1	1		
18	Edinburgh	1			
19	Edinburgh	1			
20	Edinburgh	3	...	1	
S. 21					
22	Edinburgh	1			
23	Edinburgh	2			
24	Edinburgh	1	...	1	
25	Edinburgh	2			
26	Edinburgh	...	...	1	
27	Edinburgh	2	...	...	2
S. 28	Edinburgh	2			
29	Edinburgh	...	...	1	
30	Edinburgh	3	1	1	
May					
W. 1	Edinburgh	1			
2	Edinburgh	2			
3	Edinburgh	...	...	...	2
4	Edinburgh	3			
S. 5					
6	Edinburgh	2	...	1	
7	Edinburgh	1			
8	Edinburgh	3	1		
9	Edinburgh	1			
10	Edinburgh	3			
11	Edinburgh	...	...	1	
S. 12	Edinburgh	3			
13	Edinburgh	...	...	1	
14	Edinburgh	9	...	1*	
15	Edinburgh	2			
16	Edinburgh	2	1	...	1
17	Edinburgh	2			
18	Edinburgh	2			

On the 11th of March—two days after Riccio's murder—she escapes at midnight from Holyrood, and on the 12th reaches Dunbar (W. i. 230 ; D. p. 92), where she remains for five days (K. ii. 421), and returns to Edinburgh on the 18th (D. p. 94). On the 3rd of April she is in Edinburgh Castle (F. C. E. viii. 44), and on the 21st both she and Darnley are there (D. p. 99).

ITINERARY

19th May 1566-   12th Aug. 1566

Date	Place	P	G	C	L	Date	Place	P	G	C	L
May						**July**					
S. 19	Edinburgh	2	...	1		2	Edinburgh	3			
20	Edinburgh	4	...	1		3	Edinburgh	1			
21	Edinburgh	...	...	1		4	Edinburgh	8			
22	Edinburgh	6	1			5	Edinburgh	3			
23	Edinburgh	1				6	Edinburgh	2	1		
24	Edinburgh	3	...	1	1	S. 7					
25	Edinburgh	4	1			8	Edinburgh	2	2		
S. 26	Edinburgh	3	1			9	Edinburgh	2			
27						10					
28	Edinburgh	3				11	Edinburgh	3	...	...	1
29	Edinburgh	2				12	Edinburgh	4			
30	Edinburgh	1				13	Edinburgh	2	1		
31	Edinburgh	5				S. 14	Edinburgh	2			
						15	Edinburgh	9	3	...	1
June						16	Edinburgh	6	...	1	1
S. 1	Edinburgh	3	...	1		17	Edinburgh	5	...	1	1
S. 2	Edinburgh	3	2	...	1	18	Edinburgh	6			
3	Edinburgh	1	...	...	1	19	Edinburgh	3	1		
4	Edinburgh	7	1			20	Edinburgh	12	1		
5	Edinburgh	1				S. 21	Edinburgh	1	...	1	2
6	Edinburgh	4				22	Edinburgh	6			
7						23	Edinburgh	3	1		
8	Edinburgh	...	...	1		24	Edinburgh	5	...	1	
S. 9	Edinburgh	1				25	Edinburgh	3			
10	Edinburgh	3	...	1*		26					
11	Edinburgh	4				27					
12	Edinburgh	2				S. 28	Alloa	...	...	1	
13	Edinburgh	1				29	{ Alloa	1			
14	Edinburgh	1					{ Edinburgh	1			
15	Edinburgh	2	...	1		30	Alloa	...	...	...	1
S. 16						31	{ Edinburgh	1	...	1	
17	Edinburgh	1					{ Holyrood	1			
18	Edinburgh	2	1	1	1		{ Alloa	...	...	...	2
19											
20	{ Perth	1				**Aug.**					
	{ Edinburgh	2				Th. 1	{ Alloa	1			
21							{ Edinburgh	1			
22	Edinburgh	1	...	1		2					
S. 23						3					
24	Edinburgh	1				S. 4					
25	Edinburgh	1				5					
26	Edinburgh	2				6					
27						7	Edinburgh	3			
28	Edinburgh	1	...	1*		8	Edinburgh	2	...	1	
29						9					
S. 30	Edinburgh	4				10	Edinburgh	1			
July						S. 11	Edinburgh	1			
M. 1	Edinburgh	1				12	Edinburgh	7			

On the 3rd of June she takes her chamber in the Castle of Edinburgh (F. C. E. viii. 81), and there on the 19th the Prince is born (D. p. 100).

ITINERARY

13th Aug. 1566-   31st Oct. 1566

Date	Place	P	G	C	L	Date	Place	P	G	C	L
Aug.						Sept.					
13	Edinburgh	4	...	...	1	S. 22					
14						23	{ Stirling	1			
15							{ Edinburgh	1			
16	{ Rodono	...	...	1		24	Edinburgh	3	...	1	
	{ Cramalt	...	...	...	1	25	Edinburgh	2	...	...	1
17						26					
S. 18						27	Edinburgh	1			
19	Traquair	1				28	Edinburgh	1			
20						S. 29	Edinburgh	1			
21	Edinburgh	1				30	Edinburgh	1	...	...	1
22	Edinburgh	2				Oct.					
23						Tu. 1	Edinburgh	3	...	...	1
24						2	Edinburgh	2			
S. 25						3	Edinburgh	4	...	1	
26						4	Edinburgh	4			
27						5	Edinburgh	...	...	1	1
28						S. 6	Edinburgh	...	...	1	
29						7	Edinburgh	1	...	...	1
30	Drymen	1				8					
31	{ Drymen	...	...	...	1	9	Edinburgh	...	...	...	1
	{ Stirling	...	...	...	1	10	Jedburgh	...	...	1	
	{ Edinburgh	1				11	Jedburgh	...	...	1	
Sept.						12					
S. 1						S. 13					
2	Stirling	1				14					
3	Stirling	1				15	Jedburgh	1			
4	Stirling	1				16	{ Jedburgh	...	...	...	1
5	Stirling	...	...	...	1		{ Hermitage	1			
6	Stirling	1				17					
7						18					
S. 8						19					
9						S. 20					
10						21					
11						22					
12	Edinburgh	4	1	...	1	23					
13	Edinburgh	1	...	1		24					
14						25	Jedburgh	1	...	1	
S. 15						26					
16	Edinburgh	5	2			S. 27					
17	Edinburgh	4	...	1		28					
18	Edinburgh	1				29	Jedburgh	1	...	...	1
19	Edinburgh	1	...	...	2	30	Jedburgh	1			
20	Edinburgh	3	2	...	1	31	Jedburgh	1			
21	Edinburgh	...	...	1							

On the 14th Aug. she is at the hunting in Megotland (F. C. E. viii. 117). On the 5th of Sept. she dines with Lethington at Stirling, and comes to Edinburgh next day (*Ibid.* viii. 128). She leaves Edinburgh for Jedburgh on the 7th of Oct. (D. p. 100), or on the 8th (B. p. 5), and arrives in Jedburgh on the 9th (F. C. E. vii. 490). On the 15th of Oct. she rides to and from the Hermitage (*Ibid.* viii. 139), and on the 25th her life is despaired of at Jedburgh (*Ibid.* viii. 141; K. iii. 286).

ITINERARY

1st Nov. 1566-   10th January 1566-7

		P	G	C	L			P	G	C	L
Nov.						**Dec.**					
F. 1	Jedburgh	...	...	...	1	6	Edinburgh	1			
2						7					
S. 3	Jedburgh	2				S. 8	Edinburgh	1			
4	Tantallon	...	...	...	1	9	{ Edinburgh	3			
5	Jedburgh	...	...	1			{ Holyrood	...	...	...	1
6						10	Edinburgh	2			
7						11					
8						12	Stirling	2			
9						13					
S. 10	Kelso	...	...	1		14	Stirling	2	...	1	
11						S. 15	Stirling	1			
12						16	Stirling	1			
13						17	Stirling	1	1		
14						18	Stirling	2			
15	{ Jedburgh	1				19					
	{ Dunbar	1				20	Stirling	2	...	...	1
16						21	Stirling	5	...	1	
S. 17						S. 22	Stirling	1			
18	Dunbar	...	...	...	2	23	Stirling	4			
19						24	Stirling	6	1		
20						25					
21						26					
22						27					
23						28	Drymen	1			
S. 24	Craigmillar	2				S. 29					
25						30	Stirling	1			
26						31	Tullibardine	1			
27						**1566-7**					
28						**Jan.**					
29						W. 1					
30						2	Stirling	2	...	1	
						3	Stirling	2	...	...	1
Dec.						4	Stirling	1	...	...	1
S. 1	Craigmillar	2				S. 5	Stirling	1			
2	Craigmillar	4	1			6	Stirling	...	...	...	1
3	Craigmillar	3	1	...	1	7					
4	Craigmillar	2	...	...	1	8	Stirling	1	1		
5	{ Craigmillar	1				9	Stirling	...	...	...	1
	{ Edinburgh	2				10	Stirling	2	...	1	

On the 2nd of Nov. she is still at Jedburgh (F. C. E. viii. 143). After leaving Jedburgh she went first to Kelso, remaining there two nights, passed next to Hume, visiting Wark on the way, from Hume she went to Langton and Wedderburn, and on the 15th rode towards Berwick, by Halidon Hill; going by Eyemouth she spent a night at Coldingham, came to Dunbar, from thence to Tantallon, and afterwards to Craigmillar (K. ii. 469-471), where she arrived on the 20th of Nov. (D. p. 102).

On the 7th of December she leaves Craigmillar for Holyrood, and on the 10th leaves Holyrood for Stirling (D. p. 102), where the Prince was baptized on the 17th (D. pp. 103, 104).

ITINERARY

Jan.		P	G	C	L
11					
S. 12	Stirling	1			
13					
14	Callendar	1			
	Edinburgh	2			
15	Edinburgh	1			
16	Callendar	...	...	...	1
	Edinburgh	2			
17	Edinburgh	...	...	...	1
18	Edinburgh	1			
S. 19					
20	Edinburgh	1	...	...	1
	Holyrood	1	1		
21					
22	Edinburgh	2			
23					
24	Edinburgh	1			
25					
S. 26					
27					
28	Linlithgow	1			
29	Linlithgow	...	...	...	1
30					
31	Edinburgh	4	2		
Feb.					
S. 1	Edinburgh	8	2		
S. 2	Edinburgh	2			
3	Edinburgh	2	1		
4	Edinburgh	10			
5	Holyrood	1			
6	Edinburgh	11	2		
7	Edinburgh	6	1		
8	Edinburgh	15	1	...	1
S. 9	Edinburgh	1			
10	Edinburgh	...	...	...	1
11	Edinburgh	2			
12	Edinburgh	1	...	1	
13	Edinburgh	3	...	...	1

Feb.		P	G	C	L
14	Edinburgh	4	1		
15	Edinburgh	5	1	...	2
S. 16	Edinburgh	2	1		
	Seton	1			
17	Seton	...	...	...	1
	Edinburgh	1			
18	Seton	3	...	...	1
	Edinburgh	2			
19	Seton	1	1		
20	Edinburgh	2			
	Seton	6			
21	Seton	1	...	...	1
22	Seton	4			
S. 23	Seton	3			
24	Seton	10	1		
	Edinburgh	1			
25	Seton	2			
26	Seton	1			
	Edinburgh	1			
27					
28	Seton	2			
	Edinburgh	...	...	...	1
Mar.					
S. 1	Edinburgh	1	...	1	
	Seton	6	...	...	1
S. 2	Seton	3	1		
3	Seton	3			
	Edinburgh	1			
4	Edinburgh	2			
5	Edinburgh	1			
6	Edinburgh	1			
7	Edinburgh	...	...	...	1
8	Edinburgh	2			
S. 9	Edinburgh	1			
10	Edinburgh	...	...	...	2
11	Edinburgh	1	...	1	1
	Holyrood	...	...	...	1
12	Edinburgh	3	...	1	
	Seton	1			

On the 13th of January she brings the Prince from Stirling to Edinburgh (B. p. 6), or on the 14th (D. p. 105). On the 20th of January she leaves Edinburgh for Glasgow (B. p. 6; D. p. 105).

She comes to Edinburgh with Darnley on the 31st of January (B. p. 6) or on the 1st of February (D. p. 105). On the 9th of February she visits Darnley at Kirk of Field (F. C. E. viii. 176), and on the 10th he is murdered (*Ibid.* viii. 177). On the 16th of February she leaves Holyrood for Seton, and on the 19th returns to Holyrood (D. p. 106), and on the 26th is at Seton again (F. C. E. viii. 180), and is there on the 28th (*Ibid.* viii. 181).

One of the documents of 1st February in the *Register of Privy Seal* bears the year-date 1567. The letter of 10th February is dated the 11th both by Keith and Labanoff.

ITINERARY

13th March 1566-7-   17th May 1567

Mar.		P	G	C	L
13	Edinburgh	8			
14	Edinburgh	2	...	1	
15	Edinburgh	4	2	...	1
S. 16	Edinburgh	2			
17	Edinburgh	4	1		
18	Edinburgh	2			
19	⌠ Edinburgh	6			
	⌊ Holyrood	1	...	...	1
20	⌠ Edinburgh	3			
	⌊ Holyrood	1			
21	⌠ Edinburgh	3	...	1	
	⌊ Holyrood	2			
22	Edinburgh	5			
S. 23	Edinburgh	...	...	...	3
24	⌠ Edinburgh	3	1		
	⌊ Holyrood	2			
1567					
25	Edinburgh	3	1	...	1
26	Edinburgh	1	1		
27	Edinburgh	2			
28	Edinburgh	2	...	1	
29	⌠ Edinburgh	2			
	⌊ Holyrood	1			
S. 30					
31	Edinburgh	1			
April					
Tu. 1	⌠ Edinburgh	12	...	...	1
	⌊ Holyrood	1			
2	⌠ Edinburgh	1			
	⌡ Dunbar	...	...	1	
	⌊ Seton	...	...	...	1
3	Edinburgh	1			
4	⌠ Edinburgh	...	...	...	1
	⌊ Seton	1	...	...	1
5	Seton	1	...	1	
S. 6					
7	⌠ Seton	1			
	⌊ Edinburgh	1			
8	Edinburgh	1			
9	Edinburgh	...	...	...	1
10	Edinburgh	6	3		
11					

April		P	G	C	L
12	Edinburgh	1			
S. 13					
14	Edinburgh	5	1		
15	Edinburgh	3	1		
16	Edinburgh	3			
17	Edinburgh	3			
18	Edinburgh	3	1		
19	Edinburgh	6	1		
S. 20	⌠ Edinburgh	3			
	⌊ Holyrood	1			
21	Edinburgh	20	1		
22	⌠ Holyrood	1			
	⌊ Stirling	2	...	...	1
23	Stirling	2			
24	Edinburgh	1			
25	Dunbar	1			
26	Dunbar	8	1		
S. 27	⌠ Dunbar	8	4		
	⌊ Edinburgh	1			
28	Dunbar	3	2		
29	Dunbar	1	...	1	
30	Edinburgh	1	1		
May					
Th. 1	Dunbar	2	1		
2					
3					
S. 4	⌠ Dunbar	1			
	⌊ Edinburgh	1			
5	Hailes	1			
6	Holyrood	1			
7	Edinburgh	2	...	1	
8	Edinburgh	3	1	1	1
9	Edinburgh	2			
10	Edinburgh	11			
S. 11	Edinburgh	2	1		
12	Edinburgh	16	1		
13	Edinburgh	6			
14	⌠ Edinburgh	1	...	...	1
	⌊ Holyrood	1	1		
15	Edinburgh	...	...	...	2
16	Edinburgh	1	...	1	
17	Edinburgh	...	...	1	

The letter of 15th March is dated 15th Feb. by mistake. Perhaps one of the letters of 23rd March should be the 24th.

On the 16th of April she is present in Parliament (F.C.E. viii. 211), leaves Edinburgh for Stirling on the 21st (*Ibid.* viii. 213), and on the 24th is seized by Bothwell at 'The Briggis,' and carried to Dunbar (D. pp. 109, 110). On the 6th of May she comes from Dunbar to Edinburgh Castle, on the 11th goes to Holyrood, and on the 15th marries Bothwell there (D. pp. 110, 111).

18th May 1567-   17th June 1567

May		P	G	C	L	June		P	G	C	L
S. 18	Edinburgh	...	...	...	1	2	Edinburgh	7			
19	Edinburgh	1	...	1		3	Edinburgh	1			
20	Edinburgh	2				4	Edinburgh	...	...	1	1
21	Edinburgh	2	1			5	{ Edinburgh	2	...	1	
22	Edinburgh	...	...	1			{ Holyrood	1			
23	Edinburgh	...	...	1		6	Edinburgh	3			
24	Edinburgh	...	...	...	1	7	Edinburgh	2			
S. 25	Edinburgh	1				S. 8	Edinburgh	1			
26	Edinburgh	1				9					
27	Edinburgh	...	...	...	1	10					
28	Edinburgh	3	...	1		11	Borthwick	...	...	...	1
29	Edinburgh	1	...	1		12					
30						13	{ Edinburgh	...	1		
31							{ Dunbar	3			
						14					
						S. 15					
June						16					
S. 1	Edinburgh	1	...	...	1	17					

The letter of 1st June is so dated in the *Foreign Calendar*; but Thorpe and Labanoff date it the 5th. In the printed *Register of Privy Council* (i. 517), the meeting of 5th June is misdated the *sext*.

On the 7th of June she leaves Edinburgh for Borthwick, and on the 11th leaves Borthwick for Dunbar (D. pp. 112, 113), which she leaves for Seton on the 14th (D. p. 114). On the 15th she surrenders at Carberry, and is brought to Edinburgh, from which she is removed on the night of the 16th, and lodged in Loch Leven on the 17th (D. pp. 114, 115).

2nd May 1568-   16th May 1568

May		L		May		L		May		L
S. 2				7				12	Hamilton	1
3				8				13	Hamilton	1
4				S. 9				14		
5	Hamilton	2		10				15		
6	Hamilton	2		11				S. 16		

On the evening of 2nd May she escapes from Loch Leven, rides to Queensferry and thence to Niddrie, where she stays for two hours, and then proceeds to Hamilton (D. p. 129). On the 3rd of May, Murray's proclamation intimates that she is then at Hamilton (K. iii. 324); and on the 9th she is at Hamilton Castle (F. C. E. viii. 452).

On the 13th of May her army is defeated at Langside. She rides all night, and does not halt until she reaches Sanquhar; from thence she went to Terregles, where she rested a few days before embarking near Dundrennan (Herries, pp. 102, 103). On the 16th, about six in the evening, she arrives at Workington (F. C. E. viii. 460).

Printed by T. and A. CONSTABLE, Printers to Her Majesty
at the Edinburgh University Press